Part of the fun of Mardi Gras is hanging out on a balcony, exchanging beads with fellow partyers and watching the throngs go by. See chapter 2. © Kunio Owaki/The Stock Market.

Jazz Fest has grown from a small celebration of New Orleans music to become a 10-day-long international extravaganza attracting top names in blues, Cajun, jazz, and zydeco. Buckwheat Zydeco (opposite) is a regular participant. See chapter 2. © Jackson Hill/Southern Lights Photography; photo opposite © George Long Photography.

The party never stops in New Orleans. Mardi Gras (top) is usually the end of February or beginning of March. The Stella! Shouting Contest (bottom), just one segment of the Tennessee Williams Festival, is in late March or early April. Top photo © Dave G. Houser Photography; bottom photo © Syndey Byrd Photography.

Jazz Fest (top) kicks up its heels during late April and early May. And on Bourbon Street (bottom), the action goes on all year. See "When to Go" in chapter 3. Top photo © Syndey Byrd Photography; bottom photo © David Perry Lawrence/Image Bank.

The James Beard Foundation named Commander's Palace (top) the best restaurant in the entire country. Our vote for the best muffalettas (Frisbee-sized hero sandwiches stuffed with Italian cold cuts and cheeses) goes to Central Grocery (bottom). For tips on where to eat in America's fattest city, see chapter 7. Both photos © Syndey Byrd Photography.

You won't have any trouble getting a drink in New Orleans—you can even grab your beer to go. See chapter 11. © Sydney Byrd Photography.

Aaron Neville is a fixture on the New Orleans music scene, and often plays in local clubs. See the box in chapter 1 for his favorite things about New Orleans. © George Long Photography.

Name a type of music and you'll find
it here: blues, Cajun, Dixieland,
gospel (*The Zion Harmonizers, left,
at the House of Blues*), jazz, rock,
R&B, or zydeco (*Nathan Williams
and the Zydeco Cha Chas, below*).
See chapter 11. Both photos
© Syndey Byrd Photography.

The air-conditioned Aquarium of the Americas is an especially appealing attraction on hot, muggy days. See chapter 8. © Mark E. Gibson Photography.

St. Louis Cemetery No. 1 is one of several graveyards around the city where bodies are not buried underground, but in ornate above-ground mausoleums. See chapter 8 for information on how to tour the cemeteries. © George Long Photography.

The Garden District, with its magnificent Victorian, Italianate, and Greek Revival houses, is home to famous residents like author Anne Rice and Nine Inch Nails singer Trent Reznor. See chapter 9 for a walking tour of the neighborhood. © Syndey Byrd Photography.

The shopping choices for art, antiques, and collectibles run from whimsical gifts to serious 18th-century pieces. P.S. The dog on the right is real. See chapter 10. Both photos © Syndey Byrd Photography.

The Laura Plantation is a popular stop along the River Road north of New Orleans. It's no sterile museum, though; renovation and restoration is an ongoing process here. See chapter 12. © Syndey Byrd Photography.

Oak Alley is everybody's image of the classic Southern plantation home. See chapter 12.
© Randy Wells/Tony Stone Images.

Frommer's® 2000

New Orleans

by Mary Herczog

with Online Directory by Michael Shapiro

MACMILLAN • USA

ABOUT THE AUTHOR

Mary Herczog is a freelance writer who also works in the film industry. She is the author of *Frommer's Las Vegas,* and covered Bali for *Frommer's Southeast Asia.* She would never leave New Orleans if it weren't for July and August.

MACMILLAN TRAVEL

Macmillan General Reference USA, Inc.
1633 Broadway
New York, NY 10019

Find us online at **www.frommers.com**

ISBN 0-02-862643-5
ISSN 0899-2908

Editor: John Rosenthal
Production Editors: Michael Thomas, Christina Van Camp
Photo Editor: Richard Fox
Design by Michele Laseau
Digital Cartography by Lenise Fraser
Staff Cartographers: John Decamillis and Roberta Stockwell
Page Creation: Eric Brinkman, Angel Perez

SPECIAL SALES

Contents

List of Maps

ACKNOWLEDGMENTS

Very special thanks to Steve Hochman (for ten hours spent waiting in a tux). Thanks to Matt Hannafin, John and Lisa and Lucy, Beverly Gianni, Ann Christian, George Hocutt, Chuck Taggart, Marc and Ann Savoy and Dave, Nettie, Diana, Robin, John and Fiona, for over the years being the collective unconscious that has absolutely influenced this book.

AN INVITATION TO THE READER

In researching this book, we discovered many wonderful places, hotels, restaurants, shops, and more. We're sure you'll find others. Please tell us about them, so we can share the information with your fellow travelers in upcoming editions. If you were disappointed with a recommendation, we'd love to know that, too. Please write to:

Frommer's *New Orleans 2000*
Macmillan Travel
1633 Broadway
New York, NY 10019

AN ADDITIONAL NOTE

Please be advised that travel information is subject to change at any time and this is especially true of prices. We therefore suggest that you write or call ahead for confirmation when making your travel plans. The authors, editors, and publisher cannot be held responsible for the experiences of readers while traveling. Your safety is important to us, however, so we encourage you to stay alert and be aware of your surroundings. Keep a close eye on cameras, purses, and wallets, all favorite targets of thieves and pickpockets.

WHAT THE SYMBOLS MEAN

✪ Frommer's Favorites

Our favorite places and experiences, outstanding for quality, value, or both.

The following abbreviations are used for credit cards:

AE	American Express	EURO	EuroCard
CB	Carte Blanche	JCB	Japan Credit Bank
DC	Diners Club	MC	MasterCard
DISC	Discover	V	Visa
ER	EnRoute		

FIND FROMMER'S ONLINE

Arthur Frommer's Budget Travel Online (www.frommers.com) offers more than 6,000 pages of up-to-the-minute travel information—including the latest bargains and candid, personal articles updated daily by Arthur Frommer himself. No other Web site offers such comprehensive and timely coverage of the world of travel.

The Best of New Orleans

New Orleans should come with a warning label.

See, there's a growing group of residents whom locals call the "never lefts." They are the people who came to New Orleans as tourists, came for Mardi Gras, came for Jazz Festival, just came. And the city worked its magic on them. They listened to street musicians around Jackson Square. They danced to brass bands in clubs at night. They gazed at lush tropical courtyards hidden behind unassuming building fronts. They strolled down streets time seemed to have forgotten. They kissed beneath flickering gas lamps. They ate incredible meals and topped them off with beignets at 3am at the Café du Monde while watching the passing human parade. They found themselves perusing newspaper ads for houses and apartments. Because as their trip's end came and went, they were still in New Orleans. They came for Mardi Gras, came for Jazz Fest, just came—and *never left.*

New Orleans does that to people.

This is one of the few cities in America (if not the only one) where you do not feel as if you are in America. It may sound clichéd to call New Orleans magical and seductive, but it's the truth. Every one of your senses is engaged from the moment you arrive. Visually, the city is superb, from the lacy ironwork wrapped around the buildings of the French Quarter, to the stately, graceful old homes of the Garden District, to the giant oaks that stretch across Esplanade Avenue or drip with ghostly Spanish moss in City Park. To call New Orleans picturesque is not doing it justice. Aurally, music pours out of every doorway or is played right in the street. Jazz, Cajun, blues, whatever—you'll find yourself moving to a rhythm, and the very streets seem to dance along with you. There are delicious smells in the air, which seems to carry a whiff of the Caribbean. The moist, honeyed air caresses your skin and almost seems alive.

And then there's the food. Don't get us started on the food.

This is a city that is fully, totally alive. It's sensual and joyous, decadent but not exploitative. Indulgences are many, but for the right reason—they are fun. This is a city where every business entirely closes for Mardi Gras; after all, "carnival" roughly means "farewell to flesh." No one's going to say good-bye to such things (as if they ever really do) without a big party.

We tell people that all we do when we go to New Orleans is eat, drink, listen to music, dance, and walk. That's it. And you can do just

Aaron Neville's New Orleans

Multiple Grammy winner Aaron Neville's unmistakably angelic voice has been a New Orleans landmark for several decades, in his career as a soloist and as one of the Neville Brothers. His latest album is entitled *To Make Me Who I Am* (A&M records). He recently recounted what he loves about his hometown.

"I'm a homebody these days, but I still like riding the St. Charles streetcar, and going to the Camellia Grill for breakfast or having blackened redfish or crawfish at K-Paul's, where there's always a line. Is the wait worth it? Oh, yeah! And I like riding the riverboat and checking out Audubon Park, now that they have the beautiful natural habitats. I used to go up there a long time ago when they had cages, and I didn't like it. The animals didn't look happy.

"New Orleans has a mystique to it, and it's got a hold on me. This place is like a melting pot, a mixture of so many cultures, with nothing pure. It's got its own attitude. And music for any occasion—people walk here with a musical rhythm. This is one place where you can walk down the street and greet people. Do that in New York or L.A. and people look at you like you are crazy. Here, people say, 'What's up?' and you say, 'Where y'at?' When I play different cities, and someone in the audience calls out 'Where y'at?' I know where they're from. When I was growing up, I thought everyone said that.

"I travel to different countries and cities all over the world, but when I'm coming back from the road, the greatest sight to me is looking out the airplane window and seeing the swamps."

that for days without getting bored. That's the kind of town New Orleans is. In fact, that may be the simplest way to sum up its appeal—which is not an easy task. For years, countless authors have tried to explain its gestalt. You could fill entire bookcases with New Orleans–based or –inspired literature, some written by natives, even more by authors who came for a visit and never left.

We won't kid you, though. There is a downside to all this fun. New Orleans has always been the city of permissive attitudes—it was the first U.S. city where prostitution was sort of legal. Today, loose liquor laws mean a party atmosphere, but also mean obnoxious drunks and disgusting displays in the streets. (Let's just say that some of the city's smells aren't all that pleasant.) Crime has been high; for a couple of years—1995 and 1996 in particular—this was the most dangerous city in America, although recent concerted efforts to fix that have paid off with lower crime rates.

But those who love New Orleans remain amused by its flaws—they're part of what makes the town real. And it is real. It only looks like a movie set because of remarkable historic preservation; the city continues to largely resist efforts to turn it into an amusement park. For every tacky souvenir store and theme restaurant, there are 10 places that defy commercialization. This town refuses to be turned into something shiny and clean. It's not the natural order of things, anyway. Thanks to the climate, the city began to decay the moment it was built. Buildings may be worn and shabby, but every brick has a story. You want tidy and sterile? Go elsewhere. You want history and character? Come here.

The best way to get inside New Orleans is to plunge right in. Don't just go for the obvious; though we've met people who never left Bourbon Street and had a terrific time, the city has so much more to offer. We've also met people who went for recognizable names and quick and easy decisions, then were disappointed that their experiences were no more than adequate.

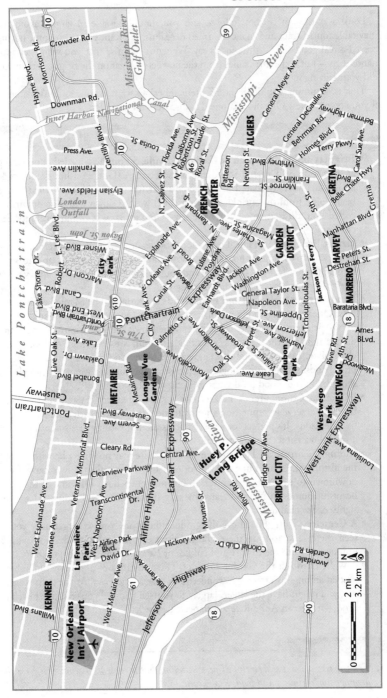

Look over the advice that follows, and you should be able to largely avoid the inevitable tourist traps and make informed decisions. We want you to go home having passed a real good time, as the locals say. We won't promise that you won't get your hands dirty—but if the dirt comes from the powdered sugar on the beignets, then you did your trip right.

That is, assuming you do go home. Remember, we warned you, so don't blame us if you come to New Orleans and one day discover you never left.

1 Frommer's Favorite New Orleans Experiences

- **Beignets and Café au Lait at Café du Monde.** Sit on the crowded patio gazing at the action on Decatur Street and Jackson Square. Gorge on hot French-style doughnuts liberally coated in powdered sugar (everyone will know what you've been doing from the sprinkles on your shirt) washed down with potent chicory coffee. And do it at any hour of the day—3pm or 3am. It's open 24 hours! See chapter 7.
- **Jazz at Preservation Hall.** Drop your 4 bucks in the hat and squeeze into one of the country's time-honored jazz institutions. You might not be able to see a thing, but your feet will be moving and your ears will be happy, even if they never knew they liked jazz before. See chapter 11.
- **Bands at the Maple Leaf and Brass Bands at Donna's.** The Maple Leaf is a very New Orleans club, and is a fun place to hang out. On nights when popular bands fill the place to hot, sweaty capacity, and the crowd spills over into the street and dances right on the sidewalk, it's sublime. Donna's exists, more or less, so the charismatic Donna herself can enjoy her favorite kind of music: New Orleans brass bands. On any given night, it's jumping and full (and we mean shoulder to shoulder full) of good local vibes. See chapter 11.
- **Dinner at Commander's Palace.** One of the legendary restaurants that continues to deserve its reputation after many decades. It's romantic, gracious, attentive, delicious. It's perfect for a special occasion, but eating there makes *any* meal a special occasion. See chapter 7.
- **Riding the Streetcar.** The streetcar named Desire may no longer be with us, but the historic St. Charles line still is. Not only is it a convenient way to travel from downtown to uptown (or vice versa), but the route shows off some of the most beautiful homes in New Orleans, making it a leisurely and delightful way to sightsee. See chapter 9.
- **A Cemetery Tour.** The above-the-ground tombs are hard to forget once you've seen them, and touring these ghostly cities of the dead provides you with a unique look into the history and culture of New Orleans. See chapter 8.
- **A Walk Through the Garden District.** These elegant but not flashy old homes, nestled among lush trees, are wonderful to gaze at and envy. At the right time of day, you might have the streets largely to yourself and feel you've slipped back in time—or into an Anne Rice novel. See chapter 9.

Impressions

The city can drive a sober-minded person insane, but it feeds the dreamer. It feeds the dreamer stories, music and food. Really great food.

—Andrei Codrescu, *The Muse Is Always Half-Dressed in New Orleans*

Inpressions

Louisiana politics exist to entertain the rest of us.

—Harry Shearer

- **A Stroll Along St. John's Bayou.** Most tourists don't get much beyond the Quarter, or else they speed past this low-slung body of water as they head for City Park. Take a left off Esplanade (if you are coming from the Quarter), and slow down, Big Easy style, finally away from the hordes, as you meander along the bayou and admire the less high-profile, but no less attractive and romantic neighborhood around it. See chapter 9.
- **Bourbon Street After Dark.** Even if you end up hating it, you have to see it at least once. Music spurts and oozes out of windows and doors, drinkers reign supreme, and sex is widely available—on paper, on stage, and on video. It's wild, disgusting, and strangely exhilarating. See chapter 11.
- **Club-Hopping in the Frenchmen Section.** This portion of the Faubourg Marigny (the neighborhood that borders the French Quarter) features at least five clubs and several bars, each with its own personality and charm, all within a few quiet blocks. Quiet, that is, except for the people strolling from one to the other, dipping in for a bit or just listening to the music pouring out the doors, before moving on to sample something farther down the street. See chapter 11.
- **Eating.** With a nearly infinite selection of outstanding restaurants and other food sources, meal planning in New Orleans is very serious indeed. There is never time to do it all; a muffaletta from Central Grocery eaten on the banks of the Mississippi, boiled crawfish or oyster shooting at Acme or Felix's, luscious seafood at Uglesich's, amazing innovative cuisine at the Upperline, Brightsen's, Emeril's, Peristyle, Bayonna. Can you eat five meals a day here? We've tried! See chapter 7.
- **A Rainy Afternoon at the Aquarium.** At times, sudden showers will send you indoors. If you find yourself dashing into the aquarium, you will probably end up enjoying yourself more than you might have thought, thanks to some first-class exhibits. See chapter 8.

2 Best Hotel Bets

Selecting just one accommodation in New Orleans is a little like picking your favorite flavor of ice cream. There are just so many great options to choose from. So in an effort to sneak a few more of our favorites onto this list, we've created several categories of accommodations. Some of the categories are a bit amorphous, but we're pretty sure you won't mind. You'll find full reviews of all these places in chapter 6, plus some other choices that we like almost as much.

- **Best for a Romantic Getaway:** The **Melrose Mansion,** 937 Esplanade Ave. (☎ **504/944-2255**), is an excellent choice. Rooms are furnished with exquisite antiques, and feature deep Jacuzzi tubs in all suites. The service is impeccable.
- **Best Moderately Priced Hotel:** The **Bourbon Orleans,** 717 Orleans St. (☎ **504/523-2222**), is the best value in its price range. It's centrally located (make sure to ask for a room *not* facing Bourbon Street; although maybe you want to keep an eye on the nonstop partying), has excellent amenities like coffeemakers and marble bathrooms, and rivals some of the city's more expensive hotels in quality of service.

- **Best Guest House Value:** At the **McKendrick-Breaux House,** 1474 Magazine St. (☎ **888/570-1700**), you get the kind of service you'd expect at a larger, more expensive hotel, and the host seems to know instinctively just how much (or how little) attention you need. Rooms and bathrooms are exceptionally large, and cable TV and telephones are standard. The claw-foot bathtubs in the main house are an added luxury.
- **Best New Hotel:** The innovative style and myriad comforts at the newly opened **International House,** 221 Camp St. (☎ **800/633-5770**), have justly made this everyone's new favorite hotel.
- **Best Location:** If you want to stay right in the French Quarter, you'll be hard-pressed to find a hotel that's better situated than the **Omni Royal Orleans,** 621 St. Louis St. (☎ **800/THE-OMNI**).
- **Best Health Club:** The hands-down winner is **Hilton New Orleans Riverside Hotel,** 2 Poydras St. (☎ **800/445-8667**). Its Rivercenter Racquet and Health Club features outdoor and indoor tennis courts, squash and racquetball courts, a rooftop jogging track, aerobics classes, tanning beds, massage, a hair salon, and a golf studio.
- **Best Little Hotel:** The **Hotel Maison de Ville,** 727 Toulouse St. (☎ **800/ 634-1600**), is listed among both the Small Luxury Hotels of the World and the Small Historic Hotels of America. Once you submit to its pampering, you'll understand why.
- **Best Classically Elegant Hotel:** The **Pontchartrain Hotel,** 2031 St. Charles Ave. (☎ **800/777-6193**), may be more worn around the edges than some of these upstarts, but it's been showing everyone how to offer discreet sophistication and ritzy style for decades—and it has the devoted clientele to show for its efforts.
- **Best Funky Little Hotels:** The **Frenchmen,** 417 Frenchmen St. (☎ **800/ 831-1781**), and the **LaMothe House,** 621 Esplanade Ave. (☎ **800/367-5858**), are small but full of pure New Orleans charm and the kind of service (with attitude) only a small hotel can provide.
- **In a Class by Itself:** Of all the hotels in New Orleans, the **Windsor Court,** 300 Gravier St. (☎ **800/262-2662**), stands head and shoulders above the rest. After all, who gets voted Best Hotel in North America by *Condé Nast Traveller*? The hotel's lovely public areas are a veritable treasure trove of fine art. Most guest rooms are suites with Italian marble bathrooms, fine fabrics, balconies or bay windows, living rooms, kitchenettes, and dressing rooms. If you choose one of the two-bedroom penthouse suites, you'll have the added luxury of a private library and a terrace that overlooks the mighty Mississippi.

3 Best Dining Bets

It's always hard to quantify such things as restaurant comparisons, particularly in a town like New Orleans, which has so many wonderful choices. But here's a list to guide you.

Some of you may wonder why there are no "Best Cajun" and "Best Creole" categories. Our feeling was that New Orleans has no exceptional Cajun restaurants (they're adequate at best), and just about everyone has a different definition of Creole cooking, so narrowing it down was nearly impossible. But we consulted with a number of hard-core New Orleans foodies, who like nothing more than debates of this nature. Serious arguments broke out in which fists were waved in the air, but when the dust settled, ultimately everyone sheepishly agreed. The compromise is "Best Contemporary Creole," and even that caused some to wail, "But those restaurants aren't Creole!" and the whole thing started up again.

For more complete listings of New Orleans restaurant by cuisine and neighborhood, see chapter 7.

- **Best Restaurant in the United States:** Actually, we haven't tried them all, so we can't say for sure, but in 1996, the James Beard Foundation, which should know, said it was **Commander's Palace,** 1403 Washington Ave. (☎ **504/899-8221**). *Food & Wine* magazine concurred in 1997. We won't argue.

- **Best Spot for a Business Lunch: Mr. B's Bistro & Bar,** 201 Royal St. (☎ **504/523-2078**). Businesspeople across the city favor its casual but classy atmosphere, not to mention the fine food.

- **Best Wine List:** The wine cellar at **Brennan's,** 417 Royal St. (☎ **504/525-9711**), is unsurpassed in New Orleans. There's a good selection of less expensive California wines, some moderately priced French wines, and some more expensive labels, as well as a lovely selection of dessert wines. (Prices range from about $20 to $1,000.)

- **Best for Kids:** Take them to **Café du Monde,** 813 Decatur St. (☎ **504/581-2914**), where getting powdered sugar all over yourself is half the fun. It's large and open-air, so it isn't confining, and there are always street performers around.

- **Best Gumbo:** More fighting words, but you can't go wrong at **Dooky Chase,** 2301 Orleans Ave. (☎ **504/821-2294**), or **Galatoire's,** 209 Bourbon St. (☎ **504/525-2021**).

- **Best French Cuisine:** The city's first French restaurant, **Louis XVI,** 730 Bienville St. (☎ **504/581-7000**), is also its best—which, in a city of French-leaning cuisine, is saying a lot. Table-side preparations add a flourish, but the food is so superior that they're not even necessary.

- **Best Contemporary Creole:** The food at **Brigtsen's,** 723 Dante St. (☎ **504/861-7610**), and the **Upperline,** 1413 Upperline St. (☎ **504/891-9822**), is consistently interesting, innovative, and delicious.

- **Best International Cuisine:** Or however the heck you want to categorize the glories served at Susan Spicer's **Bayona,** 430 Dauphine St (☎ **504/525-4455**), which has justly leapt on to the list of can't-miss places to eat.

- **Best Italian:** There is a strong Italian presence in New Orleans, so don't feel you aren't enjoying local cuisine when you go to **Bacco,** 310 Chartres St. (☎ **504/522-2426**), where the Brennan family delivers up yet another marvelous restaurant, this one featuring, in addition to grin-inducing entrees, possibly the best bread in town.

- **Best Classic New Orleans Restaurant:** Of the three mainstays of New Orleans dining (the others being Galatoire's and Antoine's), **Arnaud's,** 813 Bienville St. (☎ **504/523-5433**), is the one where you can count on getting a consistently good (and maybe even great) meal, the same way, and in the exact same surroundings, that generations of New Orleanians have done before you.

- **Best Desserts:** Desserts in New Orleans due to tend to run to the familiar; everyone serves bread pudding or flourless chocolate cake. But there are places (curiously, most often run by people named Brennan) that stray into more interesting territory with practically Bacchanalian rich choices. **Commander's Palace** (see above) serves a justifiably famous bread pudding soufflé, but don't ignore other possibilities served there, including the chocolate Sheba. Then there is the banana cream pie at **Emeril's,** 800 Tchoupitoulas St. (☎ **504/528-9393**), which reduces grown men to quivering fools. Others are brought to their knees by the white chocolate bread pudding at the **Palace Café,** 605 Canal St. (☎ **504/523-1661**). Try 'em all and decide for yourself.

- **Best Local Dive with Outstanding Food: Uglesich's Restaurant & Bar,** 1238 Barrone St. (☎ **504/523-8571**), is nearly always crowded, is only slightly better than a dump, and features food so sublime you won't care a bit. (Secretly, we think this is the best restaurant in New Orleans.)
- **Best Burgers:** Locals swear by **Port of Call,** 838 Esplanade Ave. (☎ **504/523-0120**), but its cow-sized half-pounder might be too much for some. We throw the vote to the more manageable third-of-a-pound juicy delight at the **Clover Grill,** 900 Bourbon St. (☎ **504/598-1010**).
- **Best Steaks:** Don't be turned off by the fact that it's a chain. The fact is, **Ruth's Chris Steakhouse,** 711 N. Broad St. (☎ **504/486-0810**), serves the best beef in town.
- **Best Outdoor Dining:** Back to **Bayona** we go (see International Cuisine, above), to eat their fabulous food in their beautiful, quiet, and fairly secluded courtyard. It's especially delightful on moonlit nights or balmy spring afternoons.
- **Best View:** The amazing moonlight view of the Mississippi makes **Bella Luna,** 914 N. Peters St. (☎ **504/529-1583**), possibly the most romantic restaurant in town.
- **Best Po' Boys:** It's hard to beat the drippy monster creations at **Mother's,** 401 Poydras St. (☎ **504/523-9656**).
- **Best Muffalettas:** You really haven't had a sandwich until you've tried a muffaletta, and though others do a good job, no one beats **Central Grocery,** 923 Decatur St. (☎ **504/523-1620**).

Mardi Gras & Other Festivals

This is a city that really loves a good party. And what happens when a party gets too big? It becomes a festival. That's what has happened over the years to the Jazz and Heritage Festival. It has evolved from an event where people were literally begged to take free tickets to a hugely crowded, multiday affair that has, relatively speaking, not that much to do with jazz (but is no less fun for it). Anything is an excuse for a party, and so you can experience festivals centered around swamps, gumbo, crawfish, frogs, tomatoes, and architecture. New Orleanians know what makes a great party: really good food and music, and lots of it. That's what you will find at any festival in Louisiana, regardless of what it is ostensibly celebrating.

This chapter covers some of the largest festivals in New Orleans and the outlying areas; others are listed in the "New Orleans Calendar of Events" in chapter 3. You can get information on many of the events mentioned in both chapters by contacting the **New Orleans Metropolitan Convention and Visitors Bureau,** 1520 Sugar Bowl Dr., New Orleans, LA 70112 (☎ **800/672-6124** or 504/566-5055; www. nawlins.com; e-mail: tourism@nawlins.com). Be sure to ask the people at the bureau if any other events are scheduled during your visit—chances are good that you'll have to choose between festivals or scramble if you want to catch portions of more than one.

1 Mardi Gras

Obviously, the granddaddy of all New Orleans celebrations is Mardi Gras. Thanks to sensational media accounts that zero in on the salacious portions, its rep has gone downhill in the last few years—while the accounts have attracted more and more participants looking for wild action rather than tradition. But despite what you may have heard, Mardi Gras remains one of the most exciting times to visit this city. You can spend several days admiring and reveling in the traditions and never even venture into the frat-party atmosphere of Bourbon Street.

Knowledge of some of the long and fascinating history of Mardi Gras may help put matters in perspective. First of all, it's not a festival; it's a "carnival," from a Latin word roughly meaning "farewell to flesh." Mardi Gras is both a day and a time period. It's French for "Fat Tuesday," the day before Ash Wednesday, when Lent begins, and historically refers to the 5- to 8-week stretch from Twelfth Night (January 6) to Mardi Gras day (which can fall as late as March 9). With Lent comes fasting and deprivation. The idea was that good Christians would take the opportunity to eat as much as they could in preparation for their impending denial.

The party's origins can be traced from that Roman excuse for an orgy, the Lupercalia festival. It will sound strangely familiar to today's Mardi Gras participant: 2 days when all sexual and social order disappeared, cross-dressing was mandatory, and the population ran riot. The early Christian church was naturally appalled by this, but was unable to stop it (as someone later said about Storyville and prostitution, you can make it illegal but you can't make it unpopular). Grafting Lupercalia to the beginning of Lent may have been a compromise to bribe everyone into observing Lent. And they may have needed that 40 days to recover!

Carnival, with lavish masked balls and other revels, became popular in Italy and France, and so naturally the tradition followed the Creoles to New Orleans. The first carnival balls occurred in 1743, but the first detailed accounts of Mardi Gras–specific festivities showed up in 1824. Informal parades and masked revelers cavorting in the streets characterized the celebrations. By the mid-1800s, Mardi Gras mischief had grown so ugly (the habit of tossing flour on revelers gradually turned into throwing bricks at them) that everyone predicted the impending end of the tradition. (The more things change, the more they stay the same.)

Everything changed in 1856. Tired of being left out of the Creoles' Mardi Gras, a group of Americans who belonged to a secret society called Cowbellians formed the Mystick Krewe of Comus (after the hero of a John Milton poem). On Mardi Gras evening, they presented a torch-lit parade, seemingly out of nowhere, that was breathtaking in its design, effects, and imagination. A new tradition was born. Every Mardi Gras night thereafter (with some exceptions) climaxed with the appearance of Comus, each time grander and more astounding.

And so the new standard was set. Mardi Gras societies became known as krewes, and most were made up of prominent society types or businessmen; the event marked the height of the social season. The next krewe to emerge was that of Rex, the king of Carnival. Rex paraded in the morning, and later paid public homage to Comus. Their meeting became the high point of Mardi Gras. Rex was born in part to celebrate the Mardi Gras appearance of the grand duke of Russia, Alexis Alexandrovich Romanov, who had followed the actress Lydia Thompson from New York when she came to star in *Bluebeard*. The city went all out to welcome him, and when it was learned that his favorite song was Lydia's burlesque tune "If Ever I Cease to Love You," every band in the Rex parade was asked to play it. That sprightly melody is now the official song of Mardi Gras, and the royal colors—purple for justice, green for faith, and gold for power—were adopted as the festival's official colors. More krewes, such as Momus and Proteus, came into being, each throwing a lavish ball along with its parade, and each with an exclusive membership.

The Civil War put a temporary halt to things, but Comus was parading again by 1866. In 1870, a krewe known as the Twelfth Night Revelers was founded and added two new customs that still endure. Members threw trinkets to onlookers (the first thrower was dressed as Santa Claus), and a "queen" reigned over their ball.

Mardi Gras and New Orleans are virtually congruent.

—Munro Edmonson

Mardi Gras ain't so much if you're broke.

—John Dos Passos, *Funiculi Funicula*

Impressions

The other day, I had the fleeting thought that everyone, dead or alive, returns to New Orleans. If people can't come back in their lifetimes, they come back when they are dead.

—Andrei Codrescu

As a classic elite Old South institution, Mardi Gras was not exactly at the forefront of promoting racial equality or harmony. Throughout the 19th century, the city's African-Americans participated in parades only by carrying torches to illuminate the route (the *flambeaux,* as the torches are known, are still around, a welcome atmospheric Mardi Gras tradition). In 1909, a black man named William Storey mocked the elaborately garbed Rex by prancing after his float wearing a lard can for a crown. Storey was promptly dubbed "King Zulu." By 1916, his followers had grown so in number that they formed the Krewe of Zulu (officially the Zulu Social Aid and Pleasure Club), developing a parody of Rex and making a mockery of racial stereotypes. The Zulu parade quickly became one of the most popular aspects of Mardi Gras. The most famous King Zulu was Louis Armstrong, who reigned in 1949.

Unfortunately, most krewes remained notable for their lack of blacks, Jews, and women, and as times changed, the public, which was not permitted to join the krewes but was supposed to be happy to pay taxes for postparade cleanup, demanded equality. It was not considered enough that some krewes had begun (grudgingly) inviting blacks to their balls. An ordinance passed in 1992 denies a parade permit to any group that discriminates on the basis of race or religion. (Krewes are still not required to integrate along gender lines, a choice of the all-female Krewes as much as the male, though men in drag are a hallmark of Mardi Gras.) Rex acceded to the new regulations, but mighty Comus, in a move that many still feel marked the beginning of the end of classic Mardi Gras, canceled its parade. Proteus and Momus soon followed suit.

Some say the flavor of Mardi Gras had already changed long before the 1992 ordinance.

Parades were always things of spectacle and beauty, with literally antique floats: 19th-century caissons with wooden wheels. But the processions had gotten so big over the years that they had to be taken out of the Quarter. The old krewes were gradually replaced by "super krewes" like Bacchus and Endymion, whose membership was nonexclusive. One of their floats was as big as an entire Comus parade. In 1997, the largest parades each had more than 20 floats, celebrity guests, marching bands, dancing groups, motorcycle squads, and a total of many thousands of participants. Celebrities are often the super krewes' kings; the 1998 Bacchus king was Drew Carey. Also in 1998, the Krewe of the Americas, completely made up of non–New Orleans residents, paraded for the first time, on Mardi Gras afternoon itself, a sacrilege to natives who long considered this Comus' day.

The throws fly thick and fast from the floats of these super krewes, but they lack the tradition of the old krewes. The exact origin of throws has been lost to time, but at some point in the 1920s, Rex began throwing trinkets to parade-watchers. Other Krewes eventually followed suit, and now throws are mandatory. The ubiquitous beads were originally glass (often from Czechoslovakia) but now are of more inexpensive plastic. Doubloons are another popular souvenir. Usually of aluminum, these oversize coins show the krewe's coat of arms on one side and the year's parade theme on the other. They are collectors' items for natives, many of whom have every krewe's doubloons from many different years. Other throws include stuffed animals, plastic Krewe cups, and especially the highly prized, hand-painted Zulu coconuts.

Alas, the traditional cry of, "Throw me something, Mister" to obtain a trinket has gradually turned into the request/demand, "Show me your tits!" But even though it seems Mardi Gras is moving ever further away from its traditions, we have to remember that Comus has in the past disappeared for several years, and that it always rose again. Indeed, as this was being written, the rumor was going around that both Comus and Proteus would return for Mardi Gras 2000.

KICKIN' UP YOUR HEELS: MARDI GRAS ACTIVITIES

One of the beautiful things about Mardi Gras, residents point out, is that with a mask on your face, you can be and do anything you want. You feel the total freedom of anonymity.

In that same way, Mardi Gras itself can be whatever you want. Don't be suckered by media reports that focus on the exhibitionism and drunken orgies. Sure, some of Mardi Gras is becoming more and more like spring break, as college kids pour into town, eager to have license to do anything. Thankfully, that kind of activity is largely confined to Bourbon Street. If that's what you want, go there. But if you avoid Bourbon Street, you will find an entirely different Mardi Gras experience.

THE SEASON   The date of Fat Tuesday is different each year, but carnival season always starts on Twelfth Night, January 6, as much as 2 months before Mardi Gras. On that night, the Phunny Phorty Phellows kick off the season with a streetcar ride from Carrollton to Canal Street and back.

Over the following weeks, the city celebrates Mardi Gras in its own inimitable fashion. For most people, this means attending a string of King Cake parties. The traditional King Cake is a round, braided confection into which a plastic baby is baked; getting the piece with the baby can be a good omen or can mean you have to throw the next King Cake party. For the high society crowd, the season brings the year's best parties, some of which hark back to the grand masked balls of the 19th century. Each krewe throws a ball, ostensibly to introduce its royalty for the year. There are dozens of these parties between Twelfth Night and Mardi Gras, but most are not traditional masked balls. (By the way, don't expect to be invited—they are quite exclusive.)

As the season progresses, the hazy outline of Mardi Gras becomes apparent, and things start to get more and more festive. Two or three weeks before Mardi Gras itself, parades begin chugging through the streets with increasing frequency. There are also plenty of parodies, like the parade of the Mystick Krewe of Barkus and the Krewe du Vieux's yearly expression of decadence (open to the public). Barkus is, as you might guess, a krewe for pets, which parades through the Quarter (some of the dogs get quite gussied up) and is a total hoot.

If you want to experience Mardi Gras but don't want to face the full force of craziness, consider coming for the weekend 10 days before Fat Tuesday (the season officially begins the Friday of this weekend). You can count on 10 to 15 parades during the weekend, by lesser-known krewes like Cleopatra, Pontchartrain, Sparta, and Camelot. The crowds are more manageable than the ones you'll find just a week later.

That following weekend there are another 15 parades—the biggies. Everything's bigger: the parades are bigger, the crowds are bigger, everything's bigger. By this point, the city has succumbed to carnival fever. After a day of screaming for beads, you'll probably find yourself heading somewhere to get a drink or three. The French Quarter will be the center of late-night revelry; all of the larger bars will be packed. If you go uptown or to Mid City to see a parade, however, you might consider staying put and spending your evening at one of the joints nearby. The last parade each day (on both weekends) usually ends around 9:30pm or later; if you have children along, they'll probably be beat by the time you get back to the hotel. You might be, too.

By the way, a good Mardi Gras activity for children is a trip to the Mardi Gras Museum in Kenner's Rivertown area (see chapter 8 for a listing).

LUNDI GRAS   In the 19th century, Rex's King of Carnival arrived downtown from the Mississippi River on this night, the Monday before Fat Tuesday. Over the years, the day gradually lost its special significance, becoming just another day of parades. In the 1980s, however, Rex revived the old tradition.

These days, festivities at the riverfront begin in the afternoon, with lots of drink and live music leading up to the King's arrival at around 6pm. Down the levee a few hundred feet, at Wolfenberg Park, Zulu has its own Lundi Gras celebration, with the king arriving at around 5pm. In 1999, for the first time, King Zulu met up with Rex, in an impressive ceremony. That night, the **Krewe of Orpheus** holds their parade. It's one of the biggest and most popular parades, thanks to their generosity with their throws. And although it's a recent addition to the Mardi Gras scene (it began in 1994) it holds fast to old Mardi Gras traditions, including floats designed by master float creator Henri Schindler.

Because Lent begins the following night at midnight, Monday is the final dusk-to-dawn night of Mardi Gras. A good portion of the city forgoes sleep so as not to waste the occasion—which only adds to the craziness.

MARDI GRAS   The day begins early, starting with the two biggest parades, **Zulu** and **Rex,** which run back to back. Zulu starts near the Central Business District at 8:30am, Rex starts Uptown at 10am.

Throughout the early morning, in between the parades, you can also see the elaborately costumed Mardi Gras **"walking clubs,"** like the Jefferson City Buzzards, the Pete Fountain Half Fast, and the Mondo Kayo Social and Marching Club (identifiable by their tropical/banana theme). They walk, they drink, they're usually accompanied by marching bands, and they probably didn't sleep the night before, so they don't move very fast. You can catch these "marchers" anywhere along their St. Charles Avenue route (between Poydras and Washington). Keep your eyes open also for the unofficial marching club, the Julus, which includes members of the New Orleans Klezmer All-Stars, and tends to follow the Zulu parade.

It will be early afternoon when Rex spills into the Central Business District. Nearby, at about this time, you can find some of the most elusive New Orleans figures, the **Mardi Gras Indians.** The "tribes" of New Orleans are small communities of African Americans and black Creoles (some of whom have Native American ancestors), mostly from the inner city. Their elaborate (and that's an understatement) beaded and feathered costumes, rivaling Bob Mackie Vegas headdresses in outrageousness and size, are entirely made by hand. The men begin working on them on Ash Wednesday, the day after Mardi Gras, to get them ready in time for next year. Throughout the day, tribes of Indians from all over town converge along the median of Claiborne Avenue, underneath the interstate, where a large crowd of locals is always milling around to see the spectacle. If two tribes meet on the median, or back in their neighborhoods, they'll stage a mock confrontation, resettling their territory and common borders. (If you're lucky, you can sometimes catch these confrontations during other times of the year, if the Indians are out to celebrate something else, like Jazz Fest or the mayor's inauguration.)

After the parades, the action picks up in the Quarter. En route, you'll see that Mardi Gras is still very much a family tradition, with whole families dressing up in similar costumes. Marvel at how an entire city has shut down so that every citizen can join in the celebrations. Some people don't bother hitting the streets; instead, they hang out on their balconies watching the action below, or have barbecues in their courtyards. If you are lucky and seem like the right sort, you might well get invited in.

In the Quarter, the frat-party action is largely confined to Bourbon Street. The more interesting activity is in the lower Quarter and the Frenchmen section of the Faubourg Marigny, where the artists and gay community really know how to celebrate Mardi Gras. The costumes are elaborate works of art, some the product of months of work. Although the people may be (okay, probably *will* be) drunk, they are boisterous and enthusiastic, not (for the most part) obnoxious.

As you make your way through the streets, keep your eyes peeled for members of the legendary Krewe of Comus. They will be men dressed in tuxes, with brooms over their shoulders, holding cowbells. Ask them if they are Comus, and they will deny it, insisting they are Cowbellians. But then they might hand you a vintage Comus doubloon, and the truth will be out.

If you can, try to stay until midnight, when the police come through the Quarter, officially shutting down Mardi Gras.

PLANNING A VISIT DURING MARDI GRAS

LODGING   You can't just drop in on Mardi Gras. If you do, you may find yourself sleeping in Jackson Square or on a sidewalk somewhere. Accommodations in the city and the nearby suburbs are booked solid, *so make your plans well ahead and book a room as early as possible.* Many people plan a year or more in advance. Prices are usually much higher during Mardi Gras, and most hotels and guest houses impose minimum-stay requirements.

CLOTHING   As with anything in New Orleans, but perhaps now more than ever, you must join in if you want to have the best time. Simply being a spectator is not enough. And that means a costume and mask. Once you are masked and dressed up, you are automatically part of it all. (Tellingly, the Bourbon Street participants usually do not wear costumes.) A mask tends to bring out the extrovert in everyone. It makes it much easier to talk to strangers or simply to jump up and down begging for beads. It's so simple—a $1.50 piece of plastic will make you part of the spectacle, rather than a spectator. As far as costumes go, you need not do anything fancy. A bad suit will suffice. You can't possibly compete with those residents who spend all year, and thousands of dollars, on their costumes, but don't feel bad. If anything, feel morally superior to those who don't bother dressing up at all. They aren't in the Carnival spirit. But you are.

If you've come unprepared, several shops in town specialize in Mardi Gras costumes and masks. One of the most reasonable is the **Mardi Gras Center,** 831 Chartres St. (☎ **504/524-4384**). If you come early enough, they can custom-make a costume to your specifications; if not, they're well stocked with new and used costumes, wigs, masks, hats, and makeup. (See "Shopping A to Z" in chapter 10 for more listings.) You might also try the second-hand stores along Magazine Street, which have a large inventory of costumes from the year before. You can usually pick up something quite snazzy for not very much money.

DINING   If you want to eat at a restaurant during Mardi Gras, make reservations as early as possible. And pay very close attention to parade routes (see the map in this

---

Handy Tip

You can always figure out **the date of Mardi Gras** because it falls exactly 47 days before Easter. If you can't find your calendar or just can't be bothered with the math, here's the next 5 years for ya: March 7, 2000; February 27, 2001; February 12, 2002; March 4, 2003; February 24, 2004.

More Information

You'll enjoy Mardi Gras more if you've done a little homework before your trip. Contact the **New Orleans Metropolitan Convention and Visitors Bureau,** 1520 Sugar Bowl Dr., New Orleans, LA 70112 (☎ **800/672-6124** or 504/566-5055; www.nawlins.com; e-mail: tourism@nawlins.com), and ask for its current Mardi Gras information.

You'll also want to get your hands on the 2000 edition of *Arthur Hardy's Mardi Gras Guide* as early as possible. Your best bet is to call the magazine directly (☎ **504/ 838-6111;** e-mail: mardihardy@aol.com). It is sold all over town, and is an invaluable guide, full of history, tips, and maps of the parade routes.

Also a terrific buy is the **MardiCard,** a combination map and Mardi Gras schedule, full of insider tips to help you find the best stuff to see during the greatest free show and party in the country. It all folds up into pocket-size and is most handy for taking around during the day. Check out their Web site for additional informational resources: www.mardicard.com. You can buy the MardiCard at, among other places, Accent Annex (633 Toulose), the House of Blues gift shop, Lenny's News (5420 Magazine and 622 Carrollton Ave.) and Martin's Wine Cellar (3827 Baronne).

---

chapter), because if there is one between you and your restaurant, you may not be able to cross the parade route and you can kiss your dinner goodbye. For those of you who don't plan in advance, this might work to your advantage; often restaurants have a high no-show rate during Mardi Gras for this reason, and so a well-timed drop-in may work nicely.

PARKING   Remember that while the huge crowds you'll find everywhere add to the general merriment, they also grind traffic to a halt all over town. So our admonition against renting a car is even stronger during Mardi Gras. *Don't drive.* Instead, relax and take a cab or walk. Go with the flow. Don't get irritated. Remember, the fun is everywhere, so you don't really have to go anywhere. Parking along a parade route is not allowed 2 hours before and 2 hours after the parade. In addition, although you'll see people leaving their cars on "neutral ground" (the median strip), it's illegal to park there, and chances are good that you'll be towed. Traffic in New Orleans is never worse than in the hour after a parade.

SAFETY   Many, many cops are out, making the walk from uptown to downtown safer than at other times of year, but, not surprisingly, the streets of New Orleans are a haven for pickpockets during Mardi Gras. Take precautions.

HOW TO SPEND THE BIG DAY

It seems there are as many ways to experience Mardi Gras as there are residents of New Orleans. While the national media focuses only on the Bourbon Street zoo, there are plenty of traditions and family-friendly fun that can be had elsewhere. What you come away with will depend on where you go and who you hang out with. Indeed, you need never see nudity if you plan your day correctly. Basically, there are three ways of doing it—nice, naughty, and nasty. See below for examples of each kind. Us? We prefer a mix of the first two.

Nice: Hang out exclusively Uptown, with the families. Find a spot on St. Charles Avenue, which is entirely closed for the day, and camp out with a blanket, a picnic lunch, and some kids if you can find any, and spend the day there. After **Rex,** there are countless smaller parades (with trucks acting as floats) put on by the Elks and other groups (Zulu, alas, doesn't go through Uptown). Dressed-up families are all around. One side of St. Charles is for the parades and the other is open only to foot traffic, so everyone can wander about and admire the costumes, with **walking groups** and everyone just milling about on the street. You might well get asked to join in a group BBQ or balcony party. New Orleans kids assure us that Mardi Gras is more fun than Halloween, and we can see why.

Naughty: In the morning, around the start of Zulu, head to Jackson Avenue or Claiborne Avenue and the neighborhoods around those main thoroughfares, and look for the **Mardi Gras Indians.** It's a hit-or-miss proposition; the Indians themselves never know when they are going to start, and where they are going to be, but running across them on their own turf is one of the great sights and experiences of Mardi Gras. Play it cool, however—this is not your neighborhood. And *do not bring your camera;* this is not an attraction put on for your benefit and the Indians do not like being treated like a sideshow carnival act. By early to midafternoon, they will gather at Indian Ground Zero, on Claiborne under the freeway, where a festival of sorts takes place.

At noon, try to be around the corner of Burgundy and St. Ann, for the **Bourbon Street** awards. You may not get close enough to actually see the judging, but the participants are all around you so you can gawk up close and personal at their sometimes "R" and "X"-rated costumes. As you wander the Quarter, keep an eye out for the **Krewe of Kosmic Debris** and the **Society of St. Anne,** marvelously costumed revelers. After the awards (about midafternoon), head over to the Frenchmen section where everyone is in costume, dancing in the street to tribal drums, drinking, and generally celebrating Carnival as it should be, often well into the night.

Nasty: Stay strictly on **Bourbon Street.** Yep, it's every bit as crowded, vulgar, and obscene as you've heard. The street is full of drunks (and the occasional bewildered soul), few (if any) in costume, with balconies full of more drunks, dangling expensive beads (some with X-rated anatomical features on them), which they will hand over in exchange for a glimpse of flesh. Sometimes, they show flesh themselves. (And they are never the people who ought to be exposing themselves.) This is the "anything goes" attitude of Carnival taken to an unimaginative extreme, and while it might be worth getting a quick peep at, it grows boring more quickly than you might think. The city has tried to keep that sort of thing confined just to Bourbon, and efforts seem to have paid off. Astonishingly, a mere one street over is like another world. Dauphine, above, is largely empty, while Royal, below, is full of naughty, not nasty, Mardi Gras participants.

PARADE WATCH

A Mardi Gras parade works a spell on people. There's no other way to explain why thousands of otherwise rational men and women scream, plead, and sometimes expose themselves for no more reward than a plastic bead necklace, a plastic cup, or a little aluminum medallion. Today's parades have become bloated affairs: Natives seem to be unimpressed with a parade of fewer than 20 major floats—and if your parade has 20 floats, it'll need many high school marching bands, the Shriners and their ilk, and a few thousand other participants just to balance it out. Krewe members and guests drop tons of trinkets off their floats in the course of a parade, leaving a trail of trash that is truly astounding. Trees on parade routes have beads hanging in their branches all year long.

In your zeal to catch beads, don't forget to actually look at the parades. Considerable effort goes into these floats, but increasingly, bead-lust blinded parade goers pay

Catch Them If You Can: Tips on Getting the Best Throws

So float-riders throw beads. "So what?" you think. That's because you've never been in the middle of a Mardi Gras mob before. Trust us, you're going to go crazy for beads, plastic cups, aluminum coins, and other "throws."

First, you stand there passively. All around you, the strands fly thick and fast. You catch a few. Hmm, you think, they look kind of good around my neck. Timidly you hold up one hand. You catch a few more. Then you notice the guy next to you/cute college girl in front of you/kid on ladder behind you is getting a lot of beads. A lot more than you. You reach more aggressively for the strands as they fly overhead. Wait, that guy/cute girl/kid got a really good strand! And another! I want one like that! How come I'm not getting any like that!

Now you find yourself shrieking, "Throw me something, Mister!" with everyone. You jump. You wail. You plead. You knock over a kid. You are completely consumed by bead lust. You think, "This is stupid. It's a 5¢ piece of plastic—oh, look, a really glittery strand! I want it I want it I want! Please, *mistah!!!*"

And that's not even discussing Zulu coconuts.

Now, if there's a trick to bead catching, we are darned if we know it. One sure-fire way is to be a small child or a cute college girl (or even better, a cute college girl sitting on a tall person's shoulders). If you are none of these, you must plead and beg and whine like everybody else. Local pros stand on ladders, which put them almost at eye level with float riders. Others bring umbrellas or nets, challenging float riders to hone their aim. Direct eye contact with a float rider also works. Sob stories invoking real and fictional ailments and family members can't hurt—if you can make yourself heard above the din of everyone else's tale of woe and deservedness.

We don't condone the popular pastime of flashing body parts in exchange for beads. Neither does the city of New Orleans, which, in an effort to reclaim Mardi Gras from the party hearty types, has sternly asked float riders not to throw to exhibitionists. This tactic hasn't entirely worked, but the hopes are that this sort of thing will largely be confined to Bourbon Street.

But if you really want to score, try positioning yourself at the end of a parade route, particularly for one of the generous super krewes, like Orpheus. Throws are of no use to float riders once the parade is over, and toward the end of the ride, they often shovel out their excess inventory in great amounts (even heaving whole packages of beads overboard). By accidentally ending up at the very last block of Zulu, we scored no less than two of the highly prized Zulu coconuts, and a man near us got three.

Note: When beads land on the ground, put your foot over them to claim them, because if you reach for them with your hands you might well get your fingers broken by someone else stepping on them. If you get lucky and are tossed a whole package of beads, don't be greedy—share with your neighbors, who might well trade you a nifty strand in exchange.

little attention. Too bad; they are missing some amazing creations, and when the nighttime ones are lit by flambeaux, you are suddenly flung back to a time when

Mardi Gras meant mystery and magic. Floats aren't drawn by mules anymore (tractors instead), but the Rex floats come on the same antique wagons the Krewe has been using since the 19th century.

There are two environments for viewing each parade. You can choose to stay downtown in the thick of the action, or you can walk out into the neighborhood the parade will traverse (see the map of major parade routes in this chapter). There are still crowds Uptown and in Mid City, but they're not as large or rowdy as those farther downtown—and they're much more family oriented. In fact, a good portion of the crowd lined up for a parade on St. Charles Avenue and Canal Street will be local children and families.

Generally, the best place to watch parades on St. Charles Avenue is between Napoleon and Jackson avenues, where the crowds are somewhat smaller and consist mostly of local families and college students. Frankly, we wouldn't attend a Mardi Gras parade (if we can help it) without children—their delight increases your enjoyment considerably. Don't forget to bring a bag to hold any throws you catch, and consider bringing moist towelettes (your hands get dirty), drinks, a blanket or chair to sit on, and a picnic.

These are just a few of the major parades of the last days of carnival (times and dates are subject to change):

- **Iris** (founded 1917): This women's krewe follows traditional carnival rules of costume and behavior. It parades on the Saturday afternoon before Mardi Gras along Napoleon Avenue to St. Charles Avenue to Canal Street and then along Convention Center Boulevard.

- **Endymion** (founded 1967): This became one of the early "super krewes" in the 1970s by featuring a glut of floats and a celebrity guest, like Doc Severinsen, Alice Cooper, Charo, Tom Jones, Dolly Parton, John Goodman, or Chuck Norris. In 1997, the parade had 28 floats. It runs Saturday evening down Canal Street to St. Charles Avenue, then on to Howard and Girod streets and into the Superdome for a big party.

- **Bacchus** (founded 1968): The original "super krewe," Bacchus was the first to host international celebrities. It traditionally runs the Sunday before Mardi Gras, from Napoleon Avenue to St. Charles Avenue to Canal Street, then along Tchoupitoulas Street and into the Convention Center.

- **Orpheus** (founded 1994): One of the youngest krewes, it was founded by a group that includes Harry Connick Jr. and tries to adhere to classic Krewe traditions. It is popular for its many amazing floats, and for the generosity of its throws. The parade is on the evening of Lundi Gras and follows the same route as Bacchus.

- **Zulu** (founded 1916): Zulu is the liveliest parade, with float riders decked out in woolly wigs and blackface. They carry the most prized of Mardi Gras souvenirs: gold-and-black painted coconuts. The parade runs on Mardi Gras morning from Claiborne Avenue to Jackson Avenue to St. Charles Avenue to Canal Street, and then along Galvez and Orleans streets to Armstrong Park.

- **Rex** (founded 1872): Rex, the original Mardi Gras parade, follows Zulu down St. Charles. It features the King of Carnival and some of the classic floats of New Orleans' Carnival. Various independent walking clubs often precede the parade along its route.

FLOAT LIKE A BUTTERFLY: MEMOIRS OF MARDI GRAS 1999

Sure, it's fun to watch a Mardi Gras parade, but we all yearn to actually be in one, to ride one of those glorious floats in a fabulous, shiny costume, wearing a mask, tossing

Major Mardi Gras Parade Routes

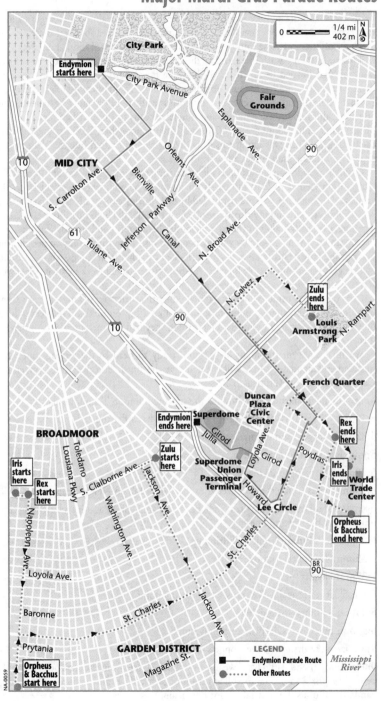

1/4 mi
402 m

City Park

Endymion starts here

City Park Avenue

Fair Grounds

Esplanade Ave.

90

MID CITY

Orleans Ave.

Bienville

S. Carrolton Ave.

Jefferson Parkway

Canal

N. Broad Ave.

Tulane Ave.

61

90

N. Galvez

Zulu ends here

Louis Armstrong Park

N. Rampart

French Quarter

BROADMOOR

Endymion ends here

Superdome

Girod
Julia

Duncan Plaza Civic Center

Rex ends here

Toledano
Lousiana Pkwy

S. Claiborne Ave.

Zulu starts here

Jackson Ave.

Superdome Union Passenger Terminal

Loyola Ave.

Girod

Poydras

Iris ends here

World Trade Center

Iris starts here

Rex starts here

Washington Ave.

Howard

Lee Circle

Napoleon Ave.

Loyola Ave.

St. Charles

Orpheus & Bacchus end here

BR 90

Baronne

St. Charles

Jackson Ave.

Prytania

GARDEN DISTRICT

Orpheus & Bacchus start here

Magazine St.

Mississippi River

LEGEND
■——— Endymion Parade Route
●····· Other Routes

NA-0059

19

beads to an adoring public. Even lifelong New Orleanians almost never get to have that experience, as only a few Krewes invite outsiders to ride. So when the Krewe of Orpheus offered to let me join their 1999 Mardi Gras parade, I didn't hesitate.

This year's theme was "Premieres of the French Opera," an homage to the beloved building that burned down in the 1920s. The floats were designed by master float designer Henri Schindler. I would be riding on "Le Cid" (an opera by Jules Massenet). I had to send in measurements for my costume (float riders must be masked and costumed throughout the parade), and purchase beads to throw. Many, many beads. How many? "Oh, about 50 or 60 gross." That's more than 7,000 strands! I said, calculating that this was going to set me back several hundred bucks. "Yeah, you're right—you might want to get a few more."

Orpheus parades on Lundi Gras night, starting at 6pm. I show up at 10am at the Convention Center to load my beads on the float. Several other float riders do the same, and before long, we are surrounded by little fortresses of beads and other throws. My neighbors, noticing my thrifty (read: cheap) beads (the better quality beads cost a lot more, especially 7,000 of them), graciously share a few good strands with me, so I may bestow them on especially worthy people. I resolve to throw only to people who don't have many beads, who've been overlooked by other float riders, who aren't cute college girls—in short, people like me. (I'd been frustrated all week by float riders who seemed to find me invisible.)

I try on my costume, which is vaguely knightlike (that is, if knights wore shiny metallic fabric and orange polyester). I look like a big pumpkin. The sleeves hang down four inches past my fingers. Good thing they had my measurements—imagine if they didn't!

We finally get on the floats at 3:30pm, ready to head to the parade route. My husband, in mandatory tux, will meet me at the finish line near the Convention Center, home of the Orpheus Ball.

4pm: The floats start to move toward the starting point on Tchoupitoulas.

4:30pm: Our float stops. The float in front of us has a flat tire.

4:31pm: Everyone around me starts drinking.

5pm: Float starts to move again.

5:20pm: Float stops moving.

5:45pm: Pizzas (dinner) are delivered to the float. Only in New Orleans.

6pm: Parade starts. It doesn't really affect us. We are float 24 and it's a long long time until we hit the starting line.

6:05pm to 7:35pm: People still drinking.

7:35pm: Float starts to move again.

7:37pm: Float stops.

8pm: Float starts again. We can see the starting point.

8:05pm: So much for moving.

8:30pm: Everyone is deeply, crushingly bored.

9pm: Even the drinkers have stopped drinking.

9:05pm: My friend Ann says, "We are only about 30 feet from the start now. It should be really soon." I say, "There's still at least four or five floats and a couple of marching bands ahead of us. I'm not falling for that again."

9:17pm: I think of my husband at the ball, and wonder if I will ever see him again.

9:30pm: Here we go! And it's mayhem. Thousands of people, waving hands, screaming, shrieking, pleading, crying, "Please, Mister, throw me something, throw me something, Mister!" I start to grin and don't stop for hours. I throw beads, feeling, at last, like a queen tossing largesse to the populace. I am sparing in my generosity, however, minding advice not to go overboard too early, lest I run out of beads. I discover my aim isn't bad, and from my upper-level vantage point, I can throw quite far out, to specific people in the back. I also learn that from atop the float, you can see everybody, no matter how small, so if it seems like float riders are ignoring you, it's because they are.

9:35pm: One heavily endowed young woman flashes me, and looks expectant, but I say, "Put those away!"

10pm: As we turn on to St. Charles, I hear someone shout my name. It's my cousin's son, a Tulane Med student, whom I've never actually met before. Of course, since I'm masked and costumed, he still doesn't know what I look like.

10:15pm: Orpheus is known for its generosity, so by now, every parade-goer's neck is already thickly covered in beads. There is no bead-challenged person to throw to. Worse, because so many floats have already gone by, everyone only wants the really good beads, not the utilitarian stuff I'm throwing. Oh, dear.

10:45pm: I notice how Ann is really good at taunting the crowd with the good beads. She holds out long, thick strands, shows them off, whips the crowd into a frenzy, then shakes her head sadly and puts them away, to await more worthy types.

11pm: The crowd impatience is high whenever the float comes to a halt—that's when riders supposedly throw the really good stuff. The crowd threatens to turn ugly when I don't. The occasional good strand given by a sympathetic corider means I can then appease the angry mob. Lacking a worthy target, I choose to turn my back and throw blindly. Meanwhile, my neat fortress of beads is now in a shambles, and I slip and slide on loose strands, frantically trying to get some to throw before revelers scale the float to rip them from me.

11:04pm: I never want to see another bead as long as I live.

11:05pm: Oh, goody, only about halfway there!

11:06pm to 12:35am: Pleasemisterthrowmesomethingpleasemisterpleasemister c'monmisterhey misterpleasemisterpleasemisterpleasepleasepleasemister!

12:40am: I make a horrifying discovery. With less than one third of the parade to go, I still have several thousand beads left. These are worthless once the parade is over (particularly my crappy cheap beads) and so as we hit Canal Street, I start to heave them at a great rate, by the dozen, and sometimes entire packages of several dozen. Suddenly, I am *very* popular. Especially fun is throwing the packages into knots of frat boys and watching them pummel each other for it.

1:30am: We arrive at the Convention Center. Although these people have been watching floats arrive for at least 3 hours, they are still surprisingly fresh and enthusiastic. This howling mob of gowned women and tuxedoed men stands on chairs and tables and shrieks for beads. Among them is my husband, who catches the camera I toss him, so he can take a picture of my dirty, bedraggled self.

1:35pm: I descend from the float and proceed to the party. "How was it?" my husband's new friends (he's been sitting there a long time) inquire. "Ask me tomorrow," I say.

CAJUN MARDI GRAS

Mardi Gras in New Orleans sounds like too much for you, no matter how low-key you keep it? Consider driving out to Cajun country, where Mardi Gras traditions are just as strong but considerably more, er, wholesome. Lafayette, the capital of French Acadiana, celebrates carnival in a different manner, one that reflects the Cajun heritage and spirit. (For the full story, see chapter 12.) Three full days of activities lead up to Cajun Mardi Gras, making it second in size only to New Orleans' celebration. There's one *big* difference, though: The Cajuns open their final pageant and ball to the general public. Don your formal wear and join right in!

Instead of Rex and his queen, the Lafayette festivities are ruled by King Gabriel and Queen Evangeline. They are the fictional hero and heroine of Henry Wadsworth Longfellow's epic poem "Evangeline," which was based on real-life lovers who were separated during the British expulsion of Acadians from Nova Scotia, around the time of the French and Indian War. Their story is still very much alive here, among the descendants of those who shared their wanderings.

Things get off to a joyous start with the Children's Krewe and Krewe of Bonaparte parades and ball, held on the Saturday before Mardi Gras, following a full day of celebration at Acadian Village. On Monday night, Queen Evangeline is honored at the Queen's Parade. The King's Parade, held the following morning, honors King Gabriel and opens a full day of merriment. Lafayette's African American community stages the Parade of King Toussaint L'Ouverture and Queen Suzanne Simonne at about noon, just after the King's Parade. Then the Krewe of Lafayette invites everyone to get into the act as its parade winds through the streets. Krewe participants trot along on foot or ride in the vehicle of their choice—some very imaginative modes of transportation turn up every year. The Mardi Gras climax, a formal ball presided over by the king and queen and their royal court, takes place that night. Everything stops promptly at midnight, as Cajuns and visitors alike depart to begin their observance of Lent.

In the Cajun countryside that surrounds Lafayette, there's yet another form of Mardi Gras celebration, one tied to the rural lifestyle. Cajuns firmly believe in sharing, so you're welcome to come along. The celebration goes like this: Bands of masked men dressed in raggedy patchwork costumes (unlike the New Orleans costumes, which are heavy on glitter and shine) and peaked hats known as *capichons* set off on Mardi Gras morning on horseback, led by their *capitaine*. They ride from farm to farm, asking at each, "*Voulez-vous reçevoir le Mardi Gras?*" ("Will you receive the Mardi Gras?") and dismounting as the invariable "Oui" comes in reply. Each farmyard then becomes a miniature festival as the revelers *faire le macaque* ("make monkeyshines") with song and dance, much drinking of beer, and other antics loosely labeled "entertainment." As payment for their show, they demand, and get, "a fat little chicken to make a big gumbo" (or sometimes a bag of rice or other ingredients).

When each band has visited its allotted farmyards, they all head back to town, where everyone else has already begun the general festivities. There'll be dancing in the streets, rowdy card games, storytelling, and the like until the wee hours, and you can be sure that all those fat little chickens go into the "gumbo gros" pot to make a very big gumbo indeed.

You can write or call ahead for particulars on both the urban and the rural Mardi Gras celebrations. For the latter, the towns of Eunice and Mamou stage some of the most enjoyable celebrations. Contact the **Lafayette Parish Convention and Visitors Commission,** P.O. Box 52066, Lafayette, LA 70505 (☎ **800/346-1958** in the U.S., 800/543-5340 in Canada, or 318/232-3808).

2 The New Orleans Jazz & Heritage Festival

What began in 1969 as a small gathering in a public park to celebrate the music of New Orleans now ranks as one of the best-attended, most-respected, and musically comprehensive festivals in the world. Although people call it "Jazz Fest," the full name is the New Orleans Jazz and Heritage Festival, and the heritage is about as broad as it can get. Stand in the right place and, depending on which way the wind's blowing, you can catch as many as 10 musical styles from several continents, smell the tantalizing aromas of a dozen or so different food offerings, and meet a U.N.-like spectrum of fellow fest-goers all at once.

While such headliners as Van Morrison, Bob Dylan, and Jimmy Buffett have drawn record-setting crowds in recent years, serious Jazz Fest aficionados savor the lesser-known acts. They range from Mardi Gras Indians to old-time bluesmen who have never played outside the Delta, from Dixieland to avant-garde, from African artists making rare U.S. appearances to the top names in Cajun, zydeco, and, of course, jazz.

Gone are the days when the event was held in Congo Square and only a few hundred people came. Now filling the infield of the Fair Grounds horse racing track up near City Park, the festival (which covers the last weekend in April and the first in May) is set up about as well as such an event can be. When the crowds get big, though—the second Saturday traditionally is the busiest—it can be tough to move around, especially if the grounds are muddy from rain. And the lines at the most popular of the several dozen food booths can be frustratingly long. However, the crowds are remarkably well behaved—to make a sweeping generalization, these are not the same types who come for Mardi Gras. Tellingly, there are few, if any, arrests during Jazz Fest.

Attending Jazz Fest means making a few decisions. Hotel and restaurant reservations, not to mention choice plane flights, fill up months (if not a year) in advance, but the schedule is not announced until a couple of months before the event. That may mean scheduling your visit around your own availability, not an appearance by a particular band. Just about every day at Jazz Fest is a good day, so this is not a hardship—at least, until you learn about an extraordinary group that is playing on a day you won't be in town. Or you could do like we do: Go for the whole 10 days, so you won't miss a thing.

The second Saturday does attract some of the top acts, and each year it sets a record for single-day attendance. But we feel the fun tends to diminish with that many people. Still, the tickets are cheap enough that going early in the day and leaving before the crowds get too big is a viable option. The Thursday before the second weekend is traditionally targeted to locals, with more local bands and generally smaller crowds, because fewer tourists are around than on the weekends. It's a great time to hit the best food booths and to check out the shopping in the crafts areas. Fans of the Neville Brothers, New Orleans' favorite sons, will be pleased to know they are the traditional closing act on Sunday, with brother Aaron Neville usually making a popular appearance in the gospel tent earlier in the day.

Whenever you decide to go, contact the **New Orleans Jazz and Heritage Festival,** 1205 N. Rampart St., New Orleans, LA 70116 (☎ **504/522-4786;** www. nojazzfest.com), to get the schedule for each weekend and information about other Jazz Fest–related shows around town.

JAZZ FEST POINTERS

Of course, going to Jazz Fest means marathon endurance. With so many stages and musical choices, your mind can almost freeze. You can plot out your day or just wander from stage to stage, catching a few songs by just about everyone. There is something to be said for the latter approach; some of the best Jazz Fest experiences come from discovering a hitherto unknown (at least to you) band, or otherwise stumbling across a gem of a musical moment. Or you can camp out at just one stage—from the big ones, which feature famous headliners, to the gospel tent, where magical moments seem to happen several times a day.

Regardless, a typical Jazz Fest day has you arriving sometime after the gates open at 11am and staying until you are pooped or when they close at around 7pm (incredibly, despite the many acts on many stages, the whole thing runs as efficiently as a Swiss train). Go back to where you are staying, get some dinner, and then hit the clubs. All night long, every club in the city has Jazz Fest–related bookings. (The increasingly popular LMNOP music industry conference, which runs concurrent with part of Jazz Fest, showcases local acts.) Bouncing from one to another can keep you out until nearly dawn. Then you get up and start all over again. This is part of the reason we think Jazz Fest is so darn fun.

There are many nonmusical aspects of Jazz Fest to distract you, particularly the crafts and the food. Local craftspeople and imported artisans fill a sizable section of the Fair Grounds with displays of their products during the festival. What's more, many of them offer demonstrations. You might get to see Louisiana Native American basket making; Cajun accordion, fiddle, and triangle making; decoy carving; boat building; and Mardi Gras Indian beading and costume making. Contemporary arts and crafts, like jewelry, furniture, hand-blown glass, and painting, are also featured. In addition, you'll find an open marketplace at Congo Square filled with contemporary and traditional African (and African-influenced) crafts and performing artists.

And then there's the food. The heck with the music—when we dream of Jazz Fest, we are often thinking more about those 50-plus food booths, filled with some of the best goodies we've ever tasted. We have friends who, at the end of every Jazz Fest, buy tickets for the very popular soft shell crab po' boy stand *for next year* so they won't suffer even a moment's delay in getting their mouths wrapped around one of the best sandwiches they've ever tasted.

The food ranges from local standbys—red beans and rice, jambalaya, étouffée, gumbo—to more interesting choices such as oyster sacks, the hugely popular sausage bread, *cochon de lait* (a mouth-watering roast pig sandwich), alligator sausage po' boys, and quail and pheasant gumbo. There's crawfish every way, including crawfish sushi, crawfish beignets, and the divine crawfish Monica (no, it has nothing to do with Ms. Lewinsky). And that's not even discussing the various Caribbean, African, Spanish, and even vegetarian dishes. And how about dessert? Lemon crêpes, Italian ice cream, key lime tarts, chocolate snowballs with condensed milk on them—oh, my! There's

Note: At any Jazz Fest, any number of *Simpsons* creators and artists will be on hand, enjoying themselves thoroughly.

More Fun on the Bayou

A possible alternative to Jazz Fest, especially for those who feel its size now outweighs the amount of fun it generates, is the **Festival International de Louisiane.** The 6-day celebration of the music and art of Southern Louisiana and its French-speaking cousins around the world is held on the blocked-off streets of Lafayette. It usually runs through the last weekend in April. Between the considerably smaller crowds and the even smaller price (it's free!), it makes for a nice change of pace from Jazz Fest, with which it overlaps.

Festival International doesn't have the budget of the big deal in New Orleans, so it has smaller offerings, but it always manages to come up with a fairly impressive lineup. For more information, call or write the Festival International de Louisiane, 735 Jefferson St., Lafayette, LA 70501 (☎ **318/232-8086;** e-mail: fil@net-connect.net).

plenty of cold beer available, too, although you'll probably have to wait on some mighty long lines to get to it.

Try to purchase tickets as early as February if possible. They're available by mail through **Ticketmaster** (☎ **504/522-5555**). To order tickets by phone, or to get ticket information, call **the Heritage Festival** (☎ **800/488-5252** outside Louisiana, or 504/522-5555; fax 504/379-3291). Admission for adults is $12 in advance and $16 at the gate; for children, $1.50 in advance and $2 at the gate. Evening events and concerts (order tickets in advance for these events as well) may be attended at an additional cost—usually between $20 and $30, depending on the concert.

JAZZ FEST PARKING & TRANSPORTATION   Parking at the Fair Grounds is next to impossible. The few available spaces cost $10 a day; however, it's rare to get a space there. We strongly recommend that you take public transportation or one of the available shuttles.

The **Regional Transit Authority** operates bus routes from various pickup points to the Fair Grounds. For schedules and information, call ☎ **504/248-3900.** Taxis, though probably scarce, will also take you to the Fair Grounds at a special event rate of $3 per person (or the meter reading if it's higher). We recommend **United Cabs** (☎ 504/524-9606). The New Orleans Jazz and Heritage Festival provides information about shuttle transportation, which is not included in the ticket price.

PACKAGE DEALS   If you want to go to Jazz Fest but would rather someone else did all the planning, consider contacting **Festival Tours International,** 15237 Sunset Blvd., Suite 17, Pacific Palisades, CA 90272 (☎ **310/454-4080;** e-mail: Fest tours@aol.com). It's the brainchild of Nancy Covey, who has superb music connections by virtue of years spent booking concerts at the famed McCabe's Guitar Shop in Santa Monica, plus her marriage to English singer-songwriter Richard Thompson. Festival Tours is the place for music lovers who don't wish to wear name tags or do other hokey tour activities. Covey's packages include not just accommodations and tickets for Jazz Fest, but also a visit to Cajun country for unique personal encounters with some of the finest local musicians. Past trips have included a visit with D. L. Menard, a shrimp boat concert by Beausoleil's Michael Doucet, and a crawfish boil at Marc and Ann Savoy's house.

If you're flying to New Orleans specifically for the Jazz and Heritage Festival, consider calling **Continental Airlines** (☎ **800/525-0280** or 504/581-2965). It's the official airline of Jazz Fest, and offers special fares during the event. You'll need the Jazz Fest promotional code, available from the festival's information line.

3 Other Top Festivals

SPRING FIESTA

The annual 5-day Spring Fiesta has been going on since 1935 and is a good opportunity to see the inside of some lovely old homes that are ordinarily closed to the public. Hostesses in antebellum dress escort you through the premises and provide all sorts of information and anecdotes. In the French Quarter, there are balcony concerts by sopranos rendering numbers sung there in the past by Jenny Lind and Adelina Patti. Out on River Road, there are plantation home tours. One highlight is the gala "Night in Old New Orleans" parade, which features carriages bearing passengers dressed as prominent figures in the city's history, as well as some of the best marching bands in town.

Spring Fiesta usually takes place over a full week in April. For full details, reservations, and a schedule of admission fees for some of the homes (around $15 for city tours, $45 for country estate tours), write to the **Spring Fiesta Association,** 826 St. Ann St., New Orleans, LA 70116 (☎ **504/581-1367**). You can order tickets by mail, or purchase them at the French Market Gift Shop, 824 Decatur St., and at Gray Line Tour Desks. For a list of locations, contact the Spring Fiesta Association.

TENNESSEE WILLIAMS FESTIVAL

In late March or early April, New Orleans honors one of its most illustrious writers. Although he was not born here, Tennessee Williams once said, "If I can be considered to have a home, it would have to be New Orleans . . . which has provided me with more material than any other city."

During the 3-day Tennessee Williams/New Orleans Literary Festival, many of his plays are performed, and there are symposiums and panel discussions on his work, as well as walking tours of his favorite French Quarter haunts. Other New Orleans–associated authors are celebrated as well (in fact, Williams has been somewhat deemphasized in recent years.)

For dates and details, contact festival organizers at 5500 Prytania St., Suite 217, New Orleans, LA 70115 (☎ **504/581-1144;** e-mail: twfest@gnofn.org).

FRENCH QUARTER FESTIVAL

The 3-day French Quarter Festival in early April is a celebration of the ingredients of French Quarter life. There are scores of free outdoor concerts, patio tours, a parade, a battle of jazz bands, art shows, children's activities, and talent and bartender competitions. As if that weren't enough, Jackson Square is transformed into the world's largest jazz brunch, with about 40 leading restaurants serving Cajun and Creole specialties such as jambalaya, gumbo, and crawfish fettuccine. Jazz aficionados are finding this festival somewhat more to their liking than Jazz Fest—despite the names, the Quarter Festival emphasizes that kind of music more.

For exact dates and other information, write to **French Quarter Festivals,** 100 Conti St., New Orleans, LA 70130 (☎ **504/522-5730**).

CREOLE CHRISTMAS

Leave it to New Orleans! A few days simply are not enough for this lively city to celebrate Christmas, so the entire month of December is designated "Creole Christmas." All sorts of gala events are sprinkled throughout the calendar, including tours of 19th-century homes decorated for the holidays, candlelight caroling in Jackson Square, cooking demonstrations, a madrigal dinner, gingerbread house demonstrations, and special Reveillon menus at select French Quarter restaurants

---

Without the Food, It's Not a Party

Just about every New Orleans celebration, from Jazz Fest to Mardi Gras and everything in between, includes food in one way or another. At a few annual events, the primary focus is local cuisine.

The **Great French Market Tomato Festival** is a daylong June event celebrating the diversity of the tomato. The **Gumbo Festival,** held in Bridge City each October, showcases that favorite New Orleans dish. In Breaux Bridge, the **Louisiana Crawfish Festival** takes place each May; if you love crawfish, this event is not to be missed. Other festivals to look out for, especially if you're a fan of international cuisine, are the **Greek Festival** in May; the **Reggae Riddums Festival,** featuring African and Caribbean cuisine, in June; and the **Carnaval Latino,** also in June.

See the "New Orleans Calendar of Events" in chapter 3 for exact dates and other details on these events.

(including Arnaud's, Begue's, the Rib Room, and Alex Patouts). Hotels offer special "Papa No'l" rates from December 5 through December 25.

For full details, contact **French Quarter Festivals,** 100 Conti St., New Orleans, LA 70130 (☎ **504/522-5730**).

FESTIVALS ACADIENS

This is a Cajun Country celebration—or rather, six celebrations—held during the third week of September in Lafayette. The festivals, lumped together under the heading "Festivals Acadiens," pay tribute to the culture and heritage of Cajun families, who have been here since the British expelled them from their Nova Scotia homes nearly 250 years ago. The festive week includes the Bayou Food Festival, the Festival de Musique Acadienne, the Louisiana Native Crafts Festival, the Acadiana Fair and Trade Show, the RSVP Senior Fair and Craft Show, and Downtown Alive.

At the **Bayou Food Festival,** you'll be able to taste the cuisine of more than 30 top Cajun restaurants. Specialties such as stuffed crabs, crawfish étouffée, oysters Bienville, shrimp Creole, oysters Rockefeller, shrimp de la Teche, catfish en brochette, jambalaya, chicken-and-sausage gumbo, smothered quail, and hot boudin are everyday eating for Cajuns, and this is a rare opportunity to try them all. The Bayou Food Festival is held in Girard Park, adjacent to the music festival. Admission is free.

The **Festival de Musique Acadienne** began in 1974 when some Cajun musicians were engaged to play briefly for visiting French newspaper editors. It was a rainy night, but some 12,000 Cajun residents showed up to listen. The walls rang for 3 solid hours with old French songs, waltzes, two-steps, Cajun rock rhythms, zydeco, and the special music some have dubbed "Cajun country." It has become an annual affair, with more than 50,000 visitors usually on hand. Because of the crowds, the festival is now held outdoors in Girard Park, where fans can listen in grassy comfort. Performed almost entirely in French, the music covers both traditional and modern Cajun styles, including zydeco. The music starts early and ends late, and there's no charge to come to the park and listen. Proceeds from sales of food and beverages go to fund public service projects of the Lafayette Jaycees.

You'll see native Louisiana artisans demonstrating their skills at the **Louisiana Native Crafts Festival.** All crafts presented must have been practiced before or during the early 1900s, and all materials used must be native to Louisiana. Meeting these criteria are such arts as woodcarving (with an emphasis, it seems, on duck decoys), soap-making, pirogue-making (pronounced *pee*-rogue, it's a Cajun canoe, one variety of which is made from a dug-out cypress log), chair-caning, doll-making, palmetto-weaving, Native American–style basket weaving, quilting, spinning, dyeing, pottery-making, jewelry-making, and alligator-skinning.

The **Acadiana Fair and Trade Show** is put on by Lafayette merchants and businesspeople, and there's an indoor display of their goods and services, plus an outdoor carnival with rides, a midway, and games. It's sponsored by the Lafayette Jaycees, and free shuttle bus service for the public from one festival to another is provided by the city.

Older artisans—who passed along their crafts to the younger Cajuns you see at the Native Crafts Festival—have their day in the sun at the **RSVP Senior Fair and Craft Show** (RSVP stands for Retired Senior Volunteer Program). They're all over 60, and it's a rare treat to meet them, see their homemade articles, and listen to them talk of the old days.

Downtown Alive (☎ **318/291-5566**) features a free band playing outside on the streets of downtown Lafayette every Friday from April through June and September through November. The show starts at 5:30pm and usually runs until 8pm. Proceeds from the refreshments benefit Downtown Lafayette Unlimited, a nonprofit organization that works to help develop the downtown and promote Cajun music.

You can visit the **Acadian Village** any time of the year, but special events are often scheduled during Festivals Acadiens. If you have any interest in Acadiana's history, you'll find this little village an interesting trip back in time. Homes and buildings are not models or reconstructions—they're all original Acadian homes that have been restored and moved to the village to create (or, as the Cajuns say, "reassemble") a typical 1800s village. It's a tranquil, charming spot. (See chapter 12 for more information.)

For exact dates and full details on Festivals Acadiens, write or call the **Lafayette Parish Convention and Visitors Commission,** P.O. Box 52066, Lafayette, LA 70505 (☎ **800/346-1958** in the U.S., 800/543-5340 in Canada, or 318/232-3808).

THE RAYNE FROG FESTIVAL

To prove that just about anything is cause for celebration in New Orleans and its environs, let us tell you about the Rayne Frog Festival, held just a few miles west of Lafayette. The Cajuns can hold their own when it comes to inventing excuses for a party—a harvest, a new season, a special tradition, or just the job of being alive. In this case they've turned to the lowly frog as an excuse for *a fais-dodo* (dance) and a waltz contest. Mindful of the reason for it all, frog races and frog-jumping contests fill the entertainment bill—and if you arrive without your amphibian, there's a "Rent-a-Frog" service. To wind up, there's a lively frog-eating contest.

The Rayne Frog Festival is held in September. For dates and full details, contact **Lafayette Parish Convention and Visitors Commission,** P.O. Box 52066, Lafayette, LA 70505 (☎ **800/346-1958** in the U.S., 800/543-5340 in Canada, or 318/232-3808).

Planning a Trip to New Orleans 3

With the possible exception of July and August (unless you thrive on heat and humidity), just about any time is the right time to go to New Orleans. Mardi Gras is, of course, the time of year when it's hardest to get a hotel room, but it can also be difficult during the various music festivals throughout the year, especially the Jazz and Heritage Festival (see chapter 2). It's important to know what's going on when; the city's landscape can change dramatically depending on what festival or convention is happening, and prices can also reflect that.

Whatever your idea of the ideal New Orleans trip, this chapter will give you the information to make informed plans, and will point you toward some additional resources.

International travelers should also consult chapter 4, "For Foreign Visitors," for information on entry requirements, getting to the United States, and more.

1 Visitor Information & Money

VISITOR INFORMATION

Even a seasoned traveler should consider writing or calling ahead to the **New Orleans Metropolitan Convention and Visitors Bureau,** 1520 Sugar Bowl Dr., New Orleans, LA 70112 (☎ **800/672-6124** or 504/566-5055; www.nawlins.com; e-mail: tourism@nawlins.com). The staff is extremely friendly and helpful, and you can easily get any information you can't find in this book from them.

Another source of information is **the Greater New Orleans Black Tourism Network,** Louisiana Superdome, 1520 Sugar Bowl Dr. 70112 (☎ **504/523-5652**); you may be particularly interested in their self-directed tours of African American landmarks.

SITE SEEING: THE BIG EASY ON THE WEB

The following Web sites offer buckets of useful information—and, in some cases, personal opinions—on New Orleans activities, lodgings, restaurants, music, nightlife, food, culture, eccentricities, and just about anything else you can think of. Also check out Frommer's Online Directory at the back of this book.

- **www.nolalive.com** The *Times-Picayune's* site for locals. The newspaper offers good food reviews and local fest information.
- **www.loveneworleans.com** The tourist version of the above, featuring the infamous "Bourbocam": a video camera trained 24 hours a day on Bourbon Street.

What Things Cost in New Orleans	U.S. $
Taxi from airport to Central Business District or French Quarter	21.00
Bus from airport to downtown	1.50
Streetcar fare (one way)	1.00
Double at Hotel Inter-Continental (very expensive)	235.00–295.00
Double at Place d'Armes Hotel (moderate)	110.00–180.00
Double at Hotel Villa Convento (inexpensive)	89.00–125.00
Lunch for one at Port of Call (moderate)	10.00
Lunch for one at Petunia's (inexpensive)	8.50
Dinner for one at Antoine's (expensive)	50.00
Dinner for one at Mike Anderson's Seafood (moderate)	30.00
Dinner for one at Camellia Grill (inexpensive)	15.00
Bottle of beer	2.50–5.00
Coca-Cola	1.00–1.75
Cup of coffee	.50–1.50
Roll of ASA 100 color film, 36 exposures	7.50
Admission to New Orleans Museum of Art	6.00
Theater ticket at Le Petit Theater	18.00–25.00

- **www.gumbopages.com**   Expatriate Chuck Taggart has packed the Gumbo Pages with nearly everything about New Orleans music and food.
- **www.neosoft.com/~offbeat**   *Offbeat* magazine's site is probably the most comprehensive source of music listings. It's chock-full of info and in-the-know local artist information, plus a dense links page.
- **http://neworleansonline.com**   The New Orleans Tourism page links you to local calendars, and has restaurant, hotel, and entertainment searches.
- **www.neworleans.com**   A commercial site with a lot of diversity.
- **www.satchmo.com/index2.html**   The Crescent City Connection lists lots of music and local happenings.
- **www.yatcom.com/neworl/vno.html**   Run by Ed Branley, this is a good overview site with many links. It's a great source of information.
- **www.gayneworleans.com**   This site provides information on lodging, dining, arts, and nightlife, and links to other information on New Orleans gay life.
- **http://citylink.neosoft.com/citylink/mardigr**   The "official" Mardi Gras site.
- **www.nojazzfest.com**   The Jazz and Heritage Festival's official site. Goes dormant after May, and starts up again a couple months before the event.

MONEY

Prices for everything from accommodations to zydeco clubs go up precipitously during major events and festivals (see chapter 2). New Orleans is also quite popular in the fall, during what has become the convention season. The heat and humidity of the summer months (July and August) keep tourism in the city to its yearly low, so if the weather doesn't bother you, you can find some incredible bargains, especially at hotels.

You can get traveler's checks at almost any bank. **American Express** offers denominations of $10, $20, $50, $100, $500, and $1,000. You'll pay a service charge ranging from 1-4 percent. You can also get American Express traveler's checks over the phone by calling ☎ **800/221-7282;** by using this number, Amex gold and platinum card-holders are exempt from the 1% fee. AAA members can obtain checks without a fee at most AAA offices.

Visa offers traveler's checks at Citibank locations nationwide, as well as several other banks. The service charge ranges between 1.5% and 2%; checks come in denominations of $20, $50, $100, $500, and $1,000. **MasterCard** also offers traveler's checks. Call ☎ **800/223-9920** for a location near you.

Most hotels will happily cash traveler's checks for you, while many stores and restaurants are equally pleased to accept them (as are even the food booths at Jazz Fest!). You can buy traveler's checks at most major banks, or from **American Express** (☎ **800/221-7282**).

There are automated-teller machines (ATMs) throughout New Orleans, most of which are connected to national ATM networks. You might want to check with your bank before you leave home to see if it can provide a list of ATM locations that will accept your card. If your bank is connected to the **Plus** network, call ☎ **800/843-7587** for its ATM locator; for **Cirrus,** call ☎ **800/424-7787.** Some centrally located ATMs in New Orleans are at the First National Bank of Commerce, 240 Royal St.; Hibernia National Bank, 701 Poydras St.; and Whitney National Bank, 228 St. Charles Ave.

2 When to Go

THE WEATHER

The average mean temperature in New Orleans is an inviting 70°, but it can drop or rise considerably in a single day. (We've experienced 40°F and rain one day, and 80°F and humidity the next.) Conditions depend primarily on two things: whether it rains and whether there is direct sunlight or cloud cover. Rain can provide slight and temporary relief on a hot day; for the most part, it hits in sudden (and sometimes dramatically heavy) showers, which disappear as quickly as they arrived. Anytime the sun shines unimpeded, it gets much warmer. The region's high humidity can make even mild warms and colds feel intense. Still, the city's semitropical climate is part of its appeal—a slight bit of moistness makes the air come sensually alive. It will be pleasant at almost any time of year except July and August, which can be exceptionally hot and muggy. If you do come during those months, you'll quickly learn to follow the natives' example, staying out of the noonday sun and ducking from one air-conditioned building to another. Winter is very mild by American standards, but is punctuated by an occasional cold snap, when the mercury can drop below the freezing point.

In the dead of summer, T-shirts and shorts are absolutely acceptable everywhere except the finest restaurants. In the spring and fall, something a little warmer is in order; in the winter, you should plan to carry a lightweight coat or jacket. Umbrellas and cheap rain jackets are available everywhere for those tourists who inevitably get caught in a sudden, unexpected downpour.

New Orleans Average Temperatures & Rainfall

	Jan	Feb	Mar	Apr	May	June	July	Aug	Sept	Oct	Nov	Dec
High (°F)	69	65	71	79	85	90	91	90	87	79	70	64
High (°C)	21	18	22	26	29	32	33	32	30	26	21	18
Days of Rainfall	10	9	9	7	8	10	15	13	10	5	7	10

New Orleans Calendar of Events

For more information on **Mardi Gras, Jazz Fest, Festivals Acadiens,** and other major area events, see chapter 2. For general information, contact the **New Orleans Metropolitan Convention and Visitors Bureau,** 1520 Sugar Bowl Dr., New Orleans, LA 70112 (☎ **800/672-6124** or 504/566-5055; www.nawlins.com; e-mail: tourism@nawlins.com).

January

- The **USF&G Sugar Bowl Classic.** First held in 1934, this is New Orleans' oldest yearly sporting occasion. The football game is the main event, but there are also tennis, swimming, basketball, sailing, running, and flag-football competitions. Fans tend to be really loud, really boisterous, and everywhere during the festivities. For information, contact USF&G Insurance Sugar Bowl, 1500 Sugar Bowl Dr., New Orleans, LA 70112 (☎ **504/525-8573**). January 1.

March

- ✪ **Lundi Gras.** An old tradition that has been revived in the last decade or so. Celebrations take place at Spanish Plaza. It's free, it's outdoors, and it features music (including a jazz competition) and the arrival of Rex at 6pm, marking the beginning of Mardi Gras. For more information, contact New Orleans Riverwalk, 1 Poydras St., New Orleans, LA 70130 (☎ **504/522-1555**). Monday before Mardi Gras (in 2000, March 6).

- ✪ **Mardi Gras.** The culmination of the 2-month-long carnival season, Mardi Gras is the big annual blowout, a city-wide party that takes place on Fat Tuesday (the last day before Lent in the Christian calendar). The entire city stops working (sometimes days in advance!) and starts partying in the early morning, and the streets are taken over by some overwhelming parades—which, these days, go through the Central Business District instead of the French Quarter. Day before Ash Wednesday (in 2000, March 7).

- **Black Heritage Festival.** Honors the various African American cultural contributions to New Orleans. Specific events usually begin about 2 weeks after Carnival. Write or call the Black Heritage Foundation, 4535 S. Prieur St., New Orleans, LA 70125 (☎ **504/827-0112**) for more info.

- **St. Patrick's Day Parades.** There are two. One takes place in the French Quarter, beginning at Molly's at the Market (1107 Decatur St.), and the other goes through the Irish Channel neighborhood, following a route that begins at Race and Annunciation streets and ends at Jackson Street. The parades have the flavor of Mardi Gras, but tinted green, with a corned-beef-and-cabbage undertone. For information on the French Quarter parade, call **Molly's at the Market** (☎ **504/525-5169**). The Irish Channel parade will be on March 13 in 2000.

- **St. Joseph's Day Parade.** In addition to the parade, which takes place March 19, you may want to visit the altar devoted to St. Joseph at the American Italian Museum and Library, 537 South Peters St. The altar is on display March 17 to 19. For more information, call ☎ **504/522-7294.**

- ✪ **Tennessee Williams New Orleans Literary Festival.** A 5-day series celebrating New Orleans' rich literary heritage, it includes theatrical performances, readings, discussion panels, master classes, musical events, and literary walking tours dedicated to the playwright. By the way, the focus is not confined to Tennessee Williams. Events take place at venues throughout the city. For information, call or write 5500 Prytania St., Suite 217, New Orleans, LA 70115 (☎ **504/581-1144**). Late March.

○ **Spring Fiesta.** The fiesta, which begins with the crowning of the Spring Fiesta queen, is more than half a century old and takes place throughout the city—from the Garden District to the French Quarter to Uptown and beyond. Historical and architectural tours of many of the city's private homes, courtyards, and plantation homes are offered in conjunction with the 5-day event. For the schedule, call or write the Spring Fiesta Association, 826 St. Ann St., New Orleans, LA 70116 (☎ **504/581-1367**). Late March and early April.

April

○ **The French Quarter Festival.** This is a relatively new event, just over a decade old, that celebrates New Orleans' history. For hard-core jazz fans, it is rapidly becoming an alternative to Jazz Fest, where actual jazz is becoming less and less prominent. It kicks off with a parade down Bourbon Street. Among other things, you can join people dancing in the streets, learn the history of jazz, visit historic homes, and take a ride on a riverboat. Many local restaurants set up booths in Jackson Square, so the eating is exceptionally good. Events are held all over the French Quarter. For information, call or write French Quarter Festivals, 100 Conti St., New Orleans, LA 70130 (☎ **504/522-5730**). Middle of the month.

○ **The New Orleans Jazz & Heritage Festival.** A 10-day event that draws musicians, music fans, cooks, and craftspeople to celebrate music and life, Jazz Fest rivals Mardi Gras in popularity. Lodgings in the city tend to sell out up to a year ahead, so book early. Events take place at the Fair Grounds Race Track and various venues throughout the city. For information, call or write the **New Orleans Jazz and Heritage Festival,** 1205 N. Rampart St., New Orleans, LA 70116 (☎ **504/522-4786;** www.nojazzfest.com). Usually held the last weekend in April and first weekend in May.

• **The Crescent City Classic.** This 10K road race, from Jackson Square to Audubon Park, brings an international field of top runners to the city. For more information, call or write the Classic, 104 Metairie Heights Ave., Metairie, LA 70001 (☎ **504/861-8686**). Saturday before Easter (in 2000, April 22).

May

• **Greek Festival.** At the Holy Trinity Cathedral's Hellenic Cultural Center, it features Greek folk dancing, specialty foods, crafts, and music. For more information about the 3-day event, call or write Holy Trinity Cathedral, 1200 Robert E. Lee Blvd., New Orleans, LA 70122 (☎ **504/282-0259**). End of the month.

June

• **The Great French Market Tomato Festival.** A celebration of tomato diversity, this day-long event features cooking and tastings in the historic French Market. For more information, call or write the French Market, P.O. Box 51749, New Orleans, LA 70151 (☎ **504/522-2621**). First Sunday in June.

• **Reggae Riddums Festival.** This 3-day gathering of calypso, reggae, and soca (a blend of soul and calypso) musicians is held in City Park, and includes a heady helping of ethnic foods and arts and crafts. For more information, call or write Ernest Kelly, P.O. Box 6156, New Orleans, LA 70174 (☎ **888/767-1317** or 504/367-1313). Second week of the month.

July

• **Go Fourth on the River.** The annual Fourth of July celebration begins in the morning at the riverfront and continues into the night, culminating in a spectacular fireworks display. For more information, call or write Anna Pepper, 610 S. Peters St., Suite 301, New Orleans, LA 70130 (☎ **504/528-9994**).

- **New Orleans Wine and Food Experience.** Antique shops and art galleries throughout the French Quarter hold wine and food tastings, wine makers and local chefs conduct seminars, and a variety of vintner dinners and grand tastings are held for your gourmandistic pleasure. More than 150 wines and 40 restaurants are featured every day. For information, call or write Mary Reynolds, P.O. Box 70514, New Orleans, LA 70172 (☎ **504/529-9463**). End of the month.

September

- **Southern Decadence.** All over the French Quarter, thousands of folks—drag queens, mostly—follow a secret parade route, making sure to stop into many bars along the way. People travel from far and wide to be a part of the festivities. There is only an informal organization associated with the festival, and it's hard to get anyone on the phone. For information, try the Web site (www.southerndecadence.com) or contact **AmBush Magazine 2000,** 828-A Bourbon St., New Orleans, LA 70116-3137 (☎ **800/876-1484** or 504/522-8047; fax 504/522-0907). Sunday of Labor Day weekend.

- **Festivals Acadiens.** This is a series of happenings that celebrate Cajun music, food, crafts, and culture in and near Lafayette, Louisiana. (Most of the events are in Lafayette.) For more information, contact the Lafayette Parish Convention and Visitors Commission, P.O. Box 52066, Lafayette, LA 70505 (☎ **800/346-1958** in the U.S., 800/543-5340 in Canada, or 318/232-3808). Third week of the month.

- **Swamp Festival.** Sponsored by the Audubon Institute, the Swamp Festival features long days of live swamp music performances (lots of good zydeco here) as well as hands-on contact with Louisiana swamp animals. Admission to the festival is free with zoo admission. For information, call or write the Audubon Institute, 6500 Magazine St., New Orleans, LA 70118 (☎ **504/861-2537**). Last weekend in September and first weekend in October.

October

- **Art for Arts' Sake.** The arts season begins with gallery openings throughout the city. Julia, Magazine, and Royal streets are where the action is. For more information, contact the Contemporary Arts Center, 900 Camp St., New Orleans, LA 70130 (☎ **504/523-1216**). Lasts throughout the month.

- **Louisiana Jazz Awareness Month.** This is one of the highlights of October. There are nightly concerts (some of which are free), television and radio specials, and lectures, all sponsored by the Louisiana Jazz Federation. For more information and a schedule, contact the Louisiana Jazz Federation, 225 Baronne St., Suite 1712, New Orleans, LA 70112 (☎ **504/522-3154**).

- **Gumbo Festival.** This festival showcases one of the region's signature dishes and celebrates Cajun culture to boot. It's 3 days of gumbo-related events (including the presentation of the royal court of King and Miss Creole Gumbo), plus many hours of Cajun music. The festival is held in Bridge City, on the outskirts of New Orleans. For more information, contact the Gumbo Festival, P.O. Box 9069, Bridge City, LA 70096 (☎ **504/436-4712**). Second weekend in October.

- **New Orleans Film and Video Festival.** This relatively young festival (it began in 1989) is well worth checking out. Canal Place Cinemas and other theaters throughout the city screen award-winning local and international films and host writers, actors, and directors over the course of a week. Admission prices range from $3 to $12. For dates, contact the New Orleans Film and Video Society, 225 Baronne St., Suite 1712, New Orleans, LA 70112 (☎ **504/523-3818;** www.neworleansfilmfest.com; e-mail: neworleansfilmfest@wordnet.att.net). Midmonth.

❂ **Halloween.** Rivaling Mardi Gras in terms of costumes, Halloween is certainly celebrated more grandly here than in any other American city. After all, New Orleans has a way with ghosts. Events include Boo-at-the-Zoo (October 30 and 31) for children, costume parties (including a Monster Bash at the Ernest N. Morial Convention Center), haunted houses (one of the best is run by the sheriff's department in City Park), the Anne Rice Vampire Lestat Extravaganza, and the Moonlight Witches Run. You can catch the ghoulish action all over the city—many museums get in on the fun with specially designed tours—but the French Quarter, as always, is the center of the Halloween-night universe. October 31.

December

- **A New Orleans Christmas.** Holiday events include candlelight caroling in Jackson Square; old New Orleans homes are dressed up especially for the occasion. Restaurants offer specially created multicourse Reveilion dinners, and hotels throughout the city offer "Papa Noël" rates. For information, contact French Quarter Festivals, 100 Conti St., New Orleans, LA 70130 (☎ **504/ 522-5730**). All month.

- **Celebration in the Oaks.** Lights and lighted figures, designed to illustrate holiday themes, bedeck sections of City Park. This display of winter wonderment is open for driving and walking tours. Driving tours are $5 per family car or van, and walking tours are $3 per person. For information, contact Celebration in the Oaks, 1 Palm Dr., New Orleans, LA 70124 (☎ **504/483-9415**). Late November to early January.

- **New Year's Eve.** The countdown takes place in Jackson Square and is one of the country's biggest and most reliable street parties. In the South-coast equivalent of New York's Times Square, revelers watch a lighted ball drop from the top of Jackson Brewery. December 31.

3 Getting There

BY PLANE

No fewer than 13 airlines fly to New Orleans' **Moisant International Airport** (airline code **MSY,** for those of you browsing fares on the Web), among them **American** (☎ 800/433-7300; www.aa.com), **Continental** (☎ 800/525-0280 or 504/581-2965; www.flycontiental.com), **Delta** (☎ 800/221-1212; www.delta-air.com), **Northwest** (☎ 800/225-2525; www.nwa.com), **Southwest** (☎ 800/435-9792; www.iflyswa. com), **TWA** (☎ 504/529-2585; www2.twa.com), and **US Airways** (☎ 800/ 428-4322; www.usairways.com). The airport is 15 miles west of the city, in Kenner. You'll find information booths scattered around the airport and in the baggage claim area. There's also a branch of the **Travelers Aid Society** (☎ **504/464-3522**).

FLYING FOR LESS: TIPS FOR GETTING THE BEST AIRFARE

1. Watch for **sales.** You'll almost never see a sale during Mardi Gras or other peak times, but in the off-season, you can save big money. If you already hold a ticket when a sale breaks, it may even pay to exchange your ticket, which usually incurs a $50 to $75 charge.

2. If your schedule is flexible, ask if you can secure a cheaper fare by staying an extra day, by staying over a Saturday night, or by flying midweek. (Many airlines won't volunteer this information.)

3. **Consolidators,** also known as bucket shops, are a good place to find low fares. Consolidators buy seats in bulk from the airlines and then sell them back to the

public at prices below even the airlines' discounted rates. Their small ads usually run in the Sunday travel section at the bottom of the page. **Council Travel** (☎ 800/226-8624; www.counciltravel.com) and **STA Travel** (☎ 800/781-4040; www.sta.travel.com) cater especially to young travelers, but their bargain basement prices are available to people of all ages. **Travel Bargains** (☎ 800/ AIR-FARE; www.1800airfare.com) was formerly owned by TWA but now offers the deepest discounts on many other airlines, with a four-day advance purchase. Other reliable consolidators include **1-800-FLY-CHEAP** (www.1800flycheap. com); **TFI Tours International** (☎ 800/745-8000 or 212/736-1140), which serves as a clearinghouse for unused seats; or "rebators" such as **Travel Avenue** (☎ 800/333-3335 or 312/876-1116) and the **Smart Traveller** (☎ 800/ 448-3338 in the U.S. or 305/448-3338), which rebate part of their commissions to you.

4. Search **the Internet** for cheap fares. (See Frommer's Online Directory at the back of the book for more guidance on this subject.) A few of the better-respected virtual travel agents are **Travelocity** (www.travelocity.com) and **Microsoft Expedia** (www.expedia.com). Great last-minute deals are also available through a free e-mail service, provided directly by the airlines, called **E-savers.** Each week, the airline sends you a list of discounted flights, usually leaving the upcoming Friday or Saturday, and returning the following Monday or Tuesday. You can sign up for all the major airlines at once by logging on to **Smarter Living** (www.smarter living.com), or go to each individual airline's web site.

5. **Arthur Frommer's Budget Travel** (www.frommers.com) offers detailed information on 200 cities and islands around the world, and up-to-the-minute ways to save dramatically on flights, hotels, car reservations, and cruises. Book an entire vacation on line and research your destination before you leave.

BY CAR

You can drive to New Orleans via **I-10, I-55, U.S. 90,** and **U.S. 61** and across the Lake Pontchartrain Causeway on **La. 25.** From any direction, you'll see the city's distinctive and swampy outlying regions; if you can, try to drive in while you can enjoy the scenery in daylight. For the best roadside views, take U.S. 61 or La. 25, but only if you have time to spare. The larger roads are considerably faster.

It's a good idea to call before you leave home to ask for directions to your hotel. Most hotels have parking facilities (for a fee); if they don't, they'll give you the names and addresses of nearby parking lots.

AAA (☎ 800/926-4222) will assist members with trip planning and emergency services.

Driving in New Orleans can be a hassle, and parking is a nightmare. Cabs are plentiful, and not too expensive, so you don't need a car in New Orleans unless you're planning several day trips.

Nevertheless, most major national car rental companies are represented at the airport, including **Alamo** (☎ 800/327-9633), **Avis** (☎ 800/331-1212), **Budget** (☎ 800/527-0700), **Dollar** (☎ 800/800-4000), **Hertz** (☎ 800/654-3131), and **National** (☎ 800/227-7368). See "Getting Around" in chapter 5 for more information on car rental and driving in New Orleans.

BY TRAIN

As with the interstates and highways into New Orleans, the passenger rail lines cut through some beautiful scenery. **Amtrak** (☎ 800/USA-RAIL or 504/528-1610) trains serve New Orleans' **Union Passenger Terminal,** 1001 Loyola Ave., from Los Angeles and intermediate points; from New York, Washington, and points in between; and from Chicago and intermediate points. Using All Aboard America fares, you'll pay $188 to $208 from New York or Chicago, $248 to $288 from Los Angeles. Amtrak frequently offers senior-citizen discounts and other packages, some with a rental car, so be sure to check when you reserve. Also, many Amtrak discounts depend on early reservations.

Amtrak also offers some appealing tour packages, which can be arranged through your local Amtrak Tour Desk. Options include a ticket with accommodations, an air-rail package—take the train and then fly back home—and eight other combinations of tour packages.

The New Orleans train station is in the Central Business District. Plenty of taxis wait outside the main entrance to the passenger terminal. Hotels in the French Quarter and the Central Business District are a short ride away.

BY BUS

Greyhound-Trailways buses (☎ **800/231-2222** or 504/524-7571) come into the **Union Passenger Terminal** from points throughout the country. The terminal is located at 1001 Loyola Ave., in the Central Business District. We recommend taking a cab from the bus terminal to your hotel. There should be taxis out front, but if there aren't, the number for **United Cabs** is ☎ **504/522-9771.**

4 Tips for Travelers with Special Needs

FOR TRAVELERS WITH DISABILITIES

A disability shouldn't stop anyone from traveling. There are more resources out there than ever before.

Rollin' by the River is a guide to wheelchair-accessible restaurants and clubs in the French Quarter prepared by the **Advocacy Center,** 225 Baronne St., Suite 2112, New Orleans, LA 70112 (☎ **504/522-2337**). The guide was prepared many years ago, and may not be entirely up to date. It's available for a handling fee of $2.25 (check or money order), though apparently only a limited supply is available. The Advocacy Center is a legal services organization, but if you have specific tourism questions, the volunteers there will likely be able to help.

For information about specialized transportation systems, call **LIFT** (☎ **504/827-7433**).

A World of Options, a 658-page book of resources for disabled travelers, costs $35 ($30 for members) and is available from **Mobility International USA,** P.O. Box 10767, Eugene, OR 97440 (☎ **541/343-1284,** voice and TDD; www.miusa.org). Annual membership for Mobility International is $35, which includes their quarterly newsletter, *Over the Rainbow.* **The Moss Rehab Hospital** (☎ **215/456-9600**) has been providing friendly and helpful phone advice and referrals to disabled travelers for years through its **Travel Information Service** (☎ **215/456-9603;** www.moss resourcenet.org).

You can join **The Society for the Advancement of Travel for the Handicapped** (SATH), 347 Fifth Ave. Suite 610, New York, NY 10016 (☎ **212/447-7284;** fax 212/725-8253; www.sath.org), for $45 annually, $30 for seniors and students, to gain access to their vast network of connections in the travel industry. They provide infor-mation sheets on travel destinations and referrals to tour operators that specialize in traveling with disabilities. Their quarterly magazine, *Open World for Disability and*

Mature Travel, is full of good information and resources. A year's subscription is $13 ($21 outside the United States).

Many of the major car rental companies now offer hand-controlled cars for disabled drivers. **Avis** can provide such a vehicle at any of its locations in the U.S. with 48-hour advance notice; **Hertz** requires between 24 and 72 hours of advance reservation at most of its locations. **Wheelchair Getaways** (☎ 800/873-4973; www.blvd.com/wg.htm) rents specialized vans with wheelchair lifts and other features for the disabled in more than 100 cities across the United States.

Travelers with disabilities may also want to consider joining a tour that caters specifically to them. One of the best operators is **Flying Wheels Travel,** 143 West Bridge (P.O. Box 382), Owatonna, MN 55060 (☎ 800/535-6790). They offer various escorted tours and cruises, with an emphasis on sports, as well as private tours in minivans with lifts.

In addition, both **Amtrak** (☎ 800/USA-RAIL; www.amtrak.com) and **Greyhound** (☎ 800/752-4841; www.greyhound.com) offer special fares and services for the disabled. Call at least a week in advance of your trip for details.

Vision-impaired travelers should contact the **American Foundation for the Blind,** 11 Penn Plaza, Suite 300, New York, NY 10001 (☎ 800/232-5463), for information on traveling with seeing-eye dogs.

FOR GAY & LESBIAN TRAVELERS

You'll find an abundance of establishments serving gay and lesbian interests, from bars to restaurants to community services to certain businesses. If you need help finding your way, you can stop by or call **the Gay and Lesbian Community Center,** 2114 Decatur St. (☎ 504/945-1103; fax 504/945-1102); hours vary, so call before stopping in.

The **NO/AIDS task force** has a 24-hour hot line (☎ 504/821-2601).

Ambush Mag 2000, 828-A Bourbon St., New Orleans, LA 70116 (☎ 504/522-8047; www.ambushmag.com), is a weekly entertainment and news publication for the Gulf South's gay, lesbian, bisexual, and transgender communities. The Web site offers plenty of links to other interesting sites. *Impact Gulf South Gay News* is another popular area publication.

Grace Fellowship, 3151 Dauphine St. (☎ 504/944-9836), and the **Vieux Carrè Metropolitan Community Church,** 1128 St. Roch Ave. (☎ 504/945-5390), are religious organizations that serve primarily gay and lesbian congregations. Both invite visitors to attend services.

One useful Web site is **www.gayneworleans.com**, which provides information on lodging, dining, arts, and nightlife, and links to other information on New Orleans gay life.

The **International Gay & Lesbian Travel Association** (IGLTA), (☎ 800/448-8550 or 954/776-2626; fax 954/776-3303; www.iglta.org), links travelers with the appropriate gay-friendly service organization or tour specialist. With around 1,200 members, it offers quarterly newsletters, marketing mailings, and a membership directory that's updated quarterly. Membership often includes gay or lesbian businesses but is open to individuals for $150 yearly, plus a $100 administration fee for new members. Members are kept informed of gay and gay-friendly hoteliers, tour operators, and airline and cruise-line representatives. Contact the IGLTA for a list of its member agencies, who will be tied into IGLTA's information resources.

General gay and lesbian travel agencies include **Family Abroad** (☎ 800/999-5500 or 212/459-1800; gay and lesbian); **Above and Beyond Tours** (☎ 800/397-2681; mainly gay men); and **Yellowbrick Road** (☎ 800/642-2488; gay and lesbian).

There are also two good, biannual English-language gay guidebooks, both focused on gay men but including information for lesbians as well. You can get the ***Spartacus International Gay Guide*** or ***Odysseus*** from most gay and lesbian book stores, or order them from Giovanni's Room (☎ **215/923-2960**), or A Different Light Bookstore (☎ **800/343-4002** or 212/989-4850). Both lesbians and gays might want to pick up a copy of ***Gay Travel A to Z*** ($16). **The Ferrari Guides** (www.q-net.com) is yet another very good series of gay and lesbian guidebooks.

Out and About, 8 W. 19th St. no. 401, New York, NY 10011 (☎ **800/929-2268** or 212/645-6922), offers guidebooks and a monthly newsletter packed with good information on the global gay and lesbian scene. A year's subscription to the newsletter costs $49.

FOR SENIORS

Don't be shy about asking for discounts, but always carry some kind of identification, such as a driver's license, that shows your date of birth. Also, mention the fact that you're a senior citizen when you first make your travel reservations. For example, both **Amtrak** (☎ **800/USA-RAIL;** www.amtrak.com) and **Greyhound** (☎ **800/ 752-4841;** www.greyhound.com) offer discounts to persons over 62, as do many airlines. And many hotels offer seniors discounts; **Choice Hotels** (Clarion Hotels, Quality Inns, Comfort Inns, Sleep Inns, Econo Lodges, Friendship Inns, and Rodeway Inns), for example, give 30% off their published rates to anyone over 50, provided you book your room through their nationwide toll-free reservations numbers (that is, not directly with the hotels or through a travel agent).

Members of the **American Association of Retired Persons (AARP),** 601 E St. NW, Washington, DC 20049 (☎ **800/424-3410** or 202/434-2277), get discounts not only on hotels but on airfares and car rentals, too. AARP offers members a wide range of special benefits, including *Modern Maturity* magazine and a monthly newsletter.

The National Council of Senior Citizens, 8403 Colesville Rd., Suite 1200, Silver Spring, MD 20910 (☎ **301/578-8800**), a nonprofit organization, offers a newsletter six times a year (partly devoted to travel tips) and discounts on hotel and auto rentals; annual dues are $13 per person or couple.

The Mature Traveler, a monthly 12-page newsletter on senior citizen travel is a valuable resource. It is available by subscription ($30 a year) from GEM Publishing Group, Box 50400, Reno, NV 89513-0400. GEM also publishes ***The Book of Deals,*** a collection of more than 1,000 senior discounts on airlines, lodging, tours, and attractions around the country; it's available for $9.95 by calling ☎ **800/460-6676.** Another helpful publication is ***101 Tips for the Mature Traveler,*** available from Grand Circle Travel, 347 Congress St., Suite 3A, Boston, MA 02210 (☎ **800/ 221-2610** or 617/350-7500; fax 617/346-6700).

Grand Circle Travel is also one of the hundreds of travel agencies specializing in vacations for seniors (347 Congress St., Suite 3A, Boston, MA 02210 (☎ **800/ 221-2610** or 617/350-7500)). Many of these packages, however, are of the tour-bus variety, with free trips thrown in for those who organize groups of 10 or more. Seniors seeking more independent travel should probably consult a regular travel agent.

4 For Foreign Visitors

This chapter will provide international travelers with specific information about getting to and into the United States as effortlessly as possible, and try to anticipate any questions you might have about the way things are done in these parts.

1 Preparing for Your Trip

ENTRY REQUIREMENTS

Immigration laws are a hot political issue in the United States these days, and the following requirements may have changed somewhat by the time you plan your trip. Check at any U.S. embassy or consulate for current information and requirements. You can also plug into the **U.S. State Department's** Internet site at **http://state.gov.**

The U.S. State Department has a **Visa Waiver Pilot Program** allowing citizens of certain countries to enter the United States without a visa for stays of up to 90 days. At press time these included Andorra, Argentina, Australia, Austria, Belgium, Brunei, Denmark, Finland, France, Germany, Iceland, Ireland, Italy, Japan, Liechtenstein, Luxembourg, Monaco, the Netherlands, New Zealand, Norway, San Marino, Slovenia, Spain, Sweden, Switzerland, and the United Kingdom. Citizens of these countries need only a valid passport and a round-trip air or cruise ticket in their possession upon arrival. If they first enter the United States, they may also visit Mexico, Canada, Bermuda, and/or the Caribbean islands and return to the United States without a visa. Further information is available from any U.S. embassy or consulate. Canadian citizens may enter the United States without visas; they need only proof of residence.

Citizens of all other countries must have (1) a valid passport that expires at least 6 months later than the scheduled end of their visit to the United States, and (2) a tourist visa, which may be obtained without charge from any U.S. consulate.

To obtain a visa, the traveler must submit a completed application form (either in person or by mail) with a 1½-inch-square photo, and must demonstrate binding ties to a residence abroad. Usually you can obtain a visa at once or within 24 hours, but it may take longer during the summer rush from June through August. If you cannot go in person, contact the nearest U.S. embassy or consulate for directions on applying by mail. Your travel agent or airline office may also be able to provide you with visa applications and instructions. The U.S. consulate or embassy that issues your visa will determine whether you will be issued a multiple- or single-entry visa and any restrictions regarding the length of your stay.

British subjects can obtain up-to-date passport and visa information by calling the **U.S. Embassy Visa Information Line** (☎ **0891/200-290**) or the **London Passport Office** (☎ **0990/210-410** for recorded information).

Telephone operators will answer your inquiries regarding U.S. immigration policies or laws at the **Immigration and Naturalization Service's Customer Information Center** (☎ **800/375-5283**). Representatives are available from 9am to 3pm, Monday through Friday. The INS also runs a 24-hour automated information service, for commonly asked questions, at ☎ **800/755-0777.**

MEDICAL REQUIREMENTS

Unless you're arriving from an area known to be suffering from an epidemic (particularly cholera or yellow fever), inoculations or vaccinations are not required for entry into the United States. If you have a disease that requires treatment with narcotics or syringe-administered medications, carry a valid signed prescription from your physician to allay any suspicions that you may be smuggling narcotics (a serious offense that carries severe penalties in the U.S.).

For HIV-positive visitors, requirements for entering the United States are somewhat vague and change frequently. For up-to-the-minute information concerning HIV-positive travelers, contact the Centers for Disease Control's **National Center for HIV** (☎ **404/332-4559;** www.hivatis.org) or the **Gay Men's Health Crisis** (☎ **212/367-1000;** www.gmhc.org).

CUSTOMS REQUIREMENTS

Every visitor over 21 years of age may bring in, free of duty, the following: (1) 1 liter of wine or hard liquor; (2) 200 cigarettes or 100 cigars (but not from Cuba) or 3 pounds of smoking tobacco; and (3) $100 worth of gifts. These exemptions are offered to travelers who spend at least 72 hours in the United States and who have not claimed them within the preceding 6 months. It is altogether forbidden to bring into the country foodstuffs (particularly fruit, cooked meats, and canned goods) and plants (vegetables, seeds, tropical plants, and the like). Foreign tourists may bring in or take out up to $10,000 in U.S. or foreign currency with no formalities; larger sums must be declared to U.S. Customs on entering or leaving. For more specific information regarding U.S. Customs, call your nearest U.S. embassy or consulate, or the **U.S. Customs** office at ☎ **202/927-1770** or www.customs.ustreas.gov.

Foreign tourists to Louisiana can receive a refund on taxes paid on tangible goods purchased within the state. You must show your passport (Canadians can show a driver's license) at the time of purchase and *request a tax refund voucher from the vendor.* You will be charged the full amount and given a sales receipt and a refund voucher. If you're leaving New Orleans by plane, go to the Louisiana Tax Free Shopping Refund Center at the airport. Present your sales receipts and vouchers from merchants, your passport, and a round-trip international ticket (the duration of the trip must be less than 90 days). To arrange your refund by mail, you'll need copies of sales receipts, copies of your travel ticket and passport, your original refund vouchers, and a statement explaining why you were not able to claim your refund at the airport. Send these to: **Louisiana Tax Free Shopping Refund Center,** P.O. Box 20125, New Orleans, LA 70141 (☎ **504/467-0723**).

INSURANCE

Although it's not required of travelers, health insurance is highly recommended. Unlike many European countries, the United States does not usually offer free or low-cost medical care to its citizens or visitors. Doctors and hospitals are expensive, and in most cases will require advance payment or proof of coverage before they render their services. Policies can cover everything from the loss or theft of your baggage and trip cancellation to the guarantee of bail in case you're arrested. Good policies will also cover the costs of an accident, repatriation, or death. Packages such as **Europ Assistance** in Europe are sold by automobile clubs and travel agencies at attractive rates. **Worldwide Assistance Services, Inc.** (☎ **800/821-2828**) is the agent for Europ Assistance in the United States. Though lack of health insurance may prevent you from being admitted to a hospital in nonemergencies, don't worry about being left on a street corner to die: the American way is to fix you now and bill the living daylights out of you later.

MONEY

CURRENCY & EXCHANGE   The U.S. monetary system is painfully simple: The most common bills (all ugly, all green) are the $1 (colloquially, a "buck"), $5, $10, and $20 denominations. There are also $2 bills (seldom encountered), $50 bills, and $100 bills (the last two are usually not welcome as payment for small purchases). The $100, $50, and $20 bills have been redesigned in the past few years, with changes to the $10 and $5 expected in 2000. Despite rumors to the contrary, both the old and the new versions of all bills are still legal tender.

There are six denominations of coins: 1¢ (1 cent, or a penny); 5¢ (5 cents, or a nickel); 10¢ (10 cents, or a dime); 25¢ (25 cents, or a quarter); 50¢ (50 cents, or a half dollar); and, prized by collectors, the rare $1 piece (the older, large silver dollar and the newer, small Susan B. Anthony coin). A new gold $1 piece will be introduced by the year 2000.

Note: The "foreign-exchange bureaus" so common in Europe are rare even at airports in the United States, and nonexistent outside major cities. It's best not to change foreign money (or traveler's checks denominated in a currency other than U.S. dollars) at a small-town bank, or even a branch in a big city; in fact, leave any currency other than U.S. dollars at home—it may prove a greater nuisance to you than it's worth.

TRAVELER'S CHECKS   Though traveler's checks are widely accepted, make sure that they're denominated in U.S. dollars, as foreign-currency checks are often difficult to exchange. The three traveler's checks that are most widely accepted are **Visa, American Express,** and **Thomas Cook.** Be sure to record the numbers of the checks, and keep that information separately in case they get lost or stolen. Most businesses are pretty good about taking traveler's checks, but you're better off cashing them at a bank.

Remember, you'll need identification, such as a driver's license or passport, to change a traveler's check.

CREDIT CARDS & ATMs   Bring at least one major credit card on your trip. Airlines and hotels usually require a credit-card imprint as a deposit against expenses, and car-rental agencies will not give you a car without a major credit card. In an emergency, you can use your credit card as identification, or to draw money at a bank. **Visa** (BarclayCard in Britain), **MasterCard** (EuroCard in Europe, Access in Britain, Chargex in Canada), **American Express, Diners Club, Discover,** and **Carte Blanche** are the most commonly accepted cards. Most businesses display a sticker near their entrance to let you know which cards they accept. There are, however, a handful of stores and restaurants that do not take credit cards, so be sure to ask in advance. (Note: Often businesses require a minimum purchase price, usually around $10, to use a credit card.)

You'll find automated-teller machines (ATMs) in almost every town in the United States. Some ATMs will allow you to draw U.S. currency against your bank and credit cards. Check with your bank before leaving home, and remember that you will need your personal identification number (PIN) to do so. Most accept Visa, MasterCard, and American Express, as well as ATM cards from other U.S. banks. Expect to be charged up to $3 per transaction, however, if you're not using your own bank's ATM.

2 Getting to the United States

THE MAJOR AIRLINES

FROM CANADA   Air Canada (☎ 800/268-7240 in Toronto or 800/663-3721 in Vancouver) flies from Toronto and Montreal to Newark, New Jersey, and from Calgary and Vancouver to Houston, Texas. From both cities, connecting flights are on Continental Airlines.

Many American carriers also serve similar routes. **American Airlines** (☎ 800/ 433-7300) connects through Chicago or Dallas; **Continental Airlines** (☎ 800/ 231-0856) flies from Montreal and Toronto, connecting through Newark (it partners with Air Canada to service other Canadian cities); **Delta** (☎ 800/241-4141) connects through Atlanta or Cincinnati; **TWA** (☎ 800/221-2000) flies from Toronto only, connecting through St. Louis; and **United Airlines** (☎ 800/241-6522) flies from Toronto, Calgary, and Vancouver, connecting through Chicago.

FROM THE UNITED KINGDOM & IRELAND   There are no direct flights from London to New Orleans, but the following airlines will book you through on a connecting flight.

American Airlines (☎ 0181/572-5555 in London or 0345/789-789 elsewhere in the U.K.) connects through Chicago; **British Airways** (☎ 0345/222-111 in Europe) connects through Philadelphia or Charlotte, North Carolina; **Continental Airlines** (☎ 0800/776-464 in the U.K.) connects through Newark, New Jersey, or Houston; **Delta Airlines** (☎ 0800/414-767 in the U.K.) connects through Atlanta or Cincinnati; **United Airlines** (☎ 0181/990-9900 in London, or 0800/888-555 elsewhere in the U.K.) connects through Washington, D.C.'s Dulles or Chicago; and **Virgin Atlantic** (☎ 01293/747-747 in the U.K.) connects through New York, Newark, Miami, or Orlando.

From Ireland, **Aer Lingus** (☎ 01/844-4777) flies to New York, where you can connect to a New Orleans flight on its partner airline, TWA.

FROM AUSTRALIA & NEW ZEALAND   Qantas (☎ 008/112-121 toll free in Sydney and Melbourne, 2/9957-0111 in Sydney, or 7/234-3747 in Brisbane) flies into Los Angeles, then puts you on a Delta or American Airlines flight to New Orleans. You can also take **United** (☎ 2/9237-8888 in Sydney, 3/9602-2544 in Melbourne, or 008/230-322 elsewhere in Australia), which connects through San Francisco or Los Angeles.

Air New Zealand (☎ 09/357-3000 in Auckland or 03/379-5200 in Christchurch) connects through Los Angeles on a local carrier such as Delta.

ARRIVING IN THE UNITED STATES

No matter which airport you connect through, you should cultivate patience and resignation before setting foot on U.S. soil. Getting through immigration control and customs may take as long as 2 to 3 hours on some days, especially on summer weekends, so keep a good book handy to help pass the time (this guidebook, for instance). Make a very generous allowance for these delays when you're planning connections between international and domestic flights.

In contrast, for the traveler arriving by car or by rail from Canada, the border-crossing formalities have been streamlined to the vanishing point. And for the traveler by air from Canada, Bermuda, and some places in the Caribbean, you can sometimes go through customs and immigration at the point of departure, which is much quicker and less painful.

See "Getting There" in chapter 3 for more information on arriving in New Orleans.

3 Getting Around the United States

BY PLANE Air travel is the fastest and most convenient means of travel in the United States, but not necessarily the most romantic. If you intend to travel a long distance within the country, you should strongly consider flying.

Some large American airlines (for example, TWA, American Airlines, Northwest, United, and Delta) offer travelers on their transatlantic or transpacific flights special discount tickets under the name **Visit USA,** allowing travel between U.S. destinations at minimum rates. They are not on sale in the United States and must, therefore, be purchased before you leave your foreign point of departure. This system is the best, easiest, and fastest way to see the United States at low cost. You should obtain information well in advance from your travel agent or the office of the airline concerned, because the conditions attached to these discount tickets can be changed without notice.

For further information about travel to and arriving in New Orleans, see "Getting There" in chapter 3.

BY TRAIN International visitors can also buy a **USA Railpass,** good for 15 or 30 days of unlimited travel on Amtrak (☎ 800/USA-RAIL). The pass is available through many foreign travel agents. Prices in 1999 for a 15-day pass are $285 off-peak, $425 peak; a 30-day pass costs $375 off-peak, $535 peak. (With a foreign passport, you can also buy passes at some Amtrak offices in the United States, including locations in San Francisco, Los Angeles, Chicago, New York, Miami, Boston, and Washington, D.C.) Reservations are generally required and should be made for each part of your trip as early as possible.

Train travel can be slower than flying or driving, but it can also be the most pleasant way to see the regions between cities. Visitors should be aware, however, of the limitations of long-distance rail travel in the United States. With a few notable exceptions (for instance, the Northeast Corridor line between Boston and Washington, D.C.), service is rarely up to European standards: Delays are common, routes are limited and often infrequently served, and fares are rarely significantly lower than discount airfares. Thus, cross-country train travel should be approached with caution.

BY BUS Bus travel is often the most economical form of public transit for short hops between U.S. cities, but it can also be slow and uncomfortable. **Greyhound/Trailways** (☎ 800/231-2222; www.greyhound.com), the sole nationwide bus line, offers an **Ameripass** for unlimited travel for 7 days at $199, 15 days at $299, 30 days at $409, and 60 days at $599. Passes must be purchased at a Greyhound terminal. Special rates are available for senior citizens and students.

SAFETY

GENERAL SAFETY TIPS While tourist areas are generally safe, crime is on the increase everywhere, and U.S. urban areas tend to be less safe than those in Europe or Japan. Visitors should always stay alert. This is particularly true of large U.S. cities. In New Orleans, avoid deserted areas (like the outer edges of the French Quarter), especially at night. Don't go into any cemeteries or city parks at night unless there's an event that attracts crowds, like a festival or concert. Generally speaking, you can feel safe in areas where there are many people and many open establishments. Contact the New Orleans Metropolitan Convention and Visitors Bureau if you're in doubt about which neighborhoods are safe.

Avoid carrying valuables with you on the street, and don't display expensive cameras or electronic equipment. Hold on to your pocketbook and place your billfold in an inside pocket. In theaters, restaurants, and other public places, keep your possessions in sight.

Remember also that hotels are open to the public, and in a large hotel, security may not be able to screen everyone entering. Always lock your room door. Don't assume that once inside your hotel you no longer need to be aware of your surroundings.

DRIVING SAFETY   Recently, more and more crime in all U.S. cities has involved cars and drivers, most notably carjacking. If you drive off a highway into a doubtful neighborhood, leave the area as quickly as possible. If you have an accident, even on the highway, stay in your car with the doors locked until you assess the situation or until the police arrive. If you're bumped from behind on the street or are involved in a minor accident with no injuries and the situation appears to be suspicious, motion to the other driver to follow you to the nearest well-lit service station or the nearest police precinct, if you happen to know where that is. *Never* get out of your car in such situations.

If you see someone on the road who indicates a need for help, do *not* stop. Take note of the location, drive on to a well-lit area, and telephone the police by dialing ☎ **911.**

Park in well-lit, well-traveled areas if possible. Always keep your car doors locked, whether the car is within your sight or not. Look around before you get out of your car, and never leave any packages or valuables in sight. If someone attempts to rob you or steal your car, do *not* try to resist the thief or carjacker. Report the incident to the police department immediately.

Ask for a brochure of traveler safety tips from the rental agent when you pick up your car. Also, ask for written directions to your destination, or a map with the route clearly marked.

Fast Facts: For the Foreign Traveler

Automobile Organizations   Auto clubs can provide maps, suggested routes, guidebooks, accident and bail-bond insurance, and emergency road service. The major auto club in the United States, with 955 offices nationwide, is the **American Automobile Association (AAA).** Members of some foreign auto clubs have reciprocal arrangements with AAA and enjoy its services at no charge. If you belong to an auto club, inquire about AAA reciprocity before you leave. AAA can provide you with an International Driving Permit, validating your foreign license. You may be able to join AAA even if you're not a member of a reciprocal club; call ☎ **800/222-4357** for information. Some automobile rental agencies now provide roadside assistance services, so you should inquire about their availability when you rent your car.

Business Hours   Banks are open weekdays from 9am to 3pm, but almost every bank has 24-hour automated-teller machines (ATMs). Generally, business offices are open weekdays from 9am to 5pm. In New Orleans, many small shops do not open until later in the morning (around 10am) and many stay open until 6pm. Stores are open 6 days a week, with many open on Sundays, too; department stores usually stay open until 9pm one day a week.

Climate   See "When to Go" in chapter 3.

Currency & Exchange   You'll find currency-exchange services in major airports with international service. Elsewhere, they may be quite difficult to come by. In New Orleans, you can find exchange services at the **Bank One,** 210 Baronne St., and the **Whitney National Bank's International Department,** 228 St. Charles Ave. In addition, most hotels will exchange currency for registered guests.

Drinking Laws   See "Liquor Laws" in "Fast Facts: New Orleans" in chapter 5.

Electric Current   The United States uses 110 to 120 volts AC (60 cycles), compared to 220 to 240 volts AC (50 cycles), used in most of Europe. Besides a 100-volt converter, small appliances of non-American manufacture, such as hair dryers or shavers, will require a plug adapter with two flat, parallel pins.

Embassies & Consulates   All embassies are located in Washington, D.C. Some consulates are located in major U.S. cities, and most nations have a mission to the United Nations in New York City. If your country isn't listed below, call directory assistance in Washington, D.C. (☎ **202/555-1212**) for the number of your national embassy.

   The embassy of **Australia** is at 1601 Massachusetts Ave. NW, Washington, DC 20036 (☎ **202/797-3000;** www.austemb.org). There are consulates in New York, Honolulu, Houston, Los Angeles, and San Francisco. The embassy of **Canada** is at 501 Pennsylvania Ave. NW, Washington, DC 20001 (☎ **202/ 682-1740;** www.cdnemb-washdc.org). Other Canadian consulates are in Buffalo (New York), Detroit, Los Angeles, New York, and Seattle. The embassy of **Ireland** is at 2234 Massachusetts Ave. NW, Washington, DC 20008 (☎ **202/ 462-3939**). Irish consulates are in Boston, Chicago, New York, and San Francisco. The embassy of **Japan** is at 2520 Massachusetts Ave. NW, Washington, DC 20008 (☎ **202/238-6700;** www.embjapan.org). Japanese consulates are located in Atlanta, Kansas City, San Francisco, and Washington D.C. The embassy of **New Zealand** is at 37 Observatory Circle NW, Washington, DC 20008 (☎ **202/328-4800;** www.emb.com/nzemb). New Zealand consulates are in Los Angeles, Salt Lake City, San Francisco, and Seattle. The embassy of the **United Kingdom** is at 3100 Massachusetts Ave. NW, Washington, DC 20008 (☎ **202/462-1340**). Other British consulates are in Atlanta, Boston, Chicago, Cleveland, Houston, Los Angeles, New York, San Francisco, and Seattle.

Emergencies   Call ☎ **911** for fire, police, and ambulance. This is a free call from pay phones. If you encounter such traveler's problems as sickness, accident, or lost or stolen baggage, call the Travelers Aid Society (☎ **504/464-3522** at New Orleans International Airport), an organization that specializes in helping distressed travelers, whether American or foreign. The main local office is at 846 Baronne St., New Orleans, LA 70113 (☎ **504/525-8726**).

Holidays   On the following national legal holidays, banks, government offices, post offices, and many stores, restaurants, and museums are closed: January 1 (New Year's Day), third Monday in January (Martin Luther King Jr. Day), third Monday in February (Washington's Birthday), last Monday in May (Memorial Day), July 4 (Independence Day), first Monday in September (Labor Day), second Monday in October (Columbus Day), November 11 (Veterans Day/Armistice Day), fourth Thursday in November (Thanksgiving Day), and December 25 (Christmas Day). Most New Orleans businesses are also closed Mardi Gras day. The Tuesday following the first Monday in November, Election Day, is a legal holiday in presidential election years. The next one is in 2000.

Information   See "Visitor Information & Money" in chapter 3. For telephone directory assistance, dial ☎ **1-411.**

Legal Aid   The foreign tourist will probably never become involved with the American legal system. If you are "pulled over" for a minor infraction (for example, of the highway code, such as speeding), never attempt to pay the fine directly to a police officer; this could be construed as attempted bribery, a much more serious crime. Pay fines by mail, or directly into the hands of the clerk of the court. If accused of a more serious offense, say and do nothing before consulting a lawyer. Here the burden is on the state to prove a person's guilt beyond a reasonable doubt, and everyone has the right to remain silent, whether he or she is suspected of a crime or actually arrested. Once arrested, a person can make one telephone call to a party of his or her choice. Call your embassy or consulate.

Mail   If you want your mail to follow you on your vacation and aren't sure where you'll be staying, your mail can be sent to you, in your name, in care of General Delivery at the main post office of the city or region where you expect to be. (In New Orleans: c/o General Delivery, New Orleans, LA 70140.) The addressee must pick it up in person at 701 Loyola Ave., near the Superdome, and produce proof of identity (driver's license, credit card, or passport).

Mailboxes are blue, carry the inscription U.S. MAIL, and are generally found at intersections. If your mail is addressed to a U.S. destination, don't forget to add the five-digit ZIP code after the city and state name.

At press time domestic postage rates were 20¢ for a postcard and 33¢ for a letter. For international mail, a first-class letter of up to one-half ounce costs 60¢ (46¢ to Canada and 40¢ to Mexico); a first-class postcard costs 50¢ (40¢ to Canada and 35¢ Mexico); and a preprinted postal aerogramme costs 50¢.

Measurements   One mile equals 1.6 kilometer. One pound equals .45 kilograms.

Medical Emergencies   For an ambulance, dial ☎ **911.** For information on hospitals and doctors in New Orleans, see "Fast Facts: New Orleans" in chapter 5.

Taxes   In the United States there is no VAT (value-added tax) or other indirect tax on a national level. Every state, and each city in it, is allowed to levy its own local tax on all purchases, including hotel and restaurant checks, airline tickets, and so on. In New Orleans, the sales tax rate is 9%. See "Customs Requirements," above, for information on receiving a refund on taxes paid on tangible goods purchased in Louisiana.

Telephone & Fax   The telephone system in the United States is run by private corporations, so rates, especially for long-distance service, can vary widely—even on calls made from public telephones. Local calls from public phones in the United States usually cost 35¢.

Generally, hotel surcharges on long-distance and local calls are astronomical. You're usually better off using a public pay telephone, which you'll find clearly marked in most public buildings and private establishments, as well as on the street. Outside metropolitan areas, public telephones are more difficult to find. Stores and gas stations are your best bets.

Most long-distance and international calls can be dialed directly from any phone.

Note that calls to numbers with the area codes 800, 888, and 877 are toll free. However, calls to numbers with the area codes 700 and 900 (chat lines, bulletin

Phone Tips

- **To call the United States from another country,** dial the international access code of that country (00 in the U.K., 0011 in Australia, 0170 in New Zealand), then the country code (1), then the three-digit area code (504 for New Orleans) and seven-digit phone number (for example, from the U.K. you'd dial **00-1-504/000-0000**).

- **For calls between different area codes in the United States and to Canada,** dial **1** followed by the area code and the seven-digit number (for example, 1-504/000-0000).

- **For calls within New Orleans,** just dial the seven-digit number (for example, **000-0000**).

- **For international calls from the United States,** dial the international access code (**011**) followed by the country code (44 for the U.K., 353 for Ireland, 61 for Australia, 62 for New Zealand, 27 for South Africa; others can be found in the telephone directory's White Pages), then the city code (if applicable), and the telephone number of the person you wish to call (for example, to call Dublin you'd dial **011+353+1/000-0000**).

- **For reversed-charge or collect calls, and for person-to-person calls,** dial **0** (zero or nil, not the letter "O") followed by the area code and number you want; an operator will then come on the line, at which point you should specify that you're calling collect, or person-to-person, or both. If your call is international, ask for the overseas operator.

- **For local directory assistance** ("Information"), dial ☎ **411;** for **long-distance information,** dial **1,** then the appropriate area code and **555-1212** (for example, New Orleans directory assistance would be 1-504/555-1212).

boards, sex lines, and so forth) can be very expensive—from 95¢ up to $5 per minute.

Most hotels have fax machines available for guests' use, and some hotel rooms are even wired for guests' fax machines. You'll probably also see signs for public faxes in the windows of local shops.

Telephone Directory   There are two kinds of telephone directories. The general directory is the **White Pages,** in which private and business subscribers are listed in alphabetical order. The inside front cover lists the emergency numbers for the police, fire department, and ambulance service, plus other vital numbers (coast guard, poison-control center, crime-victims hot line, and so on). The first few pages are devoted to community-service numbers, including a guide to long-distance and international calling, complete with country codes and area codes.

The second directory, printed on yellow paper (hence its name, the **Yellow Pages**), lists all local services, businesses, and industries by type of activity, with an index at the back. The listings cover not only such obvious items as automobile repair shops and drugstores (pharmacies), but also restaurants by type of cuisine and geographical location, bookstores by special subject, places of worship by religious denomination, and other information that the tourist might otherwise not readily find. The Yellow Pages also include city plans or detailed area maps, often showing postal ZIP codes and public transportation routes.

Temperature   To convert degrees Fahrenheit to degrees Celsius, subtract 32 from °F, multiply by 5, then divide by 9 (example: 85°F – 32 × $^5/_9$

= 29.4°C). A simpler method, producing a pretty close approximation, is to subtract 30 from °F and divide by two.

Time   The United States is divided into six time zones, each separated by an hour. From east to west these are: eastern time (ET), central time (CT), mountain time (MT), Pacific time (PT), Alaska time (AT), and Hawaii time (HT). New Orleans is in the central time zone.

Always keep time zones in mind if you're traveling (or even telephoning) long distances in the United States. For example, noon in New York City (ET) is 11am in New Orleans (CT), 10am in Denver (MT), 9am in Los Angeles (PT), 8am in Anchorage (AT), and 7am in Honolulu (HT). When it's noon in London (GMT, or Greenwich mean time), it's 7am in New York.

Daylight saving time is in effect from 1am on the first Sunday in April (turn your clocks ahead 1 hour) until 2am on the last Sunday in October (turn 'em back again), except in Arizona, Hawaii, part of Indiana, and Puerto Rico.

Tipping   Waiters and taxi drivers are tipped between 15% and 20%. Bellhops and airport porters should be tipped $1 per bag. Leave $1 to $2 per day for the maid at most hotels, more if you've left a disaster area for her to clean up, and even more ($3 to $4) if you're traveling with kids and/or pets.

Toilets   Often euphemistically referred to as rest rooms, public toilets are nonexistent on the streets of New Orleans. They can be found, though, in bars, restaurants, hotel lobbies, museums, department stores, and service stations— and will probably be clean (except those in service stations, which can sometimes be frighteningly filthy). Some restaurants and bars display a notice that "Toilets are for use of patrons only," but you can ignore this sign—or, better yet, avoid arguments by paying for a cup of coffee or soft drink, which will qualify you as a patron. The cleanliness of toilets at railroad stations and bus depots may be questionable; some public places are equipped with pay toilets that will require you to insert one or two dimes (10¢) or a quarter (25¢) into a slot on the door before it will open. In rest rooms with attendants, leaving at least a 25¢ tip is customary.

5

Getting to Know New Orleans

New Orleans is a very user-friendly city—that is, except for the unusual directions and the nearly impossible-to-pronounce street names. (More on that later.) It's a manageable size (only about 7 miles long) with most of what the average tourist would want to see concentrated in a few areas.

However, it is easy to just fall into the Big Easy and dream your vacation away, if you even remember to leave. Some find spending the entire time in a haze of delightful decadence a perfectly acceptable way to enjoy a trip. But for those of you who feel that there is a lot to see and do, not to mention eat and drink, in perhaps too short a time, a little planning is in order. This chapter contains some of the ins and outs of New Orleans navigation, and gives you some local sources to contact for specialized information.

1 Orientation

ARRIVING

From the airport, you can reach the **Central Business District** by bus for $1.50 (exact change required). Buses run from 6am to 6:30pm. From 6 to 9am and 3 to 6pm, they leave the airport every 12 to 15 minutes and go to the downtown side of Tulane Avenue between Elks Place and South Saratoga Street; at other times, they leave every 23 minutes. For more information, call the **Louisiana Transit Company** (☎ 504/737-9611).

You can also get to your hotel on the **Airport Shuttle** (☎ 504/522-3500). For $10 per person (one way), the van will take you directly to your hotel. There are Airport Shuttle information desks (staffed 24 hours) in the airport.

Note: If you plan to take the Airport Shuttle to the airport when you depart, you must call a day in advance and let them know what time your flight is leaving. They will tell you what time they will pick you up.

A **taxi** from the airport will cost about $21; if there are three or more passengers, the fare is $8 per person.

If you want to ride in style from the airport to your hotel, contact **Olde Quarter Livery** (☎ 504/945-3796). Express transfer service costs $50 for a four-passenger stretch limousine, plus $10 per extra person (up to eight, total). You'll be greeted by a uniformed chauffeur and escorted to the car, just outside the airport's baggage claim area. The drivers are prompt and efficient.

VISITOR INFORMATION

The **New Orleans Metropolitan Convention and Visitors Bureau,** 1520 Sugar Bowl Dr., New Orleans, LA 70112 (☎ **504/566-5055;** www.nawlins.com; e-mail: tourism@nawlins.com), is one of the most helpful tourist centers in any major city. Not only does it have a wide array of well-designed and well-written brochures that cover everything from the usual sightseeing questions to cultural history, but the incredibly friendly and helpful staff can answer almost any random question you may have. If you're having trouble making decisions, they can give you good advice; if you have a special interest, they'll help you plan your visit around it.

Once you've arrived in the city, you also might want to stop by the **Visitor Information Center,** 529 St. Ann St. (☎ **504/566-5031**), in the French Quarter. The center is open daily 9am to 5pm and has walking- and driving-tour maps and booklets on restaurants, accommodations, sightseeing, special tours, and pretty much anything else you might want to know about. The staff is friendly and knowledgeable about both the city and the state. You also might keep an eye out for the mobile **Info a la Cart** sites around town.

CITY LAYOUT

"Where y'at?" goes the traditional local greeting. "Where" is easy enough when you are in the French Quarter, the site of the original settlement. A 13-block-long grid between Canal Street and Esplanade Avenue, running from the Mississippi River to North Rampart Street, it's the closest the city comes to a geographic center.

After that, all bets are off. Because of the bend in the river, the streets are laid out at angles and curves that render north, south, east, and west useless. It's time to readjust your thinking: In New Orleans, the compass points are *riverside, lakeside, uptown,* and *downtown.* You'll catch on quickly if you keep in mind that North Rampart Street is the *lakeside* boundary of the Quarter, and that St. Charles Avenue extends from the French Quarter, *downtown,* to Tulane University, *uptown.*

Canal Street forms the boundary between new and old New Orleans. Street names change when they cross Canal (Bourbon Street, for example, becomes Carondelet Street), and addresses begin at 100 on either side of Canal. In the Quarter street numbers begin at 400 at the river because 4 blocks of numbered buildings were lost to the river before the levee was built).

MAPS   Don't think you can get along without one in New Orleans! Call the Convention and Visitors Bureau (see above) or stop by the Visitor Information Center for a free one, or pay for one at any major bookstore. If you rent a car, be sure to ask

---

Impressions

"Is it the part of the police department to harass me when this city is the flagrant vice capital of the civilized world?," Ignatius bellowed. "This city is famous for its gamblers, prostitutes, exhibitionists, anti-Christs, alcoholics, sodomites, drug addicts, fetishists, onanists, pornographers, frauds, jades, litterbugs and lesbians, all of whom are only too well protected by graft. If you had a moment, I shall endeavor to discuss the crime problem with you, but don't make the mistake of bothering me."
—John Kennedy Toole, *A Confederacy of Dunces*

for maps of the city—the rental agents have good ones. If you're planning excursions outside the city, the places listed above also supply state maps.

STREET NAMES As if the streets themselves weren't colorful enough, there are the street names, from Felicity to the jaw-breaker Tchoupitoulas (say chop-i-*too*-las). How did they get these fanciful monikers? Well, in some cases, from overeducated city fathers, who named streets after Greek muses (Calliope and Terpsichore). Some immortalize long-dead and otherwise forgotten women: Julia was a free woman of color, but who was Felicity? Many streets in the French Quarter—Burgundy, Dauphine, Toulouse, and Dumaine—honor French royalty or nobility, while St. Peter and St. Ann were favorite baptismal names of the Orleans family. The Faubourg Marigny (Faubourg being the local word for *suburb*) was once part of the Marigny (say *Mare-i-nee*) family plantation. After scion Bernard squandered his family's fortune (mostly on gambling), he sold off parcels to the city, naming the streets after his favorite things: Desire, Piety, Poets, Duels, Craps, and so forth.

By the way, if pronunciation seems a mystery, try it with a French accent and you might actually get it right. Unless it's Chartres (*chart*-ers) or Burgundy (bur-*gun*-dee) Street. Oh, never mind. When in doubt, just ask a local. They're used to it.

The Neighborhoods in Brief

The French Quarter Made up of about 90 square blocks, this section is also known as the *Vieux Carré* ("Old Square") and is enclosed by Canal Street, North Rampart Street, the Mississippi River, and Esplanade Avenue. The Quarter is full of commercial establishments, residences, and museums; its major public area is Jackson Square, bounded by Chartres, Decatur, St. Peter, and St. Ann streets. The most historic and best-preserved area in the city, it's likely to be the focal point of your stay.

Esplanade Ridge (Mid City) Stretching from the French Quarter to City Park, the Ridge hugs either side of Esplanade Avenue. This area encompasses a few distinct neighborhoods, all of which have certain things in common. In the 19th century, Esplanade was the grand avenue of New Orleans Creole society—the St. Charles Avenue of downriver. Many sections of the avenue and houses along it have seen better days, but there is still evidence of those times, especially in the ancient oak trees forming a canopy above the road. If you drive or stroll toward the park along Esplanade (see chapter 9), you can measure the progress of the avenue's development in the styles of its houses.

The oldest section of Esplanade Ridge, **Faubourg Tremé,** is located directly across Rampart Street from the French Quarter. Like the Quarter, it was a dense 19th-century Creole community. Unlike the Quarter, Tremé has remained almost untouched by preservationists and so has continued to be an organic residential community. Today, it is one of the most vibrant African American neighborhoods in New Orleans, home to more than a few of the city's best brass bands. Unfortunately, Tremé is also plagued by severe crime, so it's not advisable to walk through at night.

Canal Street/Central Business District Historically, Canal Street has been New Orleans' main street, and in the 19th century it also divided the French and American sections of the city. (By the way, there's no canal—the one that was planned for the spot never came off.)

The **Central Business District (CBD)** is roughly bounded by Canal Street and the elevated Pontchartrain Expressway (Business Route U.S. 90), between Loyola Avenue and the Mississippi River. Some of the most elegant luxury hotels are in this area. Most of the district was known as Faubourg St. Mary when Americans began settling here after the Louisiana Purchase. Lafayette Square was the center of life here during the 19th century.

Within the CBD is the **Warehouse District.** Twenty years ago, this area was full of abandoned warehouses and almost nothing else. With the efforts of some dedicated individuals and institutions, however, it's steadily evolving into a residential neighborhood with some commercial activity. Furthermore, this area also serves as the city's art gallery district, with most of the premier galleries concentrated along **Julia Street** (see chapter 10). Most of these show the works of local and regional contemporary artists. The Contemporary Arts Center and Louisiana Children's Museum (see chapter 8) are also in this area.

Uptown/The Garden District   Bounded by St. Charles Avenue (lakeside) and Magazine Street (riverside) between Jackson and Louisiana avenues, the Garden District remains one of the most picturesque areas in the city. Originally the site of a plantation, the area was subdivided and developed as a residential neighborhood for wealthy Americans. Throughout the middle of the 19th century, developers built the Victorian, Italianate, and Greek Revival homes that still line the streets. Most of the homes had elaborate lawns and gardens, but few of those still exist. The Garden District is located uptown (as opposed to the CBD, which is downtown); the neighborhood west of the Garden District is often called **Uptown.** (See chapter 9 for a suggested stroll through this area.)

The Irish Channel   The area bounded by Magazine Street and the Mississippi River, Louisiana Avenue, and the Central Business District got its name during the 1800s, when more than 100,000 Irish immigrated to New Orleans. As was true elsewhere in the country, the Irish of New Orleans were often considered "expendable" labor. Many were killed while employed at dangerous construction work and other manual labor. These days, the Channel is significantly less Irish, but it retains its lively spirit and distinctive neighborhood flavor. Much of the area is run-down, but just as much is filled with quiet residential neighborhoods. To get a glimpse of the Irish Channel, go to the antique shop district on Magazine Street and stroll between Felicity Street and Jackson Avenue.

Basin Street   You remember Basin Street, of course—it's the birthplace of jazz. Or at least that's the legend. In fact, jazz probably predates the rise of **Storyville** (the old red-light district along Basin Street), where it is said to have been born, by a good number of years. To give credit where credit is due, Storyville's "sporting houses" did provide a place for the music to grab the ear of a wide segment of the public, who came to enjoy the houses', uh, services. King Oliver, Jelly Roll Morton, and Louis Armstrong were among the jazz greats who got their start on Basin Street in the brothels between Canal Street and Beauregard Square.

Apart from a couple of nondescript buildings, no trace of the old Storyville survives. A low-income public housing project now sprawls over much of the site, and statues depicting Latin American heroes—Simón Bolívar, Benito Juárez, and Gen. Francisco Morazán—dot the landscape.

Faubourg Marigny   *Faubourg* means "suburb," and *Marigny* is the name of a prominent early New Orleans family. This area is between the French Quarter (along Esplanade Avenue) and Bywater (along Press Street). Over the past decade, the Marigny has emerged as one of the city's vital centers of activity. You can still find the outlines of a small Creole suburb, and many old-time residents remain. Younger urban dwellers have moved into the area in significant numbers recently. Today, some of the best bars and nightspots in New Orleans are along Frenchmen Street, the Marigny's main drag. Along with the adjacent sections of the French Quarter, the Marigny is also a social center for the city's gay and lesbian communities.

Algiers Point   Directly across the Mississippi River from the Central Business District and the French Quarter, and connected by the Canal Street Ferry, the point is the old town center of Algiers. It is another of New Orleans' original Creole suburbs, but probably the one that has changed the least over the decades. Today, you can't see many signs of the area's once-booming railroad and dry-docking industries, but you can see some of the best-preserved small gingerbread and Creole cottages in New Orleans. The neighborhood has recently begun to attract attention as a historic landmark, and it makes for one of the city's most pleasant strolls (see chapter 9).

Bywater   This riverside neighborhood is past the Faubourg Marigny and bounded on the east by an industrial canal. It is tempting to misspeak and call it "Backwater," because at first glance it seems like a wasteland of light industry and run-down homes. In fact, Bywater has plenty of nice, modest residential sections. Furthermore, it's home to the city's artists-in-hiding, and many local designers have shops among the urban decay. That is in keeping with the history of the area, which early on was home to artisans and communities of immigrants and free people of color.

SAFETY

The city's high crime rate has made headlines over the past few years. New Orleans has worked hard on the problem, and an increased police force and vigilance have led to a decrease in crime.

However, problems still remain, and we want to help you avoid them as best you can. We consulted with the Convention and Visitors Bureau and a 7-year member of the New Orleans Police Department, and have these tips to offer. Mostly, it's a matter of relying on common sense and taking a few precautions.

STREET SMARTS   The **French Quarter** is fairly safe, thanks to the number of people present at any given time, but some areas are better than others. On **Bourbon Street,** be careful when socializing with strangers, and be alert to distractions by potential pickpocket teams. Dauphine and Burgundy streets are in quiet, lovely old parts of the Quarter, but as you near Esplanade, watch out for purse snatchers. At night, stay in lighted areas with street and pedestrian traffic, and take cabs down Esplanade Avenue and into the **Faubourg Marigny.** Do not walk alone much past Bourbon toward Rampart after dark. Stay in a group or see if you can get a beat cop to escort you. In the **Garden District,** as you get past Magazine toward the river, the neighborhoods can be rough, so exercise caution.

At all times, try to avoid looking distracted or confused. If you appear confident and alert, you will look less like a target.

TRAVEL SMARTS   Don't hang that expensive camera around your neck when it's not in use. Put it out of sight, if you can, in a camera bag or other case. If the bag or case has a shoulder strap, carry it so the bag is on your hip with strap over the opposite shoulder, so a simple tug won't dislodge it. That goes for purses as well. You might consider using a money belt or other hidden, pickpocket-proof type of travel wallet. (Women probably won't want to bring purses to clubs where they plan on dancing.) And never leave valuables in the outside pocket of a backpack. Should you stop for a bite to eat, keep everything within easy reach—of you, not a purse snatcher. If you're traveling in a car, place your belongings in the trunk, not under the seat. And it's

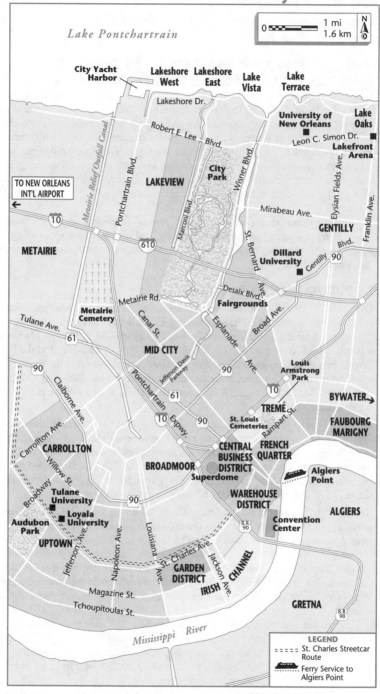

Lake Pontchartrain

0 [scale] 1 mi
1.6 km

N

City Yacht Harbor
Lakeshore West
Lakeshore East
Lake Vista
Lake Terrace

Lakeshore Dr.

University of New Orleans
Lake Oaks
Leon C. Simon Dr.
Lakefront Arena

Robert E. Lee Blvd.

Metairie Relief Outfall Canal

Pontchartrain Blvd.

LAKEVIEW

City Park

Marconi Blvd.

Wisner Blvd.

TO NEW ORLEANS INT'L AIRPORT ←

10

610

METAIRIE

Mirabeau Ave.

GENTILLY

St. Bernard Ave.

Elysian Fields Ave.

Franklin Ave.

Gentilly Blvd.
90

Dillard University

Tulane Ave.

61

Metairie Cemetery

Metairie Rd.

Canal St.

Desaix Blvd.

Fairgrounds

Esplanade Ave.

Broad Ave.

MID CITY

Jefferson Davis Parkway
90

Pontchartrain Expwy
61

10

90

Louis Armstrong Park

BYWATER →

10

TREMÉ

Rampart St.

St. Louis Cemeteries

FAUBOURG MARIGNY

CARROLLTON

Claiborne Ave.

Carrollton Ave.

Willow St.

Broadway

90

BROADMOOR

CENTRAL BUSINESS DISTRICT

FRENCH QUARTER

Superdome

Algiers Point

Tulane University

Loyala University

Audubon Park

UPTOWN

90

WAREHOUSE DISTRICT

ALGIERS

B.R. 90

Convention Center

Jefferson Ave.

Napoleon Ave.

Louisiana Ave.

St. Charles Ave.

Jackson Ave.

GARDEN DISTRICT

IRISH CHANNEL

GRETNA

B.R. 90

Magazine St.

Tchoupitoulas St.

Mississippi River

LEGEND
===== St. Charles Streetcar Route
Ferry Service to Algiers Point

always a good idea to leave expensive-looking jewelry and other conspicuous valuables at home, anyway.

2 Getting Around

You really don't need to rent a car during your stay. Not only is the town just made for walking (thanks to being so flat—and so darn picturesque), but most places you want to go are easily accessible on foot or by some form of the largely excellent public transportation system. Indeed, we find a streetcar ride as much entertainment as practical means of getting around. At night, when you need them most, cabs are easy to come by. Meanwhile, driving and parking in the French Quarter bring grief. The streets are narrow and crowded, and many go one way only. Street parking is minimal (and likely to attract thieves), and parking lots are fiendishly expensive.

Sure, everything takes a bit longer when you are depending on the kindness of strangers to get around, but driving and parking headaches take time too, and are not conducive to a pleasant vacation. Besides, you need to walk off all those calories (we hope) you will be ingesting!

BY PUBLIC TRANSPORTATION

DISCOUNT PASSES   If you won't have a car in New Orleans, we strongly encourage you to invest in a **VisiTour** pass, which entitles you to an unlimited number of rides on all streetcar and bus lines. It costs $4 for 1 day, $8 for 3 days. Many visitors think this was the best tip they got about their New Orleans stay, and the finest bargain in town. Passes are available from VisiTour vendors—to find the nearest one, ask at your hotel or guest house or call **the Regional Transit Authority** (☎ **504/ 248-3900**). You can call the RTA for information about any part of the city's public transportation system.

BUSES   New Orleans has an excellent public bus system, so chances are there's a bus that runs exactly where you want to go. Local fares at press time are $1 (you must have exact change, in bills or coins), transfers are an extra 10¢, and express buses are $1.25. You can get complete route information by calling the RTA (☎ **504/248-3900**) or by picking up one of the excellent city maps available at the Visitor Information Center, 529 St. Ann St. (☎ **504/568-5661**), in the French Quarter.

STREETCARS   Besides being a national historic landmark, the **St. Charles Avenue streetcar** (see "A Streetcar Tour" in chapter 9) is also a convenient and fun way to get from downtown to Uptown and back. The trolleys run 24 hours a day at frequent intervals, and the fare is $1 each way (you must have exact change in bills or coins). It can get crowded at rush hour and when school is out for the day. Board at Canal and Carondelet streets (directly across Canal from Bourbon Street in the French Quarter), or anywhere along St. Charles, sit back, and look for landmarks or just enjoy the scenery.

The streetcar line extends beyond the point where St. Charles Avenue bends into Carrollton Avenue. The end of the line is at Palmer Park and Playground at Clairborne Avenue, but you'll want to mount a shopping expedition at the Riverbend Shopping Area (see chapter 10). It will cost you another $1 for the ride back to Canal Street. It costs 10¢ to transfer from the streetcar to a bus.

The **riverfront streetcar** runs for 1.9 miles, from the Old Mint across Canal Street to Riverview, with stops along the way. It's a great step-saver as you explore the riverfront. The fare is $1.25, and there's ramp access.

A Bus Named Desire

"They told me to take a streetcar named Desire, and then transfer to one called Cemeteries and ride six blocks and get off at Elysian Fields!"

Although Blanche's directions wouldn't actually have gotten her to Stella and Stanley's house (Tennessee Williams fiddled with streetcar lines to make his metaphor work), there were indeed once streetcars called Desire and Cemeteries. The signs indicated their ultimate destinations (a street and a district, respectively). However, Blanche's later question, "Is that streetcar named Desire still grinding along the tracks?" must now be answered no. (Unless we are still using that metaphor.)

The streetcar in question, which used to run through the French Quarter along Bourbon and Royal streets, has, like all but two of its brethren, been replaced by buses. That means you can't take a whirl on the legendary streetcar, but you can still ride buses called Desire and Cemeteries.

BY CAR

If you absolutely have to have a car, try one of the following car-rental agencies: **Avis,** 2024 Canal St. (☎ **800/331-1212** or 504/523-4317); **Budget Rent-A-Car,** 1317 Canal St. (☎ **800/527-0700** or 504/467-2277); **Dollar Rent-A-Car,** 1910 Airline Hwy., Kenner (☎ **800/800-4000** or 504/467-2285); **Hertz,** 901 Convention Center Blvd., No. 101 (☎ **800/654-3131** or 504/568-1645); **Swifty Car Rental,** 2300 Canal St. (☎ **504/524-7368**); **Value Rent-A-Car,** 1806 Airline Hwy., Kenner (☎ **800/GO-VALUE** or 504/469-2688).

Rental rates vary according to the time of your visit and from company to company, so call ahead and do some comparison shopping. Ask lots of questions, try different dates and pickup points, and ask about corporate or organizational discounts. And if you're staying for a week or more, be sure to ask about weekly rates, which are cheaper.

New Orleans drivers are often reckless, so drive defensively. The meter maids are an efficient bunch, so take no chances with parking meters. Carry change with you, as many meters take only quarters. It's probably best to use your car only for longer jaunts away from congested areas. Most hotels provide guest parking, often for a daily fee; smaller hotels or guest houses (particularly in the French Quarter) may not have parking facilities but will be able to direct you to a nearby public garage.

The narrow streets and frequent congestion make driving in the French Quarter more difficult than elsewhere in the city. The streets are one way, and on weekdays during daylight hours, Royal and Bourbon streets between the 300 and 700 blocks are closed to automobiles. Also, the blocks of Chartres Street in front of St. Louis Cathedral are closed at all times. Driving is also trying in the Central Business District, where congestion and limited parking make life difficult for the motorist. Do yourself a favor: Park the car and use public transportation in both areas.

Once you get into more residential areas, like the Garden District, and off main drags like St. Charles, finding where you are going becomes quite the challenge. Street

Factoid

Most **taxis** can be hired for a special rate for up to five passengers. It's a hassle-free and economical way for a small group to tour far-flung areas of the city (the lakefront, for example). Within the city you pay an hourly rate; out-of-town trips cost double the amount on the meter.

signs are often no bigger than a postcard, and hard to read at that. At night, they aren't even lit, so deciphering where you are can be next to impossible. If you must drive, we suggest counting the number of streets you have to cross to tell you when to make any turns, rather than relying on street signs.

BY TAXI

Taxis are plentiful in New Orleans. They can be hailed easily on the street in the French Quarter and some parts of the Central Business District, and are usually lined up at taxi stands at larger hotels. Otherwise, telephone and expect a cab to appear in 3 to 5 minutes. The rate is $2.10 when you enter the taxi and $1.20 per mile thereafter. During special events (like Mardi Gras and Jazz Fest), the rate is $3 per person (or the meter rate if it's greater) no matter where you go in the city. The city's most reliable company is **United Cabs** (☎ **504/524-9606**).

ON FOOT

We can't stress this enough: Walking is by far the best way to see this town. There are too many unique and sometimes glorious sights to want to whiz past them. Slow down. Have a drink to go. Get a snack. Stroll. Take one of our walking tours. Sure, sometimes it's too darn hot or humid—or raining too darn hard—to make walking attractive, but there is always a cab or bus nearby. Do remember to drink lots of water if it's hot, and pay close attention to your surroundings. If you enter an area that seems unsafe, retreat.

BY FERRY

The Canal Street ferry is one of the city's secrets—and it's free for pedestrians. The ride takes you across the Mississippi River from the foot of Canal to Algiers Point (25 minutes round-trip), and affords great views of downtown New Orleans and of the commerce on the river. Once in Algiers, you can take a walking tour of the old Algiers Point neighborhood (see chapter 9). At night, with the city's glowing skyline reflecting on the river, a ride on the ferry can be quite romantic. The ferry also does carry car traffic, in case you'd like to do some West Bank driving.

Fast Facts: New Orleans

Airport   See "Getting There" in chapter 3, and "Orientation," earlier in this chapter.

American Express   The local office (☎ **504/586-8201**) is at 158 Baronne St. in the Central Business District. It's open weekdays 9am to 5pm.

Area Code   The area code for New Orleans is **504.**

Baby-sitters   It's best to ask at your hotel about baby-sitting services. If your hotel doesn't offer help finding child care, try calling **Accent on Children's Arrangements** (☎ **504/524-1227**).

Convention Center   The **Ernest N. Morial Convention Center** (☎ **504/ 582-3000**) is at 900 Convention Center Blvd. It was built in anticipation of the World's Fair, held in New Orleans in 1984, under "Dutch" Morial's administration. Morial, father of the current mayor, Marc Morial, was the city's first black mayor.

Emergencies   For fire, ambulance, and police, dial ☎ **911.** This is a free call from pay phones.

Hospitals   Should you become ill during your visit, most major hotels have in-house doctors on call 24 hours a day. If no one is available at your hotel or guest house, call or go to the emergency room at **Ochsner Medical Institutions,** 1516 Jefferson Hwy. (☎ **504/842-3460**), or the **Tulane University Medical Center,** 1415 Tulane Ave. (☎ **504/588-5800**).

Information   See "Visitor Information" earlier in this chapter.

Liquor Laws   The legal drinking age in Louisiana is 21, but don't be surprised if people much younger take a seat next to you at the bar. Alcoholic beverages are available around the clock, 7 days a week. You're allowed to drink on the street, but not from a glass or bottle. Bars will often provide a plastic "go cup" so you can transfer your drink as you leave (and some have walk-up windows for quick and easy refills).

One warning: Although the police may look the other way if they see a pedestrian who's had a few too many (as long as he or she is peaceful and not bothering anyone), they have no tolerance at all for those who are intoxicated behind the wheel.

Maps   See "City Layout" earlier in this chapter.

Newspapers & Magazines   To find out what's going on around town, you might want to pick up a copy of the daily *Times-Picayune* or *Offbeat*—a monthly guide (probably the most extensive one available) to the city's evening entertainment, art galleries, and special events. It can be found in most hotels, though it's often hard to find toward the end of the month. The *Gambit Weekly* is the city's free alternative paper, and has a good mix of news and entertainment information. It comes out every Thursday. The paper conducts an annual **"Best of New Orleans"** reader poll; results are posted at www.gambit-no.com.

Pharmacies   The 24-hour pharmacy closest to the French Quarter is **Walgreens,** at 3311 Canal St., at Jefferson Davis (☎ **504/822-8072**).

Photographic Needs   Two good options for 1-hour film processing are **Fox Photo Labs,** 414 Canal St. (☎ **504/568-0198**), and **French Quarter Camera,** 809 Decatur St. (☎ **504/529-2974**). Disposable and inexpensive cameras, film, and batteries can be found in any **Rite Aid** pharmacy. You'll find one on almost every other corner in New Orleans.

Police   Dial ☎ **911** for emergencies.

Post Office   The main post office is at 701 Loyola Ave. There's also a post office in the World Trade Center. If you're in the Quarter, you'll find a post office at 1022 Iberville St. There's another one at 610 S. Maestri Place. If you have something large or fragile to send home and don't feel like hunting around for packing materials, go to **Prytania Mail Services,** 5500 Prytania St. (☎ **504/897-0877**), uptown.

Radio   WWOZ FM 90.7 is *the* New Orleans radio station. They say they are the best in the world, and we aren't inclined to disagree. New Orleans jazz, R&B, brass bands, Mardi Gras Indians, gospel, Cajun, zydeco—it's all here. Don't miss music historian (and former White Panther activist, memorialized in a song by John Lennon) John Sinclair's shows (at press time, Wednesday 11am to 2pm and Sunday 2 to 5am) which recently got him named Best DJ in *OffBeat's* annual poll.

Safety   Be careful while visiting any unfamiliar city. In New Orleans in particular, don't walk alone at night, and don't go into the cemeteries alone at any time during the day or night. Ask around locally before you go anywhere. People will tell you if you should take a cab instead of walking or using public transportation. Most important, if someone holds you up and demands your wallet, purse, or other personal belongings, don't resist.

Taxes   The **sales tax** in New Orleans is 9%. An additional 2% tax is added to hotel bills, for a total of 11%.

Taxis   See "Getting Around," earlier in this chapter.

Time Zone   New Orleans observes central time, the same as Chicago. Between the first Sunday in April and the last Saturday in October, daylight saving time is in effect. During this period, clocks are set 1 hour ahead of standard time. Call ☎ **504/976-1111** for the correct local time.

Transit Information   Local bus routes and schedules can be obtained from the **RTA Ride Line** (☎ **504/248-3900**). **Union Passenger Terminal,** 1001 Loyola Ave., provides bus information (☎ **504/524-7571**) and train information (☎ **504/528-1610**).

Traveler's Aid Society   You can reach the local branch of the society at ☎ **504/ 525-8726.**

Weather   For an update, call ☎ **504/828-4000.**

Accommodations 6

If you're doing your New Orleans trip right, you shouldn't be doing much sleeping. But you do have to put your change of clothes somewhere. New Orleans is bursting with hotels of every variety, so you should be able to find something that fits your preferences. However, during crowded times (Mardi Gras, for example), just finding anything might have to be good enough. After all, serious New Orleans visitors often book a year in advance for popular times. That's competition!

Given a choice, we tend to favor slightly faded, ever-so-faintly-decayed, just-this-side-of-elegant locales; a new, sterile chain doesn't seem right for New Orleans, where atmosphere is all. Slightly tattered lace curtains, faded antiques, mossy courtyards with banana trees and fountains, a musty, Miss Havisham air—to us, it's all part of the fun. We prefer to stay in a Tennessee Williams play, if not an Anne Rice novel (though in summertime, we'll take air-conditioning, thank you very much). Understandably, this may not appeal to you. (It may in fact describe your own home, and who wants her own home on vacation?) Regardless of whether you want the anonymous familiarity of a chain (where every room is identical but a certain level of quality is assured), serious pampering, major antiques, or a good location, there's a place for you.

However, here are a few tips. Don't stay on Bourbon Street unless you absolutely have to, or don't mind getting no sleep. The open-air frat party that is that thoroughfare does mean a free show below your window, but is hardly conducive to . . . well, just about anything other than participation in same. (On the other hand, making a night of it on your balcony, people-watching—and people-egging-on—is an activity with its own merits, one enjoyed by a number of happy tourists.) If you must stay on Bourbon Street, try to get a room away from the street.

A first-time visitor might also strongly consider not staying in the Quarter at all. Most of your sightseeing will take place there, but you may want to get away from it all after dinner, or simply see a neighborhood whose raison d'être isn't to entertain first-time visitors. Try the beautiful Garden District instead. It's an easy streetcar ride away from the Quarter, and closer to a number of wonderful clubs and restaurants. Conventioneers and businesspeople tend to favor the Central Business District. It is closer to their kind of action, but has not produced much in the way of colorful hotels, and is a largely sterile location otherwise.

All of the guest houses in this chapter are first rate. If you want more information, we highly recommend the ✪ **Bed and Breakfast, Inc. Reservation Service,** 1021 Moss St. (P.O. Box 52257), New Orleans, LA 70152 (☎ **800/729-4640** or 504/488-4640). The domain of Hazell Boyce, a leading personality in the local tourism industry, it was one of the first licensed registration services in the nation. It represents around 50 establishments in every section of the city, among them 19th-century, turn-of-the-century, and modern residences, offering suites, rooms, and cottages. Hazell's staff knows every property inside and out (they make sure all of the B&Bs stay up to snuff) and can pick the perfect place for you—just tell them what you want. Prices range from $35 to $225 a night. The service can also often find a room for you on relatively short notice.

As a general rule, just to be on the safe side, always book ahead during spring, fall, and winter. And if your trip will coincide with Mardi Gras or Jazz Fest, book way ahead—up to a year in advance, if you want to be sure of a room. Sugar Bowl week and other festival times when visitors flood New Orleans also require planning for accommodations, and there's always the chance that a big convention will be in town, making it difficult to find a room. You might conceivably run across a cancellation and get a last-minute booking, but the chances are remote at best. You should also be aware that rates frequently jump more than a notch or two for Mardi Gras and other festival times (sometimes they even double), and in some cases there's a 4- or 5-night minimum requirement.

If you want to miss the crowds and the lodgings squeeze that mark the big festivals, consider coming in the month immediately following Mardi Gras, or, if you can stand the heat and humidity, in the summer, when the streets are not nearly as thronged. December, before the Sugar Bowl and New Year's activities, is a good time, too, but perhaps a bit rainy.

There are no recommendable inexpensive hotels in the French Quarter. If you're on a budget and must stay there, consider a guest house. On the whole, however, you'll have a better selection of inexpensive lodgings outside the Quarter. There are two hostels in New Orleans; both are listed at the end of this chapter.

At press time, a new promising property was **The Jockey Club,** due to open at 125 St. Charles Ave. (☎ **504/671-8000;** fax 504/671-8003), in the first quarter of 2000. It will be a high-end boutique hotel, taking over and entirely revitalizing the old Kolb Restaurant building and the next door Whitney Bank, and will have well-appointed luxury rooms and guest suites in a classic New Orleans structure.

You'll find a list of our favorite accommodations in a variety of eclectic categories in chapter 1.

The hotels and guest houses listed in this chapter are divided first by neighborhood, and then into four price categories. Those listed as **very expensive** will cost upwards of $200 a night for a double room; **expensive** hotels start in the neighborhood of $160 a night; **moderate** hotels offer rooms for $80 to $160. A hotel where you can get a comfortable room for under $80 is considered **inexpensive.** Rates are for double rooms and do not include the city's 11% hotel tax. Reduced single-occupancy rates are often offered; inquire when you make reservations. Unless otherwise noted, all accommodations in New Orleans have private bathrooms.

1 The French Quarter

VERY EXPENSIVE

✪ **Melrose Mansion.** 937 Esplanade Ave., New Orleans, LA 70116. ☎ **800/650-3323** or 504/944-2255. Fax 504/945-1794. 10 units. A/C MINIBAR TV TEL. $225–$250 double; $325–$425 suite. Rates include champagne breakfast and cocktail hour. AE, DISC, MC, V. Parking available on street.

Factoid

There is, of course, considerable concern about personal safety in New Orleans. Your hotel choice, for the most part, need not be influenced by that. Daytime is mostly safe, and at night, you will probably be in cabs or, if you're in the French Quarter, in fairly well-populated areas. If you stay above Bourbon Street, closer to Rampart, you should not walk back to your hotel alone at night; take a cab, or be sure to follow along with other groups.

Even on a street full of envy-inducing mansions, in a town full of pampering guest houses, the Melrose Mansion (and soon to be Spa) is an experience. Think luxury resort living, combined with the best of guest house offerings, and you should get the idea. A charming old mansion, beautifully renovated, is the setting, where full-time butlers, soft music, evening candles, and other touches (including cocktail hour wine and cheese) combine for a rarified, but not snooty atmosphere. The rooms vary, from classic Victorian antiques to lighter country-style decor; we love the bright yellow Miss Kitty's Room (named for a former tenant and burlesque dancer), and the more classic Burgundy Room. Bathrooms can be small, but plush bathrobes and linens help. The Parc Henry suite overlooks the year-round heated pool, and between that and its large dining room and kitchen, seems perfect for entertaining and hanging out. Don't miss the crawfish quiche at breakfast. Plans are to create a full spa right next door, but in the meantime, they have someone on call for all your massage and herbal scrub needs.

✪ **Omni Royal Orleans.** 621 St. Louis St., New Orleans, LA 70140. ☎ **800/THE-OMNI** in the U.S. and Canada, or 504/529-5333. Fax 504/529-7089. www.omnihotel.com. 346 units. A/C MINIBAR TV TEL. $129–$309 double; $269–$649 suite; $949 penthouse. Children under 18 stay free in parents' room. AE, CB, DC, DISC, MC, V. Valet parking $15.

Despite being part of a chain, this is a most elegant hotel that, unlike others in its class, escapes feeling sterile and generic. This is only proper, given that it is on the former site of the venerable 1836 St. Louis Exchange Hotel, one of the country's premier hostelries and a center of New Orleans social life until the final years of the Civil War. The original building was finally destroyed by a 1915 hurricane, but the Omni, built in 1960, is a worthy successor. It enjoys a prime location, smack in the center of the Quarter. Truman Capote and William Styron have stayed here, and there is a Tennessee Williams Suite. The lobby is a small sea of marble and brass and crystal chandeliers. Furnishings in the guest rooms are equally elegant, full of muted tones and plush furniture, with windows that let you look dreamily out over the Quarter. All rooms come equipped with umbrellas, irons, and ironing boards, and bathrooms include such amenities as terry robes and makeup mirrors. Service varies between exceptional and slightly lacking when the place is busy.

Dining: The classic Rib Room is a favorite dining spot for many natives (see chapter 7), and there's soft music after 8pm in the sophisticated Esplanade Lounge. Touché Bar offers light meals and excellent mint juleps. The rooftop, poolside La Riviera bar and restaurant is a terrific lunch spot, with palm trees and unobstructed views of the French Quarter.

Amenities: Health club, heated outdoor pool, concierge, baby-sitting, emergency mending and pressing, complimentary shoe shine, nightly turndown, 24-hour room service, beauty and barber shops, florist, sundries shop and newsstand, business center.

Ritz-Carlton, New Orleans. 921 Canal St., New Orleans, LA 70112. ☎ **800/241-3333** or 504/524-1331. 452 units. A/C MINIBAR TV TEL. $335 double. Suites $685 and way, way up. AE, DC, MC, V.

New Orleans Accommodations

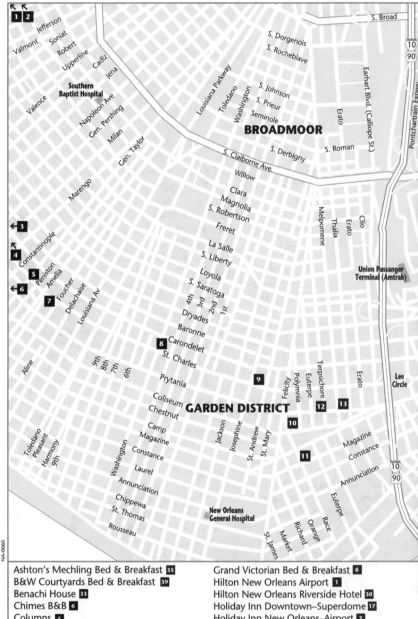

Ashton's Mechling Bed & Breakfast **35**
B&W Courtyards Bed & Breakfast **39**
Benachi House **33**
Chimes B&B **6**
Columns **5**
Courtyard by Marriott **22**
Crowne Plaza New Orleans **29**
Depot at Madame Julia's **15**
Fairmont Hotel **19**
Frenchmen **38**

Grand Victorian Bed & Breakfast **8**
Hilton New Orleans Airport **1**
Hilton New Orleans Riverside Hotel **30**
Holiday Inn Downtown–Superdome **17**
Holiday Inn New Orleans–Airport **2**
Hotel Inter-Continental **23**
Hotel La Salle **18**
House on Bayou Road **34**
Hyatt Regency **16**
International House **24**

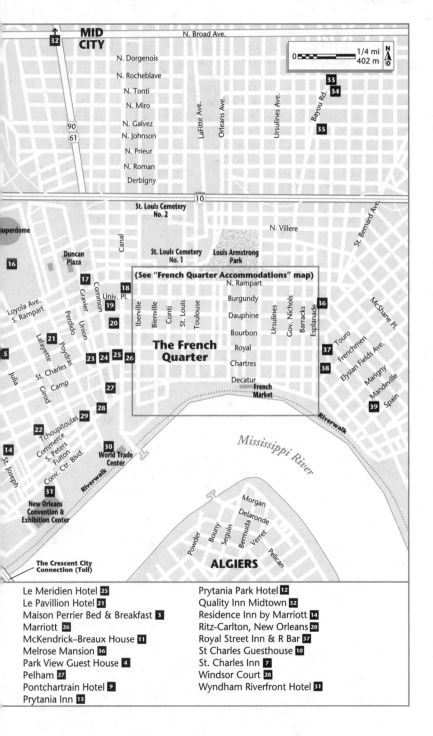

MID CITY

N. Broad Ave.

N. Dorgenois
N. Rocheblave
N. Tonti
N. Miro
N. Galvez
N. Johnson
N. Prieur
N. Roman
Derbigny

90
61
32

33
34
35

LaFitte Ave.
Orleans Ave.
Ursulines Ave.
Bayou Rd.

0   1/4 mi
    402 m
N

Superdome

16

I-10

St. Louis Cemetery No. 2

Canal

N. Villere

St. Bernard Ave.

Duncan Plaza

17

St. Louis Cemetery No. 1

Louis Armstrong Park

Common
Gravier
Univ. Pl.
18
19
20

(See "French Quarter Accommodations" map)

N. Rampart
Burgundy
Dauphine
Bourbon
Royal
Chartres
Decatur

The French Quarter

Ursulines
Gov. Nichols
Barracks
Esplanade

McShane Pl.

36

Touro
Frenchmen
Elysian Fields Ave.

37
38

Marigny
Mandeville
Spain

39

Iberville
Bienville
Conti
St. Louis
Toulouse

Loyola Ave.
S. Rampart

Perdido
Union
Poydras

21

5

Julia
St. Charles
Girod
Camp

23 24 25 26

27

28

French Market

Riverwalk

Lafayette

Tchoupitoulas
Commerce
S. Peters
Fulton
Conv. Ctr. Blvd.

22

14

St. Joseph

29

30
World Trade Center

Mississippi River

Riverwalk

31

New Orleans Convention & Exhibition Center

The Crescent City Connection (Toll)

Morgan
Delaronde
Bermuda
Verret
Powder
Bouny
Seguin
Pelican

ALGIERS

Le Meridien Hotel 25
Le Pavillion Hotel 21
Maison Perrier Bed & Breakfast 3
Marriott 26
McKendrick–Breaux House 11
Melrose Mansion 36
Park View Guest House 4
Pelham 27
Pontchartrain Hotel 9
Prytania Inn 13

Prytania Park Hotel 12
Quality Inn Midtown 32
Residence Inn by Marriott 14
Ritz-Carlton, New Orleans 20
Royal Street Inn & R Bar 37
St Charles Guesthouse 10
St. Charles Inn 7
Windsor Court 28
Wyndham Riverfront Hotel 31

Sentimentalists that we are, we were deeply sad to see the venerable Maison Blanche department store go the way of Woolworth's, D. H. Holmes, and other Canal Street shopping landmarks. But for New Orleans' sake, we are pleased to have a Ritz-Carlton take its place, preserving the classic glazed terra-cotta building and bringing a high-end luxury hotel to the Quarter. The hotel is due to open at the end of 1999, and should bring plenty of Ritz luxury. They also promise other touches, like safes and dual-line telephones and modems in the rooms, plus "interior design and furnishings that pay homage to the Garden District."

Dining: Breakfast, lunch, and dinner can be had at the Library Lounge, while afternoon tea, cocktails, and hors d'oeuvres are served in the Lobby Lounge.

Amenities: Large spa and fitness center, 24-hour room service, turndown, business center, shops, ballroom and meeting rooms.

Westin Canal Place. 100 Rue Iberville, New Orleans, LA 70130. ☎ **800/228-3000** or 504/566-7006. www.westin1.com. 437 units. A/C MINIBAR TV TEL. $289–$319 double. AE, CB, DC, DISC, MC, V. $15 valet parking, $13 self-parking.

At the foot of Canal Street, the Westin Canal Place is in the French Quarter, but not quite *of* it. It is, literally, *above* the Quarter: The grand-scale lobby, with its fine paintings and antiques, is on the 11th floor of the Canal Place tower. The hotel completed major renovations in the spring of 1996, redesigning the lobby and guest rooms in a nicely muted neoclassical style. The guest rooms are on the floors above; each has a marble foyer and bathroom, fine furnishings (including particularly good pillows), and phones with call waiting and voice mail. Needless to say, this hotel provides some of the city's most expansive views of the river and the French Quarter.

Of particular appeal to business travelers (who often rave about the hotel) is the Westin Guest Office program (available for an additional $20), which includes free office supplies, a coffeemaker, and use of an in-room copier/printer/fax.

Dining: The lobby makes an impressive setting for afternoon tea. The Green Bar and the Riverbend Grill restaurant are just steps away. There is also a Sunday jazz brunch.

Amenities: Heated pool, privileges at nearby 18-hole golf course, tour desk, concierge, 24-hour room service, multilingual staff, dry cleaning and laundry, newspaper delivery. There's direct elevator access to Canal Place shopping center, where guests can use the health center free of charge or visit the barber shop, beauty salon, and stores.

EXPENSIVE

Best Western Inn on Bourbon Street. 541 Bourbon St., New Orleans, LA 70130. ☎ **800/535-7891** or 504/524-7611. Fax 504/568-9427. www.innonbourbon.com. 186 units. A/C MINIBAR TV TEL. $195–$275 double. AE, CB, DC, DISC, MC, V. Valet parking $13.

This hotel is on the site of the 1859 French Opera House, the first built in the United States (it burned down in 1919). Party animals and party animal-phobes should note this location is right in the middle of the liveliest action on Bourbon, and many rooms have balconies overlooking the mayhem below. If you have a serious commitment to sleeping, you might want to choose another place to stay, or at least request an interior room. On the other hand, there are worse ways to spend a N'Awlins evening than having a pizza on your balcony while enjoying the free show on Bourbon Street below. All rooms have Deep South decor and king or double beds.

Dining: There's a lounge in the lobby. The Bourbon Street Cafeteria serves breakfast.

Amenities: Fitness room, outdoor pool, concierge, dry cleaning and laundry, newspaper delivery, baby-sitting by arrangement, express checkout, jewelry shop, gift shop.

French Quarter Accommodations

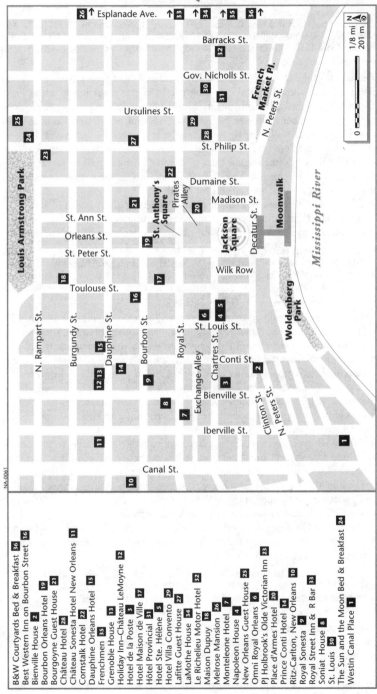

Esplanade Ave. 26 33 34 35 36

Barracks St. 32

Gov. Nicholls St. 30 31

Ursulines St. 29

27 28

St. Philip St.

25

24

23

Louis Armstrong Park

Dumaine St. 22

Pirates Alley

Madison St.

21 St. Anthony's Square 20

St. Ann St.

Orleans St. 19

St. Peter St.

Jackson Square

Decatur St.

Moonwalk

French Market Pl.

N. Peters St.

Mississippi River

Wilk Row

18 Toulouse St. 17

16

N. Rampart St.

Burgundy St.

Dauphine St.

15

14

12 13

Bourbon St.

9

6 4 5

St. Louis St.

Royal St.

Chartres St.

Conti St. 2

3

8

7

Exchange Alley

Bienville St.

Woldenberg Park

11

Iberville St.

Clinton St.

N. Peters St.

1

Canal St.

10

NA-0061

B&W Courtyards Bed & Breakfast 36
Best Western Inn on Bourbon Street 16
Bienville House 2
Bourbon Orleans Hotel 19
Bourgoyne Guest House 21
Château Hotel 28
Château Sonesta Hotel New Orleans 11
Cornstalk Hotel 22
Dauphine Orleans Hotel 15
Frenchmen 35
Grenoble House 13
Holiday Inn–Château LeMoyne 12
Hotel de la Poste 3
Hotel Maison de Ville 17
Hôtel Provincial 31
Hotel Ste. Hélène 5
Hotel Villa Convento 29
Lafitte Guest House 27
LaMothe House 34
Le Richelieu Motor Hotel 32
Maison Dupuy 18
Melrose Mansion 26
Monteleone Hotel 7
Napoleon House 4
New Orleans Guest House 25
Omni Royal Orleans 6
PJ Holbrook's Olde Victorian Inn 23
Place d'Armes Hotel 20
Prince Conti Hotel 14
Ritz-Carlton, New Orleans 10
Royal Sonesta 9
Royal Street Inn & R Bar 33
Soniat House 8
St. Louis 30
The Sun and the Moon Bed & Breakfast 24
Westin Canal Place 1

67

Château Sonesta Hotel New Orleans. 800 Iberville St., New Orleans, LA 70112. ☎ **800/ SONESTA** or 504/586-0800. Fax 504/586-1987. 251 units. A/C MINIBAR TV TEL. $160–$260 double; $350–$550 suite. Extra person $40. AE, CB, DC, DISC, MC, V. Valet parking $15, self-parking $12.

On the site of the D. H. Holmes Canal Street Department Store (1849), the Château Sonesta Hotel opened in 1995, making it one of the newer hotels in the French Quarter. While the building maintains the 1913 facade, inside it is a generic high-end hotel, popular among business groups for its meeting rooms and location. At the Canal Street entrance is a newly erected statue of Ignatius Reilly, hero of *A Confederacy of Dunces,* whom we first met when he was waiting, as all of New Orleans once did, under the clock (the original clock is now in a bar inside). Guest rooms are large, and many feature balconies overlooking Bourbon or Dauphine street. In addition to in-house movies, videos are available for rental.

Dining: La Chatelaine Restaurant and the Clock Bar are open daily.

Amenities: Heated outdoor pool, exercise room, concierge, room service till at least midnight, laundry and dry cleaning, baby-sitting, nightly turndown, gift shop, tour desk.

Dauphine Orleans Hotel. 415 Dauphine St., New Orleans, LA 70112. ☎ **800/521-7111** or 504/586-1800. Fax 504/586-1409. www.dauphineorleans.com. 111 units. A/C MINIBAR TV TEL. $149–$199 double; $149–$259 patio room; $179–$359 suite. Rates include continental breakfast and afternoon tea. Extra person $15. Children under 17 stay free in parents' room. AE, CB, DC, DISC, MC, V. Valet parking $12.

On a relatively quiet and peaceful block of the Quarter, the Dauphine Orleans Hotel sports a casual elegance. It's just a block from the action on Bourbon Street, but you wouldn't know it if you were sitting in any of its three secluded courtyards. The hotel's buildings have a colorful history. The license a former owner took out to make the place a bordello is proudly displayed in the bar, and its proprietors are happy to admit that ghosts have been sighted on the premises. The hotel's back buildings were once the studio of John James Audubon, and the "patio rooms" across the street from the main building were originally built in 1834 as the home of New Orleans merchant Samuel Herrmann.

All rooms have recently been upgraded with marble bathrooms (equipped with robes and hair dryers), irons and ironing boards, new solid-wood headboards and feather pillows, and new furnishings, either modern or upgraded period pieces.

Dining: May Baily's, the hotel bar, was once a notorious "sporting house" (brothel), and guests are given a copy of the 1857 license. Breakfast is served from 6:30 to 11am in the Coffee Lounge. Afternoon tea is served daily from 3 to 5pm.

Amenities: Outdoor pool, small fitness room, concierge, dry cleaning and laundry, baby-sitting, complimentary French Quarter and downtown transportation, newspaper delivery, guest library, Jacuzzi.

Grenoble House. 329 Dauphine St., New Orleans, LA 70112. ☎ **800/722-1834** or 504/522-1331. 17 suites. A/C TV TEL. $199–$279 1-bedroom suite; $199–$279 2-bedroom suite. Rates include continental breakfast. Weekly rates available. AE, MC, V. Parking available at nearby lot. No children under 12.

The Grenoble House is an old French Quarter town house built around a courtyard, small, quiet and close to everything. Rooms are all apartments (the most private are in the old slave quarters in the back), with a totally full kitchen (including microwave), a sitting/living area, and a bedroom recently refitted with expensive new mattresses. Furnishings can be disappointingly modern—it clashes with the frequently exposed brick walls, if you ask us. Businesspeople like the apartment-like convenience, while families with teenagers (children under 12 aren't allowed) might look into the two-bedroom accommodations. There is a small unheated pool for dipping, plus a Jacuzzi.

A special plus here is the personal, attentive service—they'll book theater tickets, restaurant reservations, and sightseeing tours, and even arrange a gourmet dinner brought to your suite or a private cocktail party on the patio if you want to entertain.

✪ **Hotel Maison de Ville.** 727 Toulouse St., New Orleans, LA 70130. ☎ **800/634-1600** or 504/561-5858. Fax 504/528-9939. www.maisondeville.com. 23 units, 5 cottages. A/C MINIBAR TV TEL. $195–$225 double; $215–$235 queen; $225–$245 king; $325–$375 suite; $235–$325 1-bedroom cottage; $535–$725 2-bedroom cottage; $770–$1,005 3-bedroom cottage. AE, DC, MC, V. Valet parking $18.

On the list of Best Small Hotels in the World, the Maison de Ville is a great splurge. Tennessee Williams was a regular guest in room no. 9. Most of the rooms surround an utterly charming courtyard (complete with fountain and banana trees), where it's hard to imagine you're in the thick of the Quarter. The hotel is elegant and antique-filled. Rooms vary dramatically in size; some can be downright tiny, so ask when you reserve, as price is no indicator of size. The more spacious Audubon Cottages, located a few blocks away in their own courtyard with a small pool, can go for less than cramped queen suites in the main hotel (and are further from the hubbub of Bourbon Street).

All accommodations are thoroughly lush, with nice touches like featherbeds, and the service is stupendous. Best of all, once you book a room, it's yours. If you have it during Jazz Fest, for example, you get first crack at the same room the following year (if you decline, then somebody else gets a chance at it). Not cheap, but certainly a case of getting what you pay for. A great romantic getaway.

Dining: Continental breakfast is served on a silver tray in your room, in the parlor, or on the patio. Complimentary sherry and port are served in the afternoon and evening. Le Bistro, the hotel's restaurant, is intimate and inviting. (See chapter 7 for a full review.)

Amenities: Outdoor pool, access to nearby health club, concierge, room service (7am to 10pm), twice-daily maid service, newspaper delivery, shoe shine, dry cleaning and laundry.

Maison Dupuy. 1001 Toulouse St., New Orleans, LA 70112. ☎ **800/535-9177** or 504/586-8000. Fax 504/525-5334. www.maisondupuy.com. 200 units. A/C MINIBAR TV TEL. $99–$269 superior double; $149–$299 deluxe double with balcony; $329–$838 suite. AE, CB, DC, DISC, MC, V. Valet parking $16 when available.

Made up of seven town houses, Maison Dupuy is well located for French Quarter sightseeing and is the perfect size for those who like privacy but don't want to be ignored. Rooms are quite large, and each has a desk, comfortable armchairs, and two double beds or one king-size bed. Some rooms have balconies that face the courtyard or the street. The maid service is perhaps the best in town. In the courtyard, you can swim, enjoy a cocktail, or just take in the beautiful surroundings.

Dining/Diversions: Dominique's is a French Caribbean restaurant serving breakfast, lunch, and dinner (see review in chapter 7). The hotel also offers a Sunday "Champagne Jazz Brunch Buffet." The Cabaret Lautrec Lounge has live entertainment and is a perfect place to relax. The courtyard patio bar is open during fair weather.

Amenities: Heated outdoor pool, health club, concierge, room service (6am to midnight), twice-daily maid service, same-day laundry and dry cleaning, newspaper delivery, baby-sitting.

Monteleone Hotel. 214 Royal St., New Orleans, LA 70130. ☎ **800/535-9595** or 504/523-3341. Fax 504/528-1019. www.hotelmonteleone.com. 600 units. A/C TV TEL. $140–$225 double or king double; $360–$900 suite. Extra person $25. Children under 18 stay free in parents' room. Package rates available. AE, CB, DC, DISC, MC, V. Valet parking $13 car, $17 van.

Opened in 1886, the Monteleone is the oldest hotel in the city. Truman Capote's parents were living here when he was born in 1924. It's also the largest hotel in the French Quarter, and seems to keep getting bigger without losing a trace of its trademark charm. Because of its size, you can almost always get a reservation here, even when other places are booked. The Monteleone is defined by its lobby, made irresistibly grand by a delicately painted ceiling, chandeliers, and a marble floor. Service is surprisingly personal for a hotel of this size, perhaps because it has been operated by four generations of Monteleones. Accommodations range in style from luxurious, antique-filled suites to more modern, comfortable family rooms.

Dining/Diversions: Le Café restaurant is a favorite with New Orleans natives; even if you stay elsewhere, stop by to see the revolving Carousel Bar (see chapter 11).

Amenities: Heated rooftop swimming pool (open year-round), hot tub, sauna, fitness center, concierge, room service 6am to 11pm, laundry, baby-sitting.

✪ **Royal Sonesta.** 300 Bourbon St., New Orleans, LA 70140. ☎ **800/766-3782** or 504/586-0300. Fax 504/586-0335. www.royalsonestano.com. 500 units. A/C MINIBAR TV TEL. $205–$340 double; $400–$1,400 suite. AE, CB, DC, DISC, MC, V. Parking $15.

This is the most upscale hotel in the French Quarter. The contrast between the hurly-burly of Bourbon Street and the Sonesta's marbled and chandeliered lobby couldn't be greater. Outside, it's raucous and boisterous and up all night. Inside, all is quiet and gracious, and if your room faces the courtyard (complete with large pool), you are in another world altogether. Some people consider this the only acceptable, top-flight Bourbon Street hotel, though noise is still a problem in rooms that face Bourbon (or even the side streets). But because the Sonesta is so large, reaching nearly to Royal Street, unless you do have one of those rooms, you won't believe you are so close to such craziness. Rooms are upscale standard hotel issue—pretty and highly comfortable, but nothing memorable. This is the best place in the Quarter to catch a cab: They line up at the corner.

Dining/Diversions: Begue's restaurant carries on the tradition of an older New Orleans eating spot of the same name; Desire offers fresh seafood and an oyster bar. The Can Can Cafe features live Dixieland jazz.

Amenities: Room service until 2am, exercise room, business center. The concierge service is primo and the pool is the largest in the Quarter.

St. Louis. 730 Bienville St., New Orleans, LA 70130. ☎ **800/537-8483** or 504/581-7300. Fax 504/679-5013. 72 units. A/C TV TEL. $159–$259 double; $329–$629 suite. Children under 16 stay free in parents' room. AE, CB, DISC, MC, V. Valet parking $16.50.

Right in the heart of the Quarter, the St. Louis is a small hotel that surrounds a lush courtyard with a fountain. But it's somewhat disappointingly dull for what ought to be a charming boutique hotel. Some rooms have private balconies overlooking Bienville Street, and all open on to the central courtyard. Rooms are undergoing a remodeling with new carpet, drapes, and furniture, which should freshen up a slightly stodgy decor by the time you read this. The otherwise uninteresting bathrooms do have bidets.

Dining: This is the home of the elegant Louis XVI restaurant (see chapter 7), which serves fine French cuisine.

Amenities: Concierge, complimentary daily newspaper, laundry, room service from Louis XVI restaurant at breakfast, baby-sitting, access to nearby healthy club.

✪ **Soniat House.** 1133 Chartres St., New Orleans, LA 70116. ☎ **800/544-8808** or 504/522-0570. Fax 504/522-7208. 33 units. A/C TV TEL. $165–$245 double; $295–$495 suite; $625 2-bedroom suite. AE, MC, V. Valet parking $16.

The recipient of a seemingly endless series of tributes from various prestigious travel journals, the Soniat House lives up to the hype. It's mighty wonderful. Keeping a low profile behind a solid wood gate, it's classic Creole, where the treasures are hidden off the street. This is the perfect little hideaway, an oasis of calm that seems impossible in the Quarter. The beyond-efficient staff will spoil you and the sweet courtyards, candlelit at night, will soothe you.

Rooms do vary, if not in quality, then at least in distinction. All have antiques, but if you want, say, high ceilings and really grand furniture (room 23 has a 17th-century bed), you are better off in the main house or the suite-filled annex across the street. The rooms in the old kitchen and other buildings are not quite as smashing by comparison. On the main property, bathrooms are small. But across the street, they gain size, not to mention Jacuzzi bathtubs, custom decor, and antique furnishings. Children over 12 are welcome only in rooms that accommodate three.

Dining: The "Southern Continental" breakfast, available every morning after 7am, costs $7 extra, but you will say it's worth it when you taste the huge fluffy biscuits, baked to order, and fresh orange juice. There is a fully stocked honor bar in the parlor next to the reception area.

Amenities: Jacuzzi, access to nearby health club and business center (for an additional charge), concierge, same-day dry-cleaning and laundry, evening turndown, newspaper delivery.

MODERATE

B&W Courtyards Bed & Breakfast. 2425 Chartres St., New Orleans, LA 70117. ☎ **800/ 585-5731** or 504/945-9418. www.bandwcourtyards.com. 5 units. $115–$225 double. Rates include breakfast. AE, D, MC, V. Parking available on street.

The deceptively simple façade hides a sweet and very hospitable little B&B, complete with two small courtyards and a fountain. It's located in the Faubourg Marigny, next to the bustling nighttime Frenchmen scene, a 10-minute walk or $5 cab ride (at most) to the Quarter. Owners Rob Boyd and Kevin Wu went to ingenious lengths to turn five oddly shaped spaces into comfortable rooms. No two rooms are alike—you enter one through its bathroom. Another room is more like a small, two-story apartment, with the bedroom upstairs and a virtually full kitchen downstairs. All are carefully and thoughtfully decorated (check out the remote-control ceiling fans!). Rob and Kevin are adept at giving advice—and strong opinions—not just about the city, but about their own local favorites. Breakfast is light (fruit, homemade breads), but beautifully presented. Prepare to be pampered. They take good care of you here.

Bienville House. 320 Decatur St., New Orleans, LA 70130. ☎ **800/535-7836** or 504/529-2345. Fax 504/525-6079. 83 units. A/C TV TEL. $89–$300 double. Rates include continental breakfast. AE, CB, DC, DISC, MC, V. Valet parking $11 cars, $15 sport utility vehicles.

The newly renovated Bienville House is in the same neighborhood as Hotel de la Poste (see below). Bienville House is more sedate, if not as impressive from the street. Its small lobby is lavish, with a chandelier, marble floors, Mediterranean-style wall paintings, and overstuffed sofas. The guest rooms have all of the standard amenities of a fine hotel (large TVs, coffeemakers, hair dryers, fine toiletries), but antique and reproduction furniture gives the rooms more personality than you find in most places. Some rooms have a small balcony overlooking the flagstone courtyard and pool area.

✪ **Bourbon Orleans Hotel.** 717 Orleans St., New Orleans, LA 70116. ☎ **504/523-2222.** Fax 504/525-8166. 216 units. A/C MINIBAR TV TEL. $119–$189 petite queen or twin; $139–$209 deluxe king or double; $179–$249 junior suite; $229–$379 town house suite; $259–$459 town house suite with balcony. Extra person $20. AE, CB, DC, DISC, MC, V. Valet parking $14.55.

A lot of hotels claim to be centrally located in the French Quarter, but the Bourbon Orleans really is. The place takes up an entire block of prime real estate at the intersection of—guess where—Bourbon and Orleans streets.

A lot of hotels also claim to have an interesting history, but this one really does. The oldest part of the hotel is the Orleans Ballroom, constructed in 1815 as a venue for the city's masquerade, carnival, and notorious quadroon balls. In 1881, the building was sold to the Sisters of the Holy Family, members of the South's first order of African American nuns. The sisters converted the ballroom into a school and remained for 80 years until the building was sold to real estate developers from Baton Rouge, who turned it into an apartment hotel.

Today, the hotel occupies three buildings and has recently undergone a $6 million renovation. You just wish it had more character to go along with its fascinating history. Public spaces are lavishly decorated but their elegant interest doesn't quite extend to the guest rooms. Bigger than average, they will give no cause for complaint about either decor (standard for this area, though even after upgrades, rooms feel tired rather than fresh and exciting) or comfort (we do like the Bath & Bodyworks amenities) but you can't help but want something a little more striking. There are also two-level suites that have a living room with a pull-out queen sofa. If you want to escape the excitement of Bourbon Street during your nonwaking hours, ask for an interior room. Bathrooms are outfitted with Italian marble, telephones, and hair dryers.

Amenities include same-day dry cleaning, room service during limited hours, optional voice mail, fax machines, data ports, nightly shoe shine, and daily morning newspaper delivery. There's a good-sized pool on the premises. Dining is in the Café Lafayette, and the elegant lobby bar features a nightly cocktail hour.

Bourgoyne Guest House. 839 Bourbon St., New Orleans, LA 70116. ☎ **504/525-3983** or 504/524-3621. 5 apts. A/C MINIBAR TEL. Studios $85 double; Blue Suite $110 double, $135 triple, $150 quad; Green Suite $120 double, $145 triple, $170 quad. MC, V. Parking (about $13) available nearby.

This is an eccentric place with an owner to match. If you dislike stuffy hotels and can happily take things a little worn at the edges in trade for a relaxed, hang-out atmosphere, come here.

Accommodations are arranged around a nicely cluttered courtyard, the right spot to visit and regroup before diving back out on to Bourbon Street (whose main action begins just a few feet away). Studios are adequate little rooms with kitchens and baths that appear grimy but are not (we saw the strong potions housekeeping uses; it's just a function of age). The Green Suite is as big and grand as one would like, with huge tall rooms, a second smaller bedroom, a bigger bath, and a balcony overlooking Bourbon Street. For price and location, it's a heck of a deal, maybe the best in the Quarter. The first floor can suffer from street noise, though, that probably depends on the time of year and how far up Bourbon the party travels.

Château Hotel. 1001 Chartres St., New Orleans, LA 70116. ☎ **504/524-9636.** Fax 504/525-2989. 45 units. A/C TV TEL. $99–$129 double. Rates include continental breakfast. 10% senior discount available. AE, CB, DC, MC, V. Free parking.

A bit removed from the well-traveled sections of the French Quarter, the Château is still only a short walk from wherever you're headed. You enter through an old carriage way into a large old Creole building. Oddly dark colors and fussy details unfortunately give you the mistaken first impression that you're in a seedy motel room, but rooms are very clean. It's better than that, though mattresses are hard and bathrooms merely okay. King rooms are bigger in size and a better value, and some rooms have living and bedroom combinations. The courtyard is very New Orleans (though it would benefit from additional greenery) and features an oval shaped swimming pool that cleverly

looks like it might once have been a fountain. The morning newspaper is complimentary.

Cornstalk Hotel. 915 Royal St., New Orleans, LA. 70116. ☎ **504/523-1515.** Fax 504/
522-5558. 14 units. A/C TV TEL. Summer $75–$155 double; winter $135–$175 double. Rates
include continental breakfast. AE, MC, V. Parking $5.

Thanks to the famous fence out front, this might be better known as a sightseeing stop
for tourists than a place to stay, but consider staying here anyway. A gorgeous Victorian home on the National Register of Historic Places, it's nearly as pretty inside as
out. The location couldn't be better. It's almost at the exact heart of the Quarter, on a
busy but not noisy section of Royal.

The requisite antiques dominate; if you are looking for period charm, look no further. The high-ceilinged rooms have fireplaces or stained-glass windows, and some
have plasterwork (ceiling medallions, scrolls, and cherubs) from old plantations. One
room (the one with the largest bed) is spectacular, while the rest are charming—you
feel as if you have gone back 100 years. Unfortunately, that also applies to things like
the plumbing. (Don't hold your breath if everyone turns the hot water on at the same
time.) The large front gallery, set unusually far back from the street, and the upstairs
balcony provide perfect spots for sipping coffee in the morning or sherry after a hard
day's shopping.

Oh, the fence? Well, it's at least 130 years old (photos indicate it might be even
older), is made of cast iron, and looks like cornstalks painted in the appropriate colors.
Legend (almost certainly apocryphal) has it that the original owner built it to ease his
homesick bride's longing for her Iowa roots. When it was a private home, Harriet
Beecher Stowe stayed here—a trip that inspired her to write *Uncle Tom's Cabin.*

✪ The Frenchmen. 417 Frenchmen St., New Orleans, LA 70116. ☎ **800/831-1781**
or 504/948-2166. Fax 504/948-2258. www.french-quarter.org. 27 units. A/C TV TEL.
$79–$155 double. Rates include breakfast. AE, DISC, MC, V. Free parking.

This small, sweet, and slightly funky inn is very popular with in-the-know regular visitors. It's not for some, but others become loyal repeat customers. It feels out of the
way, but in some respects, the location can't be beat. At the intersection of Esplanade
Avenue and Frenchmen Street, it's just across from the Quarter and a block away from
the main drag of the Frenchmen section of the Faubourg Marigny, where there are all
sorts of clubs and happenings at night.

Housed in two 19th-century buildings that were once grand New Orleans homes,
the rooms are each individually decorated and furnished with antiques. They vary in
size considerably, however, and some are very small indeed. Standard rooms have one
double bed, some rooms have private balconies, and others have a loft bedroom with
a sitting area. A small pool (which is currently undergoing a badly needed face-lift)
and Jacuzzi are in the inn's tropical courtyard, where you can often find guests hanging
out at night, talking over the day's activities, planning what they are about to do now,
or just making a night of it right there.

Holiday Inn-Château LeMoyne. 301 Dauphine St., New Orleans, LA 70112. ☎ **800/
HOLIDAY** or 504/581-1303. Fax 504/523-5709. 171 units. A/C TV TEL. $159–$244 double;
$259–$459 suite. Extra person $15. AE, CB, DC, DISC, MC, V. Valet parking $17.

The Château LeMoyne is in a good location, just around the corner from Bourbon
Street, but away from the noise, and not far from Canal. It's a nice surprise to find a
Holiday Inn housed in century-plus old buildings, but the ambience stops at your
room's threshold. Once inside, matters look pretty much like they do in every Holiday
Inn. Too bad. One of these 19th-century buildings was by famed architect James Gal-
lier, and you can still see bits of old brick, old ovens, and exposed cypress beams here

and there, along with a graceful curving outdoor staircase. You wish they'd made more of their space, but instead, even the spacious courtyard feels oddly sterile. Maybe it's the new brick, which seems sandblasted free of pesky (but atmosphere-inducing) moss.

Bedrooms feature coffee makers, hair dryers, irons, and ironing boards. Suites aren't much different, just with frillier furniture, though the enormous Executive Suite is probably worth budget busting, for its four large (if dark) rooms, including a Jacuzzi and sauna.

The restaurant on the premises serves breakfast only, but room service is available until 10pm. There's also a bar, and an outdoor swimming pool. Daily weather is posted in the lobby.

Hotel de la Poste. 316 Chartres St., New Orleans, LA 70130. ☎ **800/448-4927** or 504/581-1200. Fax 504/523-2910. 100 units. A/C TV TEL. $109–$229 standard double; $134–$254 deluxe double; $279 suite. Children under 16 stay free in parents' room. AAA and senior discounts available. AE, CB, DC, DISC, MC, V. Valet parking $18.

The nonbusiness crowd looking for a small family hotel is usually pleased with the Hotel de la Poste. It's on a busy stretch of Chartres (late sleepers should beware the 10am garbage trucks) and Bienville and rooms overlook these streets. Accommodations are mostly spacious (including big dressing areas and closets), though rooms with king-sized beds lose much of their floor space to same. Fresh air fanatics will be pleased that the windows actually open. The courtyard is a fine gathering spot, with piped in music and a small unheated pool. Unfortunately, it shares boundaries with the parking garage driveway. *USA Today* is delivered to your room; your phone will feature voice mail and a data port; and you'll get a hair dryer, iron, and ironing board. Complimentary coffee, tea, and apples are available 24 hours a day. Services include valet laundry, room service 7am to 11pm, a 24-hour bellman, and baby-sitting. Also within the hotel is Bacco (see chapter 7).

Hôtel Provincial. 1024 Chartres St., New Orleans, LA 70116. ☎ **800/535-7922** or 504/581-4995. Fax 504/581-1018. www.hotelprovincial.com. 100 units. A/C TV TEL. $119–$289 double. Summer packages available. AE, CB, DC, DISC, MC, V. Valet parking $11.

Don't mention this to the owners, who are sensitive about it, but word from the ghost tours is that the Provincial is haunted, mostly by soldiers treated here when it was a Civil War hospital. It must not be too much of a problem, because guests rave about the hotel and never mention ghostly visitors. With flickering gas lamps, no elevators, no fewer than five patios, and an overall tranquil setting, this feels less like a hotel than a guest house. Both the quiet and the terrific service belie its size, so it seems smaller and more intimate than it is. It's also in a good part of the Quarter, on a quiet street off the beaten path. Rooms have high ceilings and all have at least a few antiques. Bathrooms are often quite large. The rectangular pool is bigger and more aesthetically pleasing than most in the Quarter. The hotel owns Nu Nu's restaurant on Decatur.

✪ Hotel Ste. Hélène. 508 Chartres St., New Orleans, LA 70130. ☎ **800/348-3888** or 504/522-5014. Fax 504/523-7140. www.stehelene.com. 26 units. A/C TV TEL. $125–$185 double. Rates include continental breakfast and champagne 5:30–6:30pm. AE, CB, DC, DISC, JCB, MC, V. Parking (about $10) in nearby lot.

Thanks to being the shadow of the Omni Royal, its grand across-the-street neighbor, Hotel Ste. Hélène could easily be overlooked. But in our opinion, this is what a slightly funky Quarter hotel should be. What it lacks in magnificence, it makes up for in character and location (less than two blocks from Jackson Square, in the heart of the Quarter). Rooms vary in size and style; front rooms have balconies overlooking the street, others have beds set in alcoves (we find it romantic, though you might find it claustrophobic) with a sort of low-rent parlor sitting area. Still others are just square rooms. Bathrooms can be tiny, but are clean and modern. If some of the "antiques" are actually mock, and the hangings and linens not high end, it all still has a good feel to it.

The property winds about several buildings, with surprises at every turn. Throughout are interior and exterior courtyards (some with flickering gas lamps), which rooms overlook (interior rooms have windows only on the atrium), and there is a rather pretty, though small, raised and brick-enclosed pool. Baby-sitting and laundry service are available.

Hotel Villa Convento. 616 Ursulines St., New Orleans, LA 70116. ☎ **504/522-1793.** Fax 504/524-1902. www.neworleansonline.com/convento.htm. 25 units. A/C TV TEL. $89–$125 double; $155 suite. Rates include continental breakfast. Extra person $10. AE, CB, DC, DISC, MC, V. Parking $12.

Local tour guides say this was the original House of the Rising Sun bordello, so if you have a sense of humor (or theater), be sure to pose in your bathrobe on your balcony so you can be pointed out to passing tour groups. With its rather small public spaces and the personal attention that its owners and operators, the Campo family, give to their guests, the Villa Convento has the feel of a small European inn or guest house. It does a lot of repeat business. The building is a Creole town house; some rooms open onto the tropical patio, others to the street, and many have balconies. The loft rooms are unique family quarters with a king-size bed on the entry level and twin beds in the loft. Breakfast is served in the courtyard; guests may take a tray to their rooms.

Lafitte Guest House. 1003 Bourbon St., New Orleans, LA 70116. ☎ **800/331-7971** or 504/581-2678. Fax 504/581-2677. www.lafitteguesthouse.com. 14 units. A/C TV TEL. $99–$179 double. Rates include continental breakfast. Extra person $25. AE, DISC, MC, V. Parking $10.

Here you'll find the best of both worlds: antique living, but just blocks from Bourbon Street (though the Lafitte's cute little parlor seems almost antithetical to rowdy merriment). The three-story brick building, with wrought-iron balconies on the second and third floors, was constructed in 1849 and has been completely restored. Thanks to new owners, there are ongoing upgrades (columns added to the lobby and so forth), plus better beds and new fixtures in the rooms. The latter each have their own Victorian flair (though rooms #5 and #40 have modern furnishings) with occasional memorable details like a cypress fireplace, plus touches like pralines on the pillow, sleeping masks, and sound machines with soothing (apparently) nature noises. Some rooms have wet bars and small fridges. Room rates include the daily newspaper, and wine and cheese in the parlor during "happy hour." Dry cleaning and baby-sitting are available.

✪ LaMothe House. 621 Esplanade Ave., New Orleans, LA 70116. ☎ **800/367-5858** or 504/947-1161. Fax 504/943-6536. www.new-orleans.org. 20 units. A/C TV TEL. $64–$275 double. Rates include breakfast. AE, DISC, MC, V. Free parking.

Somehow, a shiny new hotel doesn't seem quite right for New Orleans. More appropriate is slightly faded, somewhat threadbare elegance. The LaMothe House neatly fits that bill. The Creole-style plain facade of the 1840s town house hides the atmosphere you are looking for—a mossy, brick-lined courtyard with a fish-filled fountain and banana trees, and rooms filled with antiques that are worn in the right places, but not shabby. A continental breakfast is served in a second-floor dining room that just screams faded gentility. (As the staff points out, it's not Victorian style, it is Victorian.) It's a short walk to the action in the Quarter and just a couple of blocks to the bustling

Frenchmen scene. On a steamy night, sitting in the courtyard breathing the fragrant air, you can feel yourself slip out of time.

Le Richelieu Motor Hotel. 1234 Chartres St., New Orleans, LA 70116. ☎ **800/535-9653** or 504/529-2492. Fax 504/524-8179. 86 units. A/C MINIBAR TV TEL. $95–$170 double; $170–$475 suite. Extra person or child $15. French Quarter Explorer and honeymoon packages available. AE, CB, DC, DISC, JCB, MC, V. Free parking.

First a row mansion, then a macaroni factory, and now a hotel, this building has seen it all. It's at the Esplanade edge of the Quarter—a perfect spot from which to explore the Faubourg Marigny. Though slightly run-down these days, it's good for families, being out of the adult action and not the sort of place that prefers you keep the kids at home. The McCartney family thought so; Paul, the late Linda, and their kids stayed here for some months long ago while Wings was recording an album. Management is proudest of the enormous VIP suite—a sort of early '70s-style apartment, with three bedrooms, a kitchen, living room, dining area, and even a steam room. Other rooms are standard high-end motel rooms. Many have balconies, and all overlook either the French Quarter or the courtyard. Bathrooms are large and outfitted with hair dryers. There's a pool in the large courtyard, with lunch service poolside. The hotel also has a restaurant and bar. Le Richelieu is the only hotel in the French Quarter with free self-parking on the premises.

Napoleon House. 500 Chartres St., New Orleans, LA 70130. ☎ **504/524-9752.** Fax 504/525-2431. 1 apt. A/C TV TEL. $125–$250. Weekly and monthly rates available. AE, DC, DISC, MC, V. No parking available.

The apartment above historic Napoleon House is, by any definition, singular. It has three rooms, with two balconies, and was the longtime residence of owner Sal Impastato's uncle. Its furnishings are what might be called New Orleans homey—several antique pieces intermingle happily with rather well-worn furnishings of indeterminate age but definite comfort. The apartment is in the heart of the Quarter and in the middle of the Napoleon House, one of the city's best pubs and light-meal restaurants. Guests can look down on (or head down to) the restaurant's courtyard, but are hidden away from the world beyond. The apartment is often booked up to a year in advance, but it's worth checking to see if there have been any cancellations.

New Orleans Guest House. 1118 Ursulines St., New Orleans, LA 70116. ☎ **800/ 562-1177** or 504/ 566-1177. Fax 504/566-1178. www.nogh.com. 14 units. A/C TV TEL. $79 double; $89 queen or twin; $99 king or 2 full beds. Rates include continental breakfast. Extra person $25. AE, MC, V. Free parking.

Run for more than 10 years by Ray Cronk and Alvin Payne, this guest house is a little off the beaten path (just outside the French Quarter, across North Rampart Street), but it's painted a startling hot pink, so it's hard to miss.

There are rooms in the old Creole main house (1848) and in what used to be the slave quarters. Each is decorated with period furniture and has a unique color scheme (not hot pink, in case you were worried). Guest rooms are restful and tastefully done. Rooms in the slave quarters are a little smaller than the ones in the main house, but they all open onto the lush courtyard. Here you'll find a veritable tropical garden, with a banana tree, more green plants than you can count, and some intricately carved old fountains that Ray and Alvin have restored to working order. There is a new covered breakfast room with an outdoor patio where you'll be served at cozy white-clothed tables. Also in the courtyard are a beer machine, a soda machine, and an ice maker.

✪ **P. J. Holbrook's Olde Victorian Inn.** 914 N. Rampart St., New Orleans, LA 70116. ☎ **800/725-2446** or 504/522-2446. Fax 504/897-0248. 6 units. A/C. $120–$175 double.

Rates include full breakfast. Senior discount and weekly rates available. AE, MC, V. Parking available on street.

Walking into P. J.'s is like walking through time. The entire house is done in Victorian style, from the "gathering room" to the dining room. P. J. has gone to the ends of the earth to find the perfect pieces, draperies, color schemes, and curios. Most of the thoughtfully decorated rooms have fireplaces, and one even has a balcony set over North Rampart Street and furnished with a cast-iron table and chairs and hanging plants. A couple of units' private bathrooms are across the hall.

P. J. herself is a most gracious host who will look after your every need and cook up a breakfast that could probably keep you going for a week—bread (usually banana or cinnamon), fruit, eggs (prepared all different ways), biscuits, some type of potato, juice, and coffee or hot tea. You can feast in the dining area just outside the kitchen, in your room, or at one of the courtyard tables.

Be sure to sit and chat with P. J. and her staff—they have some great stories to tell. If you ask nicely, they might even tell you about Uncle Leo.

Place d'Armes Hotel. 625 St. Ann St., New Orleans, LA 70116. ☎ **800/366-2743** or 504/524-4531. Fax 504/571-3803. www.frenchquarter.com. 80 units. A/C TV TEL. $110–$180 double; $170–$180 patio. Rates include continental breakfast. AE, CB, DC, DISC, MC, V. Parking (next door) $14.

Parts of this hotel seem a bit grim and old, though its quite large courtyard and amoeba-shaped pool are ideal for hanging out and may make up for it. Plus, it's only half a block from the Café du Monde—very convenient when you need a beignet at 3am. This also makes it a favorite for families traveling with kids. Rooms are homey and furnished in traditional style; however, 32 of them do not have windows and can be cell-like. Be sure that you ask for a room with a window when you reserve. Breakfast is served in a breakfast room, and the location, just off Jackson Square, makes sightseeing a breeze.

Prince Conti Hotel. 830 Conti St., New Orleans, LA 70112. ☎ **800/366-2743** or 504/529-4172. Fax 504/581-3802. 53 units. A/C TV TEL. $120–$175 double; $195–$215 suite. AE, DC, DISC, MC, V. Valet parking $14.

This tiny but friendly hotel with a marvelously helpful staff (some of whom are docent tour guides on their off-hours) is in a great location right off Bourbon, and is not generally noisy. Second floor rooms all have fresh striped wallpaper and antiques, but quality varies from big canopy beds to painted iron bedsteads. Bathrooms can be ultra-tiny, with the toilet virtually on top of the sink. Travelers with kids should stay at their sister location, the Place D'Armes, because it is farther from Bourbon and has a pool. The restaurant is open Tuesday through Saturday from 5pm.

✪ **Royal Street Inn & R Bar.** 1431 Royal St., New Orleans, LA 70116. ☎ **800/449-5535** or 504/948-7499. Fax 504/943-9880. www.royalstreetinn.com. 5 units. A/C TV TEL. $75 double; $100 suite. Rates include bar beverage.

This is a funky, happening little establishment in a residential neighborhood with plenty of street parking and regular police patrols. It's a loose, but not disorganized place and there couldn't be a better choice for laid-back travelers. They don't serve breakfast here, but they still bill themselves as a B&B. That's for Bed and Beverage— the lobby is the highly enjoyable R Bar (see chapter 11). You check in with the bartender, and you get two complimentary cocktails at night. (As if you will stop there.) The right guests—the only kind who will be happy here—will want to hang out in the bar all night. And why not? It's that kind of place.

Regular rooms are small but cute, like a bedroom in a real house, but with doors that open directly to the street. Suites are the best value near the Quarter. They're well sized, accommodating up to four, though not without some loss of privacy, and feature kitchenettes, as well as their own names and stories. "The Ghost in the Attic" is a big room (complete with a mural of said ghost) with sloping ceilings, pleasing for those with starving artists garret fantasies who don't like to give up good furniture.

The Sun & the Moon Bed & Breakfast. 1037 N. Rampart St., New Orleans, LA 70116. ☎ **800/638-9169** or 504/529-4652. www.sunandmoon.qpg.com. 2 units. A/C MINIBAR TV. $85–$100 double. Rates include continental breakfast. AE, MC, V.

Also known by its Spanish name, El Sol y la Luna, the Sun & Moon got a new proprietor (Mary Pat Van Tine) and hostess (Kathleen Barrow) a few years back. The guest rooms, decorated in Southwestern style, have been renovated recently. Each has a separate entrance, roomy and comfortable sleeping and sitting areas, and a full bathroom. The Sun suite has a balcony and the Moon suite a deck; both overlook the courtyard, in which you'll find a large fruit-bearing banana tree and a fountain. Breakfast can be served in your room or on the deck.

2 Mid City/Esplanade

EXPENSIVE

✪ **The House on Bayou Road.** 2275 Bayou Rd., New Orleans, LA 70119. ☎ **800/ 882-2968** or 504/945-0992. Fax 504/945-0993. www.houseonbayouroad.com. 8 units, 2 cottages. A/C MINIBAR TEL. $150–$295 double. Rates include full breakfast. AE, MC, V. Free parking.

If you want to stay in a rural plantation setting but still be near the French Quarter, try the House on Bayou Road. Just off Esplanade Avenue, this intimate Creole plantation home, built in the late 1700s for a colonial Spanish diplomat, has been restored by owner Cynthia Reeves. As you enter the antique-filled double parlor, you'll feel as if you're stepping back in time.

The individually decorated rooms are named for bayous and have a light, airy quality. The Bayou St. John Room (the old library) holds a queen-size four-poster bed and has a working fireplace; the Bayou Delacroix has the same kind of bed and a wonderfully large bathtub. Bayou Cocodrie holds a brass-and-iron half-canopy bed with mosquito netting and can be joined with the Bayou Barataria Room, which has a queen-size pencil-post bed. The large cottage has three rooms that can be rented separately or together. It's perfect for a large family. The small Creole cottage is a great romantic getaway spot. It has a queen-size four-poster bed, a queen sleeper sofa, Jacuzzi tub, wet bar, and a porch with a swing and rocking chairs.

The grounds are beautifully manicured, and there's an outdoor pool, Jacuzzi, patio, and screened-in porch. The House on Bayou Road serves a plantation-style breakfast, and during the day and in the evening there's access to a minirefrigerator filled with beverages. The House also offers cooking classes as part of a special package (see chapter 7).

MODERATE

Ashton's Mechling Bed & Breakfast. 2023 Esplanade Ave., New Orleans, LA 70116. ☎ **800/725-4131** or 504/942-7048. Fax 504/944-9382. 4 units. A/C. $125–$155 double. Rates include full breakfast. AE, MC, V. Free parking.

This 1860s mansion was restored over several years by Keith and Claudine Mechling (pronounced *mek-ling*) and their son and daughter-in-law, Kelly and Taina, who now own and operate the place. It's along the Esplanade Ridge—a beautiful setting, but somewhat removed from most of the places you'll want to visit. You'll be within walking distance of the French Quarter and City Park, but don't walk alone at night, and keep the number for **United Cab** handy (☎ **504/522-9771**).

The guest rooms, on the first floor of the house, are quite large and retain as many of the original fixtures, windows, and woodwork as could be salvaged—including a leaded-glass front door window and black onyx marble fireplace mantels.

Benachi House. 2257 Bayou Rd., New Orleans, LA 70119. ☎ **800/308-7040** or 504/525-7040. Fax 504/525-9760. 4 units, 2 with private bathroom. A/C TEL. $105–$150 double. AE, DISC, MC, V. Free parking.

The house was constructed in 1858 for Nicholas M. Benachi, a cotton broker, consul of Greece, and founder of the New Orleans Greek Orthodox Congregation. From the public roof patio, you can easily imagine how grand it must have been. The immediate neighborhood, near the intersection of Bayou Road and Esplanade Avenue (then the outskirts of town), is still one of the most exotic in the city.

Under the care of current owner Jim Derbes, the house was brought up to its current award-winning condition. Furnishings in the downstairs public rooms are of Victorian, rococo revival, Gothic, classical, and Empire styles. The guest rooms are named for the Benachi children and have ceiling fans. Marie's room, at the front of the house, features a balcony with outdoor seating and connects to Irene's room, making them a good choice for families. The rooms share a bathroom and are furnished with reproduction antiques. The stand-out is Pandia's room, on the first floor. Its rococo revival dresser and American mahogany double bed are quite beautiful. Televisions are available on request. (*Note:* If the big black dog Magnus is there, it's best not to play with him. He can get overly rough.)

Quality Inn Midtown. 3900 Tulane Ave., New Orleans, LA 70119. ☎ **800/486-5541** or 504/486-5541. Fax 504/488-7440. 104 units. A/C TV TEL. $69–$300 double; $180–$350 suite. Extra person $10–$25. AE, CB, DC, DISC, MC, V. Free parking.

The Quality Inn Midtown is removed from most of the heavily visited areas, and is a good 5-minute drive from the Central Business District. The free shuttle service to the French Quarter and convention center makes up for the distance. All the rooms have balconies; many face the courtyard, are spacious, and have double beds. The hotel's French Quarter–style courtyard features a swimming pool and Jacuzzi. Guests also have use of coin-operated laundry facilities. Francesco's restaurant serves breakfast, lunch, and dinner; seafood and Italian dishes are the specialty. The Mardi Gras lounge overlooks the pool and is open daily.

3 Central Business District

VERY EXPENSIVE

✪ **Fairmont Hotel.** At University Place, 123 Baronne St., New Orleans, LA 70122. ☎ **800/527-4727** or 504/529-7111. Fax 504/529-4764. www.fairmont.com. 700 units. A/C TV TEL. $229–$289 double. Extra person $25. AE, DC, DISC, MC, V. Valet parking $15.

New Orleanians still sometimes think of this as the Roosevelt, and today's Fairmont Hotel upholds its predecessor's tradition of elegance. The marbled and columned lobby was renovated in 1993, and the guest rooms—all spacious, with high ceilings and such extras as an electric shoe buffer—were overhauled in 1996. Beds are luxuriously turned out, with the finest all-cotton sheets and down pillows. Bathrooms have scales, oversized towels, and custom-made fixtures. For the business traveler, the Fairmont offers in-room computer hookups and fax machines in the suites. The Fairmont is a "grand hotel" in the old manner, but it's in a less than desirable neighborhood, so be very careful at night.

Dining: Perhaps you remember those old radio broadcasts "from the Blue Room of the Hotel Roosevelt in downtown New Orleans." This is the place. The blue-and-gold decor and French period furnishings have changed very little over the years. On Sunday, there's a sumptuous brunch. Bailey's, a casual bistro, serves three meals daily, and for fine dining, there's the romantic Sazerac Bar and Grill (see chapter 7).

Amenities: Rooftop health club, pool, tennis courts, 24-hour room service, twice-daily maid service, concierge, multilingual staff, tour desk, baby-sitting, activities desk, laundry service, beauty shop, business center, gift shop, newsstand, currency exchange.

✪ Hotel Inter-Continental. 444 St. Charles Ave., New Orleans, LA 70130. ☎ **800/ 327-0200** or 504/525-5566. Fax 504/523-7310. 482 units. A/C MINIBAR TV TEL. $235–$295 single; $305–$325 double; $500–$2,000 suite. AE, CB, DC, DISC, MC, V. Valet parking $17.

The red granite Hotel Inter-Continental rises from the heart of the Central Business District, within walking distance of the French Quarter and the Mississippi River attractions. It's a favorite of groups (including rock groups; the Stones stayed here two tours ago) and conventions. You should consider it, too. Ongoing renovations should have all the rooms redecorated by fall 2000. A strong, fresh decor features custom furniture, deep rich colors (not precisely gaudy, but strong), dark woods and lots of marble, with better bathrooms and many nice touches including "the best beds in town" (the mattresses are quite comfortable indeed) and some classy looking amenities. These handsome rooms feel quite luxurious and are the best in the immediate area, though probably too stuffy for families. Some rooms have balconies that overlook the courtyard, although said courtyard is modern and industrial in appearance.

The Governor's Floor (the 14th) is reminiscent of Louisiana's romantic past, with suites featuring period antiques and reproductions, artifacts, and decorations that represent the six heads of state for whom the rooms are named. The floor has a VIP lounge, where guests can have continental breakfast and evening cocktails. The Governor's Lounge is stocked with popular periodicals.

Dining: The large marble lobby showcases a cocktail lounge, gourmet meals are served in the Veranda Restaurant (see chapter 7), and Pete's Pub serves lunch daily.

Amenities: A good-looking health club focuses on cardiovascular machines. There is a basic pool, plus a barber shop and beauty salon, gift shop, business center, 24-hour room service, laundry and dry cleaning service, concierge, shoe shine service.

Le Meridien Hotel. 614 Canal St., New Orleans, LA 70130. ☎ **800/543-4300** or 504/ 525-6500. Fax 504/586-1543. www.meridienneworleans.com. 494 units. A/C MINIBAR TV TEL. $180–$300 double; $700–$2,000 suite. AE, CB, DC, DISC, MC, V. Valet parking $16.

This hotel is so committed to appearing classy that it covers the electrical cords of its lamps with shirred designer fabric. You can't fault the location on Canal, right across from the Quarter, but ultimately it is anonymously ritzy, with the public areas far more grand than the actual rooms. The latter are good-sized, with faux-luxe furniture. But the mattresses are overly stiff and closets are small, adding up to a comfortable, but not particularly special experience. Bathrooms can be cramped, but the ergonomically designed amenities are eye-catching. Each room has multiple-line

Spending the Night in Chains

For those of you who prefer the predictability of a chain hotel, there's a **Marriott** at 555 Canal St., at the edge of the Quarter (☎ **800/228-9290** or 504/581-1000), and a **Crowne Plaza** at 333 Poydras St., in the Central Business District (☎ **800/ 747-3279** or 504/525-9444). And if all the rooms in town are booked, you might try to see if one of these chains down by the airport has something for you.

telephones and a desk and sitting area. The hotel's location is excellent for viewing Mardi Gras festivities.

Dining/Diversions: La Gauloise is a Parisian-style bistro. The Jazz Meridien Club, in the large central atrium and lobby, features entertainment Monday through Saturday.

Amenities: Health club (offering free aerobics and spinning classes), sauna, heated outdoor pool, massage, concierge, 24-hour room service, laundry and dry cleaning, baby-sitting, complimentary shoe shine, newspaper delivery, nightly turndown, business center, beauty salon, gift shop, jewelry store, art gallery.

Residence Inn by Marriott. 345 St. Joseph St., New Orleans, LA 70130. ☎ **800/ 331-3131** or 504/522-1300. Fax 522-6060. 105 units. A/C MINIBAR TV TEL. $249 double. AE, DC, DISC, MC, V.

The Residence Inn line was designed as potential long-term apartments, and so each unit here is practically a regular-sized small apartment, with a good-sized living room area; a utensil-stocked kitchenette with full fridge, small stove, and at least a toaster oven; a large bedroom; plus dressing area and modern bathroom. Comforts of home include TVs in living area and bedroom, hair dryers, irons and ironing boards, a table ready set for two, and popcorn. They even offer to do your grocery shopping. (As if! You're in New Orleans, and you're going to cook?) Sure, the mattress and pillow feel like foam rubber, and it's hard to find a trash can, but the couch is nice, there's a big desk to work on and somehow, the cookie-cutter uniformity of the rooms also allows you to put your own stamp and vibe on the place, and though sterile, it does not come off drearily anonymous.

The often harried staff is nonetheless efficient and practical and enjoy getting to know their long-term guests. While this would lack the style of a Vieux Carré flat, it's much more suited to the practical aspects that probably brought you long-term to New Orleans anyway (including a two block walk to the Convention Center, and less than that to Emeril's). You can always throw a few cheap masks around to add some N'Awlins flavor.

Note: For the same idea, but a little more style, try the even newer **Courtyard by Marriott,** 300 Julia St. (☎ **504/598-9898**), which makes good use of its former warehouse space and is even more convenient to the Convention Center.

Amenities: Swimming pool, a little workout room, newspapers, dry cleaning, laundry, grocery shopping, meeting rooms.

✪ **Windsor Court.** 300 Gravier St., New Orleans, LA 70130. ☎ **800/262-2662** or 504/523-6000. Fax 504/596-4749. www.windsorcourthotel.com. 319 units. A/C MINIBAR TV TEL. $275–$385 standard double; $365–$485 junior suite; $425–$675 full suite; $700–$1,150 2-bedroom suite. Children under 12 stay free in parents' room. AE, CB, DC, DISC, MC, V. Valet parking $18.

Condé Nast Traveler voted the Windsor Court the Best Hotel in North America (and probably did it a disservice, because who could ever live up to such hype?). In any case, there may be a finer hotel on the continent, but it can't be found in New Orleans. The unassuming, somewhat office-building exterior is camouflage for the quiet but posh delights found within. Two corridors downstairs are minigalleries that display original 17th-, 18th-, and 19th-century art, and there's a plush reading area with an international newspaper rack on the second floor. Everything is very, very chic. It's not too stiff for restless children, but this still feels more like a grownup hotel. The level of service is extraordinarily high; we doubt it could be much better were this Windsor Castle rather than Windsor Court.

The accommodations are exceptionally spacious, with classy, not flashy decor. All are suites, featuring large bay windows or a private balcony overlooking the river (get a river view if at all possible) or the city, a private foyer, a large living room, a bedroom with French doors, a large marble bathroom with particularly luxe amenities (plush robes, high-quality personal care items, thick towels, hamper, extra hair dryers), two dressing rooms, and a "petite kitchen."

Dining/Diversions: The Polo Club Lounge has the ambience of a private English club; the exceptional Grill Room Restaurant (see chapter 7) serves breakfast, brunch, lunch, and dinner. Le Salon, the lobby lounge, serves afternoon tea, cocktails, and sweets, and has chamber music and piano music during the day and evening.

Amenities: Health club with resort-size pool, sauna, and steam room; 24-hour suite service (much more than your average room service); concierge; laundry and dry cleaning; newspaper delivery; in-room massage. Numerous conveniences for business travelers, in rooms and in conference areas, which are as luxurious as the guest accommodations.

EXPENSIVE

✪ **Hilton New Orleans Riverside Hotel.** 2 Poydras St., New Orleans, LA 70140. ☎ **800/ 445-8667** or 504/561-0500. Fax 504/568-1721. www.neworleans.hilton.com. 1,600 units. A/C MINIBAR TV TEL. $174–$314 double; $540–$2,000 suite. Special packages available. AE, CB, DC, DISC, JCB, MC, V. Valet parking $16; self-parking $12.

The Hilton is in the neighborhood of the Windsor Court, but in a more central location—right at the riverfront, near the World Trade Center of New Orleans, the New Orleans Convention Center, and the Aquarium. It's a self-contained complex of nearly a dozen restaurants, bistros, and bars; two gift shops; a full racquet and health club; a huge exhibition space; and no fewer than 38 conference rooms. In addition, Hilton's Flamingo Casino and the Riverwalk Marketplace are accessible from the hotel's lobby, which contains a nine-story atrium. Inside, the hotel is decorated with Italian oak and mahogany paneling, travertine marble, and deep-pile hand-woven carpeting. Guest rooms are spacious, and most have fabulous views of the river or the city.

Dining/Diversions: The atrium is broken up into attractive centers, such as the English Bar, Le Café Bromeliad, and the French Garden Bar. Pete Fountain moved his jazz club from the Quarter to a third-floor replica here (see chapter 11). The Flamingo is currently the only casino operating in the downtown area.

Amenities: 24-hour room service, concierge, laundry, dry cleaning, and pressing service, airport transportation, newspaper delivery, shoe-shine service. Guests are eligible for membership ($20 for 3 days) in the hotel's Rivercenter Racquet and Health Club, which has outdoor and indoor tennis courts, squash and racquetball courts, an outdoor basketball court, a rooftop jogging track, aerobics classes, saunas, whirlpools, tanning beds, massage, a hair salon, and a golf studio. There's an extra charge for things like golf ($13 per hour for an indoor studio) and racquet sports ($35 for 1½ hours on an indoor tennis court and $15 for an hour on a racquetball court).

Hyatt Regency. 500 Poydras Plaza, New Orleans, LA 70113. ☎ **800/233-1234** or 504/561-1234. Fax 504/587-4141. www.hyatt.com. 1,184 units. A/C TV TEL. $219–$244 double; $400–$625 suite. AE, DC, DISC, MC, V. Valet parking $15.

If your trip to New Orleans revolves around an event at the Superdome, you should consider the Hyatt. The hotel occupies a 32-story building, with guest rooms surrounding a seemingly bottomless central atrium. The public spaces are in grand corporate style, and so, as you'd expect, the lobby cafes generally attract a lunchtime crowd from the Central Business District. (If there's a Saints home game, however, expect to find a football crowd—the hotel's Hyttops Sports Bar & Grill is a popular hangout.) Guest rooms were clearly designed with the business traveler and the conventioneer in mind. You could probably run a Fortune 500 company from one of the deluxe suites, which have a meeting table, desk, fax machine, and lounge area.

Dining/Diversions: The Courtyard serves regional fare at breakfast, lunch, and dinner. Top of the Dome Steakhouse is an upscale, revolving rooftop steak and seafood restaurant, open for dinner only. Hyttops Sports Bar & Grill serves pizza and burgers at lunch and dinner. The Mint Julep Lounge sometimes features live jazz.

Amenities: Heated rooftop pool, whirlpool, exercise room, free shuttle service to the French Quarter, concierge, room service during limited hours, baby-sitting, currency exchange, business center, multilingual staff. gift shop, hair salon, florist.

☼ International House. 221 Camp St., New Orleans, LA 70130. ☎ **800/633-5770** or 504/553-9550. Fax 504/200-6532. www.ihhotel.com. 119 units. A/C MINIBAR TV TEL. $180–$289 double; $359–$439 suite. Rates include continental breakfast. AE, MC, V. Valet parking.

Everyone's favorite new hotel, the International House, with creative design and meticulous attention to detail, has set a new standard, and other hotels in the area should be paying careful attention. The bar has been raised. Record company and film execs should love it, but so should anyone whose had enough of Victorian sweetness and needs a palate cleanser. A wonderful old beaux arts bank building has been transformed into a modern space that still pays tribute to its locale. Consequently, in the graceful lobby, classical pilasters stand next to modern wrought iron chandeliers.

Interiors are the embodiment of minimalist chic. Rooms are simple, with muted, monochromatic (okay, beige) tones, tall ceilings and ceiling fans, up-to-the-minute bathroom fixtures, but also black-and-white photos of local musicians and characters, books about the city, and other clever decorating touches that anchor the room in its New Orleans setting. (This is significant; without them, you could easily plant this hotel in L.A. and not notice a difference.) The commitment to hip, neat, cool, and groovy means dark corridors and hard-to-read room numbers, and while the big bathrooms boast large tubs or space-age glassed-in showers, they do come off a bit industrial. But they are made up for by cushy touches like fine towels, feather pillows, rather large TVs with movie channels, your own private phone number in your room, data ports, CD players with CDs, and hair dryers.

Dining: Lemon Grass is a branch of a popular local restaurant (see chapter 7). The bar is a hip hangout already, particularly at night as candles flicker and music plays.

Amenities: Room service, newspapers, fitness center, gift shop, dry cleaning, meeting rooms.

The Pelham. 444 Common St., New Orleans, LA 70130. ☎ **800/659-5621** or 504/ 522-4444. Fax 504/539-9010. www.decaturhotel.com. 60 units. A/C TV TEL. $164–$325 double. AE, DC, DISC, MC, V. Parking $15.

This small hotel, in a renovated building that dates from the late 1800s, is one of the new wave of boutique hotels. From the outside and in its public areas, the Pelham feels like an upscale apartment building. Centrally located rooms are generally less bright than those on the exterior of the building. If you're not interested in staying right in the French Quarter, or if you're looking for something with less public atmosphere than a hotel and more anonymity than a B&B, the Pelham is a good option.

Dining: Specializing in contemporary American and Creole cuisine, Graham's Restaurant is chef Kevin Graham's original restaurant. It's not your average hotel dining room.

Amenities: Concierge, room service during restaurant hours, newspaper delivery, laundry service, express check-in, twice-daily maid service, in-room safes.

Wyndham Riverfront Hotel. 701 Convention Center Blvd., New Orleans, LA 70130.
☎ **800/WYNDHAM** or 504/524-8200. Fax 504/524-0600. www.wyndham.com. 202 units.
A/C TV TEL. $175–$220 double. AE, CB, DC, DISC, MC, V. Valet parking $15.

There couldn't be a better location for the Convention Center: It's right across the
street. But the rooms feel less business hotel and more, well, "use-convention-as-
excuse-for-New Orleans-junket." Not that there's a party-hearty vibe, but the rooms
aren't as much set up for real business travelers as those in your average Marriott.
Instead, rooms are prefab elegant, with stately wallpaper and armchairs, far more aesthetically pleasing than most big hotels. Some can be small, but the second floor has
quite tall ceilings, which offsets that. Bathrooms are nothing special, but the many
fruity/flowery amenities are made by Bath & Bodyworks. Towels are thick, but pillows
rubbery. We did get a sense that the staff can be somewhat overwhelmed when a convention is staying there, but they were never less than gracious.

Dining: E's Restaurant serves Creole and continental fare at breakfast, lunch, and
dinner. There's a lounge in the lobby.

Amenities: Room service until 11pm, laundry and dry cleaning, newspaper
delivery, express checkout, concierge, exercise room, gift shop.

MODERATE

Holiday Inn Downtown-Superdome. 330 Loyola Ave., New Orleans, LA 70112. ☎ **800/
535-7830** or 504/581-1600. Fax 504/522-0073. www.holidayinn.com/hotels/msydt. 297
units. A/C TV TEL. $94–$209 double; $350 suite. Extra person $15. Children under 20 stay
free in parents' room. AE, CB, DC, DISC, JCB, MC, V. Parking $11.

The 18-story Holiday Inn Downtown-Superdome is centrally located, with easy access
to the business and financial centers, the Louisiana Superdome (duh!), and the French
Quarter. Each room has a balcony and city view, and the hotel has a collection of jazz
scene murals available for public viewing. The dining room holds an interesting collection of New Orleans streetcar paintings. The Mardi Gras Lounge offers cocktails
and after-dinner drinks nightly. There's a heated pool on the roof.

Le Pavillion Hotel. 833 Poydras St., New Orleans, LA 70140. ☎ **800/535-9095** or
504/581-3111. Fax 504/522-5543. www.lepavillion.com. 226 units. A/C MINIBAR TV TEL.
$105–$370 double; $495–$1,495 suite. AE, CB, DC, DISC, MC, V. Valet parking $18.

Established in 1907 in a prime Central Business District location, Le Pavillion was the
first hotel in New Orleans to have elevators. It's now a member of Historic Hotels of
America. The building is a long, slender rectangle with a prominent columned motor
entrance. The lobby is stunning, with high ceilings, grand columns, plush furnishings,
Oriental rugs, detailed woodwork, and 11 crystal chandeliers imported from Czechoslovakia. Each hall features massive Louisiana antiques and has 14 original paintings
from the hotel's fine-arts collection.

The standard guest rooms all have similar furnishings, but they differ in size. "Bay
Rooms" are standard, with two double beds and bay windows. Some fine suites are
available for reasonable rates; each has a mini-refrigerator and a microwave. Antique
lovers will enjoy the Antique Suite, decorated in—you guessed it—antiques, including
pieces by Mallard, C. Lee (who, as a slave, studied under Mallard), Mitchell Ram-
melsberg, Belter, Badouine, and Marcotte.

The hotel offers 24-hour room service, laundry and dry cleaning, newspaper
delivery, baby-sitting, complimentary shoe shine, and a concierge. The large Gold
Room dining room serves three meals daily and has a working fireplace. Complimentary hors d'oeuvres are served weekdays from 4 to 7pm in the Gallery lounge, and
peanut-butter-and-jelly sandwiches and milk are served each evening in the lobby.
There's a heated pool on the roof, plus a fitness center and whirlpool spa.

INEXPENSIVE

The Depot at Madame Julia's. 7048 O'Keef St., New Orleans, LA 70130. ☎ **504/ 529-2952.** Fax 504/529-1908. 14 units, all with shared bathroom. $55 single; $65 double. AE, personal checks (if rooms are paid in advance).

A new establishment from the couple that runs the St. Charles Guesthouse in the Garden District, The Depot is an alternative to more commercial hotels in the CBD, and takes up part of a whole complex of buildings dating from the 1800s.

Low prices and a guest house environment mean a number of good things— including rooms with character and a proprietor who loves to help guests with all the details of their stay—but it also means shared bathrooms, rooms on the small and cozy side, and a location that, while quiet on the weekends, can get noisy in the mornings as the working neighborhood gets going. (Still being gentrified, the neighborhood is hit or miss, though more of the former than the latter, thanks to arty Julia Street.) A mere 7 blocks (safe in the daytime) from the Quarter, it's a quick walk or a short streetcar ride, which makes it an affordable alternative to the Quarter's much more expensive accommodations. Air-conditioning is still in the planning stages—as are up to 50 more rooms, a small pool, and a proper lobby/meeting area—but the budget-conscious and those who prefer their hotels with personality will consider this a find.

Hotel La Salle. 1113 Canal St., New Orleans, LA 70112. ☎ **800/521-9450** or 504/523-5831. Fax 504/525-2531. www.neworleans.com/hotels/lasalle. 57 units, 42 with private bathroom. A/C TV TEL. $34–$70 double without bathroom; $60–$100 double with bathroom. Children under 12 stay free in parents' room. AE, DISC, JCB, MC, V. Parking $5.

The Hotel La Salle is only half a block outside the French Quarter and is probably the least expensive place downtown with comfortable quarters. The no-frills rooms are plainly furnished. There's an old-fashioned air to the small lobby, with its high ceilings, overhead fans, carved Austrian wall clock, and old-time wooden reception desk. Free coffee is always available in the lobby, and guests receive a complimentary newspaper daily. This place is a favorite with European visitors who appreciate bathroom-down-the-hall savings.

The Prytania Inn. 1415 Prytania St., New Orleans, LA 70130. ☎ **504/566-1515.** Fax 504/566-1518. 130 units, 8 without bathroom. A/C TEL. $49–$69 double. Extra person $10–$15. AE, DISC, MC, V. Limited free off-street parking available.

As you linger over breakfast at the Prytania, you'll notice the diversity of the guests: a fair number of young international budget travelers, couples enjoying a romantic weekend, a family in town to visit a university student. All seem equally at home. The Prytania manages to seem like a hotel, a hostel, a guest house, and a B&B all at the same time—and all while providing quaint, comfortable accommodations at rock-bottom rates. As one manager put it, "You can always bargain with us." You can shave a few bucks off the prices listed above, for example, if you don't mind sharing a bathroom or if you forgo the $5 breakfast (but don't be too quick to give up this breakfast). The hotel consists of three buildings that share an office and a dining area, both in the main building. There isn't really a standard room here; while they differ in size, furnishings, and decor, they all seem equally comfortable. Just ask for what you want—they probably have it.

The same folks who own and operate the Prytania recently opened **St. Vincent's Guest House,** 1507 Magazine, on the corner of Race (☎ **504/523-3411**), also in the Lower Garden District. The atmosphere there is a bit more refined and the rooms a little more expensive—around $69, but, as they told me, they can be a "little lower sometimes, up to $125 Mardi Gras time."

4 Uptown/Garden District

VERY EXPENSIVE

✪ **Pontchartrain Hotel.** 2031 St. Charles Ave., New Orleans, LA 70140. ☎ **800/ 777-6193** or 504/524-0581. Fax 504/529-1165. 104 units. A/C TV TEL. $95–$380 double. Extra person $10, except special events $25. Seasonal packages and special promotional rates available. AE, CB, DC, DISC, MC, V. Parking $13.

This dignified hotel has long been a local landmark, and if other, newer hotels make it seem slightly worn at the edges (though upgrades are fixing that), it still feels like the most romantic and elegant hotel in the world. There is a style here no other hotel can match. Back in the day, it was the place for the likes of Rita Hayworth and Aly Kahn to tryst (courtesy of adjoining suites; Ms. Hayworth's still has the fanciful floral murals on walls and woodwork). Its discreet ambience and pampering still make it a choice for celebrities and dignitaries (Tom Cruise and Nicole Kidman honeymooned here; Anne Rice was a long-term resident while her Garden District home was being remodeled, and so she made it the base for Michael and Rowan in *The Witching Hour*). Throughout, you can find some utterly fabulous furnishings (up to and including Ming vases) that date from the hotel's early days.

The regular rooms, which are larger than most, have all gotten facelifts, including cedar-lined closets, cushy towels, and pedestal washbasins. The suites are named for prestigious guests of the past (Evelyn Waugh, Mary Martin, Cyd Charisse), but many may be turned into regular rooms during the ongoing renovations.

Dining/Diversions: Café Pontchartrain has a solid reputation among locals (judges and ex-debutantes haunt the place) for its food, and they can even recreate certain dishes from the glory days of the Pontchartrain's now closed famous Caribbean Room. Stop for a drink in the Bayou Bar, which features live entertainment at night.

Amenities: 24-hour room service, complimentary shoe shine, complimentary newspaper, nightly turndown, access to nearby spa with health club and outdoor pool.

EXPENSIVE

✪ **The Grand Victorian Bed & Breakfast.** 2727 St. Charles Ave., New Orleans, LA 70130. ☎ **504/895-1104.** Fax 504/896-8688. E-mail: Brabe2727@aol.com. 8 units. A/C TV TEL. $150–$350 double. Rates include breakfast. AE, DISC, MC, V. Limited free off-street parking.

Owner Bonnie Rabe confounded and delighted her new St. Charles neighbors when she took a crumbling Queen Anne–style Victorian mansion right on the corner of Washington (2 blocks from Lafayette cemetery and Commander's Palace with a streetcar stop right in front) and over the course of many arduous months, resurrected it into a showcase B&B. The location makes its porches and balconies a perfect place to spend Mardi Gras; parade viewing doesn't come any more comfortable or convenient.

The stunning rooms are full of antiques (each has a breathtaking four-poster or wood canopy bed), with the slightly fussy details demanded by big Victorian rooms. Linens, pillows, and towels are ultra plush, and some bathrooms have big Jacuzzi tubs. The largest room—our favorite—overlooks the street corner (and has its own St. Charles view balcony) and so is potentially noisy. You can always request one towards the back. A generous continental breakfast is served and friendly Bonnie is ready with suggestions on how to spend your time. All these amenities make the establishment seem to cross the line into inn territory, but though Bonnie does live on the third floor, she is not always there, so as in any B&B, do not expect 24-hour service.

MODERATE

☼ The Chimes B&B. 1146 Constantinople St., New Orleans, LA 70115. ☎ **800/ 729-4640** (for reservations only) or 504/488-4640. Fax 504/899-9858. 5 units. A/C TV TEL. $99–$175 double; June to mid-Sept $65–$125 double. AE, MC, V. Rates include breakfast. Limited off-street free parking. Well-behaved pets accepted.

This is a real hidden gem that really allows you to experience the city away from the typical tourist experience. The Chimes is in a less fashionable, but more neighborhoody portion of the Garden District, just 2 blocks off St. Charles. Your hosts are the ever-charming and friendly Jill and Charles Abbyad, and the rooms are behind their house, surrounding a small, sweet, and yes, chime-filled courtyard. (The tinkles of same are not irritating.)

Rooms vary in size from a generous L-shape, to a two-story loft type (with a very small bathroom), to some that are downright cozy. All have antiques (including romantic old beds), but are so tastefully underdecorated, particularly in contrast to other B&Bs, they are positively Zen. An ambitious continental breakfast is served in the hosts' house, and chatting with them can be so enjoyable you might get off to a late start. Rooms have private phone lines, cable TV, irons, hair dryers, and bottled water. The hosts also speak French and Arabic. RTA passes can be purchased here.

The Columns. 3811 St. Charles Ave., New Orleans, LA 70115. ☎ **800/445-9308** or 504/899-9308. 20 units. A/C TEL. $90–$175 double. Rates include continental breakfast. AE, MC, V. Parking available on street.

New Orleans made a mistake when it tore down its famous bordellos. If somebody had turned one of the grander ones into a hotel, imagine how many people would stay there! The next best thing is the Columns, whose interior was used by Louis Malle for his film about Storyville, *Pretty Baby.* Please don't lounge around the lobby in your underwear, however, even if it is Victorian (the underwear, not the lobby). Built in 1883, the building is one of the greatest examples of a late 19th-century Louisiana residence. The grand, columned porch is a highly popular evening scene thanks to the bar inside. The immediate interior is utterly smashing; we challenge any other hotel to match this grand staircase and stained glass window combination.

Unfortunately, the magnificence of the setting is hurt by the relentlessly casual attitude towards the public areas. Cheesy furniture downstairs, an empty neglected ballroom and stale cigarette smoke in that gorgeous stairway (courtesy of the bar) detract mightily from the experience, making it perilously close to seedy in some spots. Too bad. This could be a deeply romantic hotel, ponderously Victorian, and we mean that in a good way. But bar revenue reigns supreme, so the smoke is probably there to stay. Consequently, the prices may not be justified, fabulous hangout or no. Low-end rooms are cozy, with quilts and old bedsteads. High-end rooms are indeed—it's the difference between the master's room and the servants quarters. We particularly like Room 16, with its grand furniture and floor-to-ceiling shutters that lead out to a private, second-story porch.

Maison Perrier Bed & Breakfast. 4117 Perrier (2 blocks riverside from St. Charles, 3 blocks downtown side from Napoleon), New Orleans, LA 70115. ☎ **504/897-1807.** Fax 504/ 897-1399. www.maisonperrier.com. E-mail: madame@maisonperrier.com. 7 units. A/C MINIBAR TV TEL. $80–$150. Rates include breakfast. AE, DISC, MC, V. Parking available on street.

A B&B so new it seems fresh out of the packaging; it hasn't quite mellowed like others in town. On the other hand, "mellowed" often means "shabby and threadbare," so this distinction may please you. This 1894 painted-lady Victorian has been restored to a gleaming fare-thee-well. It may or may not have been a turn of the century "gentlemen's club." Rooms now sport the names of the former landlady's "nieces." Every room is themed—in color, if nothing else (though we can do without "Desiree," the wild animal print room). And each has some special detail: a high four-poster bed, fabulous old tile around its (nonworking) fireplace, a whirlpool tub, a balcony, and so on. You'll get complimentary bottled water and soft drinks, a hair dryer, private voice mail, office supplies and machines available for your use, laundry service, irons and ironing boards, and even breakfast in bed by arrangement.

Downstairs is a warm parlor, and a rec room that is more modern than not, but the hosts ply you with beverages and evening hors d'oeuvres and the vibe is convivial. Breakfast is fresh and filling, and prepared by their resident cook—when was the last time you had a voodoo queen cook for you?

☼ The McKendrick-Breaux House. 1474 Magazine St., New Orleans, LA 70130. ☎ **888/ 570-1700** or 504/586-1700. Fax 504/522-7138. 7 units. www.mckendrick-breaux.com. A/C TV TEL. $95–$175 double. Rates include breakfast. AE, MC, V. Limited free off-street parking available.

Owner Eddie Breaux saved this 1865 building just as it was about to fall down and turned it into one of the city's best B&Bs. It's not just that the antique-filled rooms are spacious (some of the bathrooms are downright huge), quaint, and meticulously decorated, but not fussy. It's not just that the public areas are simple, elegant, and comfortable. It's Breaux himself. You would be hard-pressed to find a better host. Not only is he utterly hospitable (fresh flowers may be waiting in your room), but he loves his city and is quite knowledgeable about it. He will help with all sorts of plans and is particularly helpful and opinionated (what good New Orleanian isn't, though?) with restaurant choices. He lives on-site, but is not intrusive, so you feel pampered but not smothered. Breakfast is usually fresh fruit and homemade breads and muffins. The location is right in the middle of the convenient Lower Garden District, named the Most Trendy Neighborhood in America by *Utne Reader* magazine.

Prytania Park Hotel. 1525 Prytania St., New Orleans, LA 70130. ☎ **800/862-1984** or 504/524-0427. Fax 504/522-2977. www.prytaniaparkhotel.com. 62 units. A/C MINIBAR TV TEL. $109 double; $119 suite. Rates include continental breakfast. Extra person $10. Children under 12 stay free in parents' room. Seasonal rates and special packages available. AE, CB, DC, DISC, MC, V. Free shuttle to Convention Center & French Quarter. Free parking.

In the historic Lower Garden District, the Prytania Park is a charming place that offers a choice of contemporary or old-world settings, and is run with the same personal attention as a guest house. The 1834 Victorian Building has been expertly restored and furnished in period hand-carved English pine. Its rooms have high ceilings and exposed-brick walls. The modern addition contains 49 streamlined rooms, which retain the New Orleans architectural ambience, but have more contemporary furnishings. Each opens onto a landscaped courtyard and has a microwave oven and a refrigerator. The St. Charles Avenue streetcar line is half a block away, providing access to the French Quarter (15 blocks away) and many of the city's major attractions.

INEXPENSIVE

Park View Guest House. 7004 St. Charles Ave., New Orleans, LA 70118. ☎ **888/ 533-0746** or 504/861-7564. Fax 504/861-1225. www.parkviewguesthouse.com. 23 units, 17 with private bathroom. A/C TEL. $85 double without bathroom, $109 double with bathroom. Rates include continental breakfast. Extra person $10. AE, DISC, MC, V. Parking available on street.

If you can't live without Bourbon Street and bars mere steps away from your hotel entrance, then this is not the place for you. But if a true getaway to you means a step back in time, then come to this quite-Uptown guest house, which feels at once like a truly old fashioned hotel (as well it should; it was built in 1881) and a glamorous Belle Epoch mansion with all the trimmings. Antique-filled rooms (including some imposing beds and armoires) are becoming plusher every minute, benefiting from the addition of down comforters, better amenities, and hair dryers. All rooms have high ceilings, while some have balconies overlooking Audubon Park, which is right across the street—go for an old-fashioned late afternoon promenade. The St. Charles streetcar stops right outside, so it's easy to get to and from the Quarter, still in a period mood. The front desk is staffed 24 hours a day, they have a tour desk, and guests have the use of a refrigerator and ice machine.

St. Charles Guesthouse. 1748 Prytania St., New Orleans, LA 70130. ☎ **504/523-6556.** Fax 504/522-6340. E-mail: dhilton111@aol.com. 35 units, 23 with private bathroom. $35–$85 double. Rates include continental breakfast. AE, MC, V. Parking available on street.

Very much worth checking out for those on a budget, the St. Charles Guesthouse—the first such accommodation in the Garden District and much-copied over the last 20 years—is not fancy, but it's one of the friendliest hotels in town. Rooms are plain and run from the low-end "backpacker" lodgings, which have no air-conditioning (even the management describes them as "small and Spartan") to larger chambers with air-conditioning and private bathrooms—nice enough, but nothing special. That's okay; the place does have the required New Orleans atmosphere elements: high ceilings, long staircase, and unvaluable antiques (there is such a fine line between "antique" and "old furniture"), not to mention the banana tree-ringed courtyard. And there's a pool. It's only a short walk through the quiet and very pretty neighborhood to the St. Charles Avenue streetcar line.

St. Charles Inn. 3636 St. Charles Ave., New Orleans, LA 70115. ☎ **800/489-9908** or 504/899-8888. Fax 504/899-8892. 40 units. A/C TV TEL. $70 double. Rates include continental breakfast. AE, DC, DISC, MC, V. Free parking.

If you want to stay uptown and don't need or want the pampering of a fancy hotel or precious guest house, you are probably looking for the St. Charles Inn. It's on the St. Charles Avenue streetcar line, and is convenient to Tulane and Loyola universities and Audubon Park. Each room has two double beds or a king-size bed. Facilities include a lounge and a restaurant. Breakfast is served in your room, and the morning newspaper is complimentary.

5 At the Airport

Downtown New Orleans is only a 15-minute drive from the airport (in Kenner). But if you've got an early-morning flight and you're worried about traffic, you might consider either of these two hotels, both of which offer airport transfer.

There's the **Hilton New Orleans Airport,** 901 Airline Dr., Kenner, LA 70062 (☎ **800/445-8667** or 504/469-5000; www.neworleansairport.hilton.com), if you want to spend a night in Kenner in style, taking advantage of their lighted tennis court, fitness center, putting green, gift shop, restaurant, and business center.

A less expensive alternative to the Hilton is the **Holiday Inn New Orleans-Airport,** 2929 Williams Blvd., Kenner, LA 70062 (☎ **800/465-4329** or 504/467-5611), with a restaurant, exercise room, pool, and sauna.

7

Dining

Within a short time during a trip to New Orleans, you will find yourself talking less about the sights and more about food—if not constantly about food. What you ate already, what you are going to be eating later, what you wish you had time to eat. We are going to take a stand and say to heck with New York and San Francisco: New Orleans has the best food in the United States. (There are natives who will gladly fight you if you say otherwise.)

This is the city where the great chefs of the world come to eat—if they don't work here already. Many people love to do nothing more than wax nostalgic about great meals they have had here, describing entrees in practically pornographic detail. It is nearly impossible to have a bad meal in this town; at worst, it will be mediocre, and with proper guidance, you should even be able to avoid that.

However, there is a reason a 1997 study of U.S. eating habits proclaimed New Orleans the fattest city in the country (a fact the locals will cheerfully volunteer to you—they are terribly proud of it). At times, it might seem that everything is fried or served with a sauce, and sometimes both. This of course defeats the potentially healthful quality of seafood, the predominant offering. "It ain't the fish, it's the battah that makes you fat," explains a local saying. Vegetables seem rare, or an afterthought at best.

Some of you may fret about this. Some of you may be watching your waistlines. To which we say, with all due understanding and respect, "So what?" You're on vacation. Vow to make it up when you get home. Even if it were possible to maintain your diet here, you'd just be miserable from the deprivation and you wouldn't have the full New Orleans experience. It's part of that all-important decadence. Give in. Sure, you might consider ordering salads whenever you can, or opting for blackened rather than fried fish, in an effort to trim those calories and fat grams. But don't go into contortions about it. If you are doing your trip properly, you will be walking and dancing so much, your scale might not be as unfriendly as you fear when you return home.

The biggest problem might be trying to cram in more meals than are physically possible into your stay. Do you return to an old, sublime favorite, or try out a brand-new, highly recommended locale? Do you check out the ecstasy-inducing creations of a famous chef at an upscale establishment, or go for a mouth-watering po' boy? Since

Living in New Orleans is like drinking blubber through a straw. Even the air is caloric.

—Andrei Codrescu, "Fantastic Fast"

we've been known to cart food onto the plane for the trip home, all we can say is, ah, gee, try it all.

Our favorite restaurants in various categories, all of them sure to incite an argument, are listed in chapter 1. In the pages that follow, you'll find a wide range of places to fill your belly, arranged first by type of cuisine and then, in greater detail, by neighborhood: the French Quarter; Mid City/Esplanade (toward the lake from the French Quarter on the same side of Canal Street); the Central Business District (CBD) (roughly the area upriver from Canal, extending to the elevated expressway); Uptown (everything upriver from the CBD as far as Carrollton), including the Garden District; Metairie (New Orleans' next-door neighbor in Jefferson Parish); and the area along the shores of Lake Pontchartrain. Turn back to the Greater New Orleans map in chapter 1 and you'll get the general idea.

1 A Taste of New Orleans

Boy, does this city love to eat. And boy, does it offer the visitor a range of choices. Thanks to influences from French provincial, Spanish, Italian, West Indian, African, and Native American cuisines, it covers the whole span, from down-home Southern cooking to the most creative and artistic gourmet dishes. New Orleans is one of the few cities in America that can justify a visit solely for cooking and cuisine.

Many of the famous dishes here started out as provincial French recipes brought to the New World by early settlers. Native Americans introduced the settlers to native herbs and filé (ground sassafras leaves); the Spanish added saffron and peppers to the mix somewhat later. From the West Indies came new vegetables, spices, and sugar cane, and when slave boats arrived, landing many black women in the kitchens of white slave owners, an African influence was added. Out of all this came the distinctive Creole culinary style unique to New Orleans. Later, Italian immigrants added yet another dimension to the city's tables, which also retained many traditional Old South dishes.

From this international past, residents of New Orleans have inherited a love of exciting culinary combinations, and from the city's Old World traditions they've retained an appreciation for fine service in elegant surroundings. There are lots of ironies here, too; you can get gourmet dishes served in the plainest of settings and plain meals (such as boiled crawfish or red beans and rice) in the fanciest of eateries. New Orleanians are voracious restaurant-goers, and are notoriously strict in the qualities they expect from a restaurant. If a place is below par, it probably won't last very long.

YOU GOT YOUR CAJUN IN MY CREOLE!

Cajun and Creole are the two classic New Orleans cuisines. What's the difference? It lies chiefly in distance between city and countryside.

Cajun cooking came from country folk—the Acadians who left France for Nova Scotia in the 1600s and, after being expelled from Canada by the British in the 1700s, made their way to the swamps and bayous of rural Louisiana. French dishes traveled with them, but along the way recipes were adapted to locally available ingredients. Their cuisine tends to be a lot like their music: spicy and robust. Étouffée, a classic dish, features sausage, duck, poultry, pork, and seafood prepared in a rich roux and served over rice. It's usually accompanied by something deep-fried. Creole dishes, on the other hand, were developed by French and Spanish city-dwellers and feature delicate sauces and ingredients of the highest quality.

In practice, however, the two cuisines have effected such a happy marriage in New Orleans that it's often difficult to distinguish between them. Because Creole is already such a hodgepodge —there are so many different ways of defining it that two entirely different restaurants might correctly call themselves Creole—it might soon swallow up Cajun food as just another influence. Paul Prudhomme of K-Paul's Louisiana Kitchen calls the result of Cajun and Creole cross-fertilization "Louisiana food." He goes on to say, "Nowhere else have all the ethnic groups merged to combine all these different tastes, and the only way you'll know the difference, honey, is to live 'em!" No matter how a New Orleans restaurant classifies its culinary offerings, you're bound to find one or two examples of Cajun and Creole cooking on the menu.

WAITER, THERE'S A FILÉ IN MY SOUP

Many of the foods in New Orleans are unique to the region, and consequently unfamiliar to first-time visitors. Here's a list that will that will help you navigate any New Orleans menu:

andouille (ahn-doo-*we*): A spicy Cajun sausage made with pork.

bananas Foster: Bananas sautéed in liqueur, brown sugar, cinnamon, and butter; drenched in rum; set ablaze; and served over vanilla ice cream.

beignet (bin-*yay*): A big, puffy, deep-fried doughnut (don't look for the hole), liberally sprinkled with powdered sugar—the more the better.

boudin (boo-*dan*): A type of sausage containing onion, spices, pork, and rice.

café brûlot (cah-*fay* brew-*low*): Coffee mixed with spices and liqueurs and served flaming.

chaurice (cho-*reece*): A hard sausage used chiefly for flavoring beans or soups.

crawfish: A tiny, lobsterlike creature plentiful in the waters around New Orleans and eaten in every conceivable way. When it's served whole and boiled, separate the head from the tail; then remove the first two sections of the tail shell. Squeeze the tail at its base—the meat should pop right out. You'll get the hang of it.

daube: Beef or sometimes veal.

dirty rice: A popular menu item, it only looks dirty because of the spices and other ingredients in which it's cooked—usually chicken livers and gizzards, onions, chopped celery, green bell pepper, cayenne, black and white peppers, and chicken stock.

dressed: Served with the works—used when ordering a sandwich.

eggs hussarde: Poached eggs with hollandaise, *marchand de vin* sauce, tomatoes, and ham. *Marchand de vin* is a wine sauce flavored with onions, shallots, celery, carrots, garlic, red wine, beef broth, and herbs.

eggs sardou: Legend has it that Antoine Alciatore created this dish especially for French playwright Victorien Sardou (author *of La Tosca*). It includes poached eggs, artichoke bottoms, anchovy fillets, hollandaise, and truffles or ham as a garnish.

étouffée (ay-too-*fay*): A Cajun stew (usually containing crawfish) served with rice.

filé (*fee*-lay): A thickener made of ground sassafras leaves. Filé is frequently used to thicken gumbo.

grillades (gree-*yads*): Thin slices of beef or veal smothered in a tomato-and-beef-flavored gravy, often served with grits.

grits: Grains of dried corn that have been ground and hulled. A staple of the Southern breakfast table, grits are most frequently served with butter and salt (not maple syrup or brown sugar) or red-eye gravy.

gumbo: A thick, spicy soup, always served with rice and usually containing crab, shrimp, sometimes oysters, and okra in a roux base

Hurricane: A local drink of rum and passion fruit punch.

hush puppies: Fried balls of cornmeal, often served as a side dish with seafood.

jambalaya (jum-ba-*lie*-ya): A jumble of yellow rice, sausage, seafood, vegetables, and spices.

lagniappe (lan-*yap*): A little something extra you neither paid for nor deserve—like the 13th doughnut when you order a dozen.

muffaletta: A mountainous sandwich made with Italian sausage, deli meats, one or two kinds of cheese, olive salad (pickled olives, celery, carrots, cauliflower, and capers), and oil and vinegar, piled onto a round loaf (about 8 inches in diameter) of Italian bread made specially for these incredible sandwiches.

oysters Rockefeller: Oysters on the half shell in a creamy sauce with spinach, so called because Rockefeller was the only name rich enough to match the taste.

pain perdu (pan *pair*-du): Literally, "lost bread," this is New Orleans' version of French toast, made with French bread. You'll find a large variety of toppings on pain perdu as you make your way around New Orleans.

po' boy: A sandwich on french bread with different fillings (similar to submarine sandwiches and grinders). Most po' boys are filled with fried seafood, but they can be anything you want, from roast beef to fried eggs to french fries. Yes, french fries.

pralines (*praw*-lines): A very sweet confection made of brown sugar and pecans; they come in "original" and creamy styles.

Ramos gin fizz: A cocktail of gin, egg whites, and orange-flavored water.

rémoulade: A spicy sauce, usually over shrimp. The one at Commander's Palace is a concoction of homemade mayonnaise, boiled egg yolks, horseradish, Creole mustard, and lemon juice. But several New Orleans restaurants claim to have invented it, and who can say who is right at this point.

sazerac: A cocktail of bourbon or rye (Canadian whiskey) with bitters.

shrimp Creole: Shrimp in a tomato sauce seasoned with what's known around town as "the trinity": onions, garlic, and green bell pepper.

tasso: A local variety of ham. No weak little honey-baked version, this one's smoked and seasoned with red pepper.

2 Restaurants by Cuisine

Whether you've a hankering for cheap Cajun in the Quarter or an expensive eclectic place near the Esplanade, this list of restaurants by cuisine might help you narrow it down. Then again, it just might further confuse things. You'll note that some places are listed in more than one category (and some in more than two), as many New Orleans restaurants defy rigid classification. The solution for the indecisive? Do what some do and simply have two dinners every night.

AMERICAN & NEW AMERICAN

Bluebird Cafe (Uptown/Garden District, *I*)
Emeril's (Central Business District, *E*)
Feelings Cafe D'Aunoy (French Quarter, *M*)
G&E Courtyard Grill (French Quarter, *M*)
The Grill Room (Central Business District, *E*)
Mike's on the Avenue (Uptown/Garden District, *E*)
Napoleon House (French Quarter, *I*)
Nola (French Quarter, *E*)
Pelican Club (French Quarter, *E*)
Peristyle (French Quarter, *E*)
Red Bike (Central Business District, *M*)
Red Room (Central Business District, *E*)
Rémoulade (French Quarter, *M*)

CAFES

Café Beignet (French Quarter, *I*)
Royal Blend Coffee & Tea House (French Quarter, *I*)

CAJUN

Bon Ton Café (Central Business District, *M*)
Bozo's (Metairie, *M*)
Brigtsen's (Uptown/Garden District, *E*)
Ernst's Café (Central Business District, *I*)
K-Paul's Louisiana Kitchen (French Quarter, *E*)
Olde N'Awlins Cookery (French Quarter, *M*)
Père Antoine Restaurant (French Quarter, *I*)
Petunia's (French Quarter, *I*)

COFFEE SHOPS

Clover Grill (French Quarter, *I*)

COFFEE, TEA & SWEETS

Café du Monde (French Quarter, *I*)
Kaldi's Coffee House and Museum (French Quarter,*I*)

La Madeleine (French Quarter, *I*)
La Marquise (French Quarter, *I*)
P. J.'s Coffee & Tea Company (French Quarter, *I*)
Royal Blend Coffee & Tea House (French Quarter, *I*)
Rue de la Course (Garden District, *I*)

CONTINENTAL

Sazerac Bar and Grill (Central Business District, *E*)
The Veranda Restaurant (Central Business District, *M*)

CREOLE

Antoine's (French Quarter, *E*)
Arnaud's (French Quarter, *E*)
Bacco (French Quarter, *E*)
Bizou (Central Business District, *E*)
Brennan's (French Quarter, *E*)
Brigtsen's (Uptown/Garden District, *E*)
Broussard's (French Quarter, *E*)
Cafe Sbisa (French Quarter, *E*)
Christian's (Mid City/Esplanade, *M*)
Clancy's (Uptown/Garden District, *E*)
Commander's Palace (Uptown/Garden District, *E*)
Court of Two Sisters (French Quarter, *E*)
Delmonico's (Central Business District, *E*)
Dooky Chase (Mid City/Esplanade, *M*)
Emeril's (Central Business District, *E*)
Ernst's Café (Central Business District, *I*)
Felix's Restaurant & Oyster Bar (French Quarter, *I*)
Gumbo Shop (French Quarter, *M*)
Kelsey's (Uptown/Garden District, *M*)
Liuzza's (Mid City/Esplanade, *M*)
Mandina's (Central Business District, *M*)
Mother's (Central Business District, *I*)
Mr. B's Bistro & Bar (French Quarter, *M*)

Key to abbreviations: *E* = Expensive *M* = Moderate *I* = Inexpensive

Nola (French Quarter, *E*)
Olde N'Awlins Cookery (French
    Quarter, *M*)
Palace Café (Central Business
    District, *M*)
Père Antoine Restaurant (French
    Quarter, *I*)
Petunia's (French Quarter, *I*)
Praline Connection (French Quarter,
    I)
Ralph & Kacoo's (French Quarter,
    M)
Rémoulade (French Quarter, *M*)
Rita's Olde French Quarter Restau-
    rant (French Quarter, *M*)
Royal Café (French Quarter, *M*)
Sazerac Bar & Grill (Central Business
    District, *E*)
Tujague's (French Quarter, *M*)
Upperline (Uptown/Garden District,
    E)
The Veranda Restaurant (Central
    Business District, *M*)
Vizard's (Uptown/Garden District,
    E)

ECLECTIC

Bella Luna (French Quarter, *E*)
Red Bike (Central Business District,
    M)
Upperline (Uptown/Garden District,
    E)
Vizard's (Uptown/Garden District,
    E)

FRENCH

Brennan's (French Quarter, *E*)
Cafe Degas (Mid City/Esplanade,
    M)
Crozier's Restaurant Français
    (Metairie, *M*)
Galatoire's (French Quarter, *E*)
La Crêpe Nanou (Uptown/Garden
    District, *M*)
Louis XVI (French Quarter, *E*)
Peristyle (French Quarter, *E*)

HAMBURGERS

Camellia Grill (Uptown/Garden
    District, *I*)
Port of Call (French Quarter, *M*)

INTERNATIONAL

Bayona (French Quarter, *E*)
Dominique's (French Quarter, *E*)
Gabrielle (Mid City/Esplanade, *M*)
Gautreau's (Uptown/Garden District,
    M)
Le Bistro (French Quarter, *E*)
Lola's (Mid City/Esplanade, *M*)
Mike's on the Avenue
    (Uptown/Garden District, *E*)

ITALIAN

Angeli On Decatur (French Quarter,
    I)
Bacco (French Quarter, *E*)
Bella Luna (French Quarter, *E*)
Figaro's Pizzeria (Uptown/Garden
    District, *I*)
Liuzza's (Mid City/Esplanade, *M*)
Louisiana Pizza Kitchen (Mid
    City/Esplanade, *I*)
Mama Rosa's (French Quarter, *I*)
Mandina's (Central Business District,
    M)
Maximo's Italian Grill (French
    Quarter, *M*)
Napoleon House (French Quarter, *I*)
Pascal's Manale (Uptown/Garden
    District, *M*)
Peristyle (French Quarter, *E*)

MEDITERRANEAN

Angeli On Decatur (French Quarter,
    I)
Mystic Cafe (Uptown/Garden
    District, *I*)

MIDDLE EASTERN

Mona's Café & Deli (Mid
    City/Esplanade, *I*)

PIZZA

Figaro's Pizzeria (Uptown/Garden
    District, *I*)
Louisiana Pizza Kitchen (Mid
    City/Esplanade,*I*)
Mama Rosa's (French Quarter, *I*)

SANDWICHES

Acme Oyster House (French Quarter,
    I)

Café Maspero (French Quarter, *I*)

Camellia Grill (Uptown/Garden District, *I*)

Johnny's Po-Boys (French Quarter, *I*)

Martin Wine Cellar and Delicatessen (Uptown/Garden District, *I*)

Mother's (Central Business District, *I*)

Uglesich's Restaurant & Bar (Central Business District, *I*)

SEAFOOD

Acme Oyster House (French Quarter, *I*)

Bozo's (Metairie, *M*)

Bruning's Seafood on the Lake (Lake Pontchartrain, *M*)

Bubba Gump Shrimp Co. (French Quarter, *M*)

Café Maspero (French Quarter, *I*)

Casamento's (Uptown/Garden District, *I*)

Felix's Restaurant & Oyster Bar (French Quarter, *I*)

Frankie and Johnny's (Uptown/Garden District, *I*)

Kabby's Seafood Restaurant (Central Business District, *M*)

Mike Anderson's Seafood (French Quarter, *M*)

Olde N'Awlins Cookery (French Quarter, *M*)

Pascal's Manale (Uptown/Garden District, *M*)

Ralph & Kacoo's (French Quarter, *M*)

Red Fish Grill (French Quarter, *M*)

Rib Room (French Quarter, *E*)

Tavern on the Park (Mid City/Esplanade, *M*)

Uglesich's Restaurant & Bar (Central Business District, *I*)

SOUL FOOD

Dooky Chase (Mid City/Esplanade, *M*)

Dunbar's Fine Food (Uptown/Garden District, *I*)

The Harbor (French Quarter, *I*)

Praline Connection (French Quarter, *I*)

SPANISH

Lola's (Mid City/Esplanade, *M*)

STEAK

Dickie Brennan's Steakhouse (French Quarter, *E*)

Pascal's Manale (Uptown/Garden District, *M*)

Rib Room (French Quarter, *E*)

Ruth's Chris Steak House (Mid City/Esplanade, *M*)

Tavern on the Park (Mid City/Esplanade, *M*)

VEGETARIAN

Old Dog New Trick (French Quarter, *I*)

VIETNAMESE

Lemon Grass (Central Business District, *M*)

3 The French Quarter

EXPENSIVE

Antoine's. 713 St. Louis St. ☎ **504/581-4422.** Reservations required. Main courses $14.25–$49. AE, CB, DC, MC, V. Mon–Sat 11:30am–2pm and 5:30–9:30pm. CREOLE.

Owned and operated by the same family for an astonishing 150 years, Antoine's is, unfortunately, beginning to show its age. With its 15 dining rooms and massive menu (more than 150 items), it was once the ultimate in fine dining in New Orleans. Thomas Wolfe said he ate the best meal of his life there, and author Frances Parkinson Keyes immortalized it in her mystery *Dinner at Antoine's*. But murmurs about a decline in quality have become open complaints. There have been discussions, in print and among locals, about how the food quality has gone sharply downhill, and how knowing your waiter has become a necessity. The waiter determines which of those 15 dining rooms you sit in, and some locals have found themselves in the front room, where only (gasp!) *tourists* get seated.

French Quarter Dining

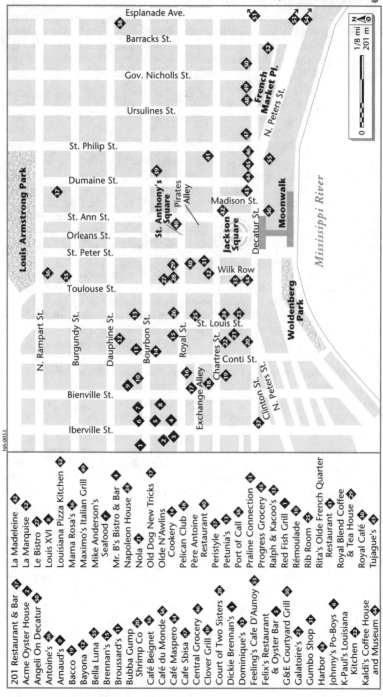

Esplanade Ave.

Barracks St.

Gov. Nicholls St.

Ursulines St.

St. Philip St.

Dumaine St.

Pirates Alley

Madison St.

St. Ann St.

Orleans St.

St. Peter St.

Wilk Row

Toulouse St.

St. Louis St.

Conti St.

Bienville St.

Exchange Alley

Iberville St.

Louis Armstrong Park

St. Anthony's Square

Jackson Square

Mississippi River

Moonwalk

Woldenberg Park

French Market Pl.

N. Peters St.

Decatur St.

Clinton St.

Chartres St.

Royal St.

Bourbon St.

Dauphine St.

Burgundy St.

N. Rampart St.

NA-0053

201 Restaurant & Bar 57
Acme Oyster House 2
Angeli On Decatur 50
Antoine's 26
Arnaud's 28
Bacco 12
Bayona 42
Bella Luna 55
Brennan's 13
Broussard's 47
Bubba Gump Shrimp Co 29
Café Beignet 31
Café du Monde 56
Café Maspero 54
Cafe Sbisa 47
Central Grocery 48
Clover Grill 32
Court of Two Sisters 28
Dickie Brennan's 3
Dominique's 43
Feeling's Cafe D'Aunoy 53
Felix's Restaurant & Oyster Bar 5
G&E Courtyard Grill 50
Galatoire's 23
Gumbo Shop 41
Harbor 34
Johnny's Po-Boys 6
K-Paul's Louisiana Kitchen 22
Kaldi's Coffee House and Museum 49

La Madeleine 42
La Marquise 32
Le Bistro 42
Louis XVI 8
Louisiana Pizza Kitchen 52
Mama Rosa's 36
Maximo's Italian Grill 51
Mike Anderson's Seafood 7
Mr. B's Bistro & Bar 24
Napoleon House 24
Nola 9
Old Dog New Tricks 47
Olde N'Awlins Cookery 47
Pelican Club 18
Père Antoine Restaurant 40
Peristyle 47
Petunia's 13
Port of Call 48
Praline Connection 51
Progress Grocery 45
Ralph & Kacoo's 33
Red Fish Grill 1
Rémoulade 10
Rib Room 25
Rita's Olde French Quarter Restaurant 1
Royal Blend Coffee & Tea House 29
Royal Café 30
Tujague's 53

Still, it's hard to ignore a legend, and so with some caution you may wish to investigate for yourself. Be sure to try the famous oysters Rockefeller (served hot in the shell, covered with a mysterious green sauce). Antoine's invented it and still won't give out the recipe. The baked Alaska is almost as famous. After he won the Nobel Prize for literature, William Faulkner got one inscribed "the Ignoble Prize."

⭐ **Arnaud's.** 813 Bienville St. ☎ **504/523-5433.** Reservations recommended. Jackets required in main dining room. Main courses $17–$28. AE, DC, MC, V, DISC. Mon–Fri 11:30am–2:30pm, Sun Jazz brunch 10am–2:30pm; Sun–Thurs 6–10pm, Fri–Sat 6–10:30pm. CREOLE.

Because we are sentimental, we are exceedingly fond of classic New Orleans restaurants, ones with venerable tradition and a menu set down when our grandparents were dating. But it's hard to maintain a reputation throughout a century. So it is a great relief to report that the food at Arnaud's is still solidly good, and often excellent. Arnaud's was founded in 1918 by "Count" Arnaud Cazenave, and due to strenuous preservation efforts by current owners Archie and Jane Casbarian, it still looks the same. The mosaic-tile floors, dark-wood paneling, ceiling medallions, and antique ceiling fans all make you feel as though you are dining in turn-of-the-century New Orleans.

Rave-producing fish dishes included snapper or trout Pontchartrain (it's topped with crabmeat), the spicy Pompano Duarte, and the Pompano David, which is a light fish dish perfect for those attempting to watch waistlines. Any filet mignon entree is superb, with the meat often better than that served in most steakhouses in town. Desserts aren't quite as magnificent, but the Chocolate Devastation is worth trying. At lunch there's an inexpensive table d'hôte (fixed-price) selection along with an à la carte menu.

Arnaud's also operates a less formal, less expensive brasserie, **Rémoulade** (see listing below), right next door.

⭐ **Bacco.** 310 Chartres St. ☎ **504/522-2426.** Reservations recommended. Main courses $19.50–$25. AE, CB, DC, MC, V. Daily 6–10pm; Sun brunch 10am–2pm. ITALIAN/CREOLE.

Don't expect spaghetti and marinara sauce here. Instead, think arresting, rich, ecstasy-inducing creations such as ravioli ripieni di formaggio, featuring four creamy cheeses all melting into a sauce of olive oil, tomatoes, and browned garlic. Or try the cannelloni con fungi, stuffed with wild mushrooms and fresh herbs covered in a goat cheese and chive sauce. The menu changes regularly, but a recent meal included a lovely insalata mista of baby greens and goat cheese with a light sun-dried tomato vinaigrette. Bacco is romantic and candlelit at night, more affordable and casual at lunchtime. Note their pizzas, which include such experiments as foie gras topped with onions, mushrooms, mozzarella, and white truffle oil. Try to charm them into a cheese sampling lagniappe to start; ours featured an impossibly creamy Gorgonzola, among other cheeses, with a slightly sweet brown sauce, served with the restaurant's hearty bread, which is the best we've had in New Orleans. Because this is a Brennan restaurant, desserts are far above average, including possibly the best version of tiramisu we've ever had.

⭐ **Bayona.** 430 Dauphine St. ☎ **504/525-4455.** Reservations required at dinner, recommended at lunch. Main courses $9–$12 at lunch, $14–$23 at dinner. AE, CB, DC, DISC, MC, V. Mon–Fri 11:30am–1:30pm; Mon–Thurs 6–9:30pm, Fri–Sat 6–10:30pm. INTERNATIONAL.

One of the city's top dining experiences, Bayona is beloved by savvy New Orleanians. In fact, two natives who were showing a visitor around the Quarter broke into spontaneous applause as they passed by. Chef Susan Spicer, who honed her considerable skills in France and at Le Bistro at the Maison de Ville, offers elegant, eclectic contemporary cuisine with Asian and Mediterranean flavors. You can sit inside the 200-year-old French Quarter Creole cottage or out in the courtyard.

Begin with one of the superb daily soups or the cream of garlic, a perennial favorite. Appetizers include grilled shrimp with cilantro sauce and black bean cakes, and delicate, flavorful veal sweetbreads sautéed with scallions and diced potatoes in a sherry vinaigrette. Knockout entrees have included a lamb chop and medallions of lamb loin with a lavender honey aïoli and Zinfandel demi-glace; a perfectly grilled pork chop with a stuffing of fontina cheese, fresh sage, and prosciutto; and yet another lamb dish, topped with goat cheese, that may have been the best lamb we've ever tasted. Heaven. Entrees come with a well-balanced selection of sides, such as gnocchi, pureed butternut squash, or fresh sweet corn. The wine selection is extensive, and the staff is extremely helpful in suggesting the right wine. After a quiet, romantic evening at Bayona, you may well applaud next time you pass by.

✪ **Bella Luna.** 914 N. Peters St. ☎ **504/529-1583.** Reservations recommended. Main courses $16–$24.75. AE, DC, DISC, MC, V. Mon–Sat 6–10:30pm, Sun 6–9:30pm. ECLECTIC/ITALIAN/CONTINENTAL.

The expansive view of the Mississippi River—probably the best reason to go here—makes this perhaps the most romantic restaurant in New Orleans. The interior, which feels like an Italian villa, suits the pasta dishes on the menu. Chef Horst Pfeifer, originally from Germany, eludes categories, however, and draws upon almost every imaginable cuisine. Appetizers might include Southwest duck enchiladas with roasted tomatillo salsa and fresh thyme. (Pfeifer grows his herbs and spices on a small plot on the grounds of the historic Ursuline Convent, so you know they are fresh.) Pastas are a specialty. Try the penne with peppers, eggplant, and Gorgonzola with a fontina sauce. The dessert menu changes frequently, but if the chocolate bellini napoleon is on the menu, give it a try.

✪ **Brennan's.** 417 Royal St. ☎ **504/525-9711.** Reservations recommended. Main courses $18–$35 at lunch, $28.50–$38.50 at dinner. AE, CB, DC, DISC, MC, V. Daily 8am–2:30pm and 6–10pm. Closed Dec 25. FRENCH/HAUTE CREOLE.

For more than 40 years, breakfast at Brennan's has been a New Orleans tradition, a feast that has surely kept many a heart surgeon busy. Expect no California health-conscious fruit-and-granola options here; this multi-course extravaganza is unashamedly sauce- and egg-intensive. It's also costly—it's not hard to drop $50 on breakfast—so you might be better off sticking with the fixed-price meal (though it often limits your choices). "Breakfast at Brennan's" has changed very little over the years, and that is part of the restaurant's charm, as is the building, constructed by Edgar Degas' great-grandfather, and childhood home to tragic chess master Paul Morphy. Dine here and you will find yourself rubbing elbows with loyal locals (including transplant Trent Reznor, Nine Inch Nails leader, who is a regular and a favorite of the staff) and tourists in search of a classic. Enjoy dishes such as eggs Portuguese (poached on top of a tomato concoction, served in puff pastry with hollandaise ladled over the whole), or their fine turtle soup and superb onion soup made with a roux. You can justify it all by making this your main meal of the day. Breakfast and lunch are quite crowded; dinner is less so (head straight to the gaslamp-lined balcony for dinner). This is probably due to a less-solid reputation for dinner. Even with a reservation, expect a wait.

Broussard's. 819 Conti St. ☎ **504/581-3866.** Reservations recommended. No jeans, shorts, sneakers, or T-shirts. Main courses $19.50–$33. AE, MC, V. Daily 5:30–10pm. CREOLE.

After a period in which it relied more on its landmark status than on its food to attract patrons, Broussard's is back. The Preuss family bought it in 1993, and breathed new life into the place just in time for it to celebrate its 75th anniversary in 1995. Along with fine French-Creole standbys like oysters Broussard's (with crabmeat and a cream sauce with Brie and artichokes), you'll find innovative creations. There's pecan-stuffed salmon de la Salle in Tabasco beurre blanc, snapper filet Pontchartrain baked with piquant crabmeat filling and topped with cayenne beurre blanc, and boneless duckling Normandy with an apple-bacon demi-glace and braised cabbage. The flaming desserts are superior, as is the chocolate marquis in raspberry sauce. The house specialty is "Delice Madam P," a plate of three desserts, such as puff pastry, cheesecake with praline sauce, and strawberries with custard sauce.

Cafe Sbisa. 1011 Decatur St. ☎ **504/522-5565.** Reservations recommended. Main courses $14.95–$24.95. AE, CB, DC, DISC, MC, V. Sun–Thurs 5:30–10:30pm; Fri–Sat 5:30–11pm; Sun brunch 10:30am–3pm. CREOLE.

Right across from the French Market, Cafe Sbisa opened in 1899 and in the 1970s was one of the first restaurants to experiment with Creole cooking. After a brief closure, it's once again a local favorite. Here's one instance where you may not want to go where the locals go, however. We found the food decidedly mediocre. Barbecued shrimp came in a sauce something like heavy Worcester. It was adequate, but disappointing. A special of wild boar was tough and chewy and its preparation bland. A salad special, however, was quite memorable, with Bibb lettuce, unusual zebra tomatoes and a lemon vinaigrette. You can't fault the atmosphere, which is classy and unpretentious, with live piano music sometimes at night. The wait staff is almost smothering in their friendly, effusive care. Sbisa also offers a Sunday jazz brunch.

Court of Two Sisters. 613 Royal St. ☎ **504/522-7261.** Reservations required at dinner. Main courses $15.50–$30; fixed-price menu $37; brunch $21. AE, CB, DC, DISC, MC, V. Daily 9am–3pm and 5:30–10pm. CREOLE.

The ambience here is more of a draw than the food, but what a draw it is. You enter through a huge courtyard filled with flowers, fountains, and low-hanging willows, with a wishing well at its center. You can dine outside amid the greenery or in the Royal Court Room. Even before you sit down, though, you know you've found a friendly establishment. A sign outside reads, "Buffet Brunch 9am to 3pm, Dinner 5:30 to 10pm. Visiting and Browsing Allowed 3:30 to 5pm. Have a Nice Day." The daily jazz brunch buffet features more than 60 dishes (meat, fowl, fish, vegetables, fresh fruits, homemade bread, and pastries) and a strolling jazz band. Delicacies such as shrimp Toulouse, crawfish Louise, and chicken Michelle are good bets at dinner. For dessert, try pecan pie or crêpes suzette. There is a $15 per person minimum at dinner.

The building and grounds were designed by an early French territorial governor of Louisiana who wanted to re-create the atmosphere of his homeland, and the unusual name comes from the Shop of the Two Sisters, operated in the late 1800s—by two sisters, of course.

Dickie Brennan's Steakhouse. 716 Iberville St. ☎ **504/522-2467.** Reservations suggested. Main courses $14.95–$32. AE, DC, DISC, MC, V. Mon–Fri 11:30am–2:30pm, 5:30–10pm. Sat–Sun 5:30–11pm. STEAK.

Carnivores should be pleased with this latest Brennan family establishment (Dickie's dad had long dreamed of opening a steakhouse), which has the feel of a contemporary clubhouse. All the meat is USDA Prime and great care is taken to cook it just as the customer dictates. The House Filet comes surrounded by quite good creamy spinach and Pontalba potatoes. We rather prefer the tender, flavorful rib eye, but do get that creamy spinach on the side. Consider starting with the napoleon of tomato and

Gorgonzola cheese topped with rémoulade sauce. It's a little busy, but you'll enjoy it. Don't miss their Bananas Foster Bread Pudding, which proves there can still be new twists on this old faithful dish.

Dominique's. 1001 Toulouse St. (in the Maison Dupuy Hotel). ☎ **504/522-8800.** Reservations recommended. Lunch main courses $11–$15, dinner main courses $20–$26. AE, MC, V. Daily 7am–10:30am, 11:30am–1:30pm, and 6–10pm. INTERNATIONAL.

Yet another reason for the New Orleans restaurant scene to be grateful to Le Bistro at the Maison De Ville. Like Bayona's Susan Spicer and others before him, Chef Dominique Macquet (originally from the Indian Ocean island of Mauritius) worked there before opening up his eponymous restaurant. Named one of the seven best new restaurants in America by *Bon Appétit* in 1998, this medium-sized bistro is well worth a little trot up the Rue Toulouse. Worth it, that is, as long as you want to try virtually cutting edge dishes like duck pastrami or duck prosciutto—and trust us, you do. Don't miss the appetizers of Aquavit-citrus cured salmon with crème fraîche, or the ahi tuna and oven-dried pineapple Napoléon. Entrees—including lamb riellette with caramelized spaghetti squash, or fire-roasted yellowfin tuna—can be a little less successful by comparison. For dessert, try the chocolate souffle or the *Cappamisu:* cappuccino flavored tiramisu in a cup.

✪ **Galatoire's.** 209 Bourbon St. ☎ **504/525-2021.** Reservations accepted Tues–Thurs only, and only for parties of 8 or more. Jackets required after 5pm and all day Sun. Main courses $14–$22. AE, MC, V, DC. Sun noon–9pm, Tues–Sat 11:30am–9pm. Closed holidays. FRENCH.

The venerated Galatoire's causes heated discussions these days among local foodies: still the best restaurant in New Orleans, or past its prime? Locals love it because they've gone for regular Sunday evening dinners for years, and all the old waiters know their names. We love it because in *A Streetcar Named Desire,* Stella took Blanche there to escape Stanley's poker game. It was Tennessee Williams' favorite restaurant (his table is the one right behind the word *Restaurant* on the window). Galatoire's has been run by the same family since 1905, and its traditions remain intact. By the time you read this, they should be finished renovating the upstairs dining room, which had been closed since World War II. The renovation will bring much-needed additional seating.

Galatoire's is worth the trip, though you may not have the same experience as a knowledgeable local, unless you get a waiter who can really guide you (ask for John). We love the lump crabmeat appetizer (think coleslaw, only with all crab instead of cabbage), the shrimp rémoulade, and the oysters Rockefeller. For an entree, get the red snapper or redfish topped with sautéed crabmeat meunière—it will probably be one of the finest fish dishes you have during your stay. Everything is à la carte, but don't miss out on the terrific creamed spinach and the puffy potatoes with béarnaise sauce, which will make you swear off regular french fries forever.

Galatoire's doesn't accept reservations except for groups of eight or more (even the Duke and Duchess of Windsor had to wait in line).

K-Paul's Louisiana Kitchen. 416 Chartres St. ☎ **504/524-7394.** Reservations recommended for upstairs dining room. Main courses $6.95–$14 at lunch, $20.95–$30 at dinner. AE, CB, DC, MC, V. Mon–Sat 11:30am–2:30pm and 5:30–10:30pm. CAJUN.

Paul Prudhomme was at the center of the Cajun revolution of the early '80s, when Cajun food became known throughout the world. His reputation and his line of spices continue today, which is probably why there is constantly a line outside his restaurant. Unfortunately, while the food is still good, it's not spectacular and certainly is not worth the wait (upwards of 1½ hours). The portions are Paul-sized, and as spicy as you might imagine, but nothing that special. Indeed, it feels as if the menu hasn't changed all that dramatically in quite some time. More interesting, innovative food is available all over town, and at some places you can get (admittedly) Prudhomme-influenced food without the long wait.

Different menu items are offered daily, but you can't go wrong with jambalaya (spicy!) or bronzed or blackened anything (really spicy!). One vegetarian friend claims the fried eggplant dish he had there was one of his lifetime outstanding meals (though you have to ask for it, as it's not regularly featured on the menu). Prudhomme's sweet potato pecan pie served with Chantilly cream is the best bet for dessert.

Le Bistro. In the Hotel Maison de Ville, 733 Toulouse St. ☎ **504/528-9206.** Reservations recommended. Main courses $19.75–$24.75. AE, DC, DISC, MC, V. Mon–Sat 11:30am–2pm, Sun brunch 11:30–2pm; daily 6–10pm. INTERNATIONAL.

This tiny bistro, part of the superb Maison De Ville hotel, is easy to overlook among the higher-profile choices in the French Quarter. But it is a favorite among in-the-know locals. They know that it is, among other things, the best training ground for new chefs, who often go on to make a splash at their own restaurants (as Susan Spicer has at Bayona). The dark, wood-paneled room—so small it can actually feel a bit cramped—almost seems like an old-fashioned men's club, which is helped along by the almost-too-attentive service. The menu changes regularly. If it's available, try pan-seared Sonoma foie gras with grilled apples and fall berry chutney; it melts in your mouth, exquisitely combining several taste sensations. Recent entrees included smoked duck breast with sun-dried cherry reduction and a ravioli of grilled quail, pine nuts, currants, and chèvre. *Wine Spectator* magazine gave Le Bistro its Award of Excellence 3 years in a row.

✪ **Louis XVI.** In the St. Louis hotel, 730 Bienville St. ☎ **504/581-7000.** Reservations required. Jacket required, tie optional. No jeans. Main courses $18–$34. AE, CB, DISC, MC, V. Mon–Fri 7am–noon, Sat–Sun 7am–2pm; daily 6–10pm. FRENCH.

Louis XVI is one of the city's premier dining experiences. The elegant dining rooms are done in 1920s Parisian style, so if you were expecting the gaudy Louis XVI style, you might be disappointed. Dining here, among impeccably tuxedoed waiters, is high and formal. The food is classically French, rich with sauces and traditional flavors—a flawless version of exactly what you would expect from a superb French restaurant. The menu will guide you toward the specialties, including fish Louisianne, beef Wellington, rack of lamb, and cream soups. Dessert is attention-grabbing, with many dishes prepared at the table and lit on fire. The *charlotte au chocolate et la banane* (chocolate and banana mousse surrounded by ladyfingers with Chantilly cream in an English rum sauce) is suggested. The bartender, Arlie, seems to be everyone's best pal, and will make you feel warm and comfortable.

Nola. 534 St. Louis St. ☎ **504/522-6652.** Reservations recommended. Main courses $16–$30. AE, DC, DISC, MC, V. Mon–Sat 11:30am–2pm; Mon–Thurs 6–10pm, Fri–Sat 6pm–midnight, Sun 6–10pm. CREOLE/NEW AMERICAN.

This modern two-story building with a glass-enclosed elevator is the more casual and less expensive of chef Emeril Lagasse's two restaurants. The same problems that plague Emeril's, however, also surface here: fine food, but often-horrible attitude, and the potential for painfully slow service (one meal that began before 9pm found the bill still not delivered at close to midnight). Still, it's conveniently located in the Quarter. And then there's the food: an appetizer that's a sort of deconstructed roast beef sandwich, unique entrees like Caribbean-style grilled free-range chicken (with a brown sugar–cayenne rub, served with sweet potato casserole, guacamole, and fried tortilla threads) and cedar-plank fish. Desserts run the gamut from Nola turtle pie with caramel sauce to coconut cream pie to banana layer cake to chicory coffee crème brûlée. The wine list is well selected.

✪ **Pelican Club.** 312 Exchange Alley. ☎ **504/523-1504.** Reservations recommended. Main courses $18.50–$24; fixed-price early dinner $17.95. AE, DC, DISC, MC, V. Mon–Thurs 5pm–closing, Fri–Sun 5:30pm–closing. Early dinner Mon–Thurs 5–5:45pm. NEW AMERICAN.

It sometimes comes as a relief to eat at a fine New Orleans establishment that is not a variation on a Brennan. Just a short stroll from the House of Blues, the Pelican Club is worth investigating, particularly for its reasonably priced three-course fixed-price meal. The appetizers are perhaps a bit more inventive than the entrees (you could easily make a meal of them), but everything is quite tasty. Escargots come in a tequila garlic butter sauce (which you will probably find yourself sopping up with bread), topped with tiny puff pastries. Oysters include apple-smoked bacon—even oyster-phobes won't have a problem. Special salads are served each evening; a recent visit produced arugula, Gorgonzola, and apple in balsamic dressing. Tender lamb comes coated in rosemary-flavored bread crumbs with a spicy pepper jelly, and fish is done to perfection. Interesting sides like wild mushroom bread pudding accompany the entrees. The desserts are certainly standouts. Try the flat (rather than puffy) white chocolate bread pudding, creamy chocolate pecan pie, or amazing profiteroles, filled with coffee ice cream and topped with three sauces. The mostly young wait staff is sassy in a good way, helpful and full of answers and opinions about the menu. Take advantage of them.

✪ **Peristyle.** 1041 Dumaine St. ☎ **504/593-9535.** Reservations recommended. Main courses $20–$24. AE, DC, MC, V. Fri 11:30am–2pm; Tues–Thurs 6–9pm, Fri–Sat 6–10:30pm. FRENCH/AMERICAN/ITALIAN BISTRO.

Chef Anne Kearney has done a beautiful job with Peristyle, which she purchased after the death of founding chef John Neal. In this dark, romantic bistro (on the site of Marti's, where Tennessee Williams liked to sit on the balcony and play poker), she continues the restaurant's fine tradition of delicious, elegant meals and attentive service. The menu changes seasonally, and there are so many interesting choices that you'll want to go back to try many of them. On a recent visit, first courses included a simple but lovely presentation of veal sweetbreads with French lentils, tomato and roasted garlic, and rich, buttery Sonoma County foie gras with a Pincau de Charentes glaze over creamy polenta. Among the entrees were marvelous grilled Maine salmon, served with a slightly pungent horseradish potato cake and a fumet of preserved lemons and dill. Seared sea scallops were huge, served with a rich truffle-thyme butter. Meats are as wonderful as the seafood, and are similarly simple but wonderfully satisfying. Desserts are interesting and unusual. The rich-rich-rich quenelles of sweetened goat's cheese came with fresh berries, heady with a drizzle of Armagnac.

Rib Room. In the Omni Royal Orleans hotel, 621 St. Louis St. ☎ **504/529-7045.** Reservations recommended. Main courses $23.50–$34. AE, MC, V, DISC, DC. Sun brunch 11:30am–2:30pm, Mon–Thurs and Sat 11:30am–2:30pm, Fri 11:30am–3pm; Sun–Thurs 6–10pm, Fri–Sat 6–10pm. SEAFOOD/STEAK.

Here is where New Orleanians come to eat beef. And who can fault their choice of surroundings? The solid and cozy Old English feel to this room is complete with natural brick and open ovens at the back. But while the meat is good, it is not outstanding, and the acclaimed prime rib is just a bit tough and more than lacking in flavor. There are also filets, sirloins, brochettes, tournedos, and steak au poivre. Veal, lamb, and duckling also appear on the menu, as do trout, crab, oysters, and shrimp. Carnivores, landlubbers, and ichthyophobes will be happier here than at one of the city's Creole restaurants, but it is not the must-do that its reputation would have you believe.

Chuck Taggart's Red Beans & Rice

Chuck Taggart is a native New Orleanian currently residing in Los Angeles. For more than 10 years he has been a music programmer and DJ, producing and hosting "Down Home" on KCSN, 88.5FM, a program featuring Louisiana music and roots and traditional music from around the world. He is the creator, author, editor, and Webmaster of the Gumbo Pages (www.gumbopages.com), a site devoted to Louisiana music, culture, and cuisine. He is also a culinary arts student at UCLA Extension, and aspires to become a chef, if he can ever tear himself away from his cushy day job.

Red beans and rice is the quintessential New Orleans dish, traditionally served on Mondays. It's going to take a little practice before you get it right. You'll probably want to fiddle with it each time you make it, and arrive at the exact combinations of seasonings you like. Feel free to alter this recipe to your taste, but don't stray too far.

1 pound dried red kidney beans

1 large onion, chopped

1 bell pepper, chopped

5 ribs celery, chopped

As much minced garlic as you like (I like lots, 5 or 6 cloves)

1 large smoked ham hock, 1 big chunk of Creole-style pickle meat (pickled pork), or ¾ pound smoked ham, diced

1 to 1½ pounds mild or hot smoked sausage or andouille, sliced

½ to 1 teaspoon dried thyme leaves, crushed

1 or 2 bay leaves

Crystal hot sauce or Tabasco, to taste

A few dashes Worcestershire sauce

Creole seasoning blend or red pepper, to taste

Salt and freshly ground black pepper, to taste

Fresh Creole hot sausage or chaurice, grilled or panfried, 1 link or patty per person, for serving (optional)

Pickled onions (optional)

White long-grain rice, for serving

MODERATE

Bubba Gump Shrimp Co. 429 Decatur. ☎ **504/522-5800.** Reservations not accepted. Main courses $9.80–$20. AE, DC, DISC, JCB, MC, V. Sun–Thurs 11am–1pm (bar open until midnight), Fri–Sat 11am–midnight (bar until 2am). SEAFOOD.

Normally we turn up our noses at theme restaurants—and heavens, it doesn't get much more theme-intensive than this national chain named after Forrest Gump's crustacean enterprise. (Yes, the movie plays on video screens nonstop.) But we make an exception here for two reasons. One, a shrimp restaurant makes sense in Louisiana (you may not be shocked to hear they serve shrimp all kinds of ways); and two, family-friendly restaurants are somewhat scarce in the French Quarter. The management brags "we have more baby chairs than any other restaurant in the Quarter."

Feelings Cafe D'Aunoy. 2600 Chartres St. ☎ **504/945-2222.** Reservations recommended. Main courses $11.75–$21.75. AE, DC, DISC, MC, V. Sun and Fri 11am–2pm; Mon–Thurs 6–10pm, Fri–Sat 6–11pm. AMERICAN.

Soak the beans overnight, if possible. The next day, drain and put fresh water in the pot. Bring the beans to a rolling boil. Make sure the beans are always covered by water, or they will discolor and harden. Boil the beans for 45 to 60 minutes, until they are tender but not falling apart. Drain.

While the beans are boiling, sauté the trinity (onions, celery, and bell pepper) until the onions turn translucent. Add the garlic and sauté for 2 more minutes, stirring occasionally. After the beans are boiled and drained, add the sautéed vegetables to the beans, then add the meat, the seasonings, and just enough water to cover.

Bring to a boil, then reduce heat to a low simmer. Cook at least 2 to 3 hours, until the whole thing gets nice and creamy. Adjust seasonings as you go along. Keep tasting it. Stir occasionally, making sure that it doesn't burn or stick to the bottom of the pot. (If the beans are old—say, more than 6 to 12 months—they won't get creamy. Make sure the beans are reasonably fresh. If they're still not getting creamy, take 1 or 2 cups of beans out and mash them, then return them to the pot and stir.)

If you can, stick the beans in the fridge overnight. Reheat with a little water, to get the right consistency, and serve for dinner the next day. They'll taste a *lot* better.

Serve generous ladles of beans over hot white long-grain rice, with good French bread and good beer. I also love to serve grilled or panfried fresh Creole hot sausage or chaurice on the side. (And pickled onions.)

Serves 8 regular people, or 6 hungry ones.

Vegetarian Red Beans & Rice

Sacrilege, you say? Maybe. But a lot of folks who don't eat pork, or meat of any kind, can still enjoy this dish. It's not the same, of course, but it's still pretty damned good. Follow the same above, except:

• Omit the meat
• Add 2 tablespoons vegetable oil along with the seasonings
• Add 1 teaspoon (or to taste) liquid smoke seasoning

This modest neighborhood joint isn't actually in the French Quarter, but a short cab ride away in the Faubourg Marigny. Friendly and funky, it serves tasty, solid, if not spectacular, food. It feels like a true local find—because it is—and can be a welcome break from the scene in the Quarter or from more intense dining. Try to get a table in the pretty courtyard or on the balcony overlooking it (particularly delightful on a balmy night), though the dining rooms are perfectly pleasant. The piano player is a neighborhood character. Be sure to have a drink at the lively bar and chat with him. A recent visit produced a dressed red snapper topped with crab claw meat and crawfish dressing, a rib-eye steak topped with bleu cheese (recommended even by nonhabitual meat eaters), and several adequate vegetarian entrees, including delicious salads. Desserts are small and overpriced, so go elsewhere for sweets.

✪ **G&E Courtyard Grill.** 1113 Decatur St. ☎ **504/528-9376.** Reservations recommended. Main courses $12.50–$26. AE, CB, DC, DISC, MC, V. Fri–Sun 11:30am–2:30pm; Sun–Thurs 6–10pm, Fri–Sat 6–11pm. NEW AMERICAN.

Cookin' Like a Cajun

Cooking is one of the prized arts in New Orleans, and if you want to learn how to prepare some local and regional specialties, you won't lack for opportunities. Many restaurants hold informal seminars, and there are several established schools in town.

The cream of the, er, crop is probably Susan Spicer's ✪ **Spice, Inc.,** 1051 Annunciation St. (☎ **504/558-9992**). Classes are held at this gourmet food and take-out shop in the Warehouse District. The schedule changes monthly, but Ms. Spicer (creator and head chef of Bayona) teaches a couple of the classes, which range from "Classical French Creole" to "New Fashioned New Orleans" to "Kitchen Basics" and "Leftovers Again?" Call for a schedule and to make a reservation. The classes are new enough that they aren't necessarily always full just yet, but that's going to change. You might also drop by for some gourmet take-out food, everything from made to order sandwiches to elaborate lamb concoctions, not to mention the famous Bayona cream of garlic soup, all perfect for a parade-watching picnic.

The **New Orleans School of Cooking,** 524 St. Louis St. (☎ **800/237-4841** or 504/525-2665), offers a great way to learn the secrets of Creole cooking. Local cooks and chefs conduct entertaining and informative demonstrations of basic techniques, then serve the dishes you've just seen prepared. The number of participants is limited, so reserve as far in advance as possible. If classes are full, inquire about the possibility of evening courses. The school is in the back of the Louisiana General Store, which is crammed full of cookbooks, Cajun and Creole seasonings, and a host of other gift items. Sessions run 10am to 1pm, Monday through Saturday.

Chef Susan Murphy runs the **Creole Delicacies and Cookin' Cajun Cooking School,** Store no. 116, Riverwalk, 1 Poydras St. (☎ **504/586-8832**), at the Mississippi River levee in the French Quarter. She and the school's staff offer daily classes where you can learn to make everything from jambalaya to pralines. Times vary, so call in advance. The gourmet shop on the premises features a great collection of hot sauces and cookbooks; it's open Monday to Thursday 9:30am to 9pm, Friday and Saturday 9:30am to 10pm, and Sunday 9:30am to 7pm.

A more intimate place for a lesson in Creole and Cajun cooking is **Cuisine Eclairée Ecole de Cuisine,** also known as Cuisine! Cuisine! (☎ **800/882-2968** or 504/945-0992). It operates at the House on Bayou Road, 2275 Bayou Rd. (see chapter 6), which offers 2- and 5-night accommodations packages in combination with the cooking school. The 2-day minicourse teaches you to plan a menu and prepare a meal. The 5-day "Grand Class" includes visits to some of the best restaurants in New Orleans, as well as the preparation of a meal. Class sizes are limited, so reserve well in advance. Prices are reasonable—as little as $45 for a 1-day course for inn guests. Courses are taught by chef Elaine Lemm, who established Cuisine Eclairée in York, England (when Lemm is out of the country, the school goes by Cuisine! Cuisine!).

The G&E has been open for nearly 10 years, but is still treated like a splashy new arrival, with a line frequently snaking out the door. Atmosphere junkies really like the covered courtyard, where cast-iron chairs and glass-topped tables rest on terra-cotta tile. The best part? The open grill at the back of the courtyard, where a dozen chickens can typically be seen spinning on the rotisserie. The soft-shell crab rolls with caviar and wasabi, or shrimp cakes with homemade goat cheese, gingered black bean puree, and garlic, tomato, and cilantro salsa are excellent starters. As an entree, rotisserie chicken in mint, garlic, tomato, and balsamic sauce is unsurpassed. Another good choice is the grilled Gulf fish with chanterelle-black lentil sauce served with a risotto cake.

Gumbo Shop. 630 St. Peter St. ☎ **504/525-1486.** Main courses $5.95–$14.95. AE, CB, DC, DISC, JCB, MC, V. Daily 11am–11pm. CREOLE.

This is the cheap and convenient way to get solid, if not particularly memorable, classic Creole food. The Gumbo Shop is 1 block off Jackson Square in a building dating from 1795. It's a bit touristy, but not unappealing. The menu reads like a textbook list of traditional local food: red beans and rice, shrimp Creole, crawfish étouffée. The seafood gumbo with okra is a meal in itself, and do try the jambalaya. Other dishes include crawfish and penne pasta, filet mignon, salads, po' boys (from regular ham and cheese to Cajun sausage), and homemade desserts such as Southern pecan pie with ice cream. In addition to the regular menu, fresh fish entrees and dessert specialties are offered daily. There's a full bar, and you can also get wine by the bottle or the glass.

Maximo's Italian Grill. 1117 Decatur St. ☎ **504/586-8883.** Reservations recommended. Main courses $8.95–$28.95. AE, DC, DISC, MC, V. Daily 6–11pm. ITALIAN.

Maximo's serves solid, if not particularly amazing, Italian food. A huge advantage is that it's open late, for dining after an early show (or lengthy afternoon nap!). On the antipasto platter, you're likely to find lovely portobello mushrooms, prosciutto-wrapped fruit, and a selection of olives. There are usually more than a dozen pastas, some smothered with tomato sauce, some tossed with garlic and oil, and others dotted with clams. The house specialty is penne Rosa, topped with sun-dried tomatoes, garlic, arugula, and shrimp. The chef's signature item is veal T-bone cattoche (pan-roasted with garlic and fresh herbs). Go for the zabaglione or the Black Max (flourless chocolate cake) for dessert. The wine list is excellent.

Mike Anderson's Seafood. 215 Bourbon St. ☎ **504/524-3884.** Reservations not accepted. Weekday lunch specials under $8.95; main courses $9.95–$17.95. AE, DISC, MC, V. Sun–Thurs 11:30am–10pm, Fri–Sat 11:30am–11pm. SEAFOOD.

This is an offshoot of the popular Baton Rouge restaurant. As the name implies, seafood is the specialty, and it comes in all varieties: fried, baked, boiled, charbroiled, or raw and on the half-shell. Especially good are the crawfish bisque and crawfish étouffée. The weekday lunch specials, which change daily, are a bargain. When oysters are in season, you can get 'em cold and raw for 25¢ apiece, Monday through Thursday before 6pm. On an average night you should be prepared to wait at least 15 minutes for a table. While you wait, you can go upstairs, have a cocktail, and sit down to some appetizers. This is not the place for a romantic evening—it's on Bourbon Street, after all, and can get pretty loud and crowded—but it serves good food at extremely reasonable prices.

They also have a location at 2712 N. Arnoult Rd. in Metarie (☎ **504/779-6453**).

✪ **Mr. B's Bistro & Bar.** 201 Royal St. ☎ **504/523-2078.** Reservations recommended. Main courses $15.50–$28. AE, DC, DISC, MC, V. Mon–Sat 11:30am–3pm; Sun brunch 10:30am–2:30pm; daily 5:30–10pm. CONTEMPORARY CREOLE.

Run by Cindy Brennan, this deceptively simple place only helps solidify the Brennan reputation. It draws a steady group of regulars for lunch several days a week, always at their regular tables—some local businesspeople just don't consider it a week without lunch here. For visitors, it's a fine place to recover from intense Royal Street shopping.

The food, mostly modern interpretations of Creole classics, is simple, but with spices that elevate the flavors into something your mouth really thanks you for. The crab cakes are about as good as that dish gets. Superb too is the not-too-spicy andouille sausage—get it in everything you can. Gumbo Ya Ya is a hearty, country-style rendition with chicken and sausage, perfect for a rainy day. The unusual pasta jambalaya is a variation on a classic dish—Gulf shrimp, andouille, duck, and chicken, tossed with spinach fettuccine. The Cajun barbecued shrimp are huge and plump, with a rich, thick, buttery sauce. It's so tasty it makes you greedy for every drop, completely oblivious to the silly bib they make you wear. Seemingly simple desserts feature just the right amount of sweet. It's hard to pick, but recent standouts were chocolate molten "up" cake with raspberry coulis, creamier-than-traditional lemon icebox pie, and a white chocolate brownie.

Olde N'Awlins Cookery. 729 Conti St. ☎ **504/529-3663.** Reservations accepted for groups of 5 or more. Breakfast items $6–$11; complete breakfast $6; main courses $5.75–$14.75 at lunch, $14.50–$20.75 at dinner. AE, MC, V. Daily 7am–11pm. CREOLE/CAJUN/SEAFOOD.

A decent standby if your first choices are full, this family-operated restaurant serves up reliably good traditional Cajun and Creole favorites such as jambalaya, blackened redfish, and shrimp Creole. Try the Cajun barbecued shrimp, and don't forget to ask for plenty of extra bread to sop up the rich, buttery, spicy sauce. Oooh, fattening. Housed in an 1849 building that's been a private house, a brothel, a bistro bar, and a disco, it makes use of the original old brick and a charming courtyard to create a very pleasant and—dare we say it?—decidedly New Orleans atmosphere. The restaurant also offers an extensive breakfast menu, with many specialty egg dishes, including Atchafalaya (poached, with alligator sausage) and des Allemandes (poached, on fried catfish). Breakfast is served until 4pm daily, and includes hash browns, grits, toast, choice of meat, coffee, and a variety of other side dishes (red beans, grilled veggies, and so forth). You may have to wait to be seated at peak hours.

✪ **Port of Call.** 838 Esplanade Ave. ☎ **504/523-0120.** Reservations not accepted. Main courses $6–$19. AE, MC, V. Sun–Thurs 11am–1am, Fri–Sat 11am–3am. HAMBURGERS.

Sometimes you just need a burger. Particularly when you've been eating many things with sauce. Locals feel strongly that the half-pound monsters served at the cozy (and we mean it) Port of Call are the best in town. We are going to take a stand and say that while they are certainly terrific, all that meat may be too much of a good thing. The Port of Call is just a half-step above a dive, but it's a convivial place with a staff that's attentive, if somewhat harried during busy hours. The hamburgers come with a baked potato (because you might not have gotten enough food), and there also are pizzas, excellent filet mignon, rib-eye steaks, and New York strip steaks. Because businesspeople come here from all over the city, it's often jammed at regular eating hours, so try it before 7pm, when people who work in the Quarter begin to gather here. Takeout service is available.

Ralph & Kacoo's. 519 Toulouse St. ☎ **504/522-5226.** Reservations recommended. Main courses $6.95–$17.95. AE, DC, DISC, MC, V. Mon–Thurs 11am–10pm, Fri–Sat 11am–11pm, Sun 11am–9:30pm. CREOLE/SEAFOOD.

This is a satisfying, reliable place for seafood, which is probably why it is usually crowded at all hours. (You can wait at the bar, though, so it's not too bad. And you'll seldom have to wait more than 15 to 20 minutes.) The Creole dishes are quite good, portions are more than ample, prices are reasonable, and the high volume of business means everything is fresh. Start with fried crawfish tails or the killer onion rings, and if you're adventurous, give the blackened alligator with hollandaise a try. For a main course, try trout Ruby (stuffed with lump crabmeat and topped with baby shrimp and hollandaise) or, when it's available, mesquite-grilled, blackened, or broiled mahimahi topped with green onions and served with a Cajun stuffed potato, coleslaw, and hush puppies. For those on restricted diets, there's a special "heart healthy" menu. Be sure to try the satin pie for dessert. It's a creamy, mousselike concoction of peanut butter and a thin layer of chocolate that will please even nonpeanut butter fans.

Red Fish Grill. 115 Bourbon St. ☎ **504/598-1200.** Reservations limited. Main courses, lunch only $8.75–$9.75, dinner $8.95–$17.75. AE, MC, V. Mon–Sat 11am–3pm, Mon–Sun 5–11pm, Sun brunch 10am–3pm. SEAFOOD.

Red Fish is far better than anything else in its price range on Bourbon Street. Ralph Brennan's—surprise, another Brennan restaurant—place serves many New Orleans specialties, with an emphasis on—surprise again—fish. Skip the dull salads in favor of appetizers like shrimp rémoulade napoleon (layered between fried green tomatoes) or grilled shrimp and shiitake mushroom quesadillas. For your entree, go right to the fish they do so well. Whatever you have should be light and flaky, with flavors that complement each other, rich (it is New Orleans) but not overly so. The signature dish is a pan-seared catfish topped with sweet potato crust and an andouille cream drizzle. It's so outstanding, we asked for the recipe so we could try to recreate it at home. You can't, not really, but it was fun trying. Also splendid is the grilled Gulf fish with a pecan butter sauce.

Rémoulade. 309 Bourbon St. ☎ **504/523-0377.** Reservations recommended. Main courses $4–$20. AE, CB, DC, MC, V, DISC. Daily 11:30am–midnight. CREOLE/AMERICAN.

If you've been wanting to go to Arnaud's but can't afford it, can't get a reservation, or just don't feel like dressing up, we have the answer: Rémoulade, a brasserie-like offshoot of the terribly formal Arnaud's, right next door. Recorded jazz plays pleasantly, and the kitchen can be seen from every table in the house. The menu is fun and eclectic, and the food, not surprisingly, is excellent. Thin-crust pizzas with a wide variety of toppings are popular, as are the seafood po' boys. Rémoulade also features some of the dishes Arnaud's made famous, like shrimp Arnaud (in a Creole mustard sauce) and oysters stewed in cream. It also pokes fun at tradition by serving a hot dog topped with rémoulade sauce (not bad, actually). The wine list comes from Arnaud's, so you won't be disappointed on that front, either.

Rita's Olde French Quarter Restaurant. 945 Chartres St. (at St. Philip St.). ☎ **504/525-7543.** Main courses $5.95–$11.95 at lunch, $13.95–$17.95 at dinner. AE, CB, DC, DISC, MC, V. Daily 11am–10pm. CREOLE.

Rita's doesn't look like much on the outside, and you're likely to walk right past without noticing it. Don't. When you walk in, you'll feel right at home. There's a big portrait of Rita, various Rita relatives often dine at the back table, and pictures on the walls hang a little crooked. The atmosphere is very casual, the staff friendly and inviting. The menu is extensive, featuring at least 20 entrees, including pasta and veal dishes. Special blackened catfish is bathed in a very tasty Lea & Perrins and lemon sauce and served with sweet potatoes in brown-sugar sauce. The oyster and artichoke soup is tasty, and the gumbo is excellent. You shouldn't miss Rita's bread pudding, and you probably won't—they often bring out a complimentary dish when you're done with your meal.

Royal Café. 700 Royal St. ☎ **504/528-9086.** Reservations recommended for parties of 6 or more. Main courses $6.75–$23.95. AE, MC, V. Mon–Fri 11am–10pm, Sat–Sun 10am–10pm. CREOLE.

The Royal Café is a casual place, with dining rooms upstairs and down, but it's the upstairs balcony that appeals to most people. Its view of the French Quarter is so good it finds its way into almost every visitor's vacation photos (as does the outside, because it's the most famous wrought-iron work in the Vieux Carré). Try French Quarter toast (New Orleans "lost bread") for breakfast (on Saturday and Sunday only), spicy shrimp Creole or a po' boy at lunch, and the famous crab cakes at dinner. Should you have difficulty choosing, the "Taste of New Orleans" sampler gives you a cup of gumbo, a small bowl of red beans and rice with sausage, and shrimp Creole served with fresh-baked French bread.

201 Restaurant & Bar. 201 Decatur St. (at Iberville). ☎ **504/561-0007.** Reservations recommended. Main courses $15–$18. AE, DC, DISC, MC, V. Mon–Fri 11am–3pm; Sun–Thurs 5–11pm, Fri–Sat 5pm–midnight. CONTEMPORARY LOUISIANA.

They do fish very nicely, with a decided Asian influence, at this casual but spiffy place. It's won praise as one of the 10 best new restaurants of the year (given the number of restaurants in town, it's tough competition). It's a simple space, a typical New Orleans high-ceilinged room, mercifully largely untampered with except for the addition of some modern and Depression-era lamps. The menu changes occasionally, but at a recent meal, I was most pleased by shrimp-and-scallop potstickers with a spicy but sweet red-pepper dipping sauce, and a macadamia-crusted fish with a ginger soy butter. There are some fine red-meat dishes, but the lighter offerings show off that Asian flair to better advantage, while making both your waistline and taste buds equally happy.

Tujague's. 823 Decatur St. ☎ **504/525-8676.** Reservations recommended. 4-course lunch $6.50–$13.95; 6-course dinner $24.95–$29.95. AE, CB, DC, DISC, MC, V. Daily 11am–3pm and 5–10:30pm. CREOLE.

Tujague's (pronounced *two-jacks*) is the second restaurant to occupy this site. The first was run by Madame Begue, who in 1856 began cooking huge and well-loved "second breakfasts" for the butchers who worked in the French Market across the way. Today, Tujague's serves only lunch and dinner, but continues the Begue's tradition of serving whatever inspiration dictates. This place is a favorite with New Orleanians, who don't seem to mind the very limited menu. At lunch, you have a choice of three entrees, which might include brisket of beef with horseradish sauce (a specialty), terrific shrimp rémoulade, or the freshest fish available that day. If something lighter appeals to you, choose gumbo served with a side dish of shrimp salad.

INEXPENSIVE

Acme Oyster House. 724 Iberville St. ☎ **504/522-5973.** Reservations not accepted. Oysters $3.50–$6; po' boys $4.75–$6.95; New Orleans specialties $5.50–$6.95; seafood $9.95–$12.95. AE, DC, DISC, JCB, MC, V. Mon–Sat 11am–10pm, Sun noon–7pm. SEAFOOD/SANDWICHES.

This joint is always loud, often crowded, and the kind of place where you're likely to run into obnoxious fellow travelers. But if you need an oyster fix, or if you've never tried oyster shooting (taking a raw oyster, possibly doused in sauce, and letting it slide right down your throat), come here. There's nothing quite like standing at the oyster bar, eating a dozen or so freshly shucked oysters on the half-shell. (You can have them at a table, but somehow they taste better at the bar.) If you can't quite stomach them raw, try the oyster po' boy, with beer, of course. Acme offers fresh-baked bread pudding and cheesecake on the dessert menu, but of course dessert is not why you come here.

☺ Angeli On Decatur. 1141 Decatur (at Gov. Nichols). ☎ **504/566-0077.** Everything under $10. AE, MC, V. 24 hours. ITALIAN/MEDITERRANEAN.

This is a brand-new, highly welcome addition to the Quarter, featuring terrific (if not particularly New Orleans–specific) food. This place has already gotten raves for round-the-clock hours and local delivery service—all things hungry locals and tourists crave. Brought to you by the team behind the Garden District's popular Mystic Cafe, Angeli's is a nice (if, at this writing, dimly lit) space that doesn't overdo the angel theme. It's conveniently accessible after a day's busy sightseeing or a night's busy club-hopping. It's perfect for a light, actually rather healthy meal, a needed alternative to some of the extravaganzas offered by more formal restaurants in town. Portions are substantial—splitting a Greek salad produced two full plates of fresh, lovely veggies and a couple of pieces of garlic bread. Couple that with a small pizza (they do them all well, but the Mystical—roasted garlic, goat cheese, onions, sun-dried tomatoes—is a top choice), and you've got a tasty, affordable meal for two, at any hour, and even in your hotel room.

Café Beignet. 334B Royal St. ☎ **504/524-5530.** All items under $7. Daily 7am–5pm. CAFE.

This is a full-service, bistro-style cafe. At breakfast you can get Belgian waffles, an omelette soufflé, bagels and lox, or brioche French toast. Items on the lunch menu include gumbo, crawfish pie, vegetable sandwiches, and salads. The cafe now serves the famous New Orleans beignets, and the exclusive Robert Mondavi wine bar is available all afternoon.

Café Maspero. 601 Decatur St. ☎ **504/523-6250.** Reservations not accepted. Main courses $4.25–$9. No credit cards. Sun–Thurs 11am–11pm, Fri–Sat 11am–midnight. SEAFOOD/SANDWICHES.

Upon hearing complaints about the increasing presence in the Quarter of "foreign" restaurants such as Subway and the Hard Rock Cafe, one local commented, "Good. That must mean the line will be shorter at Café Maspero." It serves burgers, deli sandwiches, seafood, grilled marinated chicken, and so on, in some of the largest portions you'll ever run into. And there's an impressive list of wines, beers, and cocktails, all delicious and all at low, low prices. Café Maspero always has a long line of locals, coming by after a concert, the opera, or the theater.

✪ Clover Grill. 900 Bourbon St. ☎ **504/598-1010.** All items under $7. AE, MC, V. Daily 24 hours. COFFEE SHOP.

The "Happiest Grill On Earth!" boasts the irreverent menu, which also claims "We're here to serve people and make them feel prettier than they are." The staff at this delightful 24-hour diner competes with the menu for fun. Juicy, perfect burgers are cooked under a hubcap; they say it seals in the juices, and it seems to work. So well, in fact, that we are going to break with tradition and declare them the best burgers in New Orleans, over the usual favorites at the Port of Call. Breakfast is served around the clock. By the way, Froot Loops is the most popular cereal, and yes, they know why. They also serve fabulous shakes, malts, classic (and painfully sweet) lemon icebox pie, and lots of coffee. Remember, as the menu says, "If you were a good customer, you would order more."

Felix's Restaurant & Oyster Bar. 739 Iberville St. ☎ **504/522-4440.** Main courses $10–$19.75. AE, MC, V. Mon–Thurs 10am–midnight, Fri 10am–1am, Sat 10am–1:30am, Sun 10am–10pm. SEAFOOD/CREOLE.

Like its neighbor the Acme Oyster House, Felix's is a crowded and noisy place, full of locals and tourists taking advantage of the late hours. It's more or less the same as the Acme. Each has its die-hard fans, convinced their particular choice is the superior one. Have your oysters raw, in a stew, in a soup, Rockefeller or Bienville style, in spaghetti, or even in an omelette. If oysters aren't your bag, the fried or grilled fish, chicken, steaks, spaghetti, omelets, and Creole cooking are mighty good, too. If you want something blackened, they'll fry it up to order. They usually also have boiled crawfish in season.

The Harbor. 2529 Dauphine St. ☎ **504/947-1819.** All items under $6. No credit cards. Daily 6am–5pm. SOUL FOOD.

Definitely out of the way (a cab ride away, in fact, in the Bywater section, past the Faubourg Marigny on the edge of the Quarter), The Harbor has been a favorite of knowledgeable locals since 1949. This is the place to go for huge portions of authentic soul food, all for ridiculously low prices. (A combination plate will set you back $4.40.) You order at the counter, where all the women call you "Baby," set yourself down at a beat-up table, admire the zero decor, note that you are the only nonlocal, and dig in. Smothered pork chops, fried chicken, barbecued ribs, turkey wings, greens, red beans and rice—this is not gourmet, and we mean that as a compliment. It is hearty and filling, and you will probably be sorry you can't try everything, though at these prices, it won't be for lack of funds. Get there early, as they tend to run out of food.

Johnny's Po-Boys. 511 St. Louis St. ☎ **504/524-8129.** Everything under $8. Cash only. Mon–Fri 8am–4:30pm, Sat–Sun 9am–4pm. SANDWICHES.

For location, right near a busy part of the Quarter, and menu simplicity, po' boys and more po' boys, you can't ask for much more than Johnny's. Oh, we could, probably, but we've come to expect so much. Anyway, they put anything you could possibly imagine (and some you couldn't) on huge hunks of French bread, including the archetypal fried seafood (add some Tabasco, we strongly advise), deli meats, cheese omelets, ham and eggs, and the starch-o-rama that is a French Fry po' boy. You need to try it. Really. Johnny boasts "even my failures are edible" and that says it all. And they deliver!

Mama Rosa's. 616 N. Rampart St. ☎ **504/523-5546.** Specials $5.50–$9.50; pizzas $8.99–$14.99. AE, DISC, MC, V. Sun–Thurs 11am–10pm, Fri–Sat 11am–midnight. ITALIAN/PIZZA.

Done in by sauces and hankering for something plain? Get a big slice of pizza here. While the decor is nothing to brag about—typical red-and-white-checked tablecloths, a jukebox, and a bar—the pizzas are. You can get a 10- or 14-inch pie with a variety of toppings for a very reasonable price. The crusts are thick—almost as thick as a pan pizza—and the more you put on them, the better they are. One of the other big draws is the homemade bread. You can also get mini muffalettas as appetizers. The staff can be a bit surly, but most people don't come for the ambience. Delivery available.

Napoleon House. 500 Chartres St. ☎ **504/524-9752.** Reservations required for parties of 8 or more. Salads, sandwiches and seafood $4.95–$19. AE, DISC, MC, V. Daily 11am–1am. CREOLE/ITALIAN.

Folklore has it that the name of this place derives from a bit of wishful thinking: Around the time of Napoléon's death, a plot was hatched here to snatch the Little Corporal from his island exile and bring him to live in New Orleans. The third floor was added expressly for the purpose of providing him with a home. Alas, it probably isn't true. The building dates from a couple of years after Napoléon's death. But let's not let the truth get in the way of a good story, or a good hangout, which this is at any time of day, but particularly late at night. Agreeably dark, it still seems like a place where plots are being hatched in the corner. Go hatch some of your own, while nursing a drink or enjoying the only heated muffaletta in town. They have recently added a full menu of moderately priced food.

Old Dog New Trick. 307 Exchange Alley. ☎ **504/522-4569.** Main courses $6.95–$9.95. AE, MC, V. Daily 11:30am–9pm. VEGETARIAN.

You'd think this tiny cafe tucked away on equally tiny Exchange Alley would be lost, but judging from the crowds, local and tourist vegetarians have managed to find it. They probably are hugely relieved when they do, given how hard it is to find something they can eat in this town. Large portions and small prices make this a pleasing, healthy stop. The cafe calls itself "vegan friendly." It does have dishes with cheese, but can make them without, and some tuna does sneak onto the menu. The desserts are absolutely vegan. Regardless of their specific denomination, the sandwiches, salads, and stuffed pitas, not to mention polenta and a variety of tofu dishes, have been voted best vegetarian by *Gambit* readers. Delivery is available. Ben the Boston Terrier, who's featured on the sign, was 11 when this place opened; he's now ancient.

Père Antoine Restaurant. 741 Royal St. ☎ **504/581-4478.** Main courses $3.95–$16.95. No credit cards. Mon–Fri 9am–midnight, Sat–Sun 8am–midnight. CAJUN/CREOLE.

Père Antoine is an attractive, European-style restaurant. Specialties include Cajun red snapper (cooked in a rich tomato sauce—a nice change from "blackened"), shrimp, and crawfish étouffée. The seafood platter, with catfish, shrimp, scallops, crab, and Cajun popcorn (deep-fried seasoned shrimp), is a real bargain. For lighter appetites, there are soups and salads, sandwiches and burgers, omelettes, and such New Orleans favorites as red beans and rice, jambalaya, and chicken Creole. Items on the breakfast menu are available all day. Try the Belgian waffles or the "Louisiana Breakfast—The Rajun Cajun Omelet," with smoked sausage, green peppers, onion, ham, and a Creole sauce.

Petunia's. 817 St. Louis St. (between Bourbon and Dauphine sts.). ☎ **504/522-6440.** Reservations recommended at dinner. Main courses $5.95–$13.95 at breakfast and lunch, $8.95–$26.95 at dinner. AE, CB, DC, DISC, MC, V. Daily 8am–11pm. CAJUN/CREOLE.

Petunias, in an 1830s town house, dishes up enormous portions of New Orleans specialties like shrimp Creole, Cajun pasta with shrimp and andouille, and a variety of fresh seafood. Breakfast and Sunday brunch are popular, with a broad selection of crêpes that, at 14 inches, are billed as the world's largest. Options include the "St. Marie," a blend of spinach, cheddar, chicken, and hollandaise, and the "St. Francis," filled with shrimp, crab ratatouille, and Swiss cheese. If you have room for dessert, try the dessert crêpes or the peanut butter pie.

Praline Connection. 542 Frenchmen St., just outside the Quarter. ☎ **504/943-3934.** Reservations not accepted. Main courses $4–$13.95. AE, DC, DISC, MC, V. Sun–Thurs 11am–10:30pm, Fri–Sat 11am–midnight. CREOLE/SOUL FOOD.

Somewhat hidden away on Frenchmen Street is a popular but perhaps overrated restaurant with little ambience. Don't go for a romantic dinner, because the noise level can be daunting and the crowds so dense you might have to share a table. Praline Connection serves solid but undistinguished Creole and soul food, which some rave about but others find rather ordinary. The fried chicken is crispy and juicy, and you can get it with almost any kind of beans and rice. There are red beans, white beans, and crowder peas, as well as okra, mustard greens, and collard greens. There are also large po' boys. Praline Connection's newest menu items include fried soft-shell crawfish and barbecued ribs. At lunch you might try the hog's head cheese (poor man's pâté) with garlic toast to start, followed by an oyster or smoked-sausage po' boy.

Praline Connection II, 901 South Peters St. (☎ **504/523-3973**), offers the same menu and a larger dining room.

Whole Lotta Muffaletta Goin' On

Muffalettas are almost mythological sandwiches, enormous concoctions of round Italian bread, Italian cold cuts and cheeses, and olive salad. One person cannot eat a whole one—at least not in one sitting. (And if you can, don't complain to us about your stomachache.) Instead, share; a half makes a good meal and a quarter is a filling snack. They may not sound like much on paper, but once you try one, you'll be hooked.

Several places in town claim to have invented the muffaletta, and also claim to make the best one. (Some fancy restaurants have their own upscale version—they are often delicious, but bear no resemblance to the real McCoy.) Popular opinion, shared by the author, awards the crown to Central Grocery. But why take our word for it? Muffaletta comparison shopping can be a very rewarding pastime.

Judging from the line that forms at lunchtime, many others agree with us that ✪ **Central Grocery,** 923 Decatur St. (☎ **504/523-1620**), makes the best muffaletta there is. There are a few seats at the back of this crowded, heavenly smelling Italian grocery, or you can order to go. Best of all, they ship, so once you're hooked—and you will be—you need not wait until your next trip for a muffaletta fix.

A small but critical minority favors the muffalettas at **Progress Grocery,** 915 Decatur. between Dumaine and St. Philip (☎ **504/525-6627**). It also has a full deli counter, and a seemingly endless variety of spices (with an emphasis on Cajun and Creole), which make great lightweight souvenirs. Take your sandwich across the street and eat it on the banks of the Mississippi for an inexpensive romantic meal (about $7 for a whole sandwich).

Then there are those who swear by the heated muffalettas served at the **Napoleon House,** 500 Chartres St. (☎ **504/524-9752**). Others find them blasphemous. We recommend that you start with cold and work up to heated—it's a different taste sensation.

4 Mid City/Esplanade

MODERATE

Cafe Degas. 3127 Esplanade Ave. ☎ **504/945-5635.** Reservations recommended. Main courses $6.25–$18.50. AE, DC, DISC, MC, V. Mon–Fri 11:30am–2:30pm; Sat 10:30am–2:30pm brunch; Sun 10:30am–3:30pm brunch; Mon–Thurs 5:30pm–10pm, Fri–Sat 6–11pm. FRENCH.

A charming French bistro, warm and friendly with upscale rustic decor. The hearty food is rustic as well, with big but simple flavors in large portions of tasty, rich food. Featured items include rack of lamb Dijonnaise, savory goat cheese tart, and pork chops with onions and Swiss cheese—wholly satisfying in a soulful kind of way. Desserts are delicious and homemade—the key lime tart is spectacular. Though it's French, this is not France, and this bistro is informal enough that you can go wearing blue jeans.

Christian's. 3835 Iberville St. ☎ **504/482-4924.** Reservations recommended. Main courses $15–$25. AE, DC, MC, V. Tues–Fri 11:30am–2pm; Tues–Sat 5:30–9:30pm. CREOLE.

Ever had a three-course meal in a church? Here's your chance. Christian's is doubly well named. It's owned by Christian Ansel (whose cuisine pedigree is strong; he's the grandson of a nephew of Jean Galatoire), and occupies a former church. Renovations preserved the architecture, including the high-beamed ceiling and (secular) stained-glass windows. The old altar is the waiters' station, and the sermon board out front lists the menu. This is one of the city's great French-Creole restaurants, with locals accounting for about 80% of its clientele. See what they like so much, with appetizers like smoked soft-shell crabs, oysters Roland (baked in a garlic-butter sauce with mushrooms, parsley, bread crumbs, and Creole seasoning), and a strong rendition of oysters en brochette. The roasted duck is heavenly, as is the gumbo. Daily fish specials include delights such as sheep's head (yes, that's a fish) stuffed with shrimp and crabmeat, lightly breaded and fried with aïoli, or broiled fillet of grouper with red onion beurre blanc and sautéed scallops. Desserts tend toward the traditional—flourless chocolate cake or classic profiteroles au chocolat. Feel free to worship at Christian's, because the setting is fairly appropriate.

✪ **Dooky Chase.** 2301 Orleans Ave. ☎ **504/821-0600** or 504/821-2294. Reservations recommended at dinner. Main courses $10–$17.50; fixed-price 4-course meal $25; Creole feast $37.50. AE, DC, MC, V. Sun–Thurs 11:30am–10pm, Fri–Sat 11:30am–11pm. SOUL FOOD/CREOLE.

African and African American influences are key components in New Orleans' multicultural cuisine. In the elegant dining rooms of Dooky Chase, classic soul food interacts gloriously with the city's French, Sicilian, and Italian traditions. Chef Leah Chase dishes up one of New Orleans' best bowls of gumbo—no small achievement—along with more esoteric dishes such as shrimp Clemenceau, an unlikely but successful casserole of sautéed shellfish, mushrooms, peas, and potatoes. The fried chicken is exquisite, as are the sautéed veal, grits, grillades, and court bouillon—a first cousin of gumbo in which okra is replaced by tomatoes, onions, and garlic, along with generous chunks of catfish. Desserts include thick, rich bread pudding filled with shredded coconut and pecans, drizzled with praline liqueur sauce and served hot. The thick chicory coffee and comfortable ambience will encourage you to linger after a deeply satisfying meal, along with the touring jazz artists or prominent black politicians who may well occupy the adjoining tables. Prices are a bit high and service less than brisk—though always friendly—but Dooky Chase offers very good food and a vintage New Orleans experience. Take a cab.

✪ **Gabrielle.** 3201 Esplanade Ave. ☎ **504/948-6233.** Reservations recommended. Main courses $16–$28; early evening special (Tues–Thurs 5:30–6:15pm) $16.98. AE, CB, DC, DISC, MC, V. Oct–May Fri 11:30am–2pm; year-round Tues–Sat 5:30–10pm. INTERNATIONAL.

This rather small, but casually elegant restaurant on Esplanade Avenue, just outside the French Quarter, is gaining a big reputation around town thanks to some superb food from a chef who studied under Paul Prudhomme and Frank Brigtsen. A foie gras with fig sauce appetizer features a generous portion that melts in your mouth. For a main course, you can't go wrong with any fish on the menu, from the pompano cooked in paper with garlic and tomatoes to the panfried trout with shrimp and roasted pecan butter. A standout was the double-thick-cut pork chop with a tomato salsa, topped with stuffed Anaheim chili—it had some masterful flavors. The adventurous might want to try the crawfish enchilada. The "Peppermint Patti" dessert seems the most popular, a concoction made of chocolate cake, peppermint ice cream, and chocolate sauce. There's a small bar here, and the wine list is quite nice. Gabrielle offers an early evening special Tuesday through Thursday from 5:30 to 6:15pm. You'll get a choice of three appetizers, two entrees, and two desserts for only $15.95.

✪ **Liuzza's.** 3636 Bienville St. ☎ **504/482-9120.** Main courses $4.95–$15.50. No credit cards. ATM on premises. Mon–Sat 10:30am–10:30pm. CREOLE/ITALIAN.

New Orleans Dining

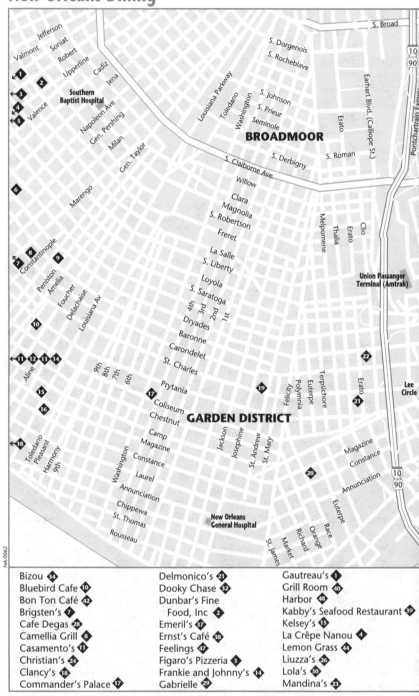

Bizou 🔷34
Bluebird Cafe 🔷10
Bon Ton Café 🔷42
Brigsten's 🔷7
Cafe Degas 🔷28
Camellia Grill 🔷8
Casamento's 🔷11
Christian's 🔷24
Clancy's 🔷18
Commander's Palace 🔷17

Delmonico's 🔷21
Dooky Chase 🔷32
Dunbar's Fine
   Food, Inc 🔷2
Emeril's 🔷37
Ernst's Café 🔷38
Feelings 🔷47
Figaro's Pizzeria 🔷3
Frankie and Johnny's 🔷14
Gabrielle 🔷29

Gautreau's 🔷1
Grill Room 🔷40
Harbor 🔷48
Kabby's Seafood Restaurant 🔷39
Kelsey's 🔷15
La Crêpe Nanou 🔷4
Lemon Grass 🔷44
Liuzza's 🔷26
Lola's 🔷30
Mandina's 🔷23

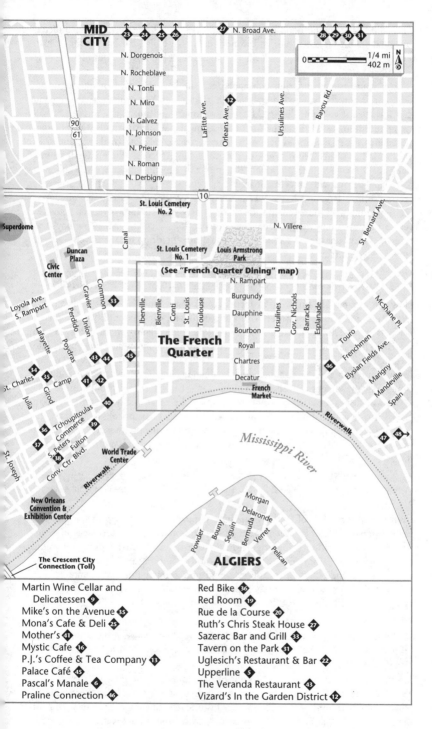

Martin Wine Cellar and
  Delicatessen ⑨
Mike's on the Avenue ㉟
Mona's Cafe & Deli ㉕
Mother's ㊶
Mystic Cafe ⑯
P.J.'s Coffee & Tea Company ⑬
Palace Café ㊺
Pascal's Manale ⑥
Praline Connection ㊻

Red Bike ㊱
Red Room ⑲
Rue de la Course ⑳
Ruth's Chris Steak House ㉗
Sazerac Bar and Grill ㉝
Tavern on the Park ㉛
Uglesich's Restaurant & Bar ㉒
Upperline ⑤
The Veranda Restaurant ㊸
Vizard's In the Garden District ⑫

This Mid City neighborhood institution (since 1947) is home to the "Frenchuletta" (a muffaletta on French bread) and wonderful Creole-Italian cuisine. It's fairly small and usually rather crowded; you'll often have to wait a bit, but you can pass the time in the bar.

Start your visit by ordering two appetizers: the heavenly fried onion rings and, believe it or not, the battered, deep-fried dill pickle slices. You won't believe how good they are, even if you don't like pickles. (One astonished visitor said, "You people will batter and deep-fry anything that isn't nailed down!") While the fried sweet potatoes available as a special sounded better than they were, the delicious fried eggplant sticks did not fail to satisfy. Don't forget to check the daily specials—there's usually something that'll make you say, "Oooh." Recommended menu items are the Galboroni pasta (spaghettini with spicy marinara sauce, pepperoni strips, and stuffed artichoke hearts), shrimp-artichoke fettuccine, and mega-rich fettuccine Alfredo. Po' boy lovers can't go wrong with the excellent fried seafood po' boys. If it's carbo overload you seek, you can get a french fried po' boy (the sandwich for which the name "po' boy" was coined). Great, inexpensive food in an establishment dripping with New Orleans atmosphere. Don't miss it.

Lola's. 3312 Esplanade Ave. ☎ **504/488-6946.** Reservations not accepted. Main courses $8.75–$14. No credit cards or out-of-town checks. Daily 6–10pm. SPANISH/INTERNATIONAL.

How can a restaurant survive if it doesn't accept reservations or credit cards, doesn't serve wine, and hardly advertises? Word of mouth, and word is that Lola's is a special place. It's a fun, funky storefront that caters to a young demographic and almost no tourists. There are only a handful of tables, each with a good view across a counter into the kitchen area. Try to arrive 15 to 30 minutes before opening time and wait in line. If you come later and there's a line, don't be discouraged: Service is attentive and food comes quickly, so your wait shouldn't be too long. Don't forget to bring cash.

Spanish dishes are a specialty here, especially the meat, seafood, and vegetarian paellas (made with Arborio rice) and fideuas (with angel hair pasta). To start, try the ceviche (white fish cured in lemon juice), or mussels in vinaigrette sauce. If you don't want a paella or a fideua, there are plenty of pasta, seafood, lamb, pork, and chicken dishes.

✪ **Ruth's Chris Steak House.** 711 N. Broad St. ☎ **504/486-0810.** Reservations recommended. Main courses $19.95–$29.95. AE, DC, MC, V. Sun–Fri 11:30am–11pm, Sat 4–11pm. STEAK.

Even though branches of Ruth's Chris have popped up everywhere in the past few years, you won't get an argument locally if you pronounce this the best steak in town. This Mid City location is the original Ruth's Chris, and if you're looking for prime beef—corn fed, custom aged, cut by hand, and beautifully prepared—this is your place. Cuts include filets, strips, rib eyes, and porterhouses (for two or more). Pork chops and one or two other meats appear on the menu, but they're vastly outnumbered by beef: This is a steak house through and through. Private dining rooms are available.

Tavern on the Park. 900 City Park Ave. ☎ **504/486-3333.** Reservations recommended. Main courses $12–$17. AE, CB, DC, JCB, MC, V. Tues–Sat 11:30am–2pm and 5–10pm or later. SEAFOOD/STEAK.

Just across from City Park, within sight of the famous "dueling oaks," the art deco Tavern on the Park is a re-creation of a Prohibition-era bistro in one of the few buildings remaining from the Storyville era. The historic structure is a marvelous setting for the restaurant's steak and seafood specialties, with broiled cold-water lobster, fresh

Nicholas Payton's Gumbo Recipe

Trumpeter Nicholas Payton is following in the tradition of New Orleans' greats from Louis Armstrong to Wynton Marsalis. His Verve recordings include *Gumbo Nouveau* and the 1998 Grammy-winning *Doc Cheatham and Nicholas Payton*.

1 pound smoked sausage

1 pound hot sausage

1 pound seasoned ham

1 pound chicken necks or gizzards

1 large onion

1 bell pepper

½ cup parsley

2 pounds shrimp

1 pound crabmeat or fresh crab

salt and pepper

1 cup flour

filé

Put all of the meats and vegetables in a large pot and sauté them. Do not add the seafood yet. In another pot, boil the shrimp heads in water for stock. After the meats and vegetables are sautéed, add the shrimp stock (without the heads) and the rest of the seafood to the pot. Brown the flour in a dry frying pan to make the roux. When the flour is browned, add a little at a time to the pot. The roux and the filé are used to thicken the gumbo, so add it according to how thick you wish to have your gumbo. Add salt and pepper to taste. Cook for about another hour, skimming the gumbo occasionally.

trout, and superb steaks high on the list of local favorites. Balcony dining is available, weather permitting.

INEXPENSIVE

Louisiana Pizza Kitchen. 95 French Market Place. ☎ **504/522-9500.** Pizzas $5.95–$7.95; pastas $4.50–$10.95. AE, CB, DC, DISC, MC, V. Sun–Thurs 5–10pm, Fri–Sat 5–11pm. ITALIAN/PIZZA.

The Louisiana Pizza Kitchen is a local favorite for its creative pies and its atmosphere. Pastas have a significant place on the menu, but diners come for the pizza and Caesar salad. Individual-sized pizzas, baked in a wood-fired oven, are featured with a wide variety of toppings (shrimp and roasted garlic are two of the most popular). The best thing about the pizza is that your toppings won't get lost in an overabundance of cheese and tomato sauce. There is another branch at 615 S. Carrollton Ave. (☎ 504/866-5900).

Mona's Café & Deli. 3901 Banks St. ☎ **504/482-7743** or 504/482-0661. Sandwiches $2.75–$3.75; main courses $5.50–$10. AE, DISC, MC, V. Mon–Thurs 11am–9pm, Fri–Sat 11am–10pm, Sun noon–6pm. MIDDLE EASTERN.

Unless you are already headed to Mid City, Mona's is out of your way; however, if you like Middle Eastern food and can't get real falafel, hummus, stuffed grape leaves, and baklava in your hometown, it's worth the trip. This restaurant and its attached grocery are in a building that must have once been a gas station, and the dining areas are very casual (the semienclosed patio is more comfortable than the newly added indoor dining room). Service is equally casual but, in my experience, has never been noticeably slow. Balancing the lack of elegance is great food at some of the lowest prices imaginable. The gyro and shish kabob sandwiches (made with lamb or beef) are standouts. For starters, my favorites are the spinach pie and lentil soup.

5 Central Business District

EXPENSIVE

Bizou. 701 St. Charles Ave. ☎ **504/524-4114.** Reservations recommended. Main courses $9.50–$22. AE, DC, MC, V. Mon–Fri 11am–3pm; Tues–Sat 5–10pm. CREOLE.

Almost directly across St. Charles from Mike's on the Avenue, Bizou (French for "little kiss") is making a strong move to become the best little bistro in the Central Business District. Celebrity chef and owner Daniel Bonnot scored an early strike by luring R. Devlin Roussel Jr. away from Mike's to be his chef de cuisine. The two have collaborated on a very strong, innovative menu. The rabbit chasseur (with mushrooms, tomatoes, and crawfish) and filet mignon (stuffed with oyster dressing, accompanied by garlic mashed potatoes and portobello mushrooms) are particularly good, but the salmon medallions with fried spinach sets an even higher standard. Some consider the atmosphere a bit sterile, but others think it romantic.

Delmonico's. 1300 St. Charles Ave. ☎ **504/525-4937.** Reservations required. Main course $18–$30. AE, DC, DISC, MC, V. Lunch Mon–Fri 11:30am–2pm; dinner Sun–Thurs 6–10pm, Fri–Sat 6–11pm, brunch Sun 10:30am–2pm. CREOLE.

This is the latest venture by the ubiquitous and spirited Emeril Lagasse. Delmonico's is less a chance for him to show off the innovative cooking that has made him a star, and more a chance to experiment with classic Creole dishes. Delmonico's was a local Italian family restaurant for 105 years, before going out of business just a couple years ago. Emeril renovated the building, and the result is one of the loveliest interiors in New Orleans, simultaneously evoking its glorious past (though surely it never looked this good), but with fresh, modern touches. It's just right for a special evening, and many locals have already jumped on the bandwagon, beginning a new tradition.

If you don't like rich, sauce-intensive food, this menu won't appeal to you. But it's fun to see what Emeril is up to in this context. You can easily blow your budget on the tasting menu, and perhaps you should, particularly when it features such decadent delights as smoked salmon and wild mushroom truffle stew topped with overeasy eggs, shaved black truffle, black truffle emulsion, crispy parsley, and a drizzle of white truffle oil. (We get dizzy just thinking about it.) We also loved the oyster brochette wrapped in apple-smoked bacon with hollandaise sauce appetizer. Entrees may include seared duck breast (a bit tough) garnished with duck confit (nicely moist) and duck crackling corn sticks, which take cornbread to new levels of nirvana. Or baked Gulf shrimp stuffed with crabmeat and served with okra and tomato, or even an individual Beef Wellington with mushroom foie gras duxelles

Impression

New Orleans is one place you can eat and drink the most, and suffer the least.
—William Makepeace Thackeray

In case you want to see the world.

At American Express, we're here to make your journey a smooth one. So we have over 1,700 travel service locations in over 130 countries ready to help. What else would you expect from the world's largest travel agency?

do more

Travel

Call 1 800 AXP-3429 or visit
www.americanexpress.com/travel

In case you want to be welcomed there.

We're here to see that you're always welcomed at establishments everywhere. That's why millions of people carry the American Express® Card – for peace of mind, confidence, and security, around the world or just around the corner.

do more **AMERICAN EXPRESS**

And in case you'd rather be safe than sorry.

We're here with American Express® Travelers Cheques. They're the safe way to carry money on your vacation, because if they're ever lost or stolen you can get a refund, practically anywhere or anytime. To find the nearest place to buy Travelers Cheques, call 1 800 495-1153. Another way we help you do more.

do more

Travelers Cheques

wrapped in puff pastry—with a sauce, of course. Haven't keeled over yet? How about a dessert like ice cream bombe, complete with dramatic tableside presenttion?

✪ **Emeril's.** 800 Tchoupitoulas St. ☎ **504/528-9393.** Reservations required at dinner. Main courses $18–$32; menu degustation $75. AE, CB, DC, DISC, MC, V. Mon–Fri 11:30am–2pm; Mon–Thurs 6–10pm, Fri–Sat 6–11pm. CREOLE/NEW AMERICAN.

Ecstasy. Emeril Lagasse isn't just the boisterous and charismatic chef who has gained nationwide popularity from his programs on cable's TV Food Network. He is one of the Crescent City's finest chefs, and one of America's finest as well.

There are arguments about the service. Some diners find it zealous and enthusiastic, others snooty and sometimes downright rude. Your mileage may vary. What is never in question is the quality of the food. Acolytes of Emeril's feel that's all that matters. Emeril's specialty is what he calls *New* New Orleans Cuisine, based upon and using key ingredients of Creole classics but taking them in new and exciting directions. His menu goes way beyond Creole, to New American cuisine at its best. Everything in his bustling, noisy warehouse district restaurant is homemade, from the bacon to the Worcestershire sauce to the andouille sausage and home-cured tasso. Portions are gargantuan, each plate dances with color and texture, and side dishes are perfectly paired with entrees (such as grilled Creole-seasoned chicken with savory corn-and-andouille bread pudding). The menu often changes, although some favorites remain, and the daily specials are always exciting and wildly varied (such as crawfish-and-morel-mushroom-stuffed artichoke bottoms with foie gras and roasted onion ragout and a drizzle of celery puree).

For one of the most luxurious dining experiences anywhere, try Emeril's degustation menu, which changes daily and presents you with a seven-movement symphony of flavors. Wines are specially chosen to go with each degustation course, and the wine list, in general, is extensive. The dessert choices, overseen by pastry chef "Mr. Lou," outnumber the entrees. His signature dessert, astonishingly rich banana cream pie with banana crust and caramel drizzle sauce, will leave you moaning and pounding on the table (we've seen it happen). Just do it.

✪ **The Grill Room.** In the Windsor Court Hotel, 300 Gravier St. ☎ **504/522-1992.** Jacket and tie required. Reservations recommended. Main courses $11–$19.50 at lunch, $28–$39 at dinner. AE, CB, DC, DISC, MC, V. Mon–Thurs 7–10:30am, Fri–Sat 7:30–10:30pm, Sun 7–9am; Mon–Sat 11:30am–2pm, Sun brunch 9am–2pm; Sun–Thurs 6–10pm, Fri–Sat 6–10:30pm. NEW AMERICAN.

This is a special-event place, where the silverware is heavy, the linens thick, and all diners dressed to the nines. The Grill Room is an elegant and stately place whose chefs constantly win culinary awards (it was the training ground for chefs like Kevin Graham, who went on to start their own, innovative restaurants) and whose cuisine, service, and wine list are all flawless. Like the Windsor Court in general, the restaurant has an upper-crust-English-meets-upper-crust-Southern character, evident in everything from its 19th-century British paintings and selection of teas to the gracious, attentive service. So sit back and enjoy what should be an exceptional meal.

A recent debauch started with creamy terrine of foie gras on crunchy apricot pecan brioche. For entrees, there was an impossibly rich and delectable roast goose with celeriac puree and foie gras croutons, and a lighter, but no less divine Dover sole, accompanied by crosne, rare vegetables from a certain part of the south of France, demonstrating how you are likely to eat something here you have never ever tasted before. The dessert cart alone is worth coming for, though narrowing down a selection is nearly impossible. One example: a ball of dense hazelnut mousse sits in a chocolate covered filo cookie, rather like a giant piece of Godiva candy. If you must have something light to end, the homemade sorbets are outstanding.

Red Room. 2040 St. Charles Ave, New Orleans. ☎ **504/528-9759.** Reservations suggested Mon–Thurs, required Fri–Sat. No jeans, T-shirts, tennis shoes or shorts. Jackets for men suggested. Main courses $18–$32. AE, MC, V. Mon–Thurs 6–10pm, Fri–Sat 6–11pm. NEW AMERICAN.

Sometimes—okay, often—we long for the days when civilized couples would go out for dinner and dancing. The Red Room supper club perfectly fills this need with delectable (albeit slightly pricey) meals that you can then dance off courtesy of their hip jazz/swing musical lineups. Don't be put off by the ugly, albeit historic industrial exterior (it was apparently lifted from the Eiffel Tower, and no wonder they wanted to get rid of it). It gives way to an interior far more evocative of 1940s swank (though we wish it were a little less 1980s).

The nouvelle cuisine is excellent, with intriguing sides such as pumpkin risotto and tomato fondue. We ate every bite of foie gras with sweet potato galette and cranberry reduction, and a carpaccio salad with roasted garlic oil, and consequently couldn't finish the enormous crispy speckled trout with meunière sauce (easily enough for two people). Should you suffer a similar problem, try to rally for their sinful desserts; you can always dance away the calories later. The Red Velvet cake is a slightly modern variation on a rich classic, and the Molten chocolate is a cake with a lava center.

Sazerac Bar and Grill. In the Fairmont Hotel, 123 Baronne St. ☎ **504/529-4167** or 504/529-4733. Reservations recommended. Jackets recommended at dinner. Main courses $16.50–$29. AE, CB, DC, DISC, MC, V. Mon–Sat 6:30am–2:30pm, Sun–Thurs 5–10pm, Fri–Sat 5–11pm. CONTINENTAL.

Note: At press time the Sazerac Bar & Grill was undergoing extensive remodeling. What was once an elegant setting for fine dining may now be a little more casual in atmosphere.

MODERATE

Bon Ton Café. 401 Magazine St. ☎ **504/524-3386.** Reservations required at dinner. Main courses $8.75–$19.75 at lunch, $19.75–$25.25 at dinner. AE, DC, MC, V. Mon–Fri 11am–2pm and 5–9:30pm. CAJUN.

At lunchtime, you'll find the Bon Ton Café absolutely mobbed with New Orleans businesspeople and their guests, but despite the crowds, that's the best time to go. Its popularity is largely due to owner Al Pierce, his nephew Wayne, and Wayne's wife, Debbie. Al and Wayne grew up in bayou country, where Al learned Cajun cooking from his mother. He came to New Orleans in 1936, bought the Bon Ton in 1953, and since then has been serving up seafood gumbo, crawfish bisque, jambalaya, crawfish omelettes, and other Cajun dishes in a manner that would make his mother proud. Wayne and Debbie are continuing the tradition. The lunch menu is partially à la carte; at dinner the menu is à la carte and fixed-price.

Kabby's Seafood Restaurant. 2 Poydras St. ☎ **504/584-3880.** Reservations recommended. Main courses $17–$28.95. AE, CB, DC, MC, V. Tues–Sat 11am–2pm, Sun 10am–2pm; Tues–Thurs 6–10pm, Fri–Sat 6–11pm. SEAFOOD.

Kabby's overlooks the river through a 200-foot-wide, 14-foot-high window. It's a spectacular view. You enter the restaurant through a New Orleans courtyard foyer with a bubbling fountain, custom-designed lampposts, and tropical plantings. At lunch, there are salads, sandwiches (oyster loaf, muffaletta, and so on), and other specialties. The dinner menu is more adventurous, with dishes like corn and crab chowder or crabmeat-stuffed oysters with a trio of dipping sauces. As a main course, the peppered duck breast (with andouille sausage dressing, sweet potato *frites*, and a natural duck reduction) is excellent, as is the salmon gratin. The warm pecan and chocolate tart is a good choice for dessert.

Lemon Grass. 221 Camp St. (in the International House). ☎ **504/553-9550.** Reservations suggested. Main courses $12.95–$18.95. AE, MC, V. Daily breakfast 7:30–9am, lunch 11:30am–2:30pm, dinner Mon–Thurs 6–10pm, Fri–Sun 6–11pm. VIETNAMESE.

Lemon Grass' Chef Minh went directly from waiting tables at Emeril's to opening up his own restaurant—a bold move in a town so fiercely competitive for dining patrons. But in less than 4 years, his modern Vietnamese cuisine has become a favorite among local foodies, and his success has been capped with a new branch at the oh-so-hip hotel of the moment, the International House.

Don't feel you're missing out on local cuisine by coming here. Chef Minh is as influenced by his adopted town as his homeland (besides, your thighs and stomach will thank you for having a light meal for a change). Crawfish can pop up in dishes, and Minh's take on Shrimp Mirliton is well worth trying. Appetizers are terrific, one and all, but a highlight is flash-fried oysters crusted with nuts and served with wasabi leek confit. We adore the spicy Chicken Roti, among the entrees, as well as the felicitously named Happy Pancake. Save room for the decidedly European desserts, including our favorite, fluffy dark and white chocolate mousse.

The original location is at 216 N. Carrollton Ave. (☎ **504/488-8335**).

✪ **Mandina's.** 3800 Canal St. ☎ **504/482-9179.** Reservations not accepted. Main courses $5.50–$13. No credit cards. Mon–Sat 11am–10:30pm, Sun noon–9:30pm. CREOLE/ITALIAN.

In a city renowned for its small, funky local joints as well as its fine dining establishments, dis is da ultimate neighbahood New Awlins restaurant. Tommy Mandina's family has owned and operated this restaurant and bar since the late 1800s, and the menu hasn't changed much in the last 50 years or so. This is a good thing. Mandina's gets crowded at lunch, so try to go a little early or late to beat the crowd. And don't be afraid of your waiter—surly or gruff as he may be, his advice is always good.

Standouts among the appetizers are the greasy but yummy fried onion rings, the excellent tangy shrimp rémoulade, and the crawfish cakes. Soups are always fine as well, especially seafood gumbo and turtle soup au sherry. Then go for the wonderful red beans and rice with Italian sausage, trout meunière, grilled trout, or whatever's on special (we order the specials whenever we can). If you're in the mood for fried seafood, you can't go wrong with the shrimp or oyster loaf, or soft-shell crab in season. Finish up with rum-soaked Creole bread pudding, and you'll have a such a taste of New Orleans, you'll feel like a native, from da old neighbahood.

✪ **Palace Café.** 605 Canal St. ☎ **504/523-1661.** Reservations recommended. Main courses $10.95–$24.95. AE, DC, DISC, MC, V. Mon–Fri 11:30am–2:30pm, Sat–Sun 7am–3pm (brunch 10:30am–2:30pm); daily 5:30–10pm. CONTEMPORARY CREOLE.

The historic Werlein's for Music building is home to one of the fine restaurants in the Brennan family empire (Dickie Brennan recently returned to town and took charge). It dishes out not sheet music, but some of the most delectable meals in the city. The Palace Café offers contemporary Creole food, with a strong emphasis on seafood. Start with the Sunburst Salad (mixed baby greens in an unusual cinnamon-Tabasco-raspberry vinaigrette, with Stilton cheese, almonds, and port-soaked cranberries), or the favorite appetizer, crabmeat cheesecake in a pecan crust. There are meat dishes on the menu, but *definitely* go for the seafood: catfish pecan meunière or andouille-crusted fish of the day, served with sides like ragout of crawfish tails, corn, peppers, and onions. Meanwhile, have fun observing the high-energy action in the open kitchen. Don't miss the near-ecstasy-inducing white chocolate bread pudding, a Palace Café original. (But be sure to remind the staff that they stopped serving the amazing Mississippi mud pie—five layers of chocolate mousse from lightest to darkest—in the hope that they will correct this error and bring it back.) Also highly recommended is the café au lait crème brûlée. And if the great food inspires you to pick up an instrument and wail out a jazz solo, Werlein's for Music is right around the corner. The Palace also has a limited bar menu available all day.

Red Bike. 746 Tchoupitoulas St. ☎ **504/529-BIKE.** Main courses $7–$11 at lunch, $9–$15 at dinner. AE, MC, V. Mon–Fri 11am–3pm, Sat–Sun Brunch 10am–3pm; Tues–Thurs 6–9:30pm; Sat–Sun 6–10pm. NEW AMERICAN/ECLECTIC.

Freshly under new management, the Red Bike is a fine choice if you are looking for a healthy alternative to the endless array of sauces offered elsewhere in the city. It's conveniently located in the warehouse district, making it a handy place for a pit stop during gallery hopping. Inside the attractive cafe setting, you will find all sorts of yummy sandwiches, on the house bread (which is for sale, along with other bakery delights, at the counter), including a recommended curried turkey salad. Salads are hearty and most menu selections use interesting cheeses, herbs, and veggies. Brunch can be particularly nice, with a variety of egg dishes. The prices here are so reasonable, the place teeters just on the edge of the "inexpensive" category.

The Veranda Restaurant. In the Hotel Inter-Continental, 444 St. Charles Ave. ☎ **504/ 585-4383.** Reservations recommended. Main courses $11.50–$22.50. AE, CB, DC, DISC, MC, V. Mon–Sun 6:30am–2pm and 5:30–10pm; Sun brunch 11am–2:30pm. CONTINENTAL/CREOLE.

Thanks to the glass-enclosed garden courtyard and private dining room, the Veranda feels like a stately New Orleans home, and Tuesday through Sunday a harpist makes dining all the more memorable.

The Veranda's chef, Willy Coln, is one of the most respected in New Orleans. The menu is varied, and it's doubtful you'll find anything to complain about. You might start with excellent Louisiana crab cakes in a light Creole mustard sauce. The oyster and artichoke soup is always good, and smoked duck and wild mushroom strudel is also a top choice. Entrees include potato-crusted redfish with baby bok choy and ginger beurre blanc. The breaded and panfried rabbit with Creole mustard sauce and the heart-healthy vegetable strudel on tomato coulis and fresh artichoke ragout are done to perfection. All the desserts are incredible.

INEXPENSIVE

Ernst's Café. 600 S. Peters St. ☎ **504/525-8544.** Main courses $6.50–$9.95. AE, DC, MC, V. Mon–Fri 11am–3pm. CAJUN/CREOLE.

The same family has run the restaurant and bar in this old brick building since 1902. Its brick walls, high ceilings, and heavy-timbered bar make it an interesting and attractive setting for excellent sandwiches, hamburgers, fried shrimp, salads, red beans and rice, and po' boys. If the weather is fine, eat outside.

✪ **Mother's.** 401 Poydras St. ☎ **504/523-9656.** Reservations not accepted. Menu items $1.75–$16.50. No credit cards. Mon–Sat 5am–10pm, Sun 7am–10pm. SANDWICHES/ CREOLE.

Perhaps the proudest of all restaurants when New Orleans was named Fattest City in the U.S. was Mother's, whose overstuffed, mountain-sized po' boys absolutely helped contribute to the results. It has long lines and zero atmosphere, but who cares when faced with a Ferdi special—a giant roll filled with baked ham, roast beef, gravy, and debris (the bits of beef that fall off when the roast is carved). There's other food, including one of the best breakfasts in the city, but the po' boys are what New Orleans goes for, and you should, too. Mother's is within walking distance of the Louisiana Superdome and a number of major hotels. Be sure to allow time to stand in line. It usually moves quickly, and there's always a seat when you get your food.

✪ **Uglesich's Restaurant & Bar.** 1238 Barrone St. ☎ **504/523-8571.** Reservations not accepted. Menu items $9–$13. No credit cards. Mon–Fri 9am–4pm, open every other Sat (seasonal). SANDWICHES/SEAFOOD.

It's dangerous to call any one place "the best in New Orleans," but it's mighty tempting to make an exception for "Ugly's," a tiny, crowded, greasy neighborhood place that serves some of the most divine seafood in town. At lunch time, especially during busy tourist times, you might have a very long wait before you order at the counter, another wait for a table, and a third wait for your food. But we swear it will be worth it. Obviously, others who should know think so; you might well end up sitting next to some of the best chefs in town, because this is where *they* go for lunch. (Although you might just want to skip Uglesich's altogether during Jazz Fest and Mardi Gras time. If you do go, at least bring a book or a bunch of chatty friends. During a recent Jazz Fest visit, the wait took from 2½ to—get this—*4 hours.* Even dedicated fans find it hard to justify that sort of time commitment.)

It's hard to narrow down the dishes, even as it's hard to try new ones when you really want to keep eating splendid old favorites. Among the musts are fried green tomatoes with shrimp rémoulade, shrimp in creamy sauce on a fried cake of grits, voodoo shrimp (in a peppery butter sauce), and trout all kinds of ways. Order extra bread to sop up sauce, but be sure to ask for it unbuttered. You'll be full, you might smell of grease, and you might well come back for more the next day.

6 Uptown/Garden District

EXPENSIVE

✪ **Brigtsen's.** 723 Dante St. ☎ **504/861-7610.** Reservations required (a week or 2 in advance). Main courses $14–$28; 3-course "Early Evening" dinner (Tues–Thurs 5:30–6:30pm) $14.95. AE, DC, MC, V. Tues–Sat 5:30–10pm. CAJUN/CREOLE.

In a setting both elegant and homey, chef Frank Brigsten serves some of the city's best contemporary Creole cuisine. Nestled in a converted 19th-century house at the Riverbend, Brigtsen's is warm, intimate, and romantic. The individual dining rooms are small and cozy, and the menu changes daily.

Brigsten has a special touch with rabbit; one of his most mouth-watering dishes is an appetizer of rabbit tenderloin on a tasso Parmesan grits cake, with sautéed spinach and a Creole mustard sauce. The rabbit and andouille gumbo is delicious, intensely flavored, and well balanced. You can't miss with any of the soups, especially the lovely butternut squash shrimp bisque, and there's an entree to please everyone. One of the most popular dishes is roast duck with cornbread dressing and pecan gravy, with the duck skin roasted to a delightful crackle. We enjoyed the broiled fish of the day (sheep's head on a recent visit) with crabmeat Parmesan crust and a delicate, tangy lemon mousseline sauce, and pan-roasted drum fish topped with lots of lump crabmeat and chanterelle mushrooms, surrounded by a wonderful crab broth. Save room for dessert, including the signature banana bread pudding with banana rum sauce. Brigtsen's offers one of the loveliest evenings you'll spend in a Crescent City restaurant. And the "Early Evening" dinner special is as good a bargain as you'll find.

Clancy's. 6100 Annunciation. ☎ **504/895-1111.** Reservations recommended. Main courses $17.75–$24.75. AE, DC, MC, V. Tues–Fri 11:30am–2pm; Sun–Thurs 5:30–10:30pm, Fri–Sat 5:30–11pm. CREOLE.

Your friendly cab driver may insist that Clancy's is "out of town," so far uptown is this locals' favorite, but it's really not that much farther than going to the zoo or Brigtsen's. The food and neighborhood vibe alone should be worth the trip; it's a relief to get off the tourist path. However, since this is not a tourist-oriented restaurant, the better service goes to the locals who nightly cram the smallish, oh-so-New Orleans room.

Said locals will make it up to you by passing along this bit of Clancy's wisdom: Order the night's specials, rather than sticking to the menu (though on the menu resides a duck dish as good as duck gets). We did, and it resulted in a perfect grouper in a tomato beurre blanc sauce, topped with crawfish, and a memorable starter salad that included lump crabmeat and crawfish in homemade mayo and horseradish, with a deviled egg made with tasso on the side. Food too heavy? What the heck—make it even more so with desserts like mocha ice cream pie and lemon icebox pie. It's what the locals would do.

✪ **Commander's Palace.** 1403 Washington Ave. ☎ **504/899-8221.** Reservations required. Jackets required at night and Sun brunch; no shorts, T-shirts, tennis shoes, blue jeans. Main courses $29–$32; full brunch $20–$32; fixed-price $29–$36. AE, CB, DC, DISC, MC, V. Mon–Fri 11:30am–1:30pm; Sat 11:30am–12:30pm; Sun brunch 10:30am–1:30pm; daily 6–9:30pm. CREOLE.

Voted the best restaurant in the United States—that's right, in the *whole country*—by the James Beard Foundation in 1996, Commander's is one place that lives up to its reputation. (And recently, the Foundation gave it their Lifetime Outstanding Restaurant award.) It's not just the food—which is never less than good—it's the whole package. In a beautiful 1880s Victorian house, it consists of a nearly endless series of dining rooms, from large to intimate, each more appealing and romantic than the last. On balmy nights, you can eat in the lovely courtyard. (A somewhat less desirable modern dining room is in the back—try to skip that one, if you can.) The wait staff is incredibly attentive; several people pamper you throughout your meal. Each night features a multicourse fixed-price menu for around $35, with evening specialties. It also allows you to mix and match off the regular menu—a good bargain and a great splurge.

The famous turtle soup with sherry is outstanding, so thick it's nearly a stew. Don't miss it. Other marvelous appetizer choices include the shrimp and tasso with five pepper jelly, carpaccio salad with roasted eggplant garlic and the hearty crawfish bisque with homemade biscuits. Main course selections change seasonally, but you are best off sticking with Creole-type offerings, such as the frequently available dreamy boned Mississippi roasted quail stuffed with Creole crawfish sausage, the Mississippi rabbit with a sauté of onions, turnips, mushrooms and concasse tomatoes topped with rabbit consommé and pastry shell, or the mixed grill (including lamb and rabbit sausage!) rather than, say, more nouvelle-cuisine such as ultimately bland panfried fish. Your serving team will tell you to try the famous bread pudding soufflé. Trust them. But all the desserts are exceptional; chocolate lovers should not overlook the chocolate Sheba, a sort of solid chocolate mousse, ever so slightly chilled, covered in nuts. And everyone should consider the Creole Cream Cheesecake, which will make you rethink your position on cheesecakes. Then there is the gorgeous rendition of pecan pie à la mode, and the not-on-the-menu-so-ask-for-it Chocolate Molten Souffle. There's an excellent wine list, and the menu offers suggestions with each entree. This is one must-do New Orleans restaurant, particularly appropriate for special occasions—but you can simply call your trip to New Orleans a special occasion, and we won't tell.

Mike's on the Avenue. In the Lafayette Hotel, 628 St. Charles Ave. ☎ **504/523-1709.** Reservations recommended. Main courses $9–$15 at lunch, $16–$30 at dinner. AE, DC, DISC, MC, V. Daily 7–10am and 6–10pm; Mon–Fri 11:30am–2pm. NEW AMERICAN/ INTERNATIONAL.

On the ground floor of the Lafayette Hotel, Mike's on the Avenue has become extremely popular with New Orleanians over the past few years. It's a fun, interesting

In New Orleans, no food is just food.

—Andrei Codrescu

place, right on the Avenue indeed (what a place to watch a Mardi Gras parade, with those broad expanses of windows looking out at St. Charles), the walls covered in canvases painted by the chef himself.

The food is Asian-influenced and clever ("East meets SouthWest New Orleans" and "perfection through spontaneous imperfection" is how they describe it), not as heavy as in many places in town, but doesn't always hit the mark as strongly as one might like. Skip the tasty-sounding sampler platter in favor of the best dish on it, the Chinese shrimp dumplings. Fish dishes can be quite spicy, while vegetarians will be pleased with the noodle pillo, a concoction of angel hair pasta, stir-fried vegetables and teriyaki glaze. Desserts are quite good, particularly the Wabi Tower, a spiral of dark chocolate filled with chocolate truffle cream, fresh raspberries and devil's food cake, with a white chocolate sauce.

✪ **Upperline.** 1413 Upperline St. ☎ **504/891-9822.** Reservations required. Main courses $16.50–$24. AE, CB, DC, MC, V. Sun brunch 11:30am–2pm; Wed–Sun 5:30–9:30pm. ECLECTIC/CREOLE.

In a small, charming house in a largely residential area, the Upperline is more low key than high-profile places such as Emeril's. In its own way, though, it's every bit as inventive. It's a great place to try imaginative food at reasonable (by fancy restaurant standards) prices. Owner JoAnn Clevenger and her staff are quite friendly, and their attitude is reflected in the part of the menu where they actually—gasp!—recommend dishes at *other* restaurants. Perhaps you can afford to be so generous when your own offerings are so strong.

Standout appetizers include their fried green tomatoes with shrimp rémoulade sauce (they invented this dish, which is now featured just about everywhere in town), spicy shrimp on jalapeño corn bread, duck confit, and fried sweetbreads. For entrees, there's moist, herb-crusted pork loin, roast duck with a sauce that tingles, and a fall-off-the-bone lamb shank. If you're lucky, there will be a special menu, like the all-garlic selection, where even dessert contains garlic. For dessert, try warm honey-pecan bread pudding or chocolate hazelnut mousse. The award-winning wine list focuses primarily on California selections.

Vizard's in the Garden District. 3226 Magazine St. ☎ **504/895-3030.** Reservations recommended. Main courses $16.95–$28.95. AE, DISC, MC, V. Mon–Fri 11:30am–2:30pm; Mon–Thurs 6–10pm, Fri–Sat 6–11pm; Sun brunch 11:30am–2:30pm. ECLECTIC/CREOLE.

Chef Kevin Vizard took over a former neighborhood barbecue joint in the Lower Garden District, cleaned it up, and turned it into what almost instantly became the hot new restaurant of the moment. In about a year's time, he had to move its location. (The previous site is now Kevin's Bar and Steakhouse.) The new space, much closer to downtown on Magazine, is a bit more formal, but simple and pretty, and seats quite a few more people, who just keep coming—will they have to move again? Who knows? In the meantime, consider joining them. The deceptively simple menu, heavy on seared entries, has dishes full of unexpected flavors and kicks. Don't miss the unusual appetizer of tuna smoked on-site. It makes your mouth come alive. Other standouts include delicious seared duck breast with a sweet garlic, rosemary, and pepper glaze, and terrifically rich crabmeat Russell, in an eggplant shell with a lemon-and-thyme hollandaise sauce. Most desserts are standard New Orleans fare, but the crème brûlée is outstanding, with a superior flavorful crust.

MODERATE

Gautreau's. 1728 Soniat St. ☎ **504/899-7397.** Reservations recommended. Main courses $14–$28. AE, DC, DISC, MC, V. Mon–Sat 6–10pm. INTERNATIONAL.

Those who knew the old Gautreau's (which closed in 1989 and reopened under new ownership) will be relieved to see that the restaurant has retained its warm and modest decor: The tin ceiling, the old New Orleans photographs, and the famous apothecary cabinet from the original drugstore have all been retained. The quality of the food has not changed, either. Rob Mitchell, a graduate of the Culinary Institute of America, has worked at Gautreau's since 1993 and became the head chef in 1995. Menus change seasonally; if you spot them on the menu, try the marinated shrimp and Dungeness crab, served with sticky rice and orange-and-honey soy sauce, or warm crisped duck confit with sherried flageolets, mustard, and sage. Recent favorite entrees include sautéed tilapia and shrimp with basmati rice, arugula, and chile mango sauce, and roasted chicken with wild mushrooms, garlic potatoes, and green beans. The pastry chef does a fine honey-orange crème brûlée and a delightful triple-layer (chocolate, maple pecan, and almond) cheesecake.

Kelsey's. 3923 Magazine St. ☎ **504/897-6722.** Reservations recommended. Main courses $6.95–$12.95 at lunch, $12.95–$24.95 at dinner. AE, DC, DISC, MC, V. Tues–Fri 11:30am–2pm; Tues–Thurs 5:30–9:30pm, Fri–Sat 5:30–10pm. CREOLE.

For nearly 5 years, Kelsey's lay hidden on the east bank of the Mississippi River in Algiers, known only to loyal patrons and restaurant critics. Then, in 1996, co-owners Randy and Ina Barlow moved Kelsey's to uptown New Orleans. The new space's light colors and attentive servers make the atmosphere nearly serene.

For 8 years Randy Barlow worked at K-Paul's with Paul Prudhomme, and the influence is apparent. The house specialty is eggplant Kelsey, a batter-fried eggplant pirogue (in the shape of a boat) stuffed with seafood seasoned with Parmesan and Romano cheeses, tomatoes, garlic, olive oil, parsley and lemon juice. Many dishes are equally elaborate, but Barlow can also make the simple stuff shine. Especially enjoyable are the tomato-and-provolone salad, a lightly panfried Gulf fish special, and apple raspberry crisp with fresh cream. There's a well-chosen selection of wines by the glass.

La Crêpe Nanou. 1410 Robert St. ☎ **504/899-2670.** Reservations not accepted. Main courses $8.95–$16.95. AE, MC, V. Sun–Thurs 6–10pm, Fri–Sat 6–11pm. FRENCH.

Voted the top French bistro in New Orleans in the Zagat survey, La Crêpe Nanou is another not-so-secret local secret. It's always crowded. It's a romantic spot (windows angled into the ceiling let you gaze at the stars) that is simultaneously 19th century and quite modern. You can order crêpes wrapped around a variety of stuffings, including crawfish. But you might want to save your crêpe consumption for dessert (big and messy, full of chocolate and whipped cream) and concentrate instead on the big healthy salads and moist, flaky fish, particularly the whole grilled fish with herbs. It's big enough for two, and is done to perfection. You can usually find knowledgeable locals ordering the mussels and extra bread to sop up the garlic white wine sauce. Meat dishes come with your choice of sauce (garlic or cognac, for example).

Pascal's Manale. 1838 Napoleon Ave. ☎ **504/895-4877.** Reservations recommended. Main courses $13.95–$22. AE, CB, DC, DISC, MC, V. Year-round Mon–Fri 11:30am–10pm, Sat 4–10pm. ITALIAN/STEAK/SEAFOOD.

Barbecued shrimp. This restaurant has made its reputation with that one dish, and you should go there if only for that. The place is crowded and noisy and verges on expensive, but it grows on you. Don't expect fancy decor—the emphasis is on food and conviviality. (Sunday nights especially feel like social gatherings.) Pascal's bills itself as an Italian–New Orleans steak house, but the presence of such specialties as veal Marsala, turtle soup, the combination pan roast, and those barbecued shrimp (a house creation) give the menu a decidedly idiosyncratic slant. By "barbecued," we don't mean on a grill, but in a rich, spicy, buttery sauce that demands that you soak up every drop with as much bread as you can get out of your waiter. Try not to think about your arteries too much; vow to walk your socks off tomorrow, lick your fingers, and enjoy.

INEXPENSIVE

Bluebird Cafe. 3625 Prytania St. ☎ **504/895-7166.** Reservations not accepted. All items under $7. No credit cards. Mon–Fri 7am–3pm, Sat–Sun 8am–3pm. AMERICAN.

Employees here tell the story of a man who awoke from an extended coma with these two words: "huevos rancheros." As soon as possible, he returned to the Bluebird for his favorite dish. A similar scene repeats each weekend morning when locals wake up with Bluebird on the brain. Why? Because this place consistently offers breakfast and lunch food that can restore and sustain your vital functions. Try the buckwheat pecan waffle, cheese grits, or homemade sausage and corned beef hash. You can also build your own omelet, or see why the huevos rancheros enjoys its reputation (if you don't like runny eggs, ask for scrambled huevos). At midmorning on weekends, there is always a wait (up to 30 minutes) out front; it's worth the wait.

✪ **Camellia Grill.** 626 S. Carrollton Ave. ☎ **504/866-9573.** Reservations not accepted. All items under $10. No credit cards. Mon–Thurs 9am–1am, Fri 9am–3am, Sat 8am–3am, Sun 8am–1am. HAMBURGERS/SANDWICHES.

Even though it's *only* been a part of New Orleans' food culture since 1946, the Camellia Grill seems to have always been there. Right off the St. Charles Avenue streetcar, it's a fixture in many people's lives. As you sit on a stool at the double-U shaped counter, white-jacketed waiters pamper you while shouting cryptic orders to the chefs. There's often a wait, because the Camellia serves some of the best breakfasts and burgers anywhere, but the wait is always worth it. The Camellia is famous for its omelettes—heavy and fluffy at the same time, and almost as big as a rolled-up newspaper. Notable choices are the chili cheese and the potato, onion, and cheese (a personal favorite). Don't forget the pecan waffle, a moan-inducing work of art. If you're feeling really decadent, go with a friend, order omelettes, and split a waffle on the side. The burgers are big and sloppy and among the best in town. Wash it all down with one of the famous chocolate freezes, then contemplate a slice of the celebrated pie for dessert (the chocolate pecan may be to die for).

✪ **Casamento's.** 4330 Magazine St. ☎ **504/895-9761.** Reservations not accepted. Main courses $4.95–$11. No credit cards. Tues–Sun 11:30am–1:30pm and 5:30–9pm. Closed mid-June to mid-Sept. SEAFOOD.

This restaurant takes oysters so seriously that it just closes down when they're not in season. It pays off—this is *the* oyster place. You pay a bit more for a dozen, but your reward is a presentation that shows the care the staff puts in; the oysters are more cleanly scrubbed and well selected. You might also take the plunge and order an oyster loaf: a big, fat loaf of bread fried in butter, filled with oysters (or shrimp), and fried again to seal it. Do your arteries a favor and only eat half (though your stomach might demand the whole thing!). Casamento's also has terrific gumbo—perhaps the best in town. It's small (you have to walk through the kitchen to get to the rest rooms), but the atmosphere is light, with the waitresses serving up jokes and poking good-natured fun at you, at each other, or at the guys behind the oyster bar.

☼ Dunbar's Fine Food, Inc. 4927 Freret St. ☎ **504/899-0734.** Main courses $5–$10. AE, DC, DISC, MC, V. Daily 7am–9pm. SOUL FOOD.

For a genuine soul food experience, come to this small, superfriendly establishment run by the very charming Tina Dunbar. A no-decor, big-kitchen place, Dunbar's caters to blue-collar locals in search of breakfast (which can run as little as $1) or lunch. You'll feast on huge, soul-warming, and generally amazing Southern dishes, including gumbo, cornbread, and bread pudding, with daily specials listed on a board. Even the health-conscious can be swayed by the red beans and rice. Service is down-home, and attire is definitely come-as-you-are.

Dunbar's has a branch at 1205 St. Charles St. (☎ **504/586-0470**), but popular opinion favors the Freret Street locale.

Figaro's Pizzeria. 7900 Maple St. ☎ **504/866-0100.** Reservations not accepted. Pizzas $6.50–$16.25; sandwiches and main courses $5.25–$9.75. AE, DC, DISC, MC, V. Mon–Thurs 11:30am–10:30pm, Fri–Sat 11:30am–11:30pm, Sun 11:30am–10pm. PIZZA/ITALIAN.

A few blocks uptown from Tulane University, Figaro's draws a semicasual crowd looking for designer pizza, cosmopolitan Italian food, and a nice outdoor patio for watching the beautiful people. Among the Neopolitan-style pies, spinach and feta is a personal favorite, but there are plenty of others from which to choose. How about a white pizza with garlic-herb butter and mozzarella, one with shrimp and cilantro, or the Margherita, with tomatoes and basil. You can also create an American-style pizza to your taste or make a meal of a calzone, an antipasto salad, a sub sandwich, or a muffaletta. I recommend any of the pasta entrees, especially the Sicilian stuffed shells. This is a good stop if you're at the university or in the Audubon Park area, especially if the weather is right for lunch outside.

Frankie and Johnny's. 321 Arabella (and Tchoupitoulas). ☎ **504/899-9146.** Everything under $10. AE, MC, V. Daily 11am–10pm. SEAFOOD.

This is a favorite local hole-in-the-wall dive neighborhood joint, with either zero atmosphere or enough for three restaurants, depending on how you view these things. And by "things" we mean plastic checked tablecloths, a ratty but friendly bar, and locals eating enormous soft shell crab po' boys with the crab legs hanging out of the bread and their mouths. You got your po' boys, your boiled or fried seafood platters with two kinds of salad, and goodness knows, you got your beer. Try that soft-shell crab po' boy, or the red beans and rice and other down-home dishes and know you are somewhere that isn't for tourists—and enjoy it all the more.

☼ Martin Wine Cellar and Delicatessen. 3827 Baronne St. ☎ **504/896-7380.** Everything under $8. AE, MC, V. Mon–Sat 9am–6:30pm, Sun 10am–2pm. SANDWICHES.

Martin's saved us one busy pre–Mardi Gras weekend, when parades and crowds prevented us from hitting a sit-down restaurant for lunch. A gourmet liquor and food store, Martin's also has a full-service deli counter. In addition to the usual deli suspects, they offer about two dozen specialty sandwiches, elaborate concoctions like the "Dave's Special:" rare roast beef, coleslaw, pâté de Campagne, special mustard, on rye. We ordered it on onion bread instead, and it made our list of the Ten Best Sandwiches of All Time. Weekdays features daily specials (lamb shanks, BBQ shrimp, garlic soup), and then there is their cheese counter, packaged salads and fresh breads. It's all inexpensive and delicious, and is the perfect Garden District spot for take-out or picnic makings (toss in a bottle of wine, if mood strikes), just 2 blocks lakeside of St. Charles.

Mystic Cafe. 3244 Magazine St. ☎ **504/891-1992.** Main courses $5.75–$11.25. AE, DISC, MC, V. Sun–Thurs 11am–11pm, Fri–Sat 11am–midnight. MEDITERRANEAN.

Local vegetarians flock here, though the cafe is technically Mediterranean (which means anything from Italy to Turkey), and some dishes include meat. The food is mostly butter-free and can be made without sugar on request. Vegans and the heart-conscious will find plenty of whole-grain, high-quality olive oil options. Some might find it a welcome relief from the usual full-fat New Orleans diet, but others might feel they are dining in California. That's fine for California, but not for New Orleans.

7 Metairie

Bozo's. 3117 21st St. ☎ **504/831-8666.** Lunch $5–$10; dinner $12–$16. MC, V. Tues–Sat 11am–3pm; Tues–Thurs 5–10pm, Fri–Sat 5–11pm. CAJUN/SEAFOOD.

New Orleanians have much affection for this plain, unpretentious fish house, and it's easy to see why, when the friendly and efficient wait staff serves heaping plates of seafood cooked to perfection. Shrimp, oysters, crawfish, crabs, and almost anything that swims or lives in nearby waters make up the bulk of the menu. Try the crisp and utterly delectable fried catfish lightly breaded with cornmeal, or "Mama Bozo's" delectable chicken andouille gumbo. There are a few other non-seafood selections, and a good list of sandwiches. Prices are unbelievably low, starting with a bargain gumbo and topping out with rib-eye steak. It's worth the trip.

Crozier's Restaurant Français. 3216 W. Esplanade North. ☎ **504/833-8108.** Reservations recommended. Main courses $16.25–$21. AE, DC, DISC, MC, V. Tues–Sat 5:30–10pm. FRENCH.

Authentic French cooking accounts for this restaurant's longstanding popularity. There are no surprises here, just good, old-fashioned French cuisine that would make any native (particularly from the south of France, like chef Gerard Crozier) feel right at home. Begin with a very tasty traditional onion soup or a salad of mixed greens. There's also a nice duck liver pâté and, of course, the ever-present escargots. Entrees might include trout with pecans, fish du jour, steak au poivre, or an incredible grilled quail with a light demi-glace. Traditional desserts like crème caramel, mousse au chocolat, and various tartlettes are a nice way to finish a meal. The wine list is limited, but good and moderately priced.

8 Lake Pontchartrain

Bruning's Seafood on the Lake. 1924 West End Pkwy. ☎ **504/282-9395.** Reservations not accepted Fri–Sat night. Main courses $7.50–$15.95. AE, DISC, MC, V. Sun–Thurs 11am–9:30pm, Fri–Sat 11am–10:30pm. SEAFOOD.

Bruning's has served a classic New Orleans seafood menu since 1859, and is now run by fifth- and sixth-generation Brunings who use traditional family recipes. The broiled seafood is especially good, as is the seafood gumbo, and fried dishes are grease free. A good buy, if you can't make up your mind, is the generous seafood platter. There's a children's menu, and all entrees come with salad, toast, and a potato.

The restaurant has had structural damage due to Hurricane Georges in 1998; it was knocked off its pilings into Lake Pontchartrain. As of press time they are serving lunch and dinner next door until they finish rebuilding.

9 Coffee, Tea & Sweets

✪ **Café du Monde.** In the French Market, 813 Decatur St. ☎ **504/581-2914.** Coffee, milk, hot chocolate, and beignets $1.10. No credit cards. Daily 24 hrs. Closed Dec 25. COFFEE, TEA & SWEETS.

Excuse us while we wax rhapsodic. Since 1862, Café du Monde has been selling café au lait and beignets on the edge of Jackson Square. A New Orleans landmark, it's *the* place for people-watching. Not only is it a must-stop on any trip to New Orleans, but you may find yourself wandering back several times a day, for your morning beignet and coffee, your afternoon snack, and, best of all, your 3am pick-me-up. What's a beignet? (Say ben-*yay*, by the way.) A square French doughnut-type object, hot and covered in powdered sugar. You might be tempted to shake off some of the sugar. Don't. Trust us. Pour more on, even. You'll be glad you did. Just don't wear black, or everyone will know what you've been eating. At three for about $1, they're a hell of a deal. Wash them down with chicory coffee, listen to the nearby buskers, ignore people trying to get your table, and try to figure out how many more stops you can squeeze in during your visit.

Kaldi's Coffeehouse and Museum. 941 Decatur St. ☎ **504/586-8989.** Sun–Thurs 7am–midnight, Fri–Sat 7am–2am. COFFEE, TEA & SWEETS.

Local alterna-youths and folkies come to this high-ceilinged, airy spot to brood over their journals and swig all kinds of coffee drinks. The menu is quite long and features everything from the traditional to the trendy (mocha drinks and whatnot) to the vaguely healthful (the blended soy drink is surprisingly tasty). They even roast the coffee beans on the premises. Poetry readings and folk music sometimes happen at night. This is a good place to drop by, not just for the addictive drinks, but also to find out what's happening in underground and alternative New Orleans.

La Madeleine. 547 St. Ann St. (at Chartres St.). ☎ **504/568-0073.** Pastries 85¢–$2.59; main courses $3.90–$9.25. AE, MC, V, DISC. Daily 7am–9pm. FRENCH BAKERY/COFFEE, TEA & SWEETS.

La Madeleine is one of the French Quarter's most charming casual eateries. One of a chain of French bakeries, it has a wood-burning brick oven that turns out a wide variety of breads, croissants, and brioches. A glass case up front holds marvelous pastries to take out or eat in the cafeteria section, where quiches, salads, soups, sandwiches, and other light entrees are available. This restaurant is delightful for a continental breakfast or light lunch.

La Marquise. 625 Chartres St. ☎ **504/524-0420.** Pastries 82¢–$5. No credit cards. Daily 7am–5:30pm. PASTRIES/COFFEE, TEA & SWEETS.

Tiny La Marquise serves French pastries in the crowded front room, which also holds the display counter, and outside on a small but delightful patio. Maurice Delechelle is the master baker and guiding hand here, and you'd be hard pressed to find more delectable goodies. There are *galettes bretonnes* (butter cookies), *pain au chocolat* (a rectangle of croissant dough wrapped around a chocolate bar, then baked), cygne swans (cream-filled éclairs in the shape of swans), *choux à la crème* (cream puffs), and *mille-feuilles* (napoleons), as well as croissants, brioches, and a wide assortment of strudels and Danish pastries. La Marquise is almost always crowded; if there are no seats on the patio, Jackson Square is just a few steps away.

   Croissant D'Or, a larger version of La Marquise operated by the same folks, is at 617 Ursulines St. (☎ **504/524-4663**). It's a quiet and calm place with the same great snacks, and you can almost always find an open table.

P. J.'s Coffee & Tea Company. 5432 Magazine St. ☎ **504/895-0273.** 95¢–$4. AE, MC, V. Mon–Fri 6:30am–11pm; Sat–Sun 7am–11pm. PASTRIES/COFFEE, TEA & SWEETS.

P. J.'s is a local institution, with 13 locations around town at last count. It offers a great variety of teas and coffees, and roasts its own coffee beans. The iced coffee is made by a cold-water process that requires 12 hours of brewing. P. J.'s also serves mochas, cappuccinos, and lattes. The granita is prepared with P. J.'s Espresso Dolce iced coffee concentrate, frozen with milk and sugar and served as a coffee "slushee"—great on hot, muggy days.

P. J.'s has branches at Tulane University (☎ 504/865-5705), Loyola University (☎ 504/865-2118), 2727 Prytania St. (☎ 504/899-0335), 637 N. Carrollton Ave. (☎ 504/482-4847), 634 Frenchmen St. (☎ 504/949-2292), and 7624 Maple St. (☎ 504/866-7031), among other locations.

Royal Blend Coffee & Tea House. 621 Royal St. ☎ **504/523-2716.** Pastries 75¢–$2.15; lunch items $2.85–$5.95. AE, MC, V ($10 minimum). Sun 7am–6pm, Mon–Thurs 7am–8pm, Fri–Sat 7am–midnight. CAFE/COFFEE, TEA & SWEETS.

This place is set back off the street; to reach it you walk through a courtyard. Order a sandwich, quiche, or salad at the counter and take it out into the courtyard. On Saturday afternoons, weather permitting, a guitarist serenades diners. (You can also eat inside, but it's not as much fun.) If you're just in the mood for coffee and pastry, they have plenty of that, too, and the pastry menu changes daily. Royal Blend has branches at 222 Carondelet St. (☎ 504/529-2005) and at 244 Metairie Rd. in Metairie (☎ 504/835-7779).

Rue de la Course. 1500 Magazine St. ☎ **504/529-1455.** Daily 7am–midnight. COFFEE-HOUSE/COFFEE, TEA & SWEETS.

This is your basic comfy boho coffeehouse, cavernous in appearance thanks to a very tall ceiling, manned by cool, friendly college kids and full of locals seeking a quick pick-me-up, lingering over the paper, or poring over their journals. In addition to prepared coffee and tea, Rue de la Course sells loose tea and coffee by the pound, as well as a few newspapers and local magazines.

Other locations: 3128 Magazine St. (☎ 504/899-0242), 219 N. Peters St. (☎ 504/523-0206), 401 Carondelet St. (☎ 504/586-0401), 535 E. Boston St. (☎ 504/893-5553). By the time you read this, the French Quarter location should have a liquor license.

8

Sights to See & Places to Be

Now, we admit that our favorite New Orleans activities involve walking, eating, listening to music, and dancing. If that's all you do while in town, we won't complain. Still, some people feel guilty if they don't take in some culture or history while on vacation. And besides, frequently you need to escape the rain or heat. New Orleans offers several fine museums and a world-class aquarium and zoo, all of which, in addition to being interesting in and of themselves, make marvelous refuges from the weather (except perhaps for the zoo).

Frankly, New Orleans itself is one big sight. It's one of the most unusual-looking cities in America, and being nice and flat, it's just made for exploring on foot. So get out there and do so. Be sure not to confine yourself to the French Quarter. While it certainly is a seductive place, to go to New Orleans and never leave the Quarter is like going to New York, remaining in Greenwich Village, and believing you've seen Manhattan. Stroll the lush Garden District or marvel at the oaks in City Park. Ride the streetcar down St. Charles Avenue and gape with jealousy at the gorgeous homes. Get really active and go visit some gators on a swamp tour.

But if you only leave the Quarter to visit clubs and restaurants, we won't blame you a bit.

Suggested Itineraries

If You Have 1 Day

If you have only 1 day in New Orleans, you might as well spend it all in the **French Quarter**—after all, you could easily spend a much longer trip entirely within its confines. (We just won't let you do so if you have the additional time.) But this is a day that will include all the important factors of a New Orleans visit: eating, walking, drinking, eating some more, listening to music, and dancing.

Start your day with beignets and coffee at **Café du Monde,** admiring as the city begins to tune up. Then take the **walking tour** in the next chapter; it gives you a bit of history in addition to pointing out individual buildings, and also helps you slow down and admire the grand architecture of this unique neighborhood. For lunch, have a muffaletta at **Central Grocery** (split it with somebody; they're gigantic), and thread your way through the buildings across the street to eat it by the banks of the **Mississippi River.** If you want something more elaborate, sample the modern Creole offerings of **Mr. B's Bistro & Bar.**

After lunch, go to the historic **Cabildo** and **Presbytère.** Each has some fine exhibits illustrating New Orleans and Louisiana history and culture. Afterward, pop in to nearby **Faulkner House Books** (see chapter 10)—not only did the author live there for a time, but you can choose a literary souvenir from the comprehensive selection of New Orleans–related books.

Then start **walking.** Walk down Royal Street and admire the antiques. Drop in at **A Gallery for Fine Photography;** it's like a museum of photos, many of which relate to local culture and history. (One of these would make a high-quality, albeit pricey, souvenir.) Swing by the shops toward the Esplanade Avenue end of Decatur Street. Be sure to check out the **Voodoo Museum;** it's more tourist voodoo than not, but there is some real information. As you wander, don't forget to admire the varying colors of buildings, the intricate iron lacework on the balconies, and so forth. This is quite a place they've got here.

As evening approaches, take a walk on **Bourbon Street.** Sure, it's gaudy, loud, and kind of disgusting, and comes off as a combination giant T-shirt shop and bar. At the right time of day, when things are starting to heat up but the real obnoxious types aren't too drunk, when different kinds of music pour from every door, when captivating smells waft from restaurants, it's also seductive and exhilarating. Have a predinner drink at the darkly mysterious **Lafitte's Blacksmith Shop** (the oldest building in town) or the darkly romantic **Napoleon House,** or sample a Hurricane at the not so dark but probably rowdy **Pat O'Brien's.**

And then get out of the Quarter. If you have one dinner to eat in New Orleans, you must eat at **Commander's Palace.** You might not totally agree with the James Beard folks who voted it best restaurant in the United States, but we doubt you will be disappointed.

Afterward, you can check out who's playing at **Tipitina's** or the **Maple Leaf** (or go to either regardless), or you may just want to head back to the Quarter. If you opt for a romantic **buggy ride,** we won't make fun of you. Do not miss hearing some jazz at **Preservation Hall**—it's cheap and it's the real McCoy. You might also want to navigate Bourbon Street, now that night has fallen, the scene will have truly kicked in. You have to see it once, even if you never want to see it again. For equal fun, less like that found at a frat party, head to the **Frenchmen section** of the Faubourg Marigny, where there are at least five clubs and a couple bars within a few blocks. Wander from one to another, sometimes never even going inside (the music can be heard outside just as easily), simply mingling with the friendly crowds. You can also drop by **Donna's** for some wild brass bands.

Suddenly feeling a bit hungry again? Grab a dozen oysters at **Acme** or **Felix's.** (Or make another trip to Café du Monde. It's been known to happen.) Have you exercised restraint and missed one of the three bars mentioned above? Go now. If you don't collapse exhausted—and full—in your bed, you haven't done your day properly.

If You Have 2 Days

Get out of the Quarter, get out of the Quarter, get out of the Quarter. Are we getting through to you? You can come back; you probably still have serious shopping (if not serious drinking) to do. But today, you must begin to see what else New Orleans has to offer.

Hop on the **St. Charles Avenue streetcar** first thing. Admire the gorgeous homes along the way (if you are awake enough), and get off at the end for breakfast at the **Camellia Grill.** The pecan waffle should get you going. It will also convince you of the need for more walking. Good. Get back on the streetcar, get off in the **Garden District,** and take the walking tour in the next chapter. Aside from its historical significance and interest, this neighborhood, full of fabulous houses and lush greenery, is just plain beautiful. Then get back on the streetcar—this time, pay attention to those beautiful houses—and get off at Lee Circle. Walk or cab to lunch at either **Uglesich's** (if you have the time to wait in line and the appetite for some of the finest, and most fattening, seafood in town) or **Mother's** (if po' boys are more your speed).

Now catch the bus to **City Park,** where you can admire the oaks and go to the **art museum.** On the way back, be sure to head **down Esplanade Avenue** (in a vehicle, please—it's too far to walk, and parts are too unsavory), perhaps even getting out to stroll along St. John's Bayou. Again, admire the beautiful homes and majestic oaks, different from what you've seen in the Garden District, but no less memorable. If you return to the Quarter for additional shopping and drinking, you can also go by the **Aquarium of the Americas**—it's a particularly good one (and open until 8pm on Friday and Saturday).

At night, sample what's new and happening in New Orleans cooking. We recommend the more-or-less-contemporary Creole food at the **Upperline** or **Brigtsen's,** but the lingering sounds of "Bam!" and "Turn it up a notch" may understandably draw you to **Emeril's.** The first two make some clubs convenient; head to Tip's or the Maple Leaf if you didn't get there the previous night, **Mid City** for some zydeco and bowling, or the **Howlin' Wolf** for serious headliners. Or all of them if you are up for it. Try to be.

If You Have 3 Days

Yes, we are dragging you out of the Quarter again, but we will let you come back later.

Get back on the St. Charles Avenue streetcar and head to **Audubon Park** and the **Zoo,** which is one of the best in the country, but small enough to see in a short time. Although we love that streetcar ride and take it whenever we can, you might want a change of scenery, in which case you can take a **riverboat** to the park. Afterward, head over to **Kelsey's** on Magazine Street and have some lunch, (or try **Pascal Manale's, Camellia Grill,** or **Martins' Wine Cellar,** which are nearby) then meander down Magazine St. for some shopping (more affordable than much you'll find in the Quarter), hopping on and off the bus as you spot stores that interest you. Finish up at the **art galleries** on Julia Street.

Sometime today, take a **walking tour.** There is one for practically every interest (from those offered by the Park Service to African American heritage tours), and we particularly like cemetery tours, which allow you to see one of New Orleans' most iconic sights in a safe and informative manner. You can fit in a tour **of Lafayette Cemetery** on your way to Magazine Street, or you can go back to the Quarter for a tour of St. Louis No. 1. (Or do these before you head over to the park.) Other possibilities include a literary heritage tour, voodoo tours, and nighttime ghost and vampire tours—though these are of dubious veracity and should be taken strictly for entertainment purposes.

If You Have 4 Days

At this point, you might consider options that take you out of New Orleans altogether. It can be hard to tear yourself away, but you will be glad you did. **Swamp tours,** at the right time of year (winter isn't the best), allow you to gawk at gators. Or you could spend a half-day at a **plantation** and learn about the realities of so-called gracious Southern living. If you have even more time, consider a 2-day trip out to **Cajun country** for some incredible music and food.

1 The French Quarter

Those who have been to Disneyland might be forgiven if they experience some déjà vu upon first seeing the French Quarter. It's somewhat more worn, of course, and, in spots, a whole lot smellier. But it's also real. However, thanks perhaps in part to Disney, many tourists treat the Quarter like a theme park, going from bar to bar instead of ride to ride, broadcasting their every move with rowdy shrieks of merriment.

Fine. Except it isn't an amusement park, constructed just for the hedonistic delight of out-of-towners. It's an actual neighborhood, one of the most visually interesting in America and one that has existed for more than 200 years. Some of the people living in the Quarter are the fifth generation of their family to do so.

There's a great deal to the French Quarter—history, architecture, cultural oddities—and to overlook all that in favor of T-shirt shops and the ubiquitous bars is a darn shame. Which is not to say we don't understand, and rather enjoy, the lure of the more playful angle. And as much as we find **Bourbon Street** tacky and often disgusting, we walk down it at least once every time we are in town. We just don't want you to end up like some tourists who never even get off Bourbon. (And when you do head there, please remember that you are walking by people's homes. You wouldn't like it if someone did something biologically disgusting on your doorstep. Afford French Quarter dwellers the same courtesy.)

The Quarter was laid out in 1718 by a French royal engineer named Adrien de Pauger, and today it's a great anomaly in contemporary America. Almost all other American cities have torn down or gutted their historic centers, but thanks to a strict preservation policy (and no thanks to the climate and the fire that destroyed the Quarter in the 1700s), the area looks exactly as it always has and is still the center of town.

Aside from Bourbon Street, you will find the most bustling activity at **Jackson Square,** where musicians, artists, fortune-tellers, jugglers, and those peculiar "living statue" performance artists (a step below mime, and that's pretty pathetic) gather, to sell their wares or entertain for change. **Royal Street** is home to numerous pricey antique shops, with other interesting stores on **Chartres and Decatur streets** and the cross streets between.

The closer you get to Esplanade Avenue and toward Rampart Street, the more residential the Quarter becomes, and buildings are entirely homes (in the business sections, the ground floors are commercial and the stories above apartments). Walk through these areas, peeping in through any open gate; surprises wait behind them in the form of graceful brick and flagstone-lined courtyards filled with foliage and bubbling fountains. Follow the French Quarter stroll in chapter 9 and you'll see a few of the nicest courtyards in the Quarter.

The Vieux Carré Commission is ever vigilant about balancing contemporary economic interests in the Quarter with concerns for historic preservation. Not only has the commission encouraged restoration, but it has also joined in the battle to hold back certain would-be intruders of the modern world. There's not a traffic light in the whole of the French Quarter—they're relegated to fringe streets—and streetlights are of the old gaslight style. In 1996, large city buses were banned from the neighborhood.

Impressions

"See Naples and die," says the proverb. My view of things is that you should see Canal Street, New Orleans, and then try to live as much longer as ever you can.
—G. A. Sala, *America Revisited* (1882)

During a good part of each day, Royal and Bourbon streets are pedestrian malls, and no vehicles are *ever* allowed in the area around Jackson Square. We also applaud the hard-drawn lines that have mostly kept out the generic chain stores that populate most city centers these days, and are threatening to turn all of America into one big mall, indistinguishable from any other.

Though much of New Orleans is made for walking, the Quarter is particularly pedestrian-friendly. The streets are laid out in an almost perfect rectangle, so it's nearly impossible to get lost. It's also so well traveled that it is nearly always safe, particularly in the central parts. Again, as you get toward the fringes (especially near Rampart) and as night falls, you should exercise caution; stay in the more bustling parts and try not to walk alone.

The French Quarter walking tour in chapter 9 will give you the best overview of the historic buildings of the area and of the city's history. Many other attractions that aren't in the walking tour are listed in this chapter, so make sure to cross-reference as you go along.

✪ **Aquarium of the Americas.** 1 Canal St., at Wells St. ☎ **800/774-7394** or 504/581-4629. www.auduboninstitute.org. Aquarium $11.25 adults, $8.75 seniors, $5 children 2–12. IMAX $7.75 adults, $6.75 seniors, $5 children. Combination tickets $15.50 adults, $12.50 seniors, $9 children. Aquarium Sun–Thurs 9:30am–6pm, Fri–Sat 9:30am–7pm. IMAX daily 10am–6pm. Shows every hour on the hour. Last ticket sold 1 hour before closing. Closed Mardi Gras and Dec 25.

With all the other delights New Orleans offers, it's easy to overlook the Audubon Institute's Aquarium of the Americas—despite its million-gallon size. Who wants to look at fish when you could be eating them? But this is a world-class aquarium, highly entertaining and painlessly educational, with beautifully constructed exhibits.

The Aquarium is on the banks of the Mississippi River, along Woldenberg Park at the edge of the French Quarter—a very easy walk from the main Quarter action. Five major exhibit areas and dozens of smaller aquariums hold a veritable ocean of aquatic life native to the region (especially the Mississippi River and Gulf of Mexico) and to North, Central, and South America. You can walk through the underwater tunnel in the Caribbean Reef exhibit and wave to finny friends swimming all around you, view a shark-filled re-creation of the Gulf of Mexico, or drop in to see the penguin exhibit. We particularly like the walk-through Waters of the Americas, where you wander in rain forests (complete with birds and piranhas) and see what goes on below the surface of swamps; one look will squash any thoughts of a dip in a bayou. *Note:* At press time, plans were being made for a sea otter exhibit.

The **IMAX theater** shows two or three films at regular intervals. The Aquarium is a great place to take the kids, though most will probably be too impatient to learn much from the educational graphics. And adults shouldn't overlook it, even if you are inclined to think it isn't your, er, bowl of chowder. In addition to its many virtues, it also makes a perfect refuge from the inevitable rain.

The Audubon Institute also runs the city's zoo at Audubon Park uptown. **Combination tickets** for the Aquarium, the IMAX theater, the zoo, and a riverboat ride to the zoo are $26.50 for adults, $13.25 for children. You can also buy tickets for different combinations of the attractions.

The Historic French Market. On Decatur St., toward Esplanade Ave. from Jackson Sq.

Legend has it that the site of the French Market was originally used by Native Americans as a bartering market. It began to grow into an official market in 1812. Circa 1840-70, it was part of Gallatin Street, an impossibly rough area so full of bars, drunken sailors, and criminals of every shape and size that it made Bourbon Street

French Quarter Attractions

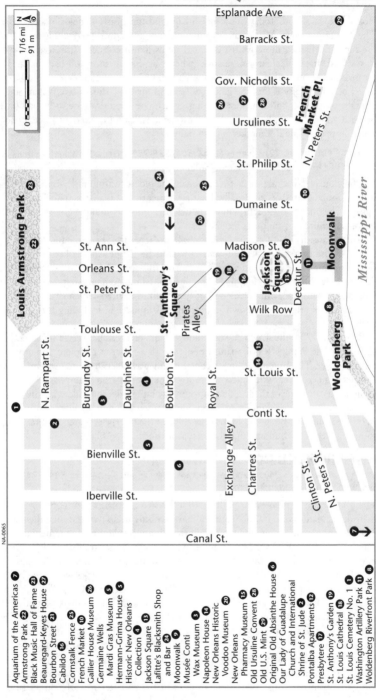

Esplanade Ave
Barracks St.
Gov. Nicholls St.
Ursulines St.
St. Philip St.
Dumaine St.
Madison St.
St. Ann St.
Orleans St.
St. Peter St.
Toulouse St.
St. Louis St.
Conti St.
Bienville St.
Iberville St.
Canal St.

Louis Armstrong Park
French Market Pl.
N. Peters St.
Mississippi River
Moonwalk
Woldenberg Park
Jackson Square
St. Anthony's Square
Pirates Alley
Wilk Row
Decatur St.
Clinton St.
N. Peters St.
Exchange Alley
Chartres St.
Royal St.
Bourbon St.
Dauphine St.
Burgundy St.
N. Rampart St.

1/16 mi
91 m

Aquarium of the Americas **7**
Armstrong Park **22**
Black Music Hall of Fame **23**
Beauregard-Keyes House **27**
Bourbon Street **21**
Cabildo **16**
Cornstalk Fence **25**
French Market **26**
Gallier House Museum **10**
Germaine Wells
Mardi Gras Museum **5**
Hermann-Grima House **5**
Historic New Orleans
Collection **4**
Jackson Square **13**
Lafitte's Blacksmith Shop
and Bar **24**
Moonwalk **9**
Musée Conti
Wax Museum **3**
Napoleon House **14**
New Orleans Historic
Voodoo Museum **20**
New Orleans
Pharmacy Museum **15**
Old Ursuline Convent **28**
Old U.S. Mint **29**
Original Old Absinthe House **6**
Our Lady of Guadalupe
Church and International
Shrine of St. Jude **2**
Pontalba Apartments **12**
Presbytere **17**
St. Anthony's Garden **19**
St. Louis Cathedral **18**
St. Louis Cemetery No. 1 **1**
Washington Artillery Park **11**
Woldenberg Riverfront Park **8**

NA-0065

139

look like Disneyland. Today, it's a mixed bag (and not nearly as colorful as its past). The 24-hour Farmer's Market makes a fun amble as you admire everything from fresh produce and fish to more tourist-oriented items like hot sauces, Cajun and Creole mixes, and snacks like gator on a stick (when was the last time you had that?). The Flea Market, a bit farther down from the Farmer's Market, is considered a must-shop place, but the reality is that the goods are kind of junky: T-shirts, jewelry, hats, belts, crystals, sunglasses, and that sort of thing. Still, some good deals are to be had (even better if you are up for bargaining), so the savvy might find it the right place for souvenir shopping. The flea market is open daily.

St. Louis Cathedral. 721 Chartres St. ☎ **504/525-9585.** Free admission. Free tours run continuously Mon–Sat 9am–5pm, Sun 2–5pm.

The St. Louis Cathedral prides itself on being the oldest continuously active cathedral in the United States. What usually doesn't get mentioned is that it is also one of the ugliest. The outside is all right, but the rather grim interior wouldn't give even a minor European church a run for its money.

Still, its history is impressive and somewhat dramatic. The cathedral formed the center of the original settlement, and it is still the major landmark of the French Quarter. This is the third building to stand on this spot. A hurricane destroyed the first in 1722. On Good Friday 1788, the bells of its replacement were kept silent for religious reasons rather than ringing out the alarm for a fire—which eventually went out of control and burned down more than 850 buildings, including the cathedral itself.

Rebuilt in 1794, the structure was remodeled and enlarged between 1845 and 1851 by J. N. B. de Pouilly. It's of Spanish design, with a tower at each end and a higher central tower. The brick used in its construction was taken from the original town cemetery and covered with stucco to protect the mortar from dampness. It's worth going in to catch one of the free docent tours; the knowledgeable guides are full of fun facts about the windows and murals and how the building nearly collapsed once from water table sinkage. Be sure to look at the slope of the floor; clever architectural design somehow keeps the building upright even as it continues to sink.

HISTORIC BUILDINGS

Old Absinthe House. 240 Bourbon St., between Iberville and Bienville. ☎ **504/523-3181.** Free admission. Daily from 9:30am.

The Old Absinthe House was built in 1806 by two Spaniards and is still owned by their descendants (who live in Spain and have nothing to do with running the place). The building now houses the Old Absinthe House bar and two restaurants, Tony Moran's and Pasta E Vino. The drink for which the building and bar were named is now outlawed in this country (it only caused blindness and madness). But you can sip a legal libation in the bar and feel at one with the famous types who came before you, listed on a plaque outside: William Makepeace Thackeray, Oscar Wilde, Sarah Bernhardt, Walt Whitman. Andrew Jackson and the Lafitte brothers plotted their desperate defense of New Orleans here in 1815. The house was a speakeasy during Prohibition, and when federal officers closed it in 1924, the interior was mysteriously stripped of its antique fixtures—including the long marble-topped bar and the old water dripper that was used to infuse water into the absinthe. Just as mysteriously, they all reappeared down the street at a corner establishment called, oddly enough, the Old Absinthe House Bar (400 Bourbon St.). The latter recently closed, and a neon-bedecked daiquiri shack opened in its stead. Needless to say, the fixtures are nowhere in sight.

Beauregard-Keyes House. 1113 Chartres St., at Ursulines. ☎ **504/523-7257.** Admission $5 adults, $4 seniors and students and AAA, $1.50 children under 13. Mon–Sat 10am–3pm. Tours on the hour.

This "raised cottage," with its Doric columns and handsome twin staircases, was built as a residence by a wealthy New Orleans auctioneer, Joseph Le Carpentier, in 1826. Confederate Gen. P. G. T. Beauregard lived in the house with several members of his family for 18 months between 1865 and 1867, and from 1944 until 1970 it was the residence of Frances Parkinson Keyes (pronounced *Cause*), who wrote many novels about the region. One of them, *Madame Castel's Lodger,* concerns the general's stay in this house. *Dinner at Antoine's,* perhaps her most famous novel, also was written here. Mrs. Keyes left her home to a foundation, and the house, rear buildings, and garden are open to the public. The gift shop has a wide selection of her novels.

Old Ursuline Convent. 1112 Chartres St., at Ursuline. ☎ **504/529-3040.** Admission $5 adults, $4 seniors, $2 students, free for children under 8. Tours Tues–Fri 10am–3pm on the hour (closed for lunch at noon), Sat–Sun 11:15am, 1, and 2pm.

Forget tales of America being founded by brawny, brave, tough guys in buckskin and beards. The real pioneers—at least, in Louisiana—were well-educated French women clad in 40 pounds of black wool robes. That's right; you don't know tough until you know the Ursuline nuns, and this city would have been a very different place without them. The Sisters of Ursula came to the mudhole that was New Orleans in 1727, after enduring a journey that several times nearly saw them lost at sea or to pirates or disease. Once in town, they provided the first decent medical care (saving countless lives), and later, founded the local first school and orphanage for girls. They also helped raise girls shipped over from France as marriage material for local men, teaching the girls everything from languages to homemaking of the most exacting sort (laying the foundation for who knows how many local families). The Convent dates from 1752 (the Sisters themselves moved uptown, where they remain to this day, in 1824) and is the oldest building in the Mississippi River Valley, and the only surviving building from the French Colonial period in the United States. It also houses Catholic archives dating back to 1718. Unfortunately, tours here can be disappointing affairs, with docents whose histories ramble all over the place, rarely painting the full, thrilling picture of these extraordinary ladies to whom New Orleans owes so much.

The Old U.S. Mint. 400 Esplanade Ave., at N. Peters (enter on Esplanade Ave. or Barracks St.). ☎ **800/568-6968** or 504/568-6968. Admission $5 adults, $4 seniors and students, free for children under 12. Tues–Sun 9am–5pm.

The Old U.S. Mint, a Louisiana State Museum complex, houses exhibits on New Orleans jazz and on the city's Carnival celebrations. The first exhibit contains a comprehensive collection of pictures, musical instruments, and other artifacts connected with jazz greats—Louis Armstrong's first trumpet is here. It tells of the development of the jazz tradition and New Orleans' place in that history. Across the hall there's a stunning array of Carnival mementos from New Orleans and other communities across Louisiana—from ornate Mardi Gras costumes to a street scene complete with maskers and a parade float. The Krewe of Zulu, one of the city's most festive Mardi Gras societies, donated costumes from years past that recently went on display.

The 1850 House, Lower Pontalba Building. 523 St. Ann St., Jackson Sq. ☎ **504/568-6968.** Admission $3 adults, $2 seniors and students, free for children under 13. Tues–Sun 9am–5pm. Closed state holidays.

James Gallier Sr. and his son designed the historic Pontalba Buildings for the Baroness Micaela Almonester de Pontalba. She had them built in 1849 (see listing number 32

Lady Bountiful: Baroness de Pontalba

New Orleans owes a great debt to Baroness Micaela Almonester de Pontalba and her family—without them, Jackson Square would be a mud hole. Her father, Don Almonester, used his money and influence to have the St. Louis Cathedral, Cabildo, and Presbytère built. The Baroness was responsible for the two long brick apartment buildings that flank Jackson Square, and for the renovation that turned the center of the square into what it is today.

The Baroness' life reads like a novel. Born in 1795 into the most influential family in New Orleans—the famous priest Pere Antoine, head of the St. Louis Cathedral and a great friend of her family, christened her and performed her wedding ceremony—she married her cousin, who stole her inheritance. When she wanted a separation, at a time when such things were unheard of, her father-in-law shot her several times, then shot himself. She survived, though some of her fingers did not. In subsequent portraits, she took care to hide the wounded hand in the folds of her dress. She did get her money back—she used it for those French Quarter improvements—and also ended up taking care of her (eventually) slightly nutty husband for the rest of his life. She died in Paris in 1874, and her home there is now the residence of the American Ambassador.

Want to know all the details about this remarkable woman? A new, well-researched book has them: *Intimate Enemies,* by Christina Vella.

in "Walking Tour 1," chapter 9) in an effort to combat the deterioration of the older part of the city. The rows of town houses on either side of Jackson Square were the largest private buildings in the country at the time. Legend has it that the Baroness, miffed that her friend Andrew Jackson wouldn't tip his hat to her, had his statue erected in the square, permanently doffing his chapeau toward her apartment on the top floor of the Upper Pontalba. It's probably not true, but we never stand in the way of a good story.

In this house, the Louisiana State Museum presents a demonstration of life in 1850, when the buildings opened for residential use. The self-guided tour uses a fact-filled sheet that explains in detail the history of the interior and the uses of the rooms, which are filled with period furnishings arranged to show how the rooms were typically used. It vividly illustrates the difference between the "upstairs" portion of the house, where the upper middle-class family lived in comfort (and the children were largely confined to a nursery and raised by servants), and the "downstairs," where the staff toiled in considerable drudgery to make their bosses comfortable. It's a surprisingly enjoyable look at life in the "good old days"; it might have you reconsidering just how good they were.

Spring Fiesta Historic House. 826 St. Ann St., at Bourbon. ☎ **504/581-1367.** $4 donation requested. By appointment only.

The New Orleans Spring Fiesta Association owns this historic mid–19th-century town house. It affords a peek back in time, furnished as it is with antiques of the Victorian era and many objets d'art from New Orleans' golden age of the 1800s. The association's fiesta, in March, coordinates tours of historic town houses, courtyards, and plantation homes around the city.

MUSEUMS

In addition to the destinations listed here, you might be interested in the **Germaine Wells Mardi Gras Museum** (☎ 504/523-5433), 813 Bienville St., on the second floor of Arnaud's restaurant. You'll find a private collection of Mardi Gras costumes and ball gowns dating from around 1910 to 1960. Admission is free, and the museum is open during restaurant hours. **The Old U.S. Mint** (see "Historic Buildings," above) displays a few Mardi Gras costumes, and also houses a collection of jazz memorabilia.

Scheduled to open in 2000 are the **National D-Day Museum,** a tribute to those who made the Normandy invasion possible; and the **Ogden Museum of Southern Art.**

✪ **The Cabildo.** 701 Chartres St. ☎ **504/568-6968.** Admission $5 adults, $4 students and seniors, free for children under 13. Tues–Sun 9am–5pm.

Constructed in 1795–99 as the Spanish government seat in New Orleans, the Cabildo was the site of the signing of the Louisiana Purchase transfer. It was severely damaged by fire in 1988, and closed for 5 years for reconstruction, which included total restoration of the roof by French artisans using 600-year-old timber-framing techniques. It is now the center of the Louisiana State Museum's facilities in the French Quarter. It's conveniently located right there on Jackson Square and is quite worth your time.

A multiroom exhibition informatively, entertainingly, and exhaustively traces the history of Louisiana from exploration through Reconstruction, from a multicultural perspective. It covers all aspects of life, not just the obvious discussions of slavery and the battle for statehood. Topics include antebellum music, mourning and burial customs (a big deal when much of your population is succumbing to yellow fever), immigrants and how they fared here, and the changing roles of women in the South (which occupies a large space). As you wander through, each room seems more interesting than the last. Throughout are portraits of nearly all the prominent figures from Louisiana history, plus other fabulous artifacts, including Napoléon's death mask.

Gallier House Museum. 1118 and 1132 Royal St., between Gov. Nicholls and Ursuline sts. ☎ **504/525-5661.** Admission $6 adults, $5.25 AAA members, $5 seniors and students, $3 children 8–18, free for children under 8. Tours begin on the half hour Mon–Sat 10am–4pm; last tour at 3:30pm.

James Gallier Jr. designed and built the Gallier House Museum as his residence in 1857. Anne Rice fans will want to at least walk by, because this is the house she was thinking of when she described Louis and Lestat's New Orleans residence in *Interview with the Vampire.* Gallier and his father were leading New Orleans architects—they designed the old French Opera House, the original St. Charles Exchange Hotel, Municipality Hall (now Gallier Hall), and the Pontalba Buildings. This carefully restored town house contains an early working bathroom, a passive ventilation system, and furnishings of the period. Leaders of local ghost tours swear Gallier haunts the place. The adjoining building houses historical exhibits as well as films on decorative plasterwork, ornamental ironwork, wood-graining, and marbling. There is also a gift shop and plenty of free parking. Special seasonal programs are available.

Hermann-Grima House. 820 St. Louis St. ☎ **504/525-5661.** Admission $6 adults, $5.25 AAA members, $5 seniors and students, $3 children 8–18, free for children under 8. Mon–Sat 10am–4pm (last tour leaves at 3:30pm).

Brought to you by the same folks who run the Gallier House, the 1831 Hermann-Grima House is a symmetrical Federal-style building (perhaps the first in the Quarter) that's very different from its French surroundings. The knowledgeable docents who give the regular tours make this a satisfactory stop at any time, but keep an eye out for the frequent special tours. At Halloween, for example, the house is draped in typical 1800s mourning, and the docents explain mourning customs; at Christmas, the house and tour reflect that season. The house, which stretches from St. Louis Street to Conti Street, passed through two different families before becoming a boarding house in the

1920s. It has been meticulously restored and researched, and the tour is one of the city's more historically accurate offerings. On Thursdays from October to May, cooking demonstrations take place in the authentic 1830s kitchen, using methods of the era. (Alas, health rules prevent those on the tour from sampling the results.) The house also contains one of the Quarter's last surviving stables, complete with stalls.

❍ **Historic New Orleans Collection—Museum/Research Center.** 533 Royal St. (between St. Louis and Toulouse). ☎ **504/523-4662.** Free admission; tours $4. Tues–Sat 10am–4:45pm; tours Tues–Sat 10am, 11am, 2pm, 3pm. Closed major holidays, Mardi Gras.

The Historic New Orleans Collection's museum of local and regional history is almost hidden away within a complex of historic French Quarter buildings. The oldest, constructed in the late 18th century, was one of the few structures to escape the disastrous fire of 1794. These buildings were owned by the collection's founders, Gen. and Mrs. L. Kemper Williams. Their former residence, behind the courtyard, is open to the public for tours. There are also excellent tours of the Louisiana history galleries, which feature choice items from the collection—expertly preserved and displayed art, maps, and original documents like the transfer papers for the Louisiana Purchase of 1803. The collection is owned and managed by a private foundation, not a governmental organization, and therefore offers more historical perspective and artifacts than boosterism. The Williams Gallery, also on the site, is free to the public and presents changing exhibitions that focus on Louisiana's history and culture.

If you want to see another grandly restored French Quarter building (and a researcher's dream), visit the **Williams Research Center,** 410 Chartres St. (☎ **504/598-7171**), which houses and displays the bulk of the collection's many thousands of items. Admission is free.

Madame John's Legacy. 632 Dumaine Street. ☎ **504/568-6968.** Admission $3 adults, $2 students and seniors. Tues–Sun 9am–5pm.

The second oldest building in the Mississippi Valley (after the Ursuline Convent), and a rare example of Creole architecture that miraculously survived the 1794 fire, Madame John's Legacy has finally been opened to the public. Built around 1788, on the foundations of an earlier home destroyed in the fire of that year, the house has had a number of owners and renters (including the son of Governor Claiborne), but none of them were named John. Or even Madame. It acquired its moniker courtesy of author George Washington Cable, who used the house as a setting for his short story "Tite Poulette." The protagonist was a quadroon named "Madame John" after her lover who willed this house to her. There are no tours, but you can enjoy two exhibits, one on the history and legends of the house (including glimpses into the style and manner of Creole life), and another of art by self taught/primitive artists.

Musée Conti Wax Museum. 917 Conti St. ☎ **504/525-2605.** www.get-waxed.com. Admission $6.25 adults, $5.50 seniors (over 62), $4.50 children 4–17, free for children under 4. Daily 10am–5:30pm. Closed Mardi Gras, Dec 25.

You might wonder about the advisability of a wax museum in a place as hot as New Orleans, but the Musée Conti is pretty neat—and downright spooky in spots. (And of course, when it is hot, this is a good place to cool off!) A large section is devoted to a sketch of Louisiana legends (Andrew Jackson, Napoléon, Jean Lafitte, Marie Laveau, Huey Long, a Mardi Gras Indian, Louis Armstrong, and Pete Fountain) and historical episodes. There's also a "Haunted Dungeon" in the true wax museum tradition, with monsters and scenes from well-known horror tales. It helps to think Vincent Price while you're here.

New Orleans Historic Voodoo Museum. 724 Dumaine St., at Bourbon. ☎ **504/ 523-7685.** www.voodoomuseum.com. Admission $6.30 adults, $5.25 students and seniors. French Quarter tour $18, cemetery tour $14, Tour of the Undead $15. Daily 10am–8pm.

Some of the hard-core voodoo practitioners in town might scoff at the Voodoo Museum, and perhaps rightly so. It is largely designed for tourists, but is also probably the best opportunity for tourists to get acquainted with the history and culture of voodoo. Don't expect high-quality, comprehensive exhibits—the place is dark, dusty, and musty (once you pass through the gift store). There are occult objects from all over the globe, plus some articles that allegedly belonged to the legendary Marie Laveau. Unless someone on staff talks you through it—which they will, if you ask—you might come away with as much confusion as facts. Still, it's an adequate introduction—and who wouldn't want to bring home a voodoo doll from here? The people who run the museum are involved in voodoo, and there is generally a voodoo priestess on site, giving readings and making personal gris-gris bags. Again, voodoo for tourists, but for most tourists, probably the right amount. (Don't confuse this place with the Marie Laveau House of Voodoo on Bourbon Street.)

The museum also offers a **guided voodoo walking tour** of the French Quarter. It leaves the museum at 1pm weekdays and 10:30am on Sunday and visits Congo Square (now Beauregard Square). Another tour takes you to **St. Louis Cemetery No. 1** to visit Marie Laveau's reputed grave. The tours might be light on verifiable facts, but they are usually entertaining. (On the St. Louis tour, please don't scratch X's on the graves; no matter what you've heard, it is not a real voodoo practice, and is destroying fragile tombs.) The museum can arrange psychic readings and visits to voodoo rituals if you want to delve deeper into the subject.

New Orleans Pharmacy Museum. 514 Chartres St., at St. Louis. ☎ **504/565-8027.** Admission $2 adults, $1 seniors and students, free for children under 12. Tues–Sun 10am–5pm.

Founded in 1950, the New Orleans Pharmacy Museum is just what the name implies. In 1823, the first licensed pharmacist in the United States, Louis J. Dufilho Jr., opened an apothecary shop here. The Creole-style town house doubled as his home, and he cultivated the herbs he needed for his medicines in the interior courtyard. Inside you'll find old apothecary bottles, voodoo potions, pill tile, and suppository molds, as well as the old glass cosmetics counter (pharmacists of the 1800s also manufactured makeup and perfumes).

Unfortunately, the old-timey atmosphere is assisted by itty-bitty information cards attached to the exhibits, with minimal facts listed in ancient typefaces or spidery handwriting. Too bad; as alternative medicine gains acceptance, it's fascinating to look back at a time when medicine was barely more than snake-oil potions. (You certainly come away with a new respect and gratitude for antibiotics.) A new exhibit that highlights "milestones in the history of pharmacy and medicine" is on the second floor, where one of the recent temporary shows was about the history of sexually transmitted disease and the dubious "cures" once available.

✪ The Presbytère. 751 Chartres St., Jackson Sq. ☎ **504/568-6968.** Admission $5 adults, $4 seniors and students, free for children under 13. Tues–Sun 9am–5pm.

The Presbytère was planned as housing for the clergy but was never used for that purpose. Currently, it's part of the Louisiana State Museum, which has announced plans to close the building in October, 1999, and reopen in January, 2000 entirely devoted to Mardi Gras.

While we will miss the witty and informative (if badly displayed) Baroness de Pontalba exhibit (and can only hope it will resurface in some other Louisiana State Museum property), the plans for this long-overdue exhibition promise something truly stunning and special. The new installation should focus on the origins and evolution of Carnival, including ancient religious festivals and Louisiana Mardi Gras' own 19th-century beginnings. The artifacts collected are staggering in variety and number. Computer and video technology will allow visitors to participate (in a virtual reality kind of way) in balls, parades, and other activities. Galleries will be devoted to themes; climb aboard a float in the Parade Gallery, or create a computer generated costume in the Masking Gallery. In short, learn about the rich history of Mardi Gras and why it's so much more than just a big debauched party. This could be quite a marvelous, if not definitive, addition to the Quarter. Time will tell.

Woldenberg Riverfront Park. ☎ **504/861-2537.**

Made up of just under 20 acres of newly repaired green space, Woldenberg Riverfront Park stretches along the Mississippi from the elevated area called the Moonwalk (for former Mayor "Moon" Landrieu) at the old Governor Nicholls Street wharf to the Aquarium of the Americas at Canal Street (see above). This has historically been the city's promenade; now, it's an oasis of greenery in the heart of the city, with numerous works by popular local artists scattered throughout. The park includes a large lawn with a brick promenade leading to the Mississippi, and is home to hundreds of trees—oaks, magnolias, willows, and crape myrtles—and thousands of shrubs.

The Moonwalk has steps that allow you to get right down to Old Muddy—on foggy nights, you feel as if you are floating above the water. There are many benches from which to view the city's main industry—its busy port (second in the world only to Amsterdam in annual tonnage). To your right you'll see the Greater New Orleans Bridge and the World Trade Center of New Orleans (formerly the International Trade Mart) skyscraper, as well as the Toulouse Street wharf, departure point for excursion steamboats. The park is open daily, dawn to dusk.

2 Outside the French Quarter

UPTOWN & THE GARDEN DISTRICT

If you can see just one thing outside the French Quarter, make it the Garden District. It has no significant historic buildings or, with one exception (below), important museums. It's simply beautiful. In some ways, even more so than the Quarter, this is New Orleans. Authors as diverse as Truman Capote and Anne Rice have been enchanted by its spell. Gorgeous homes of superb design stand quietly amidst lush foliage, elegant, but ever-so-slightly (or more) decayed. You can see why this is the setting for so many novels; it's hard to imagine that anything real actually happens here.

But it does. Like the Quarter, this is a neighborhood, so please be courteous as you wander around. Seeing the sights consists mostly of looking at nice houses, so we suggest that you turn to "Walking Tour 2" or the streetcar tour in chapter 9, which will help guide you to the Garden District's treasures and explain a little of its history. And while you're at it, use the listings in chapter 10 to clue you in to the best shops, galleries, and bookstores on Magazine Street, the main shopping strip that bounds the Garden District.

Meanwhile, a little background. Across Canal Street from the Quarter, "American" New Orleans begins. After the Louisiana Purchase of 1803, an essentially French-Creole city came under the auspices of a government determined to develop it as an American city. As American citizens moved in, tensions between Creole society and the newcomers began to increase. Some historians lay this at the feet of Creole snobbery; others blame the naive and uncultured Americans. In any case, Creole society succeeded in maintaining a relatively distinct social world, deflecting American settlement upriver of Canal Street (uptown); the Americans in turn came to dominate the city with sheer numbers of immigrants. Newcomers bought up land in what had been the old Gravier Plantation (now the uptown area), and began to build a parallel city. Very soon Americans came to dominate the local business scene, centered along Canal Street. In 1833, the American enclave that we now know as the Garden District was incorporated as Lafayette City, and—thanks in large part to the New Orleans–Carrollton Railroad, which covered the route of today's St. Charles Avenue streetcar—the Americans kept right on expanding until they reached the tiny resort town of Carrollton. It wasn't until 1852 that the various sections came together officially as a united New Orleans.

✪ **St. Elizabeth's Orphanage.** 1314 Napoleon Ave. ☎ **504/899-6450.** Tues–Sun 11am–3pm. Tours on the hour only. $7 adults, $5 children. Note: days and hours subject to change without notice so calling ahead is strongly advised.

After 118 years as a girls' orphanage (and boarding school), this grand mid-1800s building fell on hard times, only to be rescued by the city's favorite building benefactors, Anne and Stan Rice. It now holds Anne's doll collection (over 900 of the variously sized suckers) and serves as the office for her Kith & Kin holding company.

Tours are offered on the hour only, and are some of the most entertaining in town. Even if you think you don't care about dolls, the displays (which also include some of the Rices' religious art collection) produce any number of good stories, particularly if the tour is being given by Bill Murphy, Anne's first cousin once removed, a long time New Orleans newspaperman and historian. The building can also be rented for weddings.

Note: **Anne Rice's actual home,** at 1239 First St., is open for a free tour on Mondays at 1pm. It's really only for Rice buffs or fans of "The Witching Hour" (which was set there), but it is most generous of Ms. Rice to let strangers troop through her home.

TROLLING ST. JOHN'S BAYOU & LAKE PONTCHARTRAIN

St. John's Bayou is a body of water that originally extended from the outskirts of New Orleans to Lake Pontchartrain, and it's one of the most important reasons New Orleans is where it is today. Jean-Baptiste Le Moyne, Sieur de Bienville, was commissioned to establish a settlement in Louisiana that would both make money and protect French holdings in the New World from British expansion. Bienville chose the spot where New Orleans now sits because he recognized the strategic importance of "back-door" access to the Gulf of Mexico provided by the bayou's linkage to the lake. Boats could enter the lake from the Gulf, then follow the bayou until they were within easy portage distance of the mouth of the Mississippi River. Area Native American tribes had used this route for years.

The early path from the city to the bayou is today's Bayou Road, an extension of Governor Nicholls Street in the French Quarter. Modern-day Gentilly Boulevard, which crosses the bayou, was another Native American trail—it led around the lake and on to settlements in Florida.

New Orleans grew and prospered, and the bayou became a suburb as planters moved out along its shores. In the early 1800s a canal was dug to connect the waterway with the city, reaching a basin at the edge of Congo Square. The basin became a popular recreation area, with fine restaurants and dance halls (as well as meeting places for voodoo practitioners, who held secret ceremonies along its shores). Gradually New Orleans reached beyond the French Quarter and enveloped the whole area—overtaking farmland, plantation homes, and resorts.

New Orleans Attractions

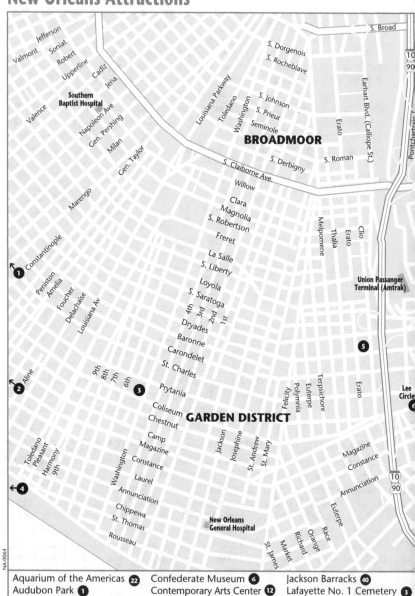

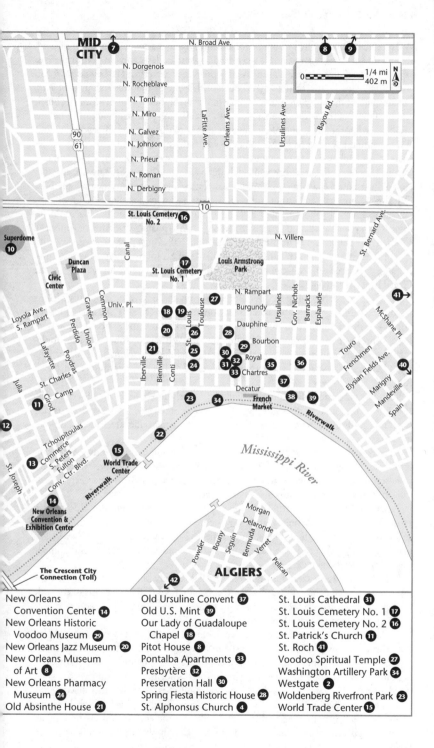

New Orleans
  Convention Center **14**
New Orleans Historic
  Voodoo Museum **29**
New Orleans Jazz Museum **20**
New Orleans Museum
  of Art **8**
New Orleans Pharmacy
  Museum **24**
Old Absinthe House **21**

Old Ursuline Convent **37**
Old U.S. Mint **39**
Our Lady of Guadaloupe
  Chapel **18**
Pitot House **8**
Pontalba Apartments **33**
Presbytère **32**
Preservation Hall **30**
Spring Fiesta Historic House **28**
St. Alphonsus Church **4**

St. Louis Cathedral **31**
St. Louis Cemetery No. 1 **17**
St. Louis Cemetery No. 2 **16**
St. Patrick's Church **11**
St. Roch **41**
Voodoo Spiritual Temple **27**
Washington Artillery Park **34**
Westgate **2**
Woldenberg Riverfront Park **23**
World Trade Center **15**

The canal is gone, filled in long ago, and the bayou is a meek re-creation of itself. It is no longer navigable (even if it were, bridges were built too low to permit the passage of boats of any size), but residents still prize their waterfront sites, and rowboats and sailboats make use of the bayou's surface. It's one of the prettiest areas of New Orleans, full of the old houses tourists love to marvel at, but without the hustle, bustle and confusion of more high profile locations. A walk along the banks and through the nearby neighborhoods is one of our favorite things to do on a nice afternoon.

The simplest way to reach St. John's Bayou from the French Quarter is to drive straight out Esplanade Avenue about 20 blocks. Or take the Esplanade Ridge walking tour in chapter 9. Right before you reach the bayou, you'll pass **St. Louis Cemetery No. 3** (just past Leda Street). It's the final resting place of many prominent New Orleanians, among them Father Adrien Rouquette, who lived and worked among the Choctaw, Storyville photographer E. J. Belloq, and Thomy Lafon, the black philanthropist who bought the old Orleans Ballroom as an orphanage for African American children and put an end to its infamous "quadroon balls." Just past the cemetery, turn left onto Moss Street, which runs along the banks of St. John's Bayou. If you want to see an example of an 18th-century West Indies–style plantation house, stop at **the Pitot House,** 1440 Moss St. (see below).

To continue, drive along Wisner Boulevard, on the opposite bank of St. John's Bayou from Moss Street, and you'll pass some of New Orleans' grandest modern homes—a sharp contrast to those on Moss Street. If you want to go all the way to Lake Pontchartrain, here's a good route: Stay on Wisner to Robert E. Lee Boulevard, turn right, and drive to Elysian Fields Avenue, then turn left. That's Louisiana State University's New Orleans campus on your left (its main campus is in Baton Rouge).

Turn left onto the broad concrete highway, Lakeshore Drive. It runs for 5½ miles along the lake, and in the summer the parkway alongside its seawall is usually swarming with swimmers and picnickers. On the other side are more luxurious, modern residences.

Lake Pontchartrain is some 40 miles long and 25 miles wide. Native Americans once lived along both sides, and it was a major waterway long before white people were seen in this hemisphere. You can drive across it over the 23¾-mile Greater New Orleans Causeway, the longest bridge in the world.

When you cross the mouth of St. John's Bayou, you'll be where **the old Spanish Fort** was built in 1770. Its remains are now nestled amidst modern homes. In the early 1800s there was a lighthouse here, and in the 1820s a railroad brought New Orleanians out to a hotel, a casino, a bandstand, bathing houses, and restaurants that made this a popular resort area.

Look for the **Mardi Gras fountain** on your left. Bronze plaques around its base are inscribed with the names of Mardi Gras krewes, and if you time your visit to coincide with sundown, you'll see the fountain beautifully lit in the Mardi Gras colors of purple (for justice), green (for faith), and gold (for power).

At the end of Lakeshore Drive, when you come to the old white Coast Guard lighthouse, you'll know you've reached **West End.** This interesting little park is home to several yacht clubs, a marina, and a number of restaurants, many of which have been here for years and look just the way you'd expect—not too fancy, and with a good view out over the water. This old fishing community has, over the years, become the main pleasure-boating center of New Orleans; the Southern Yacht Club here was established in 1840, making it the second oldest in the country. After the railroad began bringing pleasure-seekers here from the city in the 1870s, showboats and floating circuses often pulled up and docked for waterside performances.

Buckstown is another small fishing community that retains its old-time atmosphere. It occupies an area of West End on the bank of a narrow canal behind the restaurants on the western side of the West End park. To reach it, turn left on Lakeshore Drive at the Coast Guard station, then turn right on Lake Avenue (the first street you come to).

WHERE THE BODIES AREN'T BURIED

The cities of the dead are part of the city's indelible landscape, along with Spanish moss and lacy iron balconies. Their ghostly and inscrutable presence enthralls visitors, who are used to traditional methods of burial—in the ground or in mausoleums.

Why above ground? Well, it rains in New Orleans. A lot. And then it floods. Soon after New Orleans was settled it became apparent that Uncle Etienne had an unpleasant habit of bobbing back to the surface (doubtless no longer looking his best). Add to that cholera and yellow fever epidemics, which helped increase not only the number of bodies, but also the infection possibility. Given that the cemetery of the time was inside the Vieux Carré, it's all pretty disgusting to think about.

So in 1789, the city opened St. Louis No. 1, right outside the city walls, on what is now Rampart Street. The "condo crypt" look—the dead are placed in vaults that look like miniature buildings—was inspired to a certain extent by the famous Pere Lachaise cemetery in Paris. Crypts were laid out haphazardly in St. Louis No. 1, which quickly filled up, even as the city outgrew the Vieux Carré and expanded around the cemetery. Other cemeteries soon followed, and also eventually were incorporated into the city proper. They have designated lanes, making for a more orderly appearance. The rows of tombs look like nothing so much as a city—a city where the dead inhabitants peer over the shoulders of the living.

These little houses of the dead, in addition to solving the problem of belowground burial, are even more functional. There are two types of crypts: the aforementioned "family vaults" and the "oven crypts"—so called because of their resemblance to bread ovens in a wall. A coffin is slid inside, and the combination of heat and humidity acts like a slow form of cremation. In a year or so, the occupant is reduced to bone. As the space is needed, the bones are pushed to the back, coffin pieces removed, and another coffin inserted. In the larger family vaults (made of whitewashed brick), there are a couple of shelves, and the same thing happens. As family members die, the bones are swept off the shelves into a pit below, and everyone eventually lies jumbled together. The result is sometimes dozens of names, going back generations, on a single spot. It's a very efficient use of cemetery space, far more so than conventional sweeping expanses of graveyard landscaping.

For many years, New Orleans cemeteries were in shambles. Crypts lay open, exposing their pitiful contents—if they weren't robbed of them—bricks lay everywhere, marble tablets were shattered, and visitors might even trip over stray bones. Thanks to local civic efforts, several of the worst eyesores have been cleaned up, though some remain in deplorable shape. A faux voodoo practice continues in some of the St. Louis cemeteries, where visitors are encouraged to scrawl X's on the tombs. Please don't do this; not only is it a made-up voodoo ritual, it destroys the fragile tombs.

For more information, we highly recommend Robert Florence's *New Orleans Cemeteries: Life in the Cities of the Dead* (Batture Press). It's full of photos, facts, and human-interest stories, and is available at bookstores throughout the city.

SAFETY FIRST

You will be warned against going to the cemeteries alone, and urged to go with a scheduled tour group (see "Organized Tours," later in this chapter). It is true that thanks to their location and layout—some are in dicey neighborhoods, and the crypts obscure threats to your safety—some cemeteries can be quite risky, making visitors prime pickings for muggers and so forth. Other cemeteries, those with better security and in better neighborhoods, not to mention layouts that permit driving, are probably safe. Ironically, two of the most hazardous, St. Louis No. 1 and Lafayette No. 1, are often so full of tour groups that you could actually go there without one and be fairly safe. On the other hand, a good tour is fun and informative, so why not take the precaution?

If you're going to make a day of the cemeteries, you should think about renting a car for the day. You won't be driving through horrendous downtown traffic, you can visit tombs at your own pace, and you'll feel safer.

THREE CEMETERIES YOU SHOULD SEE WITH A TOUR

St. Louis No. 1. Basin St. between Conti and St. Louis sts.

The oldest extant cemetery (1789), and the most iconic. Here lie Marie Laveau, Bernard Marigny, and assorted other New Orleans characters. Louis the vampire from Anne Rice's *Vampire Chronicles* even has his (empty) tomb here. The acid-dropping scene from *Easy Rider* was shot here.

St. Louis No. 2. North Claiborne Ave. between Iberville and St. Louis sts.

Established in 1789, the city's next-oldest cemetery, unfortunately, is in such a terrible neighborhood (next to the so-called Storyville Projects) that regular cemetery tours don't usually bother with it. If there is a tour running when you are in town, go—it's worth it. Marie Laveau II, some Storyville characters, and others lie within its 3 blocks.

Note: As of this writing, there is no regular tour of St. Louis No. 2, which is absolutely unsafe. Do not go there, even in a large group, without an official tour.

Lafayette No. 1. 1427 Sixth St.

Right across the street from Commander's Palace restaurant, this is the lush uptown cemetery. Once in horrible condition, it's been beautifully restored. Anne Rice's Mayfair witches have their family tomb here.

SOME CEMETERIES YOU COULD SEE ON YOUR OWN

But if you do, please exercise caution. Take a cab (albeit expensive) to and from, or consider renting a car for the day. Most of these cemeteries (such as St. Louis 3 and Metairie) have offices that can sometimes provide maps; if they run out, they will give you directions to any grave location you like. All have sort of regular hours—figure 9am to 4pm is a safe bet.

St. Louis No. 3. 3421 Esplanade Ave.

Conveniently located next to the Fair Grounds racetrack (home of the Jazz Fest), St. Louis No. 3 was built on top of a former graveyard for lepers. Storyville photographer E. J. Belloq lies here. The Esplanade Avenue bus will take you there.

Metairie Cemetery. 5100 Pontchartrain Blvd. ☎ **504/486-6331.** By car, take Esplanade north to City Park Ave., turn left until it becomes Metairie Ave.

Don't be fooled by the slightly more modern look—some of the most amazing tombs in New Orleans are here. Not to be missed is the pyramid-and-Sphinx Brunswig mausoleum and the "ruined castle" Egan family tomb, not to mention the former resting place of Storyville madam Josie Arlington.

Cypress Grove and Greenwood Cemeteries. 120 City Park Ave. and 5242 Canal Blvd. By car, take Esplanade north to City Park Ave., turn left until it becomes Metairie Ave.

Located across the street from each other, both were founded in the mid-1800s by the Firemen's Charitable and Benevolent Association. Each has some highly original tombs; keep your eyes open for the ones made entirely of iron. These two cemeteries are an easy bus ride up Canal from the Quarter.

HERE'S THE CHURCH & HERE'S THE STEEPLE . . .

Church and religion are not likely to be the first things that jump to mind in a city known for its debauchery. But New Orleans remains a very Catholic city. Don't forget that Mardi Gras is a pre-Lenten celebration. In fact, religion of one form or another directed much of the city's early history and molded its culture in countless ways.

St. Alphonsus Church. 2045 Constance St., at St. Andrews. ☎ **504/522-6748.**

The Irish built St. Alphonsus Church in 1855, because they refused to worship with their German-speaking neighbors. The gallery and columns may vaguely remind you of the St. Louis Cathedral in the French Quarter, though we find it more spooky and atmospheric. That's probably why portions of Anne Rice's "The Witching Hour" take place here. The church no longer holds Mass. Ironically, when St. Mary's was restored, St. Alphonsus was closed and the congregation moved across the street. Hopes for similar restoration here are high. Currently, the church operates an Arts and Cultural Center, which includes an Irish Art museum. You can tour in the interior and the museum 2 days a week, Thursday and Saturday, from 10am to 2pm, with a self-guided audiotape (live tour guides must be arranged in advance.) For information, call the Friends of St. Alphonsus at ☎ **504/522-7420** or 504/482-0008.

St. Mary's Assumption. 2030 Assumption (at Josephine). ☎ **504/522-6748.**

Built in 1860 by the German Catholics, this is a more baroque and grand church than its Irish neighbor across the street, complete with dozens of life-size saints statues, and the beneficiary of a major restoration project. The two churches make an interesting contrast to each other. The hero of the yellow fever epidemic of 1867, Fr. Francis Xavier Seelos, is buried in the church. Credited with the working of many miracles, he will be beatified in 2000—and to say this is a big deal is to make an understatement. if you visit the church, you're likely to see letters of petition on his tomb. Still more "Witching Hour" action takes place here, including Rowan and Michael's wedding. The church is only open during Mass; call the office for times.

St. Patrick's Church. 724 Camp St., at Girod. ☎ **504/525-4413.**

The original St. Patrick's was a tiny wooden building founded to serve the spiritual needs of Irish Catholics. The present building, begun in 1838, was constructed around the old one, which was then dismantled. The distinguished architect James

Gallier Sr., designed much of the interior, including the altar. It opened in 1840, proudly proclaiming itself as the "American" Catholics' answer to the St. Louis Cathedral in the French Quarter (where, according to the Americans, God spoke only in French).

St. Roch and the Campo Santo. 1725 St. Roch Ave., at N. Derbigny. ☎ **504/945-5961.**

St. Roch is the patron saint of plague victims; a local priest prayed to him to keep his flock safe during an epidemic in 1867. When everyone came through all right, the priest made good on his promise to build St. Roch a chapel. The Gothic result is fine enough, but what is best is the small room just off the altar, where successful supplicants to St. Roch leave gifts, usually in the form of plaster anatomical parts or medical supplies, to represent what the saint healed for them. The resulting collection of bizarre artifacts (everything from eyeballs and crutches to organs and false limbs) is either deeply moving or the greatest creepy spontaneous folk art installation you've ever seen. The chapel is not always open, so call first.

Church of St. John the Baptist. 1139 Dryades St., at US90. ☎ **504/525-1726.**

You may have noticed a large gilded dome prominently set in the New Orleans skyline (especially as you drive on the elevated expressway). That's the Church of St. John the Baptist, built by the Irish in 1871. Its most noteworthy features (besides the exceptional exterior brickwork) are the beautiful stained-glass windows crafted by artists in Munich, and the Stations of the Cross and sacristy murals painted during and after World War II by Belgian artist Dom Gregory Dewit.

Our Lady of Guadeloupe Chapel—International Shrine of St. Jude. 411 N. Rampart St., at Conti. ☎ **504/525-1551.**

This is known as the "funeral chapel." It was erected (in 1826) conveniently near St. Louis Cemetery No. 1, specifically for funeral services, so as not to spread disease through the Quarter. We like it for three reasons: the catacomb-like devotional chapel, with plaques thanking the Virgin Mary for favors granted; the gift shop full of religious medals, including a number of obscure saints; and the statue of St. Expedite. He got his name, according to legend, when his crate arrived with no identification other than the word *expedite* stamped on the outside. Now he's the saint you pray to when you want things in a hurry. We are not making this up. Expedite has his cults in France and Spain, and is also popular among the voodoo folks. He's just inside the door on the right—go say hi.

BUILDINGS WITH A HISTORY (& ONE WITH BULK)

Degas House. 2306 Esplanade Ave. ☎ **504/821-5009.** Admission and self-guided tour, free; guided tours, $5 donation requested. Daily 9am–6pm.

Legendary French impressionist Edgar Degas felt very tender toward New Orleans; his mother and grandmother were born here and he spent several months in 1872–73 visiting his brother at this house. It was a trip that resulted in a number of paintings, and this is the only residence or studio associated with Degas anywhere in the world that is open to the public. One of his paintings showed the garden of the house behind his brother's. His brother liked that view, too; he later ran off with the wife of the Judge who lived there. His wife and children later took back her maiden name, Musson. The Musson home, as it is formally known, was erected in 1854 and has since been sliced in two and redone in an Italianite manner. Currently, only the building on the right is open to the public (including a very nice B&B set up), but the owner is busy restoring the building on the left, with plans to open it up as well, and even grander plans to one day reunite the two.

Pitot House. 1440 Moss St., near Esplanade. ☎ **504/482-0312.** Fax 504/482-0312. Admission $5 adults, $4 seniors and students, $2 children under 12. Parties of 10 or more $3 each. Wed–Sat 10am–3pm. Last tour begins at 2pm.

The Pitot House is a typical West Indies–style plantation home, restored and furnished with early 19th-century Louisiana and American antiques. Dating from 1799, it originally stood where the nearby modern Catholic school is. In 1810 it became the home of James Pitot, the first mayor of incorporated New Orleans (he served 1804–05). It has wide galleries on the sides and large columns supporting the second floor.

Jackson Barracks. 6400 St. Claude Ave. ☎ **504/271-6262,** ext. 242. Free admission. Museum hours Mon–Fri 7:30am–4pm.

On an extension of Rampart Street downriver from the French Quarter is this series of fine old brick buildings with white columns. They were built in 1834–35 for troops who were stationed at the river forts. Some say Andrew Jackson, who never quite trusted New Orleans Creoles, planned the barracks to be as secure against attack from the city as from outside forces. The barracks now serve as headquarters for the Louisiana National Guard, and there's an extensive military museum in the old powder magazine and in a new annex, which has a large collection of military items from every American war. Call before you go to confirm that the barracks and museum are open.

Superdome. 1500 block of Poydras St., near Rampart. ☎ **504/587-3808** for tour information. Admission $6 adults, $5 seniors, $4 children 5–10, free for children under 5. Guided tours daily 10am–4pm on the hour (except during events). Tours subject to change and cancellation.

Completed in 1975 (at a cost of around $180 million) the Superdome is a landmark civic structure. It's a 27-story windowless building with a seating capacity of 76,000 and a computerized climate-control system that uses more than 9,000 tons of equipment. It's one of the largest buildings in the world in diameter (680 feet), and its grounds cover some 13 acres. Inside, no posts obstruct the spectator's view of sporting events, be they football, baseball, or basketball, while movable partitions and seats allow the building to be configured for almost any event. Most people think of the Superdome as a sports center only (the Super Bowl will be held there again in 2002), but this flying saucer of a building plays host to conventions (most notably the 1988 Republican Convention), trade shows, the Krewe of Endymion's annual massive Mardi Gras ball, and large theatrical and musical productions as well.

MUSEUMS & GALLERIES

Confederate Memorial Museum. 929 Camp St., at St. Joseph's. ☎ **504/523-4522.** Fax 504/523-8595. Admission $5 adults, $4 students and seniors, $2 children under 12. Mon–Sat 10am–4pm.

Not far from the French Quarter, the Confederate Museum was established in 1891 (giving it a claim to being the oldest surviving museum in Louisiana) and currently houses the second-largest collection of Confederate memorabilia in the country. It opened so soon after the end of the war that many of the donated items are in excellent condition. Among these are 125 battle flags, 50 Confederate uniforms, guns, swords, photographs, and oil paintings. You'll see personal effects of Confederate Gen. P. G. T. Beauregard and Confederate Pres. Jefferson Davis (including his evening clothes), part of Robert E. Lee's silver camp service, and many portraits of Confederate military and civilian personalities. The museum also has a series of detailed pictures tracing Louisiana's history from secession through Reconstruction.

❂ **Contemporary Arts Center.** 900 Camp St., at St. Joseph's. ☎ **504/523-1216.** Admission $5 adults, $3 seniors and students, free for members; free to all Thurs. Tickets $3–$25. Mon–Sat 10am–5pm, Sun 11am–5pm.

Redesigned in the early '90s to much critical applause, the Contemporary Arts Center is a main anchor of New Orleans' young arts district (once the city's old warehouse district, now home to a handful of leading local galleries). In fact, having recently celebrated its 20th anniversary, the CAC is a veritable old-timer in the area. Over the past 2 decades, the center has consistently exhibited influential and groundbreaking work by regional, national, and international artists in various mediums. The CAC staggers its shows, so there should always be something worth seeing hanging on the walls; it also presents theater, performance art, dance, and music concerts. Individual exhibitions hang for 6 to 8 weeks, and performances are weekly.

❂ **New Orleans Museum of Art.** 1 Collins Diboll Circle, at City Park and Esplanade. ☎ **504/488-2631.** Admission $6 adults, $5 seniors (over 64), $3 children 3–17; free to Louisiana residents Thurs 10am–noon. Tues–Sun 10am–5pm. Closed most major holidays.

Often called NOMA, this museum is located in an idyllic section of City Park. A $23 million expansion in 1994 tripled its size, and allowed NOMA to attract a variety of international and touring exhibits. Recent spectacles have included "Monet: Late Paintings of Giverny" and "Fabergé in America." The front portion of the museum is the original large, imposing neoclassical building ("sufficiently modified to give a subtropical appearance," said the architect, Samuel Marx); the rear portion is a striking contrast of curves and contemporary styles. The museum opened in 1911 after a gift to the City Park Commission from Isaac Delgado, a sugar broker and Jamaican immigrant. Today, it houses a 40,000-piece collection: pre-Columbian and Native American ethnographic art; 16th- through 20th-century European paintings, drawings, sculptures, and prints; early American art; Asian art; and one of the six largest decorative glass collections in the United States. Be sure to pick up a guide pamphlet from the information desk at the entrance.

The changing exhibits frequently have regional resonance, such as the one devoted to religious art and objects collected from local churches, or the one—how's this for a complete change of pace—that focused on "dirty pictures" throughout the modern era! Make sure you leave time to visit any temporary exhibits.

Westgate. 5219 Magazine St., at the corner of Belcastle and Magazine. ☎ **504/899-3077.** Free admission; donations accepted. Tues–Sat noon–5pm.

Death buffs and other morbid types will be thrilled to visit Westgate (also known as "the House of Death"), while others will come down with a serious case of the creeps. The hard-to-miss purple-and-black building is a gallery of "necromantic art" run by Leilah Wendell and Daniel Kemp, who inaugurated this project in 1979. Both are authors of metaphysical books about the personification of death, and the gallery is dedicated to Azrael, the embodiment of "what Western cultures refer to as the Angel of Death," says Wendell. The art, much of it by Wendell, uses plenty of death imagery, with a heavy emphasis on its romance. The results are graphic and powerful. Some will find this deeply disturbing, but it certainly is one of the most unusual galleries in town, and worth a trip for the open-minded and curious. The owners are actually far more friendly and helpful than you might think. They also offer occasional performances and readings—call for a schedule.

A BEER RUN TO ABITA SPRINGS

Abita Springs is on the opposite side of Lake Pontchartrain from New Orleans, deep in the Piney Woods section of the state, in what also used to be called the Ozone Belt.

The area was developed in 1810 on lands that had been significant to Native American tribes; many tribe members stayed in the region long after it was colonized. The Ozone Belt got its name because it is pocketed with artesian springs of ozone water, which for years have been considered to have restorative or healing power. Because of the water, Abita Springs became a health resort for New Orleanians during the 19th century. Today, the small town attracts visitors who want to hike through the Piney Woods along the Tammany Trace, those who are on their way to the Honey Island Swamp, and those who are looking to take a deep draught of its famous liquid—and we don't mean the water. We're referring to the . . .

Abita Brewing Company. 21084 Hwy. 36, Covington. ☎ **800/737-2311** or 504/ 893-3143. Free tours Sat 1pm and 2:30pm, Sun 1pm. Take I-10 west from New Orleans to the Causeway, go east on I-12 toward Slidell (3 miles), take the Abita Springs exit (Exit 65), and drive north along Hwy. 59 (4 miles).

The same spring waters that invigorated elite society in the 19th century have helped make Abita Beer one of the most successful regional microbrew brands in the country. The first Abita brew was served in 1986 in a small pub in Mandeville, Louisiana. Ten years later, Abita's standard beers (Amber, Golden, Turbodog, and Purple Haze) and seasonal brews (Bock, Red Ale, Wheat, Fallfest, and XXXMAS Ale) are served in bars and sold in convenience stores throughout Louisiana and across the South. All of the brews were designed to complement the region's cuisine, and they really do. In 1994, the brewery moved down the road and its original building was converted into the Abita Brewpub, a restaurant and Abita product central store; you can find six-packs, half-gallon containers, kegs, and souvenirs. Despite the much larger scale of the overall brewing operation, the beer is still made in small batches. Tours of the brewery are free but offered only on weekends. This is a great excuse to drive the Causeway across Lake Pontchartrain.

FLOATING ACROSS THE RIVER TO ALGIERS POINT

Algiers, annexed by New Orleans in 1870, stretches along the western side of the Mississippi River and is easily accessible via the free ferry that runs from the base of Canal Street. *Take note:* The ferry is one of New Orleans' best-kept secrets. It's a great way to get out onto the river and see the skyline. With such easy access (a ferry leaves every 15 to 20 minutes), who knows why the Point hasn't been better assimilated into the larger city, but it hasn't. Though it's only about 400 meters (and 10 minutes) across the river from downtown and the French Quarter, it still has the feel of an undisturbed turn-of-the-century suburb. Strolling around here is a delightfully low-key way to spend an hour or two.

See chapter 9 for a walking tour that shows off the character of this neighborhood. The last ferry returns at around 11:15pm, but be sure to check the schedule before you set out, just in case. While you're over there, you might want to stop in at . . .

✪ **Blaine Kern's Mardi Gras World.** 223 Newton St., Algiers Point. ☎.**800/362-8213** or 504/361-7821. Fax 504/361-3164. www.mardigrasworld.com. Admission $9.50 adults, $6.50 seniors (over 62), $4 children 3–12. Daily 9:30am–4:30pm. Closed Mardi Gras, Easter, Thanksgiving, Dec 25. Cross the river on the Canal St. Ferry and take the free shuttle from the dock (it meets every ferry).

Few cities can boast a thriving float-making industry. New Orleans can, and no float-maker thrives more than Blaine Kern, who makes more than three-quarters of the floats used by the various krewes every Carnival season. Blaine Kern's Mardi Gras World offers tours of its collection of float sculptures and of its studios, where you can see floats being made year-round. Visitors see sculptors at work, doing everything from making small "sketches" of the figures to creating and painting the enormous sculptures that adorn Mardi Gras floats each year. You can try on dozens of different costumes, wear a giant Marilyn Monroe mask, and even climb on some of the floats from last year's parades and pretend to toss beads, cups, and other throws into the crowd. The real attractions here, though, are the huge sculptures of cartoon and comic book characters, mythological figures, and imaginary creatures.

3 Parks & Gardens

PARKS

✪ **Audubon Park.** 6500 Magazine St., between Broadway and Exposition. ☎ **504/ 581-4629.**

Across from Loyola and Tulane universities, Audubon Park and the adjacent Audubon Zoo sprawl over 340 acres, extending from St. Charles Avenue all the way to the Mississippi River. This tract once belonged to city founder Jean-Baptiste Le Moyne, and later was part of the Etienne de Boré plantation, where sugar was granulated for the first time in 1794. The city purchased it in 1871 and used much of the land for the World's Industrial and Cotton Centennial Exposition in 1884–85. Despite having the (then) largest building in the world as its main exhibition hall (33 acres under one roof), the exposition was such a financial disaster that everything except the Horticultural Hall had to be sold off—and that hall fell victim to a hurricane a little later. After that, serious work to make this into a park began.

Although John James Audubon, the country's best-known ornithologist, lived only briefly in New Orleans (in a cottage on Dauphine Street in the French Quarter), the city has honored him by naming both the park and the zoo after him. There is no historical evidence to suggest that Audubon was much of a golfer; nevertheless, a golf course now fills the middle of the park that bears his name.

The huge trees with black bark are live oaks; some go back to plantation days, and more than 200 additional ones were recently planted here. They're evergreens and shed only once a year, in early spring. With the exception of the trees, it's not the most visually interesting of parks—it's just pretty, and a nice place to be. Visitors can enjoy a picnic in the shade of the trees, feed ducks in a lagoon, and pretend they're Thoreau. Or they can look with envy at the lovely old houses whose backyards literally bumps up against the park. The park includes the Odgen Entrance Pavilion and Garden (at St. Charles Avenue), and a smattering of gazebos, shelters, fountains, and statuary.

Without question, the most utilized feature of the park is the 1¾-mile paved traffic-free road that loops around the lagoon and golf course. It was estimated a few years ago that between 2,000 and 3,000 joggers use the track each day, joined by cyclists, walkers, and in-line skaters. Along the track are 18 exercise stations; tennis courts and horseback riding facilities can be found elsewhere in the park. Check out the pavilion on the riverbank for one of the most pleasant views of the Mississippi you'll find. The Audubon Zoo is toward the back of the park, across Magazine Street.

Horseback rides through the park strike us as an appropriate way to see the grounds. Rides are available (organized, with a guide) from **Cascade Stables,** 700 East Drive (directly next to the zoo; ☎ **504/891-2246**) daily (except major holidays) from 9am to 4pm and cost $20 for 45 minutes. Call in advance.

Note: The park opens daily at 6am. Even though it officially closes at 10pm, it's not advisable to be there any time after dark.

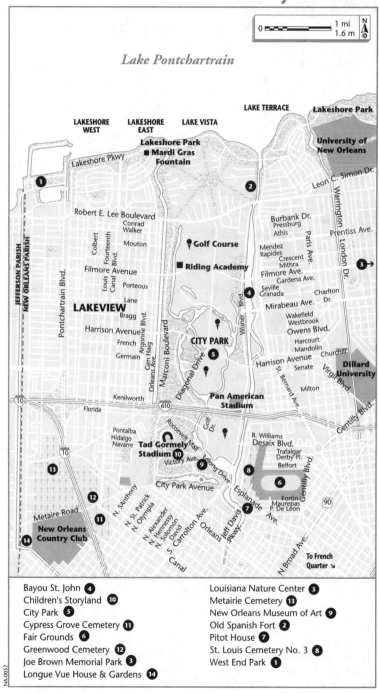

Lake Pontchartrain

LAKE TERRACE
Lakeshore Park

LAKESHORE WEST
LAKESHORE EAST
LAKE VISTA

University of New Orleans

Lakeshore Park
Mardi Gras Fountain

Lakeshore Pkwy

Leon C. Simon Dr.

Robert E. Lee Boulevard

Conrad Walker

Mouton

Burbank Dr.
Pressburg
Athis

Warrington London Dr.

Prentiss Ave.

Colbert
Fourteenth Blvd.

Louis Canal
Filmore Avenue
Porteous
Lane

Golf Course

Riding Academy

Mendez
Rapides
Crescent
Mithra
Filmore Ave.
Gardena Ave.
Seville
Granada

Paris Ave.

Charlton Dr.

LAKEVIEW

Bragg

Harrison Avenue

French
Germain

Gen Haig
Orleans Ave.
Argonne Blvd.

Pontchartrain Blvd.

JEFFERSON PARISH
NEW ORLEANS PARISH

Marconi Boulevard

Diagonal Drive

CITY PARK

Wisner Blvd.

Mirabeau Ave.
Wakefield
Westbrook
Owens Blvd.
Harcourt
Mandolin
Harrison Avenue
Senate

Churchill

Dillard University

St. Bernard Ave.

Virgil Blvd.

Milton

Kenilworth

Florida

Pan American Stadium

Golf Dr.

Gentilly Blvd.

Pontalba
Hidalgo
Navarre

Roosevelt Mall

Tad Gormely Stadium

Victory Ave.

Long Drive

R. Williams
Desaix Blvd.
Trafalgar
Derby Pl.
Belfort

City Park Avenue

N. SAnthony
N. St. Patrick
N. Olympia
N. Alexander
N. Hennessy
N. Solomon
N. David

Esplanade Ave.

Fortin
Maurepas
P. De Leon

Gentilly Blvd.

Metaire Road

New Orleans Country Club

Carrollton Ave.

Jeff Davis Pkwy

Orleans

S. Canal

To French Quarter ↘

N. Broad Ave.

NA-0057

City Park's Dueling Oaks

Dueling is a lost art, but one that nobody seems to miss—at least not enough to risk their necks reviving it. In past eras, however, one's honor was to be defended from even the suggestion of a slight. In New Orleans, disputes often ended with a heated challenge to meet "under the oaks at sunrise"—in City Park, under what came to be called the Dueling Oaks. (St. Louis Cathedral was another popular spot for these clashes.)

The practice persisted into the 1800s (10 duels were fought on just one Sunday morning in 1837), but duels changed in character after Americans arrived on the scene. Creoles observed a very formal and strict dueling etiquette, using the meetings to demonstrate their expertise with rapiers, broadswords, or pistols (fists were never used among gentlemen), and only seldom was either party actually killed. With the Americans, however, came a whole new concept—duels became a fight to the death, using such "rude" weapons as rifles, shotguns, clubs, and even axes. Dueling had always been forbidden by both church and law, but after the Civil War there was stricter enforcement, and the official line was that dueling died out. Legends of 20th-century duels among the gentry persist, however.

The oaks in City Park outlasted the sport, and during the bleak Reconstruction era, one of them became known as the "Suicide Oak" because of its popularity as a setting for that action. Another, McDonogh Oak, is believed to be more than 600 years old, and has a 142-foot branch spread.

✪ **City Park.** 1 Palm Dr. ☎ **504/482-4888.**

Once part of the Louis Allard plantation, City Park has been here a long time and has seen it all—including that favorite pastime among 18th-century New Orleans gentry: dueling (see the box above).

At the entrance you'll see a statue of Gen. P. G. T. Beauregard, whose order to fire on Fort Sumter opened the Civil War and whom New Orleanians fondly call "the Great Creole." The extensive, beautifully landscaped grounds hold botanical gardens and a conservatory, four golf courses, picnic areas, a restaurant, lagoons for boating and fishing, tennis courts, horses for hire and lovely trails to ride them on, a band-stand, two miniature trains, and Children's Storyland, an amusement area with a carousel ride for children (see "Especially for Kids," below). At Christmastime, the mighty oaks, already dripping with Spanish moss, are strung with lights—quite a magical sight—and during Halloween, there is a fabulous haunted house. You'll also find the New Orleans Museum of Art at Collins Diboll Circle, on Lelong Avenue, in a building that is itself a work of art (see "Museums & Galleries," above). The park's main office is in the casino building. The park is open daily 6am to 7pm.

Chalmette National Historical Park. 8606 W. St. Bernard Hwy. ☎ **504/589-4430.** Free admission. Daily 8:30am–4:30pm.

On the grounds of what is now Chalmette National Historical Park, the bloody Battle of New Orleans was waged on January 14, 1815. Ironically, the battle should never have been fought, because a treaty signed 2 weeks before in Ghent, Belgium, had ended the War of 1812. But word had not yet reached Congress, the commander of the British forces, or Andrew Jackson, who stood with American forces to defend New Orleans and the mouth of the Mississippi River. The battle did, however, succeed in uniting Americans and Creoles in New Orleans and in making Jackson a hero in this city.

To reach the park, take St. Claude Avenue southeast from the French Quarter until it becomes St. Bernard Highway, approximately 7 miles. You can visit the battleground and see markers that allow you to follow the course of the battle. The Beauregard plantation house on the grounds contains exhibits on the battle, and the Visitor Center presents a film and other exhibits. There's a National Cemetery in the park, established in 1864. It holds only two American veterans from the Battle of New Orleans, but some 14,000 Union soldiers who fell in the Civil War are buried here. For a terrific view of the Mississippi River, climb the levee in back of the Beauregard House.

GARDENS

Longue Vue House & Gardens. 7 Bamboo Rd., near Metairie. ☎ **504/488-5488.** Admission $7 adults, $6 seniors, $3 children and students. Mon–Sat 10am–4:30pm, Sun 1–5pm. Closed Jan 1, Mardi Gras, July 4, Labor Day, Thanksgiving, Dec 25.

The Longue Vue mansion is a unique expression of Greek Revival architecture, set on an 8-acre estate. It was constructed from 1939 to 1942 for Edgar Stern, who had interests in cotton, minerals, timber, and real estate, and was also a noted philanthropist and a founder (with his son) of local television station WDSU-TV. His wife, born Edith Rosenwald, was the daughter of Julius Rosenwald, the Sears, Roebuck magnate. Styled in the manner of an English country house, their mansion was designed to foster a close rapport between indoors and outdoors, with vistas of formal terraces and pastoral woods. Some parts of the enchanting gardens were inspired by those of Generalife, the former summer house of the sultans in Granada, Spain. Besides the colorful flowering plants, there are formal boxwood parterres, fountains, and a colonnaded loggia. Highlights are the Canal Garden, the Walled Garden, the Wild Garden (which features native irises), and the Spanish Court, with its pebbled walkways, fountains, and changing horticultural displays. Longue Vue House and Gardens is listed on the National Register of Historic Places and is accredited by the American Association of Museums.

Louisiana Nature Center (in Joe Brown Memorial Park). Nature Center Dr., New Orleans East. ☎ **504/246-5672** or 504/246-9381. www.audoboninstitute.org. Admission $4.75 adults, $3.75 seniors, $2.50 children. Tues–Fri 9am–5pm, Sat 10am–5pm, Sun noon–5pm. Take I-10 to Exit 244; pass Plaza Shopping Center and turn left onto Nature Center Dr.

Part of the Audubon Institute, Joe Brown Park is an 86-acre tract of Louisiana forest where guided walks are given daily (except Monday). A nature film is shown on weekdays, and weekends offer additional activities (canoeing, bird watching, arts and crafts workshops, and others). Three miles of trails are available for public use. There is a wheelchair-accessible raised wooden walkway for shorter excursions. The Louisiana Nature Center offers changing exhibits and hands-on activities. It has a planetarium where there are shows on Saturday and Sunday, and on Friday and Saturday nights there are laser rock shows. Call ☎ 504/246-STAR for the current planetarium schedule.

A DAY AT THE ZOO

✪ **Audubon Zoo.** 6500 Magazine St. ☎ **504/581-4629.** Admission $8.75 adults, $4.75 seniors (over 64) and $4.50 children 2–12. Daily 9:30am–5pm; 9:30am–6pm weekends in the summer. Last ticket sold 1 hour before closing. Closed holidays.

It's been more than 20 years since the Audubon Zoo underwent a total renovation that turned it from one of the worst zoos in the country into one of the best. The achievement is still worth noting, and the result is a place of justifiable civic pride that delights even nonzoo buffs. It is also a terrific destination for visitors with children.

Here, in a setting of subtropical plants, waterfalls, and lagoons, some 1,800 animals (including rare and endangered species) live in natural habitats rather than cages. Don't miss the replica of a Louisiana swamp or the new "Butterflies in Flight" exhibit, where more than 1,000 butterflies live among lush, colorful vegetation. A memorable way to visit the zoo is to arrive on the sternwheeler *John James Audubon* (see "Organized Tours," later in this chapter) and depart on the St. Charles Avenue streetcar. You can reach the streetcar by walking through Audubon Park or by taking the free shuttle bus. During your visit to the zoo, look for the bronze statue of naturalist John James Audubon, standing in a grove of trees with a notebook and pencil in hand. Also look for a funny-looking mound near the river—it was constructed so that the children of this flatland city could see what a hill looked like.

4 Voodoo

Voodoo's mystical presence is one of the most common motifs in New Orleans. The problem is, that presence is mostly reduced to a tourist gimmick. Every gift shop seems to have voodoo dolls for sale, there is a Voodoo Museum (see "Museums," above), and Marie Laveau, the famous voodoo queen, comes off as the town's patron saint. But lost among the kitsch is a very real religion, with a serious past and considerable cultural importance.

Voodoo's roots can be traced in part back to the African **Yoruba** religion, which incorporates the worship of several different spiritual forces, including a supreme being, deities and the spirits of ancestors. When people were kidnapped, enslaved, and brought to Brazil—and, ultimately, Haiti—beginning in the 1500s, they brought their religion with them.

By the 1700s, 30,000 slaves a year were brought to Haiti. Voodoo began to emerge at this time, as different African religions met and melded. Slaves were forced to convert to Catholicism, but found it easy to practice both religions. Voodoo gods were given saints' names, and voodoo worship more or less continued, appropriating certain Catholic rituals and beliefs. The word "voodoo" comes from an African word meaning "god" or "spirit." Rituals involved participants dancing in a frenzy to increasingly wild drum beats, and eventually falling into a trance-like state, during which a **loa** (a spirit and/or lower level deity intermediary between humans and gods) would take possession of them.

Voodoo didn't immediately take root in New Orleans, thanks to repressive slaveholders and an edict banning its practice. But the edict was repealed after the Louisiana Purchase, in 1803, and in 1804, when slaves in Haiti revolted and overthrew the government, free blacks came to New Orleans in great numbers, as did fleeing plantation owners with their own slaves, all bringing a fresh infusion of voodoo.

Napoleonic Law forced slave owners to give their slaves Sundays off and to provide them with a gathering place. **Congo Square,** on Rampart Street, part of what is now Armstrong Park, became the place for slaves to gather for voodoo or drumming rituals. Voodoo then was a way for slaves to have their own community and a certain amount of freedom. The religion emphasized knowledge of family and gave power to ancestors. Further, women were usually the powerful forces in voodoo—priestesses ran matters more often than priests—and this appealed to women in a time when women simply didn't have that kind of authority and power.

These gatherings naturally attracted white lookie-loos, as did the rituals held (often by free people of color) along St. John's Bayou. The local papers of the 1800s are full of lurid accounts of voodoo "orgies," and of whites being possessed by spirits,

That Voodoo That You Do

Voodoo is a nature-based traditional African religion. It is the religion that the slaves brought here when they were taken from Africa. The word literally means "spirit deity and God, the creator of the universe." The word itself means God, but it was taken out of context. African people were not brought to the New World to have themselves or their culture glorified. Anything that was not white and Protestant or Catholic was looked upon as demonic. And it was not. All people, we are all worshipping God in our own way. And it is every culture's prerogative to do so. People confuse negative magic with voodoo. It is not. That is not dealing with the religion of voodoo, but the intent to harm. That is hoodoo. And it is not voodoo.

I was drawn to it by my family. My mother used to do candles, and she was very psychic and she would tell me about spirits and ghosts, and how to protect myself from spirits. And I grew up in a neighborhood where people would hoodoo each other. Being born on Halloween, I've always been drawn to spiritual things. Actively, I started becoming involved in traditional African religions 25 years ago, but it was always part of my culture. I had to go through levels of study and initiation, with elders here and in Haiti. My Yoruba/Santeria initiation was in Atlanta. Additionally, I am a priestess of Oya, the goddess of hurricanes, the queen of the spirit world and the queen of the marketplace. I did her initiation about 10 years ago.

Voodoo is a viable religion because people feel that by using the rituals and the prayers and all of the implements, they can do things, and have power and control over their own lives. People lack something in their lives and there is a void that traditional religions do not seem to fill, at least, the way they practice it. Voodoo a lot of times fills that void, helps a person get more in touch with their spiritual self.

The voodoo dolls are greatly overrated. They are used to help you focus, and you can use them in healing. I do not sell pins with my dolls. In Haiti, I've seen the dolls and they are never with pins. It's Hollywood to think that. People will use them that way, but it's black magic. The focal point can be positive or negative but negative work will come back to you.

You can definitely be another religion along with voodoo, any religion. I have a lot of Jewish people who work with me, and also go to synagogue. I am Catholic, I go to church, I take Communion, I sing in the choir for midnight Mass. Everyone in my church knows I'm very Catholic but also I'm a voodoo and Yoruba priestess.

by Ava Kay Jones

Ava Kay Jones has a law degree from Loyal University, and is a practicing Voodoo and Yoruba priestess. Additionally, she also heads the Voodoo Macumba dance troupe and her booth at Jazz Fest is annually one of the most popular. She is available for readings, gris-gris bags, and other items of voodoo interest at ☎ **504/484-6499** by appointment only.

otherwise losing control, or being arrested after being caught in a naked pose. Thanks to the white scrutiny, the Congo Square gatherings became more like performance pieces, emphasizing drumming and music, rather than religious rituals. Because of the square's proximity to what became Storyville, legend has it, madams from the houses would come down to the Sunday gatherings and hire some of the performers to entertain at their houses.

It was during the 1800s that the famous voodoo priestesses came to some prominence. Mostly free women of color, they were devout religious practitioners and very good businesswomen, who had a steady clientele of whites secretly coming to them for help in love or money matters. During the 1900s, voodoo largely went back underground.

It is estimated that today as much as 15% of the New Orleans population practices voodoo. The most common public perception of voodoo involves casting spells or sticking pins in voodoo dolls. Most of that is Hollywood nonsense. Voodoo dolls do exist, as do gris-gris bags—little packets of herbs, stones, and other bits and pieces designed to bring luck, love, health, or what have you (*gris* means "gray," to symbolize a magic somewhere between white and black). Other rituals more or less incorporate magic, but most of it is done for good, not for evil. Ask a real practitioner about helping you with the latter, and you will probably get some nasty looks.

Most of the stores and places in New Orleans that advertise voodoo are set up strictly for tourism. This is not to say that some facts can't be found there, or that you shouldn't buy a mass-produced gris-gris bag or voodoo doll as a souvenir. For an introduction to voodoo, check out the New Orleans Historic Voodoo Museum (see "Museums," above). If you want to know about true voodoo, however, you need to seek out real voodoo temples or practitioners, of which there are several in New Orleans. If you want to know still more, check out Robert Tallant's book *Voodoo in New Orleans* (Pelican Pocket). For more about Haitian voodoo, *Voodoo In Haiti* by Alfred Metraux (Shocken Books) takes a scholarly look, and *Mama Lola* by Karen Brown (California Press) describes a personal encounter.

VOODOO TEMPLES

Here are two authentic voodoo temples, attached to two botanicas selling everything you might need for potions and spells. The public is welcome, and the employees are happy to educate the honestly curious, but don't go if you just want to giggle and gawk.

The Island of Salvation Botanica and the **Temple Simbi-sen Jak,** 835 Piety St. (☎ **504/948-9961**), are run by Sallie Glassman, voodoo priestess and author of a deck of voodoo tarot cards. The staff at the well-stocked botanica is very interested in educating the public. If you demonstrate the right enthusiasm, they might show you the temple, or you might be invited to their Saturday night ceremony—but be aware that you will be required to participate. It is not something to observe as a performance. The botanica is open Wednesday to Saturday 10am to 5:30pm.

The **Voodoo Spiritual Temple,** 828 Rampart St. (☎ **504/522-9627**), is the real McCoy—interested tourists are welcome, but please be respectful. Priestess Miriam belonged to the Spiritual Church in Chicago before setting up this spiritual house, which has a store attached. The main room is a temple, full of fascinating, complex altars. There are both personal and open rituals; the curious might try the Thursday night drumming workshops, which sometimes turn into rituals. The staff wants to increase knowledge of voodoo and sweep away myths and ignorance, so the honestly inquisitive are quite welcome. It's open daily 10am to 6pm.

MARIE LAVEAU

Marie Laveau is the most famous New Orleans voodoo queen. Though she was a real woman, her life has been so mythologized that it is nearly impossible to separate fact from fiction. But who really wants to? Certainly we know that she was born a free woman of color in 1794 and married Jacques Paris in 1819. Paris disappeared about 4 years later, and Marie later took up with Christophe Glapion.

Along the way, Marie, a hairdresser by trade, became known for her psychic abilities and powerful gris-gris. It didn't hurt that her day job allowed her into the best houses, where she heard all the good gossip and could apply it to her other clientele. In one famous story, Marie was approached by a young woman about to be forced into a marriage with a much older, wealthy man. She wanted to marry her young lover instead. Marie counseled patience. The marriage went forward, and the happy groom died from a heart attack while dancing with his bride at the reception. After a respectable time, the wealthy widow was free to marry her lover.

Marie wholeheartedly believed in voodoo, and turned it into a good business too. Her home at what is now 1020 St. Ann St. was purportedly a gift from a grateful client. A devout Catholic, Marie continued to attend daily Mass, and was publicly noted for her charity work, including regular visits to inmates awaiting execution.

Her death, in 1881, was noted by *the Times-Picayune,* though voodoo was not mentioned. Her lookalike daughter, Marie II, took over her voodoo work, leading some to believe (mistakenly) that Marie I lived a very long time, looking quite well indeed—which only added to her legend. But Marie II allegedly worked more for the darker side than her mother. Her eventual reward, the story goes, was death by poison. Today, visitors can bring Marie tokens (candles, Mardi Gras beads, change) and ask her favors—she's buried in St. Louis Cemetery No. 1.

5 Anne Rice's New Orleans

Love her or loathe her, Anne Rice is a one-woman cottage industry in New Orleans, and one of the town's biggest boosters. Many tourists come here just because they have read her books—she writes seductive descriptions of her hometown that actually are pretty accurate, minus the vampires, witches, and ghosts, of course. Rice uses many real locales; the Gallier House, for example, was the inspiration for the home of vampires Lestat and Louis. Her own childhood homes and present dwelling turn up in *Violin* and *The Witching Hour.* Even her nonhorror novel *Exit to Eden* sent its protagonists on a romantic trip to New Orleans, exulting in the sensual tropical air and gorging on barbecued shrimp at Pascal Manale.

Anne Rice (née O'Brien) was born on October 4, 1941, in New Orleans to Irish parents. When she was 16, her family moved to Texas, where she met her husband, Stan Rice. They married in 1961 and moved to California a few years later, living for years in the San Francisco area. *Interview with the Vampire* was published in 1976, and in the 1980s the Rices and their son packed up and moved back to New Orleans.

Rice continues to put out about one novel a year, often set at least in part in the city she loves. She always does her first book signing at the **Garden District Book Shop,** and as her fortunes have grown, she has bought a number of significant buildings from her youth. This has earned praise from some, who see the salvation of decaying landmarks, and the ire of others, who see it as the consumption of pieces of local history for someone's private enjoyment.

Rice herself has recently been involved in a war of words with flamboyant restaurant owner Al Copeland (founder of the chain), who bought a long-vacant car dealership and turned it into the "California Creole" restaurant Straya. Copeland's gaudy (to put it charitably) approach to decoration offended Rice, partly because of the restaurant's location on otherwise stately and dignified St. Charles Avenue, and partly because that was where we caught a last glimpse of her most beloved vampire, Lestat. Rumor has it that Rice was also miffed because she wanted to buy the site for her own cafe.

Regardless, the verbiage the combatants have exchanged (Rice has a habit of taking out wordy ads in the newspaper whenever she has a bone to pick) has amused the town. Rice also throws an increasingly elaborate Halloween ball each year; tickets are much sought after.

Between her personal life and her novels (and the overlap therein), there are any number of Anne Rice landmarks around town, including tours of one of her buildings, and, once a week, of her home itself. The faithful could make a day of it; vampire spotting is strictly up to you.

ANNE RICE IN THE FRENCH QUARTER

The romance of the French Quarter seems to attract vampires, who found easy pickin's in its dark corners in the days before electricity.

St. Louis Cemetery No. 1, 400 Basin St. A tomb (empty, of course) with Louis the vampire's name is located here in the "Vampire Chronicle" books, and Louis occasionally goes to sit on it and brood. Rumor has it that Rice has purchased a tomb here for her eventual use. *Note:* Keep your wits about you here, not because of vampires, but because this isn't the safest neighborhood.

Gallier House, 1132 Royal St. This famously preserved museum (see "The French Quarter," above) is said by Rice scholars to be the model for the house on Rue Royal that was home to vampires Lestat and Louis in *Interview with the Vampire.*

The stretch of 700 to 900 Royal St. Quite a few of the exteriors for the *Interview* movie were filmed along this stretch—though the set decorators had to labor long and hard to erase all traces of the 20th century. Try to imagine the streets covered in mud. Then try to imagine how folks who live around here felt about it.

Madame John's Legacy, 632 Dumaine St. In the *Interview* movie, this is the house from which the caskets are being carried as Brad Pitt's voice-over describes Lestat and the little vampire Claudia going out on the town: "An infant prodigy with a lust for killing that matched his own. Together, they finished off whole families."

Café du Monde, 800 Decatur St. Lestat visits this restaurant in *The Tale of the Body Thief,* and Michael and Rowan snack here in *The Witching Hour.* (See listing in chapter 7.)

Jackson Square. It's here that Claudia makes an important decision regarding Lestat's fate in *Interview,* and that Raglan James meets Lestat in *The Tale of the Body Thief.*

Omni Royal Orleans hotel, 621 St. Louis St. Katherine and Julien Mayfair stay here—it's still the St. Louis Hotel—in *The Witching Hour.* (See listing in chapter 6.)

Court of Two Sisters, 613 Royal St. Characters in *The Witching Hour* dine here.

Galatoire's, 209 Bourbon St. Characters from several books, including *The Witching Hour,* dine here as well.

Hotel Monteleone, 214 Royal St. This was Aaron Lightner's house in *The Witching Hour.*

Boyer Antiques and Doll Shop, 241 Chartres St. In the *Interview* movie, this is the shop where Claudia admires a doll and then deals with the patronizing shopkeeper in typical vampire fashion. (See listing in chapter 10.)

Marsoudet-Caruso House, 1519 Esplanade Ave. A few blocks north of the French Quarter at the intersection of Esplanade and Claiborne avenues, this is the house where Louis scents the smell of old death in the *Interview* movie and finds the moldering Lestat shrinking from helicopters in a musty chair.

Jackson Barracks, south of the French Quarter along the Mississippi. This area was used for numerous exteriors in the *Interview* movie, including the scene where Louis and Claudia run for their ship after setting Lestat on fire.

Anne Rice's New Orleans

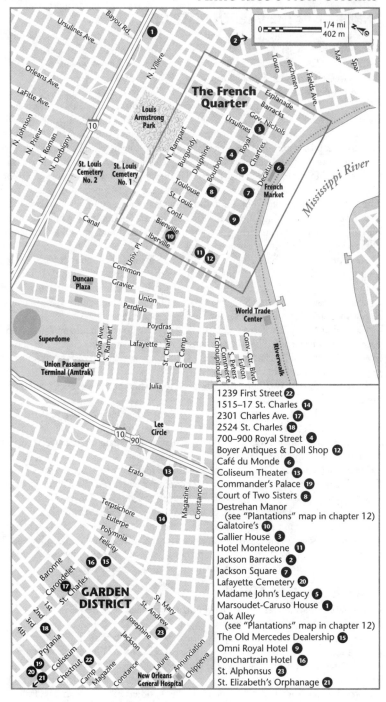

1239 First Street **22**
1515–17 St. Charles **14**
2301 Charles Ave. **17**
2524 St. Charles **18**
700–900 Royal Street **4**
Boyer Antiques & Doll Shop **12**
Café du Monde **6**
Coliseum Theater **13**
Commander's Palace **19**
Court of Two Sisters **8**
Destrehan Manor
  (see "Plantations" map in chapter 12)
Galatoire's **10**
Gallier House **3**
Hotel Monteleone **11**
Jackson Barracks **2**
Jackson Square **7**
Lafayette Cemetery **20**
Madame John's Legacy **5**
Marsoudet-Caruso House **1**
Oak Alley
  (see "Plantations" map in chapter 12)
The Old Mercedes Dealership **15**
Omni Royal Hotel **9**
Ponchartrain Hotel **16**
St. Alphonsus **23**
St. Elizabeth's Orphanage **21**

ANNE RICE IN THE GARDEN DISTRICT

Rice's books increasingly have featured the Garden District and the area around it, perhaps because she and her family live there and own a number of properties.

Coliseum Theater, 1233 Coliseum St. In the film version of *Interview,* this is the theater where Louis sees *Tequila Sunrise.*

The property at 1515–17 St. Charles Ave. Rice recently told the New Orleans City Council that she had purchased this property and that she plans to use it for a commercial venture. She had previously said she was considering opening a theme restaurant called **Cafe Lestat** sometime in the future. Draw your own conclusions.

Pontchartrain Hotel, 2031 St. Charles St. This upscale hotel (see listing in chapter 6) and its restaurant, the Caribbean Room (now closed), appear in *The Witching Hour.*

The old Mercedes dealership (now Al Copeland's Straya restaurant), 2001 St. Charles Ave. As mentioned, this is the center of the Rice-Copeland dispute. The v ampire Lestat disappeared from this world through an image of himself in the window of this building. When Straya opened, Rice criticized Copeland with a full-page ad in the daily newspaper. Lestat then mysteriously returned to this realm and bought an ad of his own, congratulating Copeland for his "stroke of genius."

St. Alphonsus Church, 2029 Constance St. This is a small church with a stunning interior (see "Here's the Church & Here's the Steeple . . . ," above). It was the O'Brien family church—Anne's parents married here, and she was baptized and received communion here. She also took Alphonsus as her confirmation name. Readers will recognize this as a setting in *The Witching Hour.*

1239 First St. This historic property (see "Walking Tour 2" in chapter 9) is Anne Rice's primary residence. The Mayfair house in *The Witching Hour* matches her home in almost every detail, including address. As of this writing, the home is open for a free tour on Mondays at 1pm.

2301 St. Charles Ave. This spacious, two-story white house was Rice's childhood home.

2524 St. Charles Ave. Rice's family moved into this traditional-style raised villa when Anne was 14. It's prominently featured in her novel *Violin.*

Commander's Palace. Rice readers will recognize this restaurant as a favorite of the Mayfair family. (See listing in chapter 7.)

Lafayette Cemetery. This centerpiece of the Garden District is also a frequent setting in Rice's work, especially as a roaming ground for Lestat and Claudia in *Interview* and the graveyard for the Mayfairs in *The Witching Hour.*

St. Elizabeth's Orphanage, 1314 Napoleon Ave. The Rice family bought this impressive building in the early 1990s. It was built in 1865 and served as an orphanage and boarding school until 1989. It houses a chapel, Anne's doll collection, and a gallery of Stan's paintings, and is also a private residence for the family. See "Outside the French Quarter," above, for information about tours of the building.

ANNE RICE OUTTA TOWN

Even vampires have to get out to the country every once in a while. For more information on the plantations, see chapter 12.

Destrehan Manor, La. 48, Destrehan, Louisiana. This plantation, the oldest in the region that's open to the public, was used as a location in the filming of *Interview.*

Oak Alley Plantation, 3645 La. 18, Vacherie, Louisiana. This popular tourist spot was also used as a location for the film version of *Interview.* Some Rice readers think this was the model for Pointe du Lac in the book; others believe it was based on the **Pitot House,** 1440 Moss St. (see "Buildings with a History," above).

6 Especially for Kids

New Orleans is one of those destinations that may be more fun *sans enfants*. Don't get us wrong—there are plenty of unusual things to do during daylight hours that will wear out everyone under 12 or over 40, but any adult confined to his or her hotel room past 9pm has entirely missed the point of vacationing here. Still, we suppose it's in everyone's best interest to introduce the little tykes to the land of big food and big music, so that they'll beg to return when they're old enough to go clubbing with Mom and Dad. In the meantime, you can entertain them with a combination of conventional and unconventional, only-in-New-Orleans activities.

The **French Quarter** in and of itself is fascinating to children over 7. A walkabout with a rest stop for beignets at **Café du Monde** will while away a pleasant morning and give you an opportunity to see the architecture and peek into the shops. Do continue (or begin) their roots music education with a visit to the **Jazz Museum** at the Old U.S. Mint (see "Historic Buildings," above) and later to **Preservation Hall** (see chapter 11) for a show. For those progeny who aren't terrifically self-conscious, a **horse-and-buggy ride** (see "Carriage Tours," below) around the Quarter is very appealing—but save it for later, when they start getting tired and you need a tiny bribe to keep them going.

The **Musée Conti Wax Museum** (see "Museums," above), which features effigies of local historical figures, holds guided tours at 11am and 2pm, is an acceptable pick if the weather turns on you. **Riverwalk Marketplace** (see chapter 10), the glass-enclosed shopping center on the edge of the Quarter on Canal Street, also appeals to kids, with its relaxed atmosphere and food vendors. Outside, the **Canal Street ferry,** which crosses the Mississippi River to Algiers, is free to pedestrians and offers views of the harbor and skyline. Shuttle service is available from the Algiers ferry landing to **Blaine Kern's Mardi Gras World** (see listing earlier in this chapter), where the floats and costumes alone should intrigue even adolescents, whether they'll admit it or not. Returning to Canal Street, you'll find the **Aquarium of the Americas** (see listing earlier in this chapter), with lots of jellyfish and other creatures from the deep and the not-so-deep. The *John James Audubon* riverboat (see "Organized Tours," below) chugs from the aquarium to lovely **Audubon Park** (see "Parks & Gardens," above) and the highly regarded **Audubon Zoological Garden** (see "A Day at the Zoo," above). The park is fronted by magnificent old oak trees

The following destinations are particularly well-suited for younger children.

Children's Storyland. City Park at Victory Ave. ☎ **504/483-9381.** Admission $2 adults and children 2 and up, free for children under 2. Wed–Fri 10am–12:30pm, Sat–Sun 10am–4:30pm. Closed weekdays Jan–Feb and Dec.

The under-8 set will be delighted with this playground (rated one of the 10 best in the country by *Child* magazine), where well-known children's stories and rhymes have inspired the decor. Kids and adults will enjoy the carousel, Ferris wheel, bumper cars, and other rides at the **Carousel Gardens,** also in City Park. It's open weekends only, 11am to 4:30pm. Admission is $1 for anyone over 2; $6 buys unlimited rides. If you happen to arrive in New Orleans during December, be sure to take a carriage ride through City Park, when thousands of lights turn the landscape and trees into fairy-tale scenery.

Louisiana Children's Museum. 420 Julia St., at Tchoupitoulis. ☎ **504/523-1357.** Admission $5. Sept–May Tues–Sat 9:30am–4:30pm, Sun noon–4:30pm; June–Aug Mon 9:30am–4:30pm.

Kenner for Grown-Ups

Going to Kenner so the kids can check out the Toy Train Museum and the Science Center? Planning to be bored out of your mind? Don't worry; among the kids' attractions there are a few places that'll appeal to adults as well.

If you were inspired by the aquarium and zoo in New Orleans, you can get more of the same at the **Louisiana Wildlife and Fisheries Museum,** 303 Williams Blvd. (☎ **504/468-7232**), where you'll find hundreds of animals as well as an aquarium. Also at the museum is **Cannes Brulee (Burnt Cane) Native American Center of the Gulf South,** where interpreters dressed in period attire (ca. 1750–1850) demonstrate their cultural heritage through folk traditions, rituals, domestic and occupational crafts, and food.

There is yet another Mardi Gras museum here as well. It's the **Mardi Gras Museum of Jefferson Parish,** 421 Williams Blvd. (☎ **504/468-4037**); and if you didn't get a chance to take part in a Mardi Gras celebration, you can simulate the experience here. Catch a throw and sample some of that famous king cake.

Finally, if you're a football fan—or, more precisely, a Saints fan—Rivertown's **Saints Hall of Fame Museum,** 409 Williams Blvd. (☎ **504/468-6617**), is the place to go. The museum exhibits all sorts of Saints memorabilia and shows video clips.

This popular two-story interactive museum is really a playground in disguise that will keep kids occupied for a good couple of hours. Along with changing exhibits, the museum offers an art shop with regularly scheduled projects, a minigrocery store, a chance to be a "star anchor" at a simulated television studio, and lots of activities exploring music, fitness, water, and life itself. If you belong to your local science museum, check your membership card for reciprocal entry privileges.

THE MUSEUMS OF KENNER

Upriver from the heart of the city, Kenner is more than just the place where they keep the airport; it's also home to some interesting attractions. The buildings known as **Rivertown** are right on the Mississippi River, and they house several small museums, all within walking distance of each other and all open Tuesday through Saturday 9am to 5pm and Sunday 1 to 5pm (except the football museum—which, as you'd expect, is closed on Sundays during football season—and the Science Center, which has observatory hours in the evening). Admission to each of the museums is $3 for adults, $2 for seniors and children 12 and under. If you plan to visit all of them, the **multimuseum ticket** will save you a few bucks. The pass, which doesn't include the Children's Castle, is $10 for adults and $5 for seniors and children 12 and under. To get there, take I-10 toward the airport to the Williams Boulevard exit, which is right before the airport.

Here's what you'll find at Rivertown:

The **Louisiana Toy Train Museum,** 519 Williams Blvd. (☎ **504/468-7223**), is a great place to take the kids. It contains six operational layouts of toy trains, as well as interesting photographs, slide shows, and a toy carousel. Behind the museum on Saturday from 10am to 3pm, you can play with remote-control cars for an additional fee.

The kids will also enjoy the planetarium and observatory at the **Freeport McMoRan Daily Living Science Center,** 409 Williams Blvd. (☎ **504/468-7229**). Shows are offered at 2pm Tuesday through Friday, four times on Saturday. The observatory is open Thursday, Friday, and Saturday from 7:30 to 10:30pm for viewing the night sky. In addition, many educational hands-on activities focus on the environment and human health.

Youngsters love the **Children's Castle,** 503 Williams Blvd. (☎ **504/468-7231,** or 504/469-3236 on Saturday), where they can see puppet shows, mimes, and magic, and take part in storytelling on Saturday afternoons.

7 Organized Tours

Though this book should give you plenty of information to help you guide yourself around the city and gain some understanding of it, another option is to hook up with a tour. A guided excursion can offer something a little more in-depth or, if you prefer, specific: Various tours cater to just about every interest, from African American history to vampires and ghosts.

There are some advantages to taking tours—someone else does the planning, it's an easy way to get to outlying areas, if the tour guide is good you should learn a lot in a fairly entertaining way—and so we do strongly suggest taking at least one at some point. But you should be warned about one thing. There has a been a problem with hotel concierges taking kickbacks from some tour companies, steering guests toward those and getting a cut of the artificially inflated price. Obviously, not every concierge is on the take, and some may have honest opinions about the merits of one company over another. The way to avoid this problem is to cut out the middleman; no matter how you learned about it, pay the fee directly to the company, not to your concierge. No reputable firm will insist you pay someone else first.

For information on organized and self-guided tours of the plantation houses outside New Orleans, see chapter 12.

IN THE FRENCH QUARTER

Note: Chapter 9 includes two French Quarter walking tours you can do on your own.

✪ **Historic New Orleans Walking Tours** (☎ 504/947-2120) is the place to go for authenticity. Tour guides are carefully chosen for their combination of knowledge and entertaining manner. They offer a "French Quarter Mystique" walking tour, focusing on Vieux Carre "history in all its outrageous glory, a distinctive gumbo of legend and fact." Now that the National Park Service has stopped doing tours, this is probably the best, straightforward, nonspecialized walking tour of the Quarter. Daily, 10:30am. Leaves from C. C.'s Coffee Shop at 528 Peter St. on Jackson Square, $12 adults/$10 students and seniors. They also offer a Voodoo tour (see "Mystical & Mysterious Tours," later in this section).

The nonprofit volunteer group **Friends of the Cabildo** (☎ 504/523-3939) offers an excellent walking tour. The organization—you guessed it—supports the Cabildo, the building on Chartres Street where the Louisiana Purchase was signed (see "Museums," above). The tour furnishes guides for a 2-hour exploration that provides a good overview of the area. It leaves from in front of the Museum Store, 523 St. Ann St. Your guide will point out and provide background on the exteriors of most of the Quarter's historic buildings and on the interiors of selected Louisiana State Museum buildings. The requested donation is $10 per adult, $8 for seniors (over 65) and children 13 to 20; it's free for children under 13. Tours leave Tuesday through Sunday at 10am and 1:30pm and Monday at 1:30pm, except holidays. No reservations are necessary—just show up, donation in hand. The Friends also offer seasonal tours—like the terrific one offered at Halloween, of local courtyards otherwise not open to the public, where guides dressed as the ghosts of local historical figures tell their tales.

Stop by the **Jean Lafitte National Park and Preserve's Folklife and Visitor Center,** 419 Decatur St. (☎ **504/589-2636**), for details on its excellent free walking tour conducted by National Park Service rangers. The History of New Orleans tour covers about a mile in the French Quarter and brings to life New Orleans' history and the ethnic roots of the city's unique cultural mix. No reservations are required for this tour but only 30 people are taken in a group. The tour starts at 10:30am daily (except for Mardi Gras), so as the office opens at 9am, it's strongly suggested you get there then to ensure you will get a ticket.

✪ **The Bienville Foundation,** run by Robert Batson (☎ **504/945-6789**), offers a number of high-quality specialty tours created by expert scholars and researchers about various aspects of New Orleans' multifaceted, dynamic, and rich culture. For variety and professionalism, this organization can't be beat. The slate of tours changes seasonally, but overall offers something for just about everyone, including a Scandal Tour, a highly popular and recommended Gay Heritage Tour, a Women's History tour (given by Mary Gehman, author of the book *Women and New Orleans*), Black History, Writers in New Orleans (given by Kenneth Holdrich; see below), Jazz History (given by Donald M. Marquis, retired curator of the jazz collection at the Louisiana State Museum and author of *The Search for Buddy Bolden*), and Architecture. Tours last roughly two hours, and generally cost $20 per person. Times and departure locations also change seasonally so call to find out what's happening when.

Kenneth Holdrich, a professor of American literature at the University of New Orleans, runs ✪ **Heritage Literary Tours,** 732 Frenchmen St. (☎ **504/949-9805**). Since 1974, Holdrich has conducted literary walking tours of the French Quarter, and unlike some tour operators, he really knows his stuff. Aside from his considerable academic credentials, he knew both Tennessee Williams and the mother of John Kennedy Toole—his introduction to Toole's second posthumous novel, *Neon Bible,* explains the controversy around its publication. In addition to a general tour about the considerable literary legacy of the French Quarter—an enormous number of authors have lived in and written about the place—you can take the Williams-specific tour (T. W. covered a lot of ground in the place he called his "spiritual home"). Some tours, arranged in advance, can be designed around a specific author. The narratives are full of facts both literary and historical, loaded with anecdotes, and often downright humorous. Tours ($20 for adults, $10 for student group rate) are "scheduled for your convenience." Holdrich also does a regularly scheduled weekly tour for the Bienville Foundation, above.

If you want something a tab naughtier, you—and by "you," we mean adults—you can try **Red Light Tours' "Historic Storyville Tour"** (☎ **504/782-1170**), covering the unique history of that much-missed district, plus burlesque history of Bourbon Street, including detailing some of the famous acts of certain notorious dancing girls of the past. Tours depart Thursday to Monday, 11:30am and 2:30pm, from A Gallery Named Desire, 315 Decatur St., and cost $20 per person (includes admission into the "gentlemen's club" of your choice).

✪ **Le Monde Creole** (☎ **504/568-1801**) offers a unique tour that uses the dramatic lives of one classic Creole family as a microcosm of the Creole world of the 19th

---

Impressions

Nothing much to say about this city. At first sight, it is too quaint, too consciously like Marseille. One would have to stay here much longer to get to know it.
—Christopher Isherwood

century. (You could call it "As The Plantation Turns," according to one of the guides.) This is the sister operation of the Laura Plantation (see chapter 12). At the city location, you can learn about Creole city life, and the extraordinary story of Laura's family, off the plantation and in the Vieux Carre, while viewing French Quarter courtyards associated with the family. Guides are some of the best in the city, and this is probably the only operation that also offers tours in French. Tours leave from 624 Royal St., Tuesday through Saturday at 10:30am and 2:30pm. Reservations are required.

BEYOND THE FRENCH QUARTER

Author Robert Florence (who has written two excellent books about New Orleans cemeteries, as well as our Garden District walking tour in chapter 9) loves his work, and his ✪ **Historic New Orleans Walking Tours** (☎ **504/947-2120**) are full of meticulously researched facts and more than a few good stories. A very thorough (more thorough even than the one in chapter 9) tour of the Garden District and Lafayette Cemetery (a section of town not many of the other companies go into) leaves daily at 11am and 1:45pm from the Garden District Book Shop (in the Rink, corner of Washington Avenue and Prytania Street). Rates are $14, students and seniors $12, free for children under 12.

Tours by Isabelle (☎ **504/391-3544**), conducts a 3-hour, 45-mile city tour for small groups in an air-conditioned minibus. The tour covers the French Quarter, the cemeteries, St. John's Bayou, City Park and the lakefront, the universities, St. Charles Avenue, the Garden District, and the Superdome. The fare is $33, and departure times are 9am and 1:30pm. Make reservations as far in advance as possible. For $37 you can join Isabelle's afternoon Combo Tour, which begins at 1pm and adds Longue Vue Gardens to all of the above.

Gray Line, 2 Canal St., Suite 1300 (☎ **800/535-7786** or 504/587-0861), offers tours of the entire city, including the French Quarter, in comfortable motor coaches. But take my word for it: The Quarter demands a more in-depth examination than a view from a bus window will provide. Take one of these excellent (and very informative) tours only after you've explored the Quarter in detail, or as a prelude to doing so.

Gray Line also offers a tour that includes a 2-hour cruise on the **steamboat Natchez**. You can have lunch on board (not included in the tour price) as you take in the sights and sounds of the world's second-busiest port. Gray Line picks up at various hotels throughout the city. You can also take the **River Road Plantation Tour,** which departs daily at 9am, or the **Oak Alley Tour,** which leaves at 1pm daily. The plantation tours operate on a different schedule during December and January, so call for details.

Gray Line has also added walking tours to its offerings, including one of the Garden District and one of the French Quarter. Call for times and departure points.

Good Old Days (☎ **504/523-0804**), offers a 3-hour van tour of the city, taking in sights in the Quarter, the Garden District, and along Esplanade Avenue; visiting a cemetery; stopping in City Park; and driving along the shore of Lake Pontchartrain. The tours begin at 9am and 2pm daily; tickets are $30. The company also offers a plantation tour and carriage tours.

SWAMP TOURS

In addition to the tour providers listed below, Jean Lafitte and Gray Line (see above) both offer swamp tours. Swamp tours can be a hoot, particularly if you get a guide who calls alligators to your boat for a little snack of chicken (please keep your hands inside the boat—they tend to look a lot like chicken to a gator). On all of the following tours you're likely to see alligators, bald eagles, waterfowl, egrets, owls, herons, ospreys, feral hogs, otters, beavers, frogs, turtles, minks, raccoons, black bears, deer, and nutria.

Half Pint's Swamp Adventures (☎ 318/280-5976 or 318/288-1544) offers private guided tours of the "beauty, serenity, and exotic wildlife" of the Atchafalaya Basin, the nation's largest swamp. Half Pint is more folk hero than man, and his tours come highly recommended.

Lil' Cajun Swamp Tours (☎ 800/725-3213 or 504/689-3213) offers a good tour of Lafitte's bayous. Captain Cyrus Blanchard, "a Cajun French-speaking gentleman," knows the bayous like the back of his hand. The tour lasts 2 hours and costs about $16 for adults, $14 for seniors, and $12 for children 6 to 12 if you drive yourself to the boat launch. With transportation from New Orleans, the cost is $30 for adults, $15 for children. (Note that the boat used on the Lil' Cajun Swamp Tours is much larger than the boat used on many of the other tours—it seats up to 67 people, and can be noisier and more crowded than you might like.)

Dr. Wagner's Honey Island Swamp Tours (☎ 504/641-1769 or 504/242-5877), take you by boat into the interior of Honey Island Swamp's "most beautiful and pristine areas" to view wildlife with native professional naturalist guides. Dr. Wagner, the primary tour guide, is a trained wetland ecologist, and provides a solid educational experience to go with the purer swamp excitement. Tours last approximately 2 hours. Prices are $20 for adults, $10 for children under 12, if you drive to the launch site yourself; the rate is $40 if you want a hotel pickup in New Orleans.

Gator Swamp Tours (☎ 800/875-4287 or 504/484-6100), also takes visitors on a ride through Honey Island Swamp. Prices are $20 for adults, $10 for children under 12. The company offers a short nature walk in addition to boat tours. Like the other tour groups, Gator Swamp Tours offers hotel pickups for a fee. Tour operators Karen and Danny have also converted an old river tugboat into a bed-and-breakfast, and are preparing an alligator exhibit as well.

MYSTICAL & MYSTERIOUS TOURS

An increased interest in the supernatural, ghostly side of New Orleans—let's go right ahead and blame Anne Rice—has meant an increased number of tours catering to the vampire set. It has also resulted in some rather humorous infighting as rival tour operators have accused each other of stealing their shtick—and customers. We enjoy a good nighttime ghost tour of the Quarter as much as anyone, but we also have to admit that what's available is really hit-or-miss in presentation (it depends on who conducts your tour), and more miss than hit with regard to facts. Go for the entertainment value, not for the education (with some exceptions—see below).

Magic Walking Tours, 1015 Iberville St. (☎ 504/588-9693), created by Richard Rochester, was apparently the first to up the ante on the evening tours, offering a bit of theatrical spectacle along with ghost stories. When others copied the concept, Rochester toned down the gimmicks (though with his long hair, top hat, and special-effect contact lenses, he makes up for it). The guides are generally good, but Richard's the best—he knows how to spin a yarn, and his history of the town is marvelous to listen to. Several guided walking tours are offered daily: St. Louis Cemetery No. 1 (which is probably the only voodoo-free cemetery tour out there), the French Quarter, the Garden District, the Voodoo Tour, and the Vampire and Ghost-Hunt Walking Tour. Reservations are not necessary, but call ahead for tour schedules. Meeting places vary according to the tour. Tours cost $13, $10 students and seniors, and are free for children under 12.

Haunted History Tours, 97 Fontainebleau Dr. (☎ 888/6-GHOSTS or 504/ 861-2727), is the Magic Walking Tours' big rival, and the place to go if you want theatrics along with facts (and we use the term very loosely). Expect fake snakes and blood, costumes, and gizmos. The Voodoo/Cemetery Tour explores St. Louis Cemetery No. 1 and provides a kind of voodoo cultural history; it departs Monday through Saturday at 10am and 1:15pm, Sunday at 10am only, and departs from Reverend Zombie's Voodoo Shop at 723 St. Peter St. The Haunted History Tour wanders the Quarter in search of its ghost stories and legends; it begins daily at 2 and 8pm departs from Reverend Zombie's Voodoo Shop at 723 St. Peter St. The nocturnal vampire tour of the Quarter starts at 8:30pm nightly and departs from the front steps of the St. Louis Cathedral. All three tours last 2 hours and cost $15 for adults and $7 for children under 13. The Garden District Tour Departs 10:30am and 1:30pm daily from the lobby of the Ramada Hotel at 2203 St. Charles Ave.

New Orleans Spirit Tours (☎ **504/566-9877**) offers a combination cemetery and voodoo tour, which leaves from 712 Orleans Ave at 10:30am and 1pm (except Sunday afternoons). It's more of same. A nightly Ghost and Vampire tour leaves from the Bourbon Orleans Hotel lobby at 8pm. Tours cost $15, children under 12 free. No reservations are needed but please arrive 10 minutes early.

Historic New Orleans Walking Tours (☎ **504/947-2120**), best known for their extremely accurate walking tours of the Quarter and the Garden District, also offers a Cemetery and Voodoo Tour. The trip goes through St. Louis Cemetery No. 1, Congo Square, and an active voodoo temple. It leaves Monday through Saturday at 10am and 1pm, Sunday at 10am only, from the courtyard at 334-B Royal St. Rates are $15, students and seniors $13, free for children under 12.

The Voodoo Museum also offers voodoo and cemetery tours; see "Museums," above.

BOAT TOURS

For those interested in doing the Mark Twain thing, a number of operators offer riverboat cruises; some cruises have specific destinations like the zoo or Chalmette, while others just cruise the river and harbor without stopping. Docks are at the foot of Toulouse and Canal streets, and there's ample parking. Call for reservations, which are required for all these tours, and to confirm prices and schedules.

The steamboat *Natchez,* 2 Canal St., Suite 1300 (☎ **800/233-BOAT** or 504/586-8777), a marvelous three-deck sternwheeler docked at the wharf behind the Jackson Brewery, offers two 2-hour daytime cruises daily. The narration is by professional guides, and there are cocktail bars, live jazz, an optional Creole buffet, and a gift shop. Daytime fares are $14.75 for adults and $7.25 for children; evening cruises (not including dinner) are $22.50 for adults, $11.25 for children. Children under 3 ride free. There's also a jazz dinner cruise with an optional buffet every evening.

Aboard the sternwheeler *John James Audubon,* 2 Canal St., Suite 1300 (☎ **800/233-BOAT** or 504/586-8777), passengers travel the Mississippi, tour the busy port, and dock to visit the Audubon Zoo and the Aquarium of the Americas. There are four trips daily, departing from the Riverwalk in front of the Aquarium at 10am, noon, 2pm, and 4pm. Return trips from the zoo leave at 11am, 1pm, 3pm, and 5pm. Tickets for one-way or round-trips can be purchased with or without aquarium and zoo admission. Combination tickets are available that will save you several dollars.

The paddle wheeler *Creole Queen,* Riverwalk Dock (☎ **800/445-4109** or 504/524-0814), departs from the Poydras St. Wharf adjacent to the Riverwalk, at 10:30am and 2pm for 3-hour narrated excursions to the port and to the historic site of the Battle of New Orleans. There is also a 7pm jazz dinner cruise. The ship has a covered promenade deck, and its inner lounges are air-conditioned and heated. Buffet and cocktail service are available on all cruises. Daytime fares are $14 for adults, $7 for children; the nighttime jazz cruise is $42 for adults, $21 for children. Children under 3 ride free.

CARRIAGE TOURS

Corny it may be, but there is a sheepish romantic lure to the old horse-drawn carriages that pick up passengers at Jackson Square and take them for day and nighttime tours of the Quarter. (They are actually mule-drawn because mules can take heat and humidity while horses can't.) The mules are decked out with ribbons, flowers, or even hats, and the drivers seem to be in a fierce competition to win the "most unusual city story" award. Once again, the "facts" presented are probably dubious, but should be most entertaining. Carriages wait at the Decatur Street end of Jackson Square from 9am to midnight in good weather; the charge is $8 per adult and $5 for children under 12.

Private horse-and-carriage tours offered by **Good Old Days Buggies** (☎ **504/ 523-0804**) include hotel or restaurant pickup and cost significantly more (between $30 and $115, depending on route and length of ride).

ANTIQUING TOURS

Antiquing in New Orleans can be an overwhelming experience, especially if you've never been to the city before, and even *more* especially if you have your heart set on something in particular. For that, you might need a little expert help, and that's why Macon Riddle founded **Let's Go Antiquing!**, 1412 Fourth St. (☎ **504/899-3027**), in the mid-1980s. She'll organize and customize antique shopping tours to fit your needs. Hotel pickup is included, and she will even make lunch reservations for you. If you find something and need to ship it home, she'll take care of that, too. There's no doubt in my mind that Macon Riddle is the best in the business.

8 Staying Active

BOATING

Surrounded by swamps, a huge lake, the nation's largest river, and the Gulf of Mexico, New Orleans is all about water, and if you want to get out on some, you have a lot of choices. If your needs are modest, you can rent pedal boats by the half-hour or hour for use on the lagoons in City Park. Pedal boats rent for $6 per half-hour or $8 an hour. Call **City Park**'s boating and fishing department (☎ **504/483-9371**) for rental hours.

One of the most spine-tingling activities in the New Orleans area is a canoe ride through a bayou. Locals will tell you that alligators are really shy and harmless ("They're more scared of you") . . .but when you see a big one up close in the wild, you *will* begin to sweat profusely. (If gator tastes like chicken, what do we taste like to gators?) In addition to gators big and small, you'll see turtles and perhaps a snake, water lilies, and Spanish moss. The most convenient way to get into a bayou is through one of the canoe rental ventures near Jean Lafitte National Park (see "Hiking," below). You can rent canoes at **Earl's Bar & Canoe Rentals** (☎ **504/ 689-3271**). Earl will drop you and your canoe off at the Jean Lafitte park bayou and let you loose. Each canoe is $25. Earl's also offers guided bayou canoe tours the night before and the night of each full moon, and guided tours each Sunday at 8am. If possible, make reservations for rentals, and especially for guided tours.

Bayou Barn "Cajun Canoeing and Dancing" (☎ **800/TO-BAYOU** or 504/ 689-2663; www.bayoubarn.com) also offers canoe rentals for use in Jean Lafitte National Historical Park. Two-person canoes go for $15 for 2 hours, or $25 per day. The Bayou Barn is also famous for its rockin' outdoor Cajun parties with live music on Sundays from 2 to 6pm.

Another good option for getting onto the water is sailing on Lake Pontchartrain. You can rent boats from **Murray Yacht Sales/Boat Rentals,** 402 S. Roadway Dr. (☎ **504/283-2507**). If you're an experienced sailor but need some help getting started, you can take a quick refresher course; there are also courses for beginners. Sailing courses are available from March to November. Boats run $100 a day week-days, $115 on weekends.

FISHING

If all that blackened redfish at dinner has you in the mood, you've come to the right place: Fishing's quite popular in the New Orleans area. Regardless of where they fish, though, nonresidents must have temporary state fishing licenses; you can get them from the **Louisiana Department of Wildlife and Fisheries** (☎ **504/568-5667**), which maintains an office at 1600 Canal St., in the University of New Orleans building, just outside the French Quarter. It's open weekdays 8:15am to 4:15pm. Separate licenses must be purchased for saltwater fishing and freshwater fishing and for motorboat registration (if you have your own boat). You may have to get another license altogether for shrimping and crabbing. Crawfishing does not require a license.

As with many of the other outdoor activities listed here, **City Park** is a good place to start. There—with a permit obtained from the park's boating and fishing depart-ment (☎ **504/483-9371**)—you can fish for bass, catfish, and perch year-round. Fishing in City Park costs $2 for a 1-day park permit ($1 for children). You can also get a temporary state fishing license (see above) here for an additional $5.50. Fishing in the park is from the shore, not from boats, and rental gear is available.

You can also fish the Mississippi River in the Carrollton/Riverbend area (where St. Charles Avenue bends into Carrollton), near the levee, where you can just drop your line.

To get a little more serious, try a fishing trip out of town. This is also a good way to see some of the most scenic corners of swamp and bayou country. *Note:* Most charter services will be able to provide you with a temporary nonresident license, but be sure to ask in advance.

To add some history and folklore to your fishing trip, call **Ripp's Inland Charters** (☎ **504/689-2665;** www.rippscharters.com). Ripp Blank, a native resident of Lafitte, organizes all-day fishing trips through the area's swamps and bayous. Trips leave from Barataria, approximately 45 minutes away from New Orleans. To get there, take Bus. 90 (the Westbank I-90 Expressway) across the Crescent City Connection; exit south on Highway 45—otherwise known as Barataria Boulevard—and continue for 15 to 20 minutes past Jean Lafitte National Historical Park. Ripp specializes in fishing for speckled trout and redfish. All gear is provided. Prices for a day trip are $300 for two people and $315 for three, plus fuel and oil costs.

In addition, several tour operators run deep-sea fishing trips in the Gulf of Mexico along with their bayou and swamp fishing excursions. Unless you have your own equipment and are an experienced boater, these charters are the way to go. **Captain Nick's Fishing Safaris** (☎ **800/375-FISH** or 504/361-3004) makes Gulf fishing as easy as it can possibly be—which is still a good challenge. It operates fishing charters daily year-round through saltwater bayous and the Gulf of Mexico. All equipment is provided, and Captain Nick's will pick you up at your hotel. The tours are personal-ized, with no more than five people per boat.

GOLF

Whether you bring your own clubs or rent them, you'll be able to get in a good round of golf at several public courses around the city. **City Park Bayou Oaks Golf Courses,**

1040 Filmore Dr. (☎ **504/483-9396**), has four 18-hole courses. Rentals are available, as are private lessons. There is a 100-tee lighted driving range and one of the top 100 golf shops in the country. Fees for nonresidents are $14 weekdays and $17 weekends. **Audubon Park** (☎ **504/865-8260**) also has an 18-hole public course; it's $9 weekdays and $12 weekends.

On the West Bank, **Joe Bartholomew Golf Course,** 6514 Congress Dr. (☎ **504/288-0928**), is a good choice and less expensive: $7.75 weekdays and $11 weekends. The **Bayou Barriere Golf Club,** 7427 Hwy. 23, Belle Chase, LA 70037 (☎ **504/394-0662** or 504/394-9500), is a 27-hole championship course about 20 minutes south of New Orleans. It's considered the best public golf course in the area and is priced accordingly—$17.50 weekdays and $28 weekends. Clubs are available for rental.

The **Bluffs at Thompson Creek,** St. Francisville La. Hwy. 965 at Freeland Road, 6 miles east of U.S. 61 (☎ **225/925-8337**), is 2 hours from the city, but it offers a great course designed by Arnold Palmer. You must reserve tee times well in advance by calling the pro shop (☎ **225/634-5551**). Monday through Thursday the fee is $60 (plus $12 for a cart); Friday through Sunday, it's $70 (plus $12 for a cart).

HIKING

The Louisiana Nature Center maintains several trails in Joe Brown Park. Additionally, **Jean Lafitte National Historical Park and Preserve,** Barataria Unit, 7400 La. Hwy. 45, Marrero (☎ **504/589-2330**), has trails maintained by the National Park Service that wind through the wetlands. You'll see water lily-dotted bayous and moss-draped cypress trees, as well as palmettos and oaks, and maybe an alligator or two. Park rangers conduct guided tours (daily at 2pm) that take visitors to some interesting historical and archaeological sites.

To get there, take Bus. 90 (the Westbank I-90 Expressway) across the Crescent City Connection bridge to the West Bank, then take state Highway 45 south approximately 12 miles to the park.

HORSEBACK RIDING

Cascade Stables in Audubon Park, 700 East Dr. (☎ **504/891-2246**), gives guided tours along a 2.2-mile route through the park. The rides ($20 per person) can be scheduled daily between 9am and 4pm.

IN-LINE SKATING

You can rent in-line skates (or old-fashioned, sedan-style skates) and safety gear at **Down South Skate Park and Pro Shop,** 341 N. Hennessey St., Mid City (☎ **504/483-8121**). After you're fully outfitted, the paved loop in Audubon Park is a safe, traffic-free space; you can also find free pavement at City Park.

We've said it before, and we will keep saying it: This town was made for walking. Except maybe at the height of the summer months, when heat and humidity—especially humidity—make you not want to do much of anything except sit gasping in the nearest shade, sipping cool drinks. But that's another story.

This unique-looking city is one of the most beautiful in the country, and to not stroll through it and marvel is a huge loss. Everywhere are gorgeous buildings, each more interesting than the last. And thanks to a colorful past, many of them have tales to tell. The French Quarter and the Garden District have their own distinct appearances, and both are easily manageable on foot.

Put on some good walking shoes, breathe in that river wind and tropical breeze, and take a walk. Go slow—there's a reason New Orleans is called the Big Easy. Don't just look at the stops on each tour; there's plenty to see in between. Admire the iron lacework on one building, and see how it differs from another. Peek through gateways, particularly in the French Quarter, where simple facades hide exquisite secrets in the form of surprising courtyards, with fountains, brickwork, and thick foliage. Gawk at the mighty oaks, some with swaying Spanish moss dripping from their branches, lining the streets.

Turn down St. John's Bayou for another kind of walk all together. If you are lucky, or if you walk at the right time of day (especially early in the morning), you might have a street or two to yourself. Imagine taking this walk 100 years ago; it would have looked almost exactly the way it does now. At certain times, ghosts seem to flit just out of sight around every corner. But don't get so carried away with daydreams and fantasies that you forget to be aware of your surroundings; these areas should be safe, but be careful just in case.

The following walking tours will give you a nice overview and are perfect for answering the "That looks interesting—what the heck *is* it?" kind of questions that arise during a casual stroll. But formal, professional walking tours (like the ones offered by **Historic New Orleans Walking Tours; ☎ 504/947-2120**) cover more ground and go into considerable more detail, though they tend to only deal with the French Quarter and Garden District. These areas, naturally, get the most attention from tourists, but below you will find three other tours well worth your time.

Walking Tour 1
The French Quarter

Start: The intersection of Royal and Bienville streets.
Finish: Jackson Square.
Time: Allow approximately 1½ hours, not including time spent in shops or historic homes.
Best Times: Any day before 8am (when it's still quiet and deserted) or 10am (when the day begins in the French Quarter).
Worst Times: At night. Some attractions won't be open and you won't be able to get a good look at the architecture.

Even if it's the only recreational time you spend in New Orleans, you owe it to yourself to experience the French Quarter, also known by the French name Vieux Carré, or "old square." Made up of just over 80 city blocks, this is perhaps the densest urban area in the country, and it's a living monument to history. Here the colonial empires of France, Spain, and, to a lesser extent, Britain intersected with the emerging American nation. Yet the place seems timeless, at once recognizably old and vibrantly alive. Today's residents and merchants are stewards of a rich tradition of individuality, creativity, and disregard for many of the concerns of the world beyond. This tour is designed to acquaint you with a bit of the style and history of this place and its important landmarks, and to lead you through some of its more picturesque regions.

From the corner of Royal and Bienville streets, head into the Quarter (away from Canal Street). As you walk along Royal, imagine that streetcar named Desire rattling along its tracks. It traveled along Royal and Bourbon streets until 1948. (It was replaced by the bus named Desire. Really.) You can also imagine how noisy these narrow streets were when the streetcars were in place.

1. **339–343 Royal St.,** also known as the Rillieux-Waldhorn House. Now the home of Waldhorn Antiques (est. 1881), it was built between 1795 and 1800 for Vincent Rillieux, the great-grandfather of the French Impressionist artist Edgar Degas. Offices of the (second) Bank of the United States occupied the building from 1820 until 1836, when, thanks to President Jackson's famous veto, its charter expired. Note the wrought-iron balconies—an example of Spanish colonial workmanship.

2. **The Bank of Louisiana,** 334 Royal St. The old bank was erected in 1826 by Philip Hamblet and Tobias Bickle, after the designs of Benjamin Fox. Its Greek Revival edifice was erected in the early 1860s, and the bank was liquidated in 1867. The building has suffered a number of fires (in 1840, 1861, and 1931) and has served as the Louisiana State Capitol, an auction exchange, a criminal court, a juvenile court, and a social hall for the American Legion. It now houses the police station for the Vieux Carré.

   Cross Conti Street to:

3. **403 Royal St.** Benjamin H. B. Latrobe died of yellow fever shortly after completing designs for the Louisiana State Bank, which opened in this building in

---

Impressions

Only in the old cities—like New Orleans—built long before cars, do walking humans still feel at home. In New Orleans, life is a pedestrian.

—Andrei Codrescu

Walking Tour—The French Quarter

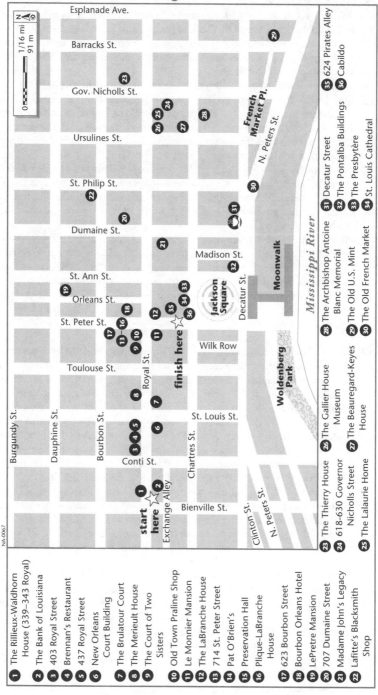

Esplanade Ave.

Barracks St.

Gov. Nicholls St.

Ursulines St.

St. Philip St.

Dumaine St.

Madison St.

St. Ann St.

Orleans St.

St. Peter St.

finish here

Toulouse St.

Royal St.

Wilk Row

St. Louis St.

Conti St.

start here

Exchange Alley

Bienville St.

Chartres St.

Clinton St.

N. Peters St.

Burgundy St.

Dauphine St.

Bourbon St.

French Market Pl.

N. Peters St.

Decatur St.

Jackson Square

Moonwalk

Mississippi River

Woldenberg Park

N ↑

1/16 mi
91 m

0

1 The Rillieux-Waldhorn House (339–343 Royal)
2 The Bank of Louisiana
3 403 Royal Street
4 Brennan's Restaurant
5 437 Royal Street
6 New Orleans Court Building
7 The Brulatour Court
8 The Merieult House
9 The Court of Two Sisters
10 Old Town Praline Shop
11 Le Monnier Mansion
12 The LaBranche House
13 714 St. Peter Street
14 Pat O'Brien's
15 Preservation Hall
16 Plique-LaBranche House
17 623 Bourbon Street
18 Bourbon Orleans Hotel
19 LePretre Mansion
20 707 Dumaine Street
21 Madame John's Legacy
22 Lafitte's Blacksmith Shop

23 The Thierry House
24 618-630 Governor Nicholls Street
25 The Lalaurie Home
26 The Gallier House Museum
27 The Beauregard-Keyes House
28 The Archbishop Antoine Blanc Memorial
29 The Old U.S. Mint
30 The Old French Market
31 Decatur Street
32 The Pontalba Buildings
33 The Presbytère
34 St. Louis Cathedral
35 624 Pirates Alley
36 Cabildo

NA-0067

181

1821. At the time of his death, Latrobe was one of the nation's most eminent architects, having designed the Bank of Pennsylvania in Philadelphia (1796) and contributed to the U.S. Capitol. Latrobe moved from Baltimore to New Orleans to design the city's custom house. You can see the monogram "LSB" on the Creole-style iron balcony railing.

4. **Brennan's Restaurant,** 417 Royal St. Brennan's opened in this building, also built by Vincent Rillieux, in 1955 (see chapter 7 for full listing). The structure was erected after the fire of 1794 destroyed more than 200 of the original buildings along this street. From 1805 to 1841, it was home to the Banque de la Louisiane. The world-famous chess champion Paul Charles Morphy moved here as a child in 1841. Edgar Degas' parents also lived here.

5. **437 Royal St.** Masonic lodge meetings were held regularly in a drugstore here in the early 1800s, but that's not what made the place famous. What did: Proprietor and druggist Antoine A. Peychaud served after-meeting drinks of bitters and cognac to lodge members in small egg cups, whose French name (*coquetier*) was Americanized to "cocktail."

6. **New Orleans Court Building,** 400 Royal St. Built in 1909, this courthouse covers the length of the block across from Brennan's. The baroque edifice, made of Georgia marble, certainly seems out of place in the French Quarter—especially considering that many Spanish-era structures were demolished to make way for it. Originally home to parish and state courts, the building is being renovated for use by the Louisiana Supreme Court and the 4th Circuit Court of Appeals.

Cross St. Louis Street to:

7. **The Brulatour Court,** 520 Royal St. This was built in 1816 as a home for François Seignouret, a furniture-maker and wine importer from Bordeaux—his furniture, with a signature "S" carved into each piece, still commands the respect of collectors. From 1870 to 1887, wine importer Pierre Brulatour occupied the building. WSDU-TV now maintains offices here, but during business hours you're welcome to walk into the courtyard. It's one of the few four-walled courtyards in the French Quarter, and one of the more exotic. Also, from the street, notice the elaborate, fan-shaped guard screen (garde de frise) on the right end of the third-floor balcony—look closely for Seignouret's "S" carved into the screen.

8. **The Merieult House,** 533 Royal St. Built for the merchant Jean François Merieult in 1792, this was the only building in the area left standing after the fire of 1794. Legend has it that Napoléon repeatedly offered Madame Merieult great riches in exchange for her hair—he wanted it for a wig to present to a Turkish sultan. She refused. Nowadays this is home to the Historic New Orleans Collection–Museum/Research Center. (See chapter 8 for tour times and more information.)

Cross Toulouse Street to:

9. **The Court of Two Sisters,** 613 Royal St. This structure was built in 1832 for a local bank president on the site of the 18th-century home of a French governor. The two sisters were Emma and Bertha Camors (whose father owned the building); from 1886 to 1906 they ran a curio store here.

10. **Old Town Praline Shop,** 627 Royal St. Walk through the shop entrance to the back of the store to see another of the French Quarter's courtyards. This 1777 building is where opera singer Adelina Patti first came for a visit and then lived after becoming something of a local heroine in 1860. The 17-year-old's popularity as a last-minute stand-in lead soprano in *Lucia di Lammermoor* saved the local opera company from financial ruin.

11. Le Monnier Mansion, 640 Royal St. This structure once towered above every other French Quarter building as the city's first "skyscraper"—all of three stories high when it was built in 1811. A fourth story was added in 1876. George W. Cable, the celebrated author of *Old Creole Days,* chose this building as the residence of his fictional hero, 'Sieur George.

Cross St. Peter Street to:

12. The LaBranche House (now the Royal Café), 700 Royal St. This is probably the most photographed building in the Quarter—and no wonder. Take a look at the lacy cast-iron grillwork, with its delicate oak leaf and acorn design, that fairly drips from all three floors. There are actually 11 LaBranche buildings, three-story brick row houses built between 1835 and 1840 for the widow of wealthy sugar planter Jean Baptiste LaBranche. Eight face St. Peter Street, one faces Royal, and two face Pirates Alley.

Turn left at St. Peter Street and continue to:

13. 714 St. Peter St. Built in 1829 by a prominent physician, this was a boarding house run by Antoine Alciatoire for several years during the 1860s. His cooking became so popular with the locals that he eventually gave up catering to open the famous Antoine's restaurant, still operated by his descendants.

14. Pat O'Brien's, 718 St. Peter St. You've probably heard of this famous New Orleans nightspot (see chapter 11). The building was completed in 1790 for a wealthy planter and was known as the Maison de Flechier. Later, Louis Tabary put on popular plays here. It's said that the first grand opera in America was performed within these walls. The courtyard is open to visitors and is well worth a look—if you can see it past the crowds consuming the famous Hurricane drink.

15. Preservation Hall, 726 St. Peter St. Scores of people descend on this place nightly to hear traditional New Orleans jazz. A daytime stop affords a glimpse, through the big, ornate iron gate, of a lush tropical courtyard in back. Erle Stanley Gardner, the author who brought us Perry Mason, lived in an apartment above the Hall.

16. Plique-LaBranche House, 730 St. Peter St. This house was built in 1825, sold to Giraud M. Plique in 1827, and sold to Jean Baptiste LaBranche in 1829. The wrought-iron balcony dates from the 1820s. This is believed to be the site of New Orleans' first theater, which burned in the fire of 1816, but that is the subject of some debate.

Turn left off St. Peter Street onto Bourbon.

17. 623 Bourbon St. Tennessee Williams and Truman Capote lived in this house, though not together (get your mind out of the gutter!). It's owned by Lindy Boggs, a much-beloved local politician (and mother of NPR and ABC commentator Cokie Roberts) who took over her husband's Congressional seat after his death. She is now the U.S. special envoy to the Vatican.

Turn around and head the other way down Bourbon. At the corner of Bourbon and Orleans, look down the street, toward the river, at:

18. The Bourbon Orleans Hotel, 717 Orleans St. This was the site of the famous quadroon balls, where wealthy white men would come to form alliances (read: acquire a mistress) with free women of color, who were one-eighth to one-fourth black. Look at the balcony and imagine the assignations that went on there while the balls were in session. The building later became a convent.

Turn left onto Orleans and follow it 1 block to Dauphine (pronounced daw-feen) Street. On the corner is:

19. Le Pretre Mansion, 716 Dauphine St. In 1839, Jean Baptiste Le Pretre bought this 1836 Greek Revival house and added the romantic cast-iron galleries. The house is the subject of a horror story: Sometime in the last century a Turk, supposedly the brother of a sultan, arrived in New Orleans and rented the Le Pretre house. He was conspicuously wealthy, and his entourage included many servants and more than a few beautiful young girls—all thought to have been stolen from the sultan. Rumors quickly spread about the situation, even as the home became the scene of lavish entertainment with guest lists that included the cream of society. One night, shrieks came from inside the house, and the next morning neighbors entered and found the tenant's body lying in a pool of blood surrounded by the bodies of the young beauties. The mystery remains unsolved. Local ghost experts say you can still hear exotic music and shrieks on the right night.

Follow Dauphine St. 2 blocks to Dumaine St. and turn right. You'll find an interesting little cottage at:

20. 707 Dumaine St. After the 1794 fire, all houses in the French Quarter were required by law to have flat tile roofs. Most have since been covered with conventional roofs, but this Spanish colonial cottage is still in compliance with the flat-roof rule.

21. Madame John's Legacy, 632 Dumaine St. This was once thought to be the oldest building on the Mississippi River. Recent research suggests, however, that only a few parts of the original building survived the 1788 fire and were used in its reconstruction. The house was originally erected in 1726, eight years after the founding of New Orleans. Its first owner was a ship captain who died in the 1729 Natchez Massacre; upon his death the house passed to the captain of a Lafitte-era smuggling ship. It has had no fewer than 21 owners since. The present structure is a fine example of a French "raised cottage." The aboveground basement is of brick-between-posts construction (locally made bricks were too soft to be the primary building material), covered with boards laid horizontally. The hipped, dormered roof extends out over the veranda. Its name, incidentally, comes from George W. Cable's fictional character who was bequeathed the house in the short story "'Tite Poulette." Now a part of the Louisiana State Museum complex, it's occasionally open for tours.

Take a left at the corner of Dumaine and Chartres streets and follow Chartres to the next corner; make a left onto St. Philip Street and continue to the corner of St. Philip and Bourbon streets.

22. Lafitte's Blacksmith Shop, 941 Bourbon St. For many years, this has been a bar (for the full story, see chapter 11), but the legend is that Jean Lafitte and his pirates posed as blacksmiths here while using it as headquarters for selling goods they'd plundered on the high seas. It has survived in its original condition, reflecting the architectural influence of French colonials who escaped St. Domingue in the late 1700s. It may be the oldest building in the Mississippi Valley, but that has not been documented. You can still see the brick-between-posts construction, which is usually covered with plaster. The modern-day owners of the building have resisted invasions of chrome and plastic, which makes the interior an excellent place to imagine life in the Quarter in the 19th century.

Turn right onto Bourbon St. and follow it 2 blocks to Governor Nicholls St. Turn right.

23. The Thierry House, 721 Governor Nicholls St., was built in 1814 and announced the arrival of the Greek Revival style of architecture in New Orleans. It was designed in part by architect Henry S. Boneval Latrobe, son of Benjamin H. B. Latrobe, when he was 19 years old.

Cross Royal Street to:

24. 618–630 Governor Nicholls St. Henry Clay's brother, John, built a house for his wife here in 1828, and in 1871 a two-story building was added at the rear of its garden. In the rear building, Frances Xavier Cabrini (now a Catholic saint) conducted a school.

Backtrack to the corner of Royal and Governor Nicholls streets. Take a left onto Royal and look for:

25. The Lalaurie Home, 1140 Royal St. Many people simply refer to this place as "the haunted house." Here's why: When Madame Delphine Macarty de Lopez Blanque wed Dr. Louis Lalaurie, it was her third marriage—she'd already been widowed twice. The Lalauries moved into this residence in 1832 and soon were impressing the city with extravagant parties. One night in 1834, fire broke out and neighbors crashed through a locked door to find seven starving slaves chained in painful positions, unable to move. The sight, combined with Delphine's stories of past slaves having "committed suicide," enraged her neighbors. Madame Lalaurie and her family escaped a mob's wrath and fled to Paris. Several years later she died in Europe, and her body was returned to New Orleans—and even then she had to be buried in secrecy. The building was a Union headquarters during the Civil War and, later, a gambling house and a home for indigents. Through the years, stories have circulated of ghosts inhabiting the building, especially that of one young slave child who fell from the roof trying to escape Delphine's cruelties.

26. The Gallier House Museum, 1132 Royal St. This was built by James Gallier Jr. as his residence in 1857. Gallier and his father were two of the city's leading architects (see chapter 8 for more details). Anne Rice was thinking of this house when she described where Lestat and Louis lived in *Interview with the Vampire.*

Turn left onto Ursulines St. toward the river.

☕ **TAKE A BREAK**   If you need a little rest or sustenance at this point, you can stop into the popular **Croissant D'Or,** 617 Ursulines St. They probably aren't actually made of gold (if so, they aren't priced accordingly), but the croissants and pastries here are very good and the ambience—inside or out on the patio—is equal to the eats.

At the corner of Ursulines and Chartres streets is:

27. The Beauregard-Keyes House, 1113 Chartres St. Notice the Doric columns and handsome twin staircases. This "raised cottage" was built as a residence in 1826 by Joseph Le Carpentier, though it has several other claims to fame (see chapter 8 for details).

28. The Archbishop Antoine Blanc Memorial, 1114 Chartres St. Completed in 1752, it includes the Old Ursuline Convent and the Archiepiscopal Residence (see chapter 8 for more information).

Continue walking along Chartres Street until you get to Esplanade (pronounced es-pla-*nade*) Avenue, which served as the parade ground for troops quartered on Barracks Street. Along with St. Charles Avenue, it is one of the city's most picturesque historic thoroughfares. Some of the grandest town houses built in the late 1800s grace the wide, tree-lined avenue. (If you're interested in viewing some of these houses, Walking Tour 4, below, concentrates on the architecture of the Esplanade Ridge.)

The entire 400 block of Esplanade is occupied by:

29. The Old U.S. Mint. This was once the site of Fort St. Charles, one of the defenses built to protect New Orleans in 1792. (Its soldiers also used Esplanade as a parade ground.) It was here that Andrew Jackson reviewed the "troops"— pirates, volunteers, and a nucleus of trained soldiers—he later led in the Battle of New Orleans. (For more information, see chapter 8.)

Follow Esplanade toward the river and turn right at the corner of North Peters Street. Follow North Peters until it intersects with Decatur Street. This is the back end of:

30. The Old French Market. This European-style market has been here for well over 150 years, and today it has a farmer's market, plus a seemingly endless number of stalls featuring everything from 'gator on a stick to somewhat tacky souvenir items. On most weekends, the Esplanade end of the market houses a flea market.

When you leave the French Market, exit on the side away from the river onto:

31. Decatur Street. Not long ago this section of Decatur—from Jackson Square all the way over to Esplanade—was a seedy, run-down area of wild bars and cheap rooming houses. Few of either remain. The strip has fallen into step with the rest of the Quarter, sporting a number of restaurants and trendier bars. (The stretch of Decatur between Ursulines and Esplanade streets has retained more of the run-down aesthetic, with secondhand shops that are worth taking a browse through, and smaller, darker bars.)

As you walk toward St. Ann Street along Decatur, you'll pass **923** and **919 Decatur St.,** where the Café de Refugies and Hôtel de la Marine were located in the 1700s and early 1800s. These were reputed to be gathering places for pirates, smugglers, and European refugees (some of them outlaws)—a far cry from today's scene.

☕ **TAKE A BREAK**   If you're walking in the area of 923 Decatur St. around lunchtime, pop into the **Central Grocery** and pick up a muffaletta sandwich. There are little tables at which to eat inside, or you can take your food and sit outside, maybe right on the riverbank. If you had something else in mind, there are a number of restaurants along this stretch. **Kaldi's,** 941 Decatur St., is a good place to get a cup of coffee or a frothy drink, or to spy on the locals.

Decatur Street will take you to Jackson Square. Turn right onto St. Ann Street; the twin four-story, redbrick buildings here and those on the St. Peter Street side of the square are:

32. The Pontalba Buildings. They sport some of the most impressive cast-iron balcony railings in the French Quarter. They also represent one of the first eras of revitalization in the Quarter. In the mid-1800s, Baroness Micaela Almonester Pontalba inherited rows of buildings along both sides of the Place d'Armes from her father, Don Almonester (who had been responsible for rebuilding the St. Louis Cathedral; see chapter 8). In an effort to counteract the emerging preeminence of the American sector across Canal Street, she decided to raze the structures and, in their place, build high-end apartments and commercial space. The Pontalba buildings were begun in 1849 under her very direct supervision; you can see her mark today in the entwined initials "a.p." in the ironwork. The buildings were designed in a traditional Creole European style with commercial space on the street level, housing above, and a courtyard in the rear. The row houses on St. Ann Street, now owned by the State of Louisiana, were completed in 1851.

The City in the Cast-Iron Mask

The use of cast iron as an architectural embellishment was introduced to this country in the 19th century by the Spanish. Wrought iron was popular earlier in the century, but it had to be worked by hand, and was significantly less durable and fire resistant than cast iron, which could be poured into molds and fashioned into almost any shape imaginable.

Using cast iron allowed blacksmiths to achieve the intricate designs seen around the Garden District and French Quarter today. Molds were hand-carved from wood, so homeowners could easily request a custom design for use on their galleries or fences. If you examine some of the ironwork carefully, you'll see a large variety of patterns and decorative motifs—everything from family crests to fruits and vegetables (like the Cornstalk Fence at the Cornstalk Hotel in the French Quarter). Everyone who was building a home in or around New Orleans in the mid- to late 1800s wanted some sort of cast-iron decoration, and during that time ships often carried up to 500 tons of pig iron a day into the city.

Baroness Pontalba is also responsible for the current design of Jackson Square, including the cast-iron fence and the equestrian statue of the general (which, legend has it, she deliberately had placed permanently saluting her own apartment).

At the corner of St. Ann and Chartres streets, turn left and continue around Jackson Square; you will see:

33. **The Presbytère,** 751 Chartres St. This, the Cabildo, and the St. Louis Cathedral—all designed by Gilberto Guillemard—were the first major public buildings in the Louisiana Territory. The Presbytère was originally designed to be the rectory of the cathedral. Baroness Pontalba's father financed the building's beginnings, but he died in 1798, leaving only the first floor done. The building was finally completed in 1813. It was never used as a rectory, but was rented and then purchased (in 1853) by the city to be used as a courthouse.

Next you'll come to:

34. **The St. Louis Cathedral.** The building standing here today is the third erected on this spot—the first was destroyed by a hurricane in 1722, the second by fire in 1788. The cathedral was rebuilt in 1794, the central tower was later designed by Henry S. Boneval Latrobe, and the building was remodeled and enlarged between 1845 and 1851. (See chapter 8 for more information.)

On the other side of the cathedral you'll come to **Pirates Alley.** Go right down Pirates Alley to:

35. **624 Pirates Alley,** Faulkner House Books. In 1925, William Faulkner lived here and worked on his first novels, *Mosquitoes* and *Soldiers' Pay.* While here, he contributed to the *Times-Picayune* and to a literary magazine, the *Double Dealer.* This is a great stop for Faulkner lovers and collectors of literature. (See chapter 10 for more information.)

Return to Jackson Square. On the right side of the cathedral (as you face the Mississippi River), also facing Jackson Square, is:

36. **The Cabildo,** on the corner of Chartres and St. Peter streets. In the 1750s, this was the site of a French police station and guardhouse. Part of that building was incorporated into the original Cabildo, statehouse of the Spanish governing body (the "Very Illustrious Cabildo"). The Cabildo was still under reconstruction when the transfer papers for the Louisiana Purchase were signed in a room on the

second floor in 1803. Since then, it has served as New Orleans' City Hall, the Louisiana State Supreme Court, and, since 1911, a facility of the Louisiana State Museum.

One further note: If you think those old Civil War cannons out front look pitifully small and ineffective by modern standards, think again. In 1921, in a near-deadly prank, one was loaded with powder, an iron ball was rammed down its muzzle, and it was fired in the dead of night. That missile traveled from the Cabildo's portico across the wide expanse of the Mississippi and some 6 blocks inland before landing in a house in Algiers, narrowly missing its occupants.

WINDING DOWN   You've finished! Now, go back across Decatur Street to **Café du Monde,** 813 Decatur St., in the French Market—no trip to New Orleans is complete without a leisurely stop here for beignets and coffee. If you still have a little bit of energy left, hike up the levee and relax on a bench for a while.

Walking Tour 2
The Garden District

Start: Prytania Street and Washington Avenue.
Finish: Lafayette Cemetery.
Time: 45 minutes to 1½ hours.
Best Times: Daylight.
Worst Times: Night, when you won't be able to get a good look at the architecture.

Walking through the architecturally phenomenal Garden District, you could get the impression that you've entered an entirely separate city from New Orleans as defined by the French Quarter—or, perhaps more specifically, entered a different time period. Although the Garden District was indeed once a separate city from the Vieux Carré (the city of Lafayette) and was established during a later period, the fact that this neighborhood was created by a different group of people most profoundly distinguishes it from the old section.

The French Quarter was initially established by Creoles during the French and Spanish colonial periods, and the Garden District was created by Americans. Antebellum New Orleans' lucrative combination of Mississippi River commerce, regional abundance of cash crops, slave trade, and national banks fueled the local economy, resulting in a remarkable building boom that extended for several square miles through Uptown New Orleans.

Although very few people from the United States lived in New Orleans during its colonial era, after the Louisiana Purchase thousands of Americans flooded the city and clashed with the Creoles. Friction arose between the two groups due to mutual snobbery, a language barrier, religious division, and, most significantly, competition over burgeoning commerce. Americans were arriving at the brink of a boom time to make fortunes. With inferior business experience, education, and organizational skills, the Creoles worried that "les Americains" would work them out of business. Americans were therefore kept out of the already overcrowded French Quarter. Feeling snubbed, they moved upriver to create a residential district of astounding opulence. The Garden District is therefore a study of a cultural clash reflected through architecture, with

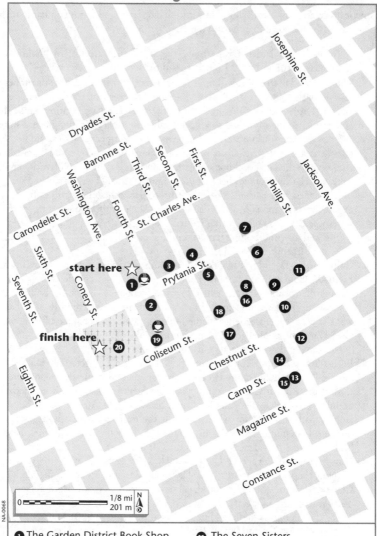

1. The Garden District Book Shop
2. Colonel Short's Villa
3. Briggs-Staub House
4. Our Lady of Perpetual Help Chapel
5. Women's Opera Guild House
6. Toby's Corner
7. Bradish Johnson House and
   Louise McGehee School
8. Archie Manning House
9. Pritchard-Pigott House
10. Morris-Israel House
11. The Seven Sisters
12. Brevard-Mahat-Rice House
13. Payne-Strachan House
14. Warwick Manor
15. 1137 Second St.
16. Joseph Merrick Jones House
17. Musson-Bell House
18. Robinson House
19. Commander's Palace Restaurant
20. Lafayette Cemetery

Americans creating an identity by boldly introducing styles and forms familiar to them and previously unknown in colonial Louisiana.

To reach the Garden District, take the St. Charles streetcar to Washington Avenue (stop 16) and walk 1 block toward the river to:

1. **The Garden District Book Shop,** 2727 Prytania St. Inside the historic property known as the Rink, you will find this store, an excellent starting point for a Garden District tour. Built in 1884 as the Crescent City Skating Rink, the building subsequently acted as a livery stable, mortuary facility, grocery store, and gas station. You probably will not view the interiors of any private homes, but the book shop's stellar collection of regional titles allows you a revealing glimpse into the neighborhood's majestic homes. It is Anne Rice's favorite bookstore, and she always holds her first book signing here. (The shop stocks a supply of her signed first editions.) Owner Britton Trice schedules signings by many regionally and nationally acclaimed authors. Along with an interesting array of stores, the Rink also offers a P.J.'s Coffee Shop, a pay phone, public benches, rest rooms, and air-conditioning (crucial in the summer).

Across Prtyatnia St., you'll find:

2. **Colonel Short's Villa,** 1448 Fourth St. Built by architect Henry Howard for Kentucky Colonel Robert Short. The story goes that Short's wife complained of missing the cornfields in her native Iowa, so he bought her the cornstalk fence. A revisionist explanation supplied by a recent owner is that the wife saw that it was the most expensive fence in the building catalog and requested it. Second Civil War occupational governor Nathaniel Banks was quartered here.

Continuing down Prytania, you'll find:

3. **Briggs-Staub House,** 2605 Prytania St. The Garden District's only example of Gothic Revival architecture. Because this style reminded the Protestant Americans of the Roman Catholicism of their Creole antagonists, it did not become popular. Original owner Charles Briggs did not hold African slaves but did employ Irish servants, for whom he built the relatively large adjacent servant quarters. Irish immigration was then starting to create the "Irish Channel" neighborhood across Magazine Street from the Garden District.

4. **Our Mother of Perpetual Help Chapel,** 2523 Prytania St. Once an active Catholic chapel, it is currently owned by Anne Rice. Rice also owns the Marigny-Claiborne House (built for the daughter-in-law of Bernard Marigny) on the other side of the block at 2524 St. Charles Ave. It's the setting for her novel *Violin.* The author's childhood home is down the street at 2301 St. Charles Ave.

5. **Women's Opera Guild House,** 2504 Prytania St. Some of the Garden District's most memorable homes incorporate more than one style. Designed by William Feret in 1858, this building combines Greek Revival and Queen Anne styles. Now owned by the Women's Opera Guild, the home can be toured by special arrangement (call ☎ **504/899-1945**).

6. **Toby's Corner,** 2340 Prytania St. The Garden District's oldest known home, it dates to at least 1838. Built for Philadelphia wheelwright Thomas Toby, it is in Greek Revival style, which was then very popular throughout the United States. Although the home represents an American attempt at creating a non-Creole architectural identity, this Anglicized style required Creole building techniques, such as raising the house up on brick piers to combat flooding and encourage air circulation.

7. **Bradish Johnson House and Louise McGehee School,** 2343 Prytania St. Paris-trained architect James Freret designed this French Second Empire–style mansion, which was built for sugar factor Bradish Johnson in 1872 at a cost of

$100,000. Contrast this house's awesome detail with the stark classical simplicity of Toby's Corner across the street—a visual indication of the effect that one generation of outrageous fortune had on Garden District architecture. Since 1929, the building has been the private Louise McGehee School for girls.

Turn down First St. (away from St. Charles) and it's less than a block to:

 8. **Archie Manning House,** 1420 First St. Home of former New Orleans Saints superstar quarterback Archie Manning and the childhood home of his son, Peyton Manning, himself an NFL quarterback for the Indianapolis Colts.

 9. **Pritchard-Pigott House,** 1407 First St. A Greek Revival double-galleried town house. As fortunes compounded, the typical Garden District house size grew. Americans introduced two house forms: the cottage (seen in Toby's Corner) and the grander town house (seen here).

10. **Morris-Israel House,** 1331 First St. As time passed, Garden District homes moved away from the simplicity of Greek Revival and became more playful with design. By the 1860s the Italianate style was popular, as seen in this double-galleried town house. Architect Samuel Jamison designed this house and the **Carroll-Crawford House** on the next corner (1315 First St.); note the identical ornate cast-iron galleries. The Morris-Israel House is reputedly haunted.

Follow Coliseum St. to the left less than half a block to:

11. **The Seven Sisters,** 2329–2305 Coliseum St. This row of "shotgun" houses gets its nickname from a story that a 19th-century Garden District resident had seven daughters whom he wanted to keep close to home, and he built these homes as wedding gifts. That story is not true. If you count the "Seven Sisters," you will find eight. (They were actually built on speculation.) An explanation for the name "shotgun" is that if you fire a gun through the front door, the bullet will go right out the back. Also, a West African word for this native African house form sounds something like "shotgun." The shotgun effectively circulates air and is commonly found in hot climates. Its relatively small size makes the shotgun house a rarity along the imposing streets of the Garden District, but it is extremely popular throughout New Orleans.

Now turn around and go back to First St. and turn left. At the corner of First and Chestnut, you'll see:

12. **Brevard-Mahat-Rice House,** 1239 First St. Designed in 1857 as a Greek Revival town house and later augmented with an Italianate bay, this house is a fine example of "transitional" architecture. It was historically called "Rosegate" for the rosette pattern on the fence. (The fence's diamond woven pattern is believed to be the precursor to the chain-link fence.) This is the home and workplace of novelist Anne Rice, and the setting for her *Witching Hour* novels.

13. **Payne-Strachan House,** 1134 First St. Jefferson Davis, president of the Confederate States of America, died here. Davis fell ill while traveling and was taken to the home of his friend Judge Charles Fenner (son-in-law of owner Jacob Payne). A stone marker in front of the house bears the date of Davis' death, December 6, 1889. Davis was buried in New Orleans' magnificent Metairie Cemetery for 2 years and then disinterred and moved to Virginia. This house is a classic antebellum Greek Revival home. Note the sky-blue ceiling of the gallery—the color is believed to keep winged insects from nesting there, and to ward off evil spirits. Many Garden District homes adhere to this tradition.

Turn left on Camp and go less than a block to:

14. **Warwick Manor,** 2427 Camp St. An example of Georgian architecture, this is one of the few homes in the vicinity that's not a single-family residence. Note the buzzers, which indicate rented apartments.

15. 1137 Second St. An example of Victorian architecture popularized in Uptown New Orleans toward the end of the 19th century. Many who built such homes were from the Northeast and left town in the summer; otherwise, it would be odd to see this kind of claustrophobic house, normally intended for cool climates, in New Orleans. Note the exquisite stained glass and rounded railing on the gallery.

Turn right onto Second St. and go 2 blocks to the corner of Coliseum, where you'll see:

16. Joseph Merrick Jones House, 2425 Coliseum St. Home of Nine Inch Nails singer Trent Reznor. When he moved in, more antinoise ordinances began being introduced into city council proceedings. Could it be a coincidence that his next-door neighbor is City Councilwoman Peggy Wilson?

Turn left onto Colisuem and go 1 block to Third Street. Turn left to get to the:

17. Musson-Bell House, 1331 Third St. This is the 1853 home of Michel Musson, one of the few French Creoles then living in the Garden District. Musson was the uncle of French Impressionist artist Edgar Degas, who once lived with Musson on Esplanade Avenue during a visit to New Orleans. On the Coliseum Street side of the house is the foundation of a cistern. The water tanks were so common in the Garden District that Mark Twain once commented that it looked as if everybody in the neighborhood had a private brewery. Cisterns were destroyed at the turn of the 20th century when mosquitoes, which breed in standing water, were found to be carriers of yellow fever and malaria.

Turn around and cross Coliseum to see:

18. Robinson House, 1415 Third St. Built between 1859 and 1865 by architect Henry Howard for tobacco grower and merchant Walter Robinson, this is one of the Garden District's most striking and unusual homes. Walk past the house on Third Street to appreciate its scale—the outbuildings, visible from the front, are actually connected to the side of the main house. The entire roof is a large vat that once collected water and acted as a cistern. Gravity provided water pressure and the Garden District's earliest indoor plumbing.

Walk down Coliseum 2 blocks to the corner of Washington. There you'll find:

19. Commander's Palace Restaurant, 1403 Washington Ave. Established in 1883 by Emile Commander, this turreted Victorian structure is now the pride of the Brennan family. Commander's is perennially rated one of the nation's top restaurants. The jazz brunch—an institution that originated here—is extremely popular. The building also housed a bordello in the 1920s.

20. Lafayette Cemetery, Washington Avenue between Prytania and Coliseum streets. Established in 1833, this "city of the dead" is one of New Orleans' oldest cemeteries. It has examples of all the classic aboveground, multipleburial techniques and features a number of interesting Anne Rice–related sites (the Mayfair witches' family tomb is here, for example). Although the cemetery gates display New Orleans Police Department signs that say "patrolled," that is not true. Be careful in this and all cemeteries, as predatory crime is a possibility. A guided tour is recommended.

☕ **WINDING DOWN**   Now go back across the street to Commander's, where you might be able to get a table (especially if you made a reservation), though proper attire is required. Or you can head back to the Rink for lighter, less formal refreshments at P.J.'s Coffee.

Walking Tour 3
Algiers Point

Start and finish: The Algiers Point ferry terminal.
Time: Approximately 1 hour.
Best Times: Between 10:30am and 4pm.
Worst Times: Try not to go during morning or evening rush hours, when the ferry can get crowded with commuters.

Algiers is considerably less high profile than the French Quarter or the Garden District, but it's every bit as much of a neighborhood, and very nearly as picturesque, if on a less grand scale. This walking tour has quickly become one of our favorite things to do, particularly as it's combined with the ferry ride, one of New Orleans' best-kept secrets. It's a perfect way to get out onto the river—you can see the city's skyline and its significant geography without any hassle, and without having to pay a dime. (It's free for pedestrians.) The ferry runs every 15 to 20 minutes, and the heart of downtown New Orleans is only a stone's throw away, yet Algiers has never been fully assimilated into the city. It retains the feel of an undisturbed turn-of-the-century suburb.

Nobody has established with certainty how Algiers got its name, although the "point" part is easy enough: It refers to the way the area juts into a bend in the Mississippi River. "Algiers" may have referred to the preponderance of slaves who worked a plantation here, or it could have been a geographical conceit (the original Algiers lies across a body of water from France). Others have speculated that the name was derived from the place's having been used as a pirates' refuge. Algiers was not developed as a town until the early 19th century. The rise of steamboat commerce spurred growth in the township; it quickly became an important dry dock and boat-building community. Later, it was a significant railroad city. Many of its earliest structures, however, were destroyed by a major fire in 1895, and the nation's railroad boom went the way of the river boat boom, leaving Algiers to languish for most of the second half of this century. Over the past decade, individual owners have painstakingly renovated many of the surviving buildings in the historic center of the Algiers township. Historical research on the area is proceeding slowly; so far, facts about the people who lived here long ago and built houses are hard to come by. Still, the houses are visually striking (if lacking in strong historical significance): This is where you'll find some of the area's best-preserved examples of late-Victorian gingerbread houses and classic Creole cottages, set in a small neighborhood relatively unmoved by modernity.

While in Algiers, you may also want to visit **Blaine Kern's Mardi Gras World** (see chapter 8 for more information), which sends a free shuttle bus to meet every ferry during the day.

When you exit the ferry, turn right to find Bounty Street. Continue down Bounty for 1 block and, turning left at Pelican Avenue, you'll find:

1. Behrman House, 228 Pelican Ave. This modest ornamental Queen Anne cottage was built by the Behrman family in 1896, 1 year after the devastating fire. Martin Behrman's parents had moved to Algiers from New York in 1865, and here they raised Martin in very modest circumstances. They did pretty well: From 1894 to 1920, he was mayor of New Orleans. Behrman lived in Algiers throughout his life (which ended in 1926), and the likes of General Pershing and Cardinal Gibbons visited him at this house. Behrman's wife lived here until 1940.

Go right at Seguin Street to:

2. 511 Seguin St. This Creole cottage was built in 1849 or 1850 and used originally as a convent and school—it was the first of both in the township. It is a celebrated example of Louisiana Colonial architecture; the French Colonial–style doors are frequently noted as well. This house is currently the residence of Sue and Richard Bond, who operate a "lifestyle tour of New Orleans," including cooking classes, in this house (for more information, call ☎ **504/362-5225**). By the way, the street is named for André Séguin, who opened Algiers' first shipyard in 1819 at what is now the foot of this street.

Turn around and follow Seguin St across Pelican Avenue to Delaronde Street and turn right.

3. 300 Block of Delaronde Street. Most of the houses on this block were built in the 1890s. It is one of Algiers' full blocks of surviving Victorian gingerbread houses. These houses have been single-family residences (and shotgun doubles) for the past century.

4. Seger-Rees House, 405–407 Delaronde St. This two-story double town house was built in 1849 for two partners in shipbuilding, Augustin Seger and Thomas Rees, and is one of the earliest structures to have survived the fire of 1895. It's a striking and Spartan example of the Greek Revival style—the only relief is the Gothic-style iron railing on the second-story porch.

As you continue along Delaronde Street across Verret Street, you will pass a narrow, nicely renovated public space, **Larkin Playground.** This strip between Delaronde and the levee was the location of Algiers' farmers' market. You can see in the architecture on either side of the playground that this was once a social and commercial center of the old township.

Turn right at Olivier Street and continue to the corner of Olivier and Pelican avenues, turning right on Pelican again to see:

5. Mt. Olivet Church. Constructed around 1866, this structure replaced an 1854 church building. This is the oldest surviving church in Algiers. Try to imagine it as it was before subsequent additions—a very modest Gothic-style wooden structure.

Continue on Pelican Avenue to Verret. Turn left at Verret, proceeding across Alix to:

6. Holy Name of Mary Church. This parish church, built in 1929, is known affectionately as the "Cathedral of the Westbank," and it really does loom over the other relatively small buildings around Algiers Point. Like Mt. Olivet Church, this structure replaced an earlier one. One important feature of the original building survives: the 75 stained-glass windows around the church. The old bell has been removed from the tower and now lies in front of the Santa Maria Council of the Knights of Columbus at the corner of Alix and Olivier streets.

☕ **TAKE A BREAK**   If you're ready for a snack or a cup of coffee, head across the street to **News & Brews,** 347 Verret St. This newly opened establishment is a coffee shop of the highest order—the coffee borders on gourmet, and muffins, sodas, juices, and some major national newspapers are on sale. The interior feels like any other urban coffee spot; if you take your snack out to a sidewalk table, however, you can enjoy the calm and character of what is still a small town.

Walking Tour—Algiers Point

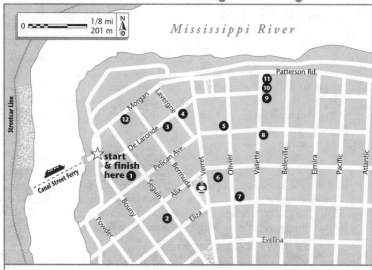

0 |———| 1/8 mi
201 m

N

Mississippi River

Streetcar Line

Canal Street Ferry

Patterson Rd.

Morgan
Lavergne
De Laronde
Pelican Ave.
Bermuda
Seguin
Alix
Bounty
Powder
Eliza
Verret
Olivier
Vallette
Belleville
Elmira
Pacific
Atlantic
Evelina

★ start
& finish
here

⓫
⓾
❾
⓬
❹
❸
❺
❽
❻
❼
❶
❷

① Behrman House
② 511 Seguin St.
③ 300 Block of Delaronde St.
④ Seger-Rees House
⑤ Mt. Olivet Church
⑥ Holy Name of Mary Church
⑦ Trinity Lutheran Church
⑧ Vallette-Barret House
⑨ Delcazel House
⑩ Vallette-Finley House
⑪ The Emporium (Reinke Store)
⑫ Algiers Courthouse

Note: If you have time, you can wander about 10 blocks out of the way to see the 1892 shotgun house at **630 Pacific Ave.** that was used as the setting for the PBS show *This Old House* in 1991. To get there, walk up Verret Street and turn left on Opelousas Avenue, continuing to Pacific Avenue. Turn left.

If you don't stop for coffee or make the detour, continue along Verret Street from Holy Name of Mary Church. Turn left at Eliza Street and left again onto Olivier Street. At the corner of Eliza and Olivier you'll find:

7. Trinity Lutheran Church. This Gothic-cum-Colonial-style church was built in the 1870s, with additions and modifications made at the turn of the century.

Continue down Olivier across Alix Street, turning right onto Pelican Avenue, to:

8. Vallette-Barret House, 705 Pelican Ave. This is one of the most impressive of the surviving 19th-century homes in Algiers, and a good example of Greek Revival architecture with a classic Louisiana center-hall construction that was popular during this period. This was the home of François Vallete, a member of one of Algiers' leading families and a partner in several local businesses in the mid-1800s. The extended Vallette family included some of the earliest developers of the old town. You'll notice the street of the same name.

Continuing along Pelican Avenue, you'll come to the **Algiers Point Public Library,** an Italianate structure built as a library in 1907. Across **Belleville Street** is Belleville School, in a building dating from the 1890s. Return to Vallette Street and turn right to:

9. **Delcazel House,** 238 Vallette St. This two-story house was once affectionately known as the Doll House. It was built in the 1870s for the Delcazel family. Notice the turret set in the corner.

10. **Vallette-Finley House,** 232 Vallette St. This is the oldest home on the block, an adaptation of the vernacular Creole cottage built in 1850. Members of the Vallette family and the relatives of a business partner of François Vallette lived here throughout the 19th century. The Finley family lived here in the early part of this century. The house is said to have been home to 17 people during the Depression.

At the corner of Vallette Street and Patterson Road you'll find:

11. **The Emporium (Reinke Store),** 2009 Patterson St. Built in 1870, this two-story brick building has a residence on the second floor and a store below. It was originally the old Emporium. Notice the early cast-iron railing on the balcony above.

Cross Patterson and walk up to the top of the **Mississippi River Levee.** Heading to your left along the levee, you will return to the ferry terminal. You will also get a good glimpse of the whole shoreline of the east bank and downtown New Orleans. As you're walking, look for:

12. **Algiers Courthouse,** 225 Morgan St. For some reason, the turrets on this building are constructed differently, upsetting the structure's symmetry. Otherwise, the 1896 courthouse boasts the finest public architecture in the city. It has been very nicely renovated, so you might want to poke around inside (if you do, try to check out the courtroom). Previously, this was the site of the Duverje Plantation house. The Duverjes were the original family of modern-day Algiers, and they helped to establish the parish, donating much of their land. Their house, constructed in 1812, burned along with much of the township in 1895.

From the courthouse, walk to the far end of Morgan Street, and on toward the terminal.

Walking Tour 4
Esplanade Ridge

Start: Esplanade Avenue and Johnson Street.
Finish: City Park.
Time: Allow approximately 1½ hours, not including museum, cemetery, and shopping stops.
Best Times: Monday through Saturday, early or late morning.
Worst Times: Sunday, when attractions are closed. Also, you certainly don't want to walk in this area after dark; if you decide to stay in City Park or in the upper Esplanade area until early evening, plan to return on the bus or by taxi.

This is another region of New Orleans that many visitors overlook—even when they drive through it on the way to City Park, the New Orleans Museum of Art, or the Jazz and Heritage Festival. If you're heading to those attractions, consider taking this stroll or leaving enough time for sightseeing from your car. We particularly enjoy the stretch along St. John's Bayou—mostly as slow and quiet as the sluggish water itself. Historically, the Esplanade Ridge area is Creole society's answer to St. Charles Avenue—it's an equally lush boulevard, with stately homes and seemingly ancient trees stretching overhead. Originally, it was the site of homes of the descendants of the earliest settlers. The avenue had its finest days toward the end of the last century, and some of the

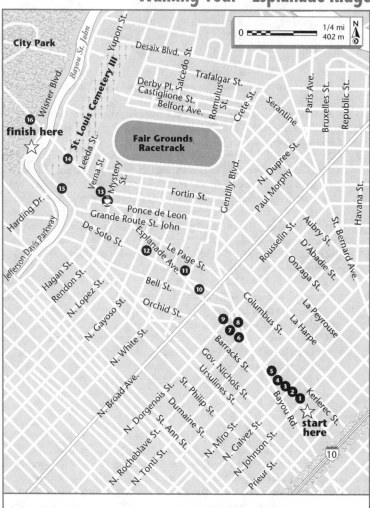

City Park

16 finish here

St. Louis Cemetery III

Wisner Blvd.

Bayou St. John

Yupon St.

Desaix Blvd.

Salcedo St.

Trafalgar St.

Derby Pl.

Castiglione St.

Belfort Ave.

Romulus St.

Crete St.

Serantine

Paris Ave.

Bruxelles St.

Republic St.

Fair Grounds Racetrack

Leeda St.

14

Verna St.

15

Mystery St.

13

Harding Dr.

Jefferson Davis Parkway

Fortin St.

Ponce de Leon

Grande Route St. John

De Soto St.

Le Page St.

Esplanade Ave.

12

11

Gentilly Blvd.

N. Dupree St.

Paul Morphy

Rousselin St.

Aubry St.

D'Abadie St.

Onzaga St.

St. Bernard Ave.

Havana St.

Hagan St.

Rendon St.

N. Lopez St.

N. Gayoso St.

Bell St.

Orchid St.

10

Columbus St.

La Peyrouse

La Harpe

N. White St.

9 **8**
7
6

Barracks St.

Gov. Nichols St.

Ursulines St.

5
4
3
2
1

Kerlerec St.

start here

N. Broad Ave.

N. Dorgenois St.

St. Philip St.

Dumaine St.

St. Ann St.

N. Miro St.

N. Galvez St.

Bayou Rd.

N. Johnson St.

N. Rocheblave St.

N. Tonti St.

Prieur St.

10

0   1/4 mi
        402 m
N

1 2023 Esplanade Avenue

2 Widow Castanedo's House

3 2139 Esplanade Avenue

4 2176 Esplanade Avenue

5 "Goddess of History– Genius of Peace"

6 2306 Esplanade Avenue

7 2326 Esplanade Avenue

8 2337 and 2341 Esplanade Avenue

9 2453 Esplanade Avenue

10 2623 Esplanade Avenue

11 2809 Esplanade Avenue

12 2936 Esplanade Avenue

13 3330 Esplanade Avenue

14 St. Louis Cemetery No. 3

15 Pitot House

16 City Park

neighborhoods along its path, especially the Faubourg Tremé, are visibly suffering. If it is a little worn compared to St. Charles Avenue, Esplanade Avenue is still closer to the soul of the city.

You can catch a bus on Esplanade Avenue at the French Quarter, headed toward the park to your starting point. Otherwise, stroll up Esplanade Avenue to:

1. 2023 Esplanade Ave. Originally a plantation home, this was designed in 1860 for A. B. Charpentier. The building is now operating as Ashton's Mechling Guest House (see chapter 6 for a full listing).

2. Widow Castanedo's House, 2033–35 Esplanade Ave. Juan Rodriguez purchased this land in the 1780s, and his granddaughter, Widow Castanedo, lived in this home until her death in 1861. At that time, the house was a smaller, Spanish colonial-style plantation home. Before Esplanade Avenue extended this far from the river, the house was located in what is now the middle of the street. The widow tried and failed to block the extension of the street. The house was moved to its present site and was enlarged sometime around the 1890s. It has a late-Italianate appearance, similar to the Mechling residence, and is split down the middle and inhabited today by two sisters.

3. 2139 Esplanade Ave. This building is a great example of the typical "Esplanade Ridge Style." The home was probably built for William Chambers, most likely a short time after the Civil War. Note the Ionic columns on the upper level.

On the opposite side of the street is:

4. 2176 Esplanade Ave., a simple, classic-style town house. It was the second Bayou Road home built by Hubert Gerard, who also built the Mechling Guest House at no. 2023.

After you cross N. Miro Street, Esplanade Avenue crosses the diagonal Bayou Road, which was the route to the French-Canadian settlements at St. John's Bayou in the late 17th century. Veer left at the fork to stay on Esplanade Avenue, and look for:

5. "Goddess of History-Genius of Peace." This monument stands on the triangular piece of land at the intersection of Bayou Road, Esplanade Avenue, and Miro Street. In 1886, the land, known to earlier generations as Gayarre Place, was given to the city by Charles Gayarre. George H. Dunbar donated the original statue to be placed there. Purchased from the Audubon Park Cotton Centennial Commission, the statue was destroyed in 1938, and the present one is a replacement.

6. 2306 Esplanade Ave. The house is known as the Musson-Degas House because it was rented for many years by the Musson family. Estelle Musson married René Degas, brother of Edgar Degas, the French Impressionist artist. (She and her descendants dropped his last name after he ran off with a neighbor's wife.) Degas is said to have painted the portrait of Estelle that is now in the New Orleans Museum of Art, as well as many other works, during the time he spent living at no. 2306. The house was built in 1854, and the Italianate decorations were added later, when it was split into two buildings. The right hand one is currently open as a homage to Degas (and is also a fine B&B; call ☎ **504/821-5009** for details), while the left hand one is being restored with the grand hopes of someday reuniting the two halves. This is the only studio or residence of Degas' open to the public in the world, so drop in (between 9am and 4pm, daily) and poke around.

7. 2326 Esplanade Ave. The current resident of this house has on display a collection of small metal houses, cinder-block sculptures, and a beautiful metal-crafted marlin on the front porch. The house is known as the Reuther House because it was owned by Joseph Reuther, a baker, in 1913.

In passing, take a look at nos. 2325, 2329, and 2331—all are interesting examples of Creole cottages. Continue to:

8. 2337 and 2341 Esplanade Ave. These houses were identical structures when they were built in 1862 for John Budd Slawson, owner of a horse-drawn streetcar company that operated along Bayou Road in the 19th century. Then, they were both single-story shotgun-style houses. Notice the unusual ironwork underneath the front roof overhang.

Cross N. Dorgenois Street to:

9. 2453 Esplanade Ave. Until the other was demolished, this house was one of a pair at the corner of Dorgenois Street. Though its architecture has been changed extensively, it's one of the few remaining mansard-roofed homes on Esplanade Ridge.

Cross Broad Avenue to:

10. 2623 Esplanade Ave. Here is a classical revival Victorian home built in 1896 by Louis A. Jung. Note the Corinthian columns. The Jungs donated the triangular piece of land at Esplanade Avenue, Broad Street, and Crete Street to the city on the condition that it remain public property. It is officially known as DeSoto Park and is graced by a fence in the art nouveau style.

11. 2809 Esplanade Ave., one of the more decorative Victorian Queen Anne center-hall houses on Esplanade Ridge.

12. 2936 Esplanade Ave., a nice example of what's known as a Gothic villa.

☕ **TAKE A BREAK**   At the intersection of Mystery Street and Esplanade Avenue you'll find a little grouping of shops and restaurants. If you're in the area at lunchtime, you might want to stop at **Café Degas** for a leisurely meal—if the weather is nice, the semioutdoors setting is exceedingly pleasant. If you just want a snack or some picnic food for City Park, we highly recommend a quick sandwich or salad from **Wholefoods.** You can also opt for a break at the **Brew Time** coffeehouse, behind Café Degas.

Continue to:

13. 3330 Esplanade Ave., a galleried frame home built in the Creole-cottage style.

14. St. Louis Cemetery No. 3, on your right. This was the site of the public Bayou Cemetery, established in 1835. It was purchased by the St. Louis diocese in 1856 and contains the burial monuments of many of the diocese's priests. If you've been putting off going into the cemeteries because of concerns over safety, this is one you can explore on your own—remember, though, to be aware of your surroundings. You can pick up brochures in the office.

From the cemetery, head back out to Esplanade Avenue and continue walking toward City Park. When you get to the bridge, you can go left, following the signs, along St. John's Bayou (one of the nicest, and least touristed areas of the city) to:

15. Pitot House, 1440 Moss St., which is open for public viewing (see chapter 8 for a description).

Or continue walking straight into:

16. **City Park,** where you can explore the amphitheater, museum, and gardens (see chapter 8 for more details).

A Streetcar Tour

Start: St. Charles Avenue and Canal Street.

Finish: Audubon Park or Carrollton Avenue.

Time: 45 minutes, not including time spent eating or wandering at any of the stops.

Best Times: Around 11am. This allows for a leisurely morning or afternoon spent wandering and exploring elsewhere, enabling you to return to the Central Business District or the Vieux Carré in time to get dressed for dinner.

Worst Times: Morning and evening rush hours and late afternoons, when the cars are packed with commuters and school-age children.

A good way to see some of the most historic and architecturally interesting sights in New Orleans is to ride the famous streetcar that runs along St. Charles Avenue. Just a few decades ago, a whole system of streetcar routes crisscrossed the city; the St. Charles line is the only one still in operation. It will take you through the Central Business District and the Garden District, past two historic universities and Audubon Park, and on to the Riverbend area at Carrollton Avenue.

The driver doesn't call out stops, so you'll have to pay attention to building numbers as you. go. The fare is $1, and you must pay every time you get on.

Before you board the streetcar, stop at the corner of Canal Street and St. Charles Avenue and have a look at:

1. **The Crescent Billiard Hall,** 115 St. Charles Ave. Built in 1826, the structure was remodeled in 1865, turning the inside into an enormous billiard hall. The Pickwick Club, founded in 1857, took over the building in 1950. (Incidentally, the members of the Pickwick Club had a hand in founding the Krewe of Comus, also in 1857.)

Now walk a block west to the streetcar stop on Common St. While you wait, notice:

2. The former **Kolb's Restaurant** (but by the time you read this, perhaps the new Jockey Club Hotel), 121–123 and 125–127 St. Charles Ave. The building at 125–127 was originally a museum (ca. 1844); it closed shortly after opening. The 121–123 structure was built in 1853. Kolb's Restaurant began as a saloon and had been in operation since 1898. It's now closed, and the new upscale Jockey Club Hotel (slated to open in the first quarter of 2000) plans to renovate the outside of both buildings to their former glory.

Board the streetcar (move to the back, please). From your perch, take note of:

3. **Lafayette Square,** on your left between streetcar stops 3 and 4 and next door to the Federal Court of Appeals. Bounded by Camp Street, North Street, South Street, and St. Charles Avenue, it's the oldest public square in New Orleans. It was named after the Marquis' visit to the city in 1825. Oddly enough, there is no monument to Lafayette in the park.

Also between stops 3 and 4, on the right, across from Lafayette Square is:

4. **Gallier Hall,** 545 St. Charles Ave. This impressive Greek Revival building was the inspiration of James Gallier Sr. Erected between 1845 and 1853, it served as City Hall for just over a century. After the completion of the building's basement,

A Streetcar Tour

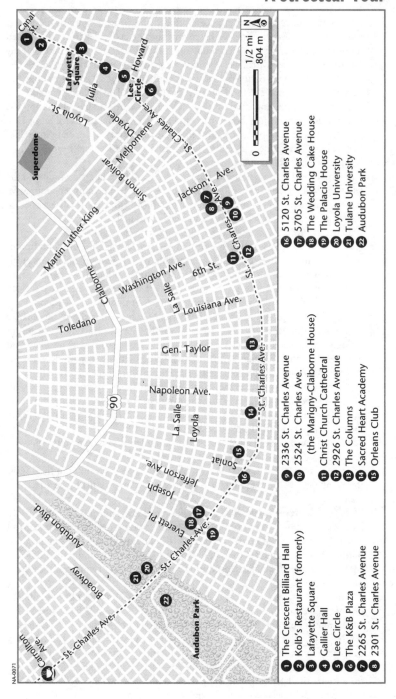

N

1/2 mi
804 m

0

Canal St.
Lafayette Square
Julia
Lee Circle
Howard
Loyola St.
Superdome
Dryades
Melpomene
St. Charles Ave.
Simon Bolivar
Martin Luther King
Jackson Ave.
Claiborne
Washington Ave.
6th St.
La Salle
Louisiana Ave.
St. Charles St.
Toledano
Gen. Taylor
Napoleon Ave.
La Salle
Loyola
Soniat
Jefferson Ave.
Joseph
Everett Pl.
St. Charles Ave.
Audubon Blvd.
Broadway
St. Charles Ave.
Audubon Park
Carrollton Ave.
90

1. The Crescent Billiard Hall
2. Kolb's Restaurant (formerly)
3. Lafayette Square
4. Gallier Hall
5. Lee Circle
6. The K&B Plaza
7. 2265 St. Charles Avenue
8. 2301 St. Charles Avenue
9. 2336 St. Charles Avenue
10. 2524 St. Charles Ave. (the Marigny-Claiborne House)
11. Christ Church Cathedral
12. 2926 St. Charles Avenue
13. The Columns
14. Sacred Heart Academy
15. Orleans Club
16. 5120 St. Charles Avenue
17. 5705 St. Charles Avenue
18. The Wedding Cake House
19. The Palacio House
20. Loyola University
21. Tulane University
22. Audubon Park

NA-0071

201

the city ran out of money to fund the project, and construction was delayed. A roof was placed over the finished basement, and the police department occupied it until money was raised for its completion. It took 2 years to finish, and on May 10, 1853, it was dedicated. The building measures 90 feet in width and 215 feet in depth, and stands 3 stories high. It is constructed of Tuckahoe marble and features two impressive rows of fluted Ionic columns. The building has been the site of many important events in New Orleans' history—especially during the Reconstruction and Huey Long eras—and has received an impressive list of U.S. presidents. Several important figures in Louisiana history lay in state in Gallier Hall before being buried, including Jefferson Davis and General Beauregard.

The streetcar will soon come to:

5. **Lee Circle,** St. Charles and Howard avenues. If you look out the window to the left, you will be able to see the statue of Robert E. Lee atop an impressive pedestal and column—note that he's facing north (so his back will never be to his enemies). It was officially raised and dedicated in 1884.

Between streetcar stops 6 and 7, you'll notice on the right side:

6. **The K&B Plaza,** St. Charles Avenue and Lee Circle. Look for the collection of sculpture outside the K&B headquarters building. There is an equally magnificent grouping inside the lobby, which is open to the public from 9am to 5pm during the week. If you're an art lover, hop off the streetcar and have a look. Inside you'll find works by many noted sculptors, including Henry Moore.

From here on, it's fun to watch as the styles of homes along the avenue change from Greek Revival to Victorian to early 1900s. The Garden District begins at Jackson Avenue, and you may want to get off the trolley to explore it fully. From the streetcar you'll see many homes in their garden settings, beginning with:

7. **2265 St. Charles Ave.,** on your right. The famed James Gallier Jr. was one of the architects of this Greek Revival mansion. It was built for Lavinia Dabney in 1856—a time when it was very rare for a woman to purchase a house, especially in the Garden District. In the nationwide recession the following year, however, Lavinia lost possession of the house.

8. **2301 St. Charles Ave.** This spacious, two-story white house, on your right, was Anne Rice's childhood home.

9. **2336 St. Charles Ave.** is on your left. When this cottage was built in the 1840s, the avenue was a dirt road known as Nyades—nothing like the broad street you see today.

10. **2524 St. Charles Ave.** (the Marigny-Claiborne House), on your left. Anne Rice's family moved into this transitional-style raised villa (part classic, part Italianate) when she was 14. The house was originally built around 1856 for Sophie Claiborne, whose husband was the son of Bernard Marigny (for whom the Faubourg Marigny is named). Finances lost during a recession the following year forced her to move out.

11. **The Christ Church Cathedral,** 2919 St. Charles Ave., on your right, is home to one of the oldest Protestant congregations in the Mississippi Valley. This Gothic structure was built in 1877; it suffered the loss of a steeple in a 1915 hurricane.

12. **2926 St. Charles Ave.** is on your left. This house was built in 1882, with a gallery for every room and an early air-conditioning system—a 12-inch space between inner and outer walls. Don't be confused by the number 710 above the front door—it's left over from an outdated numbering system.

On your right between stops 21 and 22, you'll see:

13. **The Columns,** 3811 St. Charles Ave. This is where *Pretty Baby* was filmed (accommodations are offered; see chapter 6). It was built in the 1880s. You'll

know it by the enormous columns and the sprawling front porch—the perfect place for a nightcap.

Soon after, you'll look out the right side of the streetcar and wonder about that huge brick building with the cupola. It's the:

14. Sacred Heart Academy, 4521 St. Charles Ave., between stops 24 and 25. This building houses a Catholic girls' school. Its Colonial Revival–style central portion was built in 1900, and the wings were added in the next 2 decades. The fountain in front dates from the late 1840s, when the academy occupied a house on this site.

15. Orleans Club, 5005 St. Charles Ave., is on the right between stops 27 and 28. Built in 1868 by William Lewis Wynn as a wedding gift for his daughter, it's now a private social and cultural women's club that's sometimes used for debut teas and wedding receptions. The local landmark is one of the oldest structures on St. Charles Avenue above the Garden District.

On your left you'll see an interesting neo-Italianate mansion:

16. 5120 St. Charles Ave. was built in 1907 by the owners of one of the largest department stores in New Orleans. It changed hands a number of times (one owner was the silent-screen star Marguerite Clark) before it was finally donated to the city of New Orleans for use as a public library. If you'd like to look at the interior, especially the painted ceiling and the paneling, get off at stop 27 or 28.

If you were swept away by *Gone With the Wind,* stop at:

17. 5705 St. Charles Ave., between stops 30 and 31 on the right side. This house was designed directly after the plans for Tara, which was only a Hollywood set in the first place. It was constructed in 1941.

On your right between stops 31 and 32 is:

18. The Wedding Cake House, 5809 St. Charles Ave., one of the most eye-catching houses in the city. Notice especially the elaborate balconies on this Victorian and Colonial Revival mansion.

Nearby on your left you'll see:

19. The Palacio House, 5824 St. Charles Ave., between stops 31 and 32. This was built in 1867 for Antonio Palacio, a native of Spain. It's the work of Henry Howard, who also designed many Garden District homes, as well as Nottoway Plantation in White Castle, Louisiana.

A few stops down is:

20. Loyola University, 6363 St. Charles Ave. The university has occupied the 6000 block of St. Charles Avenue since 1911. From 1904 to 1911, this was a preparatory school, Loyola Academy. The university campus covers some 14 acres. Its redbrick main buildings form three sides of a square facing the avenue. On the left (also facing the avenue) is the school's church, reflecting hints of Canterbury. It, like the others on St. Charles Avenue, is in Tudor-Gothic style. Behind these buildings, the modern Dana Center student union is a popular gathering spot, and its cafe and snack bar are open to visitors. Loyola, incidentally, is the largest Catholic university in the South.

Right next door is:

21. Tulane University, 6823 St. Charles Ave., between stops 36 and 37. It dates from 1834, when the Medical College of Louisiana was founded. The University of Louisiana, begun in 1847, was merged with the medical school. In 1884, when Paul Tulane left a bequest of $1 million to the combined schools, the name was changed. In 1918, Sophie Newcomb College—a college for women founded in 1886—moved to this campus. Today, Newcomb is a college within the Tulane University system. The university's academic departments have produced many leading scholars and community leaders across the South; its medical and law schools are among the best in the country. (The medical school occupies a downtown campus on Tulane Avenue.)

As you pass by Tulane and Loyola, you'll come to:

22. **Audubon Park,** the entrance to which can be seen on your left (it's also between stops 36 and 37). The park extends all the way to the levee at the Mississippi. For more information about the park, see chapter 8.

🍵 **WINDING DOWN**   The Riverbend (stops 43 and 44) area is a nice spot for a rest, a bit of shopping, a bite to eat, and some exploring. You might want to get a burger at the **Camellia Grill** or coffee and pastries at **La Madeleine** (a branch of the one in the French Quarter). **Lenny's,** a newsstand just down from the Camellia Grill, is a great place to get papers, magazines, and other traveler's paraphernalia.

Shopping 10

Shopping in New Orleans is a highly evolved leisure activity, with a shop for every strategy and a fix for every shopaholic—and every budget. Don't assume those endless T-shirt shops on Bourbon, or even the costly antique stores on Royal, are all New Orleans has to offer. The range is as good as it gets—many a clever person has come to New Orleans just to open up a quaint boutique filled with strange items gathered from all parts of the globe, or produced by local, somewhat twisted, folk artists.

Want to totally redecorate your house? You can do that here, whether you want a complete Victorian look or top-to-bottom folk art. Want to double your record or CD collection? This town is made of music. Want to bring home the perfect souvenir? From an antique sofa that costs about as much as a semester at college, to 50¢ Mardi Gras beads, you'll have plenty of options.

Searching for these treasures will be part of what contributes to your calorie-burning walks. Many a well-spent day, or even days, can be had strolling the Quarter, window shopping. But don't forget the many options down on Magazine Street. Antique aficionados eschew exorbitant Royal Street for Magazine, because they know the best buys are found there.

New Orleans has always been a place for fine homes and fine furnishings, and as people trade up, they leave some great antiques for the rest of us. Many came from Europe in the early days, while others were crafted right in the city by cabinetmakers internationally known for their exquisite pieces. Antiquing has become so popular in New Orleans that there are even people who will take you on a personalized guided tour of city shops (for more information, see "Organized Tours" in chapter 8). In addition, the **Royal Street Guild** (☎ **504/ 524-1260**), an association of some of the city's antique dealers, has put together brochures that are available at most hotels.

You'll also notice below that the city's art galleries are clustered around the antiques, and on Julia Street as well. Over the past 20 years (notice that's about as long as the Contemporary Arts Center has been open), New Orleans has grown to be an important regional and national market for contemporary fine arts.

Of course, if you're just looking for some souvenirs, there are whole colonies of shops in the French Quarter selling postcards, posters, sunglasses, and T-shirts. Most of them are cheap and ghastly, if not in flamingly bad taste. You might also consider bringing home Cajun spices, pralines, a Cajun or zydeco CD or two, or a box of beignet mix; these are the things that truly say you've been to New Orleans.

1 The Shopping Scene

CANAL PLACE   At the foot of Canal Street (365 Canal St.), where it reaches the Mississippi River, this shopping center holds more than 50 shops, many of them branches of some of this country's most elegant retailers. The three-tiered mall has polished marble floors, a landscaped atrium, fountains, and pools. Stores in this sophisticated setting include Brooks Brothers, Bally of Switzerland, Saks Fifth Avenue, Gucci, Williams-Sonoma, and Jaeger. Open Monday to Wednesday 10am to 6pm, Thursday 10am to 8pm, Friday and Saturday 10am to 7pm, and Sunday noon to 6pm.

THE FRENCH MARKET   Shops within the Market begin on Decatur Street across from Jackson Square; offerings include candy, cookware, fashion, crafts, toys, New Orleans memorabilia, and candles. It's open 10am to 6pm (and the Farmer's Market Café du Monde is open 24 hours). Quite honestly, there is a lot of junk, but there are some good buys mixed in, and it's always fun to stroll through—and grab a nibble.

JACKSON BREWERY   Just across from Jackson Square at 600–620 Decatur St., the old brewery building has been transformed into a jumble of shops, cafes, delicatessens, restaurants, and entertainment. The wares at the 125 shops, restaurants, and cafes within its walls include fashion, gourmet and Cajun-Creole foodstuffs, toys, hats, crafts, pipes, posters, and souvenirs. The latest addition to this mall is a branch of the theme restaurant Planet Hollywood. Keep in mind that many shops in the Brewery close at 5:30 or 6pm, before the Brewery itself. Open Sunday to Thursday 10am to 9pm, Friday and Saturday 10am to 10pm.

JULIA STREET   From Camp Street down to the river on Julia Street, you'll find many of the city's best contemporary art galleries. Of course, some of the works are a bit pricey, but there are good deals to be had if you're collecting, and fine art to be seen if you're not. You'll find many of them listed below.

MAGAZINE STREET   This is the Garden District's premier shopping street. More than 140 shops (some of which are listed below), line the street in 19th-century brick storefronts and quaint cottagelike buildings. Among the offerings are antiques, art galleries, boutiques, crafts, and dolls. The greatest concentration of stores is between Felicity and Washington streets, but if you're so inclined, you could shop your way from here all the way to Audubon Park. Or hop on and off the bus every time you reach a dry stretch (you'll have to pay a new fare each time, however).

NEW ORLEANS CENTRE   New Orleans' newest shopping center, at 1400 Poydras St., features a glass atrium and includes upscale stores like Lord & Taylor and Macy's. There are three levels of specialty shops and restaurants. Open Monday to Saturday 10am to 8pm and Sunday noon to 6pm.

RIVERBEND   The Riverbend district is in the Carrollton area. To reach it, ride the St. Charles Avenue streetcar to stop 44, then walk down Maple Street 1 block to Dublin Park, the site of an old public market once lined with open stalls. Nowadays, renovated shops inhabit the old general store, a produce warehouse made of barge board, and the town surveyor's raised-cottage home. Among the outstanding shops are Yvonne LaFleur, whose romantic fashions have appeared on TV and movie screens, and the Cache Pot, with a concentration of unusual, high-quality gifts.

RIVERWALK MARKETPLACE   This popular shopping development at 1 Poydras St. is an exciting covered mall that runs right along the river from Poydras Street to the Convention Center. If you have to go to a mall, it's a mighty pretty one (and a decent place to get out of the rain). In December 1996, the market made big news around the world when it was struck by a grain freighter descending the river; a number of shops were damaged, but there were no fatalities and everything was back in place shortly afterward. Among the 140 specialty shops, you'll find Eddie Bauer, the Limited, the Sharper Image, and Banana Republic, plus several places to eat and periodic free entertainment. Open Monday to Thursday 10am to 9pm, Friday and Saturday 10am to 10pm, and Sunday 12:30 to 5:30pm.

2 Shopping A to Z

ANTIQUES

Audubon Antiques. 2025 Magazine St. ☎ **504/581-5704.** Mon–Sat 10:30am–5pm, Sun 11am–5pm.

Audubon has everything from collectible curios to authentic antique treasures at reasonable prices. There are two floors of goods, so be prepared to lose yourself.

Boyer Antiques-Dolls & Buttons. 241 Chartres St. ☎ **504/522-4513.** Mon–Sat 11am–5pm.

In addition to an assortment of antiques, you'll find an enchanting collection of old dolls, doll houses and furniture, and toys. Most date from the 19th and early 20th centuries.

✪ **Bush Antiques and Beds Au Beau Reve.** 2109–2111 Magazine St. ☎ **504/581-3518.** Mon–Sat 10am–5pm.

This wonderful treasure trove features impressive European religious art and objects and a beautiful array of beds. An extra treat is the collection of folk art on the rear patio.

Charbonnet & Charbonnet. 2728 Magazine St. ☎ **504/891-9948.** Mon–Sat 9am–5pm.

If country pine is what you're looking for, you'll find it here. Charbonnet & Charbonnet has some beautiful English and Irish pieces. In addition, custom furnishings are made on-site.

Dixon & Dixon of Royal. 237 Royal St. ☎ **800/848-5148** or 504/524-0282. Mon–Sat 9am–5:30pm, Sun 10am–5pm.

Dixon & Dixon features 18th- and 19th-century European fine art and antiques, jewelry, grandfather clocks, and Oriental rugs. The collection of tall-case clocks is one of the largest in the country; the individual clocks are awe-inspiring. The Dixon & Dixon company is a long-standing family run business; the firm has helped many younger collectors make some of their initial purchases.

Jack Sutton Antiques. 315 Royal St. ☎ **504/522-0555.** Daily 10am–5pm.

In some ways, the Suttons are to jewelry and antiques what the Brennans are to food: same family, different businesses. There are a number of Suttons around New Orleans, mostly on Royal. This one, our favorite, specializes in jewelry and objects. The selection of estate jewelry ("estate" meaning "older than yesterday but less than 100 years") is often better than that at other antique stores—the author's engagement ring came from here—but thanks to the ebb and flow of the estate business, you can never be sure what may be offered. The store encourages special requests and has a room devoted to "men's gift items" such as antique gambling, cigar, and drinking paraphernalia.

Kiel's Antiques. 325 Royal St. ☎ **504/522-4552.** Mon–Sat 9am–5pm.

Kiel's was established in 1899 and is currently run by the fourth generation of the founding family. The shop has a considerable collection of 18th- and 19th-century French and English furniture, chandeliers, jewelry, and decorative items.

Le Wicker Gazebo. 3715 Magazine St. ☎ **504/899-1355.** Mon–Sat 10am–5pm.

The name gives this one away. Get your wicker furniture here, folks. At Le Wicker, you can find antique wicker, new and custom-built wicker furniture, and wicker baskets, plus new and antique quilts, miniature furnishings for children, and domestic repair and painting items.

✪ **Lucullus.** 610 Chartres St. ☎ **504/528-9620.** Mon–Sat 9:30am–5pm.

An unusual shop, Lucullus has a wonderful collection of culinary antiques as well as 17th-, 18th-, and 19th-century furnishings to "complement the grand pursuits of cooking, dining, and imbibing." They have recently opened a second shop at 3932 Magazine St.

Magazine Arcade Antiques. 3017 Magazine St. ☎ **504/895-5451.** Mon and Wed–Sat 10am–5pm.

This large, fascinating shop once housed the Garden District's classiest merchant. Today, it holds an exceptional collection of 18th- and 19th-century European, Asian, and American furnishings as well as music boxes, dollhouse miniatures, European and Oriental porcelain, cloisonné, lacquer, cameos, opera glasses, old medical equipment, windup phonographs, antique toys, and scores of other items. Try to allow plenty of time to browse through it all.

Manheim Galleries. 403–409 Royal St. ☎ **504/568-1901.** Mon–Sat 9am–5pm.

At Manheim Galleries you'll find an enormous collection of continental, English, and Oriental furnishings sharing space with porcelains, jade, silver, and fine paintings. Manheim Galleries is also the agent for Boehm Birds.

Miss Edna's Antiques. 2035 Magazine St. ☎ **504/524-1897.** Tues–Sat 10am–5pm; Mon by appointment.

Miss Edna's carries eclectic antiques—furniture, specialty items, curios—and paintings, with a focus on 19th-century works. Miss Edna recently moved a few feet up Magazine, doubling her inventory and expanding her art collection.

✪ **Rothschild's Antiques.** 241 and 321 Royal St. ☎ **504/523-5816** or 504/523-2281. Mon–Sat 9:30am–5:30pm; Sun by appointment.

Rothschild's is a fourth-generation furniture merchandiser. Some of the most interesting things you'll find here are antique and custom-made jewelry (the store is also a full-service jeweler). There's a fine selection of antique silver, marble mantels, porcelains, and English and French furnishings. Rothschild's devotes tens of thousands of square feet to displaying and warehousing antiques.

Sigle's Antiques & Metalcraft. 935 Royal St. ☎ **504/522-7647.** Mon–Sat 10am–4pm.

If you've fallen in love with the lacy ironwork that drips from French Quarter balconies, this is the place to pick out some pieces to take home. In addition, Sigle's has converted some of the ironwork into useful household items, such as plant holders.

Whisnant Galleries. 222 Chartres St. ☎ **504/524-9766.** Mon–Sat 9:30am–5:30pm, Sun 10am–5pm.

The quantity and variety of merchandise in this shop is mind-boggling. You'll find all sorts of unusual and unique antique collectibles, including items from Ethiopia,

Russia, Greece, South America, Morocco, and other parts of North Africa, and the Middle East.

ART GALLERIES

With one major exception, galleries in New Orleans follow the landscape of antique shops: Royal and Magazine streets. Since the opening of the Contemporary Arts Center, galleries also have kept popping up around Julia Street and the warehouse district. Some are listed below, and there are others. All are strong contemporary fine art galleries, but it can be hard to tell them apart. The brochure "Arts in the Warehouse District" (call for it at ☎ 504/394-1515) lists all of the galleries on Julia Street and some of the surrounding streets. If you're contemplating a gallery-hopping jaunt, start at Julia Street.

Ariodante. 535 Julia St. ☎ **504/524-3233.** Mon–Sat 11am–5pm. Closed Mon during daylight saving time.

A contemporary craft gallery, Ariodante features hand-crafted furniture, glass, ceramics, jewelry, and decorative accessories by nationally acclaimed artists. Rotating shows offer a detailed look at works by various artists.

Arius Art Tiles. 504 St. Peter St. ☎ **504/529-1665.** Daily 9:30am–5:30pm.

Arius designs and sells art tiles of the sort you might have seen if you've ever been to Santa Fe, New Mexico. In fact, many of the tiles are made in Santa Fe, and Arius has a sister gallery in New Mexico. This is no trend-chasing or fly-by-night operation; the proprietors have been in the business for 25 years. Both Southwest and Louisiana designs are made here, and new designs come out every 6 months. You can also place a custom order.

✪ **Arthur Roger Gallery.** 432 Julia St. ☎ **504/522-1999.** www.artroger.com. Mon–Sat 10am–5pm.

Arthur Roger sets the pace for the city's fine art galleries. Since opening in New Orleans 20 years ago, Roger has played a major role in developing the art community and in tying it to the art world in New York. Time and again he has taken chances—moving early into the warehouse district and briefly opening a second gallery in New York—and he continues to do so, scheduling shows that range from strongly regional work to the far-flung. The gallery represents many artists, including Francis Pavy (who did the 1997 Jazz Fest poster), Ida Kohlmeyer, Douglas Bourgeois, Ersy Schwartz, Paul Lucas, Clyde Connell, Willie Birch, Gene Koss, and George Dureau.

Bergen Galleries. 730 Royal St. ☎ **800/621-6179** or 504/523-7882. www.bergen galleries.com. Sun–Thurs 9am–9pm, Fri–Sat 9am–10pm.

Bergen Galleries has the city's largest selection of posters and limited-edition graphics, on such subjects as Mardi Gras, jazz, and the city itself, and by such artists as Erté, Icart, Nagel, Maimon, and Tarkay. Bergen also features a large collection of works by sought-after African American artists. The service by Margarita and her staff is friendly and extremely personable.

Berta's and Mina's Antiquities. 4138 Magazine St. ☎ **504/895-6201.** Mon–Sat 10am–6pm, Sun 11am–6pm.

In years past, Antiquities was just another place that bought and sold antiques and secondhand furniture and art. That all ended on the day in 1993 that Nilo Lanzas (Berta's husband and Mina's dad) began painting. Now you can barely see the furniture in the shop for all the new art. Dubbed "folk art" or "outsider art," Lanzas' works are colorful scenes from life in New Orleans or his native Latin America, stories out of the Bible, or images sprung from his imagination. His paintings are on wood with titles or commentaries painted on the frames; he also makes some tin sculptures and wood carvings. If you drop in, don't be surprised to find Lanzas quietly painting away near the counter—he paints 10 to 12 hours a day.

Bryant Galleries. 316 Royal St. ☎ **800/844-1994** or 504/525-5584. Sun–Thurs 10am–5:30pm, Fri–Sat 10am–9pm.

This gallery represents renowned artists Ed Dwight, Fritzner Lamour, and Leonardo Nierman, and other American, European, and Haitian artists. The varied work on display here may include jazz bronzes, glasswork, and graphics. The staff is very friendly and helpful; if you can't get here during the hours listed, ask nicely and chances are they'll make arrangements for you.

✪ **Casey Willems Pottery.** 3919 Magazine St. ☎ **504/899-1174.** Mon–Sat 10am–5pm.

Watch Casey Willems create functional art on his pottery wheel as you browse his gallery. You'll find bowls, lamps, pitchers, vases, and teapots, all created in the shop.

Cole Pratt Gallery, Ltd. 3800 Magazine St. ☎ **504/891-6789.** Tues–Sat 10am–5:30pm. July–Sept closes at 5pm.

This gallery showcases the work of 35 Southern artists whose creations include abstract and realist paintings, sculptures, and ceramics. The art is of the highest quality and the prices surprisingly reasonable.

✪ **The Davis Galleries.** 3964 Magazine St. ☎ **504/897-0780.** Tues–Sat 10am–5pm.

One of two world-class galleries in New Orleans (the other being A Galley for Fine Photography), this may be the best place in the world for Central and West African traditional art. The owner makes regular trips to Africa for collecting. Works on display might include sculpture, costuming, basketry, textiles, weapons, and jewelry.

Diane Genre Oriental Art and Antiques. 431 Royal St. ☎ **504/595-8945.** www.dianegenreorientalart.com. By appointment only.

If all of the 18th- and 19th-century European antiques in the stores along Royal are starting to look the same, it's time to step into Diane Genre's shop. By comparison, the atmosphere in here seems as delicate as one of the ancient East Asian porcelains on display. Hold your breath and get an eyeful of furniture, 18th-century Japanese woodblock prints, and a world-class collection of Chinese and Japanese textiles. There are also scrolls, screens, engravings, and lacquers.

Dyansen Gallery. 433 Royal St. ☎ **800/211-6984** or 504/523-2902. Sun–Thurs 10am–6pm, Fri–Sat 10am–8pm, and by appointment.

A branch of the Dyansen family galleries (there are others in San Francisco and New York), this location features graphics, sculpture, and original gouaches by Erté. Other artists represented include Richard Estes, LeRoy Neiman, and Paul Wegner.

Galerie Royale, Ltd. 728 St. Louis St. ☎ **504/523-1588.** Daily 10am–6pm (11am–6pm on some Sun).

This gallery's collection is built around the works of William Tolliver, an African American artist from Mississippi. Tolliver came to painting relatively late in his life and without formal training. Despite this, he's quickly become an internationally recognized contemporary Impressionist painter. (He was chosen to create the official poster for the 1996 Summer Olympics.) At Galerie Royale, you can find a selection of Tolliver's museum-quality pieces, as well as work by other artists, including Salvador Dalí, Bonny Stanglmaier, and Verna Hart.

Galerie Simonne Stern. 518 Julia St. ☎ **504/529-1118.** Mon Noon–5pm, Tues–Sat 10am–5pm.

Galerie Simonne Stern features paintings, drawings, and sculptures by contemporary artists. Recent shows have included the works of Sam Gilliam, George Dunbar, Richard Johnson, James McGarrell, Lynda Benglis, Albert Paley, and Arthur Silverman.

❍ **A Gallery for Fine Photography.** 322 Royal St. ☎ **504/568-1313.** Mon–Sat 10am–6pm, Sun 11am–6pm.

It would be a mistake to skip this incredibly well-stocked photography gallery. Even if you aren't in the market, it's worth looking around. Owner Joshua Mann Pailet (a photographer) calls this "the only museum in the world that's for sale." It really is like a museum of photography, with just about every period and style represented, and frequent shows of contemporary artists. When they aren't swamped, the staff is more than happy to show you some of the many photos in the files. The gallery emphasizes New Orleans and Southern history and contemporary culture (you can buy Ernest Bellocq's legendary Storyville photos) as well as black culture and music. There is something in just about every price range, as well as a terrific collection of photography books, if that better fits your budget.

Hanson Gallery. 229 Royal St. ☎ **504/524-8211.** Mon–Sat 10am–6pm, Sun 11am–5pm.

Hanson Gallery shows paintings, sculpture, and limited-edition prints by contemporary artists such as Peter Max, Frederick Hart, Pradzynski, Anoro, Thysell, Deckbar, Zjawinska, Erickson, LeRoy Neiman, Richard MacDonald, and Behrens.

Hilderbrand Gallery. 4524 Magazine St. ☎ **504/895-3312** or 504/897-3905. By appointment only.

Hilderbrand Gallery represents a number of international, national, and local artists, including Ding Massimo Boccuni, Manfred Egender, Jim Sohr, Walter Rutkowski, Christian Stock, Cort Savage, Mark Westervelt, and Karl Heinz-Strohle. The gallery is a private showroom; call to get information about the artists and to schedule a visit.

Kurt E. Schon, Ltd. 510 St. Louis St. and 523 Royal St. ☎ **504/524-5462.** Mon–Sat 9am–5pm.

Here you'll find the country's largest inventory of 19th-century European paintings. Works include French and British Impressionist and post-Impressionist paintings as well as art from the Royal Academy and the French Salon. Only a fraction of the paintings in the gallery's inventory are housed at this location, but if you're a serious collector, you can make an appointment to visit the St. Louis Street gallery.

LeMieux Galleries. 332 Julia St. ☎ **504/522-5988.** Mon–Sat 10am–5:30pm.

LeMieux represents contemporary artists and fine craftspeople from Louisiana and the Gulf Coast. They include Dr. Bob, Charles Barbier, Pat Bernard, Mary Lee Eggart, Leslie Elliottsmith, JoAnn Greenberg, David Lambert, Shirley Rabe Masinter, Evelyn Menge, Dennis Perrin, Kathleen Sidwell, Leslie Staub, and Kate Trepagnier.

Marguerite Oestreicher Fine Arts. 626 Julia St. ☎ **504/581-9253.** Tues–Sat 10am–5pm and by appointment.

Like the other Julia Street galleries, this one concentrates on contemporary painting, sculpture, and photography. It also consistently shows work by emerging artists. The gallery's recent shows have included works by Milton Avery, Balthus, Joseph Cornell, and Tony Fitzpatrick.

Mario Villa. 3908 Magazine St. ☎ **504/895-8731.** Mon 11–5pm, Tues–Sat 10am–5pm.

Mario Villa is New Orleans' undisputed king of design, or at least the city's most ubiquitous designer. You can see his hand (or mind, anyway) at work in the fancy new Kevin Graham restaurant, Sapphire, and on the exterior columns of the new Wyndham Riverfront Hotel (see chapter 6). To get the full experience, drop into Villa's uptown showroom. Within 5 minutes, you can get a good idea of his aesthetic. There are canvas rugs; plush sofas; wrought-iron chairs, lamps, and tables with organic twists and turns; and a liberal spray of photographs and paintings. It may not be to your taste, but Villa's work is certainly provocative and visually stimulating. Take a moment to look at one of the beds in the front rooms—if they won't enhance your dreams, for good or ill, nothing will.

New Orleans School of Glassworks and Printmaking Studio. 727 Magazine St. ☎ **504/529-7277.** Mon–Sat 11am–5pm. Closed Sat July–Aug.

This institution serves multiple purposes. Here, within 20,000 square feet of studio space, are a 550-pound tank of hot molten glass and a pre–Civil War press. Established glasswork artists and master printmakers display their work in the on-site gallery and teach classes in glassblowing, kiln-fired glass, hand-engraved printmaking, papermaking, and bookbinding. Absolutely unique to the area, the place is worth a visit during gallery hours. Daily glassblowing, fusing, and slumping demonstrations are open for viewing.

✪ **Peligro.** 305 Decatur St. ☎ **504/581-1706.** Mon–Thurs 10am–6pm, Fri–Sat 10am–10pm, Sun noon–6pm.

A bit out of the way but worth checking out, Peligro is one of the best folk art galleries in the city, with an emphasis on primitive and outsider art (but also work from Latin American countries). The owners have a terrific eye for up-and-coming artists. Unfortunately, they seem to have de-emphasized the smaller items that made for marvelous, original gifts.

The Rodrigue Gallery of New Orleans. 721 Royal St. ☎ **504/581-4244.** Daily 10am–6pm.

Blue Dog is the Freddie Krueger of New Orleans; once you've seen Cajun artist George Rodrique's creation, it invades your consciousness and torments your life. Oh, the staring, otherwordly, bordering-on-kitsch canine has its fans, but it scares us. This gallery is the source for all your Blue Dog needs.

Shadyside Pottery. 3823 Magazine St. ☎ **504/897-1710.** Mon–Sat 10am–5pm.

If you want to see a master potter at work, Shadyside Pottery is an excellent place to stop. Charles Bohn, who apprenticed in Japan, can be seen at his wheel all day Tuesday through Friday and until midafternoon on Saturday. He specializes in the Japanese tradition of *Raku,* a type of pottery that has a "cracked" look. In addition to his own work, Bohn carries some glass pieces and a selection of Japanese kites by Mitsuyoshi Kawamoto.

Still-Zinsel Contemporary Fine Art. 328 Julia St. ☎ **504/588-9999.** Mon–Sat 10am–5pm.

This fine art gallery shows paintings, sculpture, photography, and works on paper by contemporary local, national, and international artists. If you're hopping along gallery row on Julia Street, be sure to hop in here; it regularly shows some of the best work on the strip.

Wyndy Morehead Fine Arts. 603 Julia St. ☎ **504/568-9754.** www.411web.com/w/ wyndymoreheadfinearts. Mon–Fri 10am–5:30pm, Sat 10am–5pm.

This gallery shows contemporary fine art in many media. It represents more than 75 local and national artists, including Nofa Dixon, Robert Rector, William Lewis, Ron Richmond, and Joan Steiman.

BEAUTY

Belladonna. 2900 Magazine St. ☎ **504/891-4393.** Mon–Fri 9am–8pm, Sat 9am–6pm.

This spacious store features a day spa for men and women as well as a market for bath products, cosmetics, incense, sleepwear, bedding, homeopathic remedies, and gifts, among other things. The New Age atmosphere is relaxing.

Earthsavers. 434 Chartres St. ☎ **504/581-4999.** Mon–Wed, Fri–Sat 10am–6pm, Thurs 10am–8pm, Sun noon–5pm.

Need some serious detoxing after days of debauching, New Orleans style? This is the place to go. It features an impressive variety of holistic and otherwise healthy body care products (including the very popular, but sometimes hard to find, Kiehl's line), everything for every part of the body. The massive selection of aromatherapy products even includes a line for your dog. Earthsavers also offers facials, massages, and other salon-type pampering services. A pick-me-up here just might help you get through the rest of that wearying round of eating, drinking, and dancing you have planned.

✪ **Hove.** 824 Royal St. ☎ **504/525-7827.** Mon–Sat 10am–5pm.

Founded in 1931, Hove is the oldest perfumery in the city. It features all-natural scents (except the musk, which is synthetic), and the selection is almost overwhelming. Strips with various options, for both men and women, are laid out to help you. The place to establish your signature scent.

BOOKS

Literary enthusiasts will find many destinations in New Orleans. **Maple Street Book Shop,** 7523 Maple St. (☎ **504/866-4916**), is an uptown mecca for bookworms; the **Maple Street Children's Book Shop** is next door at 7529 Maple St. (☎ **504/861-2105**); and **Beaucoup Books** is at 5414 Magazine St. (☎ **504/895-2663**). **Little Professor Book Center of New Orleans,** 1000 S. Carrollton Ave. (☎ **504/866-7646**), stocks one of the best general selections.

Beckham's Bookshop. 228 Decatur St. ☎ **504/522-9875.** Daily 10am–6pm.

Beckham's has two entire floors of old editions, rare secondhand books, and thousands of classical LPs that will tie up your whole afternoon or morning if you don't tear yourself away. The owners also operate **Librairie Bookshop,** 823 Chartres St. (☎ **504/525-4837**), which has a sizable collection of secondhand books.

Faubourg Marigny Bookstore. 600 Frenchmen St. ☎ **504/943-9875.** Mon–Fri 10am–8pm, Sat–Sun 10am–6pm.

This well-stocked gay and lesbian bookstore also carries some local titles. It has a used section, CDs, posters, cards, and gifts (all with a more or less gay or lesbian slant), and holds regular readings and signings. The staff makes this a fine resource center—you can call them for local gay and lesbian info.

✪ **Faulkner House Books.** 624 Pirates Alley. ☎ **504/524-2940.** Daily 10am–6pm.

This shop is on a lot of walking tours of the French Quarter, because it's where Nobel Prize–winner William Faulkner lived while he was writing his early works *Mosquitoes* and *Soldiers' Pay.* Those who step inside instead of just snapping a photo and walking on find something remarkable: possibly the best selection per square foot of any bookstore in the whole wide world, with every bit of shelf space occupied by a book that's both highly collectible and of literary value. The shop holds a large collection of Faulkner first editions and rare and first-edition classics by many other authors, and has a particularly comprehensive collection of New Orleans–related work. Taking up one room and a hallway, Faulkner House feels like a portion of somebody's private home—which it is—but the selection of books here is almost magical.

✪ Garden District Book Shop. 2727 Prytania St. (in the Rink). ☎ **504/895-2266.** Mon–Sat 10am–6pm, Sun 11am–4pm.

The two best bookstores in town dealing in new books are Faulkner's, downtown, and this uptown favorite. Owner Britton Trice has stocked his medium-sized shop with just about every regional book you can think of; if you want a New Orleans or Louisiana-specific book, no matter what the exact focus (interiors, exteriors, food, Creoles, you name it), you should be able to find it here. This is also the place where Anne Rice does book signings whenever she has a new release. They usually have autographed copies of her books, plus fancy special editions of Rice titles they publish themselves.

George Herget Books. 3109 Magazine St. ☎ **504/891-5595.** Mon–Sat 10am–5:30pm, Sun 11am–5pm.

George Herget Books is another of New Orleans' great bookstores. More than 20,000 rare and used books covering absolutely every subject imaginable await browsers and collectors. If you're interested in a particular book on local subjects or by local artists, put this shop on your list—the local and regional selection may be limited, but some of the hardest-to-find books surface here.

Kaboom. 915 Barracks St. ☎ **504/529-5780.** Daily 11am–6pm.

On the edge of the Quarter, Kaboom is a bit off the beaten path, but bibliophiles should make the trek. This is a reader's bookstore, thanks to an owner who is almost scary in his knowledge of literature. The stock (used books only) tends to lean heavily on fiction, but there is little you won't find here.

CANDIES & PRALINES

Aunt Sally's Praline Shop. 810 Decatur St. ☎ **800/642-7257** or 504/944-6090. Daily 8am–8pm.

At Aunt Sally's, in the French Market, you can watch skilled workers perform the 150-year-old process of cooking the original Creole pecan pralines right before your eyes. You'll know they're fresh. The large store also has a broad selection of regional cookbooks, books on the history of New Orleans and its environs, Creole and Cajun foods, folk and souvenir dolls, and local memorabilia. In addition, Aunt Sally's has a collection of zydeco, Cajun, R&B, and jazz CDs and cassettes. They'll ship any purchase.

✪ Laura's Candies. 600 Conti St. ☎ **800/992-9699** or 504/525-3880. Daily 10am–7pm.

Laura's is said to be New Orleans' oldest candy store, established in 1913. (It was previously located on Royal Street.) It has fabulous pralines, but it also has rich, delectable golf-ball-sized truffles—our personal favorite indulgence.

✪ Leah's Candy Kitchen. 714 St. Louis St. ☎ **504/523-5662.** Mon–Sat 10am–10pm, Sun 10am–6pm.

After you've tried all of New Orleans' Creole candy shops, you might very well come to the conclusion that Leah's tops the list. Everything here, from the candy fillings to the chocolate-covered pecan brittle, is made from scratch by second- and third-generation members of Leah Johnson's praline-cookin' family.

COSTUMES & MASKS

Costumery is big business in New Orleans, and not just in the days before Lent. A number of shops in the city specialize in props for Mardi Gras, Halloween, and other occasions. In New Orleans, you never know when you're going to want or need a costume. Here's a tip: New Orleanians often sell their costumes back to these shops after Ash Wednesday, and you can sometimes pick up a one-time-worn outfit at a small fraction of its original cost.

✪ **Little Shop of Fantasy.** 523 Dumaine St. ☎ **504/529-4243.** Mon–Tues and Thurs–Sat 10am–6pm, Sun 1–6pm.

In the Little Shop of Fantasy, owners Mike Stark, Laura and Anne Guccione, and Jill Kellys sell the work of a number of local artists and more than 20 mask makers. Mike creates the feathered masks, Jill does the velvet hats and costumes, and Laura and Anne produce homemade toiletries. Some of the masks and hats are just fun and fanciful, but there are many fashionable ones as well. There are lots of clever voodoo items here, too.

Mardi Gras Center. 831 Chartres St. ☎ **504/524-4384.** Mon–Sat 10am–5pm, Sun 10am–3pm.

Mardi Gras Center carries sizes 2 to 50 and has a wide selection of new, ready-made costumes as well as used outfits. It also carries accessories, such as beads, doubloons, wigs, masks, hats, makeup, jewelry, and Mardi Gras decorations. Mardi Gras Center is also a good place to stop for Halloween supplies.

Uptown Costume & Dance Company. 5533 Magazine St. ☎ **504/895-7969.** Tues–Sat 10am–6pm.

The walls of this small store are covered with spooky monster masks, goofy arrow-through-the-head-type tricks, hats, wigs, makeup, and all other manner of playfulness. It draws a steady, year-long stream of loyal customers: kids going to parties, dancers, clowns, actors. Conventioneers come here for rental disguises. At Mardi Gras, though, things really get cooking. The shop designs party uniforms for a number of Mardi Gras krewe members. Owner Cheeryll Berlier also creates a limited number of wacky Mardi Gras tuxedo jackets, which get gobbled up quick.

FASHION

Billy Bob's. 225 N. Peters St. ☎ **504/524-5578.** Mon–Sat 10am–6pm, Sun 11am–6pm.

This is a clothing store featuring cool men's and women's contemporary clothing, plus a fun atmosphere thanks to hip music and Romeo the dog. Everything is under $100—Billy Bob's shoots for affordable, but not cheesy. (T-shirts are funky and fun, not the "I've fallen and I can't reach my beer" kind found elsewhere in the Quarter.)

Body Hangings. 835 Decatur St. ☎ **800/574-1823** or 504/524-9856. Daily 10am–6pm.

Cloaks have seen more favorable eras. Ever-hopeful, though, this place is keeping the flame alive until the Sherlock Holmes look comes back in style. It has a good collection of capes, scarves, and cloaks. Men's and women's cloaks are available in wool, cotton, corduroy, and velveteen.

The Grace Note. 900 Royal St. ☎ **504/522-1513.** Mon–Sat 10am–6pm, Sun 11am–5pm.

Primarily a clothing store, Grace Note also features some gifts. It's a bit pricey, but the clothes are stunning. The designers here work with vintage and new materials, and what they come up with is usually lush, memorable, and very touchable. If you want to swan around town, feeling as though you've stepped out of an 1800s novel, this is the place for you. The gift items come from "architectural or religious fragments"—think distressed wood and peeling paint—producing one-of-a-kind objects that evoke turn-of-the-century through '40s styles.

Jazz Rags. 1215 Decatur St. ☎ **504/523-2942.** Thurs–Mon noon–6pm.

Stuffed full of stylish, upscale, but reasonably priced, men's and women's vintage clothes. You can find locals combing the racks here for Mardi Gras and Halloween costumes. The snazzily dressed owner, usually accompanied by Ardvis the friendly hound (who hangs out at several nearby stores), is clearly a fashion plate—ask her advice for picking out an outfit.

Jim Smiley Fine Vintage Clothing. 2001 Magazine St. ☎ **504/528-9449.** Daily 11am–5pm.

Jim Smiley has attracted national media recognition as one of the best shops in the world. It features exceptional men's and women's attire, accessories, linens, and textiles from the 19th and 20th centuries. Even if you are not particularly interested in vintage clothing, it's worth a look.

Paisley Babylon. 1319 Decatur St. ☎ **504/529-3696.** Daily 1pm till dark except Tues.

Almost as soon as it opened, this vintage clothing shop at the Esplanade end of Decatur became a regular stop for all funky but chic bohemians, punks, and other style mavens. It's also a fun hangout, with great music blasting away. The prices are higher than at the Salvation Army, but lower than at other trendy vintage boutiques, and the buyers have a good eye for style. There is also a decent collection of costume jewelry and accessories. Any vintage shop is hit and miss, but Paisley Babylon is consistent enough to make it well worth the walk down Decatur.

Trashy Diva. 829 Chartres St. ☎ **504/581-4555.** Mon–Sat noon–6pm, Sun 1–6pm.

Despite the name, there is nothing trashy about the vintage clothes found here. They are absolute treasures, not the usual hit-and-miss bulk found at other vintage shops, unique and in terrific shape, dating from the turn of the century to the 1960s. The drawback is that you will pay through the nose for them. Many items are at least three figures—indeed, there was one showpiece 1920's flapper dress on display behind the counter recently, made of pure gold cloth, all yours for a mere $700.

Violet's. 808 Chartres St. ☎ **504/569-0088.** Daily 9:30am–9pm.

Our greatest temptation among French Quarter shops, given how we feel about romantic, Edwardian, and '20s inspired clothes, in lush fabrics like velvet and satin. There are some dazzling creations here, with appropriate accessories (jewelry, hats, scarves) as well.

Yvonne LaFleur-New Orleans. 8131 Hampson St. ☎ **504/866-9666.**

Yvonne LaFleur, a confessed incurable romantic, is the creator of beautifully feminine original designs. Her custom millinery, silk dresses, evening gowns, lingerie, and sportswear are surprisingly affordable, and all are enhanced by her signature perfume. Her store is in the Riverbend district.

FOOD & DRINK

Brew Ha Ha. 4505 Magazine St. ☎ **504/895-5745.** Mon–Fri 11am–6pm, Sat 11am–5pm.

It used to be the reserve of borderline fanatics and dreamers, but home brewing has become a mass-market phenomenon. Call it microbrewing for the masses. From a small storefront crammed full of supplies, the folks at Brew Ha Ha can get you started. You can get a starter kit for around $30—and, yes, they come with instructions.

Café du Monde Coffee Shop. 800 Decatur St. ☎ **504/581-2914.** Daily 24 hours.

If you want to try your hand at making those scrumptious New Orleans beignets, you can buy the mix at the Café du Monde, in the French Market. To make it complete, pick up a can of the cafe's famous coffee, a special blend of coffee and chicory. The shop also has a very good mail-order service (☎ 800/772-2927; fax 504/587-0847).

Creole Delicacies Gourmet Shop. Riverwalk Marketplace. ☎ **504/523-6425.** www.cooking cajun.com. Mon–Sat 10am–9pm, Sun 10am–7pm.

You'll find Cajun and Creole packaged foods and mixes here. Fill your shopping basket with everything from jambalaya and gumbo mix to rémoulade and hot sauces. They also have a 2 hour cooking class daily that includes a free meal for $17.50. There's another branch of Creole Delicacies at 533 St. Ann St. (☎ **504/525-9508**).

Martin Wine Cellar. 3827 Baronne St. ☎ **504/899-7411.** Mon–Sat 10am–7pm, Sun 10am–2pm.

If you're a wine lover or connoisseur—or if you want to become one—Martin Wine Cellar may be your most significant find in New Orleans. It carries an eye-popping selection of wines, spirits, and Champagnes at surprisingly reasonable prices. It's not rare to find a $10 wine recommended and described in baffling detail. The store has an extensive selection of preserves, coffees, teas, crackers, biscotti, cookies, cheeses, and even cigars that are a perfect accompaniment to drinks (and that are often imported and hard to find elsewhere). There's also a deli in the store.

Orleans Coffee Exchange. 712 Orleans Ave. ☎ **504/522-5710.** www.orleanscoffee.com. Mon–Fri 8am–6pm, Sat–Sun 9am–6pm.

Java junkies should know about the Orleans Coffee Exchange. The 500 varieties of coffee beans here come from all over the world. There are also more than 350 flavored coffees, as well as scores of exotic teas.

GIFTS

Accent Annex Mardi Gras Headquarters. 633 Toulose. ☎ **504/592-9886.** 10am–6pm daily.

Need some Mardi Gras beads, masks, and other accoutrements? This is one of the biggest suppliers of such things, and has just about everything you need to properly celebrate Mardi Gras in New Orleans, or to stock up for that party you want to throw back home. String some green, gold, and purple beads around your neck, and everyone will know where you've been. Note the reasonably priced bags of used beads.

Angele Parlange Design. 5419 Magazine St. ☎ **504/897-6511.** Mon–Fri 10am–5:30pm, Sat 10am–5pm.

Angele Parlange is a textile and interior designer of national renown, and has been featured in countless magazines such as *Elle* and *Vogue.* She gleans much of her inspiration from her illustrious ancestors who built Parlange Plantation in New Roads, Louisiana. The shop features Parlange's collection of interior furnishings, including hand-printed pillows, fabrics, furniture, and bedding, and imaginative items for entertaining.

The Anne Rice Collection. 2727 Prytania St. (in the Rink). ☎ **504/899-5996.** Mon–Sat 10am–6pm, Sun 11am–4pm.

Want to dress like Lestat? Want to buy vampire or ghost related tchotchkes? Yearning to stock up on Anne Rice paraphernalia? This is a must-stop for the faithful, as Rice brings you all manner of Gothic-related items, from clothes to knickknacks, including her old shoes and T-shirts with her personal slogans on them (taken in all at once, it seems she careens between taking matters all too seriously, and being completely in on the joke), plus skeletons, vampire dolls, and crosses. What did you expect, Hummel figures and flowery pottery?

Artifacts. 5515 Magazine St. ☎ **504/899-5505.** Mon–Sat 11am–5pm.

This gallery and shop is an eye feast, featuring finely crafted one-of-a-kind furniture, lamps, mirrors, and jewelry by local and national artists. There is also a nice selection of decorative hardware.

Aux Belles Choses. 3912 Magazine St. ☎ **504/891-1009.** Mon–Sat 10am–5pm.

From the inside, this shop feels as though it could be located at a lonely crossroads in rural France. Maybe it's all of the pretty dried plants and flowers (you can get arrangements made here). Or perhaps it's the endless variety of country French home, kitchen, and garden items. If you like creamy French soaps, especially with exotic scents, you'll probably leave with a handful—this place has many that are hard to find on this side of the Atlantic.

The Black Butterfly. 727 Royal St. ☎ **504/524-6464.** www.blackbutterfly.com. Mon–Sat 11am–6pm.

The Black Butterfly is a place for any collector or admirer of miniatures. This third-generation shop is filled with porcelain, brass, wood, and pewter figures, as well as dollhouse furniture and accessories. For men and boys (and militant women and girls), the store has a collection of miniature soldiers, and is adding a selection of trains and cars.

Casa del Corazon. 901 Chartres St. ☎ **504/569-9555.** Daily 10am–5pm

Gifts, sundries, and folk arts "from the warm latitudes" with an emphasis on Latin America are here, with some Spanish, Italian, and African items. The owner says, "We have everything from antique Mexican silver to gear shift knobs." This is true. Among recent choices were Day of the Dead figures, pottery, crosses with milagro figures on them, some small furniture pieces (including antique Mexican wedding chests), ceremonial masks, religious amulets, and good luck soaps.

Hempstead Company Store. 515 Dumaine St. ☎ **504/529-HEMP.** Mon–Fri 10am–6pm, Sat–Sun 10am–7pm.

The operative word in this store's name is *hemp*, which is what everything on sale is made from—even the soap (from hemp oil). Because hemp growing is problematic in the United States, the raw materials come from China and Hungary. The store hours are a bit loose around the edges (gee, wonder why?), so you might want to give a call first.

Importicos. 736 Royal St. ☎ **504/523-3100.** Daily 10am–6pm.

You might think there is plenty of exotica for sale in New Orleans, but this store goes well beyond the bounds—literally, as the owners regularly travel to Indonesia, among other countries, for high-quality ethnic imports. If you've been to Bali, you will recognize some of the carved wooden doodads for sale here (and may be quite pleased to find a source for them closer to home). Selections include hand-crafted silver jewelry, pottery, textiles, antique and museum reproduction earrings, and leather, wood, stone, and metal items, often made especially for the shop. You'll also find teak, mahogany, and wrought-iron furniture, and reproductions of 17th- and 18th-century mirrors. There are branches at 517 St. Louis St. (☎ **504/523-0306**) and 5523 Magazine St. (☎ **504/891-6141**).

Latin's Hand. 1025 N. Peters St. ☎ **504/529-5254.** Daily 9am–7pm.

All of the items in this shop are made, not surprisingly, in Latin America. You'll find goods from Brazil, El Salvador, Guatemala, Bolivia, and Mexico. It's easy to get lost amid the hammocks, dresses, jackets, sandals, and leather goods here.

Living Room. 927 Royal St. ☎ **504/595-8860.** Mon–Sat 10am–6pm, Sun noon–6pm.

The fine job the friendly owner has done here with her original folk craft store almost makes up for the loss of the site's former occupant, the beloved Olive Book Store. Living Room holds an eclectic assortment of old and new furnishings, knickknacks (think frames made of wood from old plantations, old spoons, and other recycled materials), fine art, and antiques. Be sure to say hi to the store dogs, Jack and Oil ("Earl" with an accent), who are neighborhood characters.

Orient Expressed Imports. 3906 Magazine St. ☎ **504/899-3060.** www.orient expressed.com Mon–Sat 10am–5pm.

This shop features a fascinating collection of antiques, santos, and objets d'art from around the world. The shop also offers its own line of hand-smocked children's clothing, plus toys and gifts.

The Private Connection and Pieces. 3927 Magazine St. ☎ **888/263-9693** or 504/899-4944. Mon–Sat 10am–5:30pm.

This shop specializes in the arts of Indonesia, including hand-crafted gifts and jewelry and unique furniture and architectural pieces. It carries both antique and contemporary furnishings. There's also a Private Connection at 1116 Decatur St. in the French Quarter.

Scriptura. 5423 Magazine St. ☎ **888/263-9699** or 504/897-1555. Mon–Sat 10am–6pm.

If you can't bear to scratch down notes with a pencil on a steno pad from the drugstore, you're a prime candidate for a romp through Scriptura. The store has everything related to the elegant art of scribbling—it's been said that the owners here love paper more than life itself. You can get designer stationery, glass fountain pens, sealing wax and wax presses, and all types of generic or specific (travel, cigar, wine, restaurant) journals. This is the kind of place where you can find a gift for that impossible-to-shop-for person in your life.

Shop of the Two Sisters. 1800 Magazine St. ☎ **504/525-2747.** Mon–Sat 10am–6pm.

Upscale "girly" items: throw pillows, lamps, sconces, accessories, unique accent pieces (with an emphasis on florals and fruits), upholstery—consumerism at its most beautiful, but be prepared to pay for it.

Thomas Mann Gallery. 1804 Magazine St. ☎ **504/581-2113.** Mon–Sat 11am–6pm.

This is a design store conceived by "techno-romantic" jewelry designer Thomas Mann. It aims at "redefining contemporary living" with its eclectic collection of jewelry, lighting, and home furnishings. They also have another location at 829 Royal St. in the French Quarter.

Three Dog Bakery. 827 Royal St. ☎ **504/525-2253.** Daily 10am–6pm.

Upon first glance, all the goodies here—cookies, petit fours, cakes—look incredibly yummy. Then you find out they are just for dogs. Which means they are made without ingredients that would appeal to human beings, like sugar or chocolate or fat or, really, anything with taste. These are strictly canine delights and are completely healthy for pooches. Cute names abound ("Snicker Poodles," "Ciao Wow Cheese Pizza," "Mini-

Beagels"—think bagels), and dogs do love them. You might sneer at those who would splurge (the treats aren't cheap) on such a gimmick. Dog owners, not to mention guilty ones away from home, go right ahead and drop lots of money. We recommend the Pawlines (the dog-friendly version of the local pralines), which went over big with some dogs we know.

Utopia. 5408 Magazine St. ☎ **504/899-8488.** Mon–Sat 10am–6pm, Sun noon–5pm.

Utopia seems to be popular with a specific demographic combination: mothers with their college-age daughters. Most of the products here are natural or organically derived, and many are meant to calm your spirits. There's a variety of women's casual clothing (much of it made of flax and flaxseed) in neutral colors. Many small earth-colored furniture items—mirrors, chests, lamps, and hanging shelves—are strewn about. You can also find things like bathing goodies, backpacks, gloves, and more.

Vintage 429. 429 Royal St. ☎ **504/529-2288.** Daily 10am–6pm.

"Fun. Funky. Fabulous" is how they bill themselves, and it is a pretty jocular place, full of autographed memorabilia, and some quite pretty antique jewelry and good old watches. It's all eye-catching, though a little too pricey for impulse buys.

HATS

Little Shop of Fantasy (see "Costumes & Masks," above) also sells fun costume hats.

Meyer the Hatter. 120 St. Charles Ave. ☎ **800/882-4287** or 504/525-1048. www. neworleans.com/meyer. Mon–Sat 10am–5:45pm.

Meyer's opened more than 100 years ago and has been in the same family since. Today, the haberdashery has one of the largest selections of fine hats and caps in the South. Men will find distinguished international labels like Stetson, Kangol, Akubra, Dobbs, and Borsalino (and there are some hats for women as well). The store is 1 block off Canal Street.

JEWELRY

Bedazzle. 635 St. Peter St. ☎ **504/529-3248.** Daily 10:30am–6pm.

If you like contemporary jewelry, head for Bedazzle, where jewelry is art. It has every-thing you'd expect to find in a traditional jewelry store, only a lot more interesting. The staff is extremely helpful and friendly, and is patient with rubbernecks.

Brass Lion. 516 Royal St. ☎ **504/525-9815.** Daily 10am–6pm.

Stuffed full of new, rather frilly jewelry from different designers. All the selections are romantic, and often have a vintage feel to them. Appropriately enough, the store recently added vintage and estate jewelry (including many very delicate rings) at some of the most affordable prices in town—often only three figures.

Hoover. 301 Royal St. ☎ **504/522-7289.** Mon–Sat 11am–6:30pm, Sun 11am–5pm.

A clever, and not unreasonably priced, collection of antique and contemporary jewelry and watches, chosen with considerable care. As *lagniappe,* owner Stacy Hoover loves to give tourists all kinds of insider New Orleans tips.

Mignon Faget Ltd. Canal Place, Level 1. ☎ **504/524-2973.** Mon and Fri–Sat 11am–7pm, Tues and Thurs 11am–6pm, Sun noon–6pm.

Mignon Faget is one of the largest personalities in New Orleans' jewelry universe. The designer is a New Orleans native; in fact, some of her ancestors moved here to escape the French Revolution, while others were longtime plantation owners. After studying fine arts and design, Faget began designing jewelry for boutiques, which proved very successful. Today, in her main studio display room, you can see some of her signature styles—gold, silver, and bronze d'oré fashioned into pendants, bracelets, rings, earrings, shirt studs, and cuff links. There's another Mignon Faget at 710 Dublin St. (☎ **504/865-7361**), uptown in the Riverbend area.

Quarter Moon. 918 Royal St. ☎ **504/524-3208.** Daily 10am–5pm, Sun noon–5pm.

Much of the jewelry in this shop is handmade on-site by owner Ellis Anderson. Her pieces are interesting and unique, because they're handmade, you won't find anything like them anywhere else. The shop also carries contemporary crafts and wearable art produced by 25 local artists. The ever-changing collection includes jewelry, hand-woven clothing, and hand-painted silks, hats, leather masks, and scarves.

Rumors, Ltd. 513 Royal St. ☎ **504/525-0292.** Daily 9:30am–6pm.

Not just an earring store—more earrings than you can possibly imagine. Unfortunately, the emphasis is on prominent (read: somewhat gaudy) styles, so the selection for those favoring a more subtle look might be a bit disappointing. A branch, Rumors Too Gallery, is at 319 Royal St. (☎ 504/523-0011).

MUSIC

In addition to the giant **Tower Records** at 408 N. Peters St. (☎ **504/529-4411**), there are a few other places you should check out for music, especially if you still have a turntable.

Beckham's Bookshop. 228 Decatur St. ☎ **504/522-9875.** Daily 10am–6pm.

It's better known for its fine collection of used books (see "Books," above), but Beckham's also has a large selection of second-hand classical LPs.

✪ **Louisiana Music Factory.** 210 Decatur St. ☎ **504/586-1094.** Daily 10am–10pm.

This popular store carries a large selection of regional music—including Cajun, zydeco, R&B, jazz, blues, and gospel—plus books, posters, and T-shirts. It also has frequent live music and beer bashes—shop while you bop!

Record Ron's. 239 Chartres St. ☎ **800/234-6889** or 504/522-2239. Daily 11am–7pm.

At Record Ron's you'll find thousands of 45s, CDs, and cassettes, plus a good selection of LPs covering classic rock, jazz, Cajun, zydeco, R&B, and blues. T-shirts, posters, sheet music, rubber stamps, music memorabilia, and jewelry are also available.

Rock & Roll Records & Collectibles. 1214 Decatur St. ☎ **504/561-5683.** www. neworleans.com/rock-n-roll. Daily 10am–10pm.

The name says it all—kind of. The owners say (and who are we to dispute?) this is the largest and best collection of vinyl "anywhere," including 45s and 78s—which means hardly just rock and roll. This is record nerd heaven. The walls are lined with classics, and floor space is at a minimum thanks to boxes and crates full of records. Prices are negotiable.

THE OCCULT

The Bottom of the Cup Tearoom. 732 Royal St. ☎ **504/523-1204.** Mon–Fri 10am–6pm, Sat–Sun 11am–7pm.

At the Bottom of the Cup Tearoom, psychics and clairvoyants specialize in palm reading, crystal gazing, tea-leaf reading, and tarot. You can also get your astrological chart done. It's been open since 1929 and bills itself as the "oldest tearoom in the United States." In addition to having a psychic consultation, you can also purchase books, jewelry, crystal balls, tarot cards, crystals, and healing wands.

Marie Laveau's House of Voodoo. 739 Bourbon St. ☎ **888/4-VOODOO** or 504/
581-3751. Sun–Thurs 10am–11:30pm, Fri–Sat 10am–12:30 or 1:30am.

The place for all your voodoo doll and gris-gris bag needs. Tourist voodoo, to be sure,
but such items make great souvenirs for the right friends, and it's a fun store to poke
around in.

Westgate—The Original Necrotorium. 5219 Magazine St. ☎ **504/899-3077.** Tues–Sat
noon–5pm.

Painted a hard-to-miss purple and black, this is the ultimate store for the right-minded
visitor, and a complete nightmare (deliberately) for others. Featuring "necromantic"
art and jewelry, which means liberal use of skeletons and other death images, some
quite graphic. Even if you aren't a death-o-phile, it's interesting to browse through, but
it might give some the creeps. The store owners are actually quite approachable.

TATTOOS
Orleans Ink. 610 Frenchmen St. ☎ **504/947-2300.** Daily noon–midnight.

Need a permanent souvenir of your trip? Stop off here for a tattoo or body piercing.
If it's fleshy, they can pierce it, and the tattoos are really quite beautiful. But you *must*
be 18!

TOYS
Le Petit Soldier Shop. 528 Royal St. ☎ **504/523-7741.** Mon–Sat 10am–4pm.

Local artists create the 2-inch-high masterpieces in this shop. The miniatures depict
soldiers from ancient Greece up to Desert Storm, and many are crafted to resemble
major figures in military history, such as Eisenhower, Grant, Lee, Hitler, and
Napoléon. There's also a large collection of medals and decorations.

The Little Toy Shoppe. 900 Decatur St. ☎ **504/522-6588.** Daily 9am–7pm.

The dolls here are quite beautiful, especially the Madame Alexander and Effanbee
creations, and the New Orleans–made bisque and rag dolls. In addition to "heroes"
wood toys from Germany and "All God's Children" collectibles, there are cuddly
stuffed animals, tea sets, toy soldiers, and miniature cars and trucks.

UMBRELLAS
The Umbrella Lady. 1107 Decatur St. ☎ **504/523-7791.** Daily 10am–8pm.

She's called "The Umbrella Lady," but her real name is Anne B. Lane. You'll find her in
her upstairs studio, above Molly's at the Market bar. A Quarter fixture, she's the creator
of wonderful Secondline umbrellas as well as fanciful "Southern belle" parasols. Look
for the umbrellas displayed on her balcony.

WOODCRAFTS
Idea Factory. 838 Chartres St. ☎ **800/524-IDEA** or 504/524-5195. Mon–Sat 10am–6pm,
Sun 10am–5pm.

The Idea Factory is one of the most distinctive shops in the French Quarter. You'll
be amazed to see what can be made without metal and plastic: toys, games, kinetic
sculptures, door harps, signs, boxes, and office supplies. These are not knickknacks;
they are impressive craft productions. The classic cars, streetcars, and riverboats could
make an adult play on the floor again. Many of the items are made right on the
premises, so if you're lucky you might get to see one of the craftspeople at work.

New Orleans After Dark

New Orleans is one of the most beautiful cities in the United States, possibly the world, but we won't mind if you never see a bit of it—provided, however, that the omission is because you are spending the daylight sightseeing hours recovering from the equally extraordinary nightlife.

This is a city of music and rhythm. It is impossible to imagine New Orleans without a soundtrack of jazz, Cajun, and zydeco. Music pours out of every doorway, and sometimes it seems people are dancing down the street. Sometimes they are. (After all, this is the town that sends you to your grave with music and then dances back from the cemetery.) You walk along Bourbon Street, for example, and with every step, you hear music of all varieties. Maybe none of it is world class, but that doesn't seem to matter too much. It's just that it's there at all, and in such variety. Plus, it's darn infectious.

This is also the city of decadence and good times rolling. Not to mention really loose liquor laws, and drinks in "to go" cups (plastic containers you can take with you; many bars and clubs even have walk-up windows for easy refills). And all this increases four-fold at night. We aren't just talking about the open-air frat party that is Bourbon Street some (okay, most) evenings. In fact, we prefer not to talk about that at all.

Much better is that virtually every night, dozens of clubs all over town offer music that can range from average to extraordinary, but is never less than danceable. In most places, cover prices vary from night to night and performer to performer, but rarely will you have to pay more than $10, and then only for more high-falutin' places like the House of Blues. When the clubs get too full, no matter; the crowd spills into the street, talking, drinking, and still dancing right there on the sidewalk (the music is often plenty audible out there). Sometimes the action outside is even more fun than inside, not to mention less hot and sweaty. Club hopping is easy, though with some exceptions some of the better choices will require leaving the Quarter, by cab or some other vehicle. Don't worry—most are a cheap cab ride away, and many are within an additional, even cheaper cab ride, if not walking distance, of each other. We strongly urge you to leave the Quarter at night to visit some of the town's better joints. However, if you aren't up to that, don't fret. Several of the best jazz and brass band clubs are right in the Quarter. And only steps away is the scene in the Frenchmen section of the Faubourg Marigny, where at least five clubs are going at once, within 3 blocks of each other. People wander from one to the other, sometimes never bothering to actually pay the cover price and go inside. If you do your evening right, those calories you consumed all day long will be gone by morning.

Or, yes, you could spend your night running from bar to bar. There is no lack. With such great music available, that seems a waste of time; if all you wanted to do was drink, you could have stayed home and enjoyed yourself just as much. Still, it is New Orleans, and some of these places are as convivial and atmospheric as you will ever find; ducking into a few isn't a bad idea at all. And of course, everything only gets livelier and wilder as the evening goes on.

And speaking of which, don't be fooled by the times given in local listings for band performances. If it says "10pm," the band will probably go on closer to midnight and keep playing until late. Really late. This isn't always true—once in a blue moon an act will go on when billed and finish up rather early—but chances are good that if you come late, even really late, you will still catch quite a bit of the act you came to see.

But however you do it, don't miss it. New Orleans at night is not New Orleans during the day, and to not take advantage of it is to miss out on half your trip. You could stay in your hotel room with the covers pulled over your head, but if that's what you want, you came to the wrong city. Just tell yourself you'll sleep when you get home.

For up-to-date information on what's happening around town, look for current editions of **Gambit, Offbeat,** and **Where,** all distributed free in most hotels and all record stores. You can also check out *Offbeat* on the Internet (www.nola.com; once you get to the Nola home page, go to the music and entertainment section). Other sources include the **Times-Picayune's** daily entertainment calendar and Friday's **"Lagniappe"** section of the newspaper. Additionally, **WWOZ** (90.7 FM) broadcasts the local music schedule several times throughout the day. If you miss the broadcasts, call ☎ **504/840-4040,** WWOZ's "Tower Records Second Line," for the same information.

1 The Rhythms of New Orleans

Ernie K-Doe has been quoted as saying, "I'm not sure, but I think all music came from New Orleans." What might be a more accurate account—and relatively hyperbole-free—is that all music came *to* New Orleans. Any style you can name, from African field hollers to industrial techno-rock, has found its way to the Crescent City, where it's been blended, shaken, and stirred into a new, distinctive, and usually frothy concoction that, it seems, could have come from nowhere else.

"Yeah," you scoff, "but what about classical music?" Well, maybe you've never heard how pianist James Booker, an eye-patched eccentric even by New Orleans standards, could make a Bach chorale strut like a second-line umbrella twirler. Or maybe you're forgetting that Wynton Marsalis has Grammy Awards for both jazz and classical recordings, not to mention a 1997 Pulitzer Prize for his slavery-themed jazz oratorio "Blood on the Fields."

On the other side of the spectrum, don't forget that Trent Reznor, the man behind the brutal sounds and imagery of the industrial act Nine Inch Nails, has chosen to live and record in New Orleans—not because of the good property values, but because the aesthetics and atmosphere suit him. (His studio is in a former funeral home, natch.)

Even more unusual is the New Orleans Klezmer All Stars ensemble, a group of musicians that plays the lively music of Eastern European Jewish troubadours, with a few New Orleans embellishments. You're not required to dance at their performances, but you'll find it impossible not to.

Of course, what you're most likely to experience is somewhere in the middle, music more truly rooted in the Crescent City—the Storyville jazz descended from Louis Armstrong and Jelly Roll Morton, the bubbly R&B transmitted via Fats Domino and Professor Longhair, the Mardi Gras Indians and the brass bands of the second lines that recently have gotten exuberant, youthful infusions of funk and hip-hop.

Finding music in New Orleans is no trick. Walk anywhere in the vicinity of Bourbon Street and your ears will be assaulted by a variety of sounds. If you're really interested, it's worth a little effort to seek out the good stuff and avoid the tourist-oriented caricatures that will be thrust at you. Consult the free monthly *Offbeat,* available at many businesses in the French Quarter and elsewhere around town, for what's playing at such clubs as the Howlin' Wolf, Donna's, the Maple Leaf, Tipitina's, or the gotta-see-it-to-believe-it Mid City Lanes bowling alley, home of the famed Rock 'n' Bowl. Listen to public radio station WWOZ-FM, which plays the best of New Orleans music and gives concert info. For planning in advance, both *Offbeat* and the radio station have easily accessible Web sites.

THE JAZZ LIFE OF NEW ORLEANS

by George Hocutt, jazz historian and executive producer of the
Grammy Award–winning album Doc Cheatham and Nicholas Payton

New Orleans did not invent jazz, but the crescents in the Mississippi River became the crucible in which jazz evolved. The city's French Catholic background has always inspired a more tolerant attitude toward the simple pleasures of the world than the Puritan fathers from Plymouth Rock. Melodic sounds of all kinds were one of those pleasures.

Music was of great importance to the Louisiana settlers and their Creole offspring, and the city early on had a fascination with marching bands and parades. As early as 1787, Governor Miro entertained a gathering of Indian leaders with a parade. Eventually, bands were required for nearly every occasion—Mardi Gras, dedications, religious holidays, cornerstone layings, weddings, funerals, ad infinitum. With this plethora of musical activities, one major ingredient was in great need: musicians.

The musicians of early New Orleans were expected to do just what the word implied—provide music. They were not categorized or labeled by any brand or style of music. They were considered tradesmen just like other skilled craftsmen, such as carpenters, shoemakers, what have you. From an afternoon parade they might be required to play at the opera, then possibly a late dance. At the dance, the program would call for waltzes, gallops, gavottes and quadrilles, among others. (The jazz song "Tiger Rag" derived from a quadrille.) Obviously these 19th-century instrumentalists were quite accomplished and versatile.

In the early 19th century, slaves were allowed to congregate in the area known as **Congo Square** for dancing to the rhythms of their homelands' drums and other percussive instruments. With the passing of time, many slaves, former slaves, and free men of color became accomplished instrumentalists. There were Negro marching bands in New Orleans before the Civil War, and many continued playing during the city's occupation by simply changing their gray uniforms for the Union blue.

Some of these musicians, possibly graduates of the Congo Square gatherings, brought to their playing a native rhythm that was likely a primitive syncopation. In an evolutionary way, many of New Orleans' musicians began absorbing this amalgam of European and African influences. Then came the addition of the very personal statements of the blues, work songs, hollers, and spirituals. The music was changing and taking on a certain American and distinctly New Orleanian aura.

In the 1870s, two men were born who were to have a profound effect on the music. **"Papa" Jack Laine** was born in 1873, and **Charles "Buddy" Bolden** in 1878, both in New Orleans.

Bolden, a cornetist who would later be known as "The First Man of Jazz," began playing dances and parties around 1895. By 1897 he had put together the band that most old-timers remember. They also remember that when Bolden put his cornet up and blew loud from Johnson Park in uptown New Orleans, he could be heard for miles around. Fans said, "Buddy's callin' his chickens home." Unfortunately, Bolden was committed to an institution for the insane in 1907, where he died in 1931, never having recorded.

At approximately the same time, Papa Jack, primarily a drummer, formed several groups simultaneously, all called the Reliance Band. They played all over the Gulf Coast and in New Orleans, and were extremely popular. Almost all the early white New Orleans jazz men played in one of Laine's groups. He withdrew from the music business around the time of the First World War, but his legacy lived on through the many greats he fostered. They were later known as Papa Jack's children.

Much of what we know of these two pioneers we have learned from taped interviews with men who were already old at the time they were interviewed—but not old enough to remember the music scene before Bolden and Laine. Names that have emerged, though dimly, include the legendary Mass Quamba, William Martin, "Picayune" Butler, and a performer known as "Old Corn Meal." All of them likely added their peculiar touches to the evolution of New Orleans music.

Concurrent with Bolden and Laine's contributions to the musical life of the city, another event that would affect the spread of jazz everywhere was unfolding. **Storyville,** the only prescribed district for legalized prostitution ever attempted in this country, operated from 1897 to 1917. The most elegant houses were along the lakeside of Rampart Street between Iberville and Conti streets. Among them were the Arlington and Lulu White's Mahogany Hall.

No documentation or mention in the taped oral histories of early New Orleans jazz men (contained in the jazz archives at Tulane) tells us of an orchestra ever playing in any of the houses, but most of them did have a piano player in the parlor. Among those entertainers were Spencer Williams, later a very successful songwriter, Tony Jackson, who wrote "Pretty Baby," and the immortal **"Jelly Roll" Morton.**

Born Ferdinand Joseph Lamothe (his actual name, established by jazz researcher Lawrence Gushee from "Jelly's" baptismal certificate) in 1890, Morton was the first true jazz composer and, next to Louis Armstrong, the most important figure in early jazz. His compositions were recorded well into the swing era and are still performed today. He was inducted into the Rock and Roll Hall of Fame in the Early Influence category.

Although the houses did not use bands for entertainment, there were many playing opportunities in the bars and clubs that dotted Storyville and the adjacent areas. These clubs—the Arlington Annex, the Cadillac, Frank Early's, 101 Ranch, the Frenchman's, Pete Lala's, and the Tin Roof Cafe, among others—all featured bands.

The great musicians of New Orleans all played in the clubs and doubled during the day in the multitude of brass bands that were always in demand. All the prominent names of early New Orleans jazz served this apprenticeship, including Freddy Keppard, King Oliver, Kid Ory, Sidney Bechet, Papa Celestin, Big Eye Louis Nelson, Buddy Petit, Bunk Johnson, Johnny and Baby Dodds, Alphonses Picou, Achille Baquet, Lorenzo Tio, and Tommy Ladnier. The list could go on and on.

As early as 1916, some New Orleans bands that included many of Papa Jack's children decided to try the musical climate in Chicago. Freddy Keppard and the Original Creole Band had been spreading music from New Orleans throughout the country in concerts and on vaudeville stages, but the groups going to Chicago made extended stays at specified clubs. The most successful group was **the Original Dixieland Jazz Band,** led by Nick LaRocca. The ODJB moved on from Chicago to open at Reisenweber's Cafe in New York City in 1917. They were a smash. Everybody loved the new music from New Orleans. After an abortive attempt by Columbia Records, they cut the first jazz record ever, released by Victor Records on February 16, 1917. The record, coupling "Livery Stable Blues" and "Dixie Jazz Band One Step," was an instant hit and was soon topping whatever hit parade existed at that time. The jazz flood had started.

In October 1917, the houses of Storyville were completely shut down by order of the U.S. Navy, and a great many jobs for entertainers and musicians started drying up. The performers began to look elsewhere. Apparently, word was filtering back to the city of the success the former New Orleanians were enjoying up north. Many decided to follow that example.

Kid Ory headed to California, where he made the first black jazz record. King Oliver traveled to Chicago in 1919, taking Johnny Dodds and other New Orleans musicians with him. After a brief sojourn in California, he returned to Chicago, and in 1922 he sent for **Louis Armstrong** to come up and join King Oliver's Creole Jazz Band—arguably the greatest aggregation ever assembled, and all but one natives of New Orleans. A young Emmett Hardy, the legendary white cornetist, went on tour with Bea Palmer and, while playing in Davenport, Iowa, was reportedly an influence on the great Bix Beiderbecke. Bix got his earliest musical experience by playing along with Nick LaRocca records. The New Orleans Rhythm Kings, all New Orleans musicians, opened at the Friars Inn in Chicago in 1922; cornetist Paul Mares certainly influenced Beiderbecke, who was attending school nearby and often sat in with the band. Jazz was spreading rapidly, and New Orleans musicians were in great demand by other groups around the country. Every other leader wanted to bring that something special to his music.

The demand continued into the swing era of the 1930s and 1940s. The big bands hired many New Orleanians; Danny Barker played with the Cab Calloway Band; Barney Bigard with Duke Ellington; Tommy Ladnier with Fletcher Henderson; Irving Pazola with Glenn Miller and Bob Crosby; Eddie Miller with the Dorseys and Crosby; Ed Hall with Teddy Wilson and Lucky Millinder; Preston Jackson with Erskine Tate, and Santa Pecora with Will Osborne. Once more the list is endless.

After leaving Oliver, Louis Armstrong, already the greatest soloist in jazz, went on to become one of the greatest entertainers and stars we have ever known. At one time, his were probably the most identifiable face and voice in the world. Nearly 30 years after his death, his records are still best-sellers. He transcended New Orleans and became a national treasure.

Sidney Bechet settled in France after World War II and became a huge star performer and prolific composer. On his wedding day a total holiday was declared in Antibes, and the entire city participated in a massive wedding party, dancing to music he had written.

New Orleans is still producing jazz greats. There is Harry Connick Jr., who is making his mark in Hollywood as well as in music. **Ellis Marsalis** has fathered a group of jazz-playing sons, the best known being trumpeter Wynton, who won a 1997 Pulitzer Prize for his composition "Blood on the Fields," the first such award for a jazz man. **Nicholas Payton** is another rising trumpet player from New Orleans. In 1998, Payton and Doc Cheatham shared the Grammy Award for best instrumental recording for their performance of "Stardust" on the album *Doc Cheatham and Nicholas Payton.* Obviously, the city still abounds with creativity.

Much remains in New Orleans for the adventurous jazz fan and explorer. Morton's home still stands on Frenchman Street. Buddy Bolden's house is on First Street, in Uptown, and a monument to him stands in Holt Cemetery, where he was buried in an unmarked grave. A plaque marks the house on Chartres Street where Danny Barker was born. At Rampart and Conti streets, one of Lulu White's buildings remains standing. Down the street is Frank Early's saloon (now a neighborhood convenience store). There is more, but that should give you an idea. Search them out.

Music still resounds around the town. Although many of the originals are gone, **Preservation Hall** continues to showcase younger players. The **Palm Court Jazz Cafe** offers good jazz five nights a week. **Donna's** books many of the brass bands that currently also perform in the streets of the city. **Snug Harbor** on Frenchman Street presents a broad spectrum of jazz, from traditional to modern. **Fritzel's** on Bourbon Street hosts weekend jam sessions. The Hilton has a sensational Sunday morning jazz brunch and is home to **Pete Fountain's club.** The Dukes of Dixieland appear nightly on the *Natchez,* a riverboat excursion joy. Other bands play for daytime sailings.

So certainly there is life in the old gal yet. Whether it's in the water, the air, or that good Creole cooking, jazz continues to grow in the fertile soil that settles on the banks of the curves of the Mississippi River.

BRASS BANDS

If your idea of New Orleans brass bands is merely the postfuneral "second line" parade of "When the Saints Go Marching In," you're in for some joyous surprises. In recent years, young African-American kids have picked up the tradition and given it new life, while also stimulating renewed interest in some of the veteran practitioners. At its roots, it's primal jazz nonpareil, with group improvisations, unexpected turns, and spirit to burn.

The key act of the current revival was the **ReBirth Brass Band,** a gaggle of teens and preteens who in the late 1980s and early 1990s tossed pop-funk tunes like "Grazin' in the Grass" and the Doobie Brothers' "Takin' it to the Streets" into their mix of New Orleans standards. They even had a local hit with "Do Whatcha Wanna." The group's still around, though trumpeter Kermit Ruffins, who as a preteen Louis Armstrong look- and sound-alike was the centerpiece, left several years ago to form his own versatile jazz band, the Barbecue Swingers. Others working today in the same vein include **New Birth** and **Olympia,** while such newer arrivals as the **Soul Rebels** and **Coolbone** have added hip-hop and reggae styles to the blend, often with terrific results. At the same time, such older ensembles as the **Olympia Brass Band** have gained from the interest. One highlight of Jazz Fest week is the free brass band showdown held at the Louisiana Music Factory record store in the Quarter. And just about any night, you can catch the best in local brass bands at **Donna's.**

CAJUN & ZYDECO

Two of the music styles often associated with New Orleans technically are not from there at all. Both Cajun and zydeco really originated in the bayou of southwest

Louisiana, a good 3 hours away. And while it's customary for the two to be named in the same breath, they are not the same thing—though they are arguably two sides of the same coin.

The foundations of the two styles lie in the arrival of two different French-speaking peoples in the swamp country: the Acadians, French migrants who were booted out of Nova Scotia by the English in 1755, and the Creole people who were jettisoned by or escaped from the Caribbean slave trade of the same era. Entwined by the pervasive poverty and hardship of the region and by their common status as underclass peoples—the white Acadians, or Cajuns as the name was eventually corrupted, were beaten by schoolteachers for speaking French well into the 20th century, while the Creoles suffered the same oppression as blacks elsewhere—the cultures blended in many ways, and nowhere more evidently than in their music.

Introduction of the button accordion and its folky, diatonic scale was a key development. It added a richness and power to what had largely been fiddle and guitar music. Early recordings of such seminal figures as Joe Falcon (a white man) and Amede Ardoin (a Creole) reveal a rough-hewn music, tied to ancient tunes rooted in France and elsewhere, with hints of influence from the sounds starting to arrive through the radio and recordings of popular tunes. Such acts as the **Hackberry Ramblers,** who still perform today with a couple of more or less original members, played the dance-hall circuits from New Orleans into Texas through the 1930s. Many added drums and amplified and steel guitars as they became available to fill out the sound.

In the postwar era, the styles began to separate more, with the Cajuns gravitating toward country and western swing, and Creole musicians heavily influenced by the urban blues. The purer music of the region was suppressed and nearly lost in the 1950s, though such figures as **D. L. Menard** ("the Cajun Hank Williams") and **Clifton Chenier** (the King of Zydeco) pioneered exciting new strains in their respective directions. Chenier, at first performing with just his brother Cleveland on washboard percussion, was among those who took up the chromatic "piano" style accordion, which suited the blues in ways the button accordion could not. Menard, as his nickname indicates, melded Cajun with the style of the country balladeer he idolized (and met once, providing a tale he's joyously told countless times). In 1959, Menard wrote "La Porte Den Arriere (The Back Door)," which along with the traditional "Jolie Blon" is certainly the most-performed song in the Cajun repertoire.

The great folk music boom of the early 1960s spilled over to Cajun music, and such figures as the **Balfa Brothers** and fiddler **Dennis McGee** suddenly had the opportunity to perform at such folk festivals as the famed Newport gathering. A turning point came when a Cajun group received a standing ovation at the 1964 Newport Festival. It was a real boost for the form and for Cajun pride, both of which seemed on the verge of extinction. With such younger musicians as **Marc Savoy,** who had begun producing homemade accordions of fine quality, providing new energy and commitment, and such entrepreneurs as Floyd Soileau recording the styles of the region, Cajun music gained new life.

This spawned a new generation, proud of their Cajun musical legacy but also fueled by rock 'n' roll. Leading the way have been fiddler **Michael Doucet** and his band, **Beausoleil,** now Cajun music's best-known band. Even if he hasn't always delighted the purists, Doucet has been a tireless ambassador for his heritage.

In zydeco, Clifton Chenier led the way from the '50s on, with a handful of others (Boozoo Chavis, John Delafose, Rockin' Sydney) adding their own embellishments. Chenier, recorded by Ville Platte's Floyd Soileau and Berkeley-based Chris Strackwitz's Arhoolie Records, became internationally famous, even playing the esteemed Montreaux Jazz Festival in Switzerland. His name loomed so large over the field that at his death in the mid-'80s, there seemed to be no one ready to step into his royal shoes.

But after a little drifting, zydeco has, arguably, grown stronger than ever. A new generation, including Chenier's son C. J. and Delafose's son Geno, is updating the old traditions, while such figures as **Beau Jocque, Keith Frank,** and **Nathan Williams** add their own variations of funk, hip-hop, and blues.

RHYTHM & BLUES

Technically, the blues is not a New Orleans form, belonging more to the rural delta and, in its urban forms, Texas and Chicago. But rhythm and blues, with its gospel and African-Caribbean bloodlines, carries a Crescent City heartbeat. In the '50s, **Fats Domino,** along with his great producer-collaborator Dave Bartholemew, fused those elements into such seminal songs as "Blueberry Hill" and "Walkin' to New Orleans"— music that still fuels much of the New Orleans R&B sound today. At the same time, such then-unheralded figures as **Professor Longhair** and **Champion Jack Dupree** developed earthier variations of the piano-based sound, contrasting mournful woe with party-time spirit. The keepers of the flame today are, of course, **the Neville Brothers,** who in their various combinations and incarnations (the Meters, Aaron Neville's solo projects, and so on) have explored and expanded just about every direction of this music. And if the Nevilles are the royal family of New Orleans music, **Irma Thomas** is its duchess of soul. Though she only had one national hit ("Wish Somebody Would Care"), her feel for a song and her magnanimous spirit have led devotees to make regular pilgrimages to her club, the Lion's Den, to hear her perform. It's well worth joining them, but take a cab—it's not in a neighborhood in which you'd want to walk around.

MARDI GRAS INDIANS

There are few stranger cultural phenomena than the "tribes" of Creoles and blacks who don colorful, elaborate faux–Native American dress for fierce singing competitions surrounding the Mardi Gras festivities. The tradition, which originated with the people segregated out of the main parades and celebrations, thrives today, with serious participants devoting remarkable parts of their lives to refining their costumes and chants. The tribes pretty much share a repertoire of call-and-response material, customized to boast about how great your tribe is and how lame the rivals are—for example: "Meet de boys on de battlefront / [tribe name here] gonna stomp some rump." Styles vary greatly, from crude percussion-driven acts to more developed musical arrangements.

The essential album of the style is ***The Wild Tchoupitoulas,*** with backing from members of the Neville Brothers (nephews of Chief George Landry) and the Meters, though Tchoupitoulases have been largely absent since Landry's death in the late '80s. The tribes you're most likely to encounter today are the **Wild Magnolias** (headed by Bo Dolis) and the **Golden Eagles.** Both have made several fine recordings. Around Mardi Gras, others perform regularly, and the Jazz Fest lineup tends to include at least one tribe per day. They're not to be missed, if you have the opportunity.

2 Jazz & Blues Clubs

This being New Orleans, jazz and blues are everywhere—though not all of it is worth hearing. Not that any of it is bad, per se. It's just that there is world-class stuff out there competing with tourist traps for your ears, so don't just settle for the first sight (or sound) of brass instruments.

French Quarter Nightlife

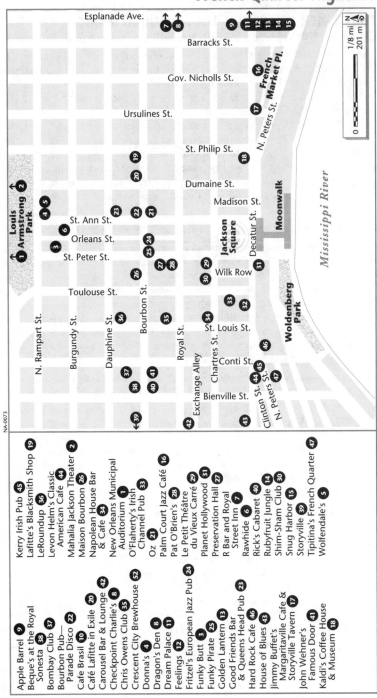

Esplanade Ave.

Barracks St.

Gov. Nicholls St.

Ursulines St.

St. Philip St.

Dumaine St.

Madison St.

St. Ann St.

Orleans St.

St. Peter St.

Toulouse St.

Wilk Row

St. Louis St.

Conti St.

Bienville St.

Louis Armstrong Park

Jackson Square

Moonwalk

Mississippi River

Woldenberg Park

French Market Pl.

N. Peters St.

Decatur St.

Royal St.

Chartres St.

Exchange Alley

Clinton St.

N. Peters St.

N. Rampart St.

Burgundy St.

Dauphine St.

Bourbon St.

NA-0073

Apple Barrel **9**
Beque's at the Royal Sonesta **38**
Bombay Club **37**
Bourbon Pub—Parade Disco **22**
Café Brasil **10**
Café Lafitte in Exile **20**
Carousel Bar & Lounge **42**
Checkpoint Charlie's **8**
Chris Owens Club **35**
Crescent City Brewhouse **52**
Donna's **4**
Dragon's Den **8**
Dream Palace **11**
Feelings **12**
Fritzel's European Jazz Pub **24**
Funky Butt **3**
Funky Pirate **25**
Golden Lantern **13**
Good Friends Bar & Queens Head Pub **23**
Hard Rock Cafe **46**
House of Blues **43**
Jimmy Buffet's Margaritaville Cafe & Storyville Tavern **17**
John Wehner's Famous Door **41**
Kaldi's Coffee House & Museum **18**

Kerry Irish Pub **45**
Lafitte's Blacksmith Shop **19**
LeRoundup **36**
Levon Helm's Classic American Cafe **44**
Mahalia Jackson Theater **2**
Maison Bourbon **26**
Napolean House Bar & Cafe **34**
New Orleans Municipal Auditorium **1**
O'Flaherty's Irish Channel Pub **33**
Oz **21**
Palm Court Jazz Café **16**
Pat O'Brien's **28**
Le Petit Théâtre du Vieux Carré **29**
Planet Hollywood **31**
Preservation Hall **27**
R Bar and Royal Street Inn **7**
Rawhide **6**
Rick's Cabaret **40**
Rubyfruit Jungle **14**
Shim-Sham Club **30**
Snug Harbor **15**
Storyville **39**
Tipitina's French Quarter **47**
Wolfendale's **5**

231

THE FRENCH QUARTER & THE FAUBOURG MARIGNY

✪ **Donna's.** 800 N. Rampart St. ☎ **504/596-6914.** Cover varies according to performer.

A corner bar at the edge of the Quarter, Donna's has become one of the top spots for the revival of the brass band experience and for a variety of jazz and blues traditions. The main asset may be Donna herself, monitoring the door to make sure you don't bring in drinks from outside, and making sure you do order something inside. She's been one of the true boosters of new generations of New Orleans music (she's managed both the hip-hop-edged brass band Soul Rebels and the new-funk ensemble Galactic) and has helped promote awareness of veteran brass bands like Treme and Olympia. As with most real New Orleans hangouts, atmosphere is minimal, but spirits (liquid and otherwise) are high. The cover charge for performances is usually no more than the cost of a good mixed drink. Well worth a stop on an evening of club hopping. *Note:* Donna's is in a transitional neighborhood, so be careful entering and leaving.

Dragon's Den. 435 Esplanade Ave. (above Siam Café). ☎ **504/949-1750.** Cover $4–$10.

Imagine a hippie-cum-opium den turned performance space and you'll have an idea of the Dragon's Den. Before show time, it's a pillows-on-the-floor, nouvelle Asian restaurant. After the lights go down, however, the place transforms into one of the funkiest jazz venues in the city. The standing-room bar and floor-bound seating area both look into the performance area, which is something short of a stage. Actually, it's the floor—be careful that the performers don't step on you. Tables are often taken by diners who don't leave, but there's room in some corner for everyone, even if it's on the balcony overlooking Esplanade. Now imagine the whole place bopping to the ReBirth Brass Band and you've got the idea.

Fritzel's European Jazz Pub. 733 Bourbon St. ☎ **504/561-0432.** No cover; 1-drink minimum per set.

You might walk right past this small establishment, but that would be a big mistake, because this 1831 building brings some of the city's best musicians to play on its tiny stage. In addition to the regular weekend program of late-night jazz (Friday and Saturday from 10:30pm, Sunday from 10pm), there are frequent jam sessions in the wee hours during the week, when performers end their stints elsewhere and gather to play "Musicians' Music." The full bar also stocks a variety of schnapps (served ice-cold) and German beers on tap and in bottles.

✪ **Funky Butt.** 714 N. Rampart St. ☎ **504/558-0872.** Cover varies.

Fret not—this is not a strip bar. Jazz aficionados will connect the name with a tune associated with New Orleans' own Buddy Boudin. There was another Funky Butt club in the early days of jazz; this one is a more recent arrival, operated by the owner of the Magic Walking Tours. (A visit is sometimes included at the end of the nighttime tours.) Downstairs is a typical funky bar; upstairs is a slightly more pleasing and mature performance space than that at other clubs in town. It's leaning toward, if not totally achieving, smoky jazz nightclub ambience. Bookings emphasize jazz but can also include anything from the Wild Magnolias (the most famous of the Mardi Gras Indians; it's something special to see them here) to an amazing Billie Holiday tribute band to the New Orleans Klezmer All Stars. Creole and vegetarian food is available, and the club is only a block from Donna's (see above). *Note:* Although the club itself is safe, the neighborhood around it isn't. Take a cab (yes, it seems silly, but even from Bourbon Street) to and from this area unless you're in a large group or during a crowded time (Mardi Gras, Jazz Fest). Better yet, get a cop to escort you.

Funky Pirate. 727 Bourbon St. ☎ **504/523-1960.** 1-drink minimum.

Decorated to resemble a pirates' den, the Funky Pirate lives up to its name—especially the "funky" part. The Pirate is as far from urbane modern jazz as you can get, so there's no chance you'll confuse it with the Funky Butt (see above). The place seems to be perpetually full of loud beer-drinkers, and at night it can get jam-packed. "Big" Al Carson and the Blues Masters hold court here, playing live blues, and "Big" Al lives up to his name—especially the "big" part.

John Wehner's Famous Door. 339 Bourbon St. ☎ **504/522-7626.** 1-drink minimum per set. Occasional cover.

Open since 1934, the Famous Door is the oldest music club on Bourbon Street. Many local jazz, pop, and rock musicians have passed through the Famous Door. One of them, Harry Connick Jr., played his first gigs here at the age of 13. The owner is actually a young musician; his group (John Wehner's Dream Band) plays at night, offering a tourist-crowd pleasing selection of Motown, funk and swing.

Maison Bourbon. 641 Bourbon St. ☎ **504/522-8818.** 1-drink minimum.

Despite its location and the sign saying the building is "dedicated to the preservation of jazz" (which seems a clear attempt to confuse tourists into thinking this is the legendary Preservation Hall), Maison Bourbon is not a tourist trap. The music is very authentic, and often superb, jazz. Stepping into the brick-lined room, or even just peering in from the street, takes you away from the mayhem outside. From about midafternoon until the wee hours, Dixieland and traditional jazz hold forth, often at loud and lively volume. Players include Wallace Davenport, Steve Slocum, and Tommy Yetta. Patrons must be at least 21 years old.

Palm Court Jazz Café. 1204 Decatur St. ☎ **504/525-0200.** Cover $5 per person at tables; no cover at bar.

This is one of the most stylish jazz haunts in the Quarter. It's an elegant setting in which to catch top-notch jazz groups Wednesday through Sunday. The music varies nightly, but is generally traditional or classic jazz. If you have a collection of jazz records at home, peek at the records for sale in a back alcove. Another tip: You might want to make reservations—it's that kind of place.

Praline Connection Gospel & Blues Hall. 907 S. Peters St. ☎ **504/523-3973** for reservations and information.

There are two Praline Connections in New Orleans, both operated by the same company. One is a restaurant on Frenchmen Street (see listing in chapter 7) that serves regional soul food. The 9,000-square-foot Praline Connection Gospel & Blues Hall is a restaurant as well (with the same cuisine), but here you get live music with dinner on Thursday, Friday, and Saturday nights. Sunday brings a great gospel buffet brunch. Reservations are strongly recommended.

✪ **Preservation Hall.** 726 St. Peter St. ☎ **504/522-2841,** or 504/523-8939 after 8pm. Cover $4.

The gray, bombed-out building that looks as if it was erected just shortly after the dawn of time (or at least the dawn of New Orleans) doesn't seem like much, but it's mecca for traditional jazz fans. This is an essential spot for anyone coming to New Orleans. It doesn't get any more authentic than this. With no seats, terrible sight lines, and constant crowds, you won't be able to see much, but you won't care, because you will be having too fun and cheerfully sweaty a time. Even if you don't consider yourself interested in jazz, there is a seriously good time to be had here, and you very probably will come away with a new appreciation for the music. Patrons start lining up at 6:15—the doors open at 8pm, so the trick to avoid the line is to get there either just as the doors open, or later in the evening. The band plays until midnight, and the first audience usually empties out around 10. A 30-year-old sign on the wall gives prices for requests, but it's out-of-date. As the doorwoman said, "If we still took $5 for 'Saints Go Marchin' In,' they'd be playing it all night." (One night, some big spenders tossed seven $100 bills for seven rounds of "Saints.") Try about $10, and for other requests, "just offer something." Thanks to the casual atmosphere, not to mention cheap cover, Preservation Hall is one of the few nightspots where it's appropriate to take kids. Early in the evening, you'll notice a number of local families doing just that.

✪ **Snug Harbor.** 626 Frenchmen St. ☎ **504/949-0696.** www.snugjazz.com. Cover $8–$20, depending on performer.

If your idea of jazz extends beyond Dixieland, and if you prefer a concert-type setting over a messy nightclub, get your hands on Snug Harbor's monthly schedule. On the fringes of the French Quarter (1 block beyond Esplanade Avenue), Snug Harbor is the city's premier showcase for contemporary jazz, with a few blues and R&B combos thrown in for good measure. Here, jazz is presented as it should be: part entertainment, part art, and, often, part intellectual stimulation. This is the surest place to find Ellis Marsalis (patriarch of the Marsalis dynasty) and Charmaine Neville (of the Neville family). Not only does Snug offer good music, but the two-level seating provides universally good viewing of the bandstand. You should buy tickets in advance, but be warned: Waiting for a show usually means hanging in the crowded, low-ceilinged bar, where personal space is at a minimum—not recommended for claustrophobes.

✪ **Storyville District.** 125 Bourbon St. ☎ **504/410-1000.** Daily 11:30am–2am. Music noon–3pm and 5pm–2am. No cover.

Nope, it's still not in (nor even all that near) the old Storyville District, nor does it have anything to do with bordellos. This is the brand-new brainchild of (in part) Quint Davis, the man who helps bring us Jazz Fest every year, and that alone inspires confidence. The idea is to bring high-quality jazz back to Bourbon Street, in a nonfrat party atmosphere, and we completely support it. Music plays much of the day, starting in the red-walled parlor room in the afternoon, with bigger bands playing in a larger, more clublike space at night. It's not stuffy or pretentious, though the clean, somewhat sophisticated atmosphere make for an almost disconcerting contrast with the rest of Bourbon Street. The level of booking, thanks to the owner, should be high. Plans are for no cover, but that may have changed by the time you read this. New Orleans–style nibbles are available, courtesy of Ralph Brennan.

OUTSIDE THE FRENCH QUARTER

The New Showcase Lounge. 1915 N. Broad St. ☎ **504/945-5612.** Cover varies.

Even though it has the patina of an age-old joint, this is indeed a new showcase—the *new* means it's one of the newest clubs in town, and the music it showcases is modern jazz with an occasional blues singer. It's in the same family of clubs with Snug Harbor, only a little looser, and it is another place to look for members of the Marsalis clan. The bar is shaped like a piano, and the room is very comfortable—just small enough to ensure that everyone pays attention to the music. If you're lucky, there will be a buffet of soul food to go with your jazz. Tuesday night is "In a Mellow Mood" night.

Pete Fountain's. In the New Orleans Hilton, 2 Poydras St. ☎ **504/523-4374** or 504/561-0500. Cover $19 (includes 1 drink).

Pete Fountain has managed to make his name synonymous with New Orleans music. He grew up playing around town, moved to Chicago with the Dukes of Dixieland, joined Lawrence Welk's orchestra, and then, for more than 20 years, held forth in his own Bourbon Street club. These days you'll find him here, in a re-creation of his former Quarter premises, with seating for more than twice as many as the old club. The plush interior—gold chairs and banquettes, red velvet bar chairs, lacy white iron-railed gallery—sets the mood for the popular nightspot. Pete is featured in one show a night, Tuesday to Saturday at 10pm. You'll need reservations.

✪ **The Red Room.** 2040 St. Charles Ave. ☎ **504/528-9759.** Jacket and tie recommended for men. No cover.

Swing has finally caught on in New Orleans, with a vengeance, helped no doubt in part by this hot, fairly new, '40s-style jazz and supper club. Live music happens every night, with jazz and swing performed by both established names and talented up and comers. It's a lively place, perfect for dancing and romancing in the way your parents (or, depending on your age, you yourself) did—and we all ought to again. It's all housed in an odd-looking structure that puts you in mind of the Eiffel Tower. That's because it once was the restaurant there; it somehow got transported to New Orleans and then was abandoned for some years before the recent transformation. Come here to dance and drink (and eat) in a sophisticated manner, but dress appropriately; the staff won't hesitate to send you on your way if you are wearing jeans.

Vaughn's Lounge. 800 Lesseps St. ☎ **504/947-5562.** Cover varies.

Tucked deep in the Bywater section of New Orleans, Vaughn's Lounge is way down home. It's in a residential neighborhood and feels almost as though you're in someone's house. The long bar takes up so much room that people almost fall over the band at the end of the room. In the back room, you might find people playing Ping-Pong. Thursday—Kermit Ruffin's night—is the night to go to Vaughn's. Go early and get some of the barbeque Kermit is usually cooking up before a show—he likes to barbeque as much as he likes to play and tends to bring his grill along with him wherever he is playing. When he isn't playing and helping out with the eats, you might catch a Mardi Gras Indian practice. Be sure to call ahead to see if there will be live music on a given night, and be sure to take a taxi.

3 Cajun & Zydeco Joints

Most of the so-called Cajun joints in New Orleans are really Cajun for tourists, in both sound and setting. If you want the real thing, you are better off going out to bayou country. Which is not to say some of the finest Cajun bands don't play in New Orleans—it's just that you are likely to find, say, the world-renowned Beausoleil at the Maple Leaf or the Grammy-nominated Hackberry Ramblers at the Mermaid Lounge, neither of which is a Cajun club. And which is also not to say that terrific and authentic Cajun bands don't play at the places below—it's just that it's hit-and-miss in terms of true quality. What these spots do offer is a place to learn to Cajun dance, which is not only a skill that comes in handy in New Orleans (trust us, when crowds start to two-step, you'll want to join in) and a dandy way to burn off calories—it's just darn fun.

Michaul's on St. Charles. 840 St. Charles Ave. ☎ **504/522-5517.** No cover.

Michaul's attempts to re-create the Cajun dance hall experience, and for a prefab kind of place, it does it well enough. If you've experienced the real thing, you'll turn up your nose, but if you haven't, it'll do. Come for the free dance lessons.

New Orleans Nightlife

Acadian Brewing Company 36
Amberjack's Down Under 35
Apple Barrel 25
Bowl Me Under 37
The Bulldog 6
Cafe Brasil 27
Carrollton Station 1
Creole Queen and the Cajun Queen 18
Dos Jefes Uptown Cigar Bar 7
Dream Palace 28
Feelings 29

Howlin' Wolf 14
Hyttops Sports Bar & Grill 22
Lion's Den 38
Madigan's 4
Maple Leaf Bar 2
Mermaid Lounge 10
Michaul's on St. Charles 21
Mid City Lanes Rock & Bowl 39
Mother-in-Law Lounge 33
Mulate's 13
Neutral Ground Coffee House 3

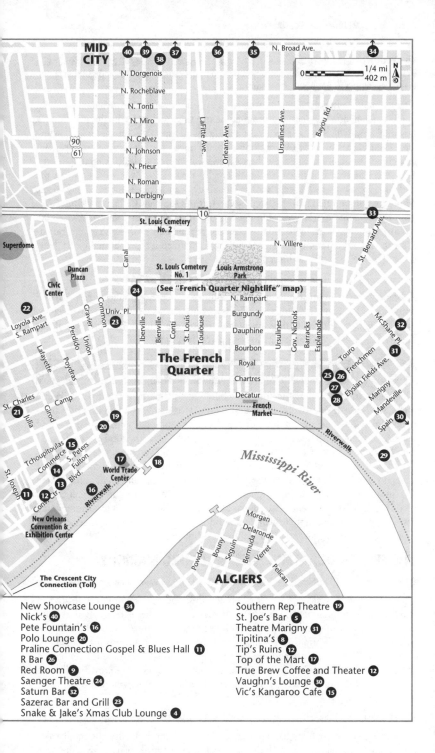

MID CITY

40 39 38 37 36 35 N. Broad Ave. 34

0 ___ 1/4 mi
   ___ 402 m
N

N. Dorgenois
N. Rocheblave
N. Tonti
N. Miro
N. Galvez
N. Johnson
N. Prieur
N. Roman
N. Derbigny

LaFitte Ave.
Orleans Ave.
Ursulines Ave.
Bayou Rd.

90 61

10

St. Louis Cemetery No. 2

33

Superdome

Canal

N. Villere

St. Louis Cemetery No. 1

Louis Armstrong Park

St. Bernard Ave.

Duncan Plaza

Civic Center

22

Loyola Ave.
S. Rampart

Gravier
Common
Univ. Pl.

24

(See "French Quarter Nightlife" map)

N. Rampart

Burgundy

Dauphine

Bourbon

Royal

Chartres

Decatur

McShane Pl.

32

23

Perdido
Union

Poydras

Iberville
Bienville
Conti
St. Louis
Toulouse

Ursulines
Gov. Nichols
Barracks
Esplanade

Touro
Frenchmen
Elysian Fields Ave.

31

The French Quarter

25 26
27
28

Marigny
Mandeville

St. Charles

21

Lafayette

Julia

Camp

Girod

French Market

19

French Market

Riverwalk

Spain

30

20

Mississippi River

29

Tchoupitoulas
Commerce
S. Peters
Fulton

15

St. Joseph

11

14

World Trade Center

17

18

Conn. Ctr.

12 13

16

Riverwalk

New Orleans Convention & Exhibition Center

Morgan

Delaronde

Powder
Bouny
Seguin
Bermuda
Verret
Pelican

The Crescent City Connection (Toll)

ALGIERS

New Showcase Lounge 34
Nick's 40
Pete Fountain's 16
Polo Lounge 20
Praline Connection Gospel & Blues Hall 11
R Bar 26
Red Room 9
Saenger Theatre 24
Saturn Bar 32
Sazerac Bar and Grill 23
Snake & Jake's Xmas Club Lounge 4

Southern Rep Theatre 19
St. Joe's Bar 5
Theatre Marigny 31
Tipitina's 8
Tip's Ruins 12
Top of the Mart 17
True Brew Coffee and Theater 12
Vaughn's Lounge 30
Vic's Kangaroo Cafe 15

✪ **Mid City Lanes Rock & Bowl**. 4133 S. Carrollton Ave. ☎ **504/482-3133.** www.cajun market.com/rock_n_bowl.html. Bowling: daytime and Sun–Thurs evening $8 per hour; Fri–Sat evening $10 per hour. Show admission $5–$7.

Everything we just said about tourist traps and nonauthentic experiences does not apply here. It does not get any more authentic than a club set in the middle of a bowling alley, which is itself set in the middle of a strip mall. Actually, as a bowling alley, Mid City is nothing to write home about, unless you like lanes that slope. But as a club, it's one of the finest and best experiences in New Orleans. Certainly it's the best place for zydeco, particularly on the nights devoted to Zydeco Wars, when the audience votes on whether, say, Boozoo Chavis or Beau Jacque is the King of Zydeco. Mid City is not limited to just zydeco; it also features top New Orleans rock and R&B groups, and some touring acts. On good nights (though we do wonder if Mid City has any that aren't), the dance floor is crowded beyond belief, the noise level is ridiculous, the humidity level is 300%, and you won't want to leave. You might even bowl a few frames. (Expect to wait for a lane.)

Mulate's. 201 Julia St. (at Convention Center Blvd.). ☎ **504/522-1492.** No cover.

A branch of the original out in Cajun country and a not-unlikely place to find authentic, and decent, Cajun bands. The stage and dance area are relatively spacious, and the food isn't bad. It's in the same neighborhood as Michaul's (see above), so if you get the Cajun bug, you can easily do both places in a night.

4 Rhythm, Rock & the Rest of the Music Scene

Most clubs in New Orleans feature an eclectic lineup that reflects the town's music scene; the ReBirth Brass Band, for example, attracts as many rock fans as it does brass band fans. Consequently, the bulk of the club scene escapes categorization (and, of course, booking policies are often subject to change)—even the local papers refer to club lineups as "mixed bags." If you want a specific sound, you have to look at listings (in *Offbeat* and *Gambit* magazines, for example) night by night. Some places are generally good fun on their own, regardless of who is playing; any night at the **Maple Leaf** is going to be a good one, while wandering from spot to spot in the Frenchmen section is a well-spent evening. Really, in New Orleans, you can't go too wrong going just about anywhere simply to hang out. And in the process, you might get exposed to a new, wonderful genre of music, or an incredible band.

THE FRENCH QUARTER & THE FAUBOURG MARIGNY

✪ **Cafe Brasil**. 2100 Chartres St. ☎ **504/949-0851.** Cover varies according to performer.

Day (when it is a great place to get a cup of coffee and hear gossip) or night (when it delivers danceable music), Cafe Brasil is the center of the increasingly lively and popular Frenchmen section of the Faubourg Marigny. It features Latin or Caribbean music, R&B, or jazz almost every night, and chances are whatever is playing will be infectious. Anticipate a hip and trendy, though still casual, crowd, and be prepared to act cool. The decent-sized dance floor fills up quickly and the crowd spills into the street, to see and be seen, and even examine the vendors who are often there hawking wares.

Checkpoint Charlie's. 501 Esplanade Ave. ☎ **504/949-7012.** No cover.

Somewhere between a biker bar and a college hangout, the dark Checkpoint Charlie's only seems intimidating—though the hard rock sounds usually blaring from the stage help. It's easy to overlook straight rock with all the other New Orleans sounds around, but this would be the place to start trying to find it. R&B and blues sneak into the mix, as well as the occasional acoustic open-mike night. A full bar, food, and pool tables help soften the ambience for the easily intimidated, and it's open 24 hours, making it a less touristy place for a quick drink during the day. Plus, there's a coin laundry, so a dusty traveler can clean up while enjoying the music. And right across the street is a fire station known for its hunky firemen, who on sultry nights sit outside and admire the views. Admire them right back.

Dream Palace. 534 Frenchmen St. ☎ **504/945-2040.** Cover varies; usually $4.

Dream Palace's decor is nothing special, but its varied schedule of Latin music, rock, R&B, and blues makes it a worthwhile stop on the Frenchmen tour. Something fine-sounding always seems to be pouring out of the doors, catching your attention and often drawing you in as you are about to pass by. Crowds tend to be young, but well beyond college age. The Reality Grill here serves dinner Wednesday through Saturday 5pm to midnight.

✪ **House of Blues.** 225 Decatur St. ☎ **504/529-2583.** Cover $5–$25.

New Orleans was a natural place for this franchise to set up shop, but its presence in the French Quarter seems rather unnatural. With all the great, funky, authentic music clubs in town, why build one with ersatz "authenticity" that wouldn't be out of place in Disneyland's Pirates of the Caribbean? And while it's noble that they've patronized many deserving Southern "primitive" artists to line the walls with colorful works, there's a certain Hearst Castle grab-bag element to that, too, which diminishes the value and cultural contexts of the individual works. That isn't to say the facility is without its qualities. The music room has adequate sight lines and good sound, and the chain's financial muscle assures first-rate bookings, from local legends like the Neville Brothers to such ace out-of-towners as Los Lobos and Nanci Griffith. The nouvelle Orleans menu in the bustling restaurant, too, is high quality, from a piquant jambalaya to fancy-schmancy pizzas. But patronizing this club rather than the real thing, like Tipitina's (which lost considerable business after the HoB opened), is akin to eating at McDonald's rather than Mother's.

Jimmy Buffett's Margaritaville Cafe & Storyville Tavern. 1104 Decatur St. ☎ **504/ 592-2565.** www.margaritavillecafe.com. No cover.

Yeah, Jimmy Buffett occasionally plays here, and yeah, they serve margaritas. Don't mind us if we sound grumpy; Buffett means well (isn't that practically his whole shtick as an artist?). But he took over a perfectly nice little jazz club (the Storyville Tavern, and, by the way, it is not in or even all that near Storyville) and made it part of the brand-name takeover of the Quarter. It's not as bad as, say, the Hard Rock Cafe, but still. Otherwise, lineups are solid, if unimaginative: blues, R&B, New Orleans roots, and zydeco bands. You'll often find local stars like Marva Wright and Charmaine Neville here, as well as the occasional nationally known act. The facility includes a bar area with a performance space and a large dining room with a main stage. There's no cover—they'll try to sell you food and merchandise instead.

Levon Helm's Classic American Cafe. 300 Dectaur. ☎ **504/522-5907.** Cover $5–$20 (if you arrive before 8pm, it's free).

Don't let the clunky name, which puts one in mind of the dreaded "theme" restaurants, fool you. Levon's is not as glitzy or oppressive as other celebrity/theme projects, though it does suffer a bit from the sterile prefab thing. They seem on their way to settling into a good groove, however. It is clear they are genuinely passionate about music, particularly New Orleans rock and R&B. The legendary Irma Thomas has made the cafe her French Quarter home, and up-and-coming chanteuse Banu Gibson has had a residency. Oh, yes, and The Band plays, too. Mr. Helm promises to appear at least 70 nights a year (the co-owner's father operated the club where Levon was working when Dylan first hired The Band.) Meanwhile, Traditional N.O. jazz will swing in the afternoons, or you can catch live sound checks and rehearsals until 6pm. They also serve "classic" American food, heavy on the meat, plus fancy martinis.

Shim-Sham Club. 615 Toulouse St. ☎ **504/565-5400.** Cover varies.

Taking over a longtime jazz club space, the new Shim-Sham only does about eight shows a month (at this writing), and its bar setting (definitely not a dive) has a good vibe. Booking is somewhat of a mixed bag, but tends toward roots, rockabilly, and swing. Seating can be either cabaret style (tables and chairs) or standing room. The lobby bar is always open for business.

✪ Tipitina's French Quarter. 233 N. Peters St. ☎ **504/891-8477.** www.tipitinas.com. Cover varies.

By gosh, they pretty much took the original Tip's, shrunk it down and stuck it in the French Quarter. Good for them. Unlike other (admittedly) tourist-geared spots, this has some ring of authenticity and so it is a most welcome addition to the Quarter. Great shows are frequent (most of them are tourist-friendly acts), and regular features include Sunday BBQ and swing sessions with Kermit Ruffins (who takes his home-made barbecue as seriously as his music), and Friday and Saturday Happy Hour (5 to 8pm) with New Orleans piano great Eddie Bo. The back is totally open to the street, so you can hear and see just fine and not bring out your wallet—though beware the sometimes overly aggressive huckster door kids whose job it is to make you understand lingering out there isn't nearly as fun as being inside. Ah, what the heck—go inside and get sweaty already. *Note:* You can often pick up business card–sized complimentary admissions to Tip's French Quarter at the Louisiana Music Factory by the cash register.

Tipitina's Ruins. 1101 Convention Center Blvd. ☎ **504/895-8477.** Cover varies.

Taking the place of the late and not lamented Tip's Big Room, this is another attempt (only just opened at press time) by the venerable club to run a big space for semi-occasional large concerts (the Neville Brothers, Isaac Hayes, the Funky Meters). It is to be profoundly hoped that this endeavor will be less oppressive and more Tip's-style good time than the previous one.

OUTSIDE THE FRENCH QUARTER

Throughout this book, we keep nagging you to be sure to leave the Quarter. At no time is this as important as at night. It's not that there aren't some worthwhile, memorable clubs in the Quarter, or at the fringes. It's just that there are so many terrific (and, in some cases, outright better) ones elsewhere. They aren't hard to find—any cab driver knows where they are. And not only do they feature some of the best music in town (if not, on some nights, in the country), but they aren't designed as tourist destinations, so your experience will be that much more legitimate.

Amberjack's Down Under. 7300 Lake Shore Dr. ☎ **504/282-6660.** Cover on Fri–Sat only.

Amberjack's is one of a number of spots at Lake Pontchartrain where you can pass a festive evening. It's on the Lake Pontchartrain marina, and most nights it's crowded with local boaters. When the weekend rolls around, Amberjack's becomes a stomping ground for young revelers with a penchant for tropical drinks. Friday and Saturday nights bring live pop, rock, and R&B bands, while Sunday is New Orleans music night—Neville Brothers covers abound. Pizzas and sandwiches are available if you get the munchies.

Bowl Me Under. 4133 S. Carrollton Ave. ☎ **504/482-3133.**

Located right under the Mid City Lanes—hence the name—this is a huge room (figure it's bowling alley size) that helps take care of the constant overflow from upstairs. Dark and bleak, thanks to the black paint job (with one large mural) and lack of windows, Bowl Me Under offers essentially the same acts as Mid City, though perhaps not as much zydeco. On some nights, the clubs split the bill—pay one price, see two bands, one upstairs and one downstairs—sometimes leading to strange, or not so, combinations of acts, such as the Latino and Southwestern-flavored Iguanas and the exuberant roots rock of Dash Rip Rock.

Carrollton Station. 8140 Willow St. ☎ **504/865-9190.** Cover $3–$10.

A long, narrow space means that folks at the back won't get to see much of what's up on stage, but hey, that puts them closer to the bar, so everyone wins. Way uptown in the Riverbend area, Carrollton Station is a gourmet beer house that schedules local and touring blues, classic New Orleans, and R&B musicians (plus some singer-songwriter types) Wednesday through Sunday, generally beginning at 10pm. (The bar opens at 3pm.) The crowd is a good mix of college students, music aficionados, and fans of whatever act is appearing on a given night.

✪ **Howlin' Wolf.** 828 S. Peters St. ☎ **504/523-2551.** Cover none–$15.

This is arguably the premier club in town in the quality and fame of its bookings, thanks to a remodeling job that increased capacity nearly fourfold—and made it a competitor with the former House of Blues powerhouse. Good. Better a local non-chain gets the business. (Unfortunately for Tipitina's, the renovations coincided with Tip's losing a large chunk of its capacity, which limited the kinds of bands willing to play there—with Howlin' Wolf ready to take up the slack.) The new look includes upstairs seating (or standing), which can be closed off for smaller shows. Howlin' Wolf draws some top touring rock acts, though it is not at all limited to rock—El Vez, the Mexican Elvis, is as likely to play as a country band or the latest in indie and alternative rock (recent performers included Frank Black, the Jon Spencer Blues Explosion and Iris DeMent). The renovations did not extend to the decor, so don't look for House of Blues–like pirate booty or something like the posters and other memorabilia Tip's uses to commemorate its history.

Lion's Den. 2655 Gravier St. ☎ **504/821-3745.** Cover varies.

A true neighborhood dive, but well worth stopping by should Miss Irma Thomas be in residence. She usually is, and sometimes, if you're lucky, she's even cooking up some red beans and rice. Thomas has only one hit to her credit ("Wish Somebody Would Care"), but she's still a great, sassy live R&B and soul act with a devoted following, who can never get enough of "You Can Have My Husband, But Please Don't Mess With My Man" and other delights. She puts on one hell of a show, and it's well worth treading into this otherwise unsavory neighborhood to see it. Heck, some come all the way from England every year during Jazz Fest just to watch her play. (*Note:* At press time, Ms. Thomas had taken up a regular residency at the new Levon Helm's Classic American Cafe. She was/is still performing regularly at the Lion's Den—and arguably, that is *the* place to see her—but the French Quarter location might be far more convenient and comfortable for the average tourist.)

✪ **Maple Leaf Bar.** 8316 Oak St. ☎ **504/866-9359.** Cover $3–$10, depending on day of week and performer.

This is what a New Orleans club is all about. It's medium-sized, but feels smaller when a crowd is packed in. And by 11pm on most nights, it is, with personal space at times becoming something you can only wistfully remember. But that's no problem. The stage is against the window facing the street, so more often than not, the crowd spills onto the sidewalk and into the street to dance and drink (and escape the heat and sweat, which are prodigious despite a high ceiling). You can hear the music just as well, watch the musicians' rear ends, and then dance some more. With a party atmosphere like this, outside is almost more fun than in. But inside is mighty fine. A good bar and a rather pretty patio (the other place to escape the crush) make the Maple Leaf worth hanging out at even if you don't care about the music on a particular night. But if Beausoleil or the ReBirth Brass Band is playing, do not miss it; go and dance till you drop.

Mermaid Lounge. 1102 Constance St. ☎ **504/524-4747.** Cover none–$10.

Although it's very hard to find thanks to a series of one-way streets (that all seem to lead away from the club) and its location in a cul-de-sac on the edge of the warehouse district, it's worth the effort. (You might call the club and ask plaintively how to get there. They might tell you.) An eclectic booking policy means everything from the Hackberry Ramblers (the Grammy-nominated Cajun band that has been playing together for nearly 70 years!) to hard-core grunge—and yet, the blue-haired pierced kids still come to dance to the Cajun bands in the tiny, cramped, dark, L-shaped space (yes, there is a mermaid motif throughout). One of the coolest vibes in town. As always, regulars avoid paying the cover charge by standing out on the sidewalk, where the music sounds just fine. Because it's not well marked even if you figure out how to get there, they might be your signpost.

Tipitina's. 501 Napoleon Ave. ☎ **504/895-8477,** or 504/897-3943 for concert line. www.tipitinas.com. Cover $4–$15, depending on the performer.

Dedicated to the late piano master Prof. Longhair, featured in the movie *The Big Easy*, Tip's was long *the* New Orleans club. But due to circumstances both external (increased competition from House of Blues and others, as well as a halving in the club's capacity imposed by city authorities) and internal (locals say the bookings have not been up to snuff for some time), its star has faded considerably. It remains a reliable place for top local bands, though. It's nothing fancy—just four walls, a wraparound balcony, and a stage. Oh, and a couple of bars, of course, including one that serves the people milling outside the club, which as at other top locales is as much a part of the atmosphere as what's inside. Bookings range from top indigenous acts (a brass bands blowout is a perennial highlight of Jazz Fest week) to touring alt-rock and roots acts, both U.S. based and international. It's a bit out of the way uptown, but definitely worth the cab ride on the right night. A stop here after dinner at the relatively nearby Upperline or as one destination in a night of club-hopping can make for a memorable experience, depending on what you're drinking.

5 The Bar Scene

You won't have any trouble finding a place to drink in New Orleans. Heck, thanks to "to go" (or "geaux") cups, you won't have to spend a minute without a drink in your hand. (It's legal to have liquor outside as long as it's in a plastic cup. Actually, given the number of people who take advantage of this law, it almost seems illegal *not* to have such a cup in your hand.) Bourbon Street comes off like a blocks-long bar—and smells like it, too. It's sort of pointless to single out any one drinking establishment there; not only are they ultimately all more or less similar, but their clientele hardly varies. The crowd is simply moving down the street from one locale to the next. If we sound a bit scornful about drinking in New Orleans, it's because so many seem to treat a visit as nothing more than a license to get blotto, and the streets as one big place to regurgitate. Not only is this obnoxious, but there's a lot more to this town than that.

Which is not to entirely dismiss drinking as a recreational activity (or, better still, as a sociological study). Certainly, New Orleans provides some of the most convivial, quaint, or downright eccentric places to do so; in many cases, the places are worth going to even if you plan to imbibe nothing stronger than a soda.

Note that many of the clubs listed above are terrific spots to hoist a few (or a dozen), while some of the bars below also provide music—but that is strictly background for their real design. Piano bars, in particular, have begun to pop up in New Orleans like mushrooms after a good rain. They're everywhere; in addition to the ones listed below, you can find a piano bar in almost every large hotel, and plenty of others off by themselves.

THE FRENCH QUARTER & THE FAUBOURG MARIGNY

In addition to the places below, you might consider the clubby bar at **Dickie Brennan's Steakhouse,** 716 Iberville St. (☎ **504/522-2467**), a place where manly men go to drink strong drinks, smoke smelly cigars (they have a vast selection for sale) and chat up girlie girls. Or you could try the low-key sophistication found at **Beque's at the Royal Sonesta,** 300 Bourbon St. (☎ **504/586-0300**), where there is usually a jazz trio playing.

Apple Barrel. 609 Frenchmen St. ☎ **504/949-9399.** No cover.

A small, dusty, wooden-floored watering hole, complete with jukebox and darts (of course) where you can find refuge from the hectic Frenchmen scene—or gear up to join in.

The Bombay Club. 830 Conti St. ☎ **504/586-0972.** No cover.

This posh piano bar features jazz Wednesday through Saturday evenings. On Fridays and Saturdays, the music runs past 1am. Apart from the piano, the Bombay Club is a restaurant and a martini bar—the drink has been a specialty here for years, so don't accuse the club of trying to ride the current martini trend. In fact, the Bombay's martinis are hailed as the best in town. The bar bills itself as casually elegant—a polite way of saying don't wear jeans and shorts.

Carousel Bar & Lounge. In the Monteleone Hotel, 214 Royal St. ☎ **504/523-3341.** No cover.

There is piano music here Tuesdays through Saturdays, but the real attraction is the bar itself—it really is a carousel, and it really does revolve. Those prone to motion sickness might well get dizzy. The music goes on until 2am, and who knows if the carousel ever stops revolving.

Crescent City Brewhouse. 527 Decatur St. ☎ **504/522-0571.**

When this place opened in 1991, it was the first new brewery in New Orleans in more than 70 years. The proprietors found a well-situated French Quarter building and installed a microbrewery—four stories of huge kettles and imposing pipes. The equipment is visible to patrons (you can't miss it) and is about as shiny and stylish as light manufacturing can possibly be. Wolfram Koehler is owner and resident brew master, and you can try one of his standard microbrews or the season's specialty. Look for art displayed on the walls in the dining room and bar area; upstairs is a popular balcony

Pat O'Brien's & the Mighty Hurricane

Pat O'Brien's, 718 St. Peter St. (☎ 504/525-4823), is world famous for the gigantic, rum-based drink with the big-wind name. The formula (according to legend) was stumbled upon by bar owners Charlie Cantrell and George Oechsner while they were experimenting with Caribbean rum during the Second World War. The drink is served in signature 29-ounce hurricane lamp–style glasses. The bar now offers a 3-gallon Magnum Hurricane that stands taller than many small children. It's served with a handful of straws and takes a group to finish (we profoundly hope)—all of whom must drink standing up. Naturally, the offerings and reputation attract the tourists and college yahoos in droves. Some nights the line can stretch out the door and down the street, which seems quite silly given how many other drinking options there are mere feet away.

Which is not to say that Pat's isn't worth a stop—it's a reliable, rowdy, friendly introduction to New Orleans. Just don't expect to be the only person who thinks so. Fortunately, it's a large enough place to (much of the time) accommodate nearly everyone—in three different bars, including a large lounge that usually offers entertainment (an emcee and alternating piano players)—with the highlight, on nonrainy days at least, being the attractive tropical patio. Don't look there for a quiet place to visit, though. The "party hearty" atmosphere thrives in that section (second only to the evening sing-alongs in the lounge), and on pretty days, tables can be hard to come by.

Even if it is a gimmick, what trip to New Orleans is complete without sampling the famous Hurricane? There's no minimum and no cover, but if you buy a drink and it comes in a glass, you'll be paying for the glass until you turn it in at the register for a $2 refund.

seating area where jazz combos play. Crescent City has a full menu and a weekday happy hour, which brings two-for-one beer specials.

Feelings. 2600 Chartres. ☎ **504/945-2222.** Cover varies.

A low-key, funky neighborhood restaurant and hangout, set around a classic New Orleans courtyard, which is where most drink—unless they are hanging out with the fabulous piano player, singing the night away. Authentic in the right ways, but also more cheerful than some of the darker, hole-in-the-wall spots that deserve that adjective. A bit out of the way, in the Faubourg Marigny, but everyone who goes there comes back raving about it.

Hard Rock Cafe. 418 N. Peters St. ☎ **504/529-5617.** No cover.

Gag. When the Hard Rock Cafe was simply a place for homesick Americans in London, longing for a real burger, it had some value. Now it's a chain—there must be one in Katmandu by this time—and particularly offensive in New Orleans, where there is real music to be had at every turn. It bemuses us to see tourists lined up outside this place when original experiences—as opposed to prefab, assembly line ones—are just feet away. Better burgers and better beer are to be found elsewhere. Go there instead.

Kerry Irish Pub. 331 Decatur St. ☎ **504/527-5954.** No cover.

In a few short years, Kerry Irish Pub has established that the French Quarter can indeed handle a little bit of the green. This traditional Irish pub has a variety of beers and other spirits, but is most proud of its properly poured pints of Guinness and hard cider. The pub is a good bet for live Irish and "alternative" folk music; it's also a place to throw darts and shoot pool. In case you want one last nightcap on your way back through the Quarter, you should know that Kerry specializes in very late-night drinking.

✪ **Lafitte's Blacksmith Shop.** 941 Bourbon St. ☎ **504/523-0066.** No cover.

It's some steps away from the main action on Bourbon, but you'll know Lafitte's when you see it. Dating from the 1770s, it's the oldest building in the Quarter—possibly in the Mississippi Valley (though that's not documented)—and looks it. Legend has it that the privateer brothers Pierre and Jean Lafitte used the smithy as a "blind" for their lucrative trade in contraband (and, some say, slaves they'd captured on the high seas). Like all legends, that's probably not true. Who cares?

The owner managed to maintain the exposed-brick interior when he rescued the building from deterioration in the '40s. At night, when you step inside and it's entirely lit by candles (*Offbeat Magazine* claims Lafitte's patented the word *dank*), the past of the Lafitte brothers doesn't seem so distant. (Unfortunately, the owner's penchant for treating good friends such as Tennessee Williams and Lucius Beebe to refreshments was stronger than his business acumen, and he eventually lost the building.) In other towns, this would be a tourist trap. Here, it feels authentic. Definitely worth swinging by, even if you don't drink.

Napoleon House Bar & Cafe. 500 Chartres St. ☎ **504/524-9752.** No cover.

Set in a landmark building, the Napoleon House is just the place to go to have a quiet drink (as opposed to the very loud drinks found elsewhere in the Quarter), and maybe hatch some schemes. (See chapter 7 for a restaurant listing, chapter 9 for information on the building.) Like Lafitte's, it's dark, dark, dark, with walls you really wish could talk. Also like Lafitte's, it seems too perfect to be real—surely this must be constructed just for the tourists. It's not. Even locals like it here.

O'Flaherty's Irish Channel Pub. 514 Toulouse St. ☎ **504/529-1317.** No cover.

Over the years, New Orleans' Irish Channel (uptown along Magazine Street) has become visibly less Irish in character. O'Flaherty's is taking up some of the slack. This is the place to go hear the best in local Celtic music, and on Saturdays there's also Irish dancing. The supposedly haunted courtyard in the 18th-century building is almost as big a draw as the Irish atmosphere.

Planet Hollywood. 620 Decatur St. ☎ **504/522-7826.** No cover.

See the description of the Hard Rock Cafe, subtract the part about how it was once valid, and add the phrase "only worse."

The R Bar and Royal Street Inn. 1431 Royal St. ☎ **504/948-7499.** No cover.

The R (short for Royal Street) Bar is a little taste of New York's East Village in the Faubourg Marigny. It is a quintessential neighborhood bar in a neighborhood full of artists, wannabe artists, punk rock intellectuals, urban gentrifiers, and well-rounded hipsters. It's a talkers' bar (crowds tend to gather in layers along the bar) and a haven for strutting, overconfident pool players. On certain nights, you can get a haircut and a drink for $10. Sometimes the cuts aren't bad, depending on how much the gal wielding the scissors has had to drink. The R Bar has a large selection of imported beers and one of the best alternative and art-rock jukeboxes in the city. Thanks to all this (or perhaps in spite of some of it), it's just a cool little local bar. You'll see a sign behind the bar for the Royal Street Inn, otherwise known as the R Bar Inn, a B&B—bed-and-beverage, that is. If you like the bar, you'll probably love the accommodations, too (see listing in chapter 6).

Special K

Tales of the blind regaining their sight are unproven, but there is a certain funky shrinelike quality to New Orleans R&B legend Ernie K-Doe's house o' himself, the **Mother-in-Law Lounge,** 1500 North Claiborne Ave. (☎ **504/947-1078**). Named after his biggest hit, a rousing 1961 number-one pop/R&B novelty, this is a true neighborhood dive bar, distinguished by the K-Doe memorabilia that lines the walls, and the nightly (maybe) presence of Mr. K-Doe himself.

New Orleans is a city of characters, so to say that K-Doe stands apart from the crowd really says something. His own biggest fan, K-Doe had a memorable radio show on WWOZ that mostly featured him yelling over records about what a genius he was and is. These tapes have become prizes among collectors of such pop culture documents, but you can see the real, bewigged thing in action, provided you don't mind treading into a grim neighborhood by the freeway. And yes, his mother-in-law—a new one he is quite fond of—is often there as well, along with his wife, the actual owner of the bar, Antoinette.

Don't worry if there are only a handful of patrons there aside from yourself; they are certainly hardcore fans who provide backing chorus to the Master's hits—because, if you are lucky (and if you ask sweetly, you probably will be), K-Doe will sing along to himself on a sort of high school principal's loudspeaker mike (call it K-Doe karaoke), as the jukebox pumps out his greatest moments. (The jukebox does have songs by other artists, but you wouldn't know it.) Call in advance to see when and if K-Doe will be in attendance (he keeps early hours these days), be careful in the neighborhood, and be sure to buy a drink (or 10) if you do go in.

OUTSIDE THE FRENCH QUARTER

In addition to those listed below, check out the bar at the International House hotel which is already becoming a lively, hip and happening hangout.

Acadian Brewing Company and Beer Garden. 201 N. Carrollton Ave. ☎ **504/ 483-9003.**

If you want to sample beers from a variety of regional brewing companies, head here. Acadian brews two brands, Acadian Pilsener and Acadian Vienna Amber, which are sold all over the city and across Louisiana. In its first few years, Acadian has won a lot of loyal beer drinkers, and the beer garden has become a favorite Mid City hangout; it serves Acadian draught beers, those from local brewing companies (Dixie, Abita, Rikenjaks, and Louisiana Brewing), and some imported beers as well.

The Bulldog. 3236 Magazine St. ☎ **504/891-1516.** No cover.

The Bulldog has become a favored hangout for uptown's young postcollege and young professional crowd (though some frat-party types can still sneak in). In the early evening, as work lets out for the day, you can see people filing in and filling up the benches out front on Magazine Street. At night, the Bulldog draws a larger, more lively group. It is likely drawn by the bar's beer selection—at more than 50 brews, probably the best in town.

Dos Jefes Uptown Cigar Bar. 5535 Tchoupitoulas St. ☎ **504/891-8500.** No cover.

Dos Jefes has a postcollege, young, yuppyish clientele. Mostly men, it seems. The patio outside has banana trees and iron chairs, and it's nicer than inside—carpet and cigars are a bad combination. The bar has a good selection of beer on tap and piano music until midnight Tuesdays through Saturdays.

Hyttops Sports Bar & Grill. In the Hyatt Regency, 500 Poydras Plaza. ☎ **504/561-1234.** No cover.

So you think you're a sports fan; well, here's your chance to prove it. Hyttops is in the lobby of the Hyatt, which is connected to the Superdome, the arena of the Sugar Bowl and New Orleans Saints home games. Everywhere you turn in the bar there's a television (many of them big-screens) featuring some athletic event; there are also plenty of electronic, video, and manual sports games for patrons. Because of its location, Hyttops is swamped with fans after Superdome events. If the arena is sold out, many fans like to go here to get as close to the action as they can.

Madigan's. 800 S. Carrollton Ave. ☎ **504/866-9455.** No cover most nights.

In the uptown section of New Orleans, Madigan's is a casual watering hole that has been home to blues musician John Mooney on Sundays. You might want to call and see if his residency is still ongoing.

Nick's. 2400 Tulane Ave. ☎ **504/821-9128.** No cover.

The slogan here is "Looks like the oldest bar in town!"—and it does. Behind the barroom you'll find billiards and occasional performances by live musicians. Special drink prices are offered on weekdays—Nick's is famous for shots of drinks with vulgar names.

The Polo Lounge. In the Windsor Court hotel, 300 Gravier St. ☎ **504/523-6000.** No cover.

The Windsor Court is, without a doubt, the city's finest hotel, and the Polo Lounge is the place to go if you're feeling particularly stylish. Sazeracs and cigars are popular here. Don't expect to find any kids; if you like to seal your deals with a drink, this is likely to be your first choice.

✪ **Saturn Bar.** 3067 St. Claude Ave. ☎ **504/949-7532.** No cover.

Genuine barflies or just slumming celebs? It's so hard to tell when they are passed out in the crumbling (and we mean it) booths or blending in with the pack-rat collection that passes as decor. The Saturn Bar is among the hipster set's most beloved dives, but it's hard to decide if the love is genuine or comes from a postmodern, ironic appreciation of the grubby, art-project (we can only hope) interior. Must be seen to be believed.

Sazerac Bar and Grill. In the Fairmont Hotel, University Place. ☎ **504/529-4733.** No cover.

In the posh Fairmont Hotel, Sazerac Bar is frequented by the city's young professionals and was featured in the movie *The Pelican Brief.* The African walnut bar and murals by Paul Ninas complete the upscale atmosphere. Wines and champagnes are available by the glass, and a dessert menu is available. *Note:* At press time the bar and restaurant were undergoing renovations. Limited food items were available at the bar.

Snake & Jake's Xmas Club Lounge. 7612 Oak St. ☎ **504/861-2802.**

Though admittedly off the beaten path, this tiny, friendly dive is the perfect place for those looking for an authentic neighborhood bar. Co-owned by local musician Dave Clements, decorated, sort of, with Christmas lights, and featuring a great juke box heavy on soul and R&B, this is the kind of place where everybody not only knows your name, they know your dog's name, 'cause you bring the dog, too. There is almost no light at all, so make friends and prepare to be surprised. Naturally, Snake & Jake's

A Bar with a View

The **Top of the Mart,** on the 33rd floor of the World Trade Center of New Orleans, 2 Canal St. (☎ **504/522-9795**), is the world's largest revolving cocktail lounge. What more is there to say? It makes a complete circle about every 90 minutes. In the evenings, the interior is dimly lit, with couples and small groups dispersed along the seats at the windows. If not for the remarkable views, people might notice that the decor is kind of tacky (they say "turn of the century"; get it?). From up here you'll see the bend in the Mississippi that makes New Orleans the "Crescent City," and the reflected lights of ships in the harbor remind you that this is not only a fun town but also a busy port. As you revolve, the layout of the city unfolds all the way to Lake Pontchartrain. There's no admission charge and no cover. Children aren't permitted. Top of the Mart is open daily until midnight or 1am.

can get really hot, crowded, and sweaty—if you are lucky. *Gambit* readers voted Jose the bartender the best in the city.

St. Joe's Bar. 5535 Magazine St. ☎ **504/899-3744.**

An agreeably dark (but not pretentious), nonseedy corner bar, this is a very typical New Orleans friendly-but-not-overbearing place. Its Upper Magazine location (across the street from Vizard's restaurant) means it's more neighborhood- than business-oriented. Folk art crosses hang from the (apparently) hammered tin ceiling, and the place is often seasonally decorated. At Halloween, the cobwebs look as if they should be permanent. There is a pleasant patio, a pool table, and a well-stocked jukebox with the likes of Ray Charles and the Grateful Dead.

Vic's Kangaroo Cafe. 636 Tchoupitoulas St. ☎ **504/524-4329.** No cover.

Really missing the brief Australia craze of the mid-'80s? Actually remember Crocodile Dundee? Drop by Vic's for a fix (or call; the last four digits of the phone number spell "g'day"). Despite the perplexing gimmick (how did Australian Vic land in New Orleans?), this is a friendly bar that caters to the local after-work crowd. On Friday and Saturday nights, decent—and occasionally better than that—blues and R&B acts play with no cover charge. Enjoy some shepherd's pie, wash it down with a sample of the nice selection of beers on tap, play a round of pool or darts, and generally have a—oh, dear, we are going to say it—g'day.

6 Burlesque & Strip Clubs

As if there weren't enough to Bourbon Street, what with the booze and the music and the booze, there is the sex industry. Kind of. In addition to numerous stores offering what we will euphemistically call marital aids, there are quite a few strip joints—some topless, some bottomless, some offering "live sex acts." If you make a habit of such places, you'll be in heaven. If you are merely curious, or simply in the mood for a naughty evening, this might be the time and place to try one. But beware: The lack of cover charges means they'll insist you buy a few overpriced, watered-down drinks. Plus, if you are looking for true risqué thrills, you'll likely be disappointed. Those "live love acts" are at best simulated, and at worst utterly tame (imagine nude aerobics done by not-half-bad dancers).

Below are a couple of recommendable institutions on this stretch of Bourbon Street (they're two of the tamer ones as well).

Chris Owens Club. 735 St. Louis St. (corner of Bourbon St.). ☎ **504/523-6400.** Cover $11 for shows Wed and Fri 10pm (includes Chris Owens show and 1 drink; $36 for shows Mon, Thurs, and Sat 9:30pm (includes Chris Owens and Al Hirt show and 1 drink). Group rates available.

If you like your entertainment on the sexy side but aren't quite game for Bourbon Street's strippers, this is the place to go. The illustrious Chris Owens, backed by a great group of musicians, puts on a show of fun-filled jazz, popular, country and western, and blues music while revealing enough of her physical endowments to make strong men bay at the moon. Between shows, there's dancing on the elevated dance floor. Audience participation is encouraged, so join the conga line. Call for reservations.

Rick's Cabaret. 315 Bourbon St. ☎ **504/524-4222.** Mon–Sat 11:30pm–4am. Cover $10, women free with male escort. No drink minimum. "Pedestal" dancing $20.

Rick's is right across the street from the Royal Sonesta, which makes it the first "gentleman's club" (euphemism for "strip joint") on Bourbon. It goes for the classy approach—the grand staircase entrance and rotating chandeliers are a dead giveaway. There are lots of mirrors and lasers, the chairs are comfortable, the interior is clean, and the girls have an on-site hairdresser to spruce them up even more. The result is a place that won't leave you feeling as if you need a shower. The topless dancers do their thing on three stages, usually to hip alternative or modern rock hits. While it certainly caters to businessmen and conventioneers, it is upscale and friendly enough that adventurous couples could go together without the women feeling too uncomfortable. Plans are in the works for a proper burlesque dinner theater show.

7 Gay Nightlife

The gay community is quite strong and visible in New Orleans, and the gay bars are some of the most bustling places in town—full of action nearly 24 hours a day. Thanks to go cups and the generally transient nature of bar activity, most New Orleans gay bars don't have a strict identity, or a specific demographic to their crowds. Though some may attract a slightly younger, or more leather crowd (as examples), that doesn't preclude a healthy mix of older patrons and suit-wearers. Below you'll find listings of New Orleans' most popular gay nightspots.

For more information, you can check *Ambush,* 828-A Bourbon St. (☎ **504/522-8049;** www.ambushmag.com), a great source for the gay community in New Orleans and for visitors. The magazine's Web site has a lot of handy-dandy links to other sites of gay interest, including info on local gay bars (www.gaybars.com/states/louisian.htm). Once you're in New Orleans, you can call the office or pick up a copy at Tower Records, 408 N. Peters St., in the French Quarter, or Lenny's News, 5420 Magazine St., uptown.

BARS

In addition to those listed below, you might also try the **Golden Lantern,** 1239 Royal St. (☎ **504/529-2860**), a nice neighborhood spot where the bartender knows the patrons by name. It's the second-oldest gay bar in town, and one longtime patron said that "it used to look like one half of Noah's Ark—with one of everything, one drag queen, one leather boy, one guy in a suit." If Levi's and leather are your scene, the **Rawhide,** 740 Burgundy St. (☎ **504/525-8106**), is your best bet; during Mardi Gras, it hosts a great gay costume contest that's not to be missed. The rest of the year, it's a hustler bar.

The Bourbon Pub-Parade Disco. 801 Bourbon St. ☎ **504/529-2107.**

This is more or less the most centrally located of the gay bars—it's right at Ground Zero and many of the other popular gay bars are nearby. The downstairs pub offers a video bar (often featuring surprisingly cutting edge, innovative stuff) and is the calmer of the two; it's open 24 hours daily and usually gets most crowded in the hour just before the Parade Disco opens. (Tip: From 5 to 9pm, a $5 cover charge gets you all the draft beer you can drink.) The Parade is upstairs and features a high-tech dance floor complete with lasers and smoke. Consistently voted by several sources as a top dance club (in all of America), it usually opens around 9pm, except on Sunday, when it gets going in the afternoon.

Café Lafitte in Exile. 901 Bourbon St. ☎ **504/522-8397.** No cover.

When Tom Caplinger left Lafitte's Blacksmith Shop behind, friends say, it broke his heart. But he rallied and opened a place down the block, bringing friends and patrons like Tennessee Williams with him. It's one of the oldest gay bars in the United States, having been around since 1953. There's a bar downstairs, and upstairs you'll find a pool table and a balcony that overlooks Bourbon Street. The whole she-bang is open 24 hours daily. This is a cruise bar, but it doesn't attract a teenybopper or Twinkie crowd. One of the most popular weekly events is the Sunday evening "Trash Disco."

Good Friends Bar & Queens Head Pub. 740 Dauphine St. ☎ **504/566-7191.** No cover.

This bar and pub is very friendly to visitors and often wins the Gay Achievement Award for Best Neighborhood Gay Bar. They describe themselves as "always snappy casual!" The local clientele is happy to offer suggestions about where you might find the type of entertainment you're looking for. Downstairs there is a mahogany bar and a pool table. Upstairs is the quiet Queens Head Pub, which was recently decorated in the style of a Victorian English pub. The bar is open 24 hours.

LeRoundup. 819 St. Louis St. ☎ **504/561-8340.** No cover.

LeRoundup attracts the most diverse crowd around. You'll find transsexuals lining up at the bar with drag queens and well-groomed men in khakis and Levi's. Expect encounters with working boys. It's open 24 hours.

DANCE CLUBS

In addition to those listed below, you might also try the **Red Room** (see "Jazz & Blues Clubs," earlier in this chapter), for some 1940s jazz swing dancing.

Oz. 800 Bourbon St. ☎ **504/593-9491.**

One of New Orleans' newest gay dance clubs, Oz is the place to see and be seen, with a primarily young crowd (as has its across the street neighbor the Bourbon Pub-Parade Disco). It was ranked the city's number-one dance club by *Gambit* magazine, and *Details* magazine named it one of the top 50 clubs in the country. The music is great, there's an incredible laser light show, and from time to time there are go-go boys atop the bar. There are frequent theme nights here, so call ahead if you're going and want to dress accordingly.

✪ **Rubyfruit Jungle.** 640 Frenchmen St. ☎ **504/947-4000.** Cover $3 Fri, $5 Sat; no cover weeknights.

Though it's technically a lesbian bar and dance club, all are welcome here—it's a very friendly, attitude-free establishment. You first enter the bar proper; the hot dance floor occupies a second room, booming with anything from techno to country and western. It almost always seems busy.

Wolfendale's. 834 N. Rampart St. ☎ **504/523-7764.**

Popular with the city's gay African-American population, Wolfendale's has a court-yard, a raised dance floor, and a pool table. Most don't come to lounge around in the courtyard or by the pool table—people come here to dance. Take a cab.

8 Gambling

The **Harrah's casino** project finally appears to be lurching toward completion. At press time, its opening was planned for October 1999. Feelings are mixed around town about this. The place could either change the tenor of the city completely, for good or for ill, or it could just be met with round indifference. New Orleans does not lack for decadence already; better you should go to Vegas for gambling of that sort. But if you feel you must go, the casino is located at 512 S. Peters St. (☎ **504/533-6016**).

There's also riverboat gambling. Outside the city you can find the **Boomtown Belle Casino** (☎ **504/366-7711** for information and directions), on the West Bank; the **Treasure Chest Casino** (☎ **504/443-8000**), docked on Lake Pontchartrain in Kenner; and **Bally's Casino** (☎ **504/248-3200**), docked on the south shore of Lake Pontchartrain.

9 The Performing Arts

New Orleans has historically been a center for all sorts of culture, especially the performing arts. In its cultural heyday, it had a thriving classical music community, many theaters, and what may have been the first opera house on the continent.

Today, after a period in which the high arts were at a pretty low ebb, things are on the mend. There are a number of local theaters and repertory groups, you'll find opera, symphony orchestras, chamber groups, ballet, and modern dance in the city, and some very good traveling musical theater companies make their way to town.

Note that ticket prices vary widely according to performance, and events are sometimes sold out; if you're interested in attending events, plan ahead.

PERFORMING ARTS COMPANIES
OPERA

Light opera appeared in New Orleans as early as 1810, and grand opera was first sung here in 1837. Opera enjoyed its peak years during the Gay Nineties and the early part of this century and thrived until a fire destroyed the famous French Opera House in 1919.

It wasn't until 1943 that the **New Orleans Opera Association** (☎ **504/529-2278**) was formed. It presents several operas a season. Stars from New York's Metropolitan Opera Company frequently appear in leading roles, supported by talented local voices. If you're an opera buff and in town during one of the local offerings, don't pass it up—there's nothing amateurish about these productions. The Met's touring company occasionally performs in New Orleans. Operas are staged in the Mahalia Jackson Theater of the Performing Arts (see below). For most performances, seats start at $30.

DANCE

The **New Orleans Ballet Association** (☎ **504/522-0996**), which merged recently with the Cincinnati Ballet, is the city's professional ballet company. The excellent performances are held at the New Orleans Theater of the Performing Arts. Check the newspapers for current performances. The ballet's season generally runs from September through April.

Classical Music

The **Louisiana Philharmonic Orchestra** (☎ 504/523-6530) plays a subscription series of concerts during the fall-to-spring season, and offers pops concerts on weekends in June and July. Concerts are held in the Orpheum Theater; tickets start at $11.

MAJOR CONCERT HALLS & AUDITORIUMS

The Mahalia Jackson Theater of the Performing Arts. 801 N. Rampart St. ☎ **504/565-7470.**

The Mahalia Jackson Theater has become the favored venue for lavish touring musical shows as well as concerts. You can catch opera and ballet in season, as well as circuses, prizefights, ice shows, and the popular summer pops symphony concerts. The theater is a part of the 32-acre New Orleans Cultural Center complex in Louis Armstrong Park, adjacent to the French Quarter.

New Orleans Municipal Auditorium. 1201 St. Peter St. ☎ **504/565-7470,** or 504/565-7490 for ticket information.

Just across a flowered walkway from the Mahalia Jackson Theatre of the Performing Arts, the auditorium has been used for just about every kind of entertainment—from the circus to touring theatrical companies to ballets and concerts.

THEATERS

In addition to the listings below, possibilities for theatrical performances and concerts include **True Brew Cafe and Theater** (see "Coffeehouses with Live Entertainment," below) and the **Louisiana Superdome** (☎ 504/587-3810), which frequently hosts entertainment that's not even remotely connected with sports.

Contemporary Arts Center. 900 Camp St. ☎ **504/523-1216.**

Located in the warehouse district, the Contemporary Arts Center is best known for its changing exhibitions of contemporary art. Also on the premises are two theaters that frequently feature dance performances and concerts, as well as experimental works by local playwrights. Call for the current schedule.

Le Petit Théâtre du Vieux Carré. 616 St. Peter St. ☎ **504/522-2081.** Tickets $18 for musicals, $14 for nonmusicals.

You may hear this place referred to as "The Little Theater in the French Quarter." It's home to one of the oldest nonprofessional theater troupes in the country. Throughout its season (early fall to late spring) the theater puts on a series of well-chosen and familiar musicals and plays. The 1998–99 season, for example, featured *42nd Street,* Noël Coward's *Hay Fever, The Innocents* (based on a Henry James story), *Ma Rainey's Black Bottom,* and *City of Angels* (the noir detective musical spoof, not the recent movie). It's community theater, but it might provide an appropriate family nighttime activity.

Saenger Theatre. 143 N. Rampart St. ☎ **504/525-1052.**

The restoration of the Saenger Theatre has been big news in New Orleans. It was regarded as a world-class venue when it first opened in 1927, and its finery has been completely restored. The decor is Renaissance Florentine, with Greek and Roman sculpture, fine marble statues, and cut-glass chandeliers. The ceiling is alive with twinkling stars and clouds so real you expect them to drift. Settings like this one are fast disappearing from the American theater scene, and New Orleans is to be congratulated for preserving such opulence. Touring Broadway productions play regularly, and popular music concerts are held here.

Southern Rep Theatre. Canal Place Shopping Centre, Level 3. ☎ **504/861-8163.** Tickets $15 Fri–Sat evening, $9 Sun 2pm.

The Southern Rep Theatre, New Orleans' newest theater, focuses on the work of Southern playwrights and actors. Located near the Canal Place movie theater, the Southern Rep is comfortable, intimate, and easily accessible from all downtown and French Quarter hotels. During the summer, novices get a chance to show their stuff as part of the theater's New Playwrights series. At other times, expect to find productions by or (occasionally) about famous Southern playwrights. Ample parking is available in the shopping center garage.

Theatre Marigny. 616 Frenchmen St. ☎ **504/944-2653.** Tickets approximately $12.

If you're looking for something in the direction of avant-garde theater, this will likely be more your speed than the places listed above. This little theater is known for its presentations of work by obscure and well-established playwrights. Shows are generally on the weekends.

10 Coffeehouses with Live Entertainment

Several coffeehouses offer live entertainment at various times throughout the week. The scene is relaxing, and a decidedly less rambunctious alternative to the city's bars. If "coffeehouses" means "poetry" to you, check out **Cafe Brasil,** 2100 Chartres St. (see "Rhythm, Rock & the Rest of the Music Scene," above). Readings happen only sporadically these days, but at least they still happen. Call ahead.

Kaldi's Coffee House and Museum. 941 Decatur St. ☎ **504/586-8989.** Sun–Thurs 7am–midnight, Fri–Sat 7am–2am.

Kaldi's frequently offers jazz and gospel music on weekends beginning at 8pm, and occasionally on Sunday afternoons. The Sunday show is often one of the best things going in New Orleans at that time.

Neutral Ground Coffee House. 5110 Danneel St., Uptown. ☎ **504/891-3381.** Tues-Sun 8pm–midnight or 1am.

The comfort level in this 1960s throwback cafe is high. Toss yourself into one of the overstuffed chairs and enjoy the music. Open-mike night brings all sorts of musicians and performers, while at other times more well-known musical talents are featured.

True Brew Coffee and Theater. 200 Julia St. ☎ **504/524-8441.** Mon–Thurs 6:30am–9pm, Fri 6:30am–closing, Sat 8am–closing, Sun 8am–9pm.

True Brew is one of the hot spots of the warehouse district, and one of the most consistent venues for entertainment. Patrons can enjoy coffee, tea, and pastries while checking out the live music and one-act plays (featuring local actors) presented weekly. Tuesday is Comedy Night.

11 An Evening Cruise

One of the loveliest evenings out in New Orleans can be found out on the water. The *Creole Queen* and the *Cajun Queen* (☎ 800/445-4109 or 504/524-0814), riverboat cruisers built in the tradition of their forebears, host superb Creole dinners and jazz cruises nightly. Both boats are operated by the same company; sometimes only one runs at a time. Departures are at 8pm (boarding at 7pm) from the Canal Street Wharf. The fare of $39 per person includes a sumptuous Creole buffet (it's $18 without the meal), and there's bar service as well as live jazz and dancing against a backdrop of the city's sparkling skyline. Schedules are subject to change, so call ahead to confirm days and times.

12 Plantation Homes & Cajun Country: Side Trips from New Orleans

As endless as the delights of New Orleans may seem, anyone could use the occasional breather—call it a palate cleanser, because after all, even the most dedicated gourmand can get dyspeptic. If you have time (to us, that means more than 3 days), you should strongly consider a trip into the countryside around the city. There are several possibilities for interesting side trips. This chapter deals with two. The first follows the River Road and the plantation homes that line the banks of the Mississippi, heading upriver from New Orleans; the second will take you a little more than 100 miles west of New Orleans to the heart of Acadiana, or Cajun country.

Even as you might feel a pang leaving the Crescent City and its wonders, once you've had a chance to soak up the beauty of the Louisiana countryside—which is entirely different from New Orleans all together—and experienced some of the hospitality of its people, you might well feel a similar pang upon returning.

How much time you devote to these trips depends on your schedule. On the River Road trip, you can see many of the highlights in a day trip, but it's quite possible to keep rambling north to visit the plantation homes in the St. Francisville area, an exploration that will call for an overnight stay. The Cajun country trip pretty much requires an overnight, and you'll have no trouble filling the time if you can spend a few more days in the region.

This chapter points out old homes where you can spend the night if you plan ahead. One recent addition along the river is Laura Plantation, which in just a short time has become one of the most popular attractions in the region. It deals with subjects (especially the experience of plantation slaves) that have generally been glossed over elsewhere along the river.

1 The Plantations Along the Great River Road

If your image of plantations comes strictly from repeated viewings of *Gone with the Wind,* you may well be disappointed when you go plantation hopping. That particular Tara was a Hollywood creation—indeed, in Margaret Mitchell's novel, Tara was quite different, a rambling structure of no particular style.

Plantation houses, at least the ones that are extant and open to public tours, are often more humble in scale (it wasn't until after 1850 that the houses got bigger in scale, and most of these predate that). They also come in two models: the Creole style, which tend to be low-slung, simple affairs (Creoles preferring to keep the goodies on the inside, where they can actually be enjoyed); and the American style, which can be closer to classic antebellum grandeur. (Isn't that just like those showy Americans?) Even so, these houses run smaller than you might think; even the "big" ones feel a bit cramped compared to certain lavish mansions built by turn-of-the-century oil barons and today's nouveau riche. If your fantasies would be dashed without pillars and porticos, you should consider sticking to Destrehan, San Francisco, Oak Alley, and Madewood.

In the beginning, the planters of Louisiana were rugged frontier people. As they spread out along the Mississippi from New Orleans, they cleared swamplands with a mighty energy. Indigo, the area's first cash crop, had to be transported downriver to New Orleans. Even as you drive on the modern highways that course through some of the bayous, you can easily imagine the challenges those early settlers faced.

In spite of all the obstacles, however, fields were cleared, swamps were drained, and crops were planted. Rough flatboats and keelboats were able to get the produce to market in New Orleans—if they weren't capsized by rapids, snags, sandbars, and floating debris, and if their cargoes weren't captured by bands of river pirates. These farming men (and a few extraordinary women) poled their boats to New Orleans, collected their pay for the journey, and then went on wild sprees of drinking, gambling, and brawling—behavior that gave the Creoles of the French Quarter their first (and lasting) impression of Americans as barbarians.

By the 1800s, Louisiana planters had introduced farming on a large scale, based primarily on their use of (and dependence on) slave labor. With cheap labor available, more and more acres went under cultivation. King Cotton, which proved to be a most profitable crop, arrived on the scene around this time. So did sugarcane, which brought huge monetary returns, especially after Etienne de Boré discovered the secret of successful granulation. Rice also became a secondary crop. There were small fortunes to be made—and then lost. Natural dangers could spell disaster for planters: A hurricane could wipe out a whole year's work, and a swift change in the capricious Mississippi's course could inundate entire plantations.

THE RIVERBOATS   After 1812, the planters turned to a newly invented water vessel for speedier and safer transportation of their crops to the market. When the first of the steamboats (the *New Orleans,* built in Pittsburgh) chugged downriver belching sooty smoke, it was so dirty, dangerous, and potentially explosive that it was dubbed a "floating volcano."

Over a 30-year period, however, as vast improvements were made, the steamboats came to be viewed as veritable floating pleasure palaces. The need to move goods to market may have floated the boat, so to speak, but the lavish staterooms and ornate "grand salons" put a whole new face on river travel and made a profound change in plantation life. A planter and his wife, children, and slaves could now travel the river with ease and comfort; many set up dual residences and spent the winters in elegant town houses in New Orleans. After months of isolation in the country, where visitors were few, the sociability of the city—with its grand balls, theatrical performances, elaborate banquets, and other entertainment—was a welcome relief. Also, it became possible to ship fine furnishings upriver to plantation homes, allowing the planters to enjoy a more comfortable and elegant lifestyle in the fields.

The riverboats did have a darker side, however. Along with families, merchants, peddlers, and European visitors, the boats were the realm of some cunning and colorful characters: the riverboat gambler and "confidence" (or "con") man. Plantation owners were drawn like magnets to the sharp-witted, silver-tongued professional gamers, crooks, and cranks. Huge fortunes were won and lost on the river, and more than a few deeds to plantations changed hands at the table on a river steamboat.

THE RISE OF THE PLANTATION HOUSES   During this period of prosperity, from the 1820s until the beginning of the Civil War, most of the impressive plantation homes were built. It was also during this time that many of the grand town houses in cities like New Orleans and Natchez were built.

The plantation home was the focal point of a self-sustaining community and generally was located near the riverfront; it may have been graced with a wide, oak-lined avenue leading from its entrance to a wharf (though some were much more modest). On either side of the avenue would frequently be *garçonnières* (much smaller houses, sometimes used to give adolescent sons and their friends privacy, or as guest houses for travelers who stopped for a night's lodging). Behind the main house, the kitchen was often separate from the house because of the danger of fire, and the overseer's office was almost always close enough for convenience. Some plantations had, behind these two structures, pigeon houses or dovecotes—and all had the inevitable slave quarters, usually in twin lines bordering a lane leading to cotton or sugarcane fields. When cotton gins and sugar mills came along, they were generally built across the fields, out of sight of the main house.

In the beginning, the main houses were much like the simple "raised cottage" known as Madame John's Legacy, on Dumaine Street in New Orleans—with long, sloping roofs, cement-covered brick walls on the ground floor, and wood and brick (brick between posts) construction in the living quarters on the second floor. These structures suited the sultry Louisiana climate and swampy building sites, and made use of native materials. Houses of the colonial period in this region were distinctly influenced by styles from the West Indies, very different from the grander revival styles that followed in the 1800s.

In the 1820s, homes that combined traces of the West Indian style with some Greek Revival and Georgian influences—a style that has been dubbed Louisiana Classic—began to appear. Large, rounded columns usually surrounded the main body of the house, wide galleries reaching from the columns to the walls encircled upper floors, and the roof was dormered. The upper and lower floors consisted of four large rooms (two on either side) flanking a wide central hall. They were constructed of native materials, with a few imported interior details, such as fireplace mantels. There were no stone quarries in Louisiana; if stone was used (which wasn't very often), it had to be shipped by sea from New England and transported up the Mississippi from New Orleans. Because the river flowed through banks of clay, however, bricks could be made on the spot. Cypress, too, was plentiful, and the water-loving wood was perfect for the hot, humid climate, which could quickly rot other woods. To protect the homemade bricks from dampness, they were plastered or covered with cement. Sometimes the outer coating was tinted, although more often it was left to mellow to a soft off-white. The columns were almost always of plastered brick, and very occasionally of cypress wood; the capitals were of these materials or, rarely, of iron.

By the 1850s, many planters were quite prosperous, and their homes became more grandiose. Many embraced extravagant Victorian architecture and gave it a unique Louisiana flavor; others tended to borrow from the features of northern Italian villas, and some plantation homes followed Gothic lines (notably the fantastic San Francisco plantation, sometimes called "steamboat Gothic"). Planters and their families traveled to Europe more frequently during this period, and they brought home ornate furnishings. European masters were imported for fine woodworking until

Louisiana artisans such as Mallard and Seignouret developed skills that rivaled or surpassed the Europeans. Ceilings were adorned with elaborate medallions from which glittering crystal chandeliers hung, and on wooden mantels and wainscoting the art of *faux marbre* ("false marble") began to appear. The wealthiest plantation owners were determined to make their country homes every bit as elegant as their New Orleans town houses.

Plantation houses also expanded in size over time, with some coming to have as many as 30 or 40 rooms. Families were quite large, and social life in the country consisted of visits from neighbors or friends, who might stay several days or weeks. After all, travel was difficult; there was very little dropping by or popping in. And certainly a Louisiana version of keeping up with the Joneses had its place as well: The Madewood house on Bayou Lafourche was built for no other reason than to outshine Woodlawn, the beautiful home of the builder's brother.

The planters' enormous wealth stemmed from an economy based on human servitude. The injustice and frequent cruelty of slavery, however, were the seeds of its own demise. Whether or not the issue of slavery caused the Civil War, it soon became a central target of the Union effort. When emancipation came, it had an inestimable effect on plantations all across the South. Farming as it had been practiced on the plantations was impossible without that large, cheap labor base. During Reconstruction, lands were often confiscated and turned over intact to people who later proved unable to run the large-scale operations; many were broken up into smaller, more manageable farms. Increasing international competition began to erode the cotton and sugar markets that had built the planters' large fortunes. The culture represented by the few houses that remain today emerged and died away in a span of less than 100 years.

THE PLANTATION HOUSES TODAY   Where once dozens of grand homes dotted the landscape along and around the river, relatively few now remain. Several houses that survived the Civil War have since fallen victim to fires or floods, and some have been torn down to make way for other things, such as industrial plants. Others, too costly to be maintained, have been left to the ravages of dampness and decay. A few, however, have been saved, preserved, and treated to the installation of modern conveniences, such as plumbing and electricity. Most of the old houses are private residences, but you can visit others for a small admission fee (which, in some instances, supplements the owner's own resources to keep up the old house).

Tours of plantations are a hit and miss affair—much depends on your guide—and if you do several, after awhile you will begin to hear many of the same facts about plantation life. The problem is that often the history of the house in question is lost in time, or it never had a particularly good story to begin with, and so consequently other details, like the practicalities of plantation living, have to be thrown in to fill out a tour. The exceptions are mostly noted below.

PLANNING YOUR TRIP

All the plantation homes shown on the map are within easy driving distance of New Orleans. How many you can tour in a day will depend on your endurance behind the wheel, your walking stamina (you'll cover a lot of ground touring the houses), how early you set out, how many of the same details you can stay to hear repeated, and how late you want to return (the small highways get a little intimidating after dark). You'll be driving through some ravaged countryside—this is oil and chemical company country now—though you will probably see more sugarcane than you've seen in your entire life. Also, don't expect to enjoy broad river views as you drive along the Great River Road (the name of the roadway on *both* sides of the Mississippi); you'll have to drive up on the levee for that. You will, however, pass through little towns that date from plantation days, and you'll have the luxury of turning off to inspect interesting old churches or aboveground cemeteries.

If you're in New Orleans on Christmas Eve, consider driving along the River Road to see the huge bonfires residents build on the levees to light the way for the Christ Child (it's an old Latin custom). They spend weeks collecting wood, trash, and anything else flammable to make the fires blaze brightly.

Not all Louisiana plantations actually bordered the Mississippi River (many were on bayous that also provided water transportation), and some of the grand old homes are too far away from New Orleans to be visited in a single day. These are listed separately, with the recommendation that you try to stay overnight at one that offers accommodations. There are also listings for lodgings in Baton Rouge and St. Francisville, either of which can serve as a convenient plantation tour base.

ORGANIZED TOURS

A plantation house bus tour is a stress-free way (someone else does the planning, and deals with directions and tricky turns) to visit the River Road region from New Orleans, though most of the tours visit only one or two of the houses described below. In general, tour guides are well informed, and the buses are an easy, comfortable way to get around in unfamiliar territory. Almost every New Orleans tour company operates a River Road plantation tour.

The 7-hour tour offered by **Gray Line,** 2 Canal St., Suite 1300 (☎ **800/535-7786** or 504/587-0861), is an especially good choice. The tour visits two plantations, Nottoway and Oak Alley, and drives by six others. The $40 price ($21 for children) includes admission fees. Tours depart at 9am on Tuesday, Thursday, and Sunday, and pick you up at and deliver you to your hotel. The cost of lunch at a country restaurant is not included and generally runs $8 to $10, sometimes more.

If you prefer a smaller tour group, **Tours by Isabelle** (☎ **504/391-3544**), takes up to 13 people in a comfortable minibus on an 8-hour expedition to visit Oak Alley, Madewood, and Nottoway plantations. The cost ($78) includes lunch in the dining room of the Madewood plantation mansion. The tour runs only when six or more people request it, so you might have to wait a day or two for a large enough group. Other Tours by Isabelle include a 4½-hour Cajun Bayou Tour (the boat tour is 1½ hours); the 5-hour Eastbank Plantation Tour (which includes guided tours of Tezcuco Plantation and Houmas House, with stops in front of Bocage and Hermitage plantations); and the Grand Tour (a visit to Oak Alley Plantation, lunch, a Cajun Bayou Tour, and a stop in front of Destrehan plantation).

PLANTATIONS BETWEEN NEW ORLEANS & BATON ROUGE

The plantations are listed in the order in which they appear on the map, running along the Mississippi north out of New Orleans. Many people choose one or two homes—Oak Alley, Nottoway, Laura, Madewood, and Tezcuco are popular ones—and find the quickest route. If you choose to follow the route along the riverbanks, you should know that you will have to cross the Mississippi a few times to see every plantation; there is a bridge just downriver from Destrehan, one between San Francisco and Laura plantations, and one a few miles downriver from Tezcuco. The river does wind, so distances along it are deceiving; give yourself more time than you think you'll need.

Destrehan Manor. La. 48 (P.O. Box 5), Destrehan, LA 70047. ☎ **504/764-9315.** Admission $7 adults, $4 teenagers, $2 children 6–12, free for children under 6. Daily 9am–4pm.

An appearance in *Interview with a Vampire*, not to mention its proximity to New Orleans (perhaps 30 minutes away) has made Destrehan Manor a popular plantation jaunt. It's also the oldest intact plantation home in the lower Mississippi Valley open to the public. It was built in 1787 by a free person of color for a wealthy Frenchman, and modified between 1830 and 1840 from its already dated French Colonial style to Greek Revival. Its warmly colored, graceful lines should please nearly everyone's aesthetic sensibilities. In addition to playing the role of Louis's ancestral home in *Interview*, it also supplied some later interiors.

The tour, lead by costumed guides who stay in character (it's better than it sounds), is worth taking. The house stayed in the original family's possession until 1910 (some female descendants are still on the board that oversees the place), so a fair amount is documented, and some of the furnishings (including a table used by Lafayette) are original. One of the rooms has been left deliberately unrenovated, and its messy deconstructed state shows you the humble rawness under the usual public grandeur.

Also of important note, this is perhaps the only plantation that is truly accessible for those with disabilities; there is an elevator to take wheelchairs up to the second floor (where the true living spaces are located).

San Francisco. La. 44 (P.O. Drawer AX), Reserve, LA 70084. ☎ **504/535-2341.** Admission $7 adults, $4 children 12–17, $3 children 6–11, free for children under 6. Daily 10am–4:30pm. Closed major holidays, Mardi Gras.

This fanciful mansion, a brightly colored creation known as steamboat Gothic, is a far-ther shlep from Destrehan (its closest neighbor) than it seems on the map. But it's worth the trip if you want to see something other than a cookie-cutter plantation home. Located 2 miles north of Reserve, the house was built between 1853 and 1856 by Edmond B. Marmillion. Unfortunately, Marmillion died shortly after its comple-tion and never occupied the home, which was willed to his sons, Valsin and Charles. In 1855, while on a grand tour of Europe, Valsin met and married Louise Seybold. Valsin and Louise undertook to decorate the home in high style, and when they were finished, Valsin jokingly declared to his friends that he was *"sans fruscin,"* or "without a cent" to his name. This is how the plantation home gained its first name, St. Frusquin. When Achille Bougere bought the estate, the name was changed to San Francisco.

The three-story Gothic house has broad galleries that look for all the world like a ship's double decks, and twin stairs lead to a broad main portal much like one that leads to a steamboat's grand salon. (Novelist Frances Parkinson Keyes visited the house and used it as the setting for her novel *Steamboat Gothic*.) Inside, the owner created beauty in every room through the use of carved woodwork and paintings alive with flowers, birds, nymphs, and cherubs on walls and ceilings of cypress tongue-and-groove boards.

✪ **Laura: A Creole Plantation.** 2247 La. 18, Vacherie, LA 70090. ☎ **225/265-7690.** Fax 225/265-7690. www.lauraplantation.com. Admission $7 adults, $4 students and children, free for children under 6. Closed major holidays.

If you see only one plantation, make it this one. Laura is the very model of a modern plantation—that is, when you figure that today's crop is tourism, not sugar cane or indigo. And it's all thanks to the vision of developer and general manager Norman Marmillion, who was determined to make this property rise above the average ante-bellum mansion. The hoopskirted tours found elsewhere are banished in favor of a comprehensive view of daily life on an 18th- and 19th-century plantation, a cultural history of Louisiana's Creole population, and a dramatic, entertaining, in-depth look at one extended Creole family.

This is a classic Creole house, simple on the outside, but with the real magic within. Unlike many other plantation homes, much is known about this house and the family that lived here, thanks to extensive records (more than 5,000 documents researched in France), particularly the detailed memoirs of Laura Local (for whom the plantation is named). On display are more than 375 original artifacts, making this the largest collection in the region of items belonging to one plantation family. They cover a 200-year period and include household items like clothes and jewelry. The property itself is a labor of love, as all the buildings are slowly being renovated (next up, the slave quarters).

Basic tours of the main building and the property last about 55 minutes and are organized around true (though spiced-up) stories from the history of the home and its residents. (Of special note: The stories that eventually became the beloved "B'r Rabbit" were first collected here by a folklorist in the 1870s.) Special tours are available on subjects including Creole architecture, Creole women, children, slaves, and the "Americanization of Louisiana." The special tours last about 1½ hours and must be scheduled in advance. Every day, they offer tours in both English and French, and have handouts in several additional languages. *Note:* To learn about Laura's family's life in the big city of New Orleans, go on the **Le Monde Creole** tours (see chapter 8.)

✪ Oak Alley Plantation. 3645 La. 18 (60 miles from New Orleans), Vacherie, LA 70090. ☎ **800/44-ALLEY** or 225/265-2151. Fax 225/265-2151. Admission $8 adults, $5 students, $3 children 6–12, free for children under 6. Mar–Oct daily 9am–5:30pm; Nov–Feb daily 9am–5pm. Closed Jan 1, Thanksgiving, Dec 25.

This is precisely what comes to mind when most people think "plantation." A splendid white house, its porch lined with giant columns, approached by a magnificent drive lined with stately oak trees—yep, it's all here. Consequently, this is the most famous (and probably most photographed) plantation house in Louisiana. (Parts of *Interview with a Vampire* and *Primary Colors* were shot here.) It's also the slickest operation, with a large parking lot, expensive lunch buffet (bring your own picnic), hoopskirted guides, and golf carts traversing the blacktopped lanes around the property. It's an interesting contrast with Laura (see above), and since they are just a mile apart, we highly recommend that you do both.

The house was built in 1839 by Jacques Telesphore Roman III and named Bon Séjour—but if you walk out to the levee and look back at the quarter-mile avenue of 300-year-old live oaks, you'll see why steamboat passengers quickly dubbed it "Oak Alley." Roman was so enamored of the trees that he planned his house to have exactly as many columns—28 in all. The fluted Doric columns completely surround the Greek Revival house and support a broad second-story gallery. Oak Alley lay disintegrating until 1914, when Mr. and Mrs. Jefferson Hardin of New Orleans bought it. Then, in 1925, it passed to Mr. and Mrs. Andrew Stewart, whose loving restoration is responsible for its National Historic Landmark designation.

Little more is known about the families who lived here, consequently tours focus on more general plantation facts. But over the last few years, renovations have given the rooms and furnishings a facelift, returning the house to its 1830s roots. The furnishings are not original, but are strict to the time period and mostly correspond to the Romans' actual inventory.

Overnight accommodations are available in five turn-of-the-century Creole cottages (complete with sitting rooms, porches, and air-conditioning), with plans to add more in 2000. Rates are $85 to $115, and include breakfast but not a tour. The overpriced restaurant is open for breakfast and lunch daily from 9am to 3pm.

Tezcuco Plantation. 3138 La. 44, Darrow, LA 70725. ☎ **225/562-3929.** Admission $7 adults; $6 seniors, students, and children 13–17; $3.25 children 4–12; free for children 4 and under. Guided tours daily 9:30am–4:30pm.

Plantations Along the Great River Road

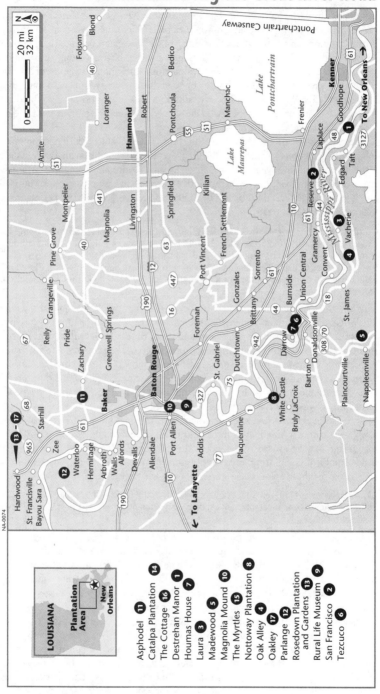

LOUISIANA

Plantation Area

New Orleans

Asphodel **11**
Catalpa Plantation **14**
The Cottage **16**
Destrehan Manor **1**
Houmas House **7**
Laura **3**
Madewood **5**
Magnolia Mound **10**
The Myrtles **15**
Nottoway Plantation **8**
Oak Alley **4**
Oakley **17**
Parlange **12**
Rosedown Plantation and Gardens **13**
Rural Life Museum **9**
San Francisco **2**
Tezcuco **6**

Just upriver from the Sunshine Bridge, 55 miles from New Orleans, Tezcuco ("Resting Place") was one of the last plantation houses built before the Civil War. It's an itty-bitty plantation house, though it's interesting to see how grand the rooms are in comparison to the very humble exterior. Although small, the raised cottage was some 5 years in the building, using slave labor, wood from surrounding swamps, and bricks from kilns on the plantation. It's surrounded by a touristy bunch of buildings, including a Civil War Museum (mostly odds and ends flung into cases), an African-American history museum (open weekends only), shops, a restaurant with a daily lunch buffet, a chapel, and a life-size dollhouse.

You can **stay overnight** in both small cabins (done in sort of ski lodge/mountain cabin rustic, complete with wood-burning fireplace) or in the main house, which seems like a great idea when you see the giant suite (bedroom, dominated by a massive wood canopy bed, parlor, bathroom). However, thanks to the tours, you can't check in until 5pm and must be out by 8:30am. Rates are $60 to $160 per night and include breakfast and wine.

Houmas House Plantation & Gardens. 40136 La. 942 Burnside (58 miles from New Orleans), Darrow, LA 70725. ☎ **888/323-8314.** Fax 225/474-0480. www.houmashouse. com. Admission (including guided tour) $8 adults, $6 children 13–17, $3 children 6–12, free for children under 6. Feb–Oct daily 10am–5pm; Nov–Jan daily 10am–4pm. Closed holidays. Take I-10 from New Orleans or Baton Rouge. Exit on La. 44 to Burnside, turn right on La. 942.

This is a different sort of plantation house, in that it is two houses joined together. The original structure was a mere four rooms, built in 1790. In 1840, a larger, Greek Revival style house was built next to it, and some time over the subsequent years, a roof was put over both, joining them together forever. The property, a former sugar plantation, has had multiple owners and little is known about them. The late Dr. George Crozat, of New Orleans, purchased the house some years ago and restored it as a comfortable home for himself and his mother, bringing in authentic period furnishings. Two of his nieces still live on the third floor.

Live oaks, magnolias, and formal gardens frame Houmas House in a way that is precisely what comes to mind when most of us think "plantation house." It so closely fits that image that its exterior was used in the film *Hush, Hush, Sweet Charlotte.* The inside is a bit disappointing, but scenes from *All My Children* were shot here, so be sure to ask for those Susan Lucci stories (they've got them).

✪ **Madewood.** 4250 La. 308, Napoleonville, LA 70390. ☎ **800/375-7151** or 225/ 369-7151. Admission $6 adults, $4 children and students. Daily 10am–4:30pm. Closed holidays.

This imposing house, a two-story Greek Revival on Bayou Lafourche, just below Napoleonville, is one of the best-preserved plantation mansions and is the place to fulfill your own plantation dreams—literally. The **overnight accommodations,** unlike those offered by other plantation homes, are in the main house, allowing you a chance to run around the 20 rooms at night, pretending it's yours, all yours. Once you hear the recent history, however, you might be rather glad it's not.

Madewood was originally built by a youngest brother for the sole purpose of outdoing his older brother's elegant mansion, Woodlawn. Four years were spent cutting lumber and making bricks, and another four were spent in actual construction. It was finally completed in 1848, but the owner never got to gloat over his brother—he died of yellow fever just before it was finished. As with many of the grand plantation homes, Madewood fell into disrepair and stood empty for awhile, until it was bought in 1964 by the parents of the present owner, Keith Marshall. When you hear the stories and see the photos of the laborious renovation (done in large part by the Marshalls and their friends), you realize how much work it is to save, and then continue to keep up, these glorious houses.

If you do **stay overnight,** you'll get the run of the place in the evening, as well as grand canopied or half tester beds, wine and cheese in the library, a multicourse dinner of Southern specialities (served by a charming woman whose family has worked at Madewood for seven generations; be sure to chat with her), brandy in the parlor, coffee in bed the next morning, followed by a full plantation breakfast. Now that's gracious Southern living. If you're lucky, Marshall and his wife, Millie Ball, will join you and share their stories. The rate ($215 for two, including meals; in January, 2000 will be going up to $225) seems like a bargain. Rooms in the elegant 1820s raised cottage are more secluded, with less formal furnishings. A bronze plaque in one tells you that Brad Pitt slept there while filming *Interview With a Vampire.*

Nottoway Plantation. Mississippi River Rd. (P.O. Box 160), White Castle, LA 70788. ☎ **225/545-2730.** Fax 225/545-8632. Admission $8 adults, $3 children under 13. Daily 9am–5pm. Last tour begins at 4:30pm. Closed Dec 25. From New Orleans, follow I-10 west to La. 22 exit, then turn left on La. 70 across Sunshine Bridge; exit onto La. 1 and drive 14 miles north through Donaldsonville. From Baton Rouge, take I-10 west to Plaquemine exit, then La. 1 south for 18 miles.

This house—69 miles from New Orleans and about 25 miles from Baton Rouge—has been likened to a castle, and you're likely to agree when you see the 22 enormous columns supporting the original slate roof. Built in 1859, the neoclassical house has 64 rooms and a total area of more than 53,000 square feet. It was saved from Civil War destruction by a northern gunboat officer who had once been a guest here, and kindness still blesses it, for the present owners have restored its rooms to their former glory. The white ballroom features hand-carved Corinthian columns of cypress wood, beautiful archways, delicate plaster frieze work, and original crystal chandeliers.

Randolph Hall restaurant serves lunch from 11am to 3pm and dinner from 6 to 9pm. You may **stay overnight** in one of the restored bedrooms with private bathroom for $125 to $250 (double occupancy), which includes a wake-up tray of hot sweet potato muffins, juice, and coffee, a full plantation breakfast served in the breakfast room, and a tour of the house.

DINING

In Vacherie
B&C Seafood Market & Cajun Deli. 2155 Hwy 18, Vacherie. ☎ **225/265-8356.** Everything under $10. MC, V. Mon–Sat 9am–6pm. CAJUN/SEAFOOD.

We believe in "when in Rome," so if you are out scouting plantations, join the locals and stop off at this decidedly low-atmosphere family operation for some fresh seafood (the house specialty) boiled or fried, gumbo, jambalaya, po' boys, and our favorite, fried boudin balls. (They make a great car snack.)

In Donaldsonville
Lafitte's Landing Restaurant. 404 Claiborne Ave. ☎ **225/473-1232.** Reservations recommended. Main courses $16.95–$27.95. AE, DISC, MC, V,. Tues–Sun 11am–3pm; Tues–Sat 6–10pm. FRENCH/CAJUN.

This long-time landmark restaurant sadly burned to the ground in late 1998, but the owners refused to let this bad luck keep them down for long. They are planning to relocate to the Bittersweet Plantation, where they intend to operate a Bed and Breakfast along with the restaurant. You should call in advance to find out operating hours and if they have indeed re-opened.

In Burnside

The Cabin. La. 44 at La. 22. ☎ **225/473-3007.** All items $2.95–$15.95. AE, DISC, MC, V. Mon 11am–3pm, Tues-Thurs 11am–9pm, Fri–Sat 11am–10pm, Sun 11am–6pm. CAJUN.

The Cabin is another good eating place appropriate to a day of plantation viewing. It is a slave cabin from the Monroe plantation, built about 1830. Nowadays its walls are covered with old newspapers, and antique farming equipment hangs throughout. Seafood lunches include blackened redfish, fried catfish, fried stuffed shrimp, and fried stuffed crab. There is also a po' boy menu. Specialties include crabmeat au gratin, broiled red snapper, and crawfish étouffée. Try the buttermilk pie or the homemade bread pudding for dessert.

PLANTATIONS FARTHER AFIELD

Many of the plantations described below are clustered in the area around St. Francisville, north of Baton Rouge. It's a good distance from New Orleans, and pretty much requires an overnight. You can get into the spirit of things and plan to stay at one of the plantations described below, or you may choose to stay in St. Francisville (they have several B&Bs there). You could also base yourself in Baton Rouge and drive the 100 miles back and forth to St. Francisville, but there is very little in Baton Rouge of interest aside from one plantation home. Besides, with the chance to stay at a genuine plantation, why bother basing yourself in what is otherwise a rather ordinary city? At the end of this section will be a listing of accommodations in both St. Francisville and Baton Rouge.

Contact the **Baton Rouge Area Convention and Visitors Bureau,** 730 North Blvd., Baton Rouge, LA 70802 (☎ **800/LA-ROUGE;** www.bracvb.com), to ask for its useful "Baton Rouge Visitors Guide," which contains maps of attractions in the city and surrounding area.

If you're visiting other houses in the area, you might want to drive by and see **Asphodel,** 4626 La. 68, north of Baton Rouge and southeast of St. Francisville. It's a charming example of the Greek Revival style popular in the 1800s, but no longer open for tours. Built about 1833, Asphodel consists of a raised central section with two identical wings of brick covered with smooth plaster made with sand from a nearby creek. Doric columns line the gallery of the central section and support its gabled roof. Each wing has its own small porch. Asphodel has been seen in films such as *The Long Hot Summer.* The old Levy house (built in the 1840s) was moved to the grounds here in recent years and is now operated by Dianne and Jerry Smith as the **Asphodel Inn** (☎ **504/654-6868**), an inn and a very fine restaurant. the leafy forest trails are open to visitors.

Magnolia Mound. 2161 Nicholson Dr., Baton Rouge, LA 70802. ☎ **225/343-4955.** Admission $5 adults, $4 seniors, $2 students, $1 children, children under 5 free. Tues–Sat 10am–4pm, Sun 1–4pm. Last tour begins at 3:15pm.

This home was built in the late 1700s as a small settler's house. As prosperity came to the lower Mississippi Valley, the house was enlarged and renovated, eventually becoming the center of a 900-acre plantation. Its single story is nearly 5 feet off the ground and has a front porch 80 feet across. The hand-carved woodwork and the ceiling in the parlor are authentically restored. Magnolia Mound takes its name from its setting within a grove of trees on a bluff overlooking the Mississippi. One of the oldest wooden structures in the state, it is typical French Creole in architecture and furnished in Louisiana and early Federal style. Costumed guides take you through. Magnolia Mound recently completed renovations of slave cabins on the site.

Rural Life Museum. 4600 Essen Lane (at I-10), Baton Rouge, LA 70808. ☎ **225/ 765-2437.** Fax 225/765-2639. Admission $5 adults, $4 seniors, $3 children under 12, free for children under 5. Daily 8:30am–5pm.

Louisiana State University's Rural Life Museum is an open-air museum on Burden Research Plantation. Authentically restored buildings include an overseer's house, slave cabins, a one-room school, a country church, and a barn that holds artifacts dealing with rural life from the 18th to the early 20th century.

Parlange Plantation. 8211 False River Rd., New Roads, LA 70760. ☎ **225/638-8410.** Admission $7 adults, $4 children 6–12. By appointment only. From Baton Rouge, take U.S. 190 19 miles west, then La. 1 10 miles north.

This plantation is one of the few that still functions as a working farm. Built in 1750 by Marquis Vincent de Ternant, the house is one of the oldest in the state, and its two stories rise above a raised brick basement. Galleries encircle the house, which is flanked by two brick *pigeonniers*. Indigo was planted here at first; in the 1800s, sugarcane became the plantation's main crop. Today, the plantation grows sugarcane, corn, and soybeans, and also supports its own cattle. During the Civil War this house was host to generals from both sides (Gen. Nathaniel Banks of the Union and Gen. Dick Taylor of the Confederacy)—not, of course, at the same time. Parlange is a National Historic Landmark and is owned by relatives of the original builders.

Oakley Plantation. La. 965 (P.O. Box 546), St. Francisville, LA 70775. ☎ **225/635-3739.** Admission $2 adults, free for seniors (over 62) and children under 12. Daily 9am–5pm. Closed Jan 1, Thanksgiving, Dec 25.

Oakley Plantation, 3 miles east of U.S. 61, features the old house where John James Audubon came to study and paint the wildlife of this part of Louisiana. Built in 1799, it is a three-story frame house with the raised basement typical of that era. A curved stairway joins the two galleries, and the whole house has a simplicity that bespeaks its age. When Audubon was here, he tutored a daughter of the family and painted some 32 of his *Birds of America* series. When you visit the house today, you will see some original prints from Audubon's elephant folio, and many fine antiques. A walk through the gardens and nature trails will explain why this location had such appeal for Audubon. Oakley is part of the 100-acre Audubon State Commemorative Area, a wildlife sanctuary that would have gladdened the naturalist's heart. There's a gift shop in the kitchen building, but you can still see the huge old fireplace where the family's meals were cooked.

⊘ **Rosedown Plantation & Historic Gardens.** 12501 Hwy. 10 (at I-10 and U.S. 61), St. Francisville, LA 70775. ☎ **225/635-3332.** Admission (house and gardens) $10 adults, $4 children under 12. Daily 9am–5pm. Closed Dec 25.

By far the most impressive and historical of the more far-flung plantations, Rosedown is notable for its dramatic gardens, and a tour stuffed with intriguing bits of facts and trivia, courtesy of more than 8,000 documents in their archives. You'll find Rosedown just east of St. Francisville. This home was completed in 1834 for Daniel Turnbull (whose son, William, married Martha Washington's granddaughter) on land granted by the Spanish in 1789 to a founder of the Port of Bayou Sara on the Mississippi River.

   The two-story house, flanked by one-story wings, combines classic and indigenous Louisiana styles. There are the typical columns and wide galleries across the front, and the house is made of cement-covered brick. A wide avenue of ancient oaks, their branches meeting overhead, leads up to the house. The 28 acres of historic gardens were begun in 1835 and came to be one of the great horticultural collections of the

19th century as well as one of the nation's most significant historical gardens in the 20th century. Fittingly, marble statues of gods and goddesses (brought back from trips to Europe by the family) dot the winding pathways. Inside is a veritable time capsule of a lost era; the house still has all its original contents (which is unusual for most of the plantation homes), thanks to members of the original family occupying the house until 1955, immediately after which the house was purchased and restored.

Rosedown is one of the best surviving examples of an antebellum plantation home, so expect to spend between 2 and 3 hours here, particularly if you wander the gardens as you should. **Overnight accommodations** are available.

Catalpa Plantation. Off U.S. 61 (P.O. Box 131), St. Francisville, LA 70775. ☎ **225/635-3372.** Admission $6 adults, $3 children 6–12, free for children under 6. Daily 1–4pm; morning tours for large groups by appointment.

Unless you are just a die-hard plantation buff, this relatively speaking humble Victorian home is probably not worth going out of your way for. It's not all that historical nor notable architecturally. On the other hand, it is still owned by the original family, which is practically unheard of among plantations these days. The oaks that line the drive up to the house grew from acorns planted by the present owner's great-great-great-grand-father, and tours do feature all sorts of curious stories about the family heirlooms that still lie within its walls. The slightly dented silver tea service, for example, lay buried in a pond during the Civil War; the lovely hand-painted china was done by none other than John James Audubon. This sense of family history and direct connection with the past is rare, so it alone may make your visit worthwhile.

The Myrtles. 7747 U.S. 61 (P.O. Box 1100), St. Francisville, LA 70775. ☎ **225/635-6277.** Fax 225/635-5837. Admission $8 adults, $4 children. Daily 9am–4:30pm. Closed major holidays.

A little over 1 mile north of the intersection with Louisiana Highway 10 along U.S. Highway 61 is this beautiful, if a tad dull, house, built in 1795. Its gallery is 110 feet long, and the elaborate iron grillwork is reminiscent of that on houses in New Orleans' French Quarter. The Myrtles is in an astonishingly good state of preservation, especially inside, where the intricate plaster moldings in each room are intact. The house is set in a grove of great old live oaks; the grounds are not as big as at Rosedown (well, nothing else really is), but still worth a ramble through. Too bad it's all set right on the noisy highway, which helps dispel any fantasy about drifting back to another era.

Overnight accommodations are available (though only the downstairs rooms have big wood canopy beds; there are at least four rooms with a decidedly modern flair), with private or shared bathrooms, for $82.50 to $143 (double occupancy), which includes a plantation breakfast and tour. Friday and Saturday nights, they offer "Mystery" tours, a chance for the guides to tell ghost stories and various legends about the Myrtles being haunted. Call for times and prices. **Kearn's Carriage House** serves fancy dinners (like chorizo and smoked Gouda-stuffed quail with apple glaze) and more simple lunches, which are available for takeout.

The Cottage. 10528 Cottage Lane (at U.S. 61), St. Francisville, LA 70775. ☎ **225/635-3674.** Admission $6. Daily 9am–5pm.

This rambling country home 5 miles north of St. Francisville is really a series of buildings constructed between 1795 and 1859. It's not that much to see, inside or out, and the accommodations pale when compared to what's offered at Madewood. Still, the low, two-story house has a long gallery out front, a nice place to sit and relax for an evening, perhaps joined by the owners' sociable dogs.

The first house was built entirely of virgin cypress taken from the grounds. Many of the outbuildings date from 1811, when Judge Thomas Butler (of the "Fighting Butlers," prominent in American history) acquired the property. After his victory in the Battle of New Orleans, Gen. Andrew Jackson, along with a troop of officers that included no fewer than *eight* Butlers, stopped off here for a 3-week stay on his way from New Orleans to Natchez. The Cottage's interior looks very much as it did when the Butlers lived here, with hand-screened wallpaper, a 19th-century loveseat (with space for a chaperone), and needlepoint fire screens made by the ladies of the family. This is a working family farm of some 360 acres.

The four **guest rooms** ($95 double, including breakfast), are a mix of elegant (huge four-poster canopy beds) and funky (icky motel room carpeting), and are not available January, February, or major holidays. But there is a small pool, and you do have breakfast in the elegant dining room of the main house.

ACCOMMODATIONS

In addition to the establishments listed below, you might consider spending the night at Madewood, Nottoway Plantation, Rosedown Plantation, or the Myrtles, described above. All should be booked well in advance.

In St. Francisville

Like many a town in this area, St. Francisville doesn't look like much on approach, but by the time you get to the center of town, you are utterly charmed. Between this, and better proximity to the plantations, we strongly suggest staying here (if not *at* one of said plantations) overnight rather than going back to Baton Rouge. In addition to the accommodations listed below, you can call the local **tourism information office** for a list of (and suggestions regarding) local B&Bs (☎ **225/635-6330** from 9am to 5pm daily).

Once in St. Francisville, do stop by ✪ **Grandmother's Buttons,** 9814 Royal St. (☎ **225/635-4107**). The owner makes jewelry from antique and vintage buttons (from Victorian brass picture buttons to 1940s Bakelite)—one of a kind, amazing creations. We've bought more earrings, brooches, and other gewgaws from here than we could ever possibly wear. Don't overlook their much-more-interesting-than-you-might-think button museum. Hours are Monday to Saturday from 10am to 5:30pm, Sunday from noon to 5:30pm.

Barrow House Inn. 9779 Royal St. (P.O. Box 2550), St. Francisville, LA 70775. ☎ **225/ 635-4791.** 8 units. A/C TV. $95–$115 double; $130–$150 suite. Extra person $30. Disc, MC, V.

The Barrow House Inn is two guest houses, the Barrow House and the Printer's House. Both are listed on the National Register of Historic Places and are located in the heart of St. Francisville's charming historic district. The Printer's House, dating from the 1780s, is the oldest in town and was built by the monks for whom St. Francisville is named. Across the street is the New England saltbox-style Barrow House (ca. 1809).

Owned and operated by Shirley Dittloff and her son Christopher, the houses have been restored and furnished with 1840s to 1880s antiques. The Dittloffs offer a choice of continental or full breakfast, and their acclaimed gourmet dinner (guests only) is served by candlelight in the historic dining room. Guests also have access to an original-edition Audubon collection and a small space museum dedicated to Shirley's father, a pioneer in American space exploration.

St. Francis Hotel on the Lake. P.O. Box 440, St. Francisville, LA 70775. ☎ **800/826-9931** in Louisiana, 800/523-6118 in the U.S., or 225/635-3821. Fax 225/635-4749. 99 units. A/C TV TEL. $65 double. AE, DC, DISC, MC, V. Free parking.

In St. Francisville, this is probably your best non-B&B bet. It's on the Highway 61 Bypass, with attractive guest rooms (some have TVs and facilities for travelers with disabilities), a restaurant, a coffee shop, a lounge, an outdoor pool, and dog kennels.

In Baton Rouge

Hilton Baton Rouge. 5500 Hilton Ave., Baton Rouge, LA 70808. ☎ **225/924-5000.** Fax 225/925-1330. 300 units. A/C TV TEL. $74–$129 double. Family discounts available. AE, DC, DISC, MC, V. Free parking.

All rooms here are Hilton quality. There is an outdoor pool, a health spa, a lounge, tennis courts, and a dining room. The hotel completed a major renovation in December 1996.

Radisson Hotel & Conference Center. 4728 Constitution Ave., Baton Rouge, LA 70808. ☎ **225/925-2244.** Fax 225/930-0140. www.radisson.com. 294 units. A/C TV TEL. $79–$139 double. Extra person $10. AE, CB, DC, DISC, MC, V. Free parking. From New Orleans, take I-10 to the College Dr. exit.

This hotel is a good stop after you've spent the day driving from plantation to plantation on the way to Lafayette. Each room has cable TV, voice mail, a coffeemaker, an ironing board, two double beds (or one king), and a desk. There is a restaurant and a bar on the premises, as well as an outdoor pool. Room service is available 24 hours a day, and there is a gift shop. In recent years, the hotel has undergone significant renovations.

DINING

In St. Francisville

Magnolia Cafe. 5687 Commerce St. ☎ **225/635-6528.** Everything under $10. MC, V. Sun–Wed 9am–4pm, Thurs–Sat 9am–9pm (or later). CAFE.

A lively, friendly place that certainly caters to plantation-hopping tourists with their decidedly nonlocal menu (though locals still come here, drawn by the good food, fine atmosphere and live music Friday nights). How else to explain an entire Mexican menu, pizza with chicken, pesto and spinach toppings, salads that don't just rely on iceberg lettuce, fat-free honey mustard dressing for same, and fat-free lemon cheesecake for dessert? The food is good and spicy, there's a kids' menu, sandwiches range from po' boys to stir-fry chicken (really). Desserts like their Snicker Blitz or Candy Bar cheesecake can send you into a sugar coma

In Baton Rouge

Mike Anderson's Seafood. 1031 W. Lee Dr. ☎ **225/766-7823.** Reservations not accepted. Main courses $10.95–$24.95. AE, DC, DISC, MC, V. Mon–Thurs 11am–2pm and 5–9:30pm, Fri–Sat 11am–10:30pm, Sun 11am–9pm. SEAFOOD.

Mike Anderson's is one of Baton Rouge's better places to get seafood, yet it's surprisingly inexpensive. The menu features fresh fish and shellfish of all kinds, prepared in every manner you can imagine. The portions are quite large, and the prices are low.

Mulate's Cajun Restaurant. 8322 Bluebonnet. ☎ **225/767-4794.** Main courses $6.95–$18.95. AE, MC, V, DISC. Daily 11am–10pm. CAJUN.

If you haven't yet gone to the Mulate's in New Orleans, try this branch near I-10, with the same Cajun friendliness, great food, and live Cajun music every night of the week.

Ruth's Chris Steak House. 4836 Constitution Ave. ☎ **225/925-0163.** Reservations strongly recommended. Main courses $19.95–$29.95. AE, MC, V. Mon–Fri 11:30am–11:30pm; Sat 4pm–midnight. STEAK.

Steak lovers who became addicted to Ruth's Chris Steak House in New Orleans (or elsewhere) will be happy to know there's a branch here, with the same high-quality meats and the same moderate price range.

2 Cajun Country

Its official name is Acadiana, and it consists of a rough triangle of Louisiana made up of 22 parishes (counties), from St. Landry Parish at the top of the triangle to the Gulf of Mexico at its base. Lafayette is its "capital," and it's dotted with such towns as St. Martinville, New Iberia, Abbeville, and Eunice. You won't find its boundaries on any map, nor the name "Acadiana" stamped across it. But those 22 parishes are Cajun country, and its history and culture are unique in America.

MEET THE CAJUNS

Their history is a sad one, but it produced a people and a culture well worth getting to know.

In the early 1600s, colonists from France began settling the southeastern coast of Canada in a region they named Acadia. They developed a peaceful agricultural society based on the values of a strong Catholic faith, deep love of family, and respect for their relatively small land holdings. The community was isolated from the mainstream of European culture for nearly 150 years. Life was defined by the company of families and friends. This pastoral existence was maintained until 1713, when Acadia became the property of the British under the Treaty of Utrecht. Though the Acadians were determined to keep to their peaceful existence under the new rulers, it became clear that it would not be possible. For more than 40 years they were continually harassed by the king's representatives, who tried to force them to pledge allegiance to the British monarch and to renounce Catholicism and embrace the king's Protestant religion. That was so abhorrent to Acadians, and they were so steadfast in their refusal, that in 1755, the British governor of the region sent troops to seize their farms and deport them. Villages were burned, husbands and wives and children were separated as ships were loaded, and a 10-year odyssey began.

Some Acadians were returned to France, some went to England, many were put ashore along America's east coast, and some wound up in the West Indies. The deportation voyages, made on poorly equipped, overcrowded ships, took a huge toll, and hundreds of lives were lost. Many of the survivors who were sent to France and England returned to America as much as 20 years later.

Louisiana, with its strong French background, was a natural destination for Acadians hoping to reestablish a permanent home, and those who were transported to the West Indies were probably the first to head there. In 1765, Bernard Andry brought a band of 231 men, women, and children to the region now known as Acadiana.

The land on which they settled differed greatly from what they had left in Nova Scotia. The swampy terrain was low-lying and boggy, interlaced with bayous and lakes, forested with live oak, willow, ash, and gum, and teeming with wildlife. Given land that mostly bounded the bayous, the Acadians built small levees (or dikes) along the banks and drained fields for small farms and pastures.

You may know about Cajuns from high school, because of Henry Wadsworth Longfellow's epic poem *Evangeline*—the story of Evangeline and Gabriel, Acadian lovers who spent their lives wandering this land searching for each other after being wrenched from their homeland. In real life, Evangeline was Emmeline Labiche, and her sweetheart was Louis Pierre Arceneaux. Their story has a different ending from the poet's—Emmeline found Louis Pierre, after many years of searching, right in Cajun country in the town of St. Martinville. The real-life tragedy was that by then Louis had given up hope of ever finding her and was pledged to another. She died of a broken heart in Louisiana, not in Philadelphia.

After many decades during which Cajuns shied away from their roots (children were beaten in school for speaking French, which was considered a sign of ignorance; Cajun music was considered primitive or hokey), the culture is experiencing a resurgence of popularity and respect, and a new sense of community pride.

CAJUN LANGUAGE

This essay was provided by Ann Allen Savoy, who is, along with her husband, Marc, a musician in the Savoy-Doucet Cajun Band and the Savoy-Smith Band, and also has her own group, the Magnolia Sisters. All three have released CDs on the Arhoolie label. She is also the author of Cajun Music Vol. 1 *(Bluebird Press), an excellent and definitive work that combines oral history with a songbook.*

The French influence in Louisiana is one of the things that sets the state apart from the rest of the United States. As soon as you get west of Baton Rouge, you can cruise down the Louisiana highways listening on your radio to French news, church services, music, and talk shows. The accent is sharp and bright, with occasional English words thrown in (*"On va revenir right back"*—"We'll be right back"), so it is fun to see how much even Anglophiles can follow the French story lines.

Though French is spoken by most of the older Cajuns (aged 60 and up), most middle-aged and young Louisianians don't speak the language. This is partially because the knowledge of the French language, from the 1930s on, became associated with a lack of business success or a lack of education, so a stigma became attached to the language. Today, however, there is a resurgence in pride at being bilingual, particularly in larger towns and metropolitan areas. French emergence programs are cropping up here and there, and educated musicians and teachers aged 30 to 50 are learning to speak French.

I recommend wandering through old grocery stores, dance halls, and feed stores, where you will hear many "natives" speaking French. This French is peppered with old words dating from Louis XIV, and the beautiful old words, no longer used in France, are historically intriguing. Cajun French is not a dialect of the French language, nor are there actual dialects of Cajun French from town to town in southwest Louisiana. The impression that there are various dialects could come from the fact that many words refer to particular items, and certain areas prefer particular words over others. For example, a mosquito can be called a *marougouin, moustique,* or *cousin.* One area might use only one of the words and never use the others. Remember that Cajun French is not a written language, so certain words that were originally mispronounced have become part of the language. Similarly, some English words are part of the language today because when the Acadians first came to Louisiana, there were no such things as pickup trucks, typewriters, and other modern inventions, so the English words are used.

Parallel to the Cajun French language, the fascinating Creole language is still spoken by many black Louisianians. The language is a compilation of African dialects and French, and is quite different from standard French. However, Cajuns and black Creoles can speak and understand both languages.

At the weekly broadcast at the Liberty Theater in Eunice, you can listen to Cajun and zydeco music and enjoy the beauty of the unique Cajun language.

—*Ann Allen Savoy*

CAJUN MUSIC

It's hard to decide which is more important to a Cajun: food or music. This is among the reasons they are such a delightful people. Cajuns love music so much that even in the early days, when instruments were scarce, they held dances, with a capella voices providing the accompaniment. With roots probably found in medieval France, traditional Cajun music is largely an orally transmitted art form. The strains usually come in the form of a brisk two-step or a waltz. The most traditional groups still play mostly acoustic—a fiddle, an accordion, a triangle, and maybe a guitar.

The best place to hear real Cajun music is on someone's back porch, the time-honored spot for gathering to eat some gumbo and listen to several generations of musicians jamming together all night long. If you don't know a Cajun and don't have access to a back-porch gathering, don't fret. Throughout Cajun country there are dance halls, with something going on just about every weekend. Locals come to dance, and so should you. Don't know how to Cajun dance? Many people will be delighted to show you. Worried everyone will be watching you because you dance so badly? Observe the couples out on the dance floor. Who are you watching? That's right—the really good couples, who fly in complex, almost jitterbug patterns. You aren't looking at the mediocre couples, and neither is anyone else. So don't be shy. And talk to the people around you. This is a social gathering, and Cajuns love to visit, telling stories and jokes.

Restaurants such as Mulate's, Randol's, and D.I.'s offer regular live music and Cajun dancing, and don't overlook Gilton's in Eunice for a true dance hall experience. The regular Saturday morning jam session at the Savoy Music Center in Eunice is not to be missed—it's the closest you will get to that back-porch experience, and it's a sheer delight.

In your search for Cajun music, please don't forget zydeco, which also thrives in this region. Zydeco bands share the bill at the weekly live show at Eunice's Liberty Theater, and they are the house specialty at such clubs as Slim's Y Ki-Ki in Opelousas and El Sido's in Lafayette.

PLANNING YOUR TRIP

A circular drive will allow you to take in one or two of the plantation homes en route to Baton Rouge (if you take the River Road instead of I-10) before turning west on I-10 to reach Lafayette and the land of the Cajuns. Go north of Lafayette on I-49 to reach Opelousas; Eunice is about 20 minutes west of there on Highway 190. A return to New Orleans on U.S. 90 is a trip through the history, legend, and romance of this region. There is more than a day's worth of interest in this area, so you'll probably want to plan at least an overnight stay. On I-10, the distance from New Orleans to Lafayette is 134 miles; Lafayette to New Orleans on U.S. 90 is 167 miles. Listed below are some of the things you should not miss, but you will find scores of other Cajun country attractions on your own. Also listed are some of the outstanding Cajun restaurants (rest assured, bad restaurants do not last long) and places to stay overnight.

Contact the **Lafayette Parish Convention and Visitors Commission,** P.O. Box 52066, Lafayette, LA 70505 (☎ **800/346-1958** in the U.S., 800/543-5340 in Canada, or 318/232-3737; fax 318/232-0161). It will send you tons of detailed information to make your trip even more fun. The office is open weekdays 8:30am to 5pm, weekends 9am to 5pm. (See "Lafayette," below, for driving directions.)

Hands down, the best time to visit Acadiana is during festival time (see chapter 2). You'll have a terrific time along with native Cajuns, who enjoy their festivals with real gusto. If you miss this, however, every weekend seems to bring a smaller festival somewhere in the area—and there is always plenty of music to go around at any time of the year.

During 1999, Louisiana will celebrate its tricentennial with **Francofete '99.** More than 400 festivals and attractions will take place during the year-long commemoration

Cajuns Today

Growing up immersed in Cajun culture was very difficult for me. My heroes weren't football jocks or rock and roll stars, but rather my old neighbors who spoke French, farmed for a living, and played the accordion or fiddle. When fiddler Dennis McGee farmed for my grandpa, it wasn't his children who were my playmates, even though they were my age—it was Dennis. I followed him in the fields while he plowed with his mule team. I wanted to hear his stories.

Needless to say, none of my classmates shared my love for what these old-timers had to offer. I guess that on my best days I could describe my peers' attitude toward me as indifference. I remember a beautiful girl who sat near my desk all during grade school. I would fantasize about being her boyfriend, which was of course totally impossible. She was very heavy into sports and cheerleader stuff and the mainstream, and I wasn't. Recently this same girl came into my store to purchase some Cajun CDs to send to her daughter, who was out of state and expressed a love for Cajun music. I recognized her immediately when she came in, even though 40 years had passed. We talked awhile, and when she was leaving she asked, "Where are you from?"

Even though it was difficult being Cajun in the '40s and '50s, I don't think I ever felt any anger toward the negativity expressed by the non-Cajuns or by those Cajuns who had given up their heritage. I think my feelings at this time were frustration and disappointment toward those people. To me, the choice they were making was really bad for themselves. They were turning away from this wonderful heritage in pursuit of the mainstream. They were turning their backs on a delicious bowl of gumbo in favor of a cold, tasteless American hot dog. I think my ulterior motive in 1966 in opening up a music store that specialized in Cajun music, rather than country or rock, was that I had an ax to grind. I wanted to destroy the stigma of being Cajun. I wanted to prove to the locals that heritage and success could coexist, that being Cajun and speaking French was okay. I wanted to tell outsiders how good our food was and about all these wonderful, warm, friendly, and sincere people who were called Cajuns.

The year was a turning point—Cajun music was first presented to the outside world. It happened at the Newport Folk Festival. A three-piece group of old Cajuns was up against names such as Bob Dylan and Joan Baez. The Cajuns played their first simple tune, "Grand Mamou," and before they were halfway through, an audience of 10,000 was giving them a standing ovation.

This experience did two things. First, it reinforced the passion that had kept the fire burning in the musicians' hearts. They came home with newspaper clippings and stories about the reception at Newport that surprised even the local non-Cajuns. Second, it called outsiders to come to Louisiana to search out all things Cajun. And this had a legitimizing effect on the people down here. The outsiders came down in droves, not for things they could see or hear back home, but for the things the Cajuns had not allowed the Americanization process to destroy. What was once considered a stigma was now considered an asset—to be Cajun.

of 300 years of French influence—and nowhere will they be more enthusiastic than in Acadiana. And because it's the Cajuns, food and music will play huge roles. To see

Although the Americanization process has not been completely successful down here, it has taken its toll, influencing many people who have become a caricature of Cajun. I find what is passed off as Cajun culture in major metropolitan areas rather yuppified. In the rural areas there are a lot of snake farms hawking the Hollywood version. But in isolated, rural areas there is also a very viable culture that exists without the slickness of the modern-day mainstream. These places can be found by getting off the interstate highways and searching out the small villages through the prairie.

It is important for the tourist to know that Cajun music is localized and never found in the forested bayou or salt marshes, but in the flat prairie region. Look at the old-timers, the first people to record—they were from Crowley. Dennis McGee and Amede Ardoin were from Eunice. There were never any recordings by musicians from bayous or marshes, because there were never any musicians living there. There were Cajuns living there, but the music came from the prairie. Where you find rice planted in Louisiana, you will find Cajun accordion music. The Germans brought the button accordion from their homeland, and some say they brought rice as well. My theory is this: I have an equation that prosperity equals permanence, and permanence equals roots. Having been raised on a rice farm, I know the topsoil in some places is 6 feet deep. The first settlers who came into this region could sustain themselves very easily in one spot and didn't have to move after the first spot was depleted. We also don't have big rivers. Big rivers bring in big industry and masses of people diluting the existing culture.

I don't think modern Cajuns are that different than they were in the past. Being a Cajun, a Mexican, a Native American, or any other ethnic group—it's not about one certain aspect of that culture. It's not about whether or not you play music, or eat spicy food, or speak a certain language. You can be a mute and still be an example of that culture. It isn't the person who wears costumes consisting of red bandannas, wide rubber boots, and big straw hats with a plucked rubber chicken hanging from his belt. That isn't Cajun either. It's about having roots or a foundation. It's about having roots that were cultivated in good times and bad times. And because of devotion and love, those roots sink deep, deep, deep and produce a strong, strong, strong tree, which gives protection and comfort to all those who come into its embrace. It's a matter of vision, being from a certain ethnic minority. It's about how you see yourself in your environment and how you relate and function in that environment. It's about having a deep sense of the past in order to know your direction. It's about having respect and love for the things that make you who you are and prevent you from being someone else. It's not about being crowd-pleasers. It's about being natural.

—*Marc Savoy*

Marc Savoy supports his Cajun heritage through the craftsmanship of accordions, as a musician with the highly acclaimed Savoy-Doucet and Savoy-Smith Cajun Bands, and by keeping Cajun community traditions alive.

what's going on where during your visit, contact **Francofete '99** (☎ **800/870-4959** or 318/262-1642).

TOURS

If you can't find time for an extended visit to Cajun country, a 1-day guided tour can provide an introduction to the area. **Tours by Isabelle** (☎ **504/391-3544**), specializes in small tours in a comfortable, air-conditioned minivan. You'll cross the Mississippi to visit Cajun country and then take a 2-hour narrated swamp tour. The Cajun Bayou Tour ($50) leaves New Orleans at 1pm and returns around 5:30pm. Isabelle's Grand Tour includes the Cajun Bayou Tour, a guided tour of Oak Alley Plantation, lunch, and a stop in front of Destrehan Plantation.

For other Cajun country tours, see "Organized Tours," in chapter 8.

A CAJUN WEEKEND

For music lovers, a trip out of New Orleans to the source of Cajun and zydeco music is practically a must. Though it's especially tempting to go during an organized event, such as Lafayette's Festival International or Breaux Bridge's Crawfish Festival, there is always plenty of music happening—so much that you can easily fill a couple of days.

FRIDAY   Drive out from New Orleans (be sure to avoid rush hour, when it can take a very long time to get through Baton Rouge). Stay in Opelousas or Washington; both are pretty towns with nice B&Bs (and some basic chain hotels). That evening, drive into Lafayette and hear whatever's going on at the Grant Street Hall, or stay in Opelousas and check out Slim's Y Ki-Ki or Richard's for the best in zydeco.

SATURDAY   Get up early and head to the Savoy Music Center in Eunice for the weekly jam session. Leave before noon and drive to Mamou, where Fred's Lounge should be jam-packed. The action at Fred's stops at 1pm, but the bar next door picks up the slack. Then head to Ville Platte and Floyd's Record Store to buy some of what you've heard. Have a bite at the Pig Stand or back in Eunice. That night, go to Eunice's Liberty Theater for the live radio broadcast featuring Cajun and zydeco groups—plus plenty of Cajun folktales and jokes. Consider dinner at D.I.'s, which also has live music. Finish up at Gilton's, outside of Eunice.

SUNDAY   Spend the morning checking out picturesque Washington, strolling the wonderful Magnolia Gardens, or combing the many antique shops, before heading back to New Orleans.

BREAUX BRIDGE

Just off I-10 on La. 31, this little town, founded in 1859, prides itself on being the "Crawfish Capital of the World." Its Crawfish Festival and Fair has drawn as many as 100,000 to the town of 4,500, and it's quite the event, with music, a unique parade, crawfish races, crawfish-eating contests, and lots more. It's held the first week in May. Some locals actually dislike the Crawfish Festival, and feel that their town is at its best the rest of the year. Consider taking them up on this challenge.

ACCOMMODATIONS

✪ **Maison Des Amis.** 1111 Washington, Breaux Bridge, LA 70517. ☎ **318/332-6966.** Fax 318/332-5273. 4 units; 2 without private bathrooms. $75–$95 double. Rates include breakfast. AE, DISC, MC, V.

Voted "Inn of the Month" in the January 1998 issue of *Travel & Leisure,* and the winner of a national preservation award, Maison des Amis offers small but gorgeously appointed rooms. They're in a one-story Creole Caribbean cabin (1860) perched almost on the bayou. The furnishings are a mix of antiques (with at least one delightful wood canopy bed from the 1700s), with modern but appropriate fabric hangings. One room has twin beds and the best view of the bayou. Some of the bathrooms are tiny

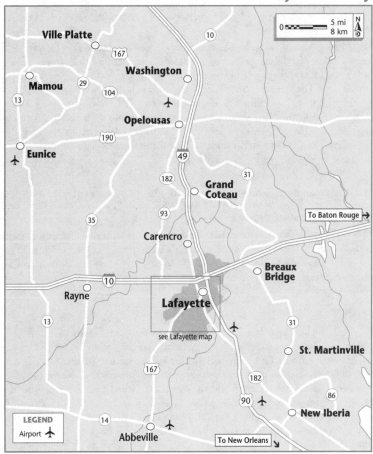

and require a walk down the glassed-in porch (robes are provided). The two front rooms have private bathrooms (they also have the biggest windows). There is one TV, with a VCR and a collection of old movies. The delightful owners are great fun and full of helpful local hints (they are among those who think the Crawfish Festival is the worst time to come to town). They live above their restaurant, Cafe Des Amis (see below), which is where Maison guests can have breakfast. It's a block away.

DINING

Cafe Des Amis. 140 E. Bridge St. ☎ **318/332-5273.** Main courses $7.95–$19.95. AE, DISC, MC, V. Tues–Wed 8am–3pm, Thurs–Fri 8am–10pm, Sat 7:30am–10pm, Sun 7:30am–3pm. Sat mornings feature "Zydeco Breakfast" 8:30–11:30am. CAJUN.

This is an airy, traditional Louisiana space turned modern cafe, with the scribbled thoughts of visitors on the walls, which also feature local folk art. There's also an interesting display of local antiquities. The civic-minded owners (who also own the inn upstairs) are often found treating honors students or local artists at the cafe. Much of what is on the menu is healthy; a grilled shrimp salad was spicy, fresh, and generous with the shrimp, while the étouffée was what that dish should be.

Crawfish Town U.S.A. 2815 Grand Point Hwy. ☎ **318/667-6148.** Reservations recommended. Main courses $4.95–$18.95. AE, DISC, MC, V. Daily 11am–closing. From Lafayette,

take I-10 to Henderson (Exit 115). Go north half a mile and follow the signs; you can't miss it.
SEAFOOD/CAJUN.

See if you can guess what the house specialty is here. The food is as pleasant as the
heavily decorated dining room, and prepared to your taste: mild, strong, or extra-
hot. The staff says they serve the biggest crawfish in the world—and who is to challenge them? The steaming platters of boiled crawfish that come out of the kitchen
by the hundreds look almost like small lobsters. The crawfish étouffée and the
gumbo are delicious. You shouldn't miss the bread pudding here. And if you just
can't decide what you want, go for the Seafood Festival Platter—a cup of gumbo,
jambalaya, crawfish étouffée, grilled catfish, shrimp, seafood pie, frogs' legs, crawfish, and a crawfish patty—all served with grilled potatoes, vegetables, and garlic
bread.

Mulate's Cajun Restaurant. 325 Mills Ave. ☎ **888/422-2586** or 318/332-4648. Reservations recommended. Main courses $5.95–$16.95. AE, MC, V. Mon–Thurs 11am–10pm,
Fri–Sun 11am–10:30pm. CAJUN.

This place has such a strong reputation that the owners were able to open a branch in
New Orleans. Come to this one. It's gotten a bit touristy, but the food is solid (and
the prices reasonable), and so is the music—Mulate's is a good introduction to Cajun
music and food. Stuffed crab is a specialty. There's live Cajun music nightly and at
noon on weekends.

EUNICE

Founded in 1894 by C. C. Duson, who named the town for his wife, Eunice is a
prairie town, not as picturesque as, say, Opelousas or Washington. However, some of
the most significant Cajun cultural happenings come out of this friendly town,
including the Saturday morning jam sessions at the Savoy Music Center, the Liberty
Theater's live radio broadcasts, and the Acadian Cultural Center, all of which will
greatly enrich your understanding of Cajun traditions and modern life. That is, if you
aren't having too much fun to notice you've also been getting an education.

On Saturday nights, **Gilton's Club,** 175 Janet Rd. (at Highway 90 East, about 3
miles east of Eunice; ☎ **318/457-1241**), is a genuine Cajun dance hall. A long, cavernous room with misspelled signs and Christmas lights passing for decor, this is
where to find the real Cajun dance tradition. Admission is as little as $3, the locals are
friendly, food is served, and the dance floor is large. By all means, use it.

ATTRACTIONS & DISTRACTIONS

✪ **Acadian Cultural Center.** 250 West Park. ☎ **318/262-6862.** Free admission; donations accepted. Mon–Sat 8am–5pm.

An almost-perfect example of a small museum, the Acadian Cultural Center is devoted
to Cajun life and culture. Exhibits explain everything from the history of the Cajuns
to how they worked, played, and got married. The graphics are lively and very readable, well combined with the objects on display (most acquired from local families
who have owned them for generations). It's all quite informative and enjoyable. In
other parts of the building, there might be quilting or other crafts demonstrations
going on. The center has a collection of videos about Cajun life and will show any and
all in the small theater (just ask). Anything by Les Blanc is a good choice, but you
might also check out "Anything I Can Catch," a documentary about the nearly lost
art of hand-fishing (you need to see someone catch a giant catfish with his bare hands).
It's well worth coming by if you are in Cajun country, even if you don't necessarily
think you want to go to a museum.

✪ Liberty Theater. 2nd and Park. ☎ **318/457-6577.** Admission $3 and up.

This classic 1927 theater has been lovingly restored and turned into a showcase for Cajun music. There's live music most nights, but Saturday attracts the big crowds, for the "Rendezvous des Cajuns" radio show. From 6 to 8pm, Cajun historian and folklorist Barry Ancelet hosts a live program, simulcast on local radio, that features Cajun and zydeco bands. It includes anything from up-and-comers to some of the biggest names, folktales, and jokes. Oh, and it's all in French. Locals and tourists alike pack the seats and aisles, with dancing on the sloped floor by the stage. Don't understand what's being said? As Barry points out, turn to your neighbors—they will be happy to translate. This is the right way (actually, *the* way) to begin your Saturday night of music in Cajun country.

✪ Savoy Music Center. Hwy. 190 East (3 miles east of Eunice). ☎ **318/457-9563.** Tues–Sat 9am–noon, Tues–Fri 1:30–5pm.

On weekdays this is a working music store, with instruments, accessories, and a small but essential selection of Cajun and zydeco CDs and tapes. In the back is the workshop where musician Marc Savoy lovingly crafts his Acadian accordions—not just fine musical instruments, but works of art—amid cabinets bearing his observations and aphorisms. On most Saturday mornings, though, this nondescript kelly green building on the outskirts of Eunice is the spiritual center of Cajun music. Keeping alive a tradition that dates from way before electricity, Marc and his wife, Ann, host a jam session where you can hear some of the region's finest music and watch the tunes being passed down from generation to generation. Here the older musicians are given their due respect, with septuagenarians and octogenarians such as Aldus Roger often leading the sessions while players as young as preteens glean all they can—if they can keep up. Meanwhile, nonmusical guests munch on hunks of boudin sausage and sip beer while listening or socializing. All comers are welcome; if they're properly respectful, they can get one of the Savoy family or shop associate Tina Pillone to show them around. But don't come empty-handed—a pound of boudin or a six-pack of something is appropriate. And if you play guitar, fiddle, accordion, or triangle, bring one along and join in. Don't try to show off. Simply follow along with the locals, or you're sure to get a cold shoulder.

ACCOMMODATIONS

If the following are booked, you might also try the **Best Western,** 1531 W. Laurel Ave., in Eunice (☎ **318/457-2800**).

Poiter's Prairie Cajun Inn. 110 W. Park, Eunice, LA 70535. ☎ **318/457-0440.** 9 units. A/C TV TEL. $60 double. AE, DC, DISC, MC, Optima, V.

Its bright pink exterior indicates that this tiny B&B is a bit heavy on the cute, but the location can't be beat—just a half-block from the Liberty Theater and the Acadian Cultural Center. A little kitsch can be tolerated for the sake of convenience. The tiny rooms are technically suites—itty-bitty sitting areas with separate, even smaller bedrooms and full kitchens, all decorated (again, think cutesy) by local Cajun craftsmen. A variety of snacks and breakfast foods (cereal, pastries, fruit, yogurt) are provided nightly. There is also a conference room, and each suite has a computer modem hookup. For a minimal fee, the inn provides transportation to and from the Lafayette airport. Baby-sitting is available.

✪ Seale Guesthouse. 125 Seale Lane (off Hwy. 13), Eunice, LA 70535. ☎ **318/457-3753.** 6 units, 4 with private bathroom (1 room's bathroom is across the hall). $75 double. Rates include continental breakfast weekdays, full breakfast weekends. MC, V.

Owner Mark Seale took an abandoned farmhouse and turned it into this wonderful B&B, perfect for a relaxing getaway. Eunice is only a 5-minute drive away, but the guest house and grounds are so inviting, sometimes it's hard to leave. Rooms are decorated with antiques, and with their high ceilings, wood trim, and cozy furniture, each is more attractive and charming than the last. The large kitchen is fully stocked for guests who wish to cook.

Wide verandas allow you to sit and gaze at the pretty landscaping, while animals galore (dogs, cats, always a fresh batch of kittens, various fowl, and who knows what else) gambol nearby or come over for attention. This is a hands-off guest house; Mark is happy to give you all kinds of good advice about local doings, but the sheets aren't changed every day, and there's no receptionist. It's perfect if you want privacy, not so good if you like hotels that pick up after you. Additional buildings are being renovated, and more rooms may be available when you visit.

DINING

D.I.'s Cajun Restaurant. Hwy. 97, Basile. ☎ **318/432-5141.** Main courses $6.75–$12.45. AE, MC, V. Lunch Mon–Fri 10:30am–1:30pm, Tues–Sat 5–11pm. Hwy. 190 to Hwy. 97, then 8 miles south. CAJUN.

Even when you follow the directions to D.I.'s Cajun Restaurant, you will think you are about to drive off the face off the earth, particularly if you drive in the dark. You'll know you're there—and that you are nowhere near alone—when you see all the cars in the gravel parking lot. Located on a back highway, D.I.'s is more or less what Mulate's was before the tourists found it: a homey family restaurant full of locals dancing to live music (except Thursday) and stuffing themselves with crawfish and catfish. Some items are not fried, but most are—or they're stuffed or topped with a sauce—and it's all good. Seasonally, you'll find some of the best boiled crawfish outside of a private home here.

Matilda's. Hwy. 190 and St. Mary. ☎ **318/546-0329.** $3.50–$10.80. MC, V. Tues–Thurs 11am–7pm, Fri 11am–10pm, Sat 11:30am–8pm, Sun 11am–3pm. BARBECUE.

For barbecue with all the fixings, this is the one sit-down place in town. It's a wood shack that some might call "quaint" but others know is authentic. The many side dishes vary in quality, but the barbecue, while not all that spicy, is agreeable.

Ruby's Cafe. 221 W. Walnut Ave. ☎ **318/457-2583.** All items under $5. Mon–Sat 5am–5pm. No credit cards. CAJUN/SOUL FOOD.

Located in the center of Eunice, Ruby's is where the real people hang out. Nothing fancy, and we mean nothing—but in the best of all ways. Got a hankering for roast chicken or, better still, ponce (stuffed cow stomach—it's better than it sounds)? Come here. Want to see local Eunicians catch up on the news? Come here for breakfast.

SHOPPING

Lejeune's Sausage Kitchen. Old Crowley Rd. 108 Tasso Circle. ☎ **318/457-8491.** Mon–Sat 7am–5:30pm.

Look for the signs or just ask, but do find your way to the Sausage Kitchen for a delicious, if perishable, souvenir. In addition to tasso (Cajun ham) and ponce (cow stomach), Lejeune's sells a variety of mouth-watering sausages, including a memorable garlic pork. It all freezes well, but alas, they don't ship.

Music Machine. 235 W. Walnut Ave. ☎ **318/457-4846.** Daily 9am to at least 7pm.

Owner Todd Ortego claims this is the "only record store, snow cone, and pool place in the area" and he gets no dispute from us. The store features a pretty good selection

Boudin Joints

Boudin is Cajun sausage, made of pork usually mixed with rice and stuffed inside a chewy casing. If it's done right, it's spicy and sublime. You can get it at just about any grocery store or gas station, and we've spent many a day driving through Cajun country taste-testing. Of course, disputes rage about who makes the best. Try for yourself—it's a cheap (just over $2 a pound), filling snack. It's easy to find, but we recommend the following places.

✪ **Superette Slaughterhouse,** Bobcat Drive and Maple Avenue, in Eunice (☎ **318/546-6041**), is open Monday to Friday from 6am to 5pm, Saturday from 6am to noon. The name is a little unnerving to those of us from urban areas, but the locals swear this is the best boudin around, and they are probably right.

Johnson's Grocery, 700 E. Maple Ave., Eunice (☎ **318/457-9314**), has darn good boudin as well, and they ship! (Overnight, at that, so if you get a craving, you can have it filled in a matter of hours.) Hours are Monday to Friday 6am to 6pm, Saturday 6am to 5pm.

Poche's, 3015-A Main Hwy., Breaux Bridge (☎ **318/332-2108**), has not only pork, but also crawfish boudin, plus tasso and other local tidbits—and they ship, too. Open Monday to Saturday 5am to 9pm, Sundays 5am to 6pm.

Ray's Grocery, Hirsh & Vine (off Hwy. 190, across from Town Center), Opelousas (☎ **318/942-9150**), has the advantage of a drive-thru window. Place your order with little interruption in your road trip. Hours are Monday to Friday from 8am to 6pm, Saturday 8am to 5pm, Sunday 8am to 2pm.

of local music (on CD and cassette), and the employees should be able to help you figure out what to buy if you need guidance. Outside of Floyd's in Ville Platte, this is probably your best music resource. The patrons are junior high and high school kids, and the snow cones are available only during spring and summer months. Todd is also a local DJ (you can find him on the radio playing zydeco and South Louisiana party music), and he's in the store during the week. If you are coming for a weekend of music, drop by and ask him where to go—by Thursday, he usually knows what's going on.

GRAND COTEAU

Grand Coteau seems like just a wide spot in the road, but it's worth exploring (it won't take you long). First see the beautiful, 175-year-old **Academy of the Sacred Heart,** 1821 Academy Rd. (☎ **318/662-5494;** tours by appointment only) and its gardens. Then there are two places to eat (one where you can also shop) that are surprising in this land of Cajun cooking.

DINING

✪ **Catahoula.** 234 Martin Luther King Ave. (Hwy. 93). ☎ **888/547-BARK** or 318/662-2275. Reservations recommended. Main courses $12.95–$19.95; specials somewhat higher. AE, DISC, MC, V. Tues–Sun 11am–2pm, Sun brunch 11am–2pm, Tues–Thurs 5–9pm, Fri 11am–10pm, Sat 5–10pm. CLASSIC & NOUVELLE LOUISIANA CUISINE.

Named for the Louisiana state dog (a hound with startling blue eyes), Catahoula is in a 1920s general store. It's a pretty, simple place with subdued lighting that at night virtually requires candles. It serves surprisingly modern fare; this is the place to get away from local specialties, assuming you need a break from fried food and crawfish. The menu features the "best of the old and best of the new," and there is almost always something experimental. Try the shrimp Caribe (marinated in papaya sauce and grilled, served over spicy black beans and rice) or the shrimp St. Charles, a traditional New Orleans dish of shrimp sautéed in white wine with sun-dried tomatoes, served over linguine. Owner John Slaughter is also a photographer, and his photos line the walls (so you can see what a Catahoula looks like).

Kitchen Shop. Corner of Cherry and King. ☎ **318/662-3500.** Tues–Sat 10am–5pm, Sun noon–4pm.

The name is misleading. This is actually a well-stocked gift store that features kitchen, cooking, and food items, and has a much larger room stuffed with local books, upscale knickknacks, jewelry (including Grandmother's Buttons, a line made from antique buttons), and vintage-looking clothes. There is also a tiny cafe with a sweet little patio. The owner is a New York–trained pastry chef who serves quiches, delicious pastries (the specialty is Gateau Nana), and terrific café au lait. It's all packed into an 1840 building that used to be a stagecoach stop.

LAFAYETTE

If you haven't written in advance, make your first stop the **Lafayette Parish Convention and Visitors Commission Center,** 1400 NW Evangeline Thruway (☎ **800/ 346-1958** in the U.S., 800/543-5340 in Canada, or 318/232-3808). The helpful staff will tell you everything you could possibly want to know about the region and send you out loaded with informative materials. Turn off I-10 at Exit 103A, go south for about a mile, and you'll find the office in the center of the median. It's open weekdays 8:30am to 5pm, weekends 9am to 5pm. Near the intersection of Willow Street and the Thruway, the attractive offices are in Cajun-style homes set on landscaped grounds that hold a pond and benches. It is a restful spot to sit and plan your Cajun country excursion.

We also highly recommend the **Festival International de Louisiane,** a 6-day music and art festival that many find a good alternative to the increasingly crowded Jazz Fest. While the scope of the bands, naturally, is nothing like the big deal in New Orleans, there's an interesting lineup each year, with an emphasis on music from other French-speaking lands. The Festival takes place in the center of town, with streets blocked off to allow easy movement from one stage to another. In contrast to Jazz Fest, it's low-key and a manageable size. Best of all, it's free! Festival International is held at the end of April; for dates, call or write the Festival International de Louisiane, 735 Jefferson St., Lafayette, LA 70501 (☎ **318/232-8086;** www.fil.net-connect.net).

Music can be found year-round at the **Grant Street Dance Hall,** 113 W. Grant St. (☎ **318/237-8513**). The warehouse-type building features the best in local music, from Cajun to brass bands, and is where out-of-towners are most likely to play. The zydeco hot spot is **El Sido's,** 1523 N. Antoine St. (☎ **318/237-1959**), where combos like Nathan & the Zydeco Cha-Cha's hold sway. Both joints jump, and any night at either is likely to be a good one.

SEEING THE SIGHTS
You shouldn't leave the area without exploring its bayous and swamps. Gliding through misty bayous dotted with gnarled cypress trees that drip Spanish moss, seeing native water creatures and birds in their natural habitat, and learning how Cajuns harvest their beloved crawfish is an experience not to be missed.

To arrange a voyage, contact Terry Angelle at **Angelle's Atchafalaya Basin Swamp Tours,** Whiskey River Landing, P.O. Box 111, Cecilla, LA 70521 (☎ **318/ 228-8567**). His tour gives you nearly 2 hours in the third-largest swamp in the United

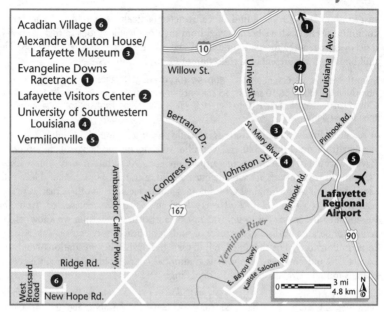

Acadian Village ⑥
Alexandre Mouton House/
    Lafayette Museum ③
Evangeline Downs
    Racetrack ①
Lafayette Visitors Center ②
University of Southwestern
    Louisiana ④
Vermilionville ⑤

States, with Cajun guides who have spent their lives thereabouts and who travel the mysterious waterways as easily as you and I walk city streets. There's a glass-enclosed boat for large groups and a small, open boat for up to 14. The fares are $12 for adults, $10 for seniors, $6 for children under 12. Departure times are 10am, 1pm, and 3pm (and 5pm during daylight saving time). Angelle's features Cajun music on Sunday beginning at around 4pm. To reach Whiskey River Landing from I-10, take Exit 115 to Henderson, go through Henderson to the levee, and turn right. The landing is the fourth exit on the left. For other swamp tours, see "Organized Tours" in chapter 8.

If you're in Cajun country between the first week in April and Labor Day and happen to be a devotee of the sport of kings, you can enjoy an evening of horse racing at **Evangeline Downs** (☎ 318/896-RACE), 3 miles north of town on U.S. 167. Post time and racing days change periodically, so be sure to check. Don't bring the kids, though—no minors are allowed.

There's a lovely natural swamp environment in the very heart of Lafayette, on the grounds of the University of Southwestern Louisiana. Although it's small, it gives the effect of being in the wild, and during the warm months you can see alligators. Several varieties of water birds, as well as turtles, are almost always on hand, and during April the swamp is abloom with Louisiana irises. If you want to know more about the lake and how it is used as a teaching tool, contact the **Public Relations and News Service,** University of Southwestern Louisiana, Lafayette, LA 70504 (☎ 318/482-6397). If you just want to get closer to the sort of swampland seen most often from highways, you'll like Cypress Lake, next to the Student Union on the USL campus, between St. Mary Boulevard and University Avenue, Hebrard Boulevard and McKinley Street.

Acadian Village. 200 Greenleaf Dr. ☎ **800/962-9133** or 318/981-2364. Admission $6 adults, $5 seniors, $2.50 children 6–14, free for children under 6. Daily 10am–5pm. Closed major holidays. Take I-10 to Exit 97. Go south on La. 93 to Ridge Rd., turn right, then turn left on West Broussard.

Just south of La. 342, you'll find a reconstructed (actually, reassembled) Cajun bayou community. Houses have been moved from their original locations to this site beside a sleepy bayou, and a footpath on its banks takes you past the historic structures. The buildings hold a representative collection of Cajun furnishings.

Vermilionville. 1600 Surrey St. ☎ **800/99-BAYOU** or 318/233-4077. Fax 318/233-1694. Admission $8 adults, $6.50 seniors, $5 students, free for children under 6. Daily 10am–5pm. Closed Jan 1, Dec 25. Take I-10 to Exit 103A. Take Evangeline Thruway south to Surrey St., then follow signs.

A recent addition to the Lafayette scene is this reconstruction of a Cajun-Creole settlement from the 1765–1890 era. Vermilionville sits on the banks of the brooding Bayou Vermilion, adjacent to the airport on U.S. 90. While it may sound like a "Cajunland" theme park, it's actually quite a valid operation. Hundreds of skilled artisans labored to restore original Cajun homes and to reconstruct others that were typical of such a village. Homes of every level in society are represented, from the humblest to the most well-to-do. (It must be authentic; one Cajun we know refuses to go, not because he dislikes the place or finds it offensive, but because "I already *live* in Vermilionville!") The costumed staff in each gives a vivid demonstration of daily life back then, and craftspeople ply their traditional crafts. In the performance center, there is music, plays, dancing, and storytelling.

Alexandre Mouton House/Lafayette Museum. 1122 Lafayette St. ☎ **318/234-2208.** Admission $3 adults, $2 seniors, $1 students. Tues–Sat 9am–5pm, Sun 3–5pm. Closed holidays.

Louisiana's first Democratic governor, Alexandre Mouton, once lived in this antebellum town house with square columns and two galleries. Today, it houses the Lafayette Museum. The main house was built in the early 1800s, and the cupola, attic, and second floor were added in 1849. Inside, in addition to the antiques, paintings, and historic documents, there's a colorful collection of Mardi Gras costumes that were worn by Lafayette's krewe kings and queens.

Chretien Point Plantation. 665 Chretien Point Rd., Sunset. ☎ **800/880-7050** or 318/233-7050. Admission $6.50 adults, $6 seniors, $3 children 4–12, free for children under 4. Daily 10am–5pm. Last tour 4pm. Closed holidays. Take I-10 west to Exit 97, then go north about 8 miles. A little over 2 miles north of Cankton, turn left onto Parish Rd. 356 (toward Bristol), then right on Chretien Point Rd.; plantation is about a mile farther, on the left.

One of Cajun country's most intriguing plantation mansions is a short drive (about 15 miles) north of Lafayette. Allow yourself at least an hour to explore the columned home, built in 1831 on a 1776 Spanish land grant. The house is fascinating, and even more so are the tales of past owners. Its history includes links to privateer Jean Lafitte, a flamboyant gambler, his equally flamboyant widow, a ghost or two, a buried treasure (never recovered), and a Civil War battle fought right out front. And if you remember the scene in *Gone With the Wind* when Scarlett O'Hara shoots a marauding Union soldier on the stairs at Tara, you'll recognize the staircase—it was copied for the movie.

The plantation also operates a **bed-and-breakfast.** The rooms are in the manor house; you get a full breakfast and a tour of the mansion, plus use of the pool and tennis courts. Rooms are $95 to $200 per night.

ACCOMMODATIONS

Bois des Chenes Inn. 338 N. Sterling (at Mudd Ave.), Lafayette, LA 70501. ☎ **318/ 233-7816.** Fax 318/233-7816. www.members.aol.com/boisdchene/bois.htm. 5 units. A/C TV. $95–$135 double. Rates include breakfast. Extra person $30. AE, MC, V.

Three suites at the Bois des Chenes Inn are in the carriage house, and two suites, one with an open fireplace, are in the 1820s Acadian-style plantation home known as the

Charles Mouton House. Now listed on the National Register of Historical Houses, Bois des Chenes was once the center of a 3,000-acre cattle and sugar plantation. Its restoration has been a labor of love, reflected in the careful selection of antique furnishings, most of Louisiana French design. All guest rooms are tastefully furnished with antiques of different periods, and each has a small refrigerator and down pillows. The rates include a Louisiana-style breakfast, a bottle of wine, and a tour of the house. The owner, a retired geologist, conducts nature and birding trips into the Atchafalaya Swamp as well as guided fishing and hunting trips. Book as far in advance as possible.

Holiday Inn Central-Holidome. 2032 NE Evangeline Thruway, Lafayette, LA 70509. ☎ **800/942-4868** or 318/233-6815. 243 units. A/C TV TEL. $69–$79 double. AE, CB, DC, DISC, JCB, MC, V.

This Holiday Inn has superior guest rooms, some of which are equipped for travelers with disabilities. There is a lounge, a coffee shop, a good restaurant, an indoor pool, a whirlpool, a sauna, a game room, lighted tennis courts, a jogging track, a playground, a picnic area, and a gift shop.

Hotel Acadiana. 1801 W. Pinhook Rd., Lafayette, LA 70508. ☎ **800/874-4664** in Louisiana, 800/826-8386 in the U.S. and Canada, or 318/233-8120. 296 units. A/C TV TEL. $79–$210 double. AE, DC, DISC, MC, V. From New Orleans, take I-10 west to Exit 103A. Follow Evangeline Thruway to Pinhook Rd., turn right, and follow Pinhook across bridge; hotel is on left.

The Hotel Acadiana is a great value. The rates are low, but you have all the modern conveniences you'd expect to find in a large chain hotel: two double beds or a king in each room, a minirefrigerator, cable TV, and a warm, friendly staff. You'll also be in a central location for sightseeing. If you really want to be in the lap of luxury, ask for a room on the Executive Floor, where you'll have access to a private lounge. Scandals is the hotel's dance club. Room service, laundry service, concierge service, and a complimentary airport shuttle are provided. Facilities include an outdoor pool and a health club.

Lafayette Hilton & Towers. 1521 Pinhook Rd., Lafayette, LA 70508. ☎ **800/33-CAJUN** or 318/235-6111. www.hilton.com. 327 units. A/C TV TEL. $105–$115 single or double; $185–$300 suite. Weekend, senior, student, faculty, military discounts available. AE, CB, DC, MC, V, DISC.

The centrally located Lafayette Hilton and Towers has nicely appointed guest rooms and suites. Some have private patios. There is a good restaurant overlooking the bayou, a lounge with live music and dancing Monday through Saturday, and a heated pool.

Dining In & Around Lafayette

Café Vermilionville. 1304 Pinhook W. Rd. ☎ **318/237-0100.** Reservations recommended. Main courses $15–$24. AE, DC, DISC, MC, V. Mon–Fri 11am–2pm; Mon–Sat 5:30–10pm. Closed holidays. INTERNATIONAL/CAJUN.

In a beautifully restored historic Acadian building of cypress and handmade brick that dates from 1799, Café Vermilionville has a glassed-in dining room overlooking the courtyard and herb garden. The superb menu represents the best of Louisiana French and Cajun cuisine, with lots of fresh seafood, including specialties like salmon au poivre and Louisiana crawfish madness (crawfish tails prepared in the chef's favorite ways—au gratin, étoufée, crawfish and mushroom sauté on couton, crawfish beignet, and fried).

Charley G's. 3809 Ambassador Caffrey Pkwy. ☎ **318/981-0108.** Reservations recommended. Main courses $13–$23. AE, DC, MC, V. Daily 11am–2pm; Mon–Thurs 5:30–10pm, Fri–Sat 5:30–11pm. LOUISIANA CUISINE.

Foodies will be happier here than at some of Lafayette's other restaurants, because not too much on the menu is fried or blackened. That also means more and fresher veggies, which is a huge relief. The bad news is that there is little crawfish. The items run closer to nouvelle, which sometimes means fussy flavors pile up on each other. Seafood is a specialty. The house crab cakes are unusual because the sauce is baked inside the lighter-than average-cake. The upscale muffaletta has shaved prosciutto, basil-infused olive oil, and a tomato-cheese-crusted loaf. Zydeco shrimp is marinated in cane syrup, red pepper, garlic, and Southern Comfort, producing an almost-bar-becue sauce. Don't miss the Angel Cream dessert, condensed milk cooked down till it caramelizes, then topped with whipped cream. Service is very attentive.

✪ **Prejean's.** 3480 I 49 North. ☎ **318/896-3247.** Reservations strongly recommended. Children's menu $3.50–$8.95; main courses $12–$24. AE, CB, DC, DISC, MC, V. Sun–Thurs 11am–10pm, Fri–Sat 11am–11pm. Take I-10 to Exit 103B, then I-49 north to U.S. 167 North. Follow the signs—it's next to the Evangeline Downs Racetrack. CAJUN.

From the outside, Prejean's hasn't changed at all over the years, and at first glance, it looks pretty much the way it always has. It's an unpretentious family restaurant with live Cajun music every night. But inside, chef James Graham has turned Prejean's from a fried seafood emporium to one of Acadiana's finest restaurants, showcasing the best ingredients and styles Cajun cuisine has to offer.

Pace yourself or dance if there's room—but do whatever's necessary to sample the full range of excellent Cajun fare. Seafood is the specialty, with large menu sections devoted to fish, shrimp and oysters, crawfish, and crab dishes, each offered at least a half-dozen ways, and a few alligator dishes. One best-seller is eggplant pirogue—half an eggplant, hollowed out, breaded, fried, and filled with shrimp, crawfish, and crab; another is cat-fish Catahoula, a fresh filet stuffed with shrimp, crawfish and crab. The extensive game menu offers exotic tastes like rack of elk and buffalo tenderloin. In the unlikely event you have room for dessert, the chocolate Grand Marnier torte is highly recommended.

Prudhomme's Cajun Cafe. 4674 NE Evangeline Thruway, near Carencro. ☎ **318/896-7964.** Reservations recommended. Main courses $6.95–$16.95. AE, DISC, MC, V. Tues–Sat 11am–10pm. Take I-10 to Exit 103B and go north on I-49 to Exit 7 (3 miles past race-track). Restaurant is on right side of Frontage Rd. CAJUN.

Set in an Acadian country home built of cypress, this restaurant is run by Enola Prud-homme, who is easily the equal of her famous brother, Paul, in the kitchen. Assisted by her son and two sons-in-law, she serves dishes from a menu that changes daily. Blackened tuna and eggplant pirogue (hollowed out and filled with seafood in a luscious cream sauce) are just two of the specialties. There's ramp access for those who need it.

Randol's Restaurant and Cajun Dance Hall. 2320 Kaliste Saloom Rd. ☎ **800/962-2586** or 318/981-7080. Reservations for 20 or more only. Main courses $7.95–$15.95. MC, V. Mon–Fri 11am–2pm and 5–10pm, Sat–Sun 5–11pm. Closed major holidays. From New Orleans, take I-10 west to Exit 103A. Follow Evangeline Thruway to Pinhook Rd., turn right, and follow Pinhook to Kaliste Saloom Rd. (on the right). Randol's will be on your right. CAJUN.

In addition to better-than-average Cajun food, Randol's offers a good-sized, popular dance floor where dancers are likely to be locals enjoying their own fais-dodo. In fact, they eagerly volunteer when owner Frank Randol needs dancers for his traveling Cajun food and dance show. Back home, the star of the menu is seafood, all fresh from bayou or Gulf waters, and served fried, steamed, blackened, or grilled. (Given how often fried is the only option at most Cajun restaurants, the other alternatives alone make Randol's an attractive stop.) A house specialty is the seafood platter, which includes a cup of seafood gumbo, fried shrimp, fried oysters, fried catfish, stuffed crab, crawfish étouffée, warm French bread, and coleslaw.

MAMOU

There is one reason to come to Mamou, and that's ✪ **Fred's Lounge,** 420 6th St. (☎ **318/468-5411**)—and it's a darn good reason. At the other end of the Cajun music scale from the Savoy Music Center, this small-town bar offers just as essential an Acadiana Saturday morning experience. Fred's has for 50 years been the site of Saturday daytime dances, for many years with Donald Thibodeaux & Cajun Fever playing from a "bandstand" that's really no more than a roped-off area in the middle of the floor. Couples waltz and two-step in the remaining space, and the whole thing airs from 8am to noon on radio station KVPI (1050 AM). While Savoy honors the folksy "house music" tradition, this is pure dance-hall stuff, a place for hardworking people to get lubricated, blow off steam, and let loose. The music leans toward the country-western side of Cajun, with the band featuring steel guitar and drums along with accordion and fiddle. Everyone's welcome, as long as you dive right in—though it might be a good idea to practice dancing with a drink in one hand before you give it a try here. When the music ends, the party often shifts to the bar next door.

OPELOUSAS

Opelousas, the third-oldest city in Louisiana, is the seat of St. Landry Parish, so the courthouse is there, but for the average tourist, there isn't that much to see. It's such a pretty town, though—particularly the main drag, Landry Street—that passers-through often find themselves pulling over to have a look around. Opelousas has a number of B&Bs and a couple of chain hotels, so accommodations are easy to come by.

The **Tourist Center,** 941 E. Vine St. (☎ **318/948-6263**), is open daily 8am to 4pm. Jim Bowie lived in the building for a (really) short time as a child, and there is a small collection of ephemera devoted to him. Don't go out of your way for that, but do drop in for other tourist and lodging advice. You can also call the **St. Landry Tourist Commission** (☎ **877/948-8004**) for more info. During the spring and fall, on Friday and Saturday nights, there's a live concert in the street in front of the courthouse (just off Landry Street, across from the Palace Cafe). Park your car and go have a two-step. And in passing, admire the 300-year-old oak across the street from City Hall; its branches have gotten so heavy that in spots they not only touch the ground, but are buried beneath the sod.

If you feel lost without proper tourist and museum going experiences, you may drop by the **Opelousas Museum and Interpetive Center,** 329 No. Main St., (☎ **318/948-2589**) Tuesday to Saturday 9am to 5pm, or the surprisingly well-appointed **Opelousas Museum of Art,** 100 No. Union St., (☎ **318/942-4991**) Tuesday to Sunday 1 to 5pm. Cajun cooking obsessives shouldn't miss making a pilgrimage to **Tony Chachere's Creole Foods,** 533 No. Lombard St., (☎ **318/551-9066**), where all the best Cajun spices are made and you can learn how (on the hour, Monday to Friday).

In the fall, Opelousas features its annual, long-lived and delightfully named **Yambilee Festival,** a salute to everyone's favorite Thanksgiving side dish. As for music, two of the best clubs in Cajun country are here. **Richard's** (4 miles west of Opelousas on Hwy. 190; no phone) is just a little shack, but it's fun. The ultimate spot for zydeco, **Slim's Y Ki-Ki** (☎ **318/942-9980**), is on Highway 81 in Opelousas. On the weekends, Slim's fills up to hot and sweaty capacity with some darn fine music. It's a must on any Cajun country weekend music tour.

ACCOMMODATIONS

Opelousas also has a **Best Western,** 1635 I-49 Service Rd. S. (☎ **318/942-5540**), and a **Quality Inn,** 4501 I-49 S. (☎ **318/948-9500**), should the following be booked.

✪ **The Estorge House.** 427 N. Market St., Opelousas, LA 70570. ☎ **318/942-8151.** www.whatbayou.com/estorage.html. 2 units. A/C TV TEL. $125 double. Rates include breakfast. MC, V.

The phrase "gracious Southern living" comes to mind as you look around the Estorge House. A Federal-style two-story home with big verandas and upstairs galleries, it dates from 1820 and is still full of interesting family heirlooms that owners Judith (an Estorge herself) and Sherl (who will give you an anecdote-packed tour) don't mind you actually using, instead of just having them admired as museum pieces. The tastefully decorated, unfussy rooms feature antiques and plump beds with fancy linens, while fresh flowers turn up when the sheets are turned down. Sherl is a talented chef whose big breakfasts (pecan-crusted french toast, egg-and-sausage casseroles, homemade biscuits) are as prettily presented as they are filling. Hopefully, you'll have your appetite back in time for her bedtime snack of homemade cookies and milk. The nearly 2-acre yard and garden are heavy with local trees, and contain a hot tub and bird bath statuary.

Maison de Saizan. 412 S. Court St., Opelousas, LA 70570. ☎ **318/948-9898.** 2 units. A/C TV TEL. $65–$75 double. Rates include breakfast. No credit cards.

This pretty white clapboard 1889 Victorian house had the first indoor bathroom plumbing in town. It has a large two-bedroom suite on the second floor, and a guest room on the ground floor. Upstairs also has a small library nook. Breakfast might feature French toast and egg dishes. The screened porch overlooks the large yard, where Dixie the dog will want to get to know you and play ball. The dark-wood trimmed downstairs was lovingly restored from scratch—and check out that spider web glass window. The owner lives on-site.

DINING

Back in Time. 145 W. Landry St. ☎ **318/942-2413.** All items under $8. MC V. Mon–Fri 10am–5pm, Sat 11am–5pm (lunch 11am–2:30pm, then desserts). SANDWICHES/SALADS.

This cafe and gift store is run by Wanda Juneau, who is only the second owner of the building since 1921. The first, shoe repairman Mr. Grecco, may still be haunting the place; ask Wanda to tell you her ghost stories. The gift store sells yummy homemade jams and kitschy local items. The cafe has homemade diner-type selections: sandwiches (including muffalettas with Back in Time's own olive dressing) and salads (with not-terribly-Cajun dressings like honey raspberry walnut vinaigrette). The gooey desserts include the "Sweet Georgia Brown," a double chocolate brownie with cream cheese filling. Come by for a snack and admire the picture from a local bar from the '20s—the man who bought the picture drank the last cup of coffee at that bar.

Palace Cafe. 167 W. Landry St. ☎ **318/942-2142.** Main courses $5.95–$13.95. AE, DISC, MC, V. Mon–Sat 6am–9pm, Sun 7am–9pm. CAJUN/GREEK.

Owned by the same family since 1927, the Palace Cafe is the place to come for your crawfish cravings—it serves a heck of an étouffée. If the tradition doesn't bring you into this no-frills place, the location (right on the main drag) surely will. There are daily lunch specials.

ST. MARTINVILLE

This historic town dates from 1765, when it was a military station known as the Poste des Attakapas. It is also the last home of Emmeline Labiche, Henry Wadsworth Longfellow's Evangeline. There was a time when it was known as "la Petite Paris"—many French aristocrats fled their homeland during the Revolution and settled here, bringing with them such traditions as fancy balls, lavish banquets, and other forms of high living.

SEEING THE SIGHTS

Three of St. Martinville's main attractions revolve around Longfellow's epic poem *Evangeline*.

The **Evangeline Monument,** on Main Street, is a statue to the side and slightly to the rear of St. Martin's Church. It was donated to the town in 1929 by a movie company that came here to film the epic. The star of that movie, Dolores del Rio, supposedly posed for the statue. This also reportedly marks the spot of the grave of the real-life Evangeline, Emmeline Labiche.

At Port Street and Bayou Teche is the ancient **Evangeline Oak,** where her descendants say Emmeline's boat landed at the end of her long trip from Nova Scotia. Legend has it that it was here, too, that she learned of her lover's betrothal to another. Truth compels us to admit that as far as a sight goes, it's just a big tree, but we like it. And it is right on the bayou, which makes for a pretty sight indeed.

Also on the banks of Bayou Teche, just north of St. Martinville on Louisiana Highway 31, is the **Longfellow-Evangeline Commemorative Area** (☎ **318/394-3754**).

The 157 acres that make up the park once belonged to Louis Pierre Arceneaux, Emmeline's real-life Gabriel. The **Olivier Plantation House** on the grounds (☎ **318/394-4284**), dating from about 1765, is typical of larger Acadian homes, with bricks made by hand and baked in the sun, a cypress frame and pegs (instead of nails), and bousillage construction on the upper floor. You can also see the *cuisine* (outdoor kitchen) and *magazin* (storehouse) out back. Admission to the house is $2 for adults, free for children, school groups, and seniors. It's open daily 9am to 5pm. Tours start every hour on the hour from 10am to 4pm.

St. Martin de Tours Church. 201 Evangeline Blvd. ☎ **318/394-6021** or 318/394-7334. Daily 8:30am–5pm.

This is the Mother Church of the Acadians; the building was constructed in 1836, on the site of a previous church building. It is the fourth-oldest Roman Catholic church in Louisiana. Father George Murphy, an Irish priest, was the first to associate it with its patron saint, St. Martin, in the 1790s, and there's a noteworthy portrait of the saint behind the main altar. You'll also see the original box pews, a replica of the grotto of Lourdes, an ornate baptismal font (which some say was a gift from King Louis XVI of France), and the lovely old altar. Outside is a cemetery that purportedly holds the grave of Evangeline herself.

The **Petit Paris Museum** (☎ **318/394-7334**), next to the church, often has some unexpectedly interesting displays—a recent visit found a terrific St. Martinsville Mardi Gras exhibit, with some splendiferous costumes and the extraordinary local story that inspired the theme that year. Guided tours of the church, antebellum rectory, and museum are available. Contact the museum for details.

ACCOMMODATIONS

Old Castillo Bed & Breakfast. 220 Evangeline Blvd., St. Martinville, LA 70582. ☎ **800/621-3017** or 318/394-4010. Fax 318/394-7983. 7 units. A/C. $50–$80 double. Daybed $10. Rates include breakfast. AE, DISC, MC, V. Free parking.

Set on the banks of the Bayou Teche, virtually under the branches of the Evangeline Oak, this Greek Revival building began life in the early 1800s as a residence and inn and for many years served as a high school for girls. It blossomed into its present incarnation—and survived the devastation caused by Hurricane Andrew in 1992—under the loving direction of Peggy and Gerald Hulin. It's listed on the National Register of Historic Places.

The spacious rooms are comfortably furnished with some antiques, and four-poster beds that are either double or queen size. There's a restaurant on the premises (see below).

DINING

La Place d'Evangeline. 220 Evangeline Blvd. ☎ **318/394-4010.** Reservations recommended. All items under $20. AE, DISC, MC, V. Mon–Tues 8am–5pm, Wed–Sat 8am–9pm, Sun 8am–2pm. FRENCH/CAJUN.

In the historic Old Castillo Bed & Breakfast (see above), La Place d'Evangeline is a warm, homey room where "friendly" certainly defines the service. Breakfast features regional favorites of beignets, *pain perdu,* and café au lait. Seafood and steaks share the à la carte menu with soup-and-salad combinations, po' boys, and such traditional homemade desserts as peach cobbler and fudge pecan pie.

Maison deVille. 100 N. Main St. ☎ **318/394-5700.** Main courses $4.95–$10.95 at lunch; $9.75–$22 at dinner. AE, DISC, MC, V. Tues–Sun 10am–3pm; Wed–Sat also 5:30–10pm. AMERICAN/CAJUN.

This pretty new restaurant in a lovely old house (lots of distressed paint on the walls) is located on the corner of the main square. It offers nice versions of the basics—salads, fish dishes, étouffée, shrimp fettuccine, and ribeye steaks.

✪ **Thibodeaux's Cafe.** 116 S. Main St. ☎ **318/394-6624.** All items under $5. No credit cards. Daily 6:30am–3pm. COUNTRY COOKING.

Now, if you want gourmet cuisine, go elsewhere. But if you want authentic, ribsticking food, not to mention something that will barely lighten your wallet, come here. This small cafe serves up huge breakfasts and lunch specials. At lunch, less than $5 (often less than $4) will buy you a plate full of such items as delicious smothered chicken or pork, rice, vegetables (out of a can, to be sure), and so forth. Nothing fancy, but pretty tasty. Chat with the friendly staff, who, if they aren't busy, will give you all kinds of local info and gossip. Those on a budget will be particularly pleased, but so will those tired of higher-profile places who want a true small-town meal.

NEW IBERIA

This town dates from 1779, when a group of 300 immigrants from the Spanish province of Málaga came up Bayou Teche and settled here. It was incorporated in 1813, and its history changed drastically after the arrival of the steamboat *Plowboy* in 1836. New Iberia became the terminal for steamboats traveling up the bayou from New Orleans, and it promptly developed the rambunctious character of a frontier town. In 1839, however, yellow fever traveled up the bayou with the steamboats and killed more than a quarter of the population. Many residents were saved through the heroic nursing of a black woman called Tante Félicité, who had come here from Santo Domingo; she went tirelessly from family to family carrying food and medicine. (She had had the fever many years before and was immune.)

During the Civil War, New Iberia was a Confederate training center that was attacked again and again. It's said that Confederate and Union soldiers alike plundered the land to such an extent that local Acadians threatened to declare war on *both* sides if any more of their chickens, cattle, and farm produce were appropriated. The steamboats continued coming up the bayou until 1947. (I'll bet you didn't know the steamboat era lasted that long anywhere in the United States.) New Iberia, known as the "Queen City of the Teche," has continued to grow.

SEEING THE SIGHTS

Take one of Annie Miller's **Swamp and Marsh Tours** (☎ **504/879-3934**) for a close-up look at the bayou and its wildlife. In a comfortable boat, you'll visit a rookery of nesting egrets and herons and say hello to the gators who come when they are called ("*Bah*-bee! *Tone*-y! *Ti*-gar!") by the friendly operators of the very personal and delightful cruises. Tours cost $15 for adults, $10 for children under 13. Be sure to call for current schedules, to find out which location (there are several) is nearest you, and to make reservations.

Note: This is also worth the drive from New Orleans. Take U.S. 90 west through Houma (about 57 miles), exit right at the tourist office on St. Charles Street, turn left at the stoplight onto Southdown/Mandalay Road, and proceed to Miller's Landing on Big Bayou Black.

Shadows-on-the-Teche Plantation. 317 E. Main St., New Iberia. ☎ **318/369-6446.** Admission $6 adults, $3 children 6–11, free for children under 6. Daily 9am–4:30pm. From New Orleans (approximately 3 hours), take U.S. 90 to La. 14, and follow La. 14 east to the intersection with La. 182.

This beautifully preserved home was built in 1834 for David Weeks, a wealthy planter. It reflects the prevailing classical taste of the times, as seen in its Greek Revival facade. The two-story house of rose-colored brick sits amid oak trees, camellias, and azaleas. One of the most authentically restored and furnished homes in the state, it is the property of the National Trust for Historic Preservation.

Tabasco Sauce Factory. La. 329, Avery Island (from Lafayette, take Hwy. 90 to Hwy 14 turn left to Hwy. 329 and turn right; it's about 7 miles down). ☎ **318/365-8173.** Free admission. Factory open Mon–Sat 9am–4pm. Parking 50¢.

Avery Island, south of New Iberia, sits atop a gigantic salt dome and the oldest salt-rock mine in the western hemisphere. It's not salt but pepper—fiery-hot peppers that grow especially well here—that's brought Avery Island its greatest fame. Tabasco brand pepper sauce, loved all over the world, is made by a close-knit family and equally close workers who cultivate and harvest the peppers, then nurse them through the fermentation process developed by Edmund McIlhenny, founder of the McIlhenny Company. You can tour the Tabasco factory and visitors center, which includes an old-fashioned Tabasco Country Store.

Jungle Gardens. La. 329, Avery Island. ☎ **318/369-6243.** Daily 8am–5:30pm.

Across the street from the Tabasco factory (but not affiliated with it), these gardens cover more than 200 acres, with something in bloom from November through June. On a driving or walking tour, you'll see a 1,000-year-old Buddha in the Chinese Garden, sunken gardens, a bird sanctuary (with egrets and herons), and tropical plants.

✪ **Rip Van Winkle Gardens.** 5055 Rip Van Winkle Rd., New Iberia. ☎ **318/365-3332.** Admission $9 adults, $8.50 seniors, $7 children 13–18 years old, $5 children 5–12 years old. Daily 9am–5pm. First tour at 10am; last tour at 4pm. Boat tours are offered at 10am, 11:30am, 1pm and 3pm. Closed holidays.

On the shores of Lake Peigneur, this is a place of huge oak trees, 350 years old or more, draped with Spanish moss. Known as Jefferson Island, it isn't a proper island, but a piece of land held up higher than its surroundings.

Actor Joseph Jefferson, who gained national fame for his portrayal of Rip Van Winkle, purchased the land in 1869 and erected an extravagant three-story home, much of which he designed himself. Although Jefferson did more than a little landscaping and gardening on the grounds, the Bayless family, which bought the estate in 1917, was responsible for the colorful panorama you see today.

The gardens were well developed when disaster struck in 1980—the lake disappeared after an oil company drilled into the salt mine, creating a gigantic whirlpool so powerful that it sucked in all the waters of the lake and huge portions of the adjacent gardens. Today, the gardens have been rebuilt (but have been reduced from their original 65 acres to a mere 25); you'll see only the glory of camellias, azaleas, crape myrtles, tulips, and a Japanese garden.

A tour takes you through Jefferson's old home and gives you an idea of (wealthy) life 100 years ago. Pirate Jean Lafitte's brother-in-law was rumored to have owned this land before Jefferson, a bit of folklore given more credence when three pots of very old silver coins were uncovered on the property. Admire the 550-year-old oak tree that Grover Cleveland snoozed under while visiting Jefferson. Then stroll around the gorgeous grounds and pretend they're yours.

Actually, for a night, they could be. The Rip Van Winkle Gardens offers **bed-and-breakfast** accommodations. It currently operates only a one-bedroom cottage, but there are plans to open up additional space. An overnight stay is an amazing experience—the cottage is extremely comfortable and beautifully decorated, with a sitting area (complete with TV and CD player), a lavish bathroom (and Jacuzzi tub), luxurious linens on the four-poster bed, and a wide veranda. A small fridge is stocked with free goodies, giving you the makings for a substantial continental breakfast. But the best part is at night, when the Gardens close for the evening, and all employees leave the grounds. The gates are locked behind them (you get a pass code should you want to leave for dinner or whatnot), and those acres of beautifully manicured gardens are all yours. Wow! Naturally, this kind of experience doesn't come cheap (it's $145 double weeknights, $175 weekends), but what a way to celebrate a special occasion such as a wedding or anniversary.

DINING

Cafe Jefferson. In the Rip Van Winkle Gardens, 5505 Rip Van Winkle Rd. ☎ **318/365-3332.** Reservations required. Main courses $11.95–$28. AE, DISC, MC, V. Daily 11am–3pm; desserts daily 3–5pm; Wed–Sat 6–10pm. CAJUN.

Featuring creative Cajun cuisine, Cafe Jefferson is worth a stop before or after strolling through the Rip Van Winkle Gardens. Also consider coming for dinner, especially right at sunset. Oaks dripping with Spanish moss frame the view of the lake, and the setting sun on the water makes for one fine romantic show. Among the menu choices are crawfish and corn beignets with Creole mustard sauce, grilled quail foccia (marinated in cane syrup, balsamic vinegar, and citrus), and slow-roasted duckling. If the prices don't fit your budget, soups and appetizers are so rich and heavenly that they will satisfy, so you don't have to skip this experience.

VILLE PLATTE

If you've fallen in love with Cajun music and want to take some home with you, you have a good reason to detour to the town of Ville Platte.

✪ **Floyd's Record Shop.** 434 E. Main St. ☎ **318/367-5622.** Mon–Sat 8:30am–5:30pm.

Floyd Soileau is in some ways the unofficial mayor of Acadiana, and certainly one of its biggest boosters—a sort of one-man chamber of commerce. But he's meant much more to the region as one of the key entrepreneurs of bayou music. Long before Cajun and zydeco were known outside the region, he was recording and releasing the music on three labels: Swallow for Cajun, Maison de Soul for zydeco, and Jin (named after his charming wife) for swamp pop, the regional offshoot of '50s and early '60s pop and soul styles. Eventually, he built a whole operation of recording, pressing (his plant was pressing vinyl well into the CD age), and selling records, by mail order and at this store. For fans of the music, this is a must-stop locale, with a fine selection of Floyd's releases by such great artists as D. L. Menard ("The Cajun Hank Williams") and Clifton Chenier (the King of Zydeco), as well as other releases that may be hard to find anywhere else.

DINING

The Pig Stand. 318 E. Main St. ☎ **318/363-2883.** $10.25 and under. No credit cards. Daily 5am–10pm. PIG.

As you might guess, the Pig Stand serves pig. A local institution, it even popped up in the recent Elvis Cole mystery *Voodoo River,* which erroneously described the place as having an outside window and serving boudin. It's a little dump of a local hangout that serves divine barbecued chicken and other Southern specialties for cheap prices. It's a treat—don't miss it. And it's just down the street from Floyd's, in case you worked up an appetite buying music.

WASHINGTON

This is a very small town—10 minutes will get you all the highlights, but even non-residents will urge you to take the quick detour from Opelousas, simply because it's so pretty. This is thanks in large part to an abundance of graceful old homes (more even than in other towns in the area) and trees. The many antique stores are also a draw. At least seven of the old homes have been converted to B&Bs; staying here is an inter-esting, and more attractive, experience than a night in some other towns in Cajun country.

If you plan only to drive through, it is worth getting out of the car for **Magnolia Ridge** (½ mile north of town on Hwy. 103; ☎ **318/826-3027**). The 1820s house is not open to the public, but its 63 acres of gardens and paths, some winding down to the bayou, are. There are also a couple of old **cemeteries,** and **Willy's Campground** (on Hwy. 10: "You come up the main drag in Washington, cross the bridge and we are right there," ☎ **318/826-9987**) has live music Friday and Saturday nights.

All B&Bs in Washington will refer callers to others in the area if they're full on a particular night. We particularly liked **Camellia Cove,** 211 W. Hill St. (☎ **318/ 826-7362**). The nicely restored old house, including the original detached kitchen (ask to see it), has its original furniture from 1905. There are three bedrooms, two with private bathrooms—the large pink bedroom with the ornate wood bedstead is probably the best. The large front porch is perfect for sitting and rocking, and the full breakfast might feature eggs Benedict or fruit crêpes, complete with fresh flowers and china.

Appendix:
New Orleans in Depth

First, there's the Gulf and the river and the lake—New Orleans, the island of Orleans, owes its existence to water. The largest city in Louisiana and one of the chief cities of the South, it's nearly 100 miles above the mouth of the Mississippi River system and stretches along a strip of land 5 to 8 miles wide, between the Mississippi and Lake Pontchartrain to the north.

1 History 101

Dateline

- **1513** Spanish explorer Juan Ponce de León lands in Florida.
- **1543** Survivors of Hernando de Soto's expedition travel down the Mississippi River, passing the present site of New Orleans.
- **1682** Sieur de la Salle stops near the present site of the city during his descent of the Mississippi River from the Great Lakes region, and plants a cross claiming the territory for Louis XIV.
- **1699** Pierre Le Moyne, Sieur d'Iberville, rediscovers and secures the mouth of the Mississippi—on Mardi Gras day, appropriately.
- **1718** The first governor of Louisiana, Iberville's brother Jean-Baptiste Le Moyne, Sieur de Bienville, founds New Orleans.
- **1723** New Orleans replaces Biloxi as the capital of Louisiana.
- **1726** Capuchin monastery erected.
- **1752** Ursuline convent completed.

continues

IN THE BEGINNING Two French-Canadian brothers found this spot at the turn of the 18th century. Pierre Le Moyne, Sieur d'Iberville, led an expedition from France to rediscover the mouth of the Mississippi in 1699. René Robert Cavelier, Sieur de la Salle, had claimed the region for France in 1682. (He was murdered in Texas in 1687, by his own party, because his lack of navigational and leadership skills risked many of their lives.) Iberville succeeded and planted a cross at a dramatic bend in the river near where La Salle had stopped almost 2 decades before. On his voyage, Iberville also established a fort at Biloxi, naming it the capital of France's new and unchartered territory. His brother, 18-year-old Jean Baptiste Le Moyne, Sieur de Bienville, stayed behind in the new capital and quickly became commanding officer of the territory. For the next 20 years, he harbored thoughts of returning up the river and establishing a new capital city at the spot where he and his brother had stopped.

In 1718, Bienville got his chance. The previous year, Louisiana had been entrusted to the Company of the West (or Company of the Indies, or the Mississippi Company) for development as a populated colony. The company was headed by John Law, a Scottish entrepreneur who had convinced the French monarch and many stockholders in his company that fortunes were to be had in the new land. The company authorized Bienville to find a suitable location for a settlement on the river, at a spot that would also protect France's holdings in the New World from British expansion. Bienville quickly settled on high ground at the site he had previously seen, and not only because the bend in the river would be relatively easy to defend: Although it was approximately 100 miles inland along the river from the Gulf of Mexico, the site was near St. John's Bayou that provided easy water transportation directly into Lake Pontchartrain. It was convenient from a military standpoint—providing a "back door" for defense or escape, should the fortunes of war turn against the French—and it gave the site great potential as a trade route, because it would allow relatively easy access to the Gulf.

The new town was named New Orleans in honor of the duc d'Orléans, then the regent of France. Following the plan of a late French medieval town, a central square (the Place d'Armes) was laid out, with streets forming a grid around it. A church, government office, priest's house, and official residences fronted the square, and earthen ramparts dotted with forts were built around the perimeter. A tiny wooden levee was raised against the river, which still flooded periodically and turned the streets into rivers of mud. Today, this area of original settlement is known as the Vieux Carré ("old square"), and the Place d'Armes as Jackson Square.

A MELTING POT   In its first few years, New Orleans was a community of French officials, adventurers, merchants, slaves, soldiers, and convicts from French prisons, all living in rude huts of cypress, moss, and clay. These were the first ingredients of New Orleans' population gumbo. The city's commerce was mainly limited to trade with native tribes and to beginning agricultural production.

To supply people and capital to the colony, John Law's company began what was essentially the first real estate scam in the New World. The territory and the city were marketed on the

- **1762** Louis XV secretly cedes New Orleans and all of Louisiana west of the Mississippi to Spain.
- **1768** French residents in New Orleans banish Spanish commissioner Don Antonio de Ulloa, proclaiming independence from Spain.
- **1769** The Spanish return.
- **1783** Treaty of Paris confirms Spanish possession.
- **1788, 1794** Fire destroys much of the city; new brick buildings replace wood.
- **1794** Planter Etienne de Boré granulates sugar from cane for the first time, spawning a boom in the industry.
- **1795** Treaty of Madrid opens port to Americans; trade thrives.
- **1800** Louisiana again becomes a French possession.
- **1803** France officially takes possession of the territory. United States then purchases it and takes possession.
- **1805** New Orleans incorporates as a city; first elections are held.
- **1812** The *New Orleans,* first steam vessel to travel the Mississippi, arrives from Pittsburgh. Louisiana admitted as a U.S. state.
- **1815** Battle of New Orleans.
- **1831** The first (horse-drawn) railway west of the Alleghenies is completed, linking New Orleans and Milneburg.
- **1832–33** Yellow fever and cholera epidemic kills 10,000 people in 2 years.
- **1834** Medical College of Louisiana (forerunner of Tulane University) founded.
- **1837** First newspaper coverage of a Mardi Gras parade.
- **1840** Antoine Alciatore, founder of Antoine's restaurant, arrives from Marseilles. New Orleans is

continues

the fourth-largest city in the United States, and second only to New York as a port.

- **1849** The Place d'Armes renamed Jackson Square.
- **1850** Booming commerce totals $200 million; cotton accounts for 45% of total trade. City becomes largest slave market in the country.
- **1852** Consolidation of municipal government; New Orleans annexes city of Lafayette.
- **1853–55** Yellow fever epidemic during the summer; 12% of the population killed in 1853 in roughly two months.
- **1861–62** Louisiana secedes from the Union; city captured by Adm. David Farragut. Gen. Benjamin Butler assumes command of the city and earns a reputation for harsh and unfriendly governance.
- **1865–77** Reconstruction; "carpetbaggers" swarm into the city, and tensions climax in clashes between the Crescent White League and government forces.
- **1870** Algiers and Jefferson City annexed.
- **1872** Carrollton annexed.
- **1884–85** Cotton Centennial Exposition (World's Fair) held at the present site of Audubon Park.
- **1890** Jelly Roll Morton born.
- **1890** Creole of color Homer Plessy gets arrested riding a train recently segregated by Jim Crow laws. He sues the state, efforts which culminate in the landmark U.S. Supreme Court decision *Plessy v. Ferguson*.
- **1892** First electric streetcar operates along St. Charles Avenue.
- **1897** Sidney Bechet born. Storyville established.
- **1900** Louis Armstrong born.
- **1911** Razzy Dazzy Spasm Band performs in New York,

continues

continent as Heaven on Earth, full of immediate and boundless opportunities for wealth and luxury. The value of real estate in the territory rose dramatically with the lies as wealthy Europeans, aristocrats, merchants, exiles, soldiers, and a large contingent of German farmers arrived—to find only mosquitoes, a raw frontier existence, and swampy land. Ultimately, the company's scheme nearly bankrupted the French nation. It did succeed, however, in swelling the population of the territory and of New Orleans; in 1723, the city replaced Biloxi as the capital of the Louisiana territory.

In 1724, Bienville approved the *Code Noir*, which set forth the laws under which African slaves were to be treated and established Catholicism as the territory's official religion. While it codified slavery and banished Jews from Louisiana, the code did provide slaves recognition and a degree of protection under the law.

One significant natural barrier to development of the population and society in Louisiana remained: a lack of potential wives. In 1727, a small contingent of Ursuline nuns arrived in the city and set about establishing a convent. While they weren't exactly eligible, they did provide a temporary home and education to many shiploads of *les filles à la cassette*. The "cassette girls" or "casket girls"—named for the government-issue *cassettes* or casketlike trunks in which they carried their possessions—were young women of appropriate character sent to Louisiana by the French government to be courted and married by the colonists. (If we're to believe the current population of the city, the plan was remarkably successful: Nearly everyone in New Orleans claims descent from the casket girls or from Spanish or French nobility, which makes one wonder at the terrible infertility of the colony's earlier population of convicts and "fallen women.")

John Law's company relinquished its governance of Louisiana in 1731, and the French monarch regained direct control of the territory. In the following decades, a number of planters established estates up and down the river from New Orleans. In the city, wealthier society began to develop a courtly atmosphere on the French model. In the midst of the rough-and-tumble frontier, families competed to see who could throw the most elegant and opulent party.

Farther afield, westward along the Gulf of Mexico, other French speakers were creating a very different kind of society in a decidedly more rural mode. During the 18th century, many French colonists displaced by British rule from Acadia, Nova Scotia, formed an outpost on the new French territory along the coastland. Today, you'll find the Acadians' descendants living a little to the west of New Orleans, still engaged in farming and trapping, some still speaking their unique brand of French, and proudly calling themselves "Cajuns."

New Orleans experienced only modest commercial development in its first decades, in large part due to trading restrictions imposed by France: The colony could only trade with the mother country. Colonists quickly found ways around the restrictions, however, and smugglers and pirates provided alternative markets and transportation for the region's agricultural products, furs, bricks, and tar.

Despite the awkward relationship with France, New Orleanians were greatly disturbed to learn in 1764 that 2 years earlier (news traveled right slow back then) Louis XV had given their city and all of Louisiana west of the Mississippi to his cousin, Charles III of Spain, in the secret Treaty of Fontainebleau. The Spanish, in turn, took 2 more years to send a governor, Don Antonio de Ulloa, who made few friends among local residents. By 1768, a large number of French residents of New Orleans and outlying areas assembled to demand Ulloa's removal. Some proposed the formation of a Louisiana republic. Ulloa was sent packing, and for nearly 2 years New Orleans and Louisiana were effectively independent of any foreign power. This episode ended in 1769 when Don Alexander O'Reilly ("Bloody O'Reilly") and 3,000 soldiers arrived in the city, dispatched by the Spanish Crown. What had been a relatively peaceful rebellion was extinguished, its leaders were executed, and Spanish rule was reimposed. With a Gallic shrug, French aristocracy mingled with Spanish nobility, intermarried, and helped to create a new "Creole" culture.

Devastating fires struck in 1788 (when more than 850 buildings were destroyed) and again in 1794, in the midst of rebuilding. From the ashes emerged a new architecture, dominated by the proud Spanish style of brick-and-plaster buildings replete with arches, courtyards, balconies, and, of course, attached slave quarters.

where its name is changed to Razzy Dazzy Jazz Band.

- **1917** Original Dixieland Jazz Band attains height of popularity.
- **1921** Inner-Harbor Navigational Canal built, connecting Lake Pontchartrain and the Mississippi.
- **1927** Levee at Poydras erected.
- **1928** Colorful Huey P. Long elected governor of Louisiana; four years later, he is elected to U.S. Senate.
- **1935** Long is shot and killed.
- **1938** Tennessee Williams arrives in New Orleans; Huey P. Long Bridge built over Mississippi River.
- **1939** French Quarter Residents Association formed as an agent for preservation.
- **1956** Lake Pontchartrain Causeway, world's longest bridge, completed.
- **1960** The city's public schools integrated.
- **1969** Clay Shaw tried by D.A. Jim Garrison and found not guilty in the country's only trial regarding the assassination of JFK.
- **1973** Parades banned in the Vieux Carré, changing the character of the city's observance of Mardi Gras.
- **1975** Superdome opens.
- **1977** Ernest N. "Dutch" Morial becomes first African American mayor.
- **1984** Louisiana World Expo draws disappointing crowds but spurs redevelopment of the riverside area between Canal and Poydras streets.
- **1988** Anne Rice moves back to New Orleans, which has enormous impact on the city.
- **1992–present** Harrah's Jazz Company opens a temporary land-based casino and begins construction of a monumental permanent structure near the Convention Center; within 2 years, the casino goes belly-up. The company now plans to complete the project on a somewhat smaller scale.

Even today you'll see tile markers giving Spanish street names at every corner in the French Quarter.

The city of New Orleans was coveted by the English and the Americans—and the French, though the trade to Spain was partly motivated because the unsuccessful colony was costing them money and they could no longer afford it. The Spanish imposed the same kind of trade restrictions on the city that the French had, with even less success (these were boom years for pirates and buccaneers like the infamous Jean Lafitte and his brother Pierre). This being a period of intense imperial conflict and maneuvering, Spain did allow some American revolutionaries to trade through the city in support of the colonists' fight against Britain.

France regained possession of the territory in 1800, with a surprisingly quiet transfer of ownership, and held on for 3 years while Napoléon negotiated the Louisiana Purchase with the United States for the paltry (as it turned out) sum of $15 million. For Creole society, the return to French rule was unpleasant enough, because France had long been facing serious financial troubles, but a sale to America was anathema. To their minds, it meant the end of a European lifestyle in the Vieux Carré.

Thus, when Americans arrived in the city, the upper crust made it known that they were welcome to settle—but across Canal Street (so named because a drainage canal was once planned along its route, although it was never constructed), away from the old city and Creole society. And so it was that New Orleans came to be two parallel cities. The American section spread outward from Canal Street along St. Charles Avenue; business and cultural institutions centered in the Central Business District, and mansions rose in what is now the Garden District, which was a separate, incorporated city until 1852. French and Creole society dominated the Quarter for the rest of the 19th century, extending toward the lake along Esplanade Avenue. Soon, however, the Americans (crass though they may have seemed) brought commercial success to the city, which quickly warmed relations—the Americans sought the vitality of downtown society, and the Creoles sought the profit of American business. They also had occasion to join forces against hurricanes, yellow fever epidemics, and floods.

FROM THE BATTLE OF NEW ORLEANS TO THE CIVIL WAR Perhaps nothing helped to cement a sense of community more than the Battle of New Orleans. The great symbol of Creole-American relations was the cooperation of Andrew Jackson and Jean Lafitte. To save the city, Jackson set aside his disdain for the pirate, and Lafitte turned down offers to fight for the British, instead supplying the Americans with cannons and ammunition that helped swing the battle in their favor. When Jackson called for volunteers, some 5,000 citizens from both sides of Canal Street responded. Battle was joined on January 8, 1815, in a field a few miles downstream from the city, and approximately 2,000 British troops and 20 Americans were killed or wounded. The dramatic battle made a local and national hero of Jackson. Ironically, though, neither Jackson nor the British had been aware that a treaty concluding the war had been signed a full 2 weeks before, on December 24, 1814.

From then until the Civil War, New Orleans was a boomtown. Colonial trade restrictions had evaporated with the Louisiana Purchase, and, more important, the era of steam-powered river travel arrived in 1812 with the first riverboat, the aptly named *New Orleans,* delivered from a Pittsburgh shipyard. River commerce exploded, peaking in the 1840s and putting New Orleans' port on a par with New York's. Cotton and sugar made many fortunes in New Orleans and its hinterlands; wealthy planters joined the city merchants in building luxurious townhouses and attending festivals, opera, theater, banquets, parades, and spectacular balls (including "Quadroon Balls," where beautiful mulatto girls were displayed to the male gentry as possible mistresses). As always, politics and gambling were dominant pastimes of these citizens and visitors.

By the middle of the century, cotton-related business was responsible for nearly half of the total commerce in New Orleans, and so it's no surprise that the city housed one of the nation's largest and most ruthless slave markets. Paradoxically, New Orleans also had one of the most extended and established populations of "free men (and women) of color" in the American South. Furthermore, racial distinctions within the city increasingly became difficult to determine; people could often trace their ancestry back to two or even three different continents. Adding to the diversity, waves of Irish and German immigrants arrived in New Orleans in this period, supplying important sources of labor to support the city's growth.

This growth—upriver and downriver from the original center, and away from the river toward Lake Pontchartrain—required extensive drainage of swamps and the construction of a system of canals and levees. The only major impediments to the development of the city in these decades were occasional yellow fever epidemics, which killed thousands of residents and visitors. Despite the clearing of swampland, the mosquito-borne disease persisted until the final decades of the 19th century.

The boom era ended rather abruptly with the Civil War and Louisiana's secession from the United States in 1861. Federal troops marched into the city in 1862 and stayed until 1877, through the bitter Reconstruction period. As was the case elsewhere in the South, this period saw violent clashes between armed white groups and the state's Reconstruction forces.

After the war, the city went about the business of rebuilding its economic life—this time without slavery. By 1880, a number of annexations had rounded out the city limits, port activity had begun to pick up, and railroads were establishing their importance to the local and national economies. Also, a new group of immigrants, Italians this time, came to put their unique mark on the city. Through it all, an undiminished enthusiasm for fun survived. Gambling again thrived in more than 80 establishments, there were almost 800 saloons, and scores of "bawdy houses" engaged in prostitution, which was illegal but uncontrolled. New Orleans was earning an international reputation for open vice, much to the chagrin of the city's polite society.

In 1897, Alderman Sidney Story thought he had figured out how to improve the city's tarnishing image. He moved all illegal (but highly profitable) activities into a restricted district along Basin Street, next door to the French Quarter. Quickly nicknamed Storyville, the district boasted fancy "sporting palaces" with elaborate decor, musical entertainment, and a wide variety of ladies of pleasure. Visitors and residents could purchase a directory (the *Blue Book*) that listed alphabetically the names, addresses, and races of more than 700 prostitutes, ranging from those in the "palaces" to the poorer inhabitants of wretched, decaying shacks (called "cribs") on the blocks behind Basin Street. African American musicians like Jelly Roll Morton played the earliest form of jazz in some of Basin Street's ornate bordellos. Although jazz predates Storyville, here it gained popularity before moving upriver and into record collections everywhere. When the secretary of the navy decreed in 1917 that armed forces should not be exposed to so much open vice, Storyville closed down and disappeared without a trace. None of the fancy sporting houses remains. Too bad; the city missed a great money-making opportunity. Think how popular a Storyville museum, set in an actual old bordello, would be!

THE 20th CENTURY The 20th century found New Orleans' port becoming the largest in the United States and the second busiest in the world (after Amsterdam), with goods coming in by barge and rail. Drainage problems were conquered by means of high levees, canals, pumping stations, and great spillways, which are opened to direct floodwater away from the city. Bridges have been built across the Mississippi River, including the Huey P. Long bridge, named after Louisiana's famous politician and demagogue. New Orleans' emergence as a regional financial center, with more than 50 commercial banks, has led to the construction of soaring office buildings, mostly in the Central Business District.

As in most other American cities, the city's population has spread outward through this century, filling suburbs and nearby municipalities. Unlike other cities, however, New Orleans has been able to preserve its original town center and much of its historic architecture. Thanks to these attractions and other tourism-related improvements, it ranks near the top in U.S. tourism (conventions alone bring in more than a million visitors each year) and is one of the country's top travel destinations for foreign visitors. The 1984 World's Fair, held in New Orleans, was a highlight in this development. Although it was not very well attended, the fair permanently elevated the spirit of the city and led to the construction of a number of high-rise and luxury hotels at the river end of Canal and Poydras Streets, and the renovation of a large portion of the previously derelict waterfront Warehouse District.

The Gulf, river, and lake have not changed much over the past 300 years—at least, not as much as the little island of Orleans. The city wears its changes proudly, and from the Vieux Carré out to the suburbs, like Metarie and Slidell, from the Garden District to the Esplanade Ridge, it invites visitors to read its history. New Orleanians certainly live by the history of their hometown, so as you navigate through the city, try to keep the likes of Iberville and Bienville, Jackson and Lafitte, Sidney Story and Jelly Roll Morton, and Don Alexander O'Reilly and the French rebels firmly in mind.

2 Recommended Books & Recordings

BOOKS

FICTION There are many examples of early fiction that give a good flavor of old-time New Orleans life. George Washington Cable's stories and novels are revealing and colorful; the collection to read is *Old Creole Days* (1879). Grace King answered Cable's not-always-flattering portrait of the Creoles in her short stories and in her novel *The Pleasant Ways of St. Medard* (1916). Perhaps the best writer to touch upon the lives of the earliest Creoles is Kate Chopin, who lived in Louisiana for only 14 years in the late 19th century, first in New Orleans and later in Cloutierville. Many of her short stories and novels, the most famous of which is *The Awakening,* are set in the region or involve characters from here.

In the next century, William Faulkner came to New Orleans, lived on Pirates Alley, and penned *Soldier's Pay.* Several other Faulkner novels and short stories are set in New Orleans. Tennessee Williams became a devoted New Orleans fan, living in the city on and off for many years. It inspired him to write *A Streetcar Named Desire,* which for many years was perhaps the best-known New Orleans tale. He also set *The Rose Tattoo* in the city. Frances

Parkinson Keyes lived on Chartres Street for more than 25 years. Her most famous works are *Dinner at Antoine's* and *Madame Castel's Lodger.*

Other notable modern New Orleans writers include Walker Percy and Shirley Ann Grau. Percy's novels, including *The Moviegoer* and *Love in the Ruins,* are classic portrayals of the idiosyncrasies of New Orleans and its residents. Grau's most famous novel, *The Keepers of the House,* won the Pulitzer Prize in 1964. John Kennedy Toole also received a Pulitzer, but he wasn't around to know about it, having committed suicide years before. At the time of his death, none of his works had even been published. Toole's *A Confederacy of Dunces* is a timeless New Orleans tragicomedy that'll have you laughing out loud. Robert Olen Butler won the Pulitzer in 1993 for his collection of stories, *A Good Scent from a Strange Mountain,* set primarily in New Orleans' Vietnamese community. Ellen Gilchrist is another nationally recognized contemporary fiction writer with roots in the city. *In the Land of Dreamy Dreams,* a collection of her short stories, portrays life in wealthy uptown New Orleans.

There are several choices in new fiction as well. Valerie Martin's *The Great Divorce* is a retelling of *Dr. Jekyll and Mr. Hyde* set in the streets of antebellum New Orleans. Other recent releases are Sheila Bosworth's *Almost Innocent* and *Slow Poison;* Nancy Levin's delightful *Lives of the Saints* and *Sportsman's Paradise;* and John Gregory Brown's critically acclaimed *Decorations in a Ruined Cemetery.* Michael Ondaatje's controversial *Coming Through Slaughter* is a fictionalized account of Buddy Bolden and the early New Orleans jazz era.

And then of course there is the cottage industry known as Anne Rice. Whatever you might think of her writing skills, she loves her native city and does arguably the best job of capturing its essence. (More than one person has come to New Orleans just because he fell in love with it from one of Rice's books.) Her "Vampire Chronicles," set in New Orleans, are her best-known work, but the city plays a significant (and seductive) role in *The Witching Hour,* and is the backdrop for a historical novel, the well-researched *Feast of All Saints,* about the free people of color.

MYSTERY Ghosts and intrigue seem to lurk around every corner, so it's no wonder so many mystery novels are set in New Orleans. A fantastic group of mystery writers currently lives in and writes about New Orleans. James Lee Burke's David Robicheaux detective series includes *Neon Rain, Black Cherry Blues,* and *Heaven's Prisoners* (recently a movie starring Alec Baldwin). Burke and Julie Smith, who wrote *New Orleans Mourning,* have won Edgar Awards as mystery novelists of the year. *With Extreme Prejudice,* by Frederick Barton, takes readers down both the mean streets of New Orleans and the picturesque ones of the Garden District. For a novel that captures the racial tension of the city, look for *Glass House* by Christine Wiltz. There are also Robert Skinner's *Skin Deep Blood Red* and Toni Fennelly's *1-900-DEAD.*

HISTORY Lyle Saxon's *Fabulous New Orleans* is the best and most charming place to start learning about the city's past. (Saxon was director of the writer's program under the WPA.) From there, move on to his collaboration with Robert Tallant, *Gumbo Ya-Ya.* Roark Bradford's Civil War novel, *Kingdom Coming,* contains a lot of information about voodoo. Mark Twain visited the city often in his riverboat days, and his *Life on the Mississippi* has a good number of tales about New Orleans and its riverfront life. *The WPA Guide to New Orleans* also contains some excellent social and historical background and provides a fascinating picture of the city in 1938. *Beautiful Crescent* by Joan Garvey and Mary Lou Widmer is a readable reference book on the history of New Orleans.

There are many guides to Mardi Gras, including Robert Tallant's *Mardi Gras* and Myron Tassin's *Mardi Gras and Bacchus: Something Old, Something New,* both published by Pelican. The definitive account is Henri Schindler's *Mardi Gras New Orleans.* Schindler produced balls and parades for Mardi Gras for 20 years and is considered carnival's foremost historian.

Those interested in Storyville need look no further than Al Rose's comprehensive *Storyville, New Orleans, Being an Authentic Illustrated Account of the Notorious Redlight District* (University of Alabama Press, 1974). Full of first-hand accounts (including those of Storyville survivors), it sweeps away the myths about that infamous neighborhood, including its relationship to the roots of jazz. It contains the only photos of Storyville, by photographer EJ Belloq, and was the inspiration for the movie *Pretty Baby.*

Other books worth reading include Facts and Legends by Raymond Martinez and Jack Holmes (Hope Publications, 1980), *and The French Quarter and Other New Orleans Scenes* by Joseph A. Arrigo (Pelican, 1980). One of the best works about the region is *Gulf Coast Country,* by Hodding Carter and Anthony Ragusin.

For the most in-depth look at the history of life on the Mississippi River between New Orleans and Baton Rouge, look for *Along the River Road: Past and Present on Louisiana's Historic Byway,* by Mary Ann Sternberg.

If you're interested in women's history, *Women and New Orleans,* by Mary Gehman, is fascinating and well written.

Literary New Orleans: Essays and Meditations and *Literary New Orleans In the Modern World* (Louisiana State University) are scholarly looks at the spell cast by the Crescent City on authors in the last century.

Finally, many of the recent books by poet and essayist Andrei Codrescu contain pieces about his adopted city of New Orleans. Codrescu has captured the city's appeal better than anyone else in recent times—we've used quotes from him liberally throughout this text. Start with *The Muse Is Always Half-Dressed in New Orleans* (St. Martin's) and go from there.

ART, ARCHITECTURE & ANTIQUES New Orleans is famous for its architecture, which is the subject of an abundance of books. *New Orleans Architecture* is a helpful and interesting series—each volume deals with a different area of the city, such as the Garden District, the lower Garden District, Esplanade Ridge, and the Vieux Carré. There is even a volume on the cemeteries. Friends of the Cabildo publishes the series and a small book on historical landmarks of New Orleans.

The National Trust Guide to New Orleans, by Roulhac Toledano, is a thorough, if somewhat dry, look at local architectural and cultural treasures. Another book you might want to refer to is *The Great Houses of New Orleans,* by Curt Bruce (Knopf, 1977).

Cemetery buffs will be delighted with Robert Florence's *New Orleans Cemeteries: Life in the Cities of the Dead* (Batture, 1997). It is the most complete look at this fascinating part of the New Orleans landscape, complete with photos of some of the less-traveled graveyards, plus colorful human-interest stories. Florence also has a guide titled (and about) *St. Louis No. 1, City of the Dead* (1996). If you are interested strictly in the aesthetics of the cemeteries, try Sandra Russell Clark's *Elysium: A Gathering of the Souls,* a collection of haunting art photos.

Antique lovers will appreciate a little book called *New Orleans Furniture* (The Knapp Press), which has color photographs and descriptive captions that help explain Louisiana antiques.

FOR KIDS The **New Orleans Metropolitan Convention and Visitors Bureau** publishes a guidebook specifically for kids, with activities and stories so your children can follow along as you sightsee. If you're interested, contact the bureau at 1520 Sugar Bowl Dr., New Orleans, LA 70112 (☎ **800/ 672-6124** or 504/566-5055).

Sharon Doucet has written two terrific books of Cajun folklore for children, *Why Lapin's Ears Are Long: And Other Tales from the Louisiana Bayou* (Orchard) and *Le Hoogie Boogie.* And the main character of Mary Alice Fontenont's series of Clovis Crawfish books (Pelican) is a crawfish struggling with everyday issues.

COOKBOOKS You can get cookbooks of all sorts at bookstores around town, and in some specialty food shops. Just about every popular New Orleans restaurant has published a cookbook or two, including Emeril's, Antoine's, K-Paul's, Commander's Palace, and Dooky Chase.

Cajun Revelation (Wimmer Companies, 1995) is a collection of award-winning recipes from modern Cajun chefs. *Le Bouche Creole* (Pelican, 1984) covers classic dishes. The Junior League has gathered local recipes in *The Plantation Cookbook* (Trice Publishing, 1989) and the *Talk About Good* series. Tony Chacere's *Second Helping* (Tony Chacere's Creole Seasonings) will tell you how to use those spices. Wimmer published a collection of Pat Mould's recipes from his CBS affiliate show *The Chef* in late 1998. Finally, John Folse's *The Encyclopedia of Cajun and Creole Cuisine* (The Encyclopedia Cookbook Committee, 1983) features simple recipes and is a good place to start if you'd like to try your hand at Cajun and Creole cooking.

BOOKS ABOUT MUSIC Scores of books discuss the music of New Orleans; the following suggestions should get you started.

We highly recommend Ann Allen Savoy's *Cajun Music Vol. 1* (Bluebird Press), a combination songbook and oral history. It features previously untranscribed Cajun music with lyrics in French (including a pronunciation guide) and English. A labor of many years, it's an invaluable resource.

John Broven's *South to Louisiana: The Music of the Cajun Bayous* (Pelican, 1987) gives an interesting and detailed introduction to the music of the Cajun people.

For a look at specific time periods, people, and places in the history of New Orleans jazz, you have a number of choices. They include William Carter's *Preservation Hall* (Norton, 1991); John Chilton's *Sidney Bechet: The Wizard of Jazz* (Oxford University Press, 1988); Gunther Schuller's *Early Jazz: Its Roots and Musical Development* (Oxford University Press, 1968); *Jazz New Orleans,* by Samuel Charters; *New Orleans Jazz: A Revised History,* by R. Collins; *Music in New Orleans* by Henry Kmen; *In Search of Buddy Bolden,* by Donald Marquis; *New Orleans Jazz: A Family Album,* by Al Rose and Edmond Souchon; *New Orleans Style,* by Bill Russell; *and Jazz Masters of New Orleans* by Martin Williams. Al Rose's *Storyville, New Orleans* (University of Alabama Press, 1974) is an excellent source of information about the very beginnings of jazz.

If you prefer primary sources, read Louis Armstrong's *Satchmo: My Life in New Orleans* (Da Capo Press, 1986) and Sidney Bechet's *Treat It Gentle* (Da Capo Press, 1960). Both autobiographies are captivating.

RECORDINGS

The selections listed below should give you a good start; if you want more advice, drop by or call the **Louisiana Music Factory,** 210 Decatur St. (☎ **504/586-1094**), in New Orleans, or **Floyd's Record Shop,** 434 E. Main

St., Ville Platte (☎ **318/363-2138**). (Floyd's is about 3 hours from New Orleans, so be sure to call before heading out, if you're making a special trip—see chapter 12 for more info.)

JAZZ   Most of Louis Armstrong's recordings are in print and can be found in many record stores. The same is true for Jelly Roll Morton, Wynton Marsalis, Harry Connick Jr., and Nicholas Payton—we particularly recommend his Grammy-winning *Doc Cheatham and Nicholas Payton* (Verve).

For the sound of early jazz, the following are recommended: *Streets and Scenes of New Orleans* (Good Time Jazz), by the Silver Leaf Jazz Band; *New Orleans Rhythm Kings* (Milestone*); King Oliver with Louis Armstrong* (Milestone); and the anthologies *New Orleans* (Atlantic Jazz), *Recorded in New Orleans* Volumes 1 and 2 (Good Time Jazz), and *New Orleans Jazz* (Arhoolie).

RHYTHM & BLUES   For sheer dancing delight, try the ReBirth Brass Band, *Take It to the Street* (Rounder, 1992). Dr. John, *Gris Gris* (Atco, 1968); *Gumbo* (Atco, 1972); and *Mos Scocious: An Anthology* (Rhino, 1993). *Wild Tchoupitoulas* (Mardi Gras Indians): *Wild Tchoupitoulas* (Antilles, 1976). The Meters, *Cissy Strut* (Island, 1975) and *Rejuvenation* (Reprise, 1974). You can't go wrong with home town heroes The Neville Brothers, *Yellow Moon* (A&M, 1989) and *Treacherous: A History of the Neville Brothers, 1955–1985* (Rhino). Allen Toussaint, *The Complete 'Tousan' Sessions* (Bear Family Records, 1992). He's a legend for a reason: Professor Longhair, *New Orleans Piano* (Atco, 1953) and *'Fess: The Professor Longhair Anthology* (Rhino, 1993). Worthwhile anthologies include *The Best of New Orleans Rhythm & Blues* Volumes 1 and 2 (Rhino, 1988), *The Mardi Gras Indians Super Sunday Showdown* (Rounder, 1992), *Mardi Gras Party* (Rounder, 1991), and *New Orleans Party Classics* (Rhino, 1992).

CAJUN & ZYDECO   One of the first Cajun musicians to be recorded was Amede Ardoin, *I'm Never Comin' Back* (Arhoolie, 1995). The Balfa Brothers were the first group to gain fame outside of Cajun country—try their *J'ai Vu La Lupe, Le Renard et La Belette* (Rounder, 1977) and *The Balfa Brothers Play Traditional Cajun Music* (Swallow, 1990). Beausoleil is currently the best known and most popular Cajun band; try their *Bayou Deluxe—the Best of Beausoleil* (Rhino, 1993*), La Danse de la Vie* (Rhino, 1993), and the Grammy-winning *L'Amour La Folie* (Rhino, 1997). Beausoleil's Michael Doucet plays alongside old friends Marc and Ann Savoy in the traditional Cajun group the Savoy-Doucet Cajun Band, *Home Music With Spirits* (Arhoolie, 1992). The Hackberry Ramblers have been playing Cajun music together since the 1930s (!) and their efforts have been rewarded with the Grammy-nominated "Deep Water" (Hot Biscuits, 1997). Other great choices include Beau Jocque, *Gonna Take You Downtown* (Rounder, 1996); Buckwheat Zydeco*, 100% Fortified Zydeco* (Black Top Records, 1988); Boozoo Chavis and Nathan & the Zydeco Cha-Cha's, *Zydeco Live!* (Rounder); Clifton Chenier, *Bogalusa Boogie* (Arhoolie, 1976) and *Clifton Chenier: Anthology* (Rhino, 1993); and Jo-El Sonnier, *Cajun Life* (Rounder, 1988). If you're looking for an anthology, seek out any of Rhino's excellent multivolume "Alligator Stomp" series.

Also, they aren't Cajun, zydeco, R&B, or jazz, but they are distinctly New Orleans: The New Orleans Klezmer All Stars. If you didn't realize how much fun it was to dance to traditional Jewish music (albeit with a funky second-line twist), here's your chance. Look for *Manichalfwitz* (Gert Town, 1996).

Frommer's Online Directory

by Michael Shapiro

Michael Shapiro is the author of *Internet Travel Planning*
(The Globe Pequot Press).

Frommer's Online Directory is a new feature designed to help you take advantage of the Internet to better plan your trip. Section 1 lists some general Internet resources that can make any trip easier, such as sites for booking airline tickets. It's not meant to be a comprehensive list—it's a discriminating selection of useful sites to get you started. In section 2, you'll find some top online guides specifically for New Orleans, which cover local lodging, the top attractions, and getting around.

We've awarded stars to the best sites, which are earned, not paid for (unlike some Web-site rankings that are based on payment).

1 The Top Travel-Planning Web Sites

Among the most popular sites are online travel agencies. The top agencies, including Expedia, Preview Travel, and Travelocity, offer an array of tools that are valuable even if you don't book online. You can check flight schedules, hotel availability, car rental prices, or even get paged if your flight is delayed.

While online agencies have come a long way over the past few years, they don't *always* yield the best price. Unlike a travel agent, for example, they're unlikely to tell you that you can save money by flying a day earlier or a day later. On the other hand, if you're looking for a bargain fare, you might find something online that an agent wouldn't take the time to dig up. Because airline commissions have been cut, a travel agent may not find it worthwhile spending half an hour trying to find you the best deal. On the Net, you can be your own agent and take all the time you want.

Online booking sites aren't the only places to book airline tickets—all major airlines have their own Web sites and often offer incentives, such as bonus frequent-flyer miles or Net-only discounts, for buying online. These incentives have helped airlines capture the majority of the online booking market.

Below are the Web sites for the major domestic airlines serving New Orleans. These site offers schedules and flight bookings, and most have pages where you can sign up for e-mail alerts on weekend deals. (New Orleans's airport is **Moisant International Airport,** airline code **MSY**).

American: www.aa.com
Continental: www.flycontiental.com
Delta: www.delta-air.com

Take a Look at Frommer's Site

We highly recommend Arthur Frommer's Budget Travel Online (**www.frommers.com**) as an excellent travel-planning resource. Of course, we're a little biased, but you will find indispensable travel tips, reviews, monthly vacation giveaways, and online booking.

Subscribe to Arthur Frommer's Daily Newsletter (**www.frommers.com/newsletters**) to receive the latest travel bargains and inside travel secrets in your mailbox every day. You'll read daily headlines and articles from the dean of travel himself, highlighting last-minute deals on airfares, accommodations, cruises, and package vacations. You'll also find great travel advice by checking our Tip of the Day or Hot Spot of the Month.

Search our Destinations archive (**www.frommers.com/destinations**) of more than 200 domestic and international destinations for great places to stay, tips for traveling there, and what to do while you're there. Once you've researched your trip, you might try our online reservation system (**www.frommers.com/book travelnow**) to book your dream vacation at affordable prices.

Northwest: www.nwa.com
Southwest: www.iflyswa.com
TWA: www.twa.com
US Airways: www.usairways.com

WHEN SHOULD YOU BOOK ONLINE?

Online booking is not for everyone. If you prefer to let others handle your travel arrangements, one call to an experienced travel agent should suffice. But if you want to know as much as possible about your options, the Net is a good place to start, especially for bargain hunters.

The most compelling reason to use online booking is to take advantage of last-minute specials, such as American Airlines' weekend deals or other Internet-only fares that must be purchased online. Another advantage is that you can cash in on incentives for booking online, such as rebates or bonus frequent-flyer miles.

Online booking works best for trips within North America; for international tickets, it's usually cheaper and easier to use a travel agent or consolidator.

Online booking is certainly not for those with a complex international itinerary. If you require follow-up services, such as itinerary changes, use a travel agent. Though Expedia and some other online agencies employ travel agents available by phone, these sites are geared primarily for self-service.

Please remember, though: The descriptions below were true at press time, but the pace of evolution on the Net is relentless, so you'll probably find some advancements by the time you visit these sites.

LEADING BOOKING SITES

Below are listings for the top travel-booking sites. The starred selections are the most useful and best designed sites.

Cheap Tickets. **www.cheaptickets.com**
Essentials: Discounted rates on domestic and international airline tickets and hotel rooms.

Sometimes discounters such as Cheap Tickets have exclusive deals that aren't available through more mainstream channels. Registration at Cheap Tickets requires

Staying Secure

Far more people look online than book online, partly due to fear of putting their credit cards through on the Net. Though secure encryption has made this fear less justified, there's no reason why you can't find a flight online and then book it by calling a toll-free number or contacting your travel agent. To be sure you're in secure mode when you book online, look for a little icon of a key (in Netscape) or a padlock (Internet Explorer) at the bottom of your Web browser.

---

inputting a credit card number before getting started, which is one reason many people elect to call the company's toll-free number rather than booking online. One of the most frustrating things about the Cheap Tickets site is that it will offer fare quotes for a route, and later show this fare is not valid for your dates of travel (other Web sites, such as Preview), consider your dates of travel before showing what fares are available. Despite its problems, Cheap Tickets can be worth the effort because its fares can be lower than those offered by its competitors.

✪ Expedia. expedia.com
Essentials: Domestic and international flights, plus hotel and rental car booking; late-breaking travel news, destination features, and commentary from travel experts; deals on cruises and vacation packages. Free registration is required for booking.

Expedia makes it easy to handle flight, hotel, and car booking on one itinerary, so it's a good place for one-stop shopping. Expedia's hotel search offers crisp, zoomable maps to pinpoint most properties; click on the camera icon to see images of the rooms and facilities. But like many online databases, Expedia focuses on the major chains, such as Hilton and Hyatt, so don't expect to find too many one-of-a-kind boutique hotels or B&Bs here.

Once you're registered (it's only necessary to do this once from each computer you use), you can start booking with the Roundtrip Fare Finder box on the home page, which expedites the process. After selecting a flight, you can hold it until midnight the following day or purchase online. If you think you might do better through a travel agent, you'll have time to try to get a lower price. And you may do better with a travel agent because Expedia's computer reservation system does not include all airlines. Most notably absent are some leading budget carriers, such as Southwest. (*Note:* At press time, Travelocity was the only major booking service that included Southwest.)

Expedia's World Guide, offering destination information, is a glaring weakness; it takes lots of page views to get very little information. However, Expedia compensates by linking to other Microsoft Network services, such as its Sidewalk city guides, which offer entertainment and dining advice.

Preview Travel. www.previewtravel.com
Essentials: Domestic and international flights, plus hotel and rental car booking; Travel Newswire lists fare sales; deals on cruises and vacation packages. Free (one-time) registration is required for booking. Preview offers express booking for members, but at press time, this feature was buried below the fold on Preview's reservation page.

Preview features the most inviting interface for booking trips, though the wealth of graphics involved can make the site somewhat slow to load. Use Farefinder to quickly find the lowest current fares on flights to dozens of major cities. Carfinder offers a similar service for rental cars, but you can only search airport locations, not city pick-up sites. To see the lowest fare for your itinerary, input the dates and times for your route and see what Preview comes up with.

In recent years Preview and other leading booking services have added features such as Best Fare Finder, so after Preview searches for the best deal on your itinerary, it will check flights that are a bit later or earlier to see if it might be cheaper to fly at a different time. While these searches have become quite sophisticated, they still occasionally overlook deals that might be uncovered by a top-notch travel agent. If you have the time, see what you can find online and then call an agent to see if you can get a better price.

With Preview's Fare Alert feature, you can set fares for up to three routes and you'll receive e-mail notices when the fare drops below your target amount. For example, you could tell Preview to alert you when the fare from New York to New Orleans drops below $250. If it does, you'll get an e-mail telling you the current fare.

Minor quibbles: When you search for a fare or hotel (at least when we went to press), Preview launches an annoying little "Please Wait" window that gets in the way of the main browser window, even when your results begin to appear. The hotel search feature is intuitive, but the images and maps aren't as crisp as those at Expedia. Also, all sorts of information that's irrelevant to travelers (such as public school locations) is listed on the maps.

Note to AOL Users: You can book flights, hotels, rental cars, and cruises on AOL at keyword: Travel. The booking software is provided by Preview Travel and is similar to Preview on the Web. Use the AOL "Travelers Advantage" program to earn a 5% rebate on flights, hotel rooms, and car rentals.

Priceline.com. **www.priceline.com**

Even people who aren't familiar with too many Web sites have heard about Priceline.com, which lets you "name your price" for domestic and international airline tickets. In other words, you select a route and dates, guarantee with a credit card, and make a bid for what you're willing to pay. If one of the airlines in Priceline's database has a fare that's lower than your bid, your credit card will automatically be charged for a ticket.

But you can't say when you want to fly—you have to accept any flight leaving between 6am and 10pm, and you may have to make a stopover. No frequent-flyer miles are awarded, and tickets are nonrefundable and can't be exchanged for another flight. So if your plans change, you're out of luck. Priceline can be good for travelers who have to take off on short notice (and who are thus unable to qualify for advance purchase discounts). But be sure to shop around first—if you overbid, you'll be required to purchase the ticket and Priceline will pocket the difference.

Travelocity. **www.travelocity.com**

Essentials: Domestic and international flight, hotel and rental car booking; deals on cruises and vacation packages. Travel Headlines spotlights latest bargain airfares. Free (one-time) registration is required for booking.

Travelocity almost got it right. Its Express Booking feature enables travelers to complete the booking process more quickly than they could at Expedia or Preview, but Travelocity gums up the works with a page called "Featured Airlines." Big placards of several featured airlines compete for your attention. If you want to see the fares for *all* available airlines, click the much smaller box at the bottom of the page labeled "Book a Flight."

Some have worried that Travelocity, which is owned by American Airlines' parent company AMR, directs bookings to American. This doesn't seem to be the case—I've booked there dozens of times and have always been directed to the cheapest listed flight, for example on Tower or ATA. But this "Featured Airlines" page seems to be Travelocity's way of trying to cash in with ads and incentives for booking certain airlines. (*Note:* It's hard to blame these booking services for trying to generate some revenue. Many airlines have slashed commissions to $10 per domestic booking for online transactions so these virtual agencies are groping for revenue streams.) There are rewards for choosing one of the featured airlines. You'll get 1,500 bonus frequent-flyer miles if you book through United's site, for example, but the site doesn't tell you about other airlines that might be cheaper. If the United flight costs $150 more than the best deal on another airline, it's not worth spending the extra money for a relatively small number of bonus miles.

On the plus side, Travelocity has some leading-edge techie tools. Exhibit A is Fare Watcher E-mail, an "intelligent agent" that keeps you informed of the best fares offered for the city pairs (round-trips) of your choice. Whenever the fare changes by $25 or more, Fare Watcher will alert you by e-mail. Exhibit B is Flight Paging: If you own an alphanumeric pager with national access that can receive e-mail, Travelocity's paging system can alert you if your flight is delayed. Finally, though Travelocity doesn't include every budget airline, it does include Southwest, the leading U.S. budget carrier, which now flies into Long Island's Islip airport.

FINDING LODGINGS ONLINE

While the services above offer hotel booking, it can be best to use a site devoted primarily to lodging; you may find properties that aren't listed on more general online travel agencies. Some lodging sites specialize in a particular type of accommodation, such as B&Bs, which you won't find on the more mainstream booking services. Other services, such as TravelWeb, offer weekend deals on major chain properties, which cater to business travelers and have more empty rooms on weekends.

All Hotels on the Web. www.all-hotels.com

Well, this site doesn't include *all* the hotels on the Web, but it does have tens of thousands of listings throughout the world. Bear in mind that each hotel listed has paid a small fee of ($25 and up) for placement, so it's not an objective list but more like a book of online brochures.

Hotel Reservations Network. www.180096hotel.com

Bargain on room rates at hotels in more than two dozen U.S. cities. The cool thing is that HRN prebooks blocks of rooms in advance, so sometimes it has rooms—at discount rates—at hotels that are "sold out." Select a city, input your dates, and you'll get a list of best prices for a selection of hotels. Descriptions include an image of the property and a locator map (to book online, click the "Book Now" button). HRN is notable for some deep discounts, even in cities where hotel rooms are expensive. The toll-free number is printed all over this site; call it if you want more options than are listed online.

InnSite. www.innsite.com

B&B listings for inns in all 50 U.S. states and dozens of countries around the globe.

Find an inn at your destination, have a look at images of the rooms, check prices and availability, and then send e-mail to the innkeeper if you have further questions. This is an extensive directory of B&Bs, but only includes listings if the proprietor submitted one (note: it's free to get an inn listed). The descriptions are written by the innkeepers and many listings link to the inn's own Web sites, where you can find more information and images.

Places to Stay. www.placestostay.com

Mostly one-of-a-kind places in the United States and abroad that you might not find in other directories, with a focus on resorts. Again, listing is selective—this isn't a comprehensive directory, but can give you a sense of what's available at different destinations.

⊙ TravelWeb. **www.travelweb.com**
TravelWeb lists more than 16,000 hotels worldwide, focusing on chains such as Hyatt and Hilton, and you can book almost 90% of these online. TravelWeb's Click-It Weekends, updated each Monday, offers weekend deals at many leading hotel chains. TravelWeb is the online home for Pegasus Systems, which provides transaction processing systems for the hotel industry.

LAST-MINUTE DEALS & OTHER ONLINE BARGAINS

There's nothing airlines hate more than flying with lots of empty seats. The Net has enabled airlines to offer last-minute bargains to entice travelers to fill those seats. Most of these are announced on Tuesday or Wednesday and are valid for travel the following weekend, but some can be booked weeks or months in advance. You can sign up for weekly e-mail alerts at airlines' sites (see above) or check sites such as WebFlyer (see below) that compile lists of these bargains. To make it easier, visit a site (see below) that will round up all the deals and send them in one convenient weekly e-mail. But last-minute deals aren't the only online bargains; some of the sites below can help you find value even if you can't wait until the eleventh hour.

⊙ 1travel.com. **www.1travel.com**
Deals on domestic and international flights, cruises, hotels, and all-inclusive resorts such as Club Med.

1travel.com's Saving Alert compiles last-minute air deals so you don't have to scroll through multiple e-mail alerts. A feature called "Drive a Little Using Low-Fare Airlines" helps map out strategies for using alternate airports to find lower fares. And Farebeater searches a database that includes published fares, consolidator bargains, and special deals exclusive to 1travel.com. *Note:* The travel agencies listed by 1travel.com have paid for placement.

BestFares. **www.bestfares.com**
Budget-seeker Tom Parsons lists some great bargains on airfares, hotels, rental cars, and cruises, but the site is poorly organized. News Desk is a long list of hundreds of bargains, but they're not broken down into cities or even countries, so it's not easy trying to find what you're looking for. If you have time to wade through it, you might find a good deal. Some material is available only to paid subscribers.

Go4less.com. **www.go4less.com**
Specializing in last-minute cruise and package deals, Go4less has some eye-popping offers, such as off-peak Caribbean cruises for under $100 per day. The site has a clean design but the bargains aren't organized by destination. However, you avoid sifting through all this material by using the Search box and entering vacation type, destination, month, and price.

Handy Tip

While most people learn about last-minute weekend deals from e-mail dispatches, it can be best to find out precisely when these deals become available and check airlines' Web sites yourself at this time. To find out when bargains will be announced, check the pages devoted to these deals on airlines' Web pages. Because these offerings are limited, seats can vanish within hours (sometimes even minutes), so it pays to log on as soon as they're available. An example: Southwest's specials are posted at 12:01am Tuesdays (central time). So if you're looking for a cheap flight, stay up late and check Southwest's site at to grab the best new deals.

Check Your E-Mail While You're on the Road

Until a few years ago, most travelers who checked their e-mail while traveling carried a laptop, but this posed some problems. Not only are laptops expensive, but they can be difficult to configure, incur expensive connection charges, and are attractive to thieves. Thankfully, Web-based free e-mail programs have made it much easier to stay in touch.

Just open an account at a free e-mail provider, such as Hotmail (hotmail.com) or Yahoo! Mail (mail.yahoo.com), and all you'll need to check your mail is a Web connection, easily available at Net cafes and copy shops around the world. After logging on, just point the browser to www.hotmail.com, enter your username and password and you'll have access to your mail.

Internet cafes have become ubiquitous, so for a few dollars an hour you'll be able to check your mail and send messages back to colleagues, friends, and family. If you already have a primary e-mail account, you can set it to forward mail to your free e-mail account while you're away. Free mail programs have become enormously popular (Hotmail claims more than 10 million members), because they enable everyone, even those who don't own a computer, to have an e-mail address they can check wherever they log onto the Web.

Moment's Notice. www.moments-notice.com
As the name suggests, Moment's Notice specializes in last-minute vacation and cruise deals. You can browse for free, but if you want to purchase a trip, you have to join Moment's Notice, which costs $25.

Smarter Living. www.smarterliving.com
Best known for its e-mail dispatch of weekend deals on 20 airlines, Smarter Living also keeps you posted about last-minute bargains on everything from Windjammer Cruises to flights to Iceland.

✪ WebFlyer. www.webflyer.com
WebFlyer is the ultimate online resource for frequent flyers and also has an excellent listing of last-minute air deals. Click on "Deal Watch" for a round-up of weekend deals on flights, hotels, and rental cars from domestic and international suppliers.

TRAVELER'S TOOLKIT

✪ CultureFinder. www.culturefinder.com
Up-to-date listings for plays, opera, classical music, dance, film, and other cultural events in more than 1,300 U.S. cities. Enter the dates you'll be in a city and get a list of events; you can also purchase tickets online.

Intellicast. www.intellicast.com
Weather forecasts for all 50 states and cities around the world.

✪ MapQuest. www.mapquest.com
Specializing in U.S. maps, MapQuest enables you to zoom in on a destination, calculate step-by-step driving directions between any two U.S. points, and locate restaurants, hotels, and other attractions on maps.

✪ Net Café Guide. www.netcafeguide.com
Locate Internet cafes at hundreds of locations around the globe. Catch up on your e-mail, log onto the Web, and stay in touch with the home front, usually for just a few dollars per hour.

Trip.com: Airport Maps and Flight Status. **www.trip.com**
A business travel site where you can find out when an airborne flight is scheduled to arrive. Click on "Guides and Tools" to peruse airport maps for more than 40 domestic cities.

Visa. **www.visa.com/pd/atm/**
MasterCard. **www.mastercard.com/atm**
Find Cirrus and Plus ATMs in hundreds of cities in the United States and around the world. Both include maps for some locations and both list airport ATM locations, some with maps. Remarkably, MasterCard lists ATMs on all seven continents (there's one at Antarctica's McMurdo Station). Tip: You'll usually get a better exchange rate using ATMs than exchanging traveler's checks at banks.

2 Top Web Sites for New Orleans

CITY & ENTERTAINMENT GUIDES

Best of New Orleans. **www.bestofneworleans.com**
This wide-ranging guide from Gambit Weekly includes staff picks for the best in dining, music, theater, events, and more.

Crescent City Connection. **www.satchmo.com/index2.html**
A detailed roundup of musical events in New Orleans. This is a great site for planning a visit to Jazz Fest, and for learning more about local musicians.

Gay New Orleans. **www.gayneworleans.com**
An extensive guide to gay-friendly bars, clubs, events, restaurants, and lodgings. This guide covers dozens of subjects, from Gay Mardi Gras to shopping.

✪ Gumbo Pages. **www.gumbopages.com**
"Remember that in Louisiana, alcohol, butter, cream and big piles of fried seafood are still good for you." So begins Nawlins native Chuck Taggart's personal guide to the Big Easy. This insider's guide captures the flavor of New Orleans and includes advice on restaurants, festivals, music, "how to tawk rite," and more.

✪ Inside New Orleans. **www.insideneworleans.com**
A well-rounded guide from Cox Communications covering dining, lodging, shopping, and much more. The Jazz Fest section is excellent as is entertainment coverage. In the dining section, locals recommend their favorite places, complementing the staff-written reviews.

New Orleans Online. **www.neworleansonline.com**
This site makes good use of the Web's search features to enable you to home in on what you're looking for. Click on "Restaurants" for example, to search for a Cajun place in the French Quarter. Up comes a list of restaurants that fit the bill, such as K'Paul's Louisiana Kitchen. Go a link deeper to see the menus, prices, and even a long

Note to AOL Users

The keyword "New Orleans" leads to **Digital City New Orleans,** which includes reviews and listings for restaurants, arts, sports, and much more. If you search for the term "New Orleans" in AOL's Find box, you'll come up with a list of other resources for New Orleans. These include B&B listings, package deals, and AOL's New Orleans Message Board, an online bulletin board that's open to any AOL member who wants to browse or ask a question. Digital City: New Orleans is also available on the Web at **neworleans.digitalcity.com.**

list of recipes from famed chef Paul Prudhomme. New Orleans Online also includes listings for hotels, tours, attractions, and events, as well as an online radio station that delivers Cajun tunes 24 hours a day.

New Orleans Travel Guide. www.neworleans.com

Though this site has sold much of its home page (and parts of many inside pages) to hotels, coupon-book companies, and others, it's still a valuable site for researching a trip. You can scan restaurant menus, see what hotels look like, get ideas about where to shop, and order free coupon books online. The attractions guide is extensive, and there are links to dozens of other New Orleans pages, such as one to the Riverwalk Marketplace.

USA Citylink: New Orleans. citylink.neosoft.com/citylink/la/new-orleans

Though this is a pretty generic city guide, it does have some good links covering hotels and events. The Mardi Gras coverage is strong.

✪ Virtually New Orleans. www.yatcom.com/neworl/vno.html

A personal and insightful guide from Ed Branley, who knows the city inside and out— this site is like having a good friend show you around the city. Ed serves up frank dining reviews, including his picks for best restaurants for breakfast, lunch, or dinner. These sightseeing pages include alluring photographs, though the hotel and shopping pages are a bit thin.

NEWSPAPERS & MAGAZINES

Louisiana Life. www.neworleans.com/lalife

A lively guide to the city's arts, history, and politics, from the print quarterly of the same name.

✪ nola Live. www.nolalive.com

From the *Times Picayune* comes this lively city guide, with tasty dining reviews and local festival information. Click on the BourboCam for live views of Bourbon Street that refresh every 20 seconds. Or drop into 24-hour Yat Chat and see what the locals are talking about.

OffBeat. www.offbeat.com

New Orleans's most thorough music magazine has extensive live music listings, and is the place to get primed for Jazz Fest. Click on "Club Listings and Events" for club listings, events, festivals, and even a tour schedule for New Orleans' leading musicians, so you can catch Cajun fever before your trip begins. You'll also find features from the magazine, such as a profile of Allen Toussaint.

DINING GUIDES

Many of the sites in the sections above include worthwhile dining guides. Below you'll find sites dedicated solely to dining or lodging.

Cuisine Net. menusonline.com

Listings and reviews for New Orleans and 15 other U.S. cities. Each restaurant has a capsule review compiled by CuisineNet and ratings based on reader surveys. For some restaurants, only two or three people have bothered to submit ratings, so they may not be statistically significant. However comments can be instructive, as CuisineNet's readers discuss service, parking, free birthday desserts, and a host of other insightful observations.

Zagat.com. www.zagat.com

Reviews of top restaurants in New Orleans and dozens of other U.S. cities. Zagat has made a name for itself as the people's choice, as its listings are based on extensive reader surveys. Use the pull-down menu on the home page to select New Orleans, where you'll find the top restaurants by food, decor, service, and type of cuisine. You can also compare restaurants in various neighborhoods or search for a place using its name. And when you find one that looks good, click on "More Like This" for similar listings.

TOP ATTRACTIONS

Not all of the city's top attractions have their own good Web sites. If you don't find what you're seeking in the list below, use one of the general city guides listed above.

✪ **Audubon Institute: Attractions. www.auduboninstitute.org/html/aa.html**
One-stop shopping for the Audubon Zoo, Aquarium of the Americas, the Living Science Museum, the Louisiana Nature Center, and IMAX Theater. The aquarium site includes a quick tour, advice for getting there, "new adventures," and even a "Creature Feature" profiling one of the inhabitants at this million-gallon aquarium. If the Web address above poses any problems, go to **www.auduboninstitute.org** and click on "Audubon Attractions." This main page also has information on local parks and an "Interactive Swamp."

Experience New Orleans: Sights. neworleansweb.org/sights.html
This guide includes descriptions and images of leading attractions, from a Natchez riverboat cruise to an essay about Jackson Square.

MardiGras.com. mardigras.com
Get the lowdown on one of the world's biggest parties and relive the festivities all year long through the words, images, and sounds of this site. Play the "Bourbon Street Game" and try to grab beads, avoid drunks, and find a bathroom—it's just like the real thing. Also see **www.mardigrasday.com**, which includes video clips, and **www.mardi grasneworleans.com**, with parade schedules and a history of the Krewes.

New Orleans Coupons. www.neworleanscoupons.com
Print out money-saving coupons for some attractions and restaurants.

✪ **New Orleans French Quarter. www.frenchquarter.com**
Laissez les bons temps roulez! This thorough and well-organized guide to the French Quarter includes an extensive calendar of events, a hotel guide, even sound files of street dancers and musicians recorded in Jackson Square. Click on "Fun Stuff" to learn about free or inexpensive activities, such as walking tours and free jazz shows.

New Orleans Jazz and Heritage Festival. www.nojazzfest.com
The official home of Jazz Fest, this site includes the line-up, sound files, ticket information, and much more. There's even a countdown to the next Jazz Fest (353 days to go when I checked!).

New Orleans Museum of Art. www.noma.org
Learn about current exhibitions, take a peek at the permanent collection, and check visitor information, such as hours and admission fees.

Preservation Resource Center. www.prcno.org
Enjoy a virtual tour of various neighborhoods and learn about the city's distinctive architectural styles.

SPORTS & RECREATION

New Orleans Saints. www.nfl.com/saints
The official NFL site for the Saints includes the team's schedule, ticket information, game stories, and player profiles.

Jean Lafitte National Historical Park and Preserve. www.nps.gov/jela
From the National Park Service's ParkNet, this site includes descriptions of attractions, visitor information (including hours and fees), and a map.

New Orleans City Park. www.neworleans.com/citypark
Known as Louisiana's family playground, this 1,500-acre park has stately oak trees, meandering hiking trails, statues, and historic buildings. Check here for maps, boating and fishing information, and events, such as the Spring Garden show.

New Orleans Jazz National Historic Park. www.nps.gov/neor
From the National Park Service comes visitor information on this park, which is dedicated to supporting and celebrating jazz music.

GETTING AROUND

Flagship Limousine Company. www.flagshiplimo.com
Service between the airport and downtown, and of course to other points in the greater New Orleans region.

New Orleans International Airport. neworleansonline.com/apt-cover.htm
If you're looking for ground transport from the airport or want to know more about airport facilities, this is the place to check.

Streetcar Named Desire. www.historicdistrict.com/bywater/strtcar.htm
Read about the streetcar line immortalized in Tennessee Williams's play and see images of a historic car currently running on the Riverfront Line.

Index

See also Accommodations and Restaurant indexes, below.
Page numbers in *italics* refer to maps.

ACCOMMODATIONS

FROMMER'S® COMPLETE TRAVEL GUIDES

Alaska
Amsterdam
Arizona
Atlanta
Australia
Austria
Bahamas
Barcelona, Madrid & Seville
Beijing
Belgium, Holland & Luxembourg
Bermuda
Boston
Budapest & the Best of Hungary
California
Canada
Cancún, Cozumel &
 the Yucatán
Cape Cod, Nantucket & Martha's Vineyard
Caribbean
Caribbean Cruises & Ports of Call
Caribbean Ports of Call
Carolinas & Georgia
Chicago
China
Colorado
Costa Rica
Denmark
Denver, Boulder & Colorado Springs
England
Europe
Florida
France
Germany
Greece
Greek Islands
Hawaii
Hong Kong
Honolulu, Waikiki & Oahu
Ireland
Israel
Italy
Jamaica & Barbados
Japan
Las Vegas
London
Los Angeles
Maryland & Delaware
Maui
Mexico
Miami & the Keys

Montana & Wyoming
Montréal & Québec City
Munich & the Bavarian Alps
Nashville & Memphis
Nepal
New England
New Mexico
New Orleans
New York City
Nova Scotia, New Brunswick &
 Prince Edward Island
Oregon
Paris
Philadelphia & the
 Amish Country
Portugal
Prague & the Best of the Czech Republic
Provence & the Riviera
Puerto Rico
Rome
San Antonio & Austin
San Diego
San Francisco
Santa Fe, Taos &
 Albuquerque
Scandinavia
Scotland
Seattle & Portland
Singapore & Malaysia
South Africa
Southeast Asia
South Pacific
Spain
Sweden
Switzerland
Thailand
Tokyo
Toronto
Tuscany & Umbria
USA
Utah
Vancouver & Victoria
Vermont, New Hampshire
 & Maine
Vienna & the Danube Valley
Virgin Islands
Virginia
Walt Disney World & Orlando
Washington, D.C.
Washington State

FROMMER'S® DOLLAR-A-DAY GUIDES

Australia from $50 a Day	Hawaii from $70 a Day	New Zealand from $50 a Day
California from $60 a Day	Ireland from $50 a Day	Paris from $85 a Day
Caribbean from $70 a Day	Israel from $45 a Day	San Francisco from $60 a Day
England from $70 a Day	Italy from $70 a Day	Washington, D.C.,
Europe from $60 a Day	London from $85 a Day	from $60 a Day
Florida from $60 a Day	New York from $80 a Day	

FROMMER'S® PORTABLE GUIDES

Acapulco, Ixtapa & Zihuatanejo	Dublin	Puerto Vallarta, Manzanillo & Guadalajara
Alaska Cruises & Ports of Call	Hawaii: The Big Island	San Diego
Bahamas	Las Vegas	San Francisco
Baja & Los Cabos	London	Sydney
Berlin	Maine Coast	Tampa & St. Petersburg
California Wine Country	Maui	Venice
Charleston & Savannah	New Orleans	Washington, D.C.
Chicago	New York City	
	Paris	

FROMMER'S® NATIONAL PARK GUIDES

Family Vacations in the National Parks	National Parks of the American West	Yellowstone & Grand Teton
Grand Canyon	Rocky Mountain	Yosemite & Sequoia/ Kings Canyon
		Zion & Bryce Canyon

FROMMER'S® GREAT OUTDOOR GUIDES

New England	Southern California & Baja
Northern California	Washington & Oregon

FROMMER'S® MEMORABLE WALKS

Chicago	New York	San Francisco
London	Paris	Washington D.C.

FROMMER'S® IRREVERENT GUIDES

Amsterdam	London	New Orleans	Seattle & Portland
Boston	Los Angeles	Paris	Vancouver
Chicago	Manhattan	San Francisco	Walt Disney World
Las Vegas			Washington, D.C.

FROMMER'S® BEST-LOVED DRIVING TOURS

America	Florida	Ireland	Scotland
Britain	France	Italy	Spain
California	Germany	New England	Western Europe

THE COMPLETE IDIOT'S TRAVEL GUIDES

Boston	Ireland	Paris
Chicago	Las Vegas	San Francisco
Cruise Vacations	London	Spain
Planning Your Trip to Europe	Mexico's Beach Resorts	Walt Disney World
Florida	New Orleans	Washington, D.C.
Hawaii	New York City	

THE UNOFFICIAL GUIDES®

Bed & Breakfast in New England	Cruises	London	San Francisco
Bed & Breakfast in the Northwest	Florida with Kids	Miami & the Keys	Skiing in the West
Beyond Disney	The Great Smoky & Blue Ridge Mountains	Mini Las Vegas	Walt Disney World
Branson, Missouri	Inside Disney	Mini-Mickey	Walt Disney World for Grown-ups
California with Kids	Las Vegas	New Orleans	Walt Disney World for Kids
Chicago		New York City	
		Paris	Washington, D.C.

SPECIAL-INTEREST TITLES

Born to Shop: France
Born to Shop: Hong Kong
Born to Shop: Italy
Born to Shop: New York
Born to Shop: Paris
Frommer's Britain's Best Bike Rides
The Civil War Trust's Official Guide to the Civil War Discovery Trail
Frommer's Caribbean Hideaways
Frommer's Europe's Greatest Driving Tours
Frommer's Food Lover's Companion to France
Frommer's Food Lover's Companion to Italy
Frommer's Gay & Lesbian Europe
Israel Past & Present
Monks' Guide to California

Monks' Guide to New York City
The Moon
New York City with Kids
Unforgettable Weekends
Outside Magazine's Guide to Family Vacations
Places Rated Almanac
Retirement Places Rated
Road Atlas Britain
Road Atlas Europe
Washington, D.C., with Kids
Wonderful Weekends from Boston
Wonderful Weekends from New York City
Wonderful Weekends from San Francisco
Wonderful Weekends from Los Angeles

WHEREVER YOU TRAVEL, *H*ELP IS NEVER FAR AWAY.

From planning your trip to providing travel assistance along the way, American Express® Travel Service Offices are always there to help you do more.

New Orleans

American Express Travel Service
201 St. Charles St.
Suite 112
504/586-8201

Travel

www.americanexpress.com/travel

American Express Travel Service Offices
are located throughout the United States.
For the office nearest you, call 1-800-AXP-3429.